P9-CCI-436

The SAGE Handbook of

Punishment and Society

The SAGE Handbook of
Punishment and Society

Edited by
Jonathan Simon
and
Richard Sparks

Los Angeles | London | New Delhi
Singapore | Washington DC

Los Angeles | London | New Delhi
Singapore | Washington DC

SAGE Publications Ltd
1 Oliver's Yard
55 City Road
London EC1Y 1SP

SAGE Publications Inc.
2455 Teller Road
Thousand Oaks, California 91320

SAGE Publications India Pvt Ltd
B 1/I 1 Mohan Cooperative Industrial Area
Mathura Road
New Delhi 110 044

SAGE Publications Asia-Pacific Pte Ltd
3 Church Street
#10-04 Samsung Hub
Singapore 049483

Editor: Natalie Aguilera
Editorial assistant: James Piper
Production editor: Rachel Eley
Copyeditor: Toynbee Editorial Services
Proofreader: Cenveo Publisher Services
Marketing manager: Sally Ransom
Cover design: Wendy Scott
Typeset by: Cenveo Publisher Services
Printed in Great Britain by the MPG Books Group

First published 2013

Library of Congress Control Number: 2012931228

British Library Cataloguing in Publication data

A catalogue record for this book is available from the British Library

ISBN 978-1-84860-675-3

Contents

About the Authors

Mary Bosworth is Reader in Criminology and Fellow of St Cross College at the University of Oxford and, concurrently, Professor of Criminology at Monash University, Australia. She has published widely on issues of race, gender, and punishment and is currently conducting research on immigration detention in Greece and the UK.

Ben Crewe is deputy director of the Prisons Research Centre, University of Cambridge. His most recent research monograph, *The Prisoner Society: Power, Adaptation and Social Life in an English Prison*, was published by Oxford University Press in 2009.

Kathleen Daly is Professor of Criminology and Criminal Justice, Griffith University, Brisbane.

David Garland is Arthur T. Vanderbilt Professor of Law and Professor of Sociology at New York University. He is the author of several works in the sociology of punishment and was the founding Editor-in-Chief of the journal *Punishment and Society*.

Alessandro De Giorgi is Associate Professor of Justice Studies at San Jose State University, California. His research interests include theories of punishment and social control, political economy, and urban ethnography. He is the author of *Re-thinking the Political Economy of Punishment: Perspectives on Post-Fordism and Penal Politics* (Aldershot, Ashgate, 2006).

Barry Goldson holds the Charles Booth Chair of Social Science at the University of Liverpool, UK and is Visiting Professorial Research Fellow at the University of New South Wales, Australia. He is the founding editor of *Youth Justice: An International Journal* (SAGE Publications).

Benjamin Goold is an Associate Professor at the Faculty of Law, University of British Columbia. In addition to writing on issues of surveillance and covert policing, he is also interested in privacy, data protection and the relationship between security and human rights.

Caitlin Goss is a doctoral student in law at the University of Oxford, writing on interim constitutions. She has degrees in law and philosophy from the University of Queensland. She has worked as a judicial associate on the Queensland Court of Appeal, and as an intern at the Office of the Co-Prosecutors at the Extraordinary Chambers in the Courts of Cambodia.

Marie Gottschalk is a professor in the Department of Political Science at the University of Pennsylvania. She is the author of, among other works, *The Prison and the Gallows: The Politics of Mass Incarceration in America* and is completing a new book on the future of penal reform.

Kelly Hannah-Moffat is Professor of Sociology and Vice Dean undergraduate at University of Toronto Mississauga. She has published several articles and books on risk, punishment, parole, gender and diversity, and decision-making. Including: 'Sacrosanct or flawed: Risk, Accountability and Gender-responsive Penal Politics,' *Current Issues in Criminal Justice*; with Maurutto (2010) 'Restructuring Pre-sentence Reports Race, Risk, and the PSR' *Punishment & Society*.

Emma Kaufman is a doctoral candidate in law at the University of Oxford. She has published on American immigration imprisonment, British penal policy and race relations in the UK.

Nicola Lacey holds a Senior Research Fellowship at All Souls College, Oxford, and is Professor of Criminal Law and Legal Theory at the University of Oxford. She is a Fellow of the British Academy. Her recent publications include *The Prisoners' Dilemma: Political Economy and Punishment in Contemporary Democracies* (Cambridge University Press, 2008), *Women, Crime and Character: From Moll Flanders to Tess of the d'Urbervilles* (Oxford University Press, 2008) and *A Life of HLA Hart: The Nightmare and the Noble Dream* (Oxford University Press, 2004).

Liora Lazarus teaches criminal justice and human rights in the Law Faculty at the University of Oxford. Her publications include *Contrasting Prisoners' Rights* and *Security and Human Rights*. Most recently she has written on the right to security and coercive duties. She has also published a number of official reports in the UK and EU on human rights policy, and is involved in the ongoing public debate on the British Bill of Rights.

Alison Liebling is Professor of Criminology and Criminal Justice and Director of the Prisons Research Centre at the University of Cambridge. She has published several books, including *Suicides in Prison* (1992), *The Prison Officer* (2001), *Prisons and their Moral Performance* (2004) and with Shadd Maruna (2005) *The Effects of Imprisonment*.

Mona Lynch is Professor of Criminology, Law and Society and Co-Director of the Center in Law, Society and Culture at University of California, Irvine. Her research focuses on the social, psychological, and cultural dynamics of contemporary adjudication and punishment processes.

Louise Mallinder is a reader at the Transitional Justice Institute, University of Ulster. She is the author of Amnesty, Human Rights and Political Transitions: Bridging the Peace and Justice Divide (Hart Publishing, 2008).

Shadd Maruna is Director of the Institute of Criminology and Criminal Justice and a Professor of Justice Studies at the Law School in Queen's University Belfast in Northern Ireland. His most recent book is *Fifty Key Thinkers in Criminology* (with Keith Hayward and Jayne Mooney).

Kieran McEvoy is Professor of Law and Transitional Justice at the School of Law, Queens University Belfast.

Fergus McNeill is Professor of Criminology and Social Work at the University of Glasgow and an associate of the Scottish Centre for Crime and Justice Research. He is a former criminal justice social worker whose work continues to intersect theory, research and practice.

Dario Melossi is Professor of Criminology at the School of Law of the University of Bologna. He has recently published *Controlling Crime, Controlling Society: Thinking About Crime in Europe and America*. His *Crime and Migration* is forthcoming.

Christopher Muller is a graduate student in the Department of Sociology at Harvard University.

John Muncie is Emeritus Professor of Criminology at the Open University, UK. He is the author of *Youth and Crime* (SAGE Publications, 3rd edition, 2009) and has published widely on issues in comparative youth justice and children's rights including the co-edited companion volumes *Youth Crime and Justice* and *Comparative Youth Justice* (Sage Publications, 2006). He is co-editor of the Sage journal *Youth Justice: An International Journal*.

Pat O'Malley is a professorial research fellow, Faculty of Law, The University of Sydney. He is the author *The Currency of Justice* (London: Routledge, 2009) and *Crime and Risk* (London: Sage Publications, 2010).

Joshua Page is Assistant Professor of Sociology at the University of Minnesota. He is the author of *The Toughest Beat: Politics, Punishment, and the Prison Officers Union in California* (Oxford University Press, 2011).

John Pratt is Professor of Criminology and James Cook Research Fellow in Social Science at the Institute of Criminology, Victoria University of Wellington, New Zealand. His latest book, *Contrasts in Punishment: an Explanation of Anglophone Excess and Nordic Exceptionalism*, will be published by Routledge in early 2013.

Gwen Robinson is Reader in Criminal Justice at the University of Sheffield, UK.

Austin Sarat is William Nelson Cromwell Professor of Jurisprudence and Political Science and the author and editor of numerous books on punishment and society, most recently, *Life Without Parole: America's New Death Penalty?* (NYU Press, 2012).

Jonathan Simon is the Adrian A Kragen Professor of Law at UC Berkeley. He is the author of several books on punishment and contemporary society and has served as co-editor-in-chief of *Punishment & Society: The International Journal of Penology*.

Philip Smith is Professor of Sociology at Yale University. Publications relevant to this book include *Punishment and Culture* (Chicago University Press), *Incivility: The Rude Stranger in Everyday Life* (co-authored, Cambridge University Press) and the textbook *Understanding Criminal Justice* (co-authored, Sage Publications).

Richard Sparks is Professor of Criminology at the University of Edinburgh and Co-Director of the Scottish Centre for Crime and Justice Research. He is the author of numerous books and articles on punishment and society and has served as editor-in-chief of *Punishment & Society: The International Journal of Penology*. His most recent book, with Ian Loader, is *Public Criminology?* (Routledge, 2010).

Dirk van Zyl Smit is Professor of Comparative and International Penal Law at the University of Nottingham. His publications in include *Principles of European Prison Law and Policy: Penology and Human Rights*, with Sonja Snacken (Oxford University Press, 2009) and *Taking Life Imprisonment Seriously in National and International Law* (Kluwer, 2002).

Christopher Wildeman is an Assistant Professor of Sociology, a Faculty Fellow of the Center for Research on Inequalities and the Life Course (CIQLE), and a Resident Fellow of the Institution for Social and Policy Studies (ISPS) at Yale University. His research interests revolve around the consequences of mass imprisonment for American inequality, with emphasis on families, health and child wellbeing.

Introduction

Punishment and Society: The Emergence of an Academic Field

Jonathan Simon and Richard Sparks

Does the academy need another Handbook? Encyclopedia? Dictionary? Or whatever other form of authoritative narrative you prefer? As occasional contributors to such enterprises, we have brought some serious scepticism to these questions as we have contemplated developing this *Handbook of Punishment and Society* for SAGE Publications. The publishers were keen, persuasive and clearly capable.[1] It was ourselves whom we needed to convince that this was the right time for such an intervention before we could commit our own time and more importantly our ever diminishing social capital in order to importune colleagues to commit their time. Why then is a *Handbook of Punishment and Society* a worthwhile project now?

Motivating us, was a sense that for a host of political, social and intellectual reasons, within our own academic lifetimes, and certainly within those of anyone younger than ourselves coming to the study of punishment, penal institutions and penal politics, or the cultural representation of those matters since the 1980s, the field we denominate here as 'punishment and society' had come into sufficient focus and achieved sufficient definition and discursive shape to provide a rallying point for our interests and concerns. It organized a certain set of puzzles, questions and explanatory problems, just as it also offered a channel for a group of ethical and political anxieties and objections. To the extent that punishment and society became a space in which we and others could form our scholarly identities this was in part because we were offered the opportunity to pick up intellectual traces already laid down by others, and in part a response to some of the peculiarities of the times in which we were living.

Of course, all such rubrics are incomplete and provisional, even to some extent arbitrary. We could just well provide a list of runners-up. Neither, when we use the term 'punishment and society' do we intend to stand on our differences from other neighbouring ways of conceptualizing related problems.

We will devote no time to stipulating what is properly considered punishment and society scholarship and what is not. We simply suggest that over the last couple of decades it has come to offer a point of congregation that enables some richly contemporary and insightful work to be done without continual anxiety over whether what we are doing is more properly thought of as belonging within the bailiwick, and thus requiring the authorization of, sociology, criminology, criminal law or some other more confident and august discipline. Punishment and society is unlikely ever to aspire to the status of a discipline. It is not a thesis or doctrine or set of claims. It is not even the answer to a determinate set of questions. If anything it consists in the questions themselves: it is a *problematique*.

We certainly do not say that 'punishment and society' exists apart from contributions made by scholars past and present who identify themselves primarily in one of those confident and august disciplines, without any of which it would be much the lesser. Neither do we assert that that our own entire work, nor anyone else's belongs only here. We simply say that we know this is viable space of scholarship just like an experienced climber knows that a line of cracks she has observed up a mountain face offers viable hand and foot holds all the way to the top. We might indeed add that we consider punishment and society to constitute an *essential* space of scholarship. The powers that are activated in the name of punishment, the resources generated and consumed, the claims made and disputed, the emotions aroused and, of course, the millions of lives around the world that are affected by the ways in which penal practices are conducted and applied, all argue for a concerted effort of understanding, clarification and critical reflection. We also know we are not alone. We have been fortunate to be taught by many of those responsible for crystallizing out this field, to have worked among a wave of similarly inspired peers and to have taught a growing body of younger colleagues. Readers will find work by members of each of these groups represented below.

Whatever 'punishment and society' is today we suspect 'it' is not likely to last forever, since it arises from, and speaks to, conditions that are themselves quite historically specific. As we will sketch briefly below, we believe it opened up as a result of particular political, cultural and epistemological developments in advanced liberal states during the period from the late 1960s to the early 1980s. Our goal is not to render this configuration permanent – far from it!, since many of the developments in question have been contentious, even destructive – but rather to take advantage of a particular moment when it seems that this somewhat improbable and incorrigibly interdisciplinary field has achieved a kind of objectivity. It is a field which simultaneously involves studies of the past and present, quantitative analyses of penal trends, and ethnographic exploration of penal experiences, work grounded in core sociological theory and work stimulated primarily by studies of literature, philosophy and law. For now, and we believe for some time to come, this will remain a highly productive – indeed, in a certain sense, an unavoidable – space for scholars from a wide variety of disciplines to explore and to extend. We hope this volume will optimize access to this field for our present and future colleagues.

THE PRE-HISTORY OF PUNISHMENT AND SOCIETY

The project of interpreting the forms of punishments in terms of the social, political, cultural and historical conditions of the society in which those forms arise goes back at least to the classic study of the penitentiary system carried out by Alexis de Tocqueville and Gustave de Beaumont, *On the Penitentiary System in America and Its Applications in France* (English translation, 1833). Durkheim's studies of penal evolution at the end of the 19th and beginning years of the 20th century in *The Division of Labor* (1893) and his essay 'Two laws of penal evolution', published in the *Annee Sociologique* (1900), offered a broad social theory of the purposes and forms of punishment. Karl Marx had referred to penal laws and sanctions in scattered fragments of his writings, but a broadly Marxist social theory of punishment would await the work of Frankfurt school scholars Georg Rusche and Otto Kirchheimer, in *Punishment and Social Structure* (1939). A separate tradition of sociology, empirical studies of small communities, began to explore the prison as an enclosed society with Donald Clemmer's (1940) *The Prison Community*, out of which emerged a sociology of the prison experience during the 1950s and 1960s in the USA (Gresham Sykes, Donald Cressey, Sheldon Messinger, John Irwin, Erving Goffman) and during the 1960s and 1970s in Europe (Thomas Mathiesen, Terence and Pauline Morris, Roy King, Stan Cohen and Laurie Taylor among others).

As this brief prospectus clearly shows, nothing that we may say about punishment and society as a distinctive field of inquiry is intended to minimize or obscure its indebtedness to, or its relations with, bodies of social and legal scholarship of longer-standing. Punishment and penal institutions play some part, if only in the margins, of each of the 'three sociologies' set in train by the work of Marx, Durkheim and Weber (Benton, 1977; Collins, 1985[2]). Moreover, if as Giddens (1984: xvii), among others, has argued, the distinctive task of sociology is the understanding of *modern* societies – the social forms brought into being by the political and economic revolutions of the 18th and 19th centuries and their still-resounding subsequent effects – then it is a relatively short step (and one that as we shall shortly see has now been extensively discussed) to suggest that changes in the prevailing modes of punishment and social control might play some significant roles among the causes and consequences of those transformations.

This is simply to note that, with the partial exception of Durkheim and his successors, punishment as such was not a principal theoretical object for any of these great sociological traditions. Their deepest explanatory concerns lay elsewhere. Durkheim represents the exception here insofar as his vision of social life presupposes a continual re-making of community through the ritual assertion of membership and exclusion. It is a vision in which emotional and ostensibly non-rational dynamics play a vital role – including reactions of censure, rejection and wrath – and for which the sharing or contagion of visceral responses (through the phenomenon that Durkheim calls 'collective effervescence') is a basic feature of human societies. For Durkheim and his successors the making and circulation of categories of dirt and pollution (Douglas, 1966), fear and loathing (Erikson, 1966), attribution and blaming (Jackson and Sunshine, 2007) are part-and-parcel of the means whereby a society comes to knowledge of itself and achieves the delineation of its membership. In these respects Durkheim may justly be seen as among the most influential precursors of the sociological study of the emotions (Scheff, 1990), of identity, and of morality (Cotterrell, 1999). The maintenance of social bonds and boundaries, for Durkheim, is in a strong and specific sense a matter of ritual. For Collins (2004) this is Durkheim's specific and most durable contribution to latter-day social theory, and is among the reasons why, for example, Goffman is in [t]his view properly thought of as a rigorously faithful follower of Durkheim. Punishment properly so-called – usually the sanctioning of proscribed behaviour by constituted authorities in ways that warrant exceptional treatment and have negative effects (sometimes drastic ones) on the social standing of the persons so censured – is the institutionalized manifestation of these very basic processes.

For the most part, however, in the case of punishment (as of most facets of social life) the task lies in demonstrating how the frameworks of explanation proposed by particular bodies of social theory may be applied or extended to account for or illuminate it (rather than claiming that the institution of punishment is integral to their construction as theory). In this regard 'the sociology of punishment' has proven to be a highly active and fruitful focus of activity, bringing to bear the explanatory tool-kits of Marxist (Spitzer, 1975; Chambliss, 1974), interactionist (Goffman, 1968; Carlen, 1976; Altheide, 1992), Weberian (Garland, 1990; Savelsberg, 1994) and other sociological perspectives on changing modes, patterns and practices of punishment. Indeed, 'the sociology of punishment' is no doubt the nearest contender for a direct synonym for 'punishment and society' that we can envisage. It signals the enormous contribution of the discipline of sociology, and the now-flourishing body of sociological work on punishment, to our current understanding of penal institutions and the politics, cultures and practices of punishment in modern societies, especially where these centrally concern – as they are commonly bound to do – the relations between punishment and the distributions of social power, opportunity, resources, status and so on.

The point of resisting capture of 'punishment and society' by sociology or any other single discipline, however, is precisely to record the primacy of the topic over the perspective. It is to insist that in the development of this field of inquiry, as we will shortly see, the contributions of scholars who do not own affiliation to sociology, but who operate as historians, anthropologists, philosophers, lawyers or practitioners of a number of other disciplines have also made contributions of the first importance. Moreover, it makes little obvious sense to restrict the range of sources from which future insight might be drawn. We know enough already about the representation of punishment in literary, cinematic and popular cultural discourses and texts, for example, to suggest that cultural theory, socio-linguistics and studies of rhetoric and metaphor might have crucial contributions to offer. Moreover, the gathering awareness of the need to extend the study of punishment-in-societies beyond the traditional heartlands of the north-Atlantic cultural space and into the global south and east promotes a parallel consciousness of the requirement of openness to new and less familiar bodies of knowledge.

Punishment and society scholarship has, we therefore suggest, come to assume its relatively distinct and solid shape now because of a convergence of substantive interest among students from a variety of disciplinary backgrounds in the enormous explanatory, normative and practical problems posed by penal questions in our times. If and to the extent that punishment and society as a field can now usefully be distinguished from criminology, or the sociology of punishment, with which it shares so much, it is just because a sufficient number of people have arrived, by their various routes, at a realization of the necessity of contemplating penal questions in a concerted manner while sharing a sense of the need to hold in view these multiple dimensions of that subject-matter without disciplinary closure.

THE 1970s AND THE EMERGENCE OF THE PUNISHMENT AND SOCIETY FIELD

The 1960s may well be recalled as a golden age for criminology, and for the sociology of the prison, but neither discourse precisely raised punishment as a fundamental problem of social order in the manner of Durkheim or Rusche and Kirchheimer. Yet within a few years in the middle of the 1970s a host of books appeared that placed the changing nature of punishment at the centre of an inquiry into the question of social order.[3]

In the UK a number of radical British social historians associated since the 1950s with the journal *Past and Present* pioneered studies of working class history. This led some of their number, perhaps most notably E. P. Thompson (1975), to undertake intensive and semi collaborative work on the role of criminal justice and especially punishment in 18th-century English society. On the European continent, Michel Foucault had offered a series of lectures at the *Collège de France* exploring the reconfiguration of punishment from sovereign to disciplinary technologies of power. He then published a monograph, *Surveiller et Punir: La Naissance de le Prison* (1975) (English translation: *Discipline and Punish: The Birth of the Prison*, 1977). Punishment, Foucault pointed out, demanded to be studied as a 'complex social function' (1977: 23), intimately related to the main vectors of social, economic and political power, but not reducible without remainder to any one of them. In Italy, at virtually the same time, two Italian sociologists, Dario Melossi and Massimo Pavarini (1978) were conducting similar research into the origins of the rationalized penal institution, which they, inspired by a rediscovery of Rusche and Kirchheimer's work saw in relation to the factory and industrial capitalism. Their book, *Carcere e Fabbrica* was published in Italian in 1977 (English translation: *The Prison and the Factory: Origins of the Penitentiary*, 1981). Also in the USA, the historian David Rothman (1972, 1980) published a monograph on the development of prisons and asylums in the first decades after the American Revolution and a follow up study of how these institutions had evolved through the 1920s. In this same period, philosophers and legal scholars in the USA began to raise moral and ethical criticisms of the form of modern correctionalism dominant at the time in which the release of prisoners was governed by administrative authorities with wide discretion and only a theoretical premise of expert knowledge on rehabilitation (Andrew Von Hirsch, 1976; Caleb Foote [American Friends Service Committee, 1971]).

Two of these books in particular, Foucault's (1977) *Discipline and Punish* and Melossi and Pavarini's (1981) *The Prison and the Factory*, seemed to revive and to reinvent the concerns of the earlier sociology of punishment of Durkheim, and Rusche and Kirchheimer. Both concern themselves with the birth of penitentiary style prison at the turn of the 19th century and its relationship to disciplinary technologies of power over the body that were circulating more widely in society along with the spread of capitalist social and economic relations. Both seemed to draw a line between the still dominant modes of penal-welfarism and this disciplinary logic. For both the major objective of the prison was a docile and productive population.

Just a few years later in Scotland, in a work that would come in retrospect to look rather like a deliberate act of foundation, two young scholars, David Garland and Peter Young (1983), assembled a collection of essays by several of the key authors that addressed a number of emergent themes. 'Penality', as Garland and Young now termed the object of their inquiry, following Foucault, was a 'specific institutional site' (1983: 21). Not only was it an object of compelling interest for reasons of traditional liberal concern – the deprivation of liberty, the imposition of compulsions – but it represented a point of intersection between social policy and the overt political deployment of state power. Garland and Young advocated an approach to questions of punishment and social regulation that was not limited by the terms of a primarily 'instrumental' penology (preoccupied with pragmatic concerns with effectiveness) nor by traditional philosophical debates over normative justifications for imposing punishments, nor yet by a purely internal history of penal ideas, but rather one that addressed the whole *ensemble* of discourses and practices ranged around the penal question. The approach was intended not only to stimulate more challenging and penetrating analysis of the articulation between regimes of punishment and regulation and wider social interests, ideologies and divisions, but also to free up that analysis to look at media discourse, political rhetoric, fictions, fables and so on – the realm of representations as well as sanctions. In other words Garland and Young sought to open a channel between

Table I.1. Punishment and society literature in the 1970s

David Rothman	*The Discovery of the Asylum: Social Order and Disorder in the New Republic*	1971
Stanley Cohen	*Folk Devils and Moral Panics: The Creation of the Mods and the Rockers*	1972
Antony Platt	*The Child Savers: The invention of delinquency, Second Edition*	1972
Thomas Mathiesen	*The Politics of Abolition*	1974
E.P. Thompson	*Whigs and Hunters: The Origins of the Black Acts*	1975
Douglas Hay, Peter Linebaugh, John G. Rule, E.P. Thompson and Cal Winslow	*Albion's Fatal Tree: Crime and Society in Eighteenth Century England*	1975
Michel Foucault	*Surveiller et Punir: La Naissance de la Prison* (1975) *Discipline and Punish: The Birth of the Prison* (1977)	1975, 1977
Dario Melossi and Massimo Pavarini	*Carcere e Fabbrica* *The Prison and the Factory: The Origins of the Penitentiary System* (1981)	1977, 1981
James B. Jacobs	*Stateville: The Penitentiary in Mass Society*	1977
Michael Ignatieff	*A Just Measure of Pain: The Penitentiary in the Industrial Revolution*	1978
Stuart Hall, Chas Critcher, Tony Jefferson, John Clarke and Brian Roberts	*Policing the Crisis: Mugging, the State, and Law and Order*	1978
David J. Rothman	*Conscience and Convenience: The Asylum and its Alternatives in Progressive America*	1980
John Irwin	*Prisons in Turmoil*	1980

studies of punishment and control and what was to become a central operative term throughout Garland's later work: *culture* (see further Garland, 2006; Sparks, 2010).

Clearly much of this work was in a dialogue with both critical criminology and prison sociology, but it also shared some distinctive features. First, and foremost, it embodied a sense that changing penal institutions were a key facet or at least clue to understanding structural change in the wider social order, at the level of culture as well as that of 'policy'. Second, in a manner quite different from most work in the adjoining fields of critical criminology and prison sociology, much of this work in the 1970s concerned itself with historical case studies. While certain key texts such as *Prisons in Turmoil* (Irwin, 1980), and *Policing the Crisis* were indeed substantially focused wholly on the present, much of the most influential work from which punishment and society scholarship arose was not only historical but on relatively distant history, with a significant focus on the 18th and early 19th centuries. Yet each of the historical studies was self-consciously related to then recent trends and developments in the criminal justice and penal fields. Third, most of these studies focused on the prison, not as part of a correctional enterprise trained on deviant individuals, but as an institution of power and social control, to be understood primarily in terms of its effects on the broader population and on governance.

Had this epistemological break happened in the late 1980s and 1990s, it would have been apparent that the renewal of interest in punishment was a direct response to the epic rise of imprisonment that took place in the USA beginning in the 1980s and in many parts of Europe in the 1990s (and as we shall see, mass incarceration has generated considerable development in the field): but, remarkably, much of this intellectual wave was produced before any evidence of a significant change in the scale of punishment was apparent.

In retrospect we can see how important social trends of the late 1960s and 1970s raised themes pursued in this emergent punishment and society literature: the emergence of a politics of law and order, most vividly in the USA; a dramatic rise in violent crime in the USA and a smaller but still distinct increase in other wealthy societies; a wave of social and political unrest, sometimes taking the form of violence in these same societies and expressing itself as well in a significant movement for prisoners' rights; and, especially in the USA, a pronounced deflation of the rehabilitative ideal and more broadly of penal-welfarism (Garland, 2001). In a variety of complex ways the prison emerged as the institution most problematized by these trends and their points of intersection including: the rising number of minorities incarcerated in American prisons at a time of widespread awakening of demands for greater social justice for minorities in the USA; the incarceration of a number of American and European radical students for protest activities during the Vietnam war years, and the reach of litigation and rights discourse into spaces of confinement as driven in the USA by the Supreme Court's 14th Amendment jurisprudence and in Europe by the European Court of Human Rights (Jacobs, 1977; Irwin, 1980; Feeley and Rubin, 1998; van Zyl Smit and Snacken, 2009). In the following two decades these tentative efforts at reform and due process were swept up and assimilated but not altogether extinguished by the turn toward punitiveness and mass incarceration, especially in the USA, but to a lesser degree in the UK and elsewhere (Garland, 2001; Pratt, 2007).

All of these factors contributed not just to an intellectual 'break' but to a kind of epistemological *break-up* of the relationship between 'scientific' knowledge[4] about punishment and what might be called the 'peno-correctional' administration (Kadish, 1960). For as long as penal-welfarism, relatively low crime rates, and a sense of optimism about the application of scientific expertise to crime control lasted, academic reflection on penal practices was almost totally swallowed up by the professional expert production of knowledge for the purpose of penal reform and improvement.[5] The trends that coalesced in the 1970s fractured this relationship between intellectuals and correctionalism in several ways. Rising crime rates and pessimism about scientific rehabilitation undercut the narrative that the prison was part of a social reform agenda which must be defended by educated elites, including academics. The emergence of abolitionism among criminologists and sociologists of the left, as expressed in books like Mathiesen's (1974) *The Politics of Abolition*, and Platt's (1969) *The Child Savers*, aligned to some extent with a prisoners' rights movement that also rejected correctionalism as degrading, framed the prison as a problem in itself, not one to be reformed but rooted out. (Among the things that subsequent decades have demonstrated is quite why that project turned out to be longer and harder, deeper and wider than many anticipated at the time, and why it would go on to suffer so many reverses of such extreme character.)

The emergence of disorder as a major social problem, exemplified by violent crime, but also evident in violent protest and violent police responses to protest, also provides a key background to the revitalization of punishment and society. Modern correctionalism had reached its apotheosis during decades of considerable stability in advanced capitalist countries. For some 40 years, under conditions of economic Depression, world war and then, unprecedented prosperity, crime and immigration had receded as urgent matters of public controversy and debate, along with revolutionary politics. In books, such as Rothman's (1972) *Discovery of the Asylum*, Cohen's *Folk Devils and Moral Panics* and Irwin's (1980) *Prisons in Turmoil*, we see quite different studies animated by an interest in reactive social responses to disorder. If much of critical theory had been preoccupied since the Frankfurt school with the rise of conformity and complacency, this new wave of studies seemed to be rediscovering social conflict and disorder as problems of government, some of them examining the ways in which social control was reasserted after the last wave of revolutionary change in the 18th and 19th centuries, while others grappled with the emerging politics of law and order and authoritarian gestures of politicians such as US President Richard Nixon.

In many ways the works produced in this period already belong to what we now call the 'punishment and society' field and with some degree of self-conscious relationship to the social theorists and empirical sociologists who had come before. Mathiesen (1974), Foucault (1977), Thompson (1975) and Melossi and Pavarini (1981) among others, sought explicitly to link their work to earlier traditions and to sketch out a future programme. What they had in common, especially, was the strategy of deliberately distancing punishment from the legal and moral apparatus that normally encapsulates it, and instead viewing the discourses and practices of punishment in relation to a myriad of other institutions and social forces.

If the epistemological break-up between scientific analysis of punishment and peno-correctional administration helps explain a new wave of differently focused studies of punishment, it does not explain fully why this emergence takes shape as a new interdisciplinary field relatively autonomous from criminology, sociology and history. If, as we think, Foucault (1975) and Melossi and Pavarini (1981) play an important role in crystallizing a sense of a new field of inquiry it is in large because their inquiries, on a topic not so different from Rothman (1971), Platt (1969) or Ignatieff (1978), made a significant break from the neo-Marxist and neo-Durkheimian orientation of most of the others. The focus on penal change and the technologies of power over the body (see Chapter 3, this volume) available in society formed an axis around which the neo-Marxist sociology of punishment of prison abolitionism, and the neo-Durkheimian sociology of disorder could coalesce and begin to form a rich mix of social theory and thick historical analysis which becomes the plane of emergence for punishment and society scholarship in the 1980s.

A theme that is evident across this body of work, but most clearly in Foucault (and arguably in Melossi and Pavarini also) is the emergence of what will later be called 'post-structuralism'. The intellectual emphasis of the 1960s in the social sciences had been toward encompassing and determinative structures, social, economic, linguistic or familial, depending on the disciplines. Foucault's work, especially from 1970 on, has been linked by many to a turn away from 'structuralism' in this sense toward what has been called 'post-structuralism' (Dreyfus and Rabinow, 1982). Regardless of whether or how one 'periodizes' Foucault's analytic approaches, *Surveiller et Punir* was for many readers a dazzling display; making original use of widely cited and discussed sources and examples to raise very new questions about the significance of penal forms and their change than Durkheim had asked or Rusche and Kirchheimer had asked. In setting up his inquiry into the prison, Foucault warmly cited the neo-Marxist approach of Rusche and Kirchheimer (1939, 2003) and emphasized the importance of political economy to his analysis (Durkheim is mysteriously not mentioned), yet economic structures seem to intrude little into the book's selection or interpretation of its materials. Likewise Melossi and Pavarini, while identifying themselves explicitly with Marxism, turn in their analysis away from the previous notion that punishment must be seen primarily as a factor in production, or in terrorizing the proletariat.[6]

The analytic approach taken in both books operated on a decidedly middle range register, neither consistently macro nor micro. Both included an historical dimension, a concern with penal change. At the same time both were explicitly histories of the present, self-conscious about the degree to which their inquiry was anchored in the problems of the present. These features help define punishment and society as an interdisciplinary field with a certain somewhat distinctive analytic structure, albeit one open to different research methodologies and theoretical traditions and variations.

Work from the mid-1980s to the early 1990s, completed the process of opening a clear field around 'punishment and society'. Pieter Spierenburg, a Dutch history student inspired by the renewed recognition of Norbert Elias, brought Elias's powerful theory of the civilizing process (1939, English translation: 1969, 1982) to close historical study of the decline of public executions and tortures in Europe and the rise of greater reliance on incarceration. In his *The Spectacle of Suffering* (1984), Spierenburg set up Elias's account as an alternative to both Foucault's power analysis and the prior tradition of celebrating the self-evident rise of humane punishment, Spierenburg helped begin a process of interpellating the study of punishment across different social theorists that has made 'punishment and society' such a dynamic and productive field for developing social theory. David Garland's (1990) *Punishment and Modern Society* brought almost all of these strands together in what amounted to a theoretical treatise on punishment and society with extensive annotation and illustration. For many of us who began to work on 'punishment and society' in the early 1990s, Garland's book was a kind of intellectual platform, promising to hold up our own construction on a foundation of classic social theory and modern empirical work.

The body of work that emerged during the 1970s and 1980s and which formed something of a canon for punishment and society scholarship was not only important to revitalizing traditions of social theorizing on punishment but also in developing models of empirical work. As noted above, much of the work was historical in nature. While social science work on punishment before the break down of penal-welfarism tended to presume that only the present and its possibilities of reform were important, much of the new work took on the character of a revisionist history of the now-problematized present (Ignatieff, 1981).

While historical studies, or studies including a pronounced historical dimension (for example: Simon, 1993; Pratt, 2002; Gottschalk, 2006), have remained a vital presence in shaping punishment and society scholarship, the field has significantly expanded and diversified in topic, method, range and scope over the intervening decades. Moreover, stimulated in large measure by the intense politicization of penal questions in the USA and some other jurisdictions, it has tended to become more concerned to interrogate contemporary conditions (and their manifold political and geographical variations), to have re-focused upon producing primary research into the scale and effects of current institutions, practices and rhetorics of punishing, and to become more involved in the reflective analysis of policy. By the 1990s, work of a distinctive punishment and society cast was visible in social science journals such as *Criminology*, *The British Journal of Criminology* and *Law & Society Review*, among many others. By the end of the decade a new journal titled *Punishment & Society: The International Journal of Penology* had been launched by SAGE seeking to encourage and cultivate this theoretical and methodological ensemble. In his opening editorial, founding editor David Garland described the ambit of the field in these terms:

> The collapse of a long-established institutional framework tends to prompt intellectual ferment and innovation as old habits of thought and recipes for action lose their epistemological privileges and institutional supports. It is not, then, surprising that the traditional assumptions of a correctionalist,

> technicist penology have been increasingly disrupted over the past two decades by more critical and diverse ways of thinking about penality. From the mid-1970s onwards, penal institutions and ideas have become a focus for path-breaking work in numerous fields as scholars have come to question the practices of mid-century penality and probe further into the social, political and cultural rationales upon which these were based. (1999: 8)

As we go on to detail below the emergence of the phenomenon of mass incarceration, especially in the USA, and the gathering realization that changes in the political cultures and economic organization of contemporary societies (see, for example, de Giorgi [Chapter 2], this volume) were likely to relate in complex and uneven but important and potentially fateful ways to their penal politics and practices, have brought more people, from more diverse starting-points, to the cross-roads of punishment and society scholarship. What they find there comprises a big series of linked explanatory puzzles, normative perplexities and political challenges.

If punishment and society scholarship was inspired by the new social histories of the 1960s and 1970s, it also had a focus on the history of ideas – or the 'history systems of thought' as Foucault had it – that would have been less central there (Foucault, 1977; Cohen and Scull, 1983; Garland, 1990). Its development was also animated by the philosophical debates about punishment (including the various abolitionist and other alternative agendas) that circulated around the same time, especially in the period of intense reflection that ensued following the collapse of the so-called rehabilitative ideal (American Friends Service Committee, 1971; von Hirsch, 1976; Allen, 1981; Feinberg, 1984; Duff, 1986). Likewise, the punishment and society scholars focused on the importance of subjectivity, and how penal practices invest the individual's identity and self-understanding consistent with earlier sociological work anchored in ethnographic observation and ethno-methodology (Garfinkel, 1956; Goffman, 1961). These concerns with the construction of penal subjects received huge impetus from the development of studies of the particular arrangements that penal systems reserve for the punishment of women (Carlen, 1983; Carlen and Worrall, 1987; Bosworth, 1999; Hannah-Moffat, 2001; Bosworth and Kaufman, Chapter 9, this volume). Such concerns have developed the founding concerns of the punishment and society tradition with modes of domination and the relationships between forms of punishment and the dimensions of inequality in the direction of a sophisticated understanding of the manifold varieties of penal social relations. In addition to the long-standing concern with gender recent work addresses the intersectional character of penal power in along the vectors of class and, especially, race (Bosworth and Flavin, 2007). The justly celebrated work of Loïc Wacquant, for example, situates the current bloating and racial disproportionality of the US prison system in terms of his wider account of the history of 'ethno-racial domination' in the USA (for example, Wacquant, 2001, 2008, 2009).

Many of these strands would suggest a heavily qualitative focus to punishment and society scholarship in contrast to the heavily quantitative focus of the scientific study of penal treatment during the era of penocorrectionalism. Certainly it is the case that the flourishing of scholarly interest in penal questions has favoured a renewed focus on the operation of penal institutions and processes, often in their hidden and intimate aspects, and that these concerns have done much to reinvent the ethnographic study of prisons and other sites of punishment, and the close study of penal ideologies and practices, not to mention the infiltration of these into popular culture and media and political rhetorics. These are all interpretive tasks, some of them focusing on the critical reading of discourses and texts, others strongly centred on in situ fieldwork. Nevertheless while qualitative work has undoubtedly been of central importance in punishment and society scholarship, a gathering concern with the shifting scale of punishment, beginning in the 1980s, has also left a deep mark on the field (Zimring and Hawkins, 1991; Greenberg and West, 2001). That concern has been most pronounced in the USA, where the rapid growth in incarceration has been both a pressing social concern and a phenomenon whose dimensions (not least its wide geographical variations, and its unequal impacts on different social groups [Western, 2006]) stand in flagrant need of documentation and analysis (Mauer and King, 2007; Zimring, 2010). More recently however growing concerns over rising penal populations in Europe, again exhibiting notable variation and unevenness have similarly stimulated a requirement for quantitative studies and for attempts to model and explain the observed differences (Cavadino and Dignan, 2006; Lappi-Seppälä, 2008).

THE 2000s AND THE MATURING OF PUNISHMENT AND SOCIETY – MASS INCARCERATION AND BEYOND

If the research agenda of the emerging punishment and society field in the 1970s was set by the politicization of prisons and the waning of intellectual solidarity with the penal-welfarist project, the mature field that has developed since the 1990s, has been largely engaged with understanding the punitive turn associated with the rise of mass incarceration.

The intellectual tool kit forged in the 1970s, and showcased by Garland's (1990) *Punishment and Modern Society* was directed towards the task of describing and explaining the punitive turn in general (which includes the resumption of regular executions in the USA during the 1990s) and mass imprisonment in particular. The first wave of such research, represented in Table I.2, concentrated on characterizing mass incarceration and explaining its rise. Mass imprisonment seemed a dramatic shift from the version of penal modernism accepted by the punishment and society scholars during the 1970s on two dimensions; the quantum shift in scale, identified by Zimring and Hawkins (1991), and the shift from prison as a tool of individualization to a tool of categoric or class control (Feeley and Simon, 1992; Garland, 2001). Others would point to the qualitative dimensions of the new incarceration practices, the loss of internal programming in favour of warehousing prisoners (Simon, 2007) and their commitment to degrading gestures (Whitman, 2003) and the racializing effects of mass imprisonment (especially in the USA) (Tonry, 1996; Wacquant, 2000; Western, 2006).

The development of mass incarceration was explained with reference to political, economic and cultural developments. In terms of politics, mass imprisonment seemed to be a crucial source of legitimacy for a state battered by the failures of welfarism and the globalization of the economy (Scheingold, 1992; Savelsberg, 1994; Garland 2001; Gottschalk, 2006; Simon, 2007). This political crisis was seen by others as part of the larger restructuring of political economy associated with the rise of neo-liberalism, with mass imprisonment as a new way to manage the poor in a context of neo-liberal restructuring of the state (Beckett and Western, 2000; Wacquant, 2009). A third approach emphasized a sense of cultural anxiety, perhaps generated by both political and economic change, creating the conditions for new penal expression of social morality (Tyler and Boeckman, 1997; Simon, 2000; Pratt, 2007). More recent work has continued all these themes while shifting the inquiry toward both comparisons across countries (Cavadino and Dignan, 2006; Tonry, 2007) and sub-national units such as the states of the USA (Greenberg and West, 2001; Barker, 2006; Lynch, 2009).

Around the problem of mass imprisonment, other punishment and society scholarship has looked at different modes of punishment. One area which has continued to receive a great deal of attention by punishment and

Table I.2. Mass incarceration as a subject of punishment and society literature

Zimring, Franklin and Hawkins, Gordon	*The Scale of Imprisonment*	1991
Scheingold, Stuart	*The Politics of Street Crime: Criminal Process and Cultural Obession*	1992
Savelsberg, Joachim	'Knowledge, domination, and criminal punishment', *American Journal of Sociology* 99: 911	1994
Tonry Michael	*Malign Neglect: Race, Crime, and Punishment in America.*	1996
Tyler, Tom and Boeckman, Robert	'Three strikes and you are out, but why? The psychology of public support for punishing rule breakers', *Law and Society Review*, 31: 237–65	1997
Beckett, Katherine	*Making Crime Pay: Law and Order in Contemporary American Politics*	1999
Caplow, Theodore and Simon, Jonathan	'Understanding prison policy and population trends', *Crime and Justice*, 26: 63–120	1999
Garland, David (editor)	'Mass imprisonment', Special Issue, *Punishment & Society* 3(1)	2000
Greenberg, David and West, Valerie	'State prison populations and their growth, 1971–1991', *Criminology*, 39: 615–53	2001
Garland, David	*The Culture of Control: Crime and Social Order in a Contemporary Society*	2001
Sarat, Austin	*When the State Kills: Capital Punishment and the American Condition.*	2002
Zimring, Franklin, Hawkins, Gordon and Kamin, Sam	*Democracy and Punishment: Three Strikes and You're Out in California*	2003
Whitman, James	*Harsh Justice: Criminal Policy and the Widening Divide between America and Europe*	2003
Cavadino, Michael and Dignan, James	*Penal Systems: A Comparative Approach London*	2006
Gottschalk, Marie	*The Prison and the Gallows: The Politics of Mass Incarceration in America*	2006
Western, Bruce	*Punishment and Inequality*	2006
Pratt, John	*Penal Populism*	2007
Gilmore, Ruth	*Golden Gulag: Prisons, Surplus, Crisis, and Opposition in Globalizing California*	2007
Simon, Jonathan	*Governing through Crime*	2007
Wacquant, Loic	*Punishing the Poor: The Neoliberal Governance of Insecurity*	2009

society scholars is capital punishment which remains a symbolic focus of contestation even as it has virtually ceased to count in the quantitative measure of punishment (Sarat, 2002; Zimring, 2003; Garland, 2010). Another is the continuing transformations of community sanctions that emerged during the era of penal welfarism, but which have survived and proliferated as an adjunct to mass incarceration (Simon, 1993; Lynch, 1998; Petersilia, 2003) sometimes with the aid of new high technology surveillance (Jones 2000; Nellis, 2009).

ORGANIZATION OF THE BOOK

Even a field as relatively young as punishment and society is already too complicated to be mapped in any precise sense within the confines of a single book, even a weighty handbook. What we have sought to identify here are main lines of inquiry out of which the field developed and along which much research in the area develops. The present handbook is intended to supplement not to replace the important monographic efforts at synthesizing theoretical and empirical work in punishment and society that continue to emerge along with multi-authored thematic volumes. Nor is our goal to provide a comprehensive synthesis of research in the field as reflected in journals like *Punishment & Society*, *Theoretical Criminology*, *Criminology*, *The British Journal of Criminology* or *Law & Society Review*. The chapters here instead aim to give the reader an intense introduction to the most productive theoretical tools and topical areas of empirical research as we see the punishment and society field today. That our view is partial should be obvious and there are quite a number of other 'tool-kits' and topic areas that could be justly included. The chapters should be read as guides to relatively safe and productive 'routes' in what remains a mountainous and unpredictable intellectual landscape.

Part I: punishment and social theory

One of the strengths of punishment and society scholarship is how often a broad range of theoretical tools are used with sensitivity to their discursive origins (and limits) but with a pragmatic willingness to create a mixed toolbox appropriate to the particular topic addressed. The chapters in Part I cover the major lines of social theory that have informed most punishment and society scholarship. As noted above, the formation of the field in the 1970s drew on neo-Marxist and neo-Durkheimian ideas along with the post-structuralism now associated with Foucault. Garland in *Punishment and Modern Society* included chapters on all three, as well as chapters on Max Weber and Norbert Elias. Since then the work of Pierre Bourdieu and cultural theory have also been drawn on by punishment and society scholars. This section is organized around avenues of approach or, as we have taken to calling them 'tool-kits' rather than particular social theorists themselves in order to enhance the value for readers wanting to continue the pragmatic tradition of mixing and matching. This is by no means comprehensive, but the chapters reflect on the most frequently used and productive approaches including 'social solidarity' (Durkheim); 'political economy' (Marxisms); 'technologies of power' (Foucault, and Melossi and Pavarini); 'civilising process' (Elias); 'culture'; 'risk' (Douglas, Beck and others); and the 'penal field' (Bourdieu).

Part II: mass imprisonment and its consequences

Although the rapid growth and transformations in imprisonment was not the main stimulus for the formation of the punishment and society field, it has very much set its research agenda over the last 20 years. This section takes up a number of topic inquiries that unfold from the problems posed by mass imprisonment including: inequality; gender; politics; social psychology; and democracy.

Part III: modes of punishment

The punishment and society field is grounded in a concern with actual forms and methods of punishment and the changing configurations of power and meaning in which they are deployed. This section takes up the major forms of punishment operating in contemporary society: the prison; capital punishment; re-entry and community corrections; youth justice; restorative justice: monetary penalties.

Part IV: new contexts

Looking beyond mass incarceration, this section seeks to describe new developments around which new work in punishment and society seems to be coalescing: human rights; migration; conflict and reconciliation; and security and terrorism.

CONCLUSION

We began by trying to give voice to our sense that punishment and society was maturing into a significant intellectual field of its own at the intersection of the social sciences and humanities as well as professions like law and public policy. That such a vision involves a degree of retrospection, by way of establishing a context is perhaps inevitable. We do consider that this recent past will continue to be a useful guide to the upcoming future and of at least some help to those joining the field now in navigating from where we find ourselves today. In conclusion, by contrast, we want to turn towards the future and to some thoughts on where the plate tectonics of this field may lead it. One very current concern is that the twin developments which seem to have formed this field, the delegitimation of penal-welfarism in the 1970s, and the build-up of mass incarceration since the 1980s, seem poised to yield to a third, the threat of descent into degrading and inhuman punishment, and the corresponding call to our conscience of dignity.

Mass incarceration, especially in the USA where it has taken root earliest and most profoundly, has enjoyed widespread legitimacy in the eyes of legislators and large sections of the public despite its visibly unbalanced racialized application and great economic costs, based on the premise that it makes communities safer without subjecting prisoners to cruel and unusual, or degrading and inhuman, punishment. 'Humane containment', as the practice of incapacitative segregation has sometimes been known (or 'warehousing as it has come more colloquially to be termed) has been assumed by many, including some who should have known better, to be compatible with basic constitutional guarantees. Or, we might more cynically suggest, the risk that it might turn out not to be so humane or lacking in cruelty after all, has been one that many politicians and voters, have been prepared to take for the sake of the presumed gains in their security, not least because it is generally visited upon people other than ourselves or those whom we know. These premises have been reinforced by a number of features of the penal field itself associated with mass incarceration, including the exclusion of researchers, journalists, and independent health professionals from the new mass incarceration prisons (Wacquant, 2002). It was also sheltered, in the USA, by Supreme Court doctrines and Congressional legislation aimed at reducing the ability of federal courts to intervene in prisons to protect constitutional rights.

Today there are signs that mass incarceration is losing its legitimacy on both sides of these assumptions. 'Supermax' prisons,[7] very high security institutions, exhibiting a tendency to rely on total lockdown isolation to control prisoners, were widely adopted by American states starting 20 years ago as a crucial supplement to mass incarceration strategies of 'supersizing' overall prison populations while at the same time reducing internal sources of legitimacy in their day-to-day management. Today these institutions are under increasing attack for their psychological effects on prisoners when used for sustained periods and for the lack of due process in assignment of prisoners to such prisons (Gawande, 2009). In California, the state with the largest prison system in the USA, and the state which led the charge into mass incarceration more than 30 years ago, litigation over health care has exposed a humanitarian crisis as prisons never designed to provide for the predictable medical needs of their inmates have been operated at nearly 200 per cent of design capacity for more than a decade (Simon, 2012). In a decision upheld by the US Supreme Court, a special three judge court condemned the inhuman treatment accorded to prisoners as cruel and unusual punishment and explicitly rejected the claim that reducing the prison population would endanger public safety in California (*Brown* v. *Plata,* 2011). Faced with billions of dollars in court ordered reforms of prison conditions, and an unprecedented order to reduce its overall population by 30,000 prisoners,

California has abruptly adopted policies designed to permanently alter the flow of new prisoners (although without the politically far more challenging work of reforming the basic sentencing laws).

In the UK, after more than a decade of expanding prison populations and changes in the administration of incarceration that have at least partly echoed some features of American mass incarceration, there are also growing signs that the project has reached its limits and can be pushed back. The UK's turn toward escalating imprisonment took a decisive upward turn under the last Conservative government in the early 1990s. The mantra articulated in 1993 by then Home Secretary Michael Howard was that 'Prison works'. The 'New' Labour governments (1997–2010) successfully out-flanked the Conservatives for much of their extended period in office in an embrace of an only slightly more nuanced rhetoric: 'tough on crime, tough on the causes of crime'. At the time of writing (October 2011) the current UK government, a coalition of Conservative and Liberal Democrat ministers, has given mixed signals but these have included a distinct lack of enthusiasm on the part of the Ministry of Justice for continuing to rely on expanding incarceration (although early signs of a consensus to reduce imprisonment have slackened with the waning of the new government's traditional 'honeymoon'). In Scotland, which a generation ago had even more punitive policies than England and older more degrading prisons, the Scottish National Party has made its rejection of over-reliance on incarceration a significant element in their vision of a distinctly Scottish public policy. In both the USA and the UK, it appears that concern about government excess (in respect of the erosion of traditional civil liberties and constitutional protections) in the name of the 'war on terror' (see Lazarus, Goold and Goss, Chapter 22, this volume) has rebounded to stimulate a growing challenge to the penal policies of the domestic war on crime.

If the legitimacy of mass incarceration in its heartlands of the USA and the UK is being undermined by recognition of its inhuman and degrading potentials, a more positive but complementary trend is the influence of human rights norms on the penal imagination, especially in Europe, South Africa and Australia. In Europe most clearly, these human rights norms have formed an important counter force to penal populism and resulting pressure for mass incarceration. The European Convention on Human Rights, and the organs created to realize its objectives, including the European Court of Human Rights, the Committee for the Prevention of Torture, and the Committee of Ministers of the Council of Europe have produced a significant body of law aimed at preventing prison conditions from becoming degrading and inhuman. These laws, while lacking in strong enforcement power, have undeniably forced governments and penal administrations to scrutinize their penal practices and to dialogue in the language of evidence based criminology, public health, and human rights to defend their records. This sets limits to the growth of prison populations not evident in the heyday of mass incarceration, and may be beginning to generate its own penal imaginary, one anchored in a vision of dignity rather than fear (van Zyl Smit and Snacken, 2009).

We think the spectre of degradation and the promise of dignity offer an exceptional opportunity for punishment and society scholarship to broaden and to become part of new policies and politics aimed at restoring balance and legitimacy to a penal field transformed by mass incarceration and penal populism (Loader and Sparks, 2010). As it does so we suspect the scholarship itself will change again. We expect quantitative research, long an important but minority strain in punishment and society work (Western, 2006; Wacquant, 2010) to become yet more important. Mass incarceration has produced social facts on the level of demography, and these require quantitative tools to gain purchase on and theorize. At the same time, we expect normative scholarship, especially philosophy, jurisprudence, and political theory, long an important influence on punishment and society (von Hirsch, 1976; Duff, 2001) to become more central as one of the key theoretical axes for punishment and society work. In this we expect humanities scholarship drawing from literature, rhetoric, and history to be an important component (Smith, 2008; Brown, 2009). We also expect the new scholarship to be more comparative (or perhaps we should say, more self-consciously and fully comparative) than it has been (Nelken, 2010) as societies struggle to replace the excesses of mass incarceration and balance the tensions of human rights and penal populism. We certainly expect the centre of gravity of such scholarship to shift away from its overwhelming historical preoccupation with the USA and other Anglophone countries and with Western Europe as more diverse voices from Asia, Africa and Latin America extend, re-shape and re-define the field (Agozino, 2004; Jefferson, 2005; Hamai and Ellis, 2008; Miyazawa, 2008; Adorno et al., 2009).

Perhaps these final reflections will seem unduly optimistic in the face of the often grim and intractable realities that punishment and society scholarship has been called upon to document and to theorize in the last several decades. We make no apologies for adopting a hopeful orientation towards the future, even in the face of the seemingly inexorable weight of the historical record. The forms of work that we wish to see and to encourage will not rest content with the mere recording of endless problems for all the dismal prospects that we survey when we consider our field. We expect (perhaps indeed we may go so far as to say that we insist upon this) emergent work to address the worlds of legal and political theory more vigorously and more consistently, as some of the best of it has already done. We hope to encourage more frequent and more mutually informed conversations across the boundaries between those who consider themselves to be mainly engaged in the work of empirical discovery and those whose concerns encompass the normative dimensions of the penal realm. Punishment and society as field of inquiry deals in matters of the most grave public interest, and it is bound to seek to address them in as responsible a manner as it can. The forms of work exemplified in this volume stand at the intersection of a range of traditional disciplines – history, sociology, social psychology, law, politics – as we have sought to explain. But since the power to punish still stands among the weightiest capacities of states in respect of citizens (and aliens), and since its consequences for all concerned can be so fateful, it is every citizen's business, whether or not they regard themselves as specialists in some part of it. In this respect it is not only the intersection between disciplines that should concern us but also that between scholarship and the more troubling dimensions of contemporary public life.

NOTES

1 Any doubts we may have entertained in no way reflected on the people or organization with whom we were working. We had great confidence in SAGE to produce a quality volume and especially in Caroline Porter's acute reading of the complex discursive field of journals, monographs, and edited volumes addressing the penal field in English today.

2 In the earlier version of this discussion Collins characterized the three sociological traditions in question as the 'conflict', 'ritual solidarity' and 'micro-interactionist' perspectives. He later (1994) concluded that there were four principal sociological traditions rather than three, adding the rational choice/utilitarian perspective as a distinct body of thought.

3 In the USA, the sociologist Erving Goffman (1961) produced an important book about total institutions that described the prison alongside institutions like mental asylums and the military and which had considerable influence on criminology and studies of mental health. Only during the 1970s would it come to seem also like a book about punishment and society.

4 In the sense of systematic, empirical, and rational inquiry.

5 That did not stop much of the work from being highly insightful about the nature of contemporary penal practices, but kept this field largely self identified with the penal-welfarist practice they studied.

6 For Melossi, Marxism itself was being reworked and re-vitalized at that time by the influence of social history and a cross fertilization from new translations of Max Weber's work (pers. comm. with Melossi).

7 For accounts of the rise of 'Supermax' prisons see inter alia King (1999), Davis (2001), Mears and Watson (2006) and Reiter (2012). For accounts of the social-psychological effects of confinement at such depth see Haney (2003) and Shalev (2008, 2009).

REFERENCES

Adorno, Sergio et al. (2009) National Institute of Science and Technology 'Violence, democracy and public security' Annual Activity Report, 2009, Sao Paolo, Brazil http://issuu.com/nevusp/docs/inct-violence-activity-report-2009.

Agozino, Biko (2004) 'Imperialism, crime and criminology: towards the decolonisation of criminology', *Crime, Law & Social Change: An Interdisciplinary Journal*, 41(4): 343–58.

Allen, Francis (1981) *The Decline of the Rehabilitative Ideal*. New Haven, CT: Yale University Press.

Altheide, David (1992) 'Gonzo justice', *Symbolic Interaction*, 51(1): 69–86.

American Friends Service Committee (1971) *Struggle for Justice: Crime and Punishment in America*. New York: Farrar Straus & Giroux.

Barker, Vanessa (2006) 'The politics of punishing: building a state governance theory of american imprisonment variation', *Punishment & Society*, 8(1): 5–33.

Beaumont, Gustave de and Tocqueville, Alexis de (1833 [1970]) *On the Penitentiary System in the United States and Its Application in France*, trans. Francis Lieber. New York: Augustus M. Kelley.

Beckett, Katherine (1999) *Making Crime Pay: Law and Order in Contemporary American Politics*. New York: Oxford University Press.

Beckett, Katherine and Western, Bruce (2001) 'Governing social marginality: welfare, incarceration, and the transformation of state policy', *Punishment and Society*, 3: 43–59.

Benton, Ted (1977) *Philosophical Foundations of the Three Sociologies*. London: Routledge & Kegan Paul.

Bosworth, Mary (1999) *Engendering Resistance: Agency and Power in Women's Prisons*. Aldershot: Ashgate.

Bosworth, Mary and Flavin, Jean (eds) (2007) *Race, Gender, and Punishment: From Colonialism to the War on Terror*. Piscataway, NJ: Rutgers University Press.

Brown, Michelle (2009) *The Culture of Punishment: Prison, Society and Spectacle*. New York: New York University Press.

Caplow, Theodore and Simon, Jonathan (1999) 'Understanding prison policy and population trends', *Crime and Justice*, 26: 63–120.

Carlen, Pat (1976) *Magistrates' Justice*. London: Martin Robertson.

Carlen, Pat (1983) *Women's Imprisonment: A Study in Social Control*. London: Routledge and Kegan Paul.

Carlen, Pat and Worrall, Anne (eds) (1987) *Gender, Crime and Justice*. Buckingham: Open University Press.

Cavadino, Michael and Dignan, James (2006) *Penal Systems: A Comparative Approach*. London: Polity.

Chambliss, William (1974) 'Toward a political economy of crime', *Theory and Society*, 2(1): 149–70.

Clemmer, Donald (1940) *The Prison Community*. New York: Holt, Rinehart and Winston.

Collins, Randall (1985) *Three Sociological Traditions*. New York: Oxford University Press.

Collins, Randall (1994) *Four Sociological Traditions*. New York: Oxford University Press.

Collins, Randall (2004) *Interaction Ritual Chains*. Princeton, NJ: Princeton University Press.

Cotterrell, Roger (1999) *Emile Durkheim: Law in a Moral Domain*. Edinburgh: Edinburgh University Press.

Davis, Angela (2001) 'Race, gender and prison history: from the convict lease system to the supermax prison', in D. Sabo, T.A. Kupers and W. J. London (eds) *Prison Masculinities*. Philadelphia, PA: Temple University Press.

Douglas, Mary (1966) *Purity and Danger*. London: Routledge and Kegan Paul.

Dreyfus, Hubert L. and Rabinow, Paul (1982) *Michel Foucault: Beyond Structuralism and Hermeneutics*. Chicago: University of Chicago Press.

Duff, Antony (1986) *Trials and Punishments*. Cambridge: Cambridge University Press.

Duff, Antony (2001) *Punishment, Communication and Community*. Oxford: Oxford University Press.

Durkheim, Emile (1893 [1997]) *The Division of Labor in Society*, trans. Lewis A. Coser. New York: Free Press.

Durkheim, Emile (1900) 'Two laws of penal evolution'. Reproduced as Chapter 4 in S. Lukes and A. Scull (eds) (1983) *Durkheim and the Law*. London: Martin Robertson.

Erikson, Kai (1966) *Wayward Puritans: a Study in the Sociology of Deviance*. New York: John Wiley and Sons.

Feeley, Malcolm and Edward Rubin (1998) *Judicial Policy Making and the Modern State: How the*

Courts Reformed America's Prisons. Cambridge: Cambridge University Press.

Feinberg, J. (1984) *The Moral Limits of the Criminal Law. Vol. 1, Harm to Others*. New York: Oxford University Press.

Foucault, Michel (1977) *Discipline and Punish: The Birth of the Prison*, trans. Alan Sheridan. New York: Pantheon.

Garfinkel, Harold (1956) 'Conditions of successful degradation ceremonies', *American Journal of Sociology*, 61(5): 420–4.

Garland, David (1990) *Punishment & Modern Society*. Oxford: Clarendon Press.

Garland, David (1999) 'Editorial: punishment and society today', *Punishment & Society*, 1(1): 5–10.

Garland, David (2001) *The Culture of Control: Crime and Social Order in a Contemporary Society*. Chicago: University of Chicago Press.

Garland, David (2006) 'Concepts of culture in the sociology of punishment', *Theoretical Criminology*, 10(4): 419–47.

Garland, David (2010) *Peculiar Institution: America's Death Penalty in an Age of Abolition*. Cambridge, MA: Harvard University Press.

Garland, David and Young, Peter (eds) (1983) *The Power to Punish*. London: Heinemann.

Gawande, Atul (2009) 'Annals of human rights: hell hole, the United States holds tens of thousands of inmates in long-term solitary confinement. Is this torture?', *The New Yorker*, 30 March. Available at: http://www.newyorker.com/reporting/2009/03/30/090330fa_fact_gawande

Giddens, Anthony (1984) *The Constitution of Society*. Cambridge: Polity Press.

Gilmore, Ruth W. (2007) *Golden Gulag: Prisons, Surplus, Crisis, and Opposition in Globalizing California*. Berkeley, CA: University of California Press.

Goffman, Erving (1961) *Asylums: Essays on the Social Situation of Mental Patients and Other Inmates*. Garden City, NY: Doubleday & Co.

Gottschalk, Marie (2006) *The Prison and the Gallows: The Politics of Mass Incarceration in America*. Cambridge: Cambridge University Press.

Greenberg, David and West, Valerie (2001) 'State prison populations and their growth, 1971–1991', Criminology 39: 615–53.

Hamai, Koichi and Ellis, Tom (2008) '*Genbatsuka*: growing penal populism and the changing role of public prosecutors in Japan?', *Japanese Journal of Sociological Criminology*, 33: 67–91.

Haney, Craig (2003) 'Mental health issues in long-term solitary and "supermax" confinement', *Crime & Delinquency*, 49(1): 124–56.

Hannah-Moffat, Kelly, (2001) *Punishment in Disguise*. Toronto: University of Toronto Press.

Ignatieff, Michael (1978) *A Just Measure of Pain: The Penitentiary in the Industrial Revolution, 1750–1850*. London: Macmillan.

Ignatieff, Michael (1981) 'State, civil society, and total institutions: a critique of recent social histories of punishment', *Crime & Justice*, 3: 153–92.

Irwin, John (1980) *Prisons in Turmoil*. Boston, MA: Little Brown & Co.

Irwin, John (2004) *The Warehouse Prison: Disposal of the New Dangerous Class*. New York: Oxford University Press.

Jackson, Jonathan and Sunshine, Jason (2007) 'Public confidence in policing: a neo-Durkheimian perspective', *British Journal of Criminology*, 47(2): 214–33.

Jacobs, James B. (1977) *Stateville: The Penitentiary in Mass Society*. Chicago: University of Chicago Press.

Jefferson, Andrew (2005) 'Reforming Nigerian prisons: rebuilding a "deviant" state', *British Journal of Criminology*, 45: 487–503.

Jewkes, Yvonne (2007) *Handbook on Prisons*. Cullompton: Willan Publishing.

Jones, Richard (2000) 'Digital rule: punishment, control and technology', *Punishment & Society*, 2(1): 5–22.

Kadish, Sanford (1960) 'Advocate and the expert – counsel in the peno-correctional process', *Minnesota Law Review*, 45: 803–42.

King, Roy (1999) 'The rise and rise of supermax: an American solution in search of a problem?', *Punishment & Society* 1(2): 163–86.

Lappi-Seppälä, Tapio (2008) 'Trust, welfare, and political culture. explaining national differences in penal severity', in M. Tonry (ed.), *Crime and Justice: A Review of Research vol 37*. Chicago: University of Chicago Press.

Lynch, Mona (1998) 'Waste managers? The new penology, crime fighting, and parole agent identity', *Law and Society Review*, 32: 839–69.

Lynch, Mona (2009) *Sunbelt Justice: Arizona and the Transformation of American Punishment*. Stanford, CA: Stanford University Press.

Mathiesen, Thomas (1974) *The Politics of Abolition*. New York: John Wiley.

Mauer, Marc and King, Ryan (2007) *Uneven Justice: State Rates of Incarceration by Race and Ethnicity*. Washington, DC: The Sentencing Project.

Mears, Daniel and Watson, Jamie (2006) 'Towards a fair and balanced assessment of Supermax prisons', *Justice Quarterly*, 23(2): 232–69.

Melossi, Dario and Pavarini, Massimo (1981) *The Prison and the Factory*. Totowa, NJ: Barnes and Noble.

Miyazawa, Setsuo (2008) 'Politics and punishment in the PRC and Japan', *Punishment & Society*, 10(1): 5–8.

Nelken, David (2010) *Comparative Criminal Justice: Making Sense of Difference*. London: SAGE Publications.

Nellis, Mike (2009) '24/7/365 mobility, locatability and the satellite tracking of offenders', in K.F. Aas, H.O. Gundhus and H.M. Lomell (eds), *Technologies of Insecurity: The surveillance of everyday life*. London: Routledge-Cavendish. pp. 105–24.

Petersilia, Joan (2003) *When Prisoners Come Home: Parole and Prisoner Reentry*. New York: Oxford University Press.

Platt, Anthony (1969) *The Child Savers: the Invention of Delinquency*. Chicago: University of Chicago Press.

Pratt, John (2002) *Punishment and Civilization*. London: SAGE Publications.

Pratt, John (2007) *Penal Populism*. London: Routledge.

Reiter, Keramet (2012) 'The Most Destructive Alternative: The Origins, Functions, Control and Ethical Implications of Super Max Prison, 19760–2010', Dissertation, Jurisprudence & Social Policy, UC Berkeley.

Rothman, David J. (1972) *The Discovery of the Asylum: Social Order and Disorder in the New Republic*. Boston, MA: Little Brown & Co.

Rothman, David J. (1980) *Conscience and Convenience: The Asylum and its Alternatives in the Progressive Era*. Boston, MA: Little, Brown & Co.

Rusche, Georg and Kirchheimer, Otto (1939 [1995]) *Punishment and Social Structure*. New Brunswick, NJ: Trans, action Publishers.

Sarat, Austin (2002) *When the State Kills: Capital Punishment and the American Condition*. Princeton, NJ: Princeton University Press.

Savelsberg, Joachim (1994) 'Knowledge, domination, and criminal punishment', *American Journal of Sociology*, 99: 911.

Scheff, Thomas (1990) *Microsociology: Discourse, Emotion and Social Structure*. Chicago: University of Chicago Press.

Scheingold, Stuart (1992) *The Politics of Street Crime: Criminal Process and Cultural Obession*. Philadelphia, PA: Temple University Press.

Shalev, Sharon (2008) *A Sourcebook on Solitary Confinement*. London: Mannheim Centre for Criminology, London School of Economics and Political Science.

Shalev, Sharon (2009) *Supermax: Controlling Risk Through Solitary Confinement*. Cullompton: Willan.

Simon, Jonathan (2000) 'Fear and loathing in late modernity: reflections on the cultural sources of mass imprisonment in the United States', *Punishment & Society*, 3(1): 21–33.

Simon, Jonathan (2007) *Governing through Crime: How the War on Crime Transformed American Democracy and Created a Culture of Fear*. New York: Oxford University Press.

Simon, Jonathan (2011) 'Editorial: mass incarceration on trial', *Punishment & Society*, 13: 251–55.

Simon, Jonathan (2012) *Mass Incarceration on Trial: America's Courts and the Future of Imprisonment*. New York: New Press, forthcoming.

Smith, Philip (2008) *Punishment and Culture*. Chicago: University of Chicago Press.

Sparks, Richard (2010) 'David Garland', in K. Hayward, S. Maruna and J. Mooney (eds), *Fifty Key Thinkers in Criminology*. London: Routledge.

Spierenburg, Pieter (1984) *The Spectacle of Suffering and the Evolution of Repression*. Cambridge: Cambridge University Press.

Spitzer, Steven (1975) 'Toward a Marxian theory of deviance', *Social Problems*, 22: 638–51.

Thompson, E. P. (1975) *Whigs and Hunters: The Origins of the Black Act*. New York: Pantheon.

Tonry, Michael (1996) *Malign Neglect: Race, Crime, and Punishment in America*. New York: Oxford University Press.

Tyler, Tom and Boeckman, Robert (1997) 'Three strikes and you are out, but why? The psychology of public support for punishing rule breakers', *Law and Society Review*, 31: 237–65.

Van Zyl Smit, Dirk and Snacken, Sonia (2009) *Principles of European Prison Law and Policy*. Oxford: Oxford University Press.

Von Hirsch, Andrew (1976) *Doing Justice: The Choice of Punishments*. New York: Hill and Wang.

Wacquant, Loïc (2001) 'Deadly symbiosis: when ghetto and prison meet and mesh', *Punishment & Society*, 3(1): 95–133.

Wacquant, Loïc (2002) 'The curious eclipse of prison ethnography in the age of mass incarceration', *Ethnography*, 3(4): 371–397. (Special issue on 'In and Out of the Belly of the Beast: Dissecting the Prison'.)

Wacquant, Loïc (2008) *Urban Outcasts: A Comparative Sociology of Advanced Marginality*. London: Polity Press.

Wacquant, Loïc (2009) *Punishing the Poor: The Neoliberal Governance of Insecurity*. London: Polity.

Western, Bruce (2006) *Punishment and Inequality in America*. New York: Russell Sage Foundation.

Zimring, Franklin (2010) 'The scale of imprisonment in the United States: twentieth century patterns and twenty-first century prospects', *Journal of Criminal Law and Criminology*, 100(3): 1225–46.

Zimring, Franklin and Hawkins, Gordon (1991) *The Scale of Imprisonment*. Chicago: University of Chicago Press.

Zimring, Franklin, Hawkins, Gordon and Kamin, Sam (2003) *Democracy and Punishment: Three Strikes and You're Out in California*. New York: Oxford University Press.

PART I

Punishment and Social Theory

1

Punishment and Social Solidarity

David Garland

Punishment and society scholarship takes as its analytic starting point Emile Durkheim's theory of punishment and social solidarity. It does so not because Durkheim was the first to write about criminal punishment in a sociological vein – Montesquieu (1762) and de Tocqueville (1833) initiated that project long before – but because Durkheim's argument best encapsulates the fundamentals of the sociology of punishment and its distinctive approach to penal phenomena.

Durkheim's foundational claim – that the punishment of offenders functions not to control crime but to enhance solidarity – is by now a familiar one. In the standard textbook formulation, it can appear somewhat glib and simplistic, but properly understood, Durkheim's theory contains within it many of the conceptual issues with which the sociology of punishment has subsequently been concerned. I will set out the argument's details in a moment, but first I want to explain why Durkheim's analytical approach to punishment has served as a model for so much of the scholarship in this field.

Durkheim's innovative move, his foundational contribution to this field, is to separate the sociological analysis of punishment from the conventional assumption that penal laws and penal practices are determined by the exigencies of crime-control-and to make this separation sharp and explicit.[1] In Durkheim's view, punishment must be understood as a *moral* institution, shaped by collective values and social relationships rather than an *instrumental* one shaped by the demands of crime-control. No doubt criminal punishments do produce crime control effects – this is, after all, their manifest function.[2] But Durkheim insists that punishment works poorly as an instrumental technique, rarely succeeding in deterring crime or reforming offenders. The 'true function' of penal sanctions, whatever the perceptions of the public or the intentions of the authorities, is the ritualized re-affirmation of collective values and the reinforcement of group solidarity.[3]

Durkheim insists on the following counter-intuitive claims: that punishment's chief functions are not penal but social; that penal sanctions generally fail to inhibit offenders though they succeed in other, less apparent, respects; that the messages punishment communicates are aimed not at criminals or potential criminals but at law-abiding citizens; and that the forms and extent of punishment are determined not by crime control exigencies but by the social values, social reactions, and social organization of the group on whose behalf punishments are imposed.

Taken together, these ideas have supplied the foundations for punishment and society scholarship. Proof of this is that these basic ideas, or something very like them, find expression in all the theoretical traditions that operate within this scholarly field, even when the theories are otherwise at odds with Durkheim's own. Marxists, Foucauldians, Eliasians, Weberians, Meadians, Bourdieuians (and of course, neo-Durkheimians) all utilize these same ideational tropes. And they all begin from the axiom that punishment's forms, functions and transformations are to be understood not (just) as an instrumental response to crime but as a constitutive aspect of larger social processes. To make this observation is not to suggest that these theories are all, in some respect Durkheimian. It is to say that they are all, in some respect, *sociological,* and that Durkheim was the first fully to articulate the fundamentals of a sociological approach to this phenomenon.

Punishment is a social process with social causes and social effects, not – or not merely – a reaction to crime. The sociological insight here is that neither individual crimes nor aggregate crime rates determine the kind or extent of penal activity that a society undertakes. It is not 'crime' that dictates penal laws, penal sentences, and penal policy decisions but rather the ways in which crime is socially perceived and problematized, together with the political and administrative decisions to which these reactions give rise. Moreover, the whole apparatus of criminal justice through which this 'reaction' is administered – the specific forms of policing and prosecution, trial and punishment, condemnation and sanctioning, penal institutions and regime management, and so on – is shaped by social conventions and historical developments rather than by the contours of criminality. So even when penal systems adapt to changing patterns of crime and problems of crime control – and they certainly do adapt to some degree – they always do so in ways that are mediated by social norms, cultural conventions, economic resources, institutional dynamics and political forces.

Durkheim's axiom is now so thoroughly taken-for-granted in the punishment and society literature that it is sometimes rendered in exaggerated versions. One occasionally reads, for instance, that punishment and penal policy are 'unrelated to' or 'utterly disconnected' from crime and crime rates. But this is an overstatement that transforms a sociological insight into an untenable claim. The phenomenon in question is, after all, the punishment of criminal offences and offenders, and the latter (offences and offenders) always operate in some relation to the former (punishment), and always exert some pressure on punishment's character and extent.[4]

Durkheim urged us to think of punishment as 'relatively autonomous' of crime (to use a concept drawn from a different tradition). He taught us to think of it as being shaped by other forces, performing other functions, and never reducible to instrumental crime control. But he did not for a moment think that punishment and crime were unrelated. On the contrary, he defined crime as deviant conduct that violates social norms to the extent of being labeled 'crime' and punished with a criminal sanction. Crimes, for Durkheim, are wrongful acts that violate deeply felt social norms and provoke punitive reactions. There is no punishment without crime, just as there is no crime without punishment. The relationship is mutually constitutive.

DURKHEIM ON PUNISHMENT AND SOLIDARITY

Durkheim argued that the punishment of crime is, archetypally, a group phenomenon of great intensity; propelled by irrational, emotive forces which sweep up group members in a passion of moral outrage. These collective reactions are channeled into ceremonial rituals of condemnation and punishment in ways that reaffirm group solidarities and restore the sacred moral order violated by the offender.

The criminal act violates sentiments and emotions that are deeply ingrained in most members of the group. It *offends* them. It shocks their 'healthy' (i.e. well-socialized) consciences. This violation of group norms calls forth strong psychological reactions, even among those not directly involved. It provokes outrage, anger, indignation, and a passionate desire for vengeance.

Although Durkheim does not say so, it should be clear that this group reaction is itself an expression of an already-existing solidarity. Without such solidarity, reacting to crime would be the sole concern of the directly affected victim. But in strongly solidaristic groups, criminal acts provoke collective reactions. They do so for one of two reasons, depending on the character of the group and the prevailing type of solidarity. (I will have more to say on types of solidarity below.)

Either, there is a collective worship for sacred values such that all true believers are outraged any time these values are violated. (The model here is the religious sect reacting to a sacrilegious act.) Or else, the collective reaction occurs because social bonds link group members together directly, producing a conductivity that transmits the victim's pain to like-minded, sympathetic others.[5] The sympathy these others feel connects them to the victim, and to each other, and draws them into a collective response. (The model here is a modern, liberal society characterized by the humanitarian sentiments that Adam Smith [1976] described.) Either way, it is the prior existence of group solidarity that ensures the victim does not suffer alone, nor are victims left to pursue their own private efforts at retaliation. The prior existence of group solidarity is what provides the basis for a collective will to punish.

The solidaristic reaction to crime is, according to Durkheim, a passionate one, whichever kind of solidarity is involved. He tells us that 'passion is the soul of punishment' and that 'vengeance', albeit a somewhat altruistic, other-regarding vengeance, is the primary motivation that drives the punishment of offenders. Durkheim acknowledges that utilitarian purposes inform modern penal practice but he considers these instrumental efforts to be superimposed upon a core reality that is quite without calculative reason. The essence of punishment, he claims, is irrational, unthinking emotion driven by outrage at the violation of sacred values or else by sympathy for fellow individuals and their suffering.[6]

That this is a *collective* response – that it is felt by each member of the group and not just by the victim – means, as we have seen, that the punitive response is grounded in solidarity, in shared values, in sympathy for the victim, in social bonds.[7] And, when these passionate responses are channeled into collective rituals of condemnation and punishment, the outcome, according to Durkheim, is the creation of a feedback loop that functions to strengthen the group and the solidarity that binds it together.

In these respects, punishment rituals are just one instance of a more general phenomenon of solidarity-producing processes, the general form of which was set out by Durkheim (1976) in his work on *Elementary Forms of the Religious Life*. In all such rituals, the group comes together to mark an important social event – a birth, a death, a marriage, a harvest, a religious feast, a holiday, a military victory, a newly appointed leader – and, in the process, to celebrate itself. Solidarity – group belonging – regenerates itself through focused group activity. The very process of coming together in this way promotes the mutual reinforcement of common beliefs, the submerging of individuality in group interaction, and the shared excitement that Durkheim calls 'collective effervescence'. The paradigmatic case is the religious ceremony, but the same processes are at work in penal rituals too.[8]

In the public processes of prosecution, trial and punishment, members of the public are brought together – as witnesses, jurors, viewers in the public gallery, or merely as onlookers who participate via news reports and conversation – in collective rituals that function to uphold legal rules, sanction lawbreakers, affirm shared social values and celebrate the authority of the group. All of this, according to Durkheim, creates a psychological excitement that increases the 'vitality' of shared values and the sense of group-belonging experienced by participating individuals and onlookers. The result is that the challenge to group norms implicit in the offender's crime is transformed into a process for the reinforcement of group solidarity. This, and not the control of crime, is for Durkheim, the real function of punishment. And this is what transforms an 'irrational', purposeless process into a socially useful one:

> Although it proceeds from a quite mechanical reaction, from movements which are passionate and in great part non-reflective, [punishment] does play a useful role. Only this role is not where we ordinarily look for it. It does not serve, or else serves only quite secondarily, in correcting the culpable or in intimidating possible followers. From this point of view, its efficacy is justly doubtful and, in any case, quite mediocre. Its true function is to maintain social cohesion intact, while maintaining all its vitality in the common conscience. (Durkheim, 1933: 108)

We can thus trace a circular process of solidarity's functional reinforcement, triggered by crimes and concluded by punishments. An initial solidarity of shared social values, cherished by well-socialized group members, is violated by a criminal act. This prompts wide-spread, visceral demands for vengeance which lead, in turn, to organized rituals of condemnation and punishment. The sanctions that result function not merely as retribution or deterrence but also as symbols of disapprobation to be read and appreciated by onlookers. These rituals of disapprobation – which uphold shared values in the process of condemning their violation – have a number of social effects. They re-instate the law and the imperative of normative compliance. They reassure law-abiding individuals that group values may not be violated with impunity. They uphold group authority. They bring together individuals in a process that generates collective effervescence, reinforces collective representations, and enlivens mutual involvement.[9] All of which, Durkheim insists, has the overall effect of reinforcing social solidarity.

TYPES OF SOLIDARITY

Solidarity is the name that Durkheim gives to 'the bonds that unite men one with another' and with the groups of which they form a part.[10] He took these bonds to be a fundamental condition for collective life and his whole research agenda revolved around the problem of how solidarity – which is to say, group-belonging and the order and cohesion that it brings to the group – could be achieved in modern, pluralistic, societies characterized by individualism and moral diversity.

Durkheim argued that the character and extent of social solidarity changes over time as societies become more developed and the division of labor becomes more complex. This change in the nature of solidarity leads, in turn, to changes in the character and extent of punishment. The key distinction he makes here is between 'mechanical' solidarity, which he takes to be a characteristic of simple societies, and 'organic' solidarity, characteristic of advanced societies.

Durkheim defined mechanical solidarity as a religiously charged 'solidarity of likeness' rooted in shared values (a 'conscience commune') and reinforced by collective rituals of the whole society. Where mechanical solidarity prevails, group boundaries are sharply defined, group members identify strongly with the group, and neither deviance nor individuality are easily tolerated.

Societies in which this form of solidarity predominates are typically simple, segmented forms of social organization with a rudimentary division of labor.

The kinship groups that form the basic units or building blocks of 'mechanical solidarity' societies are each quite similar to one another and are relatively self-sufficient. These segmental units form a larger society not via interdependence, functional integration, and networks of overlapping interests but by means of a common set of values and the common observance of shared rites and taboos. Societies of this type offer limited scope for individuality, insist on rigid conformity to group norms, and impose harsh punishments on anyone who deviates from the fixed orthodoxies of tradition.

In contrast, 'organic solidarity' is described by Durkheim (1933) as the 'solidarity of unlikeness'. This is an oddly oxymoronic phrase, but what he means by it is that social cohesion in modern society is not a matter of shared values (differentiation and individuation having rendered the moral world fragmentary and diverse) but is created instead by means of crisscrossing social bonds and economic reciprocities. These more complex networks of interaction – generated by a complex division of labor and the imperatives of interdependence and cooperation that it sets up – operate to bind together the differentiated groups and individuated persons that form the basic units of modern societies. It is in this way, according to Durkheim's first theorization, that the coming of an extended division of labor – in which occupational tasks are specialized, social roles are differentiated, moral experience is pluralistic, and persons are increasingly individuated – creates a more complex but still cohesive form of social organization.

This idea of a 'solidarity of unlikeness' based on interdependence does not stand up to much scrutiny. Interdependence can promote cooperation but it can also result in rivalry and conflict (Lockwood, 1992: 7). We need not feel positively towards those upon whom we depend – masters and slaves, colonies and empires, employers and employees are all examples of conflictual interdependence. And we may seek to subordinate or dispossess those whose resources we need, rather than work with them cooperatively and harmoniously.

In later work, Durkheim revised his initial understanding, coming to view 'organic solidarity' not as an automatic product of interdependencies but as the contingent result of a new kind of shared value – the cult of the individual. The distinctive feature of this specific value was that it could be embraced as a common ideal by people who otherwise lead very different lives and believe very different things. Together with the local, group-specific, solidarity-building work of professional associations, occupational groups, and 'intermediate associations', it is this morality of 'individualism' (and its insistence on the sacredness of human life and the autonomy and dignity of individual persons) that allows a unifying solidarity to co-exist with diversity and variation.[11]

On this revised account, the organic solidarity of modern societies revolves – like the earlier mechanical solidarity – around the sharing of values, and is upheld by institutions of socialization and ritual reinforcement that inculcate these values and sanction their violation.[12] However, unlike the rigid conformity demanded by ancient religious codes and traditional folkways, the morality of individualism embraces diversity, difference and disagreement and imposes somewhat looser controls on individual conduct. The 'conscience collective' of modern societies ceases to be a pervasive, all-powerful force demanding conformity in every sphere of life and comes to operate as a guardian of the values of individualism around which moral and social diversity can flourish. Because of these more tolerant, more diverse, more individualistic aspects of organic solidarity, Durkheim argued that modern, individuated societies would punish less harshly and be more oriented towards restitution.[13]

PUNISHMENT AND THE TYPES OF SOLIDARITY

According to Durkheim, simple societies resort to draconian penal measures because of the intensity of the conscience collective that prevails in these societies. Their characteristic social morality is itself severe, rigid, and demanding, being wholly religious in form and representing all of its rules as transcendental laws, authorized by the Gods. Within such societies, individuals are imbued with a sense of the sacred character of social rules, and conformity to the rules is regarded as a sacred duty to be rigidly policed. Since social solidarity here rests mainly on the sharing of collective beliefs and participation in collective rituals – there being no extended division of labor capable of generating what Lockwood (1992) calls 'system integration' – Durkheim suggests that the very existence of society itself depends upon the strict enforcement of these norms. In these circumstances any violation of the common conscience becomes a grave threat to social cohesion and a serious affront to deeply held beliefs. This provokes an intense reaction that manifests itself as harsh, repressive punishment. The vehemence of penal law in early societies is thus the product of a religious moral order that can brook no opposition for fear of avenging gods and social collapse.

In contrast, the collective sentiments which exist in more advanced societies are less demanding and occupy a less central place in social life. Modern organic societies are characterized by moral diversity and the interdependence of cooperating groups and individuated persons, each of whom is to some extent differentiated and unique. The collective beliefs that these individuals share do not have the character of intensive religious prohibitions. Instead, common beliefs emphasize the value of the individual and the correlative virtues of freedom, human dignity, reason, tolerance and diversity. Such values, being collective and rooted in the foundations of social life, are, like their religious predecessors, accorded a kind of transcendental status and are deeply inscribed in the consciences of individuals. But the tone and quality of these sentiments are markedly different from the stern, religiously sanctioned beliefs of earlier times. By its very nature, this new moral faith invites reflection and rational consideration in ethical matters. It no longer represents itself as the imperious will of gods who must be unquestioningly obeyed. As a consequence, social morality has a different psychological resonance, a different place in the psychic structure, and gives rise to a more moderate reaction whenever its tenets are violated. The more lenient, more individualized, more liberty-focused, and more critically contested punishments of modern societies are thus a reflection of the type of solidarity that underlies them.[14]

CRITICISMS, MODIFICATIONS AND FURTHER RESEARCH

Durkheim sets out two kinds of arguments about punishment and solidarity. First, an argument about how punishment functions to promote social solidarity. (He insists that this functional process is unchanging. Punishment may be harsh or lenient, expressing mechanical solidarity or organic solidarity: in each case its role is to reinforce social solidarity.) Second, an argument about the historical development of penal law and about punishment's changing forms, intensity, and institutions. (He insists that punishment continues to express and reinforce social solidarity, but changes its form and extent as social solidarity changes its character.) Both of these arguments have been challenged or refined in the years since Durkheim wrote and we ought to take note of these developments.

One question that arises concerns the concept of 'collective' as it applies to punishment (recall Durkheim's references to 'collective reactions' and 'collective rituals'). In modern societies we generally think of punishment as a *state* function, a governmental activity, licensed by state law and carried out by state officials. Is that not somewhat distinct from the *social* activity that Durkheim describes?

Durkheim insists that modern state punishment is generally rooted in the passions of individual members of the public, whose outraged reactions to crime provide the elemental force and energy that drive the state response. He acknowledges that state officials channel and direct these passions, routinizing them in institutional processes, and in doing so, calibrating and moderating their expression. But he insists that, except where political authorities are completely out of touch with popular sentiment, state punishment will generally express and convey the social sentiments of group members. So although much writing about penality proceeds as if there were only two parties involved – the state and the offender; the punishing and the punished – Durkheim insists that there is always a crucial third element: the members of the public whose outraged sentiments supply both motivating energy and social support.

Durkheim takes this relationship between public sentiment and state punishment to be largely unproblematic. He makes this assumption because his theory of the (well-functioning) state assumes that governments embody, express and crystalize the norms and collective representations that characterize the group as a whole. He acknowledges exceptions to this pattern – for instance where governments become absolutist and impose an imperious sovereignty upon their subjects (Durkheim, 1983). But he insists that such situations are 'pathological' and temporary and that the normal relationship is one where state officials give concrete form and legal expression to the norms and sentiments that group members hold dear.[15]

Unsurprisingly, many scholars have been skeptical of this aspect of Durkheim's argument and questions about the relationship between public sentiment and state punishment have become a major topic of research. Where democratic nations are concerned, it is generally assumed that there must be some correspondence between penal law and majority social sentiment, but scholars dispute the precise extent and nature of this correspondence. Recent work on the phenomenon of 'penal populism' has brought this question to the fore.[16]

A second aspect of Durkheim's work that has been frequently challenged is his account of the 'evolution' of punishment. Durkheim argued – in *The Division of Labour*, and again in the later essay, 'Two laws of penal evolution' – that there had been a long-term shift from the harsh, repressive, bodily sanctions that he took to be characteristic of pre-modern societies to more lenient, carceral or restitutive measures that he believed dominated in modernity.

It has been persuasively demonstrated that Durkheim was too quick to generalize from the few pre-modern societies about which he was informed to 'simple' societies in general. In contrast to Durkheim's description of ancient cruelties and primitive repression, the ethnographic data gathered by 20th century anthropologists suggests that pre-modern societies often relied more on restitutive measures and compensation than upon harsh punitive repression (Sheleff, 1975; Spitzer, 1975).

More recently, it has also become apparent that penality in many modern societies bears little resemblance to the relatively lenient, restitutive regimes that Durkheim imagined. Durkheim (1983) did allow that modern societies with a developed division of labor might 'revert' to penal repression, but he reasoned that this would occur only where the state was an absolutist one and governing authorities assumed a religious character that brooked no opposition and cared little for the lives of their subjects. But the emergence of mass imprisonment in the USA in recent decades has made it clear that liberal, democratic societies are quite capable of imposing harsh, repressive punishment – despite, or even because of, their commitment to the cult of the individual. Why did Durkheim assume otherwise?

Durkheim's assumption was that societies that embraced the morality of individualism would tend to limit the extent of punishment because of their concern for the offender's individuality and personal worth. According to Durkheim, the cult of the individual is the central moral commitment of modern societies and, as a consequence, the valuation of individual life – even the life of a criminal – would work to stay the hand of vengeance and limit the degree of punishment imposed.

It appears, however, that Durkheim failed to reckon with the tendency of some societies to divide individuals into victims and offenders, 'us' and 'them', and to anathematize those who appear to endanger others. So the cult of the individual can become the cult of 'deserving' individuals, just as the culture of life can become the culture of 'innocent' life. Despite the categorical overlap between 'offenders' and 'victims' – many offenders have themselves been victimized, some victims have criminal records – there is often a tendency to classify offenders as dangerous and undeserving, especially if they belong to low-status social groups, while thinking of victims as fellow citizens with whom we identify. Once established, divisive frames of this kind can operate as justifications for punishing without mercy or restraint.

How could Durkheim have missed this? As is often the case in his sociology, he failed to acknowledge the extent to which a society might be divided not just between the group and the individual but also between conflicting groups. In other words, he failed to recognize the extent to which societies are characterized by schism as well as by solidarity (Lockwood, 1992). Where society is divided in this respect – between racial groups, or status groups, or religious groups – the generalized respect for persons dictated by the morality of individualism may, in practice, be limited by group boundaries. In such circumstances, individualism becomes compatible with a disregard for those out-group individuals who have shown themselves unworthy of dominant group membership and protection.

Durkheim wrote as if solidarity is a property of societies and varies only in *type*. Empirical evidence suggests that solidarity also varies in *extent* and that, in divided societies, may operate *within* but not *between* specific social groups. One might say, for example, that modern America exhibits an organic solidarity built upon a cult of the free individual (and the free market). America also contains social groups – ethnic, racial, religious and regional groupings, for example – that exhibit a more 'mechanical' solidarity of shared values and hostility to outsiders. As a consequence, the solidarity born of individualism extends only so far. Some groups – most notably poor, urban, African Americans – are regarded by other groups with suspicion rather than solidarity. And certain individuals – sex offenders, violent criminals, recidivists – are excluded from the solidarities of citizenship and accorded an outcast, outlaw status. A 'criminology of the other' traces this dividing line and a massive infrastructure of imprisonment segregates those who fall on its wrong side (Garland, 2001).[17] That group solidarity can co-exist with social division, inclusion with exclusion, is a feature of social organization about which Durkheim has little to say.

Other criticisms do not seek to challenge Durkheim's claims, so much as moderate them.[18] So, where Durkheim writes as if the punishment of crime *always* succeeds in enhancing solidarity, subsequent work has shown that the actual effects of any particular punishment – whether on group solidarity, or crime control, or anything else – are necessarily subject to contingency and variation. Penal measures come in a variety of different forms, are mobilized in different contexts, and address themselves to different audiences. Not all punishments are heavily ritualized or symbolically rich. Modern criminal justice systems use behind-the-scenes guilty pleas in the vast majority of cases.

The processing and punishment of misdemeanors more often resembles a conveyor belt than a religious ritual. Plea bargains and police court justice involve little in the way of symbolic communication and the 'negotiated justice' they administer is more a matter of costs and convenience than of moral communication and social solidarity.

Like any other rituals, penal rituals can backfire. The prosecution may present a flawed case, or lack credibility, or behave unethically. The sentence may seem too lenient or too severe. Penal officials may allow a prisoner to escape or botch the execution of a condemned man. In such cases punishment's intended message will likely be spoiled (Smith 2008). Similarly, certain cases will provoke hostile reactions from sections of the on-looking public – because the offender is sympathetic, because the criminal law is controversial, because the authorities are not trusted, and so on. In these instances, the solidarity effect will be limited in its reach, impacting certain groups and not others.

Even where rituals of punishment are properly staged and performed, the solidarity effect is not guaranteed. Durkheim's account assumes that in most cases the onlookers are unified in their values and in their reaction to the case. He assumes they share a common conscience, a horror of the crime, and a collective reaction of passionate outrage. But in pluralistic societies, with their characteristic social divisions and moral fragmentation, this unitary effect is rarer than Durkheim supposed. Today's liberal democracies exhibit considerable disagreement about what should constitute a crime and what counts as an appropriate punishment. Some sections of the American public support harsh prison sentences for drug use. Others feel that drug problems ought not to be dealt with by the criminal law. Many Americans view capital punishment as the appropriate penalty for murder. Others regard the death penalty as wicked in itself. In such circumstances, crime and punishment may reinforce social divisions rather than reaffirm social unity.

Commentators have also observed punishment does not *create* solidarity merely expresses and reinforces a solidarity that already exists and which has been produced by other, more positive social processes – such as kin-group socialization, education, group activities, religious rituals, political rituals and so on.[19] To employ Durkheim's favorite society-as-a-body metaphor, each round of punishment is a form of health-giving exercise that produces a flow of blood and oxygen to the connective tissues of the social body. But even when one considers punishment's solidarity effect in that more limited way, one should acknowledge that this effect will always depend on the performative success of the penal ritual, the receptivity of the onlookers, and the nature of the social relations and group dynamics that characterize the group in question.[20]

Other commentators have granted that punishment can promote solidarity but have raised questions about the nature of the solidarity produced by these means, contrasting it with more positive forms of group-belonging and attachment. So, for example, George Herbert Mead (1918) pointed out that the solidarity-effect Durkheim describes is a particularly aggressive, exclusionary one. It evokes an upsurge of outraged, vengeful emotions that view the offender with an unforgiving resentment while embracing the group and its norms with unquestioning acceptance. It is a solidarity of 'us' against 'them'. *We*, the upstanding citizens unreservedly condemn *them*, the public enemies. Instead of reasoned disagreement, constructive problem-solving, and the re-integration of errant individuals – the approach preferred by Mead and his fellow Progressives – this reaction to crime reproduces intolerance and moral absolutism.[21]

Durkheim views punishment-fueled solidarity as a functional phenomenon that promotes social health, but in Mead's view the social psychology of punitive reaction is too conformist, too absolutist, and too uncritical to contribute to social wellbeing in a liberal democracy. According to Mead, to stage criminal punishment as the condemnation and exclusion of heretics is to accept, without demur, the criminal law and whatever punishments the authorities impose. Fundamentalist zeal and submission to authority lack the critical engagement that Mead saw as essential to post-Enlightenment liberal morality, and he argued that a progressive criminal justice system ought not to promote them.[22] In his sociological interpretation of the criminal trial as a 'degradation ceremony,' Harold Garfinkel (1956) developed a similar critique of Durkheim, though without elaborating so explicitly. As Garfinkel points out, the anthematization and degradation of the offender in the criminal trial is purchased at the cost of abandoning liberal doubt and embracing moral absolutes.

This critique leads to another criticism of the solidarity produced by retributive penal processes. In Durkheim's account, the offending individual is generally excluded from the process of solidaristic bonding that his punishment promotes.[23] The solidarity that results from punishment is not one that includes the person punished. Rather, the offending individual is the sacrifice that makes solidarity possible for others. His anathematization, punishment and exclusion is a sacrificial process in which he is cast out in order that others may be brought together.

With his characteristic moral severity, Durkheim simply assumes that criminal offenders are beyond redemption (because they suffer from pathological defects or have never been properly socialized) and that efforts to correct or redeem them are largely a waste of time. This may or may not be the case – it surely depends on the individual offender and the circumstances – but it is notable that Durkheim's attitude is echoed in the practices of modern societies where remarkably few efforts are made to re-integrate offenders.[24]

It is therefore quite in keeping with Durkheim's account that virtually all of the rituals associated with criminal justice in contemporary western societies are condemnatory, exclusionary ones. In the institutional practices of modern state punishment, the rituals of excommunication, stigmatization, and expulsion of the offender are elaborate and well-established. These exclusionary rituals are nowhere balanced by compensating rites of re-inclusion, rehabilitation or re-entry.

The near-total absence of such rituals suggests that criminal offenders, qua offenders, are largely excluded from the scope of social solidarity. The widespread use of long-term imprisonment certainly points in this direction, as do the various collateral consequences that nowadays attach to conviction and imprisonment.[25] When the population of prisoners and former prisoners reaches into the tens of millions, and is heavily patterned by race and class, as is true of the USA today, then this mass exclusion takes on the character of a major social division.[26] Western (2007) captures the deeply divisive quality of today's penal processes when he characterizes the effects of imprisonment as a diminution of citizenship – a curtailment of the solidarity that connects individuals to the nation.

Let me add a final word about Durkheim's punishment-and-solidarity argument and its continuing importance in punishment and society scholarship. Durkheim studied punishment and penal institutions not because these were of compelling interest to him but because they provided a way to get at the deeper question of solidarity, which lay at the core of his sociological concerns. But despite this – or perhaps because of it – he succeeded to a remarkable degree in illuminating the phenomenon of punishment and its social and psychological characteristics. In addition to his insights about punishment's ritual ceremonies, symbolic meanings, and functional effects, his analyses have opened up a rich seam of inquiry about the expressive qualities of punishment, about its emotional aspects, about its connection to reciprocity and group formation, and about its operation as a theme in culture and mythology. A quick perusal of the leading works in the contemporary sociology and philosophy of punishment reveals that these Durkheimian insights now form the basis for some of the most advanced work in this field.[27] Indeed, as Richard Sparks has remarked Emile Durkheim has recently come to displace Immanuel Kant as the intellectual force behind contemporary theories of retributivist and expressive punishment (pers. comm.).

BEYOND DURKHEIM: RETHINKING SOLIDARITY AND PUNISHMENT

Recent research on punishment and solidarity has taken some of these Durkheimian themes and developed them in a new way. Comparative studies of punishment and society have suggested that societies exhibiting lower levels of punishment are those that also exhibit higher levels of solidarity; and those with higher levels of punishment have lower levels of solidarity (Greenberg, 1999; Lappi-Seppala, 2008; Pratt, 2008; see also Cavadino and Dignan, 2006). Related research finds a similar (inverse) correlation between levels of punishment and levels of welfare provision (Beckett and Western, 2001; Downes and Hansen, 2006). As David Greenberg puts it, 'differences among the European countries in prison populations can be substantially explained as a consequence of the degree to which the country embraces an incorporative stance towards its less well-off citizens'(1999: 89).[28]

At first sight, these findings might seem to be at odds with Durkheim's theory. Did not Durkheim suggest that punishment generates solidarity? And would not one expect that more punishment would be associated with more solidarity, rather than the opposite?

It seems to me that these findings – provisional as they are – are not, in fact, anomalous with respect to Durkheim's theory. It also seems to me that the concept of solidarity operationalized by this new research is somewhat under-theorized and ought to be more carefully thought through. In the remainder of this chapter I will discuss this new research and connect it more directly to Durkheim's thought and to recent work in the theory of solidarity.

On a certain reading, Durkheim's account might lead one to suppose there is a positive correlation between solidarity and punishment. The formula might go as follows: more intense solidarity leads to more intense punishment, and the imposition of punishment, in turn, gives rise to more solidarity. However, empirically, at least in developed societies, we find the opposite: an *inverse* correlation between the two. Where there is more solidarity there is less punishment, and where there is more punishment, there is less solidarity. This is an important insight, and one that has emerged as the sociology of punishment has become more comparative and more interested in researching why some nations punish more than others.

To unravel this apparent anomaly, we have to take care to distinguish, as Durkheim did, between types of solidarity. In particular, we have to distinguish between intra-group solidarity – a mechanical solidarity that Durkheim associates with intense punishment – and inter-group solidarity – an organic solidarity that Durkheim links to lower rates of punishment and more restitutive sanctions.

Somewhat surprisingly, the comparative penological literature generally neglects to distinguish between types of solidarity. Solidarity is taken to be a quality of well-integrated societies, associated with other attributes such as low levels of inequality and high levels of welfare provision. This, it seems to me, is a misleading simplification. To understand what is at stake, we have to return to Durkheim's distinction between types of solidarity and introduce these long-established categories into this newly developing research agenda.

We can get at this issue more clearly if we look at the causal processes at work rather than just the correlations they produce.

The existing comparative research tends to be large scale correlation analyses but its findings are given support by studies using other methods and pitched at a more micro-level of analysis. Thus research on jury decisions in American death penalty cases finds that punishment is harsher where sentencing authorities are white and perpetrators are black, the effect being increased where victims are white (Baldus and Woodward, 2003; Garland, 2010). Sentencing a person to death –a discretionary decision left to the subjective judgment of lay jurors – involves a determination that he or she is irredeemable and lacks human worth. Such a judgment is more probable where there is no sympathy or fellow-feeling connecting the sentencer and the person sentenced. So, is this a case of punishment being enabled by a lack of solidarity? Not quite.

Notice that there are actually two kinds of solidarity involved in this encounter. There is the presence of an intra-group solidarity linking the (white) jury with the (white) victim, and the absence of an inter-group solidarity linking the (white) jury and the (black) offender. In other words – and in keeping with Durkheim's thesis – the presence of tightly knit groups exhibiting mechanical solidarity leads to intense punishment where a group member is wronged by an outsider. And this outcome is made more likely by the absence of organic, inter-group solidarity encouraging fellow-feeling to extend across differentiated groups and individuals. In other words, it is not 'solidarity' as such that varies inversely with punishment, but rather organic solidarity – the solidarity of individualism, intra-group cooperation and a tolerance of diversity.[29]

We find the same thing when we examine research on punishment and welfare. Comparative studies have found that levels of punishment, measured by imprisonment rates, vary inversely with welfare provision measured by income support for the indigent (Beckett and Western, 2001; Downes and Hansen, 2006). Commentary on these findings has generally assumed that the explanation of this effect lies in the greater levels of solidarity exhibited by strong welfare states. Once again, though, we need to be more precise. Societies in which welfare state institutions are well-developed and levels of welfare provision are high are not usually characterized by strong social ties and mechanical solidarity. Instead, they exhibit weak ties, high levels of individualism, and an organic solidarity that builds bridges between groups and provides the intra-group coalitions necessary for a strong welfare state. Again, what this suggests is that it is not 'solidarity' as such, but organic solidarity that inversely co-varies with punishment. Generous welfare and lenient state punishment may not be a product of collectivism and strong solidarity but may instead be produced by societies in which state institutions successfully bridge diverse social groups characterized by weaker social ties and stronger individualism. A little conceptual refinement here will allow us to better understand the mechanisms involved.

SOLIDARITY IN MODERN SOCIOLOGY

Durkheim's basic distinction between a tight-knit solidarity of shared substantive beliefs and a looser, crisscrossing network of ties within the framework of liberal individualism remains at the core of contemporary sociological work on solidarity – though it is sometimes understood as a continuum of weaker and stronger ties rather than as two sharply distinguished types. But the modern literature has deepened our understanding of this rather elusive phenomenon and has developed some insights that go beyond what Durkheim had to say.

In studying solidarity in various group settings, sociologists have sometimes focused on sentiment – love, fellow-feeling, attachment – and sometimes on behavior – the proportion of an individual's time, energy and resources devoted to collective ends. (The first of these gets at the phenomenon but is difficult to measure, while the second is more easily measurable but it is only a proxy for the thing itself.[30]) They have also stressed – more than did Durkheim – that solidarity is always a matter of extent as well as type, and that different groups exhibit quite different degrees of cohesiveness. Solidarity, they point out, is a variable and some groups are more solidary than others.

Hechter (1988) describes this variable quality as 'groupness' and conceptualizes it as a group's variable capacity to affect its members conduct. The more solidary the group, the greater the influence it exerts over the behavior of its members. Thus families will tend to exhibit more solidarity than clubs and voluntary associations; just as nation-states will tend to be more solidaristic than transnational polities such as the European Union.

The causes of this 'groupness' are a matter of debate but it is generally assumed that groups form in order to provide social goods that cannot be individually obtained (security, shelter, love, sociability, etc.) and that dependence and control are two of the fundamental processes that sustain the group over time and deal with problems such as exit and free-riding. Solidarity will be greater where groups exert more control (including the internalized controls of socialization) and individuals are more dependent on the group for needed resources (including identity) that are otherwise unavailable.[31]

So, to use an example that Hechter (1988: 57) develops, solidarity was strong in the families of pre-industrial societies – whether measured by beliefs or by behavior – and is considerably weaker in most families today. Why? Because individual members depended on traditional households not just for security, sustenance and shelter but also for education, employment and general welfare; heads of households exerted a powerful set of controls; and the absence of alternative sources of support made exit costs high for disaffected family members. In modern welfare states, on the other hand, the availability of alternative forms of provision make it possible for spouses or children to quit the family, thereby reducing dependency and weakening control.[32] (Hechter's example reminds us that 'solidarity' need not be a warm, communitarian experience of fellowship and mutuality: for many individuals, the strong solidarity of the pre-industrial family was largely a matter of power, dependency, and subservience.)

Just as Durkheim insisted that 'organic' solidarity was not a diluted form of 'mechanical' solidarity but was instead a different kind of social bond, contemporary theorists deny that modern societies have moved from a strong to a weak solidarity. As Lindenberg puts it:

> [D]ue to technological developments in production and to increasing wealth, strong and weak solidarities have given way to a stronger (atomized) individualism with a wide-spread incidence of arms-length relationships ... Only as a reaction against this kind of individualism did we get a wide-spread development of weak solidarity and its embedding in flanking measures in policies of the state (including income policies). (1998: 106–7)

In modern, pluralistic societies, welfare states depend not on strong, in-group solidarity but instead upon the willingness of diverse groups to work with one another – a willingness that is facilitated where individuals simultaneously belong to many groups and are capable of bridging boundaries and sustaining coalitions.[33] As Lindenberg argues, 'When compared with weak solidarity, strong solidarity is bad for business between groups' (1998:106). Or as Mark Granovetter (2003: 307) explained, in a classic essay on the subject, 'weak ties, often denounced as generative of alienation ... are ... indispensable to individuals' opportunities and to their integration into communities; strong ties, breeding local cohesion, lead to overall fragmentation.'

Recent work by Berggren and Trägårdh (2006) on the Swedish welfare state makes the same point. Sweden's welfare state is not, they argue, the expression of an underlying collectivism nor of a strong solidarity.

Rather it is a social democratic form of organization adapted to a deeply entrenched individualism. The Swedish welfare state, they argue, establishes forms of social provision that secure individuals while relieving them of their local dependencies – upon other family members, upon local communities, upon employers or the labor market – by forming a nation-wide risk pool and ensuring transfers between members. The solidarity here is a weak but tenacious one that reproduces strongly independent individuals and effective cross-group coalitions. In Durkheim's terms, it is an organic solidarity that presupposes weak social ties at the level of specific groups and mobilizes collective (state) provision in the service of individual autonomy and choice. If Sweden's punishment rates are low (Pratt, 2008) it is not a consequence of a mechanical solidarity that tightly binds the Swedish people but rather of effective coalition-building between loosely formed groups for the benefit of individuals.

CONCLUSION

In revisiting Emile Durkheim's account of the relationship between punishment and solidarity I have sought to show the foundational character of Durkheim's argument for 'punishment and society' scholarship, and to restore to the theory some of its original power and subtlety – characteristics that are often lost when the theory is briefly reproduced in criminology textbooks and introductory courses.

I have argued that, in Durkheim's theory, the social processes of punishment, insofar as they are social, *presuppose* solidarity as well as *reinforce* it. I have also re-stated the important but much misunderstood distinction between 'mechanical' and 'organic' solidarity. As I explained, Durkheim's later work corrected his original (and erroneous) account of 'organic' solidarity as interdependence and developed, instead, a more satisfactory account based around the cult of the individual as an overarching moral framework. Within this capacious, flexible framework of moral individualism, the diverse 1 group codes of modern, liberal, pluralistic society can be fostered by intermediate associations and made to co-exist.

Thereafter I addressed the implications for Durkheim's theory of recent comparative work showing a correlation between low levels of punishment and high levels of solidarity. I argued that these empirical findings do not disconfirm Durkheim's thesis because the concept of 'solidarity' that these studies mobilize is, in fact, closer to Durkheim's account of organic solidarity than to the mechanical solidarity associated with harsh punishment.

Finally, I took up the question of the relationship between solidarity and welfare – a topic of relevance here because of the inverse correlation reported between levels of punishment and levels of welfare. I argued that strong welfare states ought not to be understood as an expression of strong solidarity in the 'mechanical' sense, but instead of weak solidarity, coalition-building between social groups, and the development of state institutions that function to enhance the autonomy of individuals and reduce their dependence on families and employers. Understood against that background, the empirical association of high levels of welfare provision with low levels of punishment is shown not just to be compatible with Durkheim's account but actually to be predicted by it.

NOTES

1 Durkheim argued, in *The Rules of Sociological Method*, that crime is a normal social fact rather than a pathological one. He used this argument to reinforce his unconventional account of the social functions of punishment: 'if crime is not pathological at all, the object of punishment cannot be to cure it' (1938: 73).

2 It was Robert Merton (1957: 61) who introduced the contrast between 'manifest' and 'latent'

functions, but the distinction is clearly present in Durkheim's work, albeit latently.

3 In modern society, vengeful passions often appear to have been displaced by utilitarian rationality. But Durkheim insists that 'the nature of a practice does not change because the conscious intentions of those who apply it are modified. It might, in truth, still play the same role as before, but without being perceived' (1933: 87).

4 It makes little sense, for example, to analyze late 20th-century American penal policy without bearing in mind the extraordinary levels of violent crime that characterized parts of that nation in the decades after 1960 , and the social, cultural and political consequences that flow from this. See Garland (2001) and Stuntz (2011).

5 These two kinds of solidarity are not entirely distinct. Sympathy for other individuals is most developed and extensive where there is a cult of the individual and the individual person is regarded as a sacred value. For a neo-Durheimian account of sympathy for the victim as the moral root of today's penal practices, see Boutelier (2000).

6 See Durkheim (1933) passim.

7 In cases where officials aren't involved, the extent of solidarity – as well as the nature of the crime and the outrage it provokes – will determine the scale of the collective response. Think of the primitive case of lynchings and "popular justice."

8 On interaction rituals, see Collins (2005) and Goffman (1982).

9 On the entertainment value of punishments, especially capital punishment, see Garland (2010).

10 Durkheim, 'Introduction a la sociologie de la famille' (1888) quoted in Lukes (1973: 139).

11 See Durkheim (1933) Preface to the second edition and Durkheim (1992). Durkheim elaborated further on his account of the kind of punishment characteristic of such societies. In 'Two laws of penal evolution' (1902) he argued that modern punishments tended to be less harsh, because the central group value is individualism, not God-worship; and group norms are understood to be socially created rather than God-given. The erring individual may be regarded as an object of sympathy, not just an enemy of God. This secular trend towards more lenient punishment – driven by changes in social solidarity – results in the fading of capital and corporal sanctions and their replacement by 'the deprivation of liberty and liberty alone' – i.e. the sanction of imprisonment that addresses itself to the modern values of liberty and individualism.

12 See Cotterell (1999) for a good discussion. Durkheim argued that intermediate associations (corporations) would encourage solidarity and the 'intellectual and moral homogeneity' which comes from the practice of the same occupation (Lukes, 1973: 540).

13 Durkheim tells us that most societies exhibit both kinds of solidarity, in varying proportions. In modern society, organic solidarity prevails – along with restitutive sanctions – but traces of mechanical solidarity persist too, and remain capable of generating more repressive punishments.

14 See Garland (1990: 37).

15 Durkheim notes that some penal laws work to uphold the authority of the state rather than the collective conscience of the people.

16 For various points in the debate see Garland (2001), Beckett (1999) and Pratt (2007). On the concept of penal populism see Garland (2009).

17 We no longer see 'them' as fellow citizens. When asked to do so people are much less punitive. Solidarity is local, intimate, specific. Hostility and distrust deal in stereotypes and abstractions – in the 'criminology of the other'.

18 See Garland (1990) for an overview.

19 See Garland (1990). Durkheim (1973) made some of these points himself, when discussing the creation of the teacher's authority in the classroom and its reinforcement through the punishment of student misconduct.

20 For empirical studies of this process see Erickson (1966), Hay (1975) and Garland (2010).

21 Durkheim made it clear that he objected to the kind of non-retributive correctionalism that Mead supported. As he wrote, 'theories which refuse to punishment any expiatory character appear as so many spirits subversive of social order' (Durkheim, 1933: 108).

22 There are indications in Durkheim (1973) that Durkheim himself sometimes embraced this more critical approach.

23 Interestingly, Durkheim (1973) allows a more integrative punishment in the context of the school classroom. The critique of much state punishment is that it abandons these solidarity concerns and brings about the exclusion and alienation of the offender. Those critics who press the state to introduce 'restorative justice' are really seeking to make punishment compatible with solidarity – a solidarity that includes the erring individual and not just the righteous onlookers.

24 See Maruna (2011). In the USA and elsewhere, there has recently been a renewed interest in what is now called 'prisoner re-entry' – the various efforts to improve the social integration of released convicts by means of housing, job, drug counseling, etc. One's impression however, is that this effort (minimal as it still is) is driven less by solidarity with execution-offenders than by a pragmatic effort at improved social control.

25 These may include felon disfranchisement; exclusion from public housing; barring from various occupations; and the continuing stigma of a criminal record.

26 On mass imprisonment, see Garland (2000).

27 See, for example, Duff (2003) on punishment as moral communication; Feinberg (1970) on expressive theories of punishment; Garland (1990, 2010) on punishment and emotion; Smith (2008) on punishment and culture; and Miller (1998) on the persistence of revenge.

28 Other studies have found an inverse association between punishment and equality, trust, and homogeneity: see Killias (1986); Greenberg (1999); Lappi-Seppala 2008; and Garland (2010).

29 In contrast, mechanical solidarity and punishment directly co-vary.

30 Welfare state effort, tax levels, transfers, etc. – which are often taken as a measure of solidarity – would be a behavioral measure. The problem is that these behaviors may indicate something other than solidarity itself – e.g. risk management.

31 A variation on this account derives from the work of Durkheim's nephew, Marcel Mauss (2000), who argued that social ties come about because individuals invest in other people (Lindenberg, 1998: 69). Gifts create obligations for return gifts, they set up reciprocities; they bind people into obligations to give and to get. Solidarity groups are 'sharing groups' in which individuals make sacrifices for the group and its other members (in the expectation that the group will, in turn, make sacrifices for the individual).

32 Hechter (1988); Lindenberg (1998).

33 Baldwin's book, *The Politics of Solidarity*, suggests that the process of group-formation and solidarity creation can be an emergent phenomenon shaped by the distribution of risks and the actuarial groupings that insurance mechanisms help create. This solidarity is not the expression of strong, pre-existing solidarity between intimates and group members but instead of calculations about common risks and about the costs and benefits of prospective mechanisms for managing these risks. It is the mobilization, in the political process, not of social classes but instead of actuarial groups that recognize their interests in particular insurance schemes or transfers. Group formation is a consequence not of relations to the means of production but of relations to the means of insurance.

REFERENCES

Baldus, D. and Woodward, G. (2003) 'Race discrimination and the death penalty: an empirical and legal overview', in J. Acker et al (eds), *America's Experiment with Capital Punishment.*

Beckett, Katherine (1999) *Making Crime Pay: Law and Order in Contemporary American Politics.* New York: Oxford University Press.

Beckett, Katherine and Western, Bruce (2001) 'Governing social marginality: welfare, incarceration, and the transformation of state policy', in D. Garland (ed.), *Mass Imprisonment: Social Causes and Consequences.* London: SAGE Publications. pp. 35–50.

Berggren, Henrik and Trägårdh, Lars (2006) *Är svensken människa? Gemenskap och oberoende i det moderna Sverige.* Stockholm: Norstedts.

Boutelier, Hans (2000) *Crime and Morality: The Significance of Criminal Justice in Post-Modern Culture.* London: Kluwer.

Cavadino, Michael and Dignan, Jim (2006) *Penal Systems: A Comparative Approach.* London: SAGE Publications.

Collins, Randall (2005) *Interaction Ritual Chains.* Princeton, NJ: Princeton University Press.

Cotterrell, Roger (1999) *Emile Durkheim: Law in a Moral Domain.* Edinburgh: Edinburgh University Press.

de Tocqueville, Alexis and de Beaumont, Gustave (1833) *On the Penitentiary System of the United States.* Philadelphia.

Downes, David (1988) *Contrasts in Tolerance: Post-war penal policy in the Netherlands and England and Wales.* Oxford: Oxford University Press.

Downes, David and Hansen, Kristine (2006) 'Welfare and punishment in comparative perspective', in S. Armstrong and L. McAra (eds), *Perspectives on Punishment.* Oxford: Oxford University Press. pp. 101–118.

Duff, Antony (2003) *Punishment, Communication and Community.* New York: Oxford University Press.

Durkheim, Emile (1933) *The Division of Labor in Society.* New York: Free Press.

Durkheim, Emile (1938) *The Rules of Sociological Method.* New York: Free Press.

Durkheim, Emile (1973) *Moral Education.* New York: Free Press.

Durkheim, Emile (1976) *The Elementary Forms of the Religious Life.* New York: Free Press.

Durkheim, Emile (1983) 'Two laws of penal evolution' in S. Lukes and A. Scull (eds), *Durkheim and the Law.* London: Martin Robertson. pp. 1–35.

Durkheim, Emile (1992) *Professional Ethics and Civic Morals.* London: Routledge.

Erickson, Kai (1966) *Wayward Puritans.* New York: Free Press.

Feinberg, Joel (1970) 'The expressive theory of punishment', in *Doing and Deserving: Essays in the Theory of Responsibility.* Princeton, NJ: Princeton University Press.

Garfinkel, Harold (1956) 'Conditions of successful degradation ceremonies', *American Journal of Sociology,* 61(5): 420–24.

Garland, David (1985) *Punishment and Welfare: A History of Penal Strategies*. Aldershot: Gower.

Garland, David (1990) *Punishment and Modern Society: A Study in Social Theory*. Oxford: Oxford University Press.

Garland, David (2001) *Mass Imprisonment*. London: SAGE.

Garland, David (2001) *The Culture of Control*. Oxford: Oxford University Press.

Garland, David (2009) 'A note on penal populism', *Japanese Journal of Sociological Criminology*, 33: 219–29.

Garland, David (2010) *Peculiar Institution: America's Death Penalty in an Age of Abolition*. Cambridge, MA: Harvard University Press.

Goffman, Erving (1982) *Interaction Rituals: Essays in Face-to-Face Behavior*. New York: Pantheon.

Granovetter, Mark (2003) 'The strength of weak ties', in M. Hechter and C. Horne (eds), *Theories of Social Order*. Stanford, CA: Stanford University Press. pp. 323–32.

Greenberg, David (1999) 'Punishment, division of Labor and social solidarity', in William S. Laufer and Freda Adler (eds), *The Criminology of Criminal Law*. New Brunswick, NJ: Transaction. pp. 283–362.

Hay, Douglas (1975) 'Property, authority and the criminal law', in Douglas Hay, Peter Linebaugh, and John G. Rule (eds), *Albion's Fatal Tree*. Harmondsworth: Penguin. pp. 17–63.

Hechter, Michael (1988) *Principles of Group Solidarity*. Berkeley, CA: University of California Press.

Killias, Martin (1986) 'Power concentration, legitimation crisis, and penal severity: a comparative perspective', *International Annals of Criminology*, 24: 181–211.

Lappi-Sepala, Tapio (2008) 'Trust, welfare and political culture: explaining differences in national penal policies', in M. Tonry (ed.), *Criminal Justice: An Annual Review of Research*. Vol 37. Chicago: University of Chicago Press. pp. 313–88.

Lindenberg, S. (1998) 'The Micro-foundations of Solidarity', in P. Doreian and T. Farar (eds), *The Problem of Solidarity*. Amsterdam: Gordon and Breach.

Lockwood, David (1992) *Solidarity and Schism: 'The Problem of Disorder' in Durkheimian and Marian Sociology*. Oxford: Oxford University Press.

Lukes, Steven (1973) *Emile Durkheim: His Life and Work*. London: Peregrine.

Maruna, Shadd (2011) 'Re-entry as a rite of passage', *Punishment & Society*, 13: 3–28.

Mauss, Marcel (2000) *The Gift: The Form and Reason for Exchange in Archaic Societies*. Norton: New York.

Mead, George Herbert (1918) 'The psychology of punitive justice'. in *American Journal of Sociology*, 23(5): 577–602.

Merton, Robert (1957) 'Social Theory and Social Structure', *The British Journal of Sociology*, 8(2): 106–20.

Miller, William (1998) 'Clint Eastwood and equity: popular culture's theory of revenge', in A. Sarat and T. Kearns (eds), *Law in the Domains of Culture*. Ann Arbor, MI: The University of Michigan Press. pp. 161–202.

Montesquieu, Baronde. (1762) *The Spirit of the Laws*. Edinburgh.

Pratt, John (2007) *Penal Populism*. London: Routledge.

Pratt, John (2008) 'Scandinavian Exceptionalism in an Age of Penal Excess', *The British Journal of Criminology*, 48(2): 119–37.

Sheleff, L.S. (1975) 'From restitutive law to repressive law: Durkheim's division of Labor revisited', *European Journal of Sociology*, 16: 16–45.

Smith, Adam (1976) *The Theory of Moral Sentiments*. Oxford: Oxford University Press.

Smith, Phillip (2008) *Punishment and Culture*. Chicago: University of Chicago Press.

Spitzer, S. (1975) 'Punishment and social organization: a study of Durkheim's theory of evolution', *Law & Society Review*, 9: 613–37.

Stuntz, William J. (2011) *The Collapse of American Criminal Justice*. Cambridge, MA: Harvard University Press.

Western, Bruce (2007) *Punishment and Inequality in America*. New York: Russell Sage.

2

Punishment and Political Economy

Alessandro De Giorgi

Since its origins in the first decades of the 19th century, and for most of the 20th century, 'criminology' has been the study of *crime* rather than the study of *punishment*: punishments, criminal policies, and strategies of social control were not the objects of criminological analysis, but rather 'tools' to govern the criminal question. The main objective of criminology, particularly in its positivist currents, was the scientific production of effective strategies for the government of deviance and criminality (Pasquino, 1980).

Between the late 1960s and the early 1970s, however, these epistemological boundaries were challenged by the emergence of radical perspectives on punishment and social control. The main target of this new critical approach was exactly the positivist paradigm that had dominated the field of criminological research since its very birth. The rejection of what David Matza famously defined as the 'correctional perspective' (1969: 15–40) concerned in the first place the theoretical and methodological tenets of positivist criminology – its presumed scientific neutrality, its assumption that social problems had objective causes that social scientists could discover through adequate methodologies, and its ambition to unveil objective truths about criminal behavior. Most importantly, the emerging 'new criminology' (Taylor et al., 1973) would question the political implications of the positivist approach – in particular, its emphasis on the elaboration of strategies that could effectively address the causes of deviance, correct criminals, and ideally eradicate crime itself.

The political context of the 1960s, with its radical critique of all 'repressive' institutions (family, university, asylum, prison), and the irruption of Marxism into the academic field, laid a fertile ground for the emergence of critical perspectives on social and penal control.[1] The forms of punishment, rather than the causes of crime, became the focus of the new criminological agenda. In particular the prison, the technology of punishment peculiar to modernity, became the object of critical inquiry. Several studies began to investigate the historical trajectory through which imprisonment had come to replace earlier forms of punishment and the reasons for its persistence in contemporary societies.

Looking beyond the rhetorical legitimation of the prison – the defense of society from crime in the name of 'public safety' – critical scholars began to reveal its latent functions.

A first direction of analysis focused on the role of penal systems in the history of capitalist societies. The new 'revisionist' histories of punishment that appeared between the late 1960s and the early 1980s deconstructed mainstream penal historiography, criticizing in particular its teleological bias – that is to say, its tendency to represent the history of punishment as an ongoing process of reform and as a linear advancement toward more humane sanctions. Against this 'reformist historiography' (Ignatieff, 1983: 76), characterized by a narrative of progress that obscured the role played by penal technologies in the consolidation of class power, revisionist historians attempted to re-politicize the history of punishment, reconstructing it from the point of view of the privileged targets of social control: the working classes, the poor, the dispossessed (Platt, 1969; Foucault, 1977; Ignatieff, 1978; Melossi and Pavarini, 1981).

A second body of research emerged toward the end of the 1970s and focused on the transformations of penality in contemporary late-capitalist social formations (Quinney, 1980). In this context, changes in penal practices – and specifically variations in the severity of punishment, as measured by rates of imprisonment – were analyzed against the background of the transformation of class relations in advanced capitalist societies (Spitzer, 1975; Quinney, 1980; Adamson, 1984). Thus, while revisionist historians of punishment unveiled the historical connections between the invention of the penitentiary and the birth of a capitalist system of production based on the extensive exploitation of wage labor, neo-Marxist critics of contemporary penal politics examined the persistence of that same connection in late-capitalist societies, analyzing the relationship between current penal forms and capitalist labor markets (for a review of this literature, see Chiricos and DeLone, 1992; Melossi, 1998; De Giorgi, 2006: 19–39).

Taken together, these two perspectives contend that penal politics plays a very different role than 'defending society' from crime: both the historical emergence of specific penal practices and their persistence in contemporary societies, are structurally linked to the dominant relations of production and to the hegemonic forms of work organization. In a society divided into classes, criminal law cannot reflect any 'general interest':

> The would-be theories of criminal law that derive the principles of penal policy from the interests of society as a whole are conscious or unconscious distortions of reality. Society as a whole does not exist, except in the fantasy of the jurists. In reality we are faced only with classes, with contradictory, conflicting interests. Every historically given system of penal policy bears the imprint of the class interests of that class which instigated it. (Pashukanis, 1978: 174)

Whether in the context of a structural critique of bourgeois legal ideologies (as in the work of Evgeny Pashukanis just quoted), of a cultural analysis of the role of moral panics in 'policing the crisis' of late-capitalist societies (Hall et al., 1978), or of a deconstruction of penal discourses as 'ideological state apparatuses' (Althusser, 1971), the ground had been set for a materialist critique of punishment as a tool of class control.

THE FOUNDATIONS OF THE POLITICAL ECONOMY OF PUNISHMENT

The sociological foundations of what would later become the political economy of punishment had already been laid down in the late 1930s by Georg Rusche and Otto Kirchheimer in the early pages of their classic *Punishment and Social Structure*:

> Every system of production tends to discover punishments which correspond to its productive relationships. It is thus necessary to investigate the origin and fate of penal systems, the use or avoidance of specific punishments, and the intensity of

> penal practices as they are determined by social forces, above all by economic and then fiscal forces. (1939 [2003]: 5)[2]

Rusche and Kirchheimer argued that a sociological understanding of the historical and contemporary transformations of penal systems should be informed by a structural analysis of the connections between penal technologies and transformations of the economy – in particular, the transition of modern societies from a pre-capitalist to a capitalist mode of production.

The birth of what Michel Foucault would later define as 'disciplinary' practices and institutions of confinement in place of the torturous 'spectacles of suffering' staged in the main squares of European cities until the 18th century (see Spierenburg, 1984), should thus be interpreted as a constitutive part of the broader shift toward a new system of production based on the 'complete separation between the workers and the ownership of the conditions for the realization of their labor' (Marx, 1867 [1976]: 874). Against the background of a new emerging class structure shaped by the relation between capital and wage labor, the political economy of proto-capitalist societies started to conceive the human body as a resource to be exploited in the process of production, rather than wasted in the symbolic rituals of corporal punishment:

> In fact the two processes – the accumulation of men and the accumulation of capital – cannot be separated; it would not have been possible to solve the problem of the accumulation of men without the growth of an apparatus of production capable of both sustaining them and using them; conversely, the techniques that made the cumulative multiplicity of men useful accelerated the accumulation of capital. (Foucault, 1991: 221)

Modern penal institutions played a decisive role in the consolidation of a process of capitalist production based on the factory and grounded in the commodification of human labor (Marx, 1867 [1976]: 896–926). At the outset of the bourgeois revolution, the 'great confinement' of beggars, criminals, prostitutes and the 'idle poor' in workhouses, poorhouses and houses of correction throughout Europe (Foucault, 1965: 38–64) contributed to transform the 'free and rightless proletariat' (Marx, 1867 [1976]: 896) created by the crisis of the feudal economy into a docile, obedient and disciplined labor force ready to be incorporated in the emerging sites of capitalist production. The historical emergence, consolidation, and ongoing transformation of modern penal practices would thus reflect capital's need to carve a docile and laborious workforce out of the unruly, undisciplined and sometimes riotous 'dangerous classes' constantly generated by capital itself as a by-product of its movement of 'accumulation by dispossession' (Harvey, 2003: 137–82).

According to this materialist framework, the specific configurations of the relationship between penal technologies and economic structures would be shaped by the logic of *less eligibility*. This concept, first developed in England in the early 19th century, had provided the main rationale for the English Poor Laws of 1834. In its early formulation, the principle held that:

> The first and most essential of all conditions, a principle which we find universally admitted, even by those whose practice is at variance with it, is, that his [the relief recipient's] situation on the whole shall not be made really or apparently so eligible [i.e., desirable] as the situation of the independent laborer of the lowest class. (Quoted in Piven and Cloward, 1993: 35)

According to this logic, public assistance should never raise the living conditions of the destitute above the standards of life available to the poorest among the working poor; otherwise, public relief would become 'more eligible' (more desirable) than waged work. Georg Rusche's intuition was to apply the principle of less eligibility to the analysis of penal change: since the aim of any penal system is to deter the most marginalized classes of society from committing 'crimes of desperation' (Rusche, 1933 [1978]: 4) – thus violating the capitalist injunction to rely only on their work to survive – it follows that the conditions of life generally available in the lowest regions of the class structure will invariably set the standards of living for those who are caught in the net of the penal system. In Rusche's words:

> Although experience shows the rich to occasionally break the law too, the fact remains that a substantial majority of those who fill the prisons come from the lower strata of the proletariat. Therefore, if it is not to contradict its goals, the penal system must be such that the most criminally predisposed groups will prefer a minimal existence in freedom, even under the most miserable conditions, to a life under the pressure of the penal system. (1930 [1980]: 42)

In Rusche's view, however, the rationality of penal practices is not limited to the negative logic of deterrence. Indeed, the function of less eligibility is not only to deter the most disadvantaged classes from resorting to crime (or public assistance) to survive, but also – and even more importantly – to force the poor to 'prefer' any available working conditions to the sanctions attached to criminal behavior and refusal to work. By setting the standards of living for those punished below 'the situation of the lowest socially significant proletarian class' (Rusche, 1933 [1978]: 4), the principle of less eligibility ensures that the most marginalized fractions of the working class will accept any level of exploitation in the capitalist labor market, as this will be in most cases preferable to being punished for refusing to work at the given conditions. In a capitalist economy, this means that the situation of the marginal proletarian class will shape criminal policies, and therefore the conditions of those who are punished:

> One can also formulate this proposition as follows: all efforts to reform the punishment of criminals are inevitably limited by the situation of the lowest socially significant proletarian class which society wants to deter from criminal acts. All reform efforts, however humanitarian and well meaning, which go beyond this restriction, are condemned to utopianism. (Rusche, 1933 [1978]: 4)

What Rusche is criticizing here is the representation of the history of punishment as a sequence of humanitarian reforms toward civility. This progressive description of penal transformation is unrealistic, Rusche argues, because the principle of less eligibility – to which any penal system must ultimately conform – sets a structural limit to any reform effort or 'civilization process.' The pace and direction of penal change are dictated by the overall situation of the working class, and in a capitalist economy that situation is determined in the first place by the labor market. The dynamics of the market will establish the 'fair price' of labor as of any other commodity: an increase in the supply of workers that are 'superfluous to capital's average requirements for its own valorization' (Marx, 1867 [1976]: 782), will lessen the value of human labor, worsening the conditions of the working class. The consequence, according to the principle of less eligibility, is that any increase in the size of the 'surplus population' will prompt harsher penal policies:

> Unemployed masses, who tend to commit crimes of desperation because of hunger and deprivation, will only be stopped from doing so through cruel penalties. The most effective penal policy seems to be severe corporal punishment, if not ruthless extermination ... In a society in which workers are scarce, penal sanctions have a completely different function. They do not have to stop hungry people from satisfying elementary needs. If everybody who wants to work can find work, if the lowest social class consists of unskilled workers and not of wretched unemployed workers, then punishment is required to make the unwilling work, and to teach other criminals that they have to content themselves with the income of a honest worker. (Rusche, 1933 [1978]: 4)

Consequently, the emergence or the demise of different penal practices cannot be ascribed to the ideas of the reformers: penal change is ultimately determined by the conditions of labor and, more specifically, of the labor market. This implies that no penal reform is irreversible, and that humane punishments will be quickly replaced by penal cruelty whenever new socioeconomic conditions will prompt this shift; and penal institutions will turn again into 'places of pure torture, suitable to deter even the most wretched' (Rusche, 1933 [1978]: 6)[3].

Rusche and Kirchheimer (1939) reinterpret the whole history of punishment institutions, from the late Middle Ages to the 1930s, according to this basic principle. Thus, when in the 16th century Europe was affected by a huge demographic crisis (in part as a consequence of the Thirty Years War), the labor force became scarce and wages started to grow. These circumstances prompted several European states to revise their policies toward the poor: those who were able-bodied had to be put to work. The imposition of work would deal with two crucial issues at once: on the one hand, the social problems created by the visible presence of beggars, and on the other hand, the decline of capitalist profits caused by rising wages. Inspired by this new philosophy of poverty, the first institutions for the confinement of the poor spread throughout Europe: the Bridewell in England, the Hôpital General in France, the Zuchtaus and the Spinnhaus in the Netherlands. Confinement emerged as an alternative to corporal punishments for the control of the marginal classes: its utility went beyond the segregation of socially undesirable populations (poor, beggars, prostitutes or criminals) from the rest of society, to include the possibility to transform – through discipline – the unruly criminal into a productive worker.

The future transformations of the penitentiary would also be influenced by changes in the labor markets. According to Rusche and Kirchheimer (1939), labor market dynamics explain the emergence of the Philadelphian model (based on solitary confinement), its later crisis, and the ultimate prevalence of the Auburn model (based on work in common during daytime and solitary confinement at night) in the USA – a country whose capitalist economy was suffering an acute shortage of labor in a period of rapid industrial development.

In Europe, by contrast, the significant size of the 'industrial reserve army of labor' throughout much of the 19th century led to an increase in penal severity and prompted the demise of the idea of a productive prison in favor of a purely punitive model of solitary confinement (Rusche and Kirchheimer, 1939 [2003]: 133–7). Toward the end of the 19th century, when the rise of an organized working class and changes in the labor market led to an improvement of the living standards of the poor, penal policies changed again: social policies were implemented in order to deal with a working class in turmoil, and a new climate of penal tolerance spread throughout European prisons.

At the end of their historical analysis, Rusche and Kirchheimer hypothesized a further shift toward the replacement of incarceration by monetary sanctions. This section, less convincing than the first part of the book, is the result of Kirchheimer's later reworking of Rusche's original manuscript.[4]

THE PRISON AND THE FACTORY: PUNISHMENT AS CLASS CONTROL

After its publication in 1939, *Punishment and Social Structure* was almost ignored for a long time, both by penal historians and criminologists. Its politico-economic critique of punishment virtually disappeared from the purview of criminological theory until a second edition of the book appeared in 1969, prompting a revival of Rusche and Kirchheimer's structural perspective within the emerging field of critical criminology. Both the initial oblivion and the subsequent interest in the political economy of punishment have a historical explanation: the first edition of Rusche and Kirchheimer's work appeared in a period characterized by a strong adversity to Marxism in the USA and to the social sciences in Europe. The emergence of totalitarian regimes, the Second World War, and later the postwar reconstruction with its technocratic approach to social problems (including crime), all conjured against the success of *Punishment and Social Structure* and its materialist perspective. It was only in the transformed cultural atmosphere of the 1960s and 1970s that the structural critique elaborated by Rusche and Kirchheimer could be rediscovered. Although not always inspired by the neo-Marxist framework, the revisionist histories of punishment that appeared between the late 1960s and the early 1980s signaled the broad influence (whether acknowledged or not) of *Punishment and Social Structure* (Platt, 1969; Foucault, 1977; Ignatieff, 1978; Melossi and Pavarini, 1981).[5]

Elsewhere I have analyzed the relationship between Marxist theory and the emergence of radical histories of punishment (De Giorgi, 2006: 9–19). Here I will concentrate specifically on Melossi and Pavarini's *The Prison and the Factory*, since this is the most systematic attempt to develop a politico-economic critique of the history of the prison. This work situates the birth of the penitentiary in the specific phase of capitalist development that Marx describes as 'primitive accumulation' (Marx, 1867 [1976]: 873–940). In its early stages, capitalism had to create the conditions for its own development, and this required first of all the creation of a capitalist labor force. In order to establish a new system of production based on wage labor, capital had first to separate the producers from the means of production, unraveling the economic structure of feudal society; then, it had to transform the dispossessed populations generated by that dissolution into a unified and disciplined working class.

Capitalism liberated labor from feudal exploitation only to subject it to a purely economic form of subordination. Thus, the 'liberation' of work took the form of an expropriation of producers, replacing one kind of enslavement with another:

> Hence, the historical movement which changes the producers into wage-workers, appears, on the one hand, as their emancipation from serfdom and from the fetters of the guilds, and this side alone exists for our bourgeois historians. But, on the other hand, these new freedmen became sellers of themselves only after they had been robbed of all their own means of production, and of the guarantees of existence afforded by the old feudal arrangements. (Marx, 1867 [1976]: 875)

The consolidation of the factory system gave birth to the process Marx defined as 'real subsumption of labor under capital' (1867 [1976]: 1034–8). In the wake of capitalism's struggle to establish itself as a new mode of production, the various typologies of pre-capitalist work are subsumed under the general form of abstract wage labor. Independent producers are transformed into a social labor force, and the 'collective worker' replaces the individual worker:

> [W]ith the development of the real subsumption of labor under capital, or the specifically capitalist mode of production, the real lever of the overall labor process is not the individual worker. Instead, labor-power socially combined and the various competing labor powers, which together form the entire production machine, participate in very different ways in the immediate process of making commodities, or, more accurately in this context, creating the product. (Marx, 1867 [1976]: 1039–40)

Penal institutions played a crucial role in the historical process of subsumption of labor under capital. The penitentiary emerged as an institution ancillary to the factory, as a penal technology whose power effects were consistent with the requirements of an emerging industrial system of production. The unfolding of a disciplinary penal regime connects the internal dynamics of the prison (both in its material and ideological forms) to the transformations taking place in the sphere of production. The logic of penal discipline characterizes all the institutions of confinement that emerged since the end of the 17th century:

> Over and above their specific functions, one overall aim united them: control over a rising proletariat. The bourgeois state assigns to all of them a directing role in the various moments of the formation, production and reproduction of the factory proletariat: for society they are essential

> instruments of social control, the aim of which is to secure for capital a workforce which by virtue of its moral attitude, physical health, intellectual capacity, orderliness, obedience, etc. will readily adapt to the whole regime of factory life and produce the maximum amount of surplus labor. (Melossi and Pavarini, 1981: 42)

A new class of individuals is shaped by the penitentiary institution. The mission of the prison is to inculcate new habits into the minds and bodies of the expropriated masses, turning these unruly subjects into a disciplined labor force that, having interiorized an entirely new concept of time and space, will be ready to obey, execute orders, and comply with the rhythms of production dictated by the capitalist division of labor (Thompson, 1967). Thus, the penal institution transforms the poor into a criminal, the criminal into a prisoner and, finally, the prisoner into a proletarian.

Outside the prison, in the factory, the disciplined body of the individual proletarian will be associated with other bodies, and the capitalist organization of labor will turn this 'collective worker' into a source of surplus-value:

> This discipline is the basic condition for the extraction of surplus-value, and is the only real lesson that bourgeois society has to propose to the proletariat. If legal ideology rules outside production, within it reign servitude and inequality. But the place of production is the factory. Thus, the institutional function of the workhouses and later of the prisons was to teach the proletariat factory discipline. (Melossi and Pavarini, 1981: 195)

Unlike Rusche and Kirchheimer (1939 [2003]), who had focused exclusively on the instrumental role of penal institutions in the material reproduction of a capitalist labor force, Melossi and Pavarini insist on the crucial contribution provided by disciplinary penal technologies to the *ideological* reproduction of capitalist relations of production. The prison is surely a repressive institution because it imposes to its confined populations a regime of deprivation and complete subordination to authority. But it is also an ideological tool because it represents the unconditional acceptance of that subordination as the only way to break free – one day – from this condition. Thus, the prison creates, on the one hand, the condition of 'prisoner', and it imposes, on the other, the prisoner's subjection to a regime of labor, obedience and discipline (elements that constitute that very condition) as the only path to freedom. In this way, the suffering generated by the prison is ideologically represented as the consequence of the prisoner's own refusal to submit to the discipline of work.

The ideological normalization of the prison is also reinforced by the contractual logic of imprisonment as a punishment whose severity is measured by time:

> Deprivation of freedom, for a period stipulated in the court sentence, is the specific form in which modern, that is to say bourgeois-capitalist, criminal law embodies the principle of equivalent recompense. This form is unconsciously yet deeply linked with the conception of man in the abstract and abstract human labor measurable in time. (Pashukanis, 1978: 180–1)

The capitalistic principle of the exchange of equivalents provides ideological legitimacy to the sanction of imprisonment through the same mystification that makes a work contract 'fair': in both cases, exploitation, violence and subordination disappear from the smooth logic of the contractual reason. The legal fiction of punishment as retribution conceals the disciplinary dimension of the prison in the same way as the economic fiction of the work contract as an exchange of equivalents conceals the exploitative dimension of wage labor.

THE LIMITS OF THE 'OLD' POLITICAL ECONOMY OF PUNISHMENT

In an excoriating review of the 1939 edition of *Punishment and Social Structure* published in the March-April 1940 issue of the

Journal of Criminal Law and Criminology, American legal theorist Jerome Hall came to the following conclusions about the significance of Rusche and Kirchheimer's work:

> [D]espite the importance of the thesis, abundant descriptive data, and many acute observations, the study falls far short of being an important contribution to our present knowledge. For it becomes rather quickly apparent that the authors' 'social situation', and 'historical-sociological analysis of penal methods' simmer down to 'economic' influence – and 'economic' becomes sometimes the conditions of the labor market, occasionally methods of production, often the bias of dominant economic classes, usually the bourgeoisie. As a consequence it is impossible to determine just what their thesis is. The most persistent current of their debate suggests, but never explicitly, Marxist determinism. (1940: 971–2)

Jerome Hall was not alone in accusing *Punishment and Social Structure* of economic determinism; indeed other early reviewers agreed, although sometimes in a less acrimonious tone, that this was the book's main theoretical flaw. For example, in a review published in *The Economic Journal*, renowned British sociologist T.H. Marshall argued that 'the authors try to press their point too far and to make everything fit in too neatly', adding in particular that as soon as their analysis focused on the 19th century (and on the emergence of modern prisons), 'the simple correlation between penal methods and economic systems breaks down' (Marshall, 1940: 126–7). A few months later, David Riesman Jr added his voice to the choir, stating that Rusche and Kirchheimer's analysis neglected the role of politics, religion and culture in penal transformation, and concluding that 'social scientists have a right to demand an analysis of the plurality of factors, and an attempt to assign a proper weight to each' (1940: 1299). Finally, Chicago sociologist Ernest W. Burgess reiterated in his own review of the book that 'the authors overemphasize the relation of crime to economic conditions and ignore or minimize cultural and psychogenic factors' (1940: 986).

Despite having attracted the early attention of such prestigious scholars, *Punishment and Social Structure* would almost disappear from the criminological landscape for almost thirty years. Once the book reemerged from oblivion, the charge of economic reductionism and/or determinism would haunt again Rusche and Kirchheimer's work, along with the materialist critique of punishment built on it. Thus, in one of the founding texts in the field of punishment and society, David Garland concluded his chapter on the political economy of punishment suggesting that:

> *Punishment and Social Structure* seriously overestimates the effective role of economic forces in shaping penal practice. It grossly understates the importance of ideological and political forces and has little to say about the internal dynamics of penal administration and their role in determining policy. It gives no account of the symbols and social messages conveyed by penal measures to the law-abiding public and hence no sense of the ways in which these symbolic concerns help shape the fabric of penal institutions. (Garland, 1990: 108–9)

It is not surprising that these critiques became particularly strong during the 1980s and 1990s, when, as Dario Melossi writes in his introduction to the third edition of Rusche and Kirchheimer's book, 'Marxism was symbolically burnt at the stake, while honoring the totem pole of "cultural insight"' (2003: ix). What is slightly more surprising, however, is that the distancing of critical sociologies of punishment from the structural approach took place despite the fact that in those years advanced capitalist societies were witnessing the most significant process of structural transformation since the Industrial Revolution. In fact, those decades witnessed the crisis of the Fordist-industrial paradigm, the demise of the Keynesian welfare state, the globalization of production and consumption, the consolidation of a neoliberal model of socioeconomic (de)regulation[6], and – particularly in the USA – the unfolding of a punitive turn that would lead to a radical reconfiguration of the penal landscape. However, with the notable exception of Stuart

Hall's analysis (Hall et al., 1978) of the role of penal discourses in the reproduction class (and racial) hegemony in late capitalism (see also Laclau and Mouffe, 1985), the 'cultural turn' in the sociology of punishment coincided with (and to some extent encouraged) a rejection of the Marxist political economy at a time when this was most needed in order to elaborate a grounded critique of penal change[7].

This is not to suggest that the traditional politico-economic analysis, with its reductive focus on the relationship between unemployment and imprisonment (Jankovic, 1977; Greenberg, 1980; Wallace, 1980; Galster and Scaturo, 1985; Inverarity and McCarthy, 1988), had been able to elaborate a persuasive structural critique of contemporary punishment; nor to argue that an exclusive emphasis on punishment as an instrument of class control would provide an exhaustive explanation of the transformations of penal politics in contemporary societies. Indeed, from the standpoint of what I would define as a 'post-reductionist' political economy of punishment, the challenge is to envision a non-orthodox critique of penal strategies that is able to overcome the false alternative between 'structure' and 'culture' while addressing the important theoretical concerns raised by other critical perspectives in the field of punishment and society.

In this respect, I would suggest that at least three main themes addressed by recent narratives of penal change (particularly in the USA) deserve the attention of neo-Marxist criminologists:

1 the already mentioned issue of the *symbolic dimension* of punishment, which points to the materialist framework's excessive focus on the instrumental side of penal practices;
2 the issue of the broader *governmental effects* generated by penal strategies, which points to the neo-Marxist paradigm's narrow focus on socioeconomic marginality as the exclusive target of penal technologies;
3 the issue of the specific *politico-institutional* contexts that define the background against which specific forms of penality unfold, which points to the tendency of the political economy of punishment to favor 'global' accounts of penal transformation over comparative analysis.

In some cases, these theoretical concerns have emerged from works directly or indirectly engaged with the neo-Marxist perspective (Cavadino and Dignan, 2006; Lacey, 2008; Wacquant, 2009), while in others they emerged from critical analyses of penality the background of which is rather distant from the materialist paradigm (Simon, 2007; Barker, 2009). I suggest that we engage with each of these themes, since they shed light on relevant dimensions of the penal question that have been left underexplored by the 'old' political economy of punishment.

The first theme points to one of the most persistent critiques addressed to neo-Marxist criminology: its apparent lack of interest for the cultural, expressive, and discursive dimensions of penality. While this critique is clearly well grounded, it is worth noting here that the emphasis on the symbolic dimensions of punishment has often come at the cost of deemphasizing (if not ignoring) the historically determined structural dimensions of penality, almost in a kind of zero-sum logic where 'more culture' seems to imply 'less structure' (see for example Garland, 1990, 2001). Recently, the issue of the culture/structure schism has resurfaced in Loic Wacquant's (2009) analysis of neoliberal penality and of the emergence of an American 'penal state'. This work aims explicitly at bridging the gap between instrumental and symbolic dimensions of punishment. In the very first pages of his *Punishing the Poor*, in fact, Wacquant states that his work 'does not belong to the genre ... of the "political economy of imprisonment" inaugurated by the classic work of Georg Rusche and Otto Kirchheimer, *Punishment and Social Structure*', since its ambition is:

> [t]o hold together the material and symbolic dimensions of the contemporary restructuring of the economy of punishment that this tradition of research has precisely been unable to wed, owing to its congenital incapacity to recognize the

> specific efficacy and the materiality of symbolic power. (2009: xvii)

Wacquant argues that the unfolding of the American penal experiment over the last three decades should not be interpreted – as the *leitmotiv* of the 'old' political economy of punishment would suggest – as a simple reflection of the transition from a Fordist-industrial model of production based on stable labor markets, extensive networks of social protection, and inclusive welfare policies, to a post-Fordist economic system based on deregulated labor markets, flexible working conditions, and weak social protections. Indeed, an exclusive focus on the instrumental dimension of the 'new punitiveness' would prevent a deeper understanding of the significance of the American penal state as a broader political project.

According to Wacquant, the emerging penal state would pursue three distinct strategies with both instrumental and symbolic outcomes. At the instrumental level, the American penal experiment would entail a massive warehousing of the surplus populations generated by the restructuring of the Fordist-industrial economy. In turn, by increasing the cost of any attempt to escape from the lowest regions of the labor market (according to the well known principle of *less eligibility*) this new 'great confinement' would contribute to impart a new discipline of labor on the marginal sectors of the post-industrial workforce. Finally, at the symbolic level, the new penal discourse would appease the growing insecurities experienced by the middle class, by staging a ritual reassertion of the state's power to neutralize the unworthy and dangerous classes.

In other words, the tentacles of the penal state would extend deeply into the fabric of American society, reshaping – both at the instrumental and symbolic level – its public sphere, its political institutions and its cultural orientations. Distancing himself from the reductionist tendency of the political economy of punishment, Wacquant suggests that the punitive turn leads not only to the consolidation of a repressive machine whose operations are functional to the reproduction of current capitalist relations, but also to the configuration of 'new categories and discourses, novel administrative bodies and government policies, fresh social types and associated forms of knowledge' (2009: 295).

Wacquant's attempt to assign proper weight to the discursive and symbolic effects of penal politics provides important insights towards a post-reductionist revision of the materialist critique of punishment. Yet, the image that emerges most often from the pages of *Punishing the Poor* is that of a penal state involved in a struggle to regulate (by repressive means) the most precarious sectors of the post-industrial labor force, while less emphasis is given to its symbolic reach across other regions of American society. Thus, despite Wacquant's insistence on the necessity to 'escape the narrowly materialist vision of the political economy of punishment' (2009: xviii), his approach risks to reproduce the much contested material/symbolic divide. Not unlike other materialist critiques of penality, indeed, Wacquant's work seems to come to the conclusion that the neoliberal penal state reveals its *instrumental* side against the new poor, while projecting its purely *symbolic* hold on the rest of society – specifically, on the middle classes it struggles to reassure by allowing them to witness the punitive excess unleashed against the new dangerous classes. In other words, *Punishing the Poor* might be less distant from the traditional politico-economic critique of punishment than its author acknowledges, since once again the symbolic and discursive dimensions of penal politics appear mostly as ideological 'outgrowths' of a penal state whose main role is to punitively regulate the poor in order to force them into the post-Fordist labor market. Finally, we are left with our unsolved dilemma: how can the symbolic and instrumental dimensions of punishment be reconnected under a comprehensive structural critique of penal change? How do penal discourses and practices consolidate themselves as powerful technologies for governing not just social marginality, but late-capitalist/neoliberal societies at large?

This question points to the issue of the broader governmental effects generated by penal discourses and practices in contemporary societies. In its basic formulation, this theme draws on the Foucauldian insight that penal practices, as historically determined technologies of power, are always inscribed within broader rationalities of government. Thus, according to Foucault's genealogy, the emergence of modern penality (with the transition from the 'spectacle of suffering' to the consolidation of disciplinary technologies) would mirror a broader shift from a *destructive* sovereign power that struggles to neutralize its enemies to a *productive* governmental rationality engaged in the efficient regulation of whole populations (Foucault, 2009: 117). It is worth emphasizing the connection, often overlooked, between Foucault's theorization of the power to punish and the neo-Marxist analysis of capitalist reproduction, particularly in light of the French philosopher's own emphasis on the role played by the emergence of a capitalist 'political economy' in the unfolding of modern governmental rationalities (Foucault, 2009: 106–7). What matters the most here, however, is Foucault's insistence that penal strategies (and governmental technologies in general) should not be seen simply as repressive tools for the control of the poor, but rather as elements of broader rationalities for the governing of entire social formations.

Following this perspective, in a recent work Jonathan Simon (2007) situates his critique of the American penal experiment within a theoretical framework that is rather distant from the one advanced by Rusche and Kirchheimer. The level privileged by Simon is that of a socio-legal and political analysis of the governmental rationalities that emerged as a consequence of the increasing centrality of the penal question in the USA. In the last 30 years, the ongoing proliferation of discourses, practices and knowledge on crime and punishment would have resulted in a distinct governmental rationality that Simon calls 'governing through crime':

> When we govern through crime, we make crime and the forms of knowledge historically associated with it … available outside their limited original subject domains as powerful tools with which to interpret and frame all forms of social action as a problem for governance. (2007: 17)

Simon offers a rigorous genealogy of this new governmental rationality, whose origins can be situated in the 'legimation crisis' affecting the liberal-welfarist forms of governance that had been hegemonic in the USA for most of the 20th century. Simon reconstructs the concatenation of 'discursive events' that provided the symbolic background for the unfolding of the American punitive turn – from Goldwater's incendiary 1964 electoral campaign, to the wars on crime and drugs launched by Nixon, Reagan and Bush Sr, to the war on terror declared by George W. Bush in the aftermath of 9/11. All these transformations have converged toward a new paradigm of social governance based on the prevention and neutralization of criminal risks as a constitutive element of governmental action at all levels of American society.

This Foucauldian perspective eschews a 'top-down' concept of penal power common to much neo-Marxist criminology, and describes the punitive turn from the point of view of both its politico-institutional consequences and the diffusion of lifestyles, cultures of work, and patterns of consumption revolving around the crime-punishment nexus. Simon deconstructs, on the one hand the peculiar governmental technologies that emerged around this punitive shift, and on the other, the discursive chains that allowed these rationalities to resonate with punitive and neo-authoritarian declinations of fear and insecurity in a neoliberal society. If analyzed under this particular lens, the punitive turn appears as a broad social dynamic whose power effects are constantly reproduced through the daily interactions between citizens (not only the poor) and a power to punish that is part of a broader strategy for regulating the social.

However, I would suggest, this reconfiguration of governmental technologies is not disconnected from the deep structural inequalities affecting the social and urban landscape of American society. The molecular diffusion of the power effects associated with this new model of 'governing through crime' does not mean that such effects spread evenly. Although we can agree with Simon that we should focus on 'both the criminal justice system that is concentrated on poor communities and the private sector of middle-class securitized environments as class-specific modes of governing through crime that interact with each other' (Simon, 2007: 7), we also need to emphasize that these rationalities of government do not generate similar (or even comparable) effects at different latitudes of the American socioeconomic hierarchy. The neo-Foucauldian argument that 'crime does not govern only those on one end of structures of inequality' (Simon, 2007: 18) needs to be qualified by the Marxist insight that penal strategies contribute to the overall reproduction of those very structures of socioeconomic inequality, in directions that resonate with current dynamics of capitalist accumulation.

Furthermore, the actual configuration of this symbiotic relationship between penal technologies and socioeconomic processes cannot be taken for granted, nor can it be presumed to unfold along the same coordinates across all late-capitalist societies. This question sheds light on the third theme I would like to discuss here: the specific politico-institutional arrangements through which the relations between punishment and social structure are mediated. Such issue also points to what recently John Sutton has identified as a serious theoretical flaw in the political economy of punishment: its tendency to assume 'that all capitalist economies are the same and that business cycles are wholly exogenous to other kinds of social processes' (Sutton, 2004: 171).

The issue of the lack of comparative institutional analysis in neo-Marxist accounts of penal change has been recently raised in particular by theoretical perspectives directly engaged with (if not internal to) the politico-economic framework (Sutton, 2004; Cavadino and Dignan, 2006; Lacey, 2008). In *The Prisoners' Dilemma*, for example, Nicola Lacey clearly situates her analysis in the materialist field, broadly accepting the politico-economic argument that current penal trends must be linked to the socioeconomic transformations affecting late capitalist societies. However, rather than assuming a global spread of the neoliberal ideology sustained by a uniform shift toward penal severity, Lacey offers a detailed comparative analysis of the different 'varieties of capitalism' existing in the Western world (Hall and Soskice, 2001), and suggests that their specific features must be given proper weight in the analysis of punishment and social structure:

> My analysis builds on structural theories inspired by Marxism, but it argues that political-economic forces at the macro level are mediated not only by cultural filters, but also by economic, political, and social institutions ... It is this institutional stabilization of and mediation of cultural and structural forces, and the impact which this has on the perceived interests of relevant groups of social actors, which produce the significant and persistent variation across systems at similar stages of capitalist development. (Lacey, 2008: 57)

According to Lacey, the American shift toward a punitive governance of social marginality has not spread to all advanced capitalist democracies, and the specific configurations of the punitive turn (where it has indeed taken place) cannot be automatically derived from the emergence of a post-industrial, neoliberal economy. Instead, different capitalist social formations show diverging trends. If some neoliberal market economies such as the USA (and to a much more limited extent, the UK) have witnessed a significant transition from social to penal means for governing the poor, this has not been the case in the social-democratic or corporatist economies of continental Europe, where in the last few decades welfare protections have not been drastically reduced and indicators of penal severity have remained relatively stable. In this sense, social-democratic and corporatist economies would seem to be better positioned than their neoliberal counterparts to resist the punitive turn (despite their own problems of rising unemployment and growing social inequality), thanks to their politico-economic and institutional structures based on stable labor markets, long-term public investments in the workforce, coalition-oriented electoral politics, and greater insulation of the judiciary from the ebbs and flows of public opinion (see also Cavadino and Dignan, 2006: 3–39). Conversely, in neoliberal economic formations – characterized by flexible labor markets, low levels of investment in public services, two-party political systems, a single-issue orientation in political debate, and a hegemonic favoring individual competitiveness over social equality – the most disruptive consequences of the crisis of the industrial economy (namely, the production of a large surplus of labor) would unfold in a politico-institutional context that facilitates the shift toward a more punitive model of social regulation. Lacey suggests that in order to be able to explain *both* the punitive shift of neoliberal societies *and* the relative penal moderation of other late-capitalist social formations, the materialist approach needs to be grounded in a comparative analysis of the institutional, political and cultural arrangements which, in each variety of capitalism, mediate (and sometimes mitigate) the effect of economic forces on penal politics.

Taken together, the three themes discussed – the symbolic dimension of penality, the governmental effects of penal politics and the different politico-institutional contexts in which penal practices unfold – can assist neo-Marxist criminology in its effort to overcome some of the old conundrums of materialist criminology. Indeed, as far as they are not seen as *alternatives* to structural explanations of penal change, these themes are not incompatible with a politico-economic critique of penality. Instead, as I will argue more extensively in the final section of this chapter, they can help us envision a conceptual roadmap for the construction of a post-reductionist, culturally sensitive political economy of punishment.

NEW DIRECTIONS IN THE POLITICAL ECONOMY OF PUNISHMENT

In the 1933 article which outlined the thesis to be later developed in *Punishment and Social Structure*, Georg Rusche had already been careful to emphasize the complexity of the relationship between economic structure and penal forms:

> The dependency of crime and crime control on economic and historical conditions does not, however, provide a total explanation. These forces do not alone determine the object of our investigation and by themselves are limited and incomplete in several ways. (1933 [1978]: 3)

This early warning against oversimplified interpretations of the economy/punishment nexus would not inoculate the political economy of punishment against the dangers of economic determinism. It must also be said that the reductionist drift would indeed become particularly evident in the neo-Marxist criminological literature of the 1970s and 1980s, whose attempts to apply Rusche and Kirchheimer's paradigm to late-capitalist societies focused on narrow statistical analyses of the relationship between changes in the labor market and variations in imprisonment rates (for a review see Chiricos and DeLone, 1992; Melossi, 1998; De Giorgi, 2006: 19–39). This literature was for the most part able to provide empirical support to the hypothesis of a positive and direct correlation between unemployment and incarceration and to show how, in accordance with Rusche and Kirchheimer's insights, penal severity tended to increase in times of economic crisis and rising unemployment. However, the narrowly quantitative approach to socioeconomic change privileged by most of these analyses (perhaps in an attempt to give 'scientific validation' to the materialist approach through the use of ever more complex statistical models), has prevented a deeper understanding of the *extra-economic* and *extra-penal* factors that contribute to structure this relationship (for notable exceptions see Box, 1987; Melossi, 1993, 2000).

The reductionist tendency of the political economy of punishment has resulted in an unnecessary oversimplification of Rusche and Kirchheimer's perspective, which in turn has deprived the materialist framework of the theoretical tools it needs in order to elaborate a comprehensive critique of the capitalist restructuring that has unfolded in Western societies since the early 1970s. This broad process of socioeconomic transformation has certainly involved (particularly in the early stage of the transition) a massive expulsion of the labor force from the industrial sectors of the economy, as shown by the vertical growth of unemployment rates between the late 1970s and the early 1980s. More importantly, however, it has resulted in a deep restructuring of the specific *regime of capitalist accumulation* that had been hegemonic in Europe and (to a lesser extent) in the USA between the 1930s and the 1960s.

The concept of 'regime of accumulation' has been elaborated by neo-Marxist political economists belonging to the so called 'regulation school' (see Aglietta, 1979; Jessop, 1990). This perspective reconstructs the historical trajectory of capitalist development in light of the contradictory tendency of capitalism to generate crises and instabilities, on the one hand, and to consolidate new institutions, new norms, and new cultural orientations in response to those crises, on the other hand.[8] According to this perspective (Jessop, 2002: 56–8), each different regime of capitalist accumulation can be described according to four main elements: (1) a distinctive type of *labor process*, which identifies the dominant form of production and the corresponding composition of the workforce (e.g. mass production, the industrial working class); (2) a specific strategy of *macroeconomic growth*, which identifies the leading sectors of an economic formation (e.g. industrial production, manufacturing); (3) a particular system of *economic regulation*, which describes the prevailing regulatory framework (e.g. collective bargaining, market regulation, monetary policies); and (4) a coherent mode of *societalization*, which identifies the hegemonic forms of cultural, institutional, and social organization (e.g. cultures of welfare, fiscal policies, patterns of consumption, etc.).

According to this perspective, the Fordist-Keynesian regime of capitalist accumulation was based on a system of mass-industrial production centered on the assembly line, stable labor markets regulated by comprehensive industrial policies, high levels of labor unionization favored by an extended system of collective bargaining, significant public interventions in the economy, cultural orientations favoring mass consumption, and a tacit social pact between labor and capital (often mediated by an interventionist state) according to which high wages and generous social protections would reward high levels of labor productivity and work discipline. Bob Jessop summarizes the internal consistency between the economic, institutional, and cultural dimensions of this specific regime of accumulation as follows:

> If the Keynesian welfare national state helped secure the conditions for Fordist economic expansion, Fordist economic expansion helped secure the conditions for the Keynesian welfare national state. Welfare rights based on national citizenship helped to generalize norms of mass consumption and thereby contributed to full employment levels of demand; and they were sustained in turn by an institutionalized compromise involving Fordist unions and Fordist firms. (Jessop, 2002: 79)

The gradual demise in Western economies of this model of capitalist development during the 1970s was prompted by several crisis-generating features of the Fordist-Keynesian paradigm, such as the steady decline in capitalist profits produced by the radicalization of class struggles, the fiscal crisis of the welfare state precipitated by increasing demands for social provisions (coupled, particularly in the USA, with the rise of anti-tax movements), the inflationary tendencies generated by high wages and high welfare expenditures, the saturation of domestic markets for durable goods, and the loss of competitive advantage suffered by Western economies in the wake of economic globalization.

In liberal societies such as the USA, whose economic history has traditionally leaned toward a *laissez-faire* model of capitalist development based on deregulated markets, minimal public interventions in the economy, and a system of social protections resembling a 'charitable state' (Wacquant, 2009: 48), the dismantling of the Fordist-Keynesian regime has unfolded in a neoliberal variant characterized by extreme labor market flexibility, a vertical decline in labor unionization, a drastic curtailment of welfare provisions and soaring levels of socioeconomic inequality (Sennett, 1998; Shipler, 2004; Katz and Stern, 2006). In this respect, the crisis of the Fordist-Keynesian paradigm and the concurring process of capitalist restructuring have involved much more than the expulsion of a significant fraction of the industrial labor force from the system of production – the only aspect captured by a narrow focus on unemployment and imprisonment. Indeed, the transition to a post-Fordist/post-Keynesian regime of accumulation has taken the form of a broad capitalist offensive against the workforce, in a successful attempt to break the Fordist-Keynesian compromise and to reestablish suitable conditions for profitable capitalist accumulation in a global economy: a stricter work discipline, higher levels of labor flexibility, more insecure working conditions, lower social protections, and an increased competition *for* work among the poor. This process of capitalist restructuring resulted in a significant shift in the balance of power from labor to capital. As Melossi puts it, 'sometimes in the mid-1970s the "social system" started squeezing the working class for the juice of production, not with only one hand, but with two hands at the same time' (2003: xxv).

It is in the context of this broader realignment of social power throughout the structure of late capitalist societies that a materialist analysis of contemporary penal change must situate its critique. And such a critique must be able to take into account not only the measurable dynamics of the labor market, but also the political, institutional, and cultural transformations that have contributed to redefine existing structures of socioeconomic inequality in the wake of a new emerging regime of capitalist accumulation.

In order to illustrate some of the theoretical implications of this 'qualitative shift', I will return once again to Rusche's original formulation of the concept of *less eligibility* as the logic governing the relation between punishment and social structure:

> All efforts to reform the punishment of criminals are inevitably limited by the *situation* of the lowest socially significant proletarian class which society wants to deter for criminal acts. All reform efforts, however humanitarian and well-meaning, which go beyond this restriction, are condemned to utopianism. (Rusche, 1933 [1978]: 4, emphasis added)

Here I would argue that Rusche's concept of the '*situation* of the lowest socially significant proletarian class' (1933: 4) lends itself to a much broader conceptualization than the narrowly economistic approach privileged by most of the literature on unemployment and imprisonment: one that encourages a productive integration between the traditional materialist critique of punishment and some of the theoretical issues raised by the recent sociologies of the punitive turn.

Indeed, if the relative power of the workforce in a capitalist economy is ultimately determined by the economic value of its labor,[9] the overall *situation* of that workforce – its contingent position inside existing hierarchies of social worthiness, or its 'social value' – is not simply the product of narrow economic dynamics. Rather, it results from the ongoing interaction between structural processes of economic transformation (modes of production, patterns of economic growth, labor market dynamics), governmental technologies of social regulation (varieties of welfare/workfare, strategies of public intervention in the economy, politico-institutional arrangements, modes of economic regulation/deregulation, patterns of wealth redistribution/concentration), and discursive/symbolic dynamics of cultural reproduction (racialized and gendered taxonomies of social worth, mainstream narratives about social deservingness and undeservingness). In other words, the overall 'situation' of marginalized social classes is determined by their place in the economic structure as much as by their position in the 'moral economy' of capitalist social formations (Sayer, 2001). It should be noted here that this ongoing process of redefinition of the economic and social worth of labor represents a constant feature in the history of capitalism, and that the trajectory of this 'repositioning' of the labor force in the social structure tends to follow a clear pattern: the overall 'situation' of the marginal classes tends to improve when a stable dynamic of capitalist valorization guarantees extended periods of economic growth and social stability, while it tends to deteriorate when the crisis of a specific mode of development prompts capitalist social formations to revolutionize the system of production and spark a new regime of accumulation (Marx, 1867 [1976]: 896–904).

Following this perspective, a post-reductionist political economy of the punitive turn in the USA should analyze the changing 'situation' of the marginal classes in America against the background of the economic *and* extra-economic processes that have redefined the position of the poor within the material *and* moral economy of American society. Over the last three decades, structural processes of capitalist transformation (deindustrialization, downsizing, outsourcing, etc.) have significantly reduced the economic value of wage labor and consolidated a tendency toward rising work insecurity, declining wages, longer working hours, and an overall increase in the socially acceptable levels of 'exploitability' of the American labor force (Schor, 1992; Sennett, 1998; Ehrenreich, 2001). At the same time, however, a broad reconfiguration of governmental strategies of social regulation – such as the transition from welfare to workfare, the growing politico-institutional emphasis on individual responsibility, and the emergence of neoliberal forms of governance that encourage the 'secession of the successful' in fields like taxation, housing, education, etc. (Reich, 1991) – has eroded the Fordist-Keynesian compromise, deepening social fractures along lines of race and class. Finally, in the field of cultural signification, the powerful neoconservative hold on public debates on socioeconomic inequality – reinforced by the cyclical emergence of racialized moral panics about the underclass, welfare dependency, street crime and drugs, illegal immigration, etc. – has helped to consolidate hegemonic representations of the poor as undeserving and potentially dangerous (Handler and Hasenfeld, 1991; Gans, 1995; Quadagno, 1995).

In the field of penal politics, the broadened materialist framework sketched above would allow the political economy of punishment to overcome its traditional emphasis on the instrumental side of penality, and to analyze the emergence of the American 'penal state' from the point of view of its impact on each of the different levels at which this broad reconfiguration of the American social structure (and of the 'situation' of its marginalized populations) has taken place since the 1970s. In this direction, a post-reductionist critique of the punitive turn should of course emphasize the structural dimension of recent penal practices, illustrating their instrumental role in 'imposing the discipline of desocialized wage work … by rising the cost of strategies of escape or resistance that drive young men from the lower class into the illegal sectors of the street economy' (Wacquant, 2009: xvii). But it should also analyze the widespread governmental effects of penal technologies – particularly in conjunction with other tools of socioeconomic regulation, such as fiscal and social policies – and illustrate their tendency to reproduce and reinforce existing structures of socioeconomic inequality. Most importantly, however, it should elaborate a culturally sensitive materialist critique of the symbolic implications of contemporary penal forms, and analyze how hegemonic representations of deservingness and undeservingness resonate with (and provide cultural legitimacy to) an emerging post-Fordist model of capitalist production whose regime of accumulation is grounded in the material and symbolic devaluation of the poor and their labor.

Finally, the epistemological shift proposed here would enable neo-Marxist criminology to approach penal politics no longer as an outgrowth of capitalist relations of production (a 'superstructure' of the capitalist economy, in the language of orthodox Marxism), but rather as a set of material and symbolic practices that contribute to the overall reproduction of capitalist social formations and of their specific regimes of accumulation.

NOTES

1 Several directions of research contributed in this period to the consolidation of 'critical' or 'radical' perspectives in criminology (radical feminism, critical race theory, postcolonial studies, etc.), not all of which can be ascribed to Marxism. The focus of this chapter, however, is the political economy of punishment, an approach that owes much to Marxist theory. For a broad reconstruction of different currents of thought in critical criminology, see Van Swaaningen (1997), Lynch et al. (2006) and DeKeseredy (2010).

2 It is worth noting here that a few years before the publication of *Punishment and Social Structure*, Georg Rusche had already exposed some of his ideas in two articles. The first article, originally published in 1930 in the German newspaper Frankfurter Zeitung, analyzed prison conditions in the USA during the Depression era (Rusche, 1930 [1978]). The second article, conceived as a research project for the Institute for Social Research in Frankfurt, was published in 1933 in the Institute's journal Zeitschrift für Sozialforschung, and outlined the main concepts of the materialist critique of punishment (Rusche, 1933 [1980]).

3 For an analysis of the return of corporal punishment in the USA during the last quarter of the 20th century, see Cusac (2009).

4 For a broad reconstruction of the complex history of *Punishment and Social Structure*, detailing both Rusche's biographic vicissitudes and the problematic reworking of the original manuscript by Otto Kirchheimer, see Melossi (1978, 1980).

5 In the first pages of *Discipline and Punish*, Michel Foucault acknowledges that 'Rusche and Kirchheimer's great work, *Punishment and Social Structure* provides a number of essential reference points', adding that 'we can surely accept the general proposition that, in our societies, the systems of punishment are to be situated in a certain "political economy" of the body' (1977: 24–5).

6 Following David Harvey's recent work, here I use the term neoliberalism to identify a political project developed by Western power elites, particularly in the USA and in the UK between the late 1970s and the early 2000s, in order 'to reestablish the conditions for capital accumulation and to restore the power of economic elites' (Harvey, 2005: 19) after the social turbulence of the 1960s and early 1970s. As a politico-economic system, neoliberalism emphasizes individual freedom over social responsibility, competition over cooperation, market forces over state intervention, capital mobility over financial regulation, and corporate interests over the rights of organized labor.

7 This statement might seem to overlook the contributions of those authors – most notably David Garland (1985, 1990; but see also Howe, 1994) – who during the 1980s and 1990s have engaged in a critical conversation with the political economy of punishment. The point I would like to make here, however, is that most of these works focused on stigmatizing the inability of the neo-Marxist perspective to grasp the symbolic and cultural dimensions of punishment, rather than on promoting any significant advancement in this approach.

8 Bob Jessop and Ngai-Ling Sum have summarized the distinctive approach of the regulation school as follows: 'The regulation approach is a variant of evolutionary and institutional economics that analyzes the economy in its broadest sense as including both economic and extra-economic factors. It interprets the economy as an ensemble of socially embedded, socially regularized and strategically selective institutions, organizations, social forces and

actions organized around (or at least involved in) capitalist reproduction' (2001: 91, original emphasis).

9 Which in turn depends on the pressure exercised on the labor market by the unemployed population that fills the ranks of the Marxian industrial reserve army of labor: 'The industrial reserve army, during the periods of stagnation and average prosperity, weighs down the active army of workers; during the periods of over-production and feverish activity, it puts a curb on their pretensions' (Marx, 1867 [1976]: 792).

REFERENCES

Adamson, C. (1984) 'Towards a marxian penology: captive criminal populations as economic threats and resources', *Social Problems*, 41(4): 435–58.

Aglietta, M. (1979) *A Theory of Capitalist Regulation*. London: New Left Books.

Althusser, L. (1971) *Lenin and Philosophy and Other Essays*. New York: Monthly Review Press.

Barker, V. (2009) *The Politics of Imprisonment: How the Democratic Process Shapes the Way America Punishes Offenders*. New York: Oxford University Press.

Box, S. (1987) *Recession, Crime and Punishment*. London: Rowman & Littlefield.

Burgess, E.W. (1940) 'Book review: Punishment and social structure, by G. Rusche and O. Kirchheimer', *The Yale Law Journal*, 49(5): 986.

Cavadino, M. and Dignan, J. (2006) *Penal Systems: A Comparative Approach*. London: SAGE Publications.

Chiricos, T. and DeLone, M. (1992) 'Labor surplus and punishment: a review and assessment of theory and evidence', *Social Problems*, 39(4): 421–446.

Cusac, A. (2009) *Cruel and Unusual. The Culture of Punishment in America*. New Haven, CT: Yale University Press.

De Giorgi, A. (2006) *Re-Thinking the Political Economy of Punishment: Perspectives on Post-Fordism and Penal Politics*. Aldershot: Ashgate.

DeKeseredy, W. (2010) *Contemporary Critical Criminology*. London: Routledge.

Ehrenreich, B. (2001) *Nickel and Dimed: On (Not) Getting by in America*. New York: Holt.

Foucault, M. (1965) *Madness and Civilization*. New York: Pantheon.

Foucault, M. (1977) *Discipline and Punish: The Birth of the Prison*. London: Penguin.

Foucault, M. (1991) 'Governmentality', in G. Burchell, C. Gordon and P. Miller (eds), *The Foucault Effect: Studies in Governmentality*. Chicago: University of Chicago Press. pp. 7–104.

Foucault, M. (2009) *Security, Territory, Population: Lectures at the Collège de France, 1977–1978*. New York: Picador.

Galster, G. and Scaturo, L. (1985) 'The US criminal justice system: unemployment and the severity of punishment', *Journal of Research in Crime and Delinquency*, 22(2): 163–189.

Gans, H.J. (1995) *The War Against the Poor*. New York: Basic Books.

Garland, D. (1985) *Punishment and Welfare: A History of Penal Strategies*. Aldershot: Gower.

Garland, D. (1990) *Punishment and Modern Society: A Study in Social Theory*. Chicago: University of Chicago Press.

Garland, D. (2001) *The Culture of Control: Crime and Social Order in Contemporary Society*. Oxford: Oxford University Press.

Greenberg, D. (1980) 'Penal sanctions in Poland: a test of alternative models', *Social Problems*, 28(2): 194–204.

Hall, J. (1940) 'Book review: Punishment and social structure, by G. Rusche and O. Kirchheimer', *Journal of Criminal Law and Criminology*, 30(6): 971–973.

Hall, P.A and Soskice, D. (eds) (2001) *Varieties of Capitalism*. Oxford: Oxford University Press.

Hall, S., Critcher, C., Jefferson, T., Clarke, J. and Roberts, B. (1978) *Policing the Crisis. Mugging, the State, and Law and Order*. London: Palgrave.

Handler, J.F. and Hasenfeld, Y. (1991) *The Moral Construction of Poverty: Welfare Reform in America*. London: SAGE Publications.

Harvey, D. (2003) *The New Imperialism*. Oxford: Oxford University Press.

Harvey, D. (2005) *A Brief History of Neoliberalism*. Oxford: Oxford University Press.

Howe, A. (1994) *Punish and Critique*. London: Routledge.

Ignatieff, M. (1978) *A Just Measure of Pain: The Penitentiary in the Industrial Revolution, 1750–1850*. New York: Pantheon.

Ignatieff, M. (1983) 'State, civil society and total institutions: a critique of recent social histories of punishment', in S. Cohen and A. Scull (eds), *Social control and the state*. Oxford: Martin Robertson. pp. 75–106.

Inverarity, J. and McCarthy, D. (1988) 'Punishment and Social Structure revisited: unemployment and imprisonment in the United States, 1948–1984', *The Sociological Quarterly*, 29(2): 263–79.

Jankovic, I. (1977) 'Labor market and imprisonment', *Crime and Social Justice*, 8: 17–31.

Jessop, B. (1990) 'Regulation theories in retrospect and prospect', *Economy & Society*, 19(2): 153–216.

Jessop, B. (2002) *The Future of the Capitalist State.* Cambridge: Polity Press.

Jessop, B. and Sum, N. (2001) 'Pre-disciplinary and post-disciplinary perspectives in political economy', *New Political Economy*, 6(1): 89–101.

Katz, M.B. and Stern, M.J. (2006) *One Nation Divisible: What America Was and What it is Becoming.* New York: Russel Sage Foundation.

Lacey, N. (2008) *The Prisoners' Dilemma: Political Economy and Punishment in Contemporary Democracies.* Cambridge: Cambridge University Press.

Laclau, E. and Mouffe, C. (1985) *Hegemony and Socialist Strategy: Towards a Radical Democratic Politics.* London: Verso.

Lynch, M.J., Michalowski, R.J. and Byron Groves, W. (2006) *Primer in Radical Criminology: Critical Perspectives on Crime, Power & Identity.* Monsey, NY: Criminal Justice Press.

Marshall, T.H. (1940) 'Book review: Punishment and social structure, by G. Rusche and O. Kirchheimer', *The Economic Journal*, 50(197): 126–7.

Marx, K. (1867 [1976]) *Capital: Volume I.* Harmondsworth: Penguin.

Matza, D. (1969) *Becoming Deviant.* Englewood Cliffs, NJ: Prentice Hall.

Melossi, D. (1978) 'Georg Rusche and Otto Kirchheimer: punishment and social structure', *Social Justice*, 9: 73–85.

Melossi, D. (1980) 'Georg Rusche: a biographical essay', *Crime and Social Justice*, 14: 51–63.

Melossi, D. (1993) 'Gazette of morality and social whip: punishment, hegemony, and the case of the U.S., 1970–1992', *Social & Legal Studies*, 2: 259–79.

Melossi, D. (2000) 'Changing representations of the criminal', *British Journal of Criminology*, 40: 296–320.

Melossi, D. (2003) 'Introduction to the Transaction Transaction edition. The simple "heuristic maxim" of an "unusual human being', in G. Rusche and O. Kirchheimer (eds), *Punishment and Social Structure.* New Brunswick, NJ: Transaction Publishers. pp. ix–xlv.

Melossi, D. (ed.) (1998) *The Sociology of Punishment.* Aldershot: Dartmouth.

Melossi, D. and Pavarini, M. (1981) *The Prison and the Factory. Origins of the Penitentiary System.* London: Macmillan.

Pashukanis, E.B. (1978) *Law and Marxism: A general Theory.* London: Ink Links.

Pasquino, P. (1980) 'Criminology: the birth of a special savoir', *Ideology & Consciousness*, 7: 17–33.

Piven, F. and Cloward, R. (1993) *Regulating the Poor. The Functions of Public Welfare.* New York: Vintage.

Platt, A. (1969) *The Child Savers: The Invention of Delinquency.* Chicago: University of Chicago Press.

Quadagno, J. (1995) *The Color of Welfare.* New York: Oxford University Press.

Quinney, R. (1980) *Class, State and Crime.* New York: Longman.

Reich, R. (1991) 'The secession of the successful', *New York Times Magazine* 20 January. Accessed March 18, 2012, from http://www-personal.umich.edu/~gmarkus/secession.html

Riesman Jr, D. (1940) 'Book review: Punishment and social structure', by G. Rusche and O. Kirchheimer, *Columbia Law Review*, 40(7): 1297–301.

Rusche, G. (1930 [1978]) 'Labor market and penal sanction: thoughts on the sociology of punishment', *Social Justice*, 10: 2–8.

Rusche, G. (1933 [1980]) 'Prison revolts or social policy: lessons from America', *Social Justice*, 13: 41–44.

Rusche, G. and Kirchheimer, O. (1939 [2003]) *Punishment and Social Structure.* New Brunswick, NJ: Transaction.

Sayer, A. (2001) 'For a critical cultural political economy', *Antipode*, 33(4): 687–708.

Schor, J. (1992) *The Overworked American.* New York: Basic Books.

Sennett, R. (1998) *The Corrosion of Character. The Personal Consequences of Work in the New Capitalism.* New York: Northon.

Shipler, D.K. (2004) *The Working Poor. Invisible in America.* New York: Vintage.

Simon, J. (2007) *Governing Through Crime. How the War on Crime Transformed American Democracy and Created a Culture of Fear.* New York: Oxford University Press.

Spierenburg, P. (1984) *The Spectacle of Suffering.* Cambridge: Cambridge University Press.

Spitzer, S. (1975) 'Toward a Marxist theory of deviance', *Social Problems*, 22(5): 638–51.

Sutton, J. (2004) 'The political economy of imprisonment in affluent western democracies, 1960–1990', *American Sociological Review*, 69: 170–9.

Taylor, I., Walton, P. and Young, J. (1973) *The New Criminology. For a Social Theory of Deviance.* London: Routledge.

Thompson, E.P. (1967) 'Time, work-discipline and industrial capitalism', *Past & Present*, 38(1): 56–97.

Van Swaaningen, R. (1997) *Critical Criminology: Visions from Europe*. London: SAGE Publications.

Wacquant, L. (2009) *Punishing the Poor. The Neoliberal Government of Social Insecurity*. Durham, NC: Duke University Press.

Wallace, D. (1980) 'The political economy of incarceration trends in late US capitalism: 1971–1977', *The Insurgent Sociologist*, 11(1): 59–66.

3

Punishment and the Political Technologies of the Body

Jonathan Simon

INTRODUCTION: REVISITING THE BIRTH OF THE PRISON AND THE REAWAKENING OF THE SOCIAL STUDY OF PUNISHMENT

In important respects the 1970s was the foundational moment for the revival of punishment and society as a distinct and productive intellectual field at the intersection of criminology, sociology, political science and history. We can point to multiple intellectual sources of emergence in the decade. In the UK, and the USA British cultural studies (Cohen, 1973; Hall et al., 1978), radical criminologies (Platt, 1977; Taylor et al., 1973) and historians studying crime and society in 18th-century England (Hay et al., 1975; Thompson, 1975) all rediscovered Durkheim's interest in the relationship between crime and social order (Garland, 1990).

On the continent, two books written quite independently helped bring punishment and its forms and methods to the fore of this new interest in criminal justice; *Discipline and Punish: The Birth of the Prison,*[1] written by French philosopher and historian Michel Foucault (1977) and published in French in 1975, and two years later, the *Prison and the Factory*[2] written by Italian sociologists Dario Melossi and Massimo Pavarini (1981). Perhaps more than any other contributions, these two books helped to awaken the sociology of punishment from its long 20th-century slumber.

Discipline and Punish and *The Prison and the Factory* shared a focus on the transformations in the form of punishment at the end of the 18th century, 'the birth of the prison' as the Foucault put it, and the 'origins of the penitentiary' as Melossi and Pavarini did. This historical moment was critical for all these themes that were reanimating punishment and society, the problematization of crime rates, the beginnings of a rehabilitative focus to punishment, a moment of profound social and political revolution. These were not the only studies at this time reexamining this phase of penal history, but compared to others historians who focused more on changes in the political and moral ideas associated with punishment at the end of the 18th century (Rothman, 1972; Ignatieff, 1979), the two books shared attention to the precise relationship between changing forms of punishment and developments in the available schemas for coordinating and controlling human bodies to produce power or political authority, or as Foucault framed it to 'try and study the metamorphosis of punitive methods on the basis of a political technology of the body in which might be read a common history of power relations and object relations' (1977: 24). Each book examined the early prison and many of the same carceral practices that had preceded it (like the work house), not from the perspective of how it is determined by either crime or law, nor even as a function of some generalized features of the social order, but for its capacity to harness effective technologies of power over the body.

This approach was a radical break from the classic works of the sociology of punishment, including both Rusche and Kirchheimer's (1939 [2003]) analysis of punishment with respect to labor markets,[3] and Durkheim's 1892 (1997) analysis of punishment with respect to social solidarity. While Rusche and Kirchheimer and Durkheim moved the study of punishment away from an exclusive focus on law and crime, they treated penal practices themselves as mostly a reflection of the social structure in which they were being deployed. Their powerful insights about the work punishment does in society are often accompanied by fairly superficial analyses of how punishment is actually carried out and what it does to those subjected to it. It is in *Discipline and Punish* and *The Prison and the Factory* that the 'how' of punishment comes sharply into focus.[4] Today this focus punishment in relation to technologies of power continues to shape a great deal of work in punishment and society (Shalev, 2009; Garland, 2010; Harcourt, 2011).

In this chapter, I want to extract the analytic approach of studying the changing forms of penal practice in relationship to technologies of power over the human body and its conduct and relations from the specific case of the birth of the prison to which both *Discipline and Punish*, and *The Prison and the Factory*, were dedicated. Both books were primarily concerned with understanding the emergence of the penitentiary in the context of the 18th and 19th centuries, and the emergence of an industrial capitalist economy. Both studies focused readers on the importance of discipline as a specific (if very broad) technology of power that was crucial to the emergence of the penitentiary as the solution to the political problems of traditional forms of outdoor physical punishment that had come under scrutiny at the end of the 18th century. This creates a significant problem for contemporary students coming to the study of punishment in the early 21st century, at a time when resurgent global capitalism has little interest in disciplining a domestic working class (finding it cheaper to search globally for culturally docile ones), and when the disciplinary logic of the prison has largely been superseded by other penal projects, especially in the USA, the exclusionary logic of 'mass incarceration'.

This chapter aims at recovering the productive potential for analyzing punishment as a political technology, by suggesting that Foucault, and Melossi and Pavarini demonstrate an analytic approach that can be useful well beyond the specific historical terms of its application in their celebrated books, and by examining the work of subsequent authors who have pursued this kind of analysis in revisiting the history of the prison, and moving forward in history through two other periods of profound change in punishment in many industrial and post industrial societies.

To speak of a technology of power, or a political technology,[5] is not to engage in a metaphor. Foucault is not suggesting that the intellectual schemas he extracts from the emerging vision of the prison can be analogized to machines. Technology comes from the Greek *techne* meaning 'art, skill or craft'; it is, in that sense nothing technological in our common sense of machine operated. It would be a mistake in this context, to conflate penal technologies, like say the electric chair, or the one piece toilet sink used in many modern cellular prisons, and the political technologies of the body upon which a broad configuration of the power to punish rests. Tools and techniques are part of technology, but it also includes 'crafts, systems, or methods, for organization in order to solve some problem or serve some purpose' (Wikipedia). A political technology of the body, then, is a craft, system, or method for organizing bodies to produce specific effects that have a political value or purpose. Punishment is a political technology in this sense, but changes in how punishment is carried out can also be related to the circulation of technologies of power from elsewhere into the penal field.

The focus on punishment and political technologies should not lead us to ignore institutions, specific techniques, or penal actors and their strategies and projects. Any particular penal institution, such as capital punishment, imprisonment or even the fine, has a history of its own and is shaped by a variety of factors. Technologies of power are only part of the ensemble of determining the features of penal institutions over time. They become particularly important, I will argue, when institutions are undergoing profound pressure for change, and activists and reformers are seeking new strategies and projects to address suddenly apparent scandals or flaws in the operation of traditional institutions and practices. In doing so they will often promote a particular technique, for example, isolation or the silent system in the early penitentiaries.

I argue that analyzing change in penal methods through political technologies provides a productive 'middle range' framework that can help identify and organize evidence about specific practices and techniques at the micro-level, and probe the relationship between changing penal institutions and practices and developments in political and economic structures of society at the macro-level. Foucault was a great generator of evocative analytic terms, writing variously of technologies, strategies and rationalities, as well as *dispositifs* the overall ensembles or structures that bring them together to anchor the exercise of power at particular times and places. However, the researcher in punishment and society does not have to adopt this whole framework, to make productive use of the analytic strategy of reading penal change through technologies of power. But rather than working this term into the broader structure of Foucault's terminology (e.g. bio-power, governmentality, etc.) it is more valuable to see the analytic work that political technologies do in Foucault's research, as comparable to what social theorists, such as Pierre Bourdieu (1986), get from their analysis of differential capitals, and sociologists of science, such as Bruno Latour (1987), get from concepts such as 'black boxing' or 'actor/network'.

Both *Discipline and Punishment* and *The Prison and the Factory* gave their central focus to 'discipline', a technology of the body which according to Foucault, combined surveillance or monitoring, corrective exercise and examination to constitute control over a group of individuals but in ways that also make them as a larger ensemble, more productive and effective. Both books identified the continuity between the disciplinary colonization of the spaces and procedures of penal justice in the 18th and 19th centuries and contemporary prisons and the broader criminal justice field (as of the 1970s). Many readers ever since have take the point to be the relationship between prison and discipline, or a disciplinary technology of power, or even, more misleadingly, 'disciplinary power'. In the first decade after both books were published, many students of punishment and society debated whether the modern correctional field, as it still existed in the early 1980s with many of the institutions of 'penal-welfarism' (Garland, 1985) still functioning, for example, parole, probation, juvenile justice, correctional prisons, were best understood as an extension of the disciplinary technologies associated with the rise of the penitentiary, or as developed through bringing in new and distinctive technologies to the field of punishment (Cohen, 1979; Bottoms, 1983; Mathiesen, 1983; Shearing and Stenning, 2003; Garland, 1985). In the intervening decades, penal welfare has itself been transformed by a new wave, especially in the USA, of prison expansion and reshaped by the imperatives of incapacitation, control, and containment (Feeley and Simon, 1992; Garland, 2001a; Wacquant, 2009).

In making sense of penal change I will argue it is most productive to think of the disciplines as just one political technology that has shaped the evolution of punishment. For any period of transformation, for example from the late 18th century to the 1830s in the USA (Meranze, 1996) and parts of Europe, or the 1880s through the 1920s in the UK (Garland, 1985), it makes sense to explore the full range of political technologies available to help rework the methods of punishment, and try to make sense of why certain ones prevail.[6] For analytic purposes, I argue that it is most productive to think about three historical periods including and following the birth of the prison, in which the array of modern penal techniques have been reworked by the introduction of new technologies of power. Table 3.1, provides a schematic over view of these periods.

These are the birth of the 'penitentiary' in the 19th century, the advent of 'penal-welfarism' (or 'the social') that includes the development of new penal institutions like probation and juvenile justice in the early 20th century, and the development of mass incarceration (Garland, 2001a; Western, 2006) in the late 20th and early 21st centuries. Reality is, of course, too complicated for matrices, whether with two rows or three, especially when we look across the variety of penal cultures in the world today. Even focusing on the advanced industrialized and liberal societies of the West (Europe, North American, parts of Asia and Australia), there is more diversity than can be artfully projected on paper. For present purposes however, the fiction of uniformity can be usefully adopted for the first two periods. The rise of the penitentiary style prison was widely adopted across the advanced societies by the middle of the 19th century. Likewise, the second wave of transformation, around penal-welfarism, was widely followed between the end of the 19th century and the middle of the 20th century. In the third period however, there is rather more divergence than can be captured by the metaphor of lagging change over time. The USA, with its mass incarceration and supermax prisons has broken decisively with second period practices, but it is far from clear that this is a road the rest of the advanced countries will follow. The account given here, of the third period, therefore, focuses heavily on the USA, with readers invited to imagine alternative paths in their own societies.

In the first section, drawing on both *Discipline and Punish* and *The Prison and the Factory,* I will try state more precisely the analytic significance of the move from a sociology of punishment, such as both Durkheim (1997) and Rusche and Kirchheimer (1939 [2003]) performed it, to a study of punishment and political technologies. Since this 'tool-kit' gets shaped in the very productivity with which both sets of authors used it to interrogate the already well-established empirical record concerning the emergence of the penitentiary and its relationship to early industrial capitalism in the 19th century, my discussion will focus on their use of this framework.

In the second section, we will examine the emergence of 'penal-welfarism' (Garland, 1985) and the emergence of new institutions like parole and probation during the maturing of industrial capitalism in the early 20th century. In the third section, we will explore mass incarceration and related practices of segregation and exile as a 'containment' technology in the context of 'neo' or 'advanced' liberal efforts to govern in the context of an increasingly global form of capitalism.

Table 3.1 Technologies of punishment and the political economy of the body

Century	*Political economy*	*Technology of control*	*Exemplary penal form*	*Target of penal technology*	*Nature of the penal subject*	*Scholarship*
18–19th	Emerging industrial capitalism	Discipline and training of the body through exacting labor	Cellular (Panoptic) Prison	'Soul'	Recalcitrant member of the 'dangerous classes' who must be made a 'docile and useful' worker	Foucault (1977); Melossi and Pavarini (1981)
19–20th	Welfare capitalism	Supervision of the body in the community through surveillance, interviews, standardized tests	Probation	'Social network'	Defective adult whose integration into society has been undermined by immigrant status, or biological/psychological defects	Garland (1985); Platt (1977); Rothman (1980); Simon (1993)
20th–21st	Neoliberalism	Containment through confinement or constant monitoring of the position of the body	Supermax prison/ electronic monitoring	'Dangerous class'	'Predator' – high risk offender prone to either repeat or violent crimes	Bottoms (1983); Feeley and Simon (1992, 1994); Garland (2001a); Wacquant (2009)

DISCIPLINE: RE-WORKING PUNISHMENT FOR CAPITALIST SOCIETY

In what can be justly thought of as a 'big bang' moment for the contemporary field of punishment and society, Foucault's book, *Discipline and Punish* was published in France in 1975 and over the next two years an English translation appeared in the UK and then the USA to largely rapturous reviews and a broad interdisciplinary audience. Far less noticed at the time (although it quickly became a classic among students of punishment) was Melossi and Pavarini's, *The Prison and the Factory*, which first appeared in Italian in 1977 and was published in English translation in 1981. It is remarkable in retrospect how close in intellectual discovery and insight these two completely independent research enterprises turned out to be.[7] Both approached the prison in the context of the larger reworking of power relations under early capitalism. Both saw the penitentiary style prison as a reworking of methods first developed in workhouses, asylums,and other sites for control over the deviant (but not necessarily criminal) populations of early modern Europe.

Technologies of power

In the case of Foucault, it has been tempting to treat his analysis of the birth of the prison as offering a power-based theory of punishment that parallels those of sociologists of punishment working in either a Marxist or Durkheimian approach.[8] Bringing Melossi and Pavarini back into the picture makes clear that the common innovation they share with Foucault, is with an attention to technologies of power, not as a rival theory of the penal field to Marx or Durkheim, but as an analytic method to the history of penal change, one that attends to the field of forces, both intellectual and material, that penal practices bring to bear on the body of penal subjects, and on the resulting power and truth effects. This is quite clear from the way each of them relate to the seminal work of Rusche and Kirchheimer (1939 [2003]) whose study published as *Punishment and Social Structure* drew on Frankfurt School Marxism (Jay, 1973) to examine the relationship between changes in the methods of punishment and changes in the demands of capitalist labor markets.[9]

For both Foucault (1977) and Melossi and Pavarini (1981) political economy was a starting point of analysis, but they do not attempt to interpret the logic of penal practices directly through an analysis of political economy. Both took ideas as central objects of inquiry, but they avoided the then standard Marxist recourse to treating ideas as 'ideology', that is, as a way of producing the consent of the exploited to their exploitation.[10] Instead both enterprises treat ideas as instruments for practical action and administration. Finally, both books treat the emergence of a distinctive penal subject behind the crime and the punishment, 'the abnormal/normal individual' (Foucault, 1977: 24) not as the reason for a reconfiguration of punishment but as its effect.

For Rusche and Kirchheimer (1939 [2003]) it is the revaluation of labor power that produces the crisis of scaffold punishments[11] at the beginning of the 19th century. With the advent of wage labor, punishments that primarily kill and wound become problematic. The criminal body can now be valued as a laboring body, whether laboring in prison or back in 'free' society under some penal status, or as an ex-prisoner, a status that has some commercial value, however low it may fall, that has some value in a capitalist market for labor that is not totally dependent on local hierarchies.[12] But Rusche and Kirchheimer have little to say about why the prison emerges as the key replacement for scaffold punishment in the 19th century, as opposed to other labor oriented punishments that preserve and exploit the labor power of penal subjects. Indeed the variability in the history of punishment seems to speak to this loose coupling. Before beginning his own account of the system of wounding and killing scaffold punishments, Foucault notes that 'Rusche and Kirchheimer are right to see it as the effect of a system of production in which labour power, and therefore the human body, has neither the utility nor the commercial value that are conferred on them in an economy of an industrial type' (1977: 54)

However, it is not an account that can explain why it is the disciplinary prison that emerges as the almost universal solution to the problem of punishing those convicted of serious crimes (or even repeated minor crimes) by the end of the 19th century throughout these societies. Capitalist England, for example, which does seem to revalue the labor power of criminal bodies, and cut its heavy reliance on the scaffold during the industrial take off in the late 18th and early 19th centuries, experiments with a number of penal methods including transportation, before settling into the penitentiary style prison in the middle of the 19th century.

Melossi and Pavarini (1981) as well, develop their account precisely to fill in this 'gap' in Marxist historiography of the prison. And both will conclude that it is the facility of prison to serve as a site for deployment of disciplinary techniques, or corrective training combined with harsh demeaning labor that primarily determines its emergence.

There were at least 'three technologies of power ...' available to recasting the exercise of the power to punish at the end of the 18th century (Foucault, 1977: 131). One was a technology of physical control and coercion of the body to produce pain, mutilation and humiliation, which remained part of the still predominant practice of punishment upon the scaffold and was utilized as well in the closely related practices of judicial torture. The scaffold may have been becoming problematic for reasons of labor markets (Rusche and Kirchheimer, 1939 [2003]) as well as for changing moral sensibilities (Durkheim 1969), but it continued to produce effects of both truth and power in the wide circulation of real and contrived sights and statements on or about the scaffold, transmitted through broadsheet newspapers as well as in the telling of the sometimes massive audiences drawn to see executions.

A second technology involved deploying bodies in highly staged public acts of useful service, which Foucault described as a 'school rather than a festival' (1977: 111), in which citizens would learn the virtue of the law through watching its execution. Some of these practices, such as wheelbarrow men who cleaned public streets in Philadelphia at the end of the 18th century were tried (Meranze, 1996), while others only reached the stage of proposals; many from the great critics of the scaffold including Beccaria, Jefferson and Montesquieu.

The third technology was discipline, the arts of surveillance, exercise and judgment these were quite visible in places like the national militaries that formed in response to the Napoleonic wars at the beginning of the 19th century. They had also been increasingly used as a punitive relief measure for the disreputable poor in institutions like the influential Amsterdam *Rasphuis*, where indigent men were set to turning logs of wood into sawdust for the burgeoning paint industry.

The question that both *Discipline and Punish* and *The Prison and the Factory* set out to answer was '[h]ow is it, that in the end, it was the third that was adopted' (Foucault, 1977: 131).[13]

In seeking to answer this very precise research question, both books followed three important methodological strategies.

Treat political economy as the horizon for penal change but as under-determining it

In addition to praising Rusche and Kirchheimer for disavowing a juristic understanding of punishment, Foucault goes further, embracing their effort to correlate the forms of punishment with the 'systems of production in which they operate' (1977: 24). Indeed, he notes, 'we can surely accept the general proposition that, in our societies,[14] the systems of punishment are to be situated in a certain 'political economy' of the body' (1977: 25). It is unclear whether he means by this to fully embrace a Marxist sort of political economy of the sort that Melossi and Pavarini do.[15] For Melossi and Pavarini, much the same gap is at issue.

> It needs to be stressed, of course, that a hypothesis restricted largely to the relationship beween the labour market and forced labour (in the sense of unfree labour) cannot exhaust the entire thematic of the workhouses. ... The function of workhouses was undoubtedly much more complex than that of being a simple regulator of free labour. To put it a different way, one could say that this last objective taken in its fullest sense means *control of the labour force*, its education and training. ... Workhouses and many other similar organizations respond especially to this need. (1981: 17, original emphasis)

Thus for both books, the study of punishment as a technology of power begins with political economy as a kind of horizon for punishment, establishing its functional imperatives and negative constraints but not specifying its form. 'Analyze punitive methods not simply as consequences of legislation or as indicators of social structures, but as techniques possessing their own specificity in the more general field of other ways of exercising power' (Foucault, 1977: 23).

It is not surprising that penal institutions respond quickly and early to profound changes in political economy. As institutions that are largely bound to fail in their own terms of suppressing crime, and which are likely to come under particular stress and scrutiny during periods of social conflict, penal institutions are always about 'reform'; either the existing ideals, still in need of proper implementation, or through proclaiming new ideals. When something important changes in the political economy, throwing into question the practicality or relevance of existing assumptions about social stability, the legitimacy of the institutions of punishment are likely to be seen as in crisis and requiring dramatic changes. While the new framework of political economy often comes with a ready critique of existing penal practices, it does not as readily incorporate a clear direction for change.

Treat penal ideas as technical rather than moral

Both *Discipline and Punish* and *The Prison and the Factory* seek to take the design of the penitentiary seriously as an intellectual rather than simply moral or economic innovation but at the same time avoid privileging the enlightenment narrative that accompanied the emergence of the penitentiary and which casts the prison as product of enlightened reasoning about punishment. The focus on punishment as a technology allows them to foreground intellectual breakthroughs in the design of the form of punishment as shaping both new penal purposes like reform and penitence and the new human sciences that begin to claim a primary role in organizing the power to punish (Foucault, 1977: 23).

It is not to the better established sciences or philosophy that one should look to find the ideas that made confinement in the cellular prison the solution which has dominated our penal imagination now for some three hundred years, but to a murkier terrain of semi-practical knowledges, associated with technical rather than academic expertise.[16] For Foucault the technologies of power are often to be discovered among those minor techniques, uncelebrated by historians compared with the great scientific technologies, contrasting the telescope and lens with the techniques of visibility at work in army camps).

To speak of a 'technology of power' does not imply that completely specified template or 'blue print' for producing practices.

> Of course, this technology is diffuse, rarely formulated in continuous, systematic discourse; it is often made up of bits and pieces; it implements a disparate set of tools or methods. In spite of the coherence of its results, it is generally no more than a multiform instrumentation. Moreover, it cannot be localized in a particular type of institution or state apparatus. (Foucault, 1977: 26)

Foucault's analysis of Bentham's *Letters on the Panopticon*, which Foucault drew on at great length in his examination of the precise mechanisms of disciplinary power may have subverted his own caution, writing that the 'Pantopicon ... is in fact a figure of political technology that may and must be detached from any specific use' (Foucault, 1977: 205). Melossi and Pavarini detect this precisely as the key insight in Foucault's *Discipline and Punish* and the link with their own project.

> The great merit of Michel Foucault's recent book is that it places the relationship between *technique* and the *ideology* of control back on its feet, demonstrating how ideology (obedience and discipline) does not come to determine the *practical* reason, the morality, but how on the contrary this is produced by specific techniques of control over the body (in military art, school, ateliers, etc.). (1981: 45, original emphasis)

Taking our lead from Melossi and Pavarini, it is crucial to focus the inquiry not on the more grandiose schemes of various penal reformers but on the precise ways in which particular mechanisms exert 'specific techniques of control over the body'.

Follow the body

The shift from scaffold to penitentiary seems to suggest a remarkable letting go of the body which had been the focus of both the scaffold ritual and its instruments. Both *Discipline and Punish* and *The Prison and the Factory*, show that just the opposite occurs; the body of the criminal becomes even more invested by the practices of punishment that now substitute the brief if intense festival of pain with a constant and more or less meticulous control of the body. If the penitentiary and its successors claimed to work on the soul or psyche, this was rather an effect of the deployment of a disciplinary power over the body. Thus in *Discipline and Punish*, Foucault famously pronounced that:[17]

> The individual is no doubt the fictitious atom of an 'ideological' representation of society; but he is also a reality fabricated by this specific technology of power that I have called 'discipline'. (1977: 194)

The relationship between punishment and political technologies then runs through the body. It is not the technology itself that punishment absorbs, but a way to control bodies. The modern delinquent, the abnormal/normal individual, the docile worker, is itself the long-run effect of a certain technology of power over the body.

History of the present

Both Foucault in *Discipline and Punish*, and Melossi and Pavarini in *The Prison and the Factory*, expressly brought to the center of their analysis, a concern with the present and the role of penal institutions in it. In this sense both are doing what Foucault called a 'history of the present'.[18] For both, the political turmoil and struggles in the early 1970s within the prisons, factories and universities, provided a grid of intelligibility for revising the standard account of the history of penal reform. The disciplinary logic of the penitentiary and its successors had been hiding in plain sight, disguised only by the Whiggish self-congratulation that saw in the shift from scaffold to reformatory the long overdue recognition of the criminal's humanity. The political struggles of prisoners and students made visible the coercive and bodily technologies of power behind that humanitarianism. As Foucault put it:

> What was at issue [in the prison revolts of the 1960s and 1970s] was not whether the prison environment was too harsh or too aseptic, too primitive or too efficient, but its very materiality as an instrument and vector of power; it is this whole technology of power over the body that the technology of the 'soul' – that of the educationalists, psychologists and psychiatrists – fails either to conceal or to compensate, for the simple reason that it is one of its tools. (1977: 30)

In their extended response to Foucault,[19] published as an appendix to the English translation of their book, Melossi and Pavarini criticized Foucault (or at least the reception of *Discipline and Punish* among students of punishment) precisely for straying from the history of the present into a more general sociological theory of punishment.

> In conclusion, without denying the extremely salutary and profound impact which Foucault's perspective has had (also) in relation to the history of the prison institution, it seems to me that the kind of detailed work required in this field is local research unconstrained by 'great visions' of an ideological nature; research which would facilitate an appreciation of local strategies and moves in the game of social control. It is, in fact, probable that such research will induce us to abandon any general hypothesis as to recurrent or fixed relationships between large-scale socio-economic data. Instead, our interest would focus on clearly defined relations valid at specific times and within specific parameters in relation to particular societies, particular periods, particular forms of social control, class composition, and so forth. (Melossi and Pavarini, 1981: Appendix p. 195)

Foucault certainly would have agreed.

The penitentiary

For both *Discipline and Punish* and *The Prison and the Factory*, the empirical focus of their analysis is the emergence of the penitentiary style prison as the dominant mode of sanctioning serious crime, a process that begins at the end of the 18th century and is largely complete in the emerging industrial societies by the middle of the 19th century. Through the 18th century imprisonment remains mostly a place of detention for those awaiting trial, execution or pardon. It rarely figured as a punishment itself. Yet throughout that century, interest had grown in using indoor relief of vagrants coupled with coercive work exercises, to discourage begging and encourage habits of work. It is the shift of these disciplinary technologies from the space of the workhouse to a space defined as punishment by the middle of the 19th century that both books consider.

Political economy

Foucault situates the crisis of scaffold punishment at the point of emergence of a capitalist economy – both in terms of wage labor and the rise of valuable commercial commodities – and in the growing democratization of public space and the concomitant increase in the regularity of mass public events. The scaffold punishments were viewed as increasingly problematic in relation to a number of specific issues arising from these transitions.[20]

Punishment was seen by this new public, especially the rising influence of those involved entrepreneurial capitalism, as needing to become more effective in protecting property from the rising importance of theft and more congruent with a general social demand for the regularity of hard work. The old scaffold punishments were increasingly inapt to respond to property crimes because their very severity encouraged forms of leniency that undermined the deterrent power of the criminal law. The scaffold, with its festival like ambience and its celebration of the excessive and the atrocious, produced an effect, interrupting both production and routine civic order. For many of the same reasons, scaffold punishment was an obstacle to producing a more orderly and businesslike public. Far from being an encouragement to a more controlled society, the rituals of the scaffold encouraged drinking, fighting and the solidarity of friendship and kinship networks, over that of the State and its agents (Linebaugh, 2011).

As Melossi and Pavarini describe the logic of workhouse labor it is clear that the effect is not just on the penal subject but on the larger milieu of working class life:

> The prominence given to order, cleanliness, uniforms, hygiene (except of course when it came to working conditions), the rules against swearing, using slang or obscene language, reading, writing or singing ballads unless allowed by the governors (in a place and time characterized by the struggle for freedom of thought!), the prohibitions on gambling and the use of nicknames, etc. - all of this constituted an attempt both to impose the newly discovered way of life and to smash a radically counterposed underground popular

> culture which combined forms of the old peasant way of life with new methods of resistance called forth by capitalism's incessant attacks on the proletariat. (1981: 22)

The triumph of a disciplinary technology of control over the body

For Foucault, the prison emerges as the dominant method of punishing serious crime in modern society, out of the three possible technologies of punishment in part because unlike the scaffold, or the 'punitive city' as a social school model of outdoor expressive punishments that some of the 18th-century reformers favored (Meranze, 1996), the prison did not aggravate these problems and indeed seemed a promising way to diminish them. The prison permits a far more graduated system of sanctions, the better to encourage full enforcement of the criminal laws protecting property. It operates to enforce discipline and self-control on those subjected to its rigors without the need or occasion for unruly publics to gather. Indeed, linked to the parallel network of metropolitan policing, which emerged in the 19th century, the penal system can operate as a continuous and unobtrusive system of control facilitating rather than interrupting the public.

However, this 'fit' of the prison is not based on its theoretical foundations, let alone on whether they turn out to be empirically correct, but instead, for Foucault, on the spread throughout society of mechanisms and institutions based on a disciplinary technology of power. This disciplinary network allows the prison to appear as able to exercise the power to punish in light of the political economic challenges facing the power to punish in the 19th century. As Barry Smart aptly put it in a helpful early interpretation:

> The self evidence which imprisonment soon assumed as the generalized form of punishment was a consequence not only of the apparent appropriateness of punishing offenders through the deprivation of their liberty ... but more significantly, it stemmed from the fact that it employed, albeit in a more explicit and intense form, all the disciplinary mechanisms found elsewhere in the social body for transforming individuals. (1983: 74)

Melossi and Pavarini (1981) also identify the spread of disciplinary technologies through a whole set of formally distinct institutions dealing with the poor. The prison is only one institution that finds in the disciplinary technology of power over the body, a reliable new platform for reconstructing punishment for an age of industrial capitalism.

> The total impoverishment of the individual takes place in manufacture and in the factory; but preparation and training is ensured by a string of ancillary institutions from which basic features of modern life have already begun to develop by this time: the nuclear family, school, prison, the hospital and later the barracks and the mental asylum ensure the production, education and reproduction of the workforce for capital. (Melossi and Pavarini, 1981: 23)

Both Foucault and Melossi and Pavarini saw the target of the disciplinary power to punish as the bodies of recalcitrant members of the lowest classes, displaced from rural areas by the new commercial agriculture. Crowded into towns and cities, most of which did not yet have ways of profitably employing them in labor, the mobile poor became the 'dangerous classes' greatly feared by the upper classes of early 19th-century Europe and in the USA (Chevalier, 1958; Vogel, 2004).

The soul of punishment

Both books argued that the penitentiary was designed to produce as an effect, a distinctive subjectivity. For Melossi and Pavarini it is the disciplined subject of industrial labor. The prison, they note, like the workshop, is less another place for production than 'a place for teaching the *discipline of production*' (1981: 21, original emphasis). For Foucault (1977) disciplinary practices produce above all, a delinquent subject, a abnormal/normal individual, whose life course of persistence in crime became the real and permanent concern of the legal system.[21]

Subsequent work would question this continuity between the disciplinary technology at work in the birth of the prison and the more overtly psychological and individualizing regime that was in full flower in the 1970s.[22] Garland (1985) argued that Foucault was wrong, at least as to the Victorian penal system, to assume that a significant degree of individualization was associated with the practice of discipline. The disciplined subject of the penitentiary remained a highly abstract and ideological figure in prison discourse and practice of 19th-century prisons. Neither the length of sentence, nor in any significant way the treatment of prisoners was varied based on assessment of their psychological condition (except at the very extreme of the insanity defense).

While the very cellular architecture of the prison was arguably a surface ready to be deepened by an individualizing knowledge of the life history of the penal subject, Garland is convincing that this is a later development. In our framework here, it is seen as part of the second phase of penal transformations discussed below.

WELFARE: THE SOCIALIZATION OF PUNISHMENT IN THE ERA OF INDUSTRIAL CAPITALISM

Historians and sociologists have long agreed that the late 19th and early 20th centuries represented a significant reorganization of the legal and organizational fields in which the power to punish operated one almost as dramatic as the one that saw the scaffold replaced by the penitentiary (Schlossman, 1977; Rothman, 1980; Sutton, 1988). Although the prison did not disappear by any means (neither for a long time did the scaffold), it was supplemented and displaced from the center of penality by a panoply of new penal institutions including probation, parole, and juvenile justice. All of these shared a focus on the offender in his or her social milieu. Rather than isolating the person engaged in criminal conduct in a space of total control, all three bring the power to punish, and now correct, out into the community.

Industrial capitalism and the early welfare state

This reconfiguration of the power to punish began in the last decades of the 19th century in the most developed capitalist countries, and gained momentum throughout the first half of the 20th century, achieving its greatest strength in the first two decades after the Second World War when the relative affluence afforded by mature industrial capitalism gives rise to an unprecedented extension of welfare measures throughout society.

If the political economic imperative behind the crisis of scaffold punishments was the need to create appropriate social conditions for the flourishing of capitalism, including the formation of an industrial working class, or 'proletariat', beginning in the late 18th century, the problem for power at the end of the 19th century is how to integrate that proletariat into the structures of an increasingly consumerist urban society and democratic polity. In Garland's (1985) classic account of the breakdown of Victorian penality[23] (which was very much anchored in the penitentiary model and its disciplinary technology) at the end of the 19th century, he pointed to twin imperatives of political economy in the world's most advanced capitalist society of that era. The first was the movement of the leading edge of British capitalism into an era of consolidation (Marxists would say Monopoly capitalism). The second was the democratization of British society, primarily the expansion of the electoral franchise to include those without property (and thus very likely) working-class voters.

For Garland, the argument is not that these very important changes in the distribution of power in the UK (and other advanced industrial countries) produced or projected a new array of penal methods, or demanded on their own the deployment of a new technology of power within the penal field. It is rather that against the background of these changes in political economy, the existing penal practices were becoming politically problematic. The prison, of course, endured, and it remained in many respects at the center of penality even as probation began to account for an equivalent or larger portion of what could now be called the 'correctional population'.[24] But the narrative of the prison, the account of how it could provide a meaningful contribution to public order was losing its currency (Simon, 1993; Bright, 1996).

For 19th-century government, prisons, as well as indoor relief for the poor in workhouses, constituted an extraordinarily expensive way to govern the poor. It was a practice premised on an alarming conception of the urban poor as 'dangerous classes', an almost alien like threat, who must be isolated to disciplinary institutions of the most coercive sort (Chevalier, 1958). As Garland's detailed account of the Victorian confinement (not only the prison but the workhouse) suggests, its legitimacy was premised on the moral virtue of treating coercively all those who failed the premises of liberal economic theory. The extension of the franchise to all male citizens regardless of property ownership and the formation of a 'respectable' working class with a claim on government responses to the predictable insecurities of market capitalism, created a growing tension with the harshness of Victorian confinement strategies. So while the prison may not have suffered as significant a status decline as scaffold execution did (the latter largely disappearing within a 50-year period), it suffered a two-sided loss of legitimacy (Sparks et al., 1996). A less demonized public image of the lower classes made its necessity less apparent, and its high costs more visible.

Probation and the power of the social

A host of new penal practices emerged to address this growing gap between the current problems of insecurity and the confinement logic of 19th-century penality; including specialized prisons for particular types of offenders and penal measures designed to be implemented in the community including probation, parole and juvenile justice. Of all the new penal techniques that emerged in the late 19th century and become widely spread among jurisdictions in the early decades of the 20th century, probation must be considered the exemplary form. Unlike its close cousin parole, probation does not await the corrective discipline of a prison sentence, but seeks to correct the offender without removing them from the community. Unlike the juvenile court, which shares the same intention to avoid the incarceration of the delinquent, probation takes on the adult convicted of crime without the premise that its subject is not truly a proper offender because of their young age or the responsibility of parents. Probation incorporates a set of elements that will be widely shared by all three including a professional penal agent, the casework method[25] (borrowed from the closely related field of social work), and the involvement of positive pro-social forces within the community itself, including clergy, teachers and employers. As Leon Radzinowicz wrote of probation in the middle of the 20th century:

> If I were to be asked what was the most significant contribution made by this country to the new penological theory and practice which struck root in the 20th century ... my answer would be probation. (1958: x, quoted in Raynor, 2007: 1062)

But as we asked of the scaffold's replacement by the prison, what makes the new penal mechanisms, probation, juvenile courts, parole, individualization in sentencing and classification, an appropriate answer to the problems of the 19th-century prison, and does it make sense to speak of this new penal style as drawing on a distinctive technology of power over the body? Garland (1985) does not use that phrase nor ever claim for the common themes among the new penal techniques of the early 20th century the coherence that Foucault (1977) and Melossi and Pavarini (1981) seemed to give to the disciplines, but he does describe four broad programs,[26] criminological, social work, social security and eugenics, out of which, and through a heavily political process subject to lots of conjunctural events, a 'penal strategy' emerges, that of 'penal-welfarism',

In reviewing Garland's account of the penal strategy that emerged during this period, we can however discern a technology of power over the body, one which was borrowed from the domain of charitable work among the poor, and which eventually was professionalized as social work in the early 20th century. Across these reform measures, most not new but an upgrading of existing private initiatives that had existed for some time around the edges of the penal field into grander public projects (Sutton, 1988), there is a common logic based on individualizing persons convicted of crimes, using the casework method, and either pursuing a corrective supervision of them in the community designed ameliorate the particular variables encouraging crime in their individual case, or assign them to a custodial institution appropriate to their classified need or risk. All of these practices would seek out and apply corrective methods to the penal subject in their actual social context (rather than in confinement) by not being tied to or down by a punitive legalistic concern with a legal conviction for a very serious criminal offense. They would intervene earlier in the life of delinquent individual but stay the hand of the most punitive consequences where the prospects for correction were good. At the same time, and seamlessly, they sought out those who posed a risk of serious criminality and segregate them as much and as early as necessary to protect the public.

Jacques Donzelot (1979), in his parallel study of social control mechanisms in France at the end of the 19th century describes the new logic of control as that of 'the social'. Like disciplinary practices that were spreading in workhouses, asylums, schools and factories in the late 18th and early 19th centuries, 'welfarism' or the 'social' technologies were drawn from the field of poor relief and helped to constitute a broad new strategy for reconstituting the penal field and addressing the political problems of insecurity and inequality in maturing capitalist societies for which penality is both a fertile ground and an opportunity for advanced development (because of the power of the legal sanction). As historians of the subject agree, the implementation of this new strategy was deeply reworked by politics and the existing institutional realities[27] into which these reform proposals were ultimately introduced (Hagan et al., 1979; Rothman, 1980; Garland, 1985; Sutton, 1988). Yet the same historians concur that they were incredibly successful in winning relatively rapid spread (easier in the UK and most European nations than in fractious nation states such as the USA) and that real redistributions occurred in the hold of institutions on bodies. This is especially true of probation, and its post-confinement sisters, which brought large numbers of people under their jurisdiction, some who would otherwise have been in penitentiaries but many more who would not have been subject to this correctional control but for the reforms.

Garland, writing after *Discipline and Punishment* and *The Prison and the Factory* had powerfully asserted the historical importance of discipline and its continued relevance in the present (the 1970s and 1980s), was confronted with the question of whether the transformations in the penal field at the start of the 20th century should be seen as an extension of the disciplinary technology of power that operated in the penitentiary. In *Discipline and Punish*, Foucault drew a direct line between the rise of the penitentiary and the 20th-century practices that remained seemingly strong in the early 1970s and suggests that they have been steadily extended into society:

> The frontiers between confinement, judicial punishment and institutions of discipline, which were already blurred in the classical age, tended to disappear and to constitute a great carceral continuum that diffused penitentiary techniques into the most innocent disciplines, transmitting disciplinary norms into the very heart of the penal system and placing over the slightest illegality, the smallest irregularity, deviation, or anomaly, the threat of delinquency. (1977: 297)

Garland (1985: 31) argued that Foucault overemphasized the continuity between the disciplines of the penitentiary, and the full blown rehabilitative correctional institutions operating in the 1970s.[28]

> In particular the work of Michel Foucault (1977) has argued, with great influence, that the [modern] form of penality was constructed a whole century earlier with the development of the modern prison and its 'disciplinary' forms. He insists that the functions of disciplinary reform and normalization were not 'added on' at a later date, but were from the outset an essential aspect of the prison. In his analysis, the prison is from the start a technique of transformation and not a punishment; directed at the criminal's nature and not his act ... I have begun to demonstrate that, at least for the British case, Foucault's thesis is incorrect. (1985: 31)

Others, including Mathiesen (1983) and Cohen (1979) argued that 20th-century measures represented continued innovation within a disciplinary technology of control; a blurring of its hard lines and a dispersal of it throughout society.[29]

Today this debate seems less central because of the developments we take up in the next section. Moreover, in arguing about whether the new institutions reflected an extension of discipline, we may be investing too much in the analytic power of our own terms.[30] To the extent that Foucault clearly missed (and was not looking for) the penal turn of the early 20th century our analysis today benefits greatly from Garland's work bringing out the distinctive features of penal-welfarism. Disciplinary technology is about corrective training of the body. It operates from fixed positions in closed institutions to produce complete surveillance and internalized obedience in the prisoner. If it distinguishes among individuals, it is only along a linear grid around the normal, which it seeks to return to, and not the '*extended grid of non-equivalent and diverse dispositions*' which Garland described (1985, 28: original emphasis).

If institutions like probation do apply methods that have their origins in the disciplinary technologies of control over the body, like surveillance, corrective training, and moments of close examination of its subjects, they also and crucially leverage this disciplinary control through activating a broader grid of relationships surrounding the subject in a way that the penitentiary very explicitly chooses not to.[31] It aims at social integration. If it operates on the body, it is the body in the natural setting of social life rather than in the artificial and abstract space of the disciplinary institution. These new methods drew on a social technology of power over the bodies of the poor that had been developed by charity workers, one based on wielding the normative power of social relationships, and none more important than the relationship between the professionalized agent of control and the subject embedded in social life.[32]

In short, Foucault was right about the significance of the disciplinary technology of power in the birth of the prison, but wrong to have assumed that there was no important interruption between that transformation and the 'modern' penal system that prisoners in the 1970s were rebelling against. Most importantly, without fully appreciating the distinctive features of the early 20th-century penal institutions that Garland traces in *Punishment and Welfare*, Foucault misunderstood the nature of those contemporary grievances which were, even as he described them in *Discipline and Punish*, less about the disciplinary nature of the prison, and more about its social and psychological dimensions.

Drawing on Foucault's later work, some have suggested that these early 20th-century innovations might be associated with the 'bio-political' technologies of power, ones that like insurance, regulation, and welfare tend to operate on larger groups or whole populations (Foucault, 1978; Smart, 1983; Bottoms, 1983: 194–5). Some of the new penal techniques introduced at the turn of the 20th century were clearly linked to these technologies of control over the body aimed at the problematic of the population, for example the eugenic effects of segregating recidivists. Anxieties about the population as a direct subject of power, so evident in these programs, associated with immigration in the USA and the imperial project in Europe, clearly defined some of the problems that penal techniques had to help solve (or at least not make worst). At the same time bio-political technologies do not seem to have influenced the form or practice of most of the techniques pushed by reformers.

A more helpful parallel may to be an altogether different kind of social technology that Foucault identified with religion, education, and generally pastoral institutions, that is, the care of the subject as a self.

> [T]echnologies of the self, which permit individuals to effect by their own means or with the help of others a certain number of operations on their own bodies and souls, thoughts, conduct, a way of being, so as to transform themselves in order to attain a certain state of happiness, purity, wisdom, perfection, or immortality. (Foucault, 1988: 18)

While disciplinary technologies of power involve small groups or individuals exercising power over larger assemblies through the use of architectures of confinement and methods of surveillance, and bio-political technologies of power involve small groups or individuals exercising power over whole segments of the population through actuarial and financial methods, probation (and most of the other early 20th century penal mechanisms) involve power being exercised from one individual to another through their ongoing relationship. The relationship between penal subject and probation officer is not a panoptic one, and least of all a form of population management, it is an ultimately a dialogic and ethical relationship, or as Mike Nellis puts it, an 'incentive-based, trust-based and threat-based means of gaining compliance' (2009: 108).[33]

Social networks and the defective adult

If the target of the penitentiary technique is the soul of the prisoner isolated in the cellular structure of the prison, the target of probation is the offender as part of a social network that has facilitated their delinquency and which, with the proper interventions of the penal agent, became a source for correction. The new penal subject had far greater depth and variation than the largely uniform individual acted upon by disciplinary prisons which in Bentham's memorable phrase worked to 'grind rogues honest' (Bentham, 1791, quoted in Garland, 1985: 17). The new science of criminology had projected a range of character defects in individuals that led to deviance, delinquency and ultimately crime including alcoholism, biological degeneration and feeble mindedness. The emerging practice and science of social work saw bad parenting and unorganized communities as causing or enhancing these kinds of character defects. All of the new techniques of penal power shared a premise that effective crime control required legal authority to be refined around such specificities by detailed case knowledge and methods of social diagnosis (Richmond, 1919).

At the center of all of these is the probation officer, who combines the social worker's methods of casework, interviewing and life history construction, with the police officers legal authority (in part) and with the court's power to punish in the form of incarceration. It is true that the probation agent is in some respects in the position of the hierarchical examiner who looms so large in the disciplinary logic of panopticism (Foucault, 1977). In its strongest sites, and against some of its weakest targets, the penal-welfarist system must have felt very coercive indeed (Simon, 1998). Yet there is little panoptic in the actual ability of probation agents to see what the penal subject is up to. To the extent they can make credible their threat of catching the subject in criminal (or better yet, pre-criminal) conduct, it is primarily because of the social institutions in which the penal subject is already embedded, the family, the school, and work (Simon, 1993; Maruna, 1997). The probation agent, in the early 20th century (and for much of it) is as much a conduit from civil society into state legal authority as she is a bridgehead of state power inside the community.

PRECAUTION: PUNISHMENT AS WASTE MANAGEMENT IN NEOLIBERALISM

Talk of penal institutions as technologies of punishment cannot help but understate the variability of reform. Both *Discipline and Punish* and *The Prison and the Factory* treated the spread of the penitentiary model as a global event, although the cases they drew on were less than representative; a problem that has afflicted almost all study of penal change ever since. But the penitentiary, and the disciplinary technology of power at work in the penitentiary style prisons was to a large extent a global phenomenon that followed efforts to modernize penal practices from the end of the 18th century in Europe and North America through the 20th century (as it spreads to Latin America, Asia and Africa). The insights both books generated by treating the disciplinary features of the penitentiary as a generic logic, were well worth the loss of greater attention to national and subnational variations.[34] Likewise the social technology of power, manifest in reforms that began in England and the United States at the end of the 19th century, continues even today to shape penal reform programs (as in the post-Communist transition in Europe). But if it is, on balance, productive to treat the penitentiary and penal-welfarism as general waves of change, the pace and direction of penal reform since 1980 is far harder to determine; either because it is still in its early stages, or because there will not be as common a path as in the past.[35]

The USA, one of the leaders in deploying both disciplinary and social technologies of power for earlier waves of reform, is very much at the forefront of creating what is arguably a new pattern of penal practices and objectives that largely abandons penal-welfarism in favor of containment and control (Deleuze, 1992; Feeley and Simon, 1992; Garland, 2001a), exclusion (Young, 1999), warehousing (Irwin, 2004) and waste management (Simon, 1993; Lynch, 1998). As with earlier waves of reform, we see both new institutions including the supermax prison (Shalev, 2009), spatial exclusion or banishment (Davis, 1990, 1998; Beckett and Herbert, 2008, 2011) and electronic monitoring (Jones, 2000; Nellis, 2009); and the reorienting of older institutions, including mass incarceration prisons (Garland, 2001b; Gottschalk, 2006; Western, 2006; Gilmore, 2007; Simon, 2007) and managerialism in parole and probation into practices of risk management (Cohen, 1985; Bottoms, 1995; Simon, 1993).

While the prison remains at the center of the power to punish, mass incarceration represents a fundamentally different use of the prison than the disciplinary penitentiary or the welfarist correctional institution; and in many respects marks a more substantial break with the past than any change since the rise of the penitentiary. Scholars of punishment and society have pointed to a number of distinguishing features of incarceration in the era of mass incarceration. The scale of incarceration, having remained relatively stable in most countries, including the USA, since the late 19th century, has dramatically surged up in the USA, by a factor of more than five (Zimring and Hawkins, 1993; Garland, 2001b; Western, 2006). Like capital punishment on the scaffold, imprisonment was historically an individualized penalty rather than an automatic sentence for the conviction of a crime (accept for the most serious), and prison sentences themselves were individualized further by the widespread application of parole release. Under mass incarceration imprisonment has been mandated far more generically to whole groups or categories (Bottoms, 1983; Mathiesen, 1983; Cohen, 1985; Feeley and Simon, 1992). The penitentiary and its successors placed great emphasis on their internal design and procedures to effectuate beneficial change in prisoners (although often more in design than in delivery). The prisons of mass incarceration are devoted exclusively to the incapacitative premise of secure containment (Zimring and Hawkins, 1997), and the practice of pure custody, or warehousing (Simon, 2000; Wacquant, 2009).

This is a pattern that has not emerged everywhere across the advanced economies of the world. Indeed, the styles and approaches of contemporary punishment have been usefully described as 'volatile and contradictory' (O'Malley, 1999). Large parts of Europe retain relatively stable prison populations (Tonry, 2007) and even in places where the prison population has grown, as for instance, in the Netherlands and in the Nordic countries, the emphasis remains distinctly welfarist. In North America, Canada has stayed largely welfarist (Meyer and O'Malley, 2005). Even in the USA, some states have retained a more substantial institutional commitment to rehabilitative programming in prisons, and virtually all states have retained the forms of welfare penality, probation, juvenile courts and parole.

Following the insights of both Foucault, and Melossi and Pavarini, we must first look to political economy to establish the horizon in which this variation plays out.

Neoliberalism

The USA is quite clearly the country that has most embraced the containment approach to punishment,[36] while the UK (but primarily England and Wales) has experienced one of the most significant rises in incarceration in Europe (Garland, 2001b; Newburn, 2007), as have the much smaller Northern Irish and Scottish prison systems as well as that of the Republic of Ireland (Kilcommins, et al., 2005). This has led some punishment and society scholars to look to the strong turn toward a neoliberal political economy by the USA, the UK and other English-speaking countries to account for their concentration in the top ranks of imprisonment growth, while the more social democratic and corporatist countries of continental Europe have thus far resisted it (Cavadino and Dignan, 2006; Western, 2006; Wacquant, 2009).

While one can question the coherence or uniformity of 'neoliberalism' as a new political and economic order,[37] it is plausible that something like the classical pattern of political economic transformation, followed by increasing doubt about the existing penal practices and institutions has happened in much of the industrialized world. As political leadership has moved away from an expansive welfare state promising more insurance of one form or another, to more people (Baker and Simon, 2002), and toward a greater emphasis on deregulated markets and greater individual responsibility for social and economic security, the logic of penal-welfarism, has almost everywhere come into question. The weakening of government commitment to expanding insurance and welfare made the very premise for penal-welfarism, that the community has greater resources of producing correctional change than the state can produce in prisons, unsustainable (Beckett, 1997; Garland, 2001a; Wacquant, 2009). The formation of an underclass and a new kind of economically isolated poverty inside the USA (Wilson, 1987; Simon, 1993; Wacquant, 2009) (and to some extent Europe as well) denuded the social networks to which welfarism promised to reintegrate those engaged in crime or delinquent conduct. The extreme reliance of the middle class (and the whole consumer economy in the USA) on property ownership, in the form of owning their home created a form of unspreadable risk that made Americans more vulnerable and more spatially conscious of crime risk and less committed to public property of all sorts (schools, city centers, parks, transportation). Homeowner capitalism made welfarist forms of penality, especially probation and parole (but also juvenile court sanctions) seem a direct danger (Davis, 1990; Simon, 2010). Increased democratization made other forms of social control, ranging from mental hospitals to aggressively policed downtowns, less politically tolerable while encouraging harsh punishments as a 'market-based' solution to crime (Harcourt, 2005, 2011).

While it is easy to see how penal-welfarism loses legitimacy in the face of a broader move away from welfarist solutions to social problems and calls for more market disciplines (especially on the poor and the middle classes), it is more difficult to explain the resulting penal institutions as direct responses to these same imperatives. The growth of the 'penal state' and its high fiscal costs is rather a direct contradiction of the premise that the state needs to shrink and become less coercively present in society. It can be argued that the rhetoric of smaller government is just that, and it disguises a shift from welfare to penal styles of government (Western and Beckett, 1999; Wacquant, 2009), or that prison is a way to channel investment toward preferred segments of society, while disinvesting others (Harcourt, 2011), but while such results may be consistent with the transformation of political economy they would have been difficult to predict from it.

An alternative approach is to view the transformation of political economy as undermining the legitimacy of penal-welfarism and promoting the need for radical reforms. Successful new institutions and practices, or reorientations of old ones, must fit the resulting critique of welfarism, but their specific forms depend on available technologies for reworking the control of bodies.

Technologies of risk management

Can we describe a new political technology or set of technologies, at work in the various elements of the new penology, for example, mass incarceration, spatial exclusion and electronic monitoring? All of these depend in one way or another on a sorting of penal bodies spatially in relation to the risk they pose and a great deal of recent scholarship in punishment and society has attended closely to the relationship between contemporary penal changes and technologies of risk (much of it summarized in O'Malley, 2010).

One risk technology, long drawn on by various governmental institutions is actuarial calculation and prediction. Certain aspects of contemporary penal practices seem to implement this actuarialism. Feeley and Simon (1992) placed these techniques at the heart of what they called the 'new penology'. In this respect, penology seemed to track the path of other fields, including civil justice (Simon, 1988), fire management (O'Malley, 2010: 3) and modern medicine once the very ideal type of social technology.

Like social insurance for work accidents, which assumes that casualties are inevitable but seeks to reduce their number and severity the new penology seems to assume that criminality is largely unchangeable and instead seeks to reduce the number and severity of crimes. The target of the new penology shifts from the discipline of individual bodies, to the control of whole categories of presumptively high-risk individuals through incapacitative custody. In place of social technologies for rehabilitating and reintegrating prisoners, contemporary penal institutions focus on achieving aggregate effects, measured through process outputs that can be objectified and tracked easily, what Bottoms (1995) called managerialism. This suggested, that Foucault's bio-political technologies of power, which seemed only marginally influential on the formation of penal-welfarism, might be reaching dominance.

Yet there is a great deal about the new penal culture of containment and control that does not correspond closely to actuarial technologies of risk assessment. Mass incarceration is not, in the end, predictively oriented, but indeed embraces generalized rather than selective incapacitation (Zimring and Hawkins, 1997). Also, at its core, insurance is a form of risk spreading and risk sharing, but in combination with spatial exclusion and electronic monitoring, mass incarceration is aimed at concentrating risk that operates to keep the most troubled individuals cycling between periods of incarceration in which human capital is degenerating and periods of freedom in which former prisoners are largely isolated from the economy in communities with already high concentrations of unemployment, drugs, and illegal activity.

Thus in addition to the application of actuarial technologies, the shift to containment and control embodies a second kind of risk based technology, one that can be described as a precautionary technology (Ewald, 2002). Instead of being borrowed from the practices of spreading the routine risks of industrializing society, this precautionary technology of power has its origins in the experience of catastrophic risks like that posed by highly toxic wastes, weapons of mass destruction, or deadly epidemic diseases. If actuarialism is abut spreading risk, precautionary technologies aim to containing it to specific locations. The prison has become a place to contain subjects who pose a risk of crime. With rare exceptions (e.g. Virginia), sentencing to prison in the USA is not selective in terms of risk nor actuarial in the lengths of time it holds on to bodies. Rather, actuarialism in the prisons of mass incarceration often follows the commitment to containment, as risk prediction is used to set custody levels, which is the dominant form of differentiation in the new penal order. Beyond the prison, electronic monitoring operates to track the body of penal subjects in real-time, not to establish process of self-discipline, but enforces zones of exclusion, a practice aptly described as the 'banopticon' (Nellis, 2009: 113; Beckett and Herbert, 2011).

As with disciplinary and welfarist practices, we can find aspects of precautionary technology across many institutions remote and near to the penal field. Industrial risk management from the end of the 19th century, especially the design of machinery and procedures to avoid accidents and injuries directly is one arena in which a prudential tinkering with both humans and machines to reduce damage done by inevitable errors took shape. In the 20th century this kind of craft became even more important in the design of plants producing or using highly toxic chemicals either as the primary objective or waste (Perrow, 1984). The shaping of private property, especially mass private property (Shearing and Stenning, 2003), as well as gated communities (Simon, 2007), toward 'situational crime prevention' (Von Hirsch et al., 2000) and other forms of 'target hardening' (Farrington et al., 1993) aim to allow individual citizens to increase their security from crime risk through personal consumption choices (Gould et al., 2010). Schools have introduced harsher discipline, more control agents and readier recourse to drug testing and in school detentions in the name of keeping students safer (Kupchik and Ellis, 2007; Hirschfield, 2008). Work places engage in various kinds of screening designed to exclude higher risk employees or even customers (Simon, 2007). The precautionary logic, always part of the penal field, has come to foreground in the era of mass incarceration. Increasingly it reflects not confidence that penal sanctions alone can create greater individual security from crime, but that containment is what the penal system can do to support these other ways in which citizens have been mobilized to protect themselves from victimization (Garland, 2001a; Simon, 2007).

Two penal practices stand out as exemplifying the penal appropriation of precautionary technology, the supermax prison (Shalev, 2009; Reiter, 2012), and the most robust forms of electronic monitoring, such as satellite tracking (Jones, 2000; Nellis, 2009). Supermax prisons build on the practice of solitary confinement, which emerged as a part of the practice of disciplinary penitentiaries and continued to be used as a more select sanction in the prisons of penal-welfarism. The supermax prison moves from solitary confinement as an individualized and episodic technique to a generalized and routine technique with whole prisons designed to keep their entire population in solitary confinement. Likewise, many prisoners are there not as a sanction for a particular disciplinary violation but based on a prediction (sometimes but not generally an actuarial prediction) that they pose a risk to guards or other inmates. The supermax does more than place the prisoner in solitary confinement, rather it creates a highly technical and computer managed form of custody in which all contact with other human beings is minimized and subjected to monitoring. The penal subject of the supermax is viewed as a form of unchangeable and extreme risk, like that posed by committed terrorist, or a predatory serial killer.

The supermax brings together in a single setting many of the specific techniques and tactics that figure in precautionary technology more broadly. It utilizes architecture and technical building materials to achieve a high level of physical isolation, not just between the prison and the outside, but throughout the prison. It refrains from disciplining the body of the prisoner, focusing instead on turning the cell into a place of complete containment and sustainability making assaults on staff or other prisoners physically unlikely. Through the use of video-cameras and computers, the supermax constitutes a panoptic gaze over the prisoners, but for the purpose of documenting control to address both managerial and even human rights objectives, rather than normalization.

As a fixture in a vastly extended array of prisons, the supermax has functioned as a point of concentration for techniques that are working on a lesser basis throughout. As a place to remove those prisoners who are deemed a threat to the order of the less securitized warehousing prisons, the supermax provides for the larger prison system a way to control their enlarged populations in the absence of any meaningful internal prison programming.

Electronic monitoring, including its most advanced and comprehensive form, satellite tracking, operates in many respects at the other end of the spectrum of risk. It is designed to enforce spatialized exclusion on those deemed low enough risk to be out in public either on a pre-trial release, or as part of a sentence of parole following imprisonment, or on probation as an alternative to imprisonment. While it is often offered as an enhancement or aid to probation, as a technology it operates in very different ways than probation as the anchor practice for penal-welfarism. In terms that echo and reverse David Garland's (1985) account of the shift from Victorian penality (individuation) to penal-welfarism (individualizing), Mike Nellis points out:

> [Electronic monitoring] *individuates* - in the sense of focusing on the movements of a single, embodied human entity - but it does not *individualise* - in the sense of seeking to know a person's inner mental life or to understand (with a view to changing) behavior, as probation officers seek to do. (2009: 106, original emphasis)

While traditional probation sought to change behavior through 'the periodic co-presence of supervisor and supervisee …; it was via their structured personal encounters (and sometimes through the relationship which grew between them) that an impact on behaviour was effected', electronic monitoring seeks to extend the spatial and temporal range of control well beyond what human controls or social relations could sustain, indeed range replaces relationships

(Nellis, 2009: 108–9). Instead of creating a matrix of surveillance and influence, electronic monitoring enforces a risk based set of spatial exclusions. At the same time electronic monitoring is valued as a managerial tool that can document the performance up to standards of control agents, and protect the human rights interests of the penal subject from the abuses of confinement or the degradation possible in other risk management tools, such as public notification (Nellis, 2009: 122). Finally, electronic monitoring operates in a systemic relationship to prison, dependent on the demand to extend containment beyond the limits of the prison.

Even as a rough sketch of recent years this does not account for much of what is going on in Europe, in Russia (Piacentini, 2004), or in China, for example, where punishment remains generally tied to penal welfare or disciplinary technologies and where the relative scale of punishment in society and as a portion of governmental power more broadly remains closer to the norms of the 20th century. In characterizing the leading technology of power for shaping the penal field in our time as containment, I am placing the American (and to a much lesser degree the UK) model at the forefront. The logic of penal change in the USA has been driven in large part by the fact that crime control as a broader strategy (including policing and adjudication as well as punishing) has in the USA become itself a more important technology of power for government (Scheingold, 1992; Beckett, 1997; Garland, 2001a; Gottschalk, 2006; Simon, 2007; Wacquant, 2009). Thus while in the early 20th century, probation agents might use the common or public school as a governing framework in which their power over the penal subject could be more effectively distributed and exercised, today schools in the USA incorporate police and probation officers as working part of their internal discipline (Simon, 2007; Hirschfield, 2008).

High risk groups: monsters and predators

Although precautionary practices, like other penal applications typically act on the bodies of people caught up in the criminal justice system, its effects lie not in the soul or the penal subject, in their social relations, but on spatial zones. Placing some penal subjects in secured confinement, and others in an electronic prison of electronic monitoring, is intended to keep them out of certain neighborhoods and locked into others. The result is to maintain a risk hierarchy of spaces from desirable safe suburbs, whose own gates and control devices are enhanced by keeping the most determined threats out of circulation altogether, to the dangerous inner city neighborhoods which lacking the 'ghettos' original wall and locked gate, now sports electronic and legal zones designed to keep penal subjects inside (Davis, 1998).

The penal subject is defined as a source of risk, at the extreme a relentless monster or predator who is driven to rape, kill or destroy. The model for this came not from science, but from the nightmare factories of Hollywood, which quickly turned the alarming serial killers of the USA in the 1970s and 1980s into a ubiquitous threat to American homes. The monster is not a defective person in the sense of someone who has diverged from the social institutions and relations that would bring him or her into conformity with law, but rather someone created by aberration, who cannot be changed and may not be discerned in advance. Violent crime, especially gun crime, and above all murder, marks a penal subject as a monster and the tendency of US law is to seek lifetime incapacitation without the possibility of parole (Dolovich, 2011). But even property or public order crimes, and especially drug crimes, may indicate that the person convicted has the aberration that will make them a predator, which creates an enduring pressure to lengthen sentences for non-violent crime and to return prisoners to incarceration for even technical violations of their release conditions.

Whether, to what degree, and how, this precautionary penality so clear in America might become predominant in Europe and other places is a subject of considerable debate (di Giorgi, 2006; Jones and Newburn, 2006; Wacquant, 2009). Supermax-style prisons are comparatively rare outside the USA (whether because of the cost or because of human rights objections), while electronic monitoring has been more fully embraced in the UK than in the USA. Fear of serial killers and other penal 'monsters' is readily apparent in Europe, even while this fear is to some extent balanced by checks on penal populism overall. In Europe there are significant competitors to containment for any possible recasting of the power to punish. Human rights is clearly an important source for the development of European penal techniques in way that it has not been in the USA (Van Zyl Smit and Snacken, 2009). In addition to preventing the predictable tilt toward degrading prisoners that the containment strategy has involved (Whitman, 2003), human rights discourse has reached well into practice and research of both national and European-wide correctional administrations. Indeed human rights, with its well developed tool box of investigatory and accountability techniques, represents its own kind of technology with broad application to the penal field. Likewise, the well noted importance of 'managerialism' in European penality represents the application of another kind of technology, with its origins in business administration, to the penal field.

LOOKING BEYOND THE WASTELAND

The aim of this chapter was to outline some of the significant analytic methods of Foucault's (1977) and Melossi and Pavarini's (1981) books on the emergence of the penitentiary style prison, with its disciplinary technology of power, and to suggest how they have been and might be applied to other phases of penal evolution. These works, which share a great deal in common, helped to revitalize punishment and society as an academic field within sociology, criminology and political science. There has been a great deal of criticism of the failings of this approach, especially Foucault's use of it. In the remaining part of this chapter I will suggest why it should remain in the tool kits of contemporary students of punishment and society, regardless of what theories guide them.

To study penal change by examining the way new technologies of power play out in the reformation of penal institutions is not to assume that punishment is only, or even primarily about the production of political power or social control. Punishment in any society serves many functions; to assuage the victims and onlookers of certain crimes, especially violent crime, to validate social authority, to incapacitate or control some people and to intimidate others. It is carried out by complicated organizations that have their own histories, values, and structures. Because Foucault and Melossi and Pavarini operated in a largely Marxist intellectual context,[38] they emphasized the role of punishment in enforcing class hegemony in modern society, but the tool kit is not limited to extending a Marxist political economy. Whatever else punishment does beyond social control, it does so dependent on the fit between penal practices and extended networks of acting on things. If punishments are to satisfy victims and community members that they are seriously capable of holding the convicted accountable for their crimes, they cannot be a singular or aberrational practice that has no resonance in the larger world (that is one problem with capital punishment is that it has so little company in the social world as a way we deal with other people). The disciplines, and in the 20th century, the family of techniques, knowledges and strategies that some have called 'welfarism' (Garland, 1985) or 'the social' (Donzelot, 1979), were becoming familiar ways of organizing social action before they were launched successfully in the penal field. Today a containment approach to reformulating penality been successful in large part because it builds on a precautionary logic widely dispersed societies experiencing the late modern concern with catastrophic risks (Ewald, 2002).

It does not follow from this that penal practices are best explained as ways of exercising power over people as individuals, or as whole classes. Indeed, the empirical study of penal practices in all three eras leads to the conclusion that punishment rarely works as planned. Disciplinary rituals end up angering and degrading those subjected to them, but regularly fail to produce an internalized commitment to self-discipline (other than that involved in behaving strategically to subvert discipline).[39] Social welfare agents tracking criminal involvement, after the fact, often with the result of cycling the subject back through the penal system it was supposed to move him beyond (Simon, 1993). It is only the strong social confidence in a technology of power that can account for the tolerance that societies have for penal failure, one that disappears very quickly indeed when that confidence wanes (Allen, 1981).

By the same token contemporary precautionary punishments, such as the mass incarceration practiced in the USA and to some degree in the UK, has quite mixed implications for the reduction of crime (Clear, 2007; Zimring, 2007). Its endurance will have much more to do with the broader social acceptance of precautionary power in broader society. As with earlier waves of penal change, the breakdown of this acceptance will be driven in large part by changes in political economy, which will raise new problems about the costs of precautionary punishment. Indeed the global economic crisis of 2008, which has continued to depress economic life in the USA and large parts of Europe, has accelerated growing criticism of mass incarceration, although it is far from clear how this will play out (Gottschalk, 2010). However, it does the actual shape of reformed penal institutions is likely to depend not just on the problematization of precautionary technology, but also on the new technologies of power over the body that reformers are able to draw into the penal field.

ACKNOWLEDGEMENTS

Thanks to David Garland, Richard Jones, Dario Melossi and Richard Sparks for their comments on earlier drafts of this chapter.

NOTES

1 I will refer throughout to first English translation dates but for the present discussion it is helpful to note the actual dates. Discipline and Punish is a translation by Alan Sheridan of *Surveiller et punir: Naissance de la Prison*, Editions Galimard 1975.

2 A translation by Helen Gyntis of *Carcere e fabbrica: Alle origini del sistema penitenziario*, 1977.

3 Both books were indebted to Rusche and Kirchheimer's *Punishment & Social Structure* (1939), which might have reignited the field, had it not been published in the midst of the Second World War and further hidden by the Cold War which cast its Marxist authors into semi-invisibility in the liberal West.

4 This was missed by many of the other important sites of revitalization of the social study of crime and its control in the 1970s, which focused more on ideas, identities, and ideologies.

5 Foucault used the term political technology and technology of power interchangeably. For example, he describes the soul as an effect of a 'certain technology of power over the body,' associated with punishment through imprisonment (Foucault, 1977: 29).

6 This is very much Foucault's strategy in *Discipline and Punish* where he discusses not one, but three quite distinct technologies of power.

7 Melossi and Pavarini read Foucault's book in French in 1976 after they had largely completed their manuscript, but managed to add some references to it in their original book and a longer response in the English translation in 1981.

8 Which is essentially how Garland (1990) treats it in his influential *Punishment and Modern Society*.

9 *Punishment and Social Structure* was first published in English in 1939, after being heavily edited by Kirchheimer to tone down its Marxism for US

readers (Melossi, 2003). The book was republished in 1968, which brought it the attention of a new generation of sociologists of punishment like Melossi and Pavarini. A new edition was published in 2003.

10 This is perhaps the most important difference with a third remarkably similar book that was published at nearly the same time (Ignatieff 1979). Michael Ignatieff's analysis of the rise of the prison, discussed discipline and penal reform, but treated it much more as a problem of ideology.

11 The elaborate execution rituals of the scaffold, as described by Foucault, and others, was far from typical, but it exemplified a whole style of punishment which emphasized the public and degrading treatment of the body, including branding, mutilation, or exposure (Spierenburg, 1984).

12 The status of being outlawed and subject to the severe punishments due 'felons' at English and colonial American common law and the equivalent in continental 18th-century procedure generally did not befall people whom the local community including its hierarchy viewed as somebody who should remain a member of the community (Simon, 1993).

13 Neither Foucault nor Melossi and Pavarini were breaking entirely new ground in focusing on disciplinary practices as an important technology in 19th-century developments. Max Weber (1978) had discussed disciplinary techniques as had historian E.P. Thompson (1967).

14 By which I take him to mean European and North American societies from the at least the late 18th century right through to those same societies (as well as many others shaped by European colonialism).

15 Melossi and Pavarini are quick to recognize the parallel between Foucault's insights and their own while returning to what they conceive as a more adequate but still Marxist political economy. 'However, what is presented to us as the 'political economy of the body [in Foucault] is "political economy" *tout court*; it is already locked in the concept of labour-power' (1981: 41, original emphasis).

16 This is consistent with his later discussion of the importance of the 'specific intellectual', for example, Robert Oppenheimer rather than Albert Einstein. See Foucault, 1984.

17 And somewhat more mysteriously, '[The soul is] the present correlative of a certain technology of power over the body' (1977: 29).

18 Of course both Durkheim and Rusche and Kirchheimer had presentist concerns that were hardly hidden, militarism and French anti-semitism/nationalist racism for Durkheim and National Socialism and fascism for Rusche and Kirchheimer, but neither placed it near the center of their analytic method.

19 Melossi and Pavarini became aware of Foucault's work as they were completing the Italian first edition of their book and included only a few complementary references. Two years later, for the publication of their book in English, they provided a more developed and critical response. Although my account here has tended to emphasize the similarities between the two projects, as the following quote suggests there were also important divergences.

20 The problematics of the scaffold as a technology of power was quite independently the focus of a group of historians lead by the late E.P. Thompson who were studying the role of criminal law and punishment in the consolidation of the Whig regime during the 18th century, see Thompson (1975) and Hay et al. (1975). Thompson and his students were also working to revitalize the Marxist approach to studying the history of punishment and develop a research strategy that is remarkably similar to the punishment as political technology approach. There seems to have been little direct influence between historians around Thompson and either Foucault or Melossi and Pavarini. Because the latter focused on the scaffold regime and not the birth of the prison as such, this chapter does not treat them at any further length, but their contributions ought to be seen as part of this moment in which the history of punishment was 'lit up', as it were, through attention to punishment as a technology of power.

21 Indeed, it was this interiorizing project that Foucault believed to be undergoing a crisis in the 1970s, around the problem of prisoners' rights.

22 It is not surprising than, that a good deal of attention since (especially to Foucault's book) has gone into trying to decide how far to extend the disciplinary concept to explain 20th-century changes in penality (Bottoms, 1983; Cohen, 1985; Mathiessen, 1983; Feeley and Simon, 1992).

23 Penality is a term introduced by Garland (1985) to describe the totality of institutions, practices and discourses that surround the power to punish.

24 Of course one should not take the endurance of a particular institution to suggest that its social meaning and role are the same (Bottoms, 1983).

25 As John Sutton (1988) points out, this term originally meant simply 'work on a case' before it was blown up into a technique during the rise of social work as an academic and policy field (Richmond, 1919; Garland, 1985). This is a good example of Foucault's (1977) admonition to look at those discourses at the margins of official respectability for the ideas that pull together a set of practices into a technology of power including the earlier and more practical meanings behind terms that have been propelled to the higher stratospheres of prestige precisely by the success of this pulling together process. Tom Baker's (1996) analysis of 'genealogy of moral hazard', is another good example of a piece of knowledge production that gravitates from a

construct of based on the categories of insurance underwriters toward formal theoretical coherence as it rockets up in prestige within the social sciences and as a policy driving term.

26 By programs Garland means distinct schemes of social action, each with distinctive discursive and technical resources as well as organizational bases and social bases of support (1985: 74).

27 It is important to recognize that existing institutions, especially the prison, and the disciplinary technology of power over the body, remained embedded in the penal field and an important source of conflict and resistance to the construction of new institutions based on welfarist or social technology.

28 But surely Garland overemphasizes the differences between Foucault's analysis and his. To be sure, Foucault seemed to view the elaboration of individualizing penal techniques associated with the turn of the 20th century as immanent within the disciplinary penitentiary, and while this misses the distinctive technologies of power at work in the latter period, it is not altogether inconsistent with Garland's own analysis to see continuities between the two (in the role of reform for instance). The panoptic prison and the penitentiary clearly and unambiguously see themselves as 'techniques of transformation' even if that objective was played down in favor of retribution and deterrence during the Victorian era in Britain. Nor does Foucault assume that the penitentiary technique is already informed by a positivist criminological knowledge of offenders, indeed he seems to suggest that it is the disciplinary prison that gives rise to criminological knowledge, a position quite consistent with the story Garland tells in *Punishment and Welfare*. And indeed, Garland sees political and ideological forces as constraining the potentially individuating logic of the disciplinary prison (1985: 32).

29 As Foucault himself had suggested at the end of *Discipline and Punish*.

30 My own account of the penal reforms of the late 19th and early 20th centuries also fails to distinguish the distinctive technologies of power at work in penal mechanisms like probation and parole. See Simon (1993: 44–5), discussing disciplinary nature of parole. There I suggest that new techniques, emphasizing therapeutic interventions, emerged only after the Second World War (see Simon, 1993: 68). While it may be true that much of the real work of parole remained oriented toward linking released prisoners to the work force, at least in California, this still ignores the distinctive technologies of power at work in the larger society at the turn of the 20th century that made the promotion of reforms like parole and probation viable.

31 Michael Meranze (1996) shows how the reformers in Philadelphia at the time of the emergence of the influential Cherry Hill penitentiary, worried that alternative penal forms, like compulsory work in the public service, was dangerous and undermined the potential to reform.

32 The parole or probation officer, and their style of relating to individuals on their 'caseload' has ever since been a central preoccupation of criminological research (Simon, 1993; Lynch, 1998; Nellis, 2009).

33 Alison Liebling suggests that this relational model also shaped the logic of control inside prisons, a strategy she argues may be coming to an end under conditions to parallel some of what we describe in the next section (Liebling and Crewe, 2013).

34 Of course attending to variations with those insights in mind is perhaps the best use of them (Bright, 1996; Meranze, 1996).

35 Perhaps because the basic political economy is diverging (more on that shortly).

36 Even within the USA there is a considerable variation at the state level, which control the largest portion of prisoners. While imprisonment rates have grown significantly since the mid-1970s almost everywhere (with a national average of 500 percent), some states have kept growth to far more modest reaches and retained a more welfarist emphasis in punishment, while others have grown dramatically and embraced containment in a totalizing way (Lynch, 2009; Simon, forthcoming).

37 This movement, sometimes described as 'neoliberalism' (Harvey, 2007) or 'advanced liberalism' (Rose, 1999) includes a lot of different changes in governance including less risk spreading and thus more economic risk for the middle classes, less security of any kind for the working poor and those without employment at all, less regulation of consumer markets (and thus more risk to everyone).

38 Foucault is more often thought of as a critic of French Marxism, but he is quite clear in *Discipline and Punish* itself that he is building on the insights of Rusche and Kirchheimer's unabashedly Marxist approach and that he views the formation of capitalism as the primary horizon in which the disciplinary technology of power was being worked into reformulated penal practices in the 19th century.

39 Jimmy Boyle's (1977) memoir of his multiple incarcerations in youth and adult prisons during the 1960s captures both the total failure of disciplinary punishment and its tremendous endurance historically.

REFERENCES

Allen, Francis (1981) *The Decline of the Rehabilitative Ideal: Penal Policy and Social Purpose*. New Haven, CT: Yale University Press.

Baker, Tom (1996) 'On the Genealogy of Moral Hazard', *Texas Law Review*, 75: 237–292.

Baker, Tom and Simon, Jonathan (2002) *Embracing Risk, in Embracing Risk: The Changing Culture of Insurance and Responsibility*. Chicago: University of Chicago Press. pp.1–26.

Beckett, Katherine (1997) *Making Crime Pay: Law and Order in Contemporary American Politics*. New York: Oxford University Press.

Beckett, Katherine and Herbert, Stephen (2008) 'Dealing with disorder. Social control in the post-industrial city', *Theoretical Criminology*, 12(1): 5–30.

Beckett, Katherine and Herbert, Stephen (2011) *Banished: The New Social Control in Urban American*. New York: Oxford University Press.

Bottoms, Anthony E. (1983) 'Neglected features of contemporary penal systems', in David Garland and Peter Young (eds), *The Power to Punish: Contemporary Penality and Social Analysis*. Atlantic Highlands, New Jersey: Humanities Press. pp. 166–202.

Bottoms, Anthony (1995) 'Philosophy and politics of punishment and sentencing', in Chris Clarkson and Rod Morgan (eds). *The Politics of Sentencing Reform*. Oxford: Oxford University Press. pp. 17–49.

Bourdieu, Pierre (1986) 'The forms of capital,' in J.E. Richardson (ed.) *The Handbook of Theory of Research for the Sociology of Education*, trans. Richard Nice. New York: Greenwood Press. pp. 241–58.

Boyle, Jimmy (1977) *A Sense of Freedom*. Edinburgh: Pan Books.

Bright, Charles (1996) *The Powers that Punish: Prison and Politics in the Era of the 'Big House', 1920–1955*. Ann Arbor, MI: University of Michigan Press.

Cavadino, Michael and Dignan, James (2006) *Penal Systems: A Comparative Approach*. London: Polity.

Chevalier, Louis (1958 [1973]) *Labouring Classes and Dangerous Classes in Paris During the First Half of the Nineteenth Century*. London: Routledge.

Clear, Todd (2007) *Imprisoning Communities: How Mass Incarceration Makes Disadvantaged Neighborhoods Worse*. New York: Oxford University Press.

Cohen, Stanley (1973) *Folk Devils and Moral Panics: The Creation of the Mods and the Rockers*. St. Albans: Paladin.

Cohen, Stanley (1979) 'The punitive city: notes on the dispersal of social control', *Contemporary Crises*, 3: 339–63.

Cohen, Stanley (1985) *Visions of Social Control: Crime, Punishment, and Classification*. London: Polity.

Davis, Mike (1990) *City of Quartz: Excavating the Future in LA*. London: Verso.

Davis, Mike (1998) *Ecology of Fear: Los Angeles and the Imagination of Disaster*. New York: Metropolitan Books.

Deleuze, Gille (1992) 'Postscript on the societies of control', *October*, 59: 3–7.

Di Giorgi, Alessandro (2006) *Re-thinking the Political Economy of Punishment: Perspectives on Post-Fordism and Penal Politics*. Burlington, VT: Ashgate.

Dolovich, Sharon (2011) 'Creating the Permanent Prisoner', in Charles J. Ogletree, Jr. and Austin Sarat (eds), *Life Without Parole: America's New Death Penalty*. New York: NYU Press.,

Donzelot, Jacques (1979) *Policing the Family*, trans. Robert Hurley. New York: Pantheon.

Durkheim, Emile (1969) 'Two laws of penal evolution', 38 U. Cin. L. Rev. 32–61. (Originally published in 1900 as *Deux Lois de L'evolution Penale*, in 4 *L'Anne Sociologique* 65–95.)

Durkheim, Emile (1997) *The Division of Labor in Society*. New York: Simon and Schuster. (Originally published in 1892.)

Ewald, Francois (2002) 'The Return of Descartes' Malicious Demon: Outline of a Philosophy of Precaution', in Tom Baker and Jonathan Simon (eds), *Embracing Risk: The Changing Culture of Insurance and Responsibility*. Chicago: University of Chicago Press. pp. 273–302.

Farrington, David, Bowen, Sean, Buckle, Abigail, Burns-Howell, Tony, Burrows, John and Speed, Martin (1993) 'An experiment on the prevention of shoplifiting', in R.V. Clarke (ed.), *Crime Prevention Studies, Vol. 1*. Monsey, NY: Criminal Justice Press. pp. 93–119.

Feeley, M. and Simon, J. (1992) 'The new penology: notes on the emerging strategy of corrections and its implications', *Criminology*, 30: 449–474.

Foucault, Michel (1977) Discipline and Punishment: The Birth of the Prison, trans. Alan Sheridan. New York: Pantheon.

Foucault, Michel (1978) *The History of Sexuality, Vol. 1: An Introduction*, trans. Robert Hurley. New York: Pantheon.

Foucault, Michel (1984) 'Truth and Power', in Paul Rabinow (ed.), *The Foucault Reader*. New York: Random House.

Foucault, Michel (1988) 'Technologies of the self,' in L.H. Martin, H. Gutman and P. H. Hutton (eds), *Technologies of the Self: A Seminar with Michel Foucault*. London: Tavistock Publications.

Garland, David (1985) *Punishment and Welfare: A History of Penal Strategies*. Aldershot: Gower.

Garland, David (1990) *Punishment and Modern Society: A Study in Social Theory*. Chicago: University of Chicago Press.

Garland, David (2001a) *The Culture of Control: Crime and Social Order in Contemporary Society*. Chicago: University of Chicago Press.

Garland, David (2001b) 'Introduction', in David Garland (ed.), *Mass Imprisonment*. London: SAGE Publications. pp. 1–3.

Garland, David (2010) *Peculiar Institution: America's Death Penalty in an Age of Abolition*. Cambridge: Harvard University Press.

Gilmore, Ruth W. (2007) *Golden Gulag: Prisons, Surplus, Crisis, and Opposition in Globalizing California*. Berkeley, CA: University of California Press.

Gottschalk, Marie (2006) *The Prison and the Gallows: The Politics of Mass Incarceration in America*. Cambridge: Cambridge University Press.

Gottschalk, Marie (2010) 'Cell blocks & red ink: mass incarceration, the great recession and penal reform', *Daedalus*, Summer: 62–73.

Gould, Benjamin, Loader, Ian and Thumala, Angelica (2010) 'Consuming security? Tools for a sociology of security consumption', *Theoretical Criminology*, 14(1): 3–30

Hagan, John, Hewitt, John D. and Alwinn, Duane F. (1979) 'Ceremonial justice: crime and punishment in a loosely coupled system', *Social Forces*, 58: 506–527.

Hall, Stuart, Critcher, Chas, Jefferson, Tony, John, Clark and Roberts, Brian (1978) *Policing The Crisis: Mugging the State, and Law and Order*. London: Macmillan.

Harcourt, Bernard (2005) 'Punishment and crime: policing L.A.'s skid row: crime and real estate redevelopment in downtown Los Angeles [an experiment in real time], *The University of Chicago Legal Forum* 2005.

Harcourt, Bernard (2011) *The Illusion of Free Markets: Punishment and the Myth of Natural Order*. Cambridge: Harvard University Press.

Harvey, David (2007) *A Brief History of Neoliberalism*. Oxford: Oxford University Press.

Hay, Douglas, Linebaugh, Peter, Rule, John G., Thompson, E.P. and Winslow, Cal (1975) *Albion's Fatal Tree: Crime and Society in Eighteenth Century England*. New York: Pantheon.

Hirschfield, Paul (2008) 'Preparing for prison? The criminalization of school discipline in the USA', *Theoretical Criminology*, 12: 79–101.

Ignatieff, Michael (1979) *A Just Measure of Pain: The Penitentiary in the Industrial Revolution*. London: Penguin Books.

Irwin, John (2004) *The Warehouse Prison: Disposal of the New Dangerous Class*. New York: Oxford University Press.

Jay, Martin (1973) *The Dialectical Imagination: A history of the Frankfurt School and the Institute of Social Research 1923–1950*. Boston, MA: Little, Brown.

Jones, Richard (2000) 'Digital rule: punishment, control and technology', *Punishment and Society*, 2(1): 5–22.

Jones, Trevor and Newburn, Tim (2006) *Policy Transfer: Exploring US Influence Over UK Crime Control Policy*. New York: McGraw Hill International.

Kilcommins, S., O'Donnell, I., O'Sullivan, E. and Vaughan, B. (2005) *Crime, Punishment and the Search for Order in Ireland*. Dublin: Institute of Public Administration.

Kupchik, Aaron and Ellis, Nicholas (2007) 'School discipline and security: fair for all students?', *Youth & Society*, 39: 549–74.

Latour, Bruno (1987) *Science in Action: How to Follow Scientists and Engineers through Society*. Cambridge, MA: Harvard University Press.

Liebling, Alison and Crewe, Ben (2013) 'Prisons beyond the New Penology: The Shifting Moral Foundations of Prison Management', in Jonathan Simon and Richard Sparks (eds), *The Sage Handbook of Punishment and Society*. London: Sage. pp. 283–307.

Linebaugh, Peter (2011) 'The Tyburn Riot Against the *Surgeons*', in Douglas Hay et al. (eds), *Albion's Fatal Tree: Crime and Society in 18th Century Britain, 2nd Edition*. pp. 65–117.

Lynch, Mona (1998) 'Waste managers? The new penology, crime fighting, and parole agent identity', *Law & Society Review*, 32: 839–70.

Lynch, Mona (2009) *Sunbelt Justice: Arizona and the Transformation of American Punishment*. Stanford, CA: Stanford University Press.

Maruna, Shadd (1997) *Going Straight: Desistance from Crime and Life Narratives of Reform*. London: SAGE Publications.

Mathiessen, Thomas (1983) 'The future of control systems - the case of Norway', in David Garland and Peter Young (eds), *The Power to Punish: Contemporary Penality and Social Analysis*.Atlantic Highlands, NJ: Humanities Press. pp. 130–45.

Melossi, Dario (2003) *Introduction, in Georg Rusche and Otto Kirschheimer, Punishment and Social Structure*. New Brunswick, NJ: Transaction Press.

Melossi, Dario and Pavarini, Massimo (1981) *The Prison and the Factory:Origins of the Penitentiary System*, trans Glynis Cousin. London: The Macmillan Press Ltd.

Meranze, Michael (1996) *Laboratories of Virtue: Punishment, Revolution and Authority in Philadelphia, 1760–1835*. Chapel Hill, NC: University of North Carolina Press.

Meyer, Jeffrey and O'Malley, Pat (2005) 'Missing the punitive turn? Canadian Criminal Justice, "Balance" and Penal Modernism', in J. Pratt and D. Brown, Mark Brown, Simon Hallsworth and Wayne Morrison (eds), *The New Punitiveness: Trends, Theories, Perspectives*. London: Willan. pp. 201–7.

Nellis, Mike (2009) '24/7/365 mobility, locatability and the satellite tracking of offenders', in Katja Franko Aas, Helene Oppen Gundhus, and Heidi Mork Lomell, eds. *Technologies of Insecurity: The Surveillance of Everyday Life*. New York: Routledge-Cavendish. pp. 105–24.

Newburn, Tim (2007) '"Tough on crime": penal policy in England and Wales', *Crime and Justice*, 36: 425–70.

O'Malley, Pat (1999) 'Volatile and contradictory punishment', *Theoretical Criminology*, 3: 175–96.

O'Malley, Pat (2010) *Crime and Risk*. London: SAGE Publications.

Perrow, Charles (1984) *Normal Accidents: Living with High Risk Technologies*. New York: Basic Books.

Piacentini, Laura (2004) 'Penal identities in Russian prison colonies', *Punishment & Society*, 6: 131–47.

Platt, Anthony (1977) *The Childsavers: The Invention of Delinquency*, 2nd Edition Chicago: University of Chicago Press.

Radzinowicz, Leon (1958) *The Results of Probation: A Report of the Cambridge Department of Criminal Science*. London: Macmillan.

Raynor, Peter (2007) 'Community penalties: probation, "what works" and offender management', in Mike Maquire, Rod Morgan and Robert Reiner (eds), *The Oxford Handbook of Criminology, 4th Edition*. Oxford: Oxford University Press. pp. 1061–99.

Reiter, Kerament (2012) 'The Most Restrictive Alternative: The Origins, Functions, Control, and Ethical Implications of the Supermax Prison, 1976–2010'. Doctoral dissertation, JSP program UC Berkeley.

Richmond, Mary (1919) *Social Diagnosis*. New York: Russell Sage Foundation.

Rose, Nikolas (1999) The Powers of Freedom: Reframing Political Thought Cambridge, UK: Cambridge University Press.

Rothman, David (1972) *The Discovery of the Asylum: Order and Disorder in the New Republic*. Boston: Little Brown & Co.

Rothman, David (1980) *Conscience and Convenience: The Asylum and its Alternatives in Progressive America*. Boston, MA: Little, Brown.

Rusche, Georg and Kirchheimer, Otto (1939 [2003]) *Punishment and Social Structure*. New York: Columbia University Press.

Scheingold, Stuart A. (1992) *The Politics of Street Crime: Criminal Process and Cultural Obsession*. Philadelphia, PA: Temple University Press.

Schlossman, Stephen (1977) *Love and the American Delinquent: The Theory and Practice of Progressive Juvenile Justice*. Chicago: University of Chicago Press.

Shalev, Sharon (2009) *Supermax: Controlling Risk Through Solitary Confinement*. London: Willan.

Shearing, Clifford and Stenning, Philip (2003) 'From the Panopticon to Disney World: the development of discipline', in Eugene McLaughlin, John Muncie and Gordon Hughes (eds), *Criminological Perspectives: Essential Readings*. London: SAGE Publications. pp. 335–349.

Simon, Jonathan (1988) 'The ideological effects of actuarial practices', *Law & Society Review*, 22: 771–800.

Simon, Jonathan (1993) *Poor Discipline: Parole and the Social Underclass, 1890–1990*. Chicago: University of Chicago Press.

Simon, Jonathan (1998) 'Ghost in the disciplinary machine: Lee Harvey Oswald, life-history, and the truth of crime', *Yale Journal of Law and the Humanities*, 10: 75–114.

Simon, Jonathan (2000) 'From the big house to the warehouse: rethinking prisons and state government in the 20th century', *Punishment & Society*, 2: 213–34.

Simon, Jonathan (2007) *Governing through Crime: How the War on Crime Transformed American Democracy and Created a Culture of Fear*. New York: Oxford University Press.

Simon, Jonathan (2010) 'Consuming Obsessions: Housing, Homicide, and Mass Incarceration since 1950', The University of Chicago Legal Forum (October 2010), 141–180.

Simon, Jonathan (forthcoming) *Mass Incarceration on Trial:* Brown v. Plata *and the Future of Imprisonment*. New York: New Press.

Smart, Barry (1983) 'On discipline and social regulation', in David Garland and Peter Young (eds), *The Power to Punish: Contemporary Penality and Social Analysis*. Atlantic Highlands, NJ: Humanities Press. pp. 62–83.

Sparks, Richard, Bottoms, Anthony and Hay, Will (1996) *Prisons and the Problem of Order*. Oxford: Oxford University Press.

Spierenburg, Pieter (1984) *The Spectacle of Suffering: Executions and the Evolution of Repression: From a Preindustrial Metropolis to the European Experience.* Cambridge: Cambridge University Press.

Taylor, Ian, Walton, Paul and Young, Jock (1973) *The New Criminology: For a Social Theory of Deviance.* London: Routledge and Kegan Paul

Sutton, John (1988) *Stubborn Children: Controlling Delinquency in the United States, 1640–1981.* Berkeley, CA: UC Press.

Thompson, E.P. (1967) 'Time, work, and discipline', *Past & Present*, 38: 56–97.

Thompson, E.P. (1975) *Whigs and Hunters: The Origin of the Black Act.* New York: Pantheon.

Tonry, M. (2007) 'Determinants of penal policies', *Crime and Justice*, 36: 1–48.

Van Zyl Smit, Dirk and Snacken, Sona (2009) *Principles of European Prison Law and Policy.* Oxford: Oxford University Press.

Vogel, Mary (2004) *Plea Bargainings Triumph: A History of Plea Bargaining in America.* Stanford: Stanford University Press.

Von Hirsch, Andrew, Garland, David and Wakefield, Alison (eds) (2000) *Ethical and Social Perspectives on Situational Crime Prevention.* London: Hart.

Wacquant, Loic (2009) *Punishing the Poor: The Neoliberal Governance of Insecurity.* London: Polity.

Weber, Max (1978) *Economy and Society: An Outline of Interpretive Sociology*, ed. Guenther Roth and Claus Wittick. Berkeley, CA: UC Press.

Western, Bruce (2006) *Punishment and Inequality in America.* New York: Russell Sage Foundation.

Western, Bruce and Katherine Beckett (1999) 'How Unregulated is the US Labor Market? The Penal System as Labor Market Institution', *American Journal of Sociology*, 104(4): 1030–60.

Whitman, James (2003) *Harsh Justice: Criminal Policy and the Widening Divide between America and Europe.* New York: Oxford University Press.

Wilson, William J. (1987) *The Truly Disadvantaged: The Inner City, the Underclass and Public Policy.* Chicago: University of Chicago Press.

Young, Jock (1999) *The Exclusive Society: Social Exclusion, Crime and Difference in Late Modernity.* London: SAGE Publications.

Zimring, Franklin E. (2007) *The Great American Crime Decline.* New York: Oxford University Press.

Zimring, Franklin E. (2011) *The City that Became Safe: New York City's Lessons for Urban Crime and its Control.* New York: Oxford University Press.

Zimring, Franklin E. and Hawkins, Gordon (1993) *The Scale of Imprisonment.* Chicago: University of Chicago Press.

Zimring, Franklin E. and Hawkins, Gordon (1997) *Incapacitation: Penal Confinement and the Restraint of Crime.* New York: Oxford University Press.

4

Punishment and 'The Civilizing Process'

John Pratt

INTRODUCTION: PRATT'S EPIPHANY

October 1991. Outside 'Old Melbourne Gaol', in the downtown shopping and restaurant area of that city. An epiphany. My own. What happened? I was waiting for a dinner engagement, after a conference, when I was struck by the thought, *what was this prison*, built in 1864, but now a National Trust building and tourist site (hence the way it advertises itself), *doing here*? How incongruous it was to find this old prison, which fell into disuse in the 1920s, in the middle of all the pleasures and extravagances of everyday inner city life. As if reminding us that such a scene belongs to the past rather than the present, the brochure I purchased on a subsequent tour of it told me that 'today the Melbourne Gaol appears gloomy, sinister and depressing. Visitors looking at it in its present condition try to imagine the poor starved ill-treated wretches who once were incarcerated in its cold dark cells. Is this really what the gaol was like when it first opened?' It almost certainly was, given that it was built as a miniature version (holding about 120 prisoners) of Pentonville model prison which had opened in London in 1842.

How, though, was it possible to build prisons in these central city locations at that time when any such suggestion in the 21st century in most of the Anglophone world would be totally inconceivable? Not just because such a building would not capitalize the real estate potential of the location, but, in addition, because of the *offensiveness* it would have for most members of the public. It is hardly the case that in these societies the public no longer have any appetite for prison building, given the dramatic increases in the size of the prison estate in most of these countries in recent years; rather, it is simply that they have come to expect such institutions, and all the connotations and symbols that they carry with them, to be hidden away out of sight. What is it, then, that has brought about such a dramatic change in public sensitivities since the building of Melbourne Gaol and the host of others like it in these societies? And what have been the consequences of this 'disappearance' of the prison in relation to the way in which the public have been able to develop an understanding of the realities of prison life? What have been its consequences in relation to the way in which the penal bureaucracies can effectively control knowledge of prisons, given the way in which the physical remoteness of most prison building since has drawn a veil across sights that were an everyday occurrence in the mid-19th century? In effect, my epiphany took the form of trying to develop a new analytical framework to understand the development of punishment in modern society, one that would give more attention to changes in values, cultures and sensitivities, and to the signs and symbols of punishment, rather than one preoccupied with Foucauldian concepts of discipline and surveillance that had dominated so much sociology of punishment scholarship in the 1980s.

However, I need to acknowledge that prior to my Melbourne gaol experience, I had already been developing an understanding of the importance of long-term cultural changes on penal development. This had been stimulated by Evans' (1982), *The Fabrication of Virtue*, a book on the history of prison architecture. It contained a lithograph (p. 24) by the 19th-century English artist Augustus Pugin, one from his 'Contrasts' series, illustrating architectural change from the 15th century to his own time. In this one, 'the modern city' is shown to have the following buildings at its epicentre: a church, a lunatic asylum, a gasworks and a prison. Here, too, we have another illustration not just of the changing economic organization of modern life but also differences in cultural sensibilities: what had been perfectly tolerable in the mid-19th century has become intolerable 150 years later. Indeed, it might be thought that if such institutions are now to have a legitimate place in city life, then they can no longer exist as prisons but have to be reinvented as museums or some other heritage site. If they do not do this, then their location is likely to have become an inner city ghetto area, derelict and rundown, long since bypassed by modern urban development.

My attention had also been brought to changing public attitudes to the visibility of prisons when undertaking historical research on the New Zealand penal system. Wellington in the 19th century had two centrally located prisons, with one described as occupying 'one of the pleasantest situations in the city', while the other was already an 'eyesore' (Cyclopedia Company Limited, 1897: 341). However, both were closed in the 1920s because of 'local agitations' and the prisons relocated to more isolated and less publicly visible parts of the Wellington region. Amidst a growing feeling that prisons should be hidden away and forgotten about, rather than remain in the centre of any modern town or city, one New Zealand MP proclaimed that the presence of prisons in cities was 'like a man having a rubbish heap on his front lawn' (Hansard [New Zealand], 1900, vol. 113, p. 599). Overall, then, this epiphany was more gradual and less instantaneous than that of the famous one of St Paul (as he became) on his way to Tarsus. Furthermore, apart from a few publications at the time that drew on these experiences,[1] it did not really manifest itself in my intellectual output for a few more years. By which time I had been provided with theoretical tools to make sense of long-term cultural change in the work of Norbert Elias' (1939 [1969], 1982) *The Civilizing Process*.

WHAT IS 'THE CIVILIZING PROCESS'?

'Being civilized' has well-known normative meanings and understandings. It is defined by Chambers Dictionary (2002: 226) as '1. Socially, politically and technically advanced; 2. Agreeably refined, sophisticated or comfortable; 3. Trained to behave and speak politely.' For most societies claiming these qualities, to be recognized as 'civilized' brings 'first world' recognition and allows them to distinguish themselves from those lacking these qualities and which are thus understood as 'uncivilized'. At the same time, it puts both demands and restraints on the conduct of those societies wanting to claim this status. They must show their 'advancement' by reference to such matters as levels of health care, literacy rates, infant mortalities – *and the way in which they punish their offenders*. As then Home

Secretary Winston Churchill explained in 1910, 'the mood and temper of the public in regard to the treatment of crime and criminals is one of the most unfailing tests of the civilisation of any country' (Hansard, col. 1354, 20 July 1910). For a society to maintain its status of 'being civilized', there must be no floggings, stonings, maimings, executions or any other penal attributes of the uncivilized world.

However, and notwithstanding some residual ambivalence in his work about the normative aspects of this term (Fletcher, 1997), for Elias 'being civilized' reflected the contingent outcome of a *long term historical process* in Western society – from the Middle Ages onwards – involving socio-cultural and psychic change. As David Garland (1990: 223) notes, this brought with it two major consequences. First, the central state gradually began to assume more authority and control over the lives of its citizens, to the point where it came to have a monopoly regarding the raising of taxes, the use of legitimate force and, by inference at least, the imposition of legal sanctions to address disputes. Second, citizens in these societies came to internalize restraints, controls and inhibitions on their conduct, as their values and actions came to be framed around increased sensibility to the suffering of others. Elias based his claims on his wide examination of literature, memoirs, artworks, engravings and, most famously, books of etiquette from the Middle Ages through to the 19th century. Through these last sources in particular he was able to trace in long term developmental changes to a range of features essential to the conduct of everyday life – toilet habits, eating, washing, preparation of food and so on.

Elias claimed that the 'civilizing process' was multi-layered, affecting both social and individual development in the following ways.

Structural processes

The increasing authority of the state meant that, when disputes arose, citizens would look increasingly to it to resolve such matters for them, rather than attempt to do this themselves. Equally, the growth of European nation states and the very formation of firm and defensible territorial boundaries were likely to bring a concomitant rise in feelings of responsibility towards and identification with fellow citizens. It would make possible the formation of 'interdependencies' that would become both wider and more firmly cemented within the heterogeneous division of labour in modern society and the attendant shift from rural to urban life. One's significant others, for whom some kind of reciprocity/obligation was owed, became more extensive and necessitated restrictions on impulsive behaviour and aggression while simultaneously fostering the converse: foresight and self-restraint.

Changes in manners/culture

From the Middle Ages onwards, the forms of 'civilized' behaviour that were practiced in the manners and etiquette of court life began to work their way through society at large, establishing, in very general terms, new standards of behaviour, sensitivities and etiquette. In these ways, the social distance between rulers and the ruled became shorter so that the habits and practices of both gradually became more interchangeable. In these respects, while there would be 'diminishing contrasts' in behaviour and conduct within a particular society, there would also be more variety. Over the last two centuries, the pace of these changes seems to have accelerated, and, with the increased democratization of modern societies, the elite groups who set standards and help to formulate opinion have become both more extensive and diverse, thereby helping to institutionalize the civilizing process across wider areas of the modern social fabric, while also incorporating significant sections of the middle and working classes into democratic systems of rule ('functional democratization').

Social habitus

Elias coined this term to refer to people's 'social character or personality make-up' (Mennell, 1990: 207). That is to say, it was as if, with the advancement of the civilizing process, these moves towards greater foresight and self-restraint would become 'second nature'. As these internalized controls on an individual's behaviour became more automatic and pervasive, more and more a taken for granted aspect of cultural life which thereby again raised the threshold of sensitivity and embarrassment, they eventually helped to produce the ideal of the fully rational, reflective and responsible citizen of the civilized world in the 19th and 20th centuries: one who would be sickened by the sight of suffering and, with their own emotions under control, one who respected the authority of the state to resolve disputes on their behalf.

Modes of knowledge

Here, Elias is referring to belief systems and ways of understanding the world. Over the last two hundred years or so, we find less and less recourse to such extra human forces as Nature, Fate and Luck as a way of understanding human behaviour. Instead, with the growth of scientific knowledge, the world became more calculable and understandable. By the same token, this produced belief systems that were no longer organized around myth and fantasy, but instead were much more objective and neutral, and more likely to be based on professional, specialized expertise of varying kinds, rather than common sense and folklore.

From society to society, the interactive sequences of the civilizing process were likely to be varied, were likely to travel at a different pace and take off at different tangents according to the predominance of what Elias referred to as 'local centrifugal forces' (for example, population levels, and geographical boundaries). Thus, if the civilizing process can be seen as taking on a very general form, it can also produce differing, localized manifestations. The same is true of its effects on the different social groupings and interdependencies, or, to use another of Elias' terms, 'figurations' or ever transforming and evolving networks. At both macro- and micro-levels of social formation, innumerable, dynamic, interchanging and intercrossing civilizing processes have taken place, reflecting the struggle for power between the different groups in any particular figuration: or, again using Eliasian concepts, reflecting the 'established – outsider' relations created by power differentials within it (Elias and Scotson, 1965). The greater the social distance between these groups in any particular figuration, the more predominant would be the world view of the established, and the more power, within the specifics of the figuration, it would have – with the converse being applied to the outsider group. Indeed, the position of the established is reinforced by the sense of 'group charisma' that comes with their status. Furthermore, the greater the social distance between the two, so the established would come to characterize the outsiders on the basis of myth and fantasy – 'real' knowledge of the outsiders being increasingly minimized.

Again, it is important to recognize that Elias' concept of 'civilization' is not a normative construct: '[it] has nothing in common with Whiggish narratives of moral improvement, nor does it imply some kind of secular decline in the quantity of bad conduct and human evil to be found in the world ... [instead it] is an analysis of how certain social and psychic changes have transformed the configurations and character of cultural life' (Garland 1990: 223). It is not, as Braithwaite (1993: 6) maintained, a theory of 'unilinear evolution'. On the contrary, the civilizing process provides no guarantees of civilized outcomes. It can lead to the most uncivilized, barbarous consequences, as Elias (1996) explained in his study of the holocaust. The efficiency, planning, foresight and technological advancement of the German nation, allied to a tendency of the German people to 'look the other way' and not ask awkward questions about what was going on in the concentration camps, along with the self-restraint of the Jewish people for fear of attracting further attention to themselves, helped to make it possible, along with elaborate reassurances and euphemisms (the Jews were being 'resettled', they needed to bring warm clothing with them and so on). As Mennell put the matter, 'that the camps were able to slaughter on such a large scale depended on a vast social organization, most people involved in which squeezed no triggers, turned no taps, perhaps saw no camps and set eyes upon few victims. They sat, like Adolf Eichmann, in a highly controlled manner at desks, working out railway timetables' (1992: 249). In these respects, rather than representing the apotheosis of barbarism, Elias provides an understanding of the holocaust that sees it as the culmination of the civilizing process within its German configuration. The reality of the genocide was successfully hidden from public view, in much the same way that mass incarceration in some Western societies and its attendant consequences (not the least being its racial overtones) has become a non-issue in the 21st century.[2]

Just as importantly, there is no inevitability to the civilizing process. Indeed, its fragile and contingent nature could – and has been – interrupted at any time by phenomena such as war, catastrophe, dramatic social change and the like. In such situations, 'the armour of civilized conduct crumbles very rapidly', with a concomitant fragmentation of centralized governmental authority and a decline in human capacity for rational action (see Elias, 1939 [1969]), making possible the re-emergence of conduct and values more appropriate to previous eras. Under these circumstances, it is possible for the civilizing process to be, as it were, 'put into reverse' and 'decivilizing forces' shape social and individual development. Fletcher (1997) provides a helpful account of the criteria necessary for decivilizing to occur. These include: 'a shift in the balance between constraints by others and self-restraint in favour of constraints by others; another would be the development of a social standard of behaviour and feeling which generates the emergence of a less even, all round, stable and differentiated pattern of self-restraint; and third we would expect a contraction in the scope of mutual identification between constituent groups and individuals' (Fletcher, 1997: 83). However, it is important to note that 'decivilizing' does not involve some wholesale 'turning the clock back'. First, the specific intensity and duration of any such 'spurt' is going to be dependent, like the pace of development of the civilizing process itself, on local contingencies. And second, the effectivity of the civilizing process as a whole seems most unlikely to be swept aside by such forces. Indeed, in the civilized world today, the longstanding trends towards bureaucratization provide an important bulwark against large-scale collapse of the existing social order.[3] Under such circumstances it becomes possible to see civilizing and decivilizing trends operating together with varying degrees of intensity: a continuity of the bureaucratic rationalism associated with the former, running alongside the more emotive and unpredictable sentiments associated with the latter.

THE CIVILIZING PROCESS AND THE SOCIOLOGY OF PUNISHMENT

Elias made very little reference to the punishment of offenders in his *magnum opus* as a way of illustrating the historical development of the civilizing process. As Garland has pointed out, he offers some brief remarks about the place of the gallows in the medieval world of the knight and he notes, on the very first page, that 'the form of judicial punishment' is one of the social facts to which 'civilization' typically refers (1990: 216). Clearly, alongside the way he charts changes in attitudes to nose blowing, table manners, bedroom activities and so on to establish the course of the civilizing process, a study of penal change over the same time span has the potential to provide a very rich tapestry. Pieter Spierenburg (1984) thus demonstrated how attitudes towards the use of capital punishment and lesser punishments to the human body changed during the course of the 17th and 18th centuries in Amsterdam. In this period, many of the brutal excesses involved in the array of punishments at its start began to be toned down or disappeared altogether (it seems, for example, that tongue-piercing, blinding and the cutting off of ears and hands did not survive the 17th century); while the execution, although it continued to be administered in public, began to take the form of a more solemn affair (for example, the execution dais was eventually draped in black; after execution, the corpses of the condemned were no longer put on display). Similar patterns are found in other European societies at this time.

In London, the riotous march from Newgate Prison to Tyburn Gallows came to an end in 1783. Thereafter, executions took place outside the prison until the abolition of public executions in 1868. The 'bloody code' which had made the death penalty available for over 300 offences at that time was steadily reduced to the point where execution, for all intents and purposes, was only available for murder after 1861. The last occasion when beheading the corpse of the condemned occurred was in 1820. In 1832, gibbeting was abolished, as was the hanging of bodies in chains in 1834 (Gatrell, 1994). Equally, we find these elite sensibilities at work in the abolition of public executions in parts of the USA and Australia in the mid-19th century (Masur, 1989; McGuire, 1998). The reasons for such changes, Spierenburg argues, are due to a growing repugnance at such 'disturbing events', including these sights of brutal pain and suffering inflicted on powerless human beings. These sensitivities were initially manifested in social elites. They looked with increasing disdain at the vulgarity of the lower classes who raucously celebrated such spectacles, a point also made by Gatrell in his work on the abolition of public executions in Britain: 'if we do discover retreats from scaffold horrors which helped mediate the birth of "modern" repertoires of feeling ... they can only be associated with the accumulating restraints upon the free ranging instincts of socialized individuals to which Elias drew attention' (1994: 17).

However, it is also important to recognize the way in which changes in state formation also played an important role in this process. For example, in the UK in the early 19th century, political power began to increasingly concentrated in the middle classes in whom these feelings of revulsion at public executions seem to have been most strongly concentrated.[4] Their new rights of representation in parliament eventually gave them the opportunity to put these sensibilities into legislative effect. Smith argues that the abolition of the pillory in 1815 'was an example of the increasing centralization of power and the monopolization of violence by removing retributive vengeance from the hands of the mob' (1996: 34). The structural changes associated with the civilizing process are also evident when we examine Franke's (1995) history of the Dutch prison system from the early 19th century to the present. Drawing on Elias, he demonstrates how increasing sensitivities to the physical and psychological suffering of prisoners gradually led to an amelioration of their conditions of confinement and an improvement in their rights, particularly post 1945 after much of the Dutch body politic had itself experienced incarceration during the Nazi occupation. The reduced social distance – reflective of the 'diminishing contrasts' associated with the civilizing process – between prisoners and prison authorities that ensued meant that prisoners became more trusted. Prison life was reconfigured on the basis that the self-restraint of prisoners was all that was needed in most cases to control their behaviour in these institutions, rather than the external controls of the authorities that had previously regulated prison life. Through this emancipation they came to be seen more as human beings than outsiders, with valid opinions of their own. Indeed, in this period, they were often able to write feature articles that appeared on the front pages of the Dutch press (Franke, 1995). The introduction of open prisons and prisoner self-reporting to prisons on the day of their admission were other features of this new, more liberal prison configuration. As a consequence, the Dutch 'prison experience' became markedly different from that, for example, in the UK. Here, too, the penal authorities, for the most part, took a more liberal approach to prison administration post 1945 (Pratt, 2002). While there was more pity for the prisoners and empathy with them, this did not really extend to granting them 'rights' and accreditation as full citizens. A much greater social distance still existed between them and policy making elites. In these respects, the differing nature of the social structural changes in the two countries, with much greater emphasis on functional democratisation in the Netherlands led to two very different prison systems.[5]

While there is intrinsic importance in the historiography of such scholarship, it also raises important theoretical issues. In particular, it undermines much of the foundations of *Discipline and Punish*. Foucault's central argument is that around 1800 there was a marked shift from corporeal to carceral punishments, in line with the changing nature of political power at this juncture. Hence the contrasts at the beginning of the book between the execution of Damiens in 1757 and the reformatory timetable from the 1830s. However, as Spierenburg (1984) shows, this change was a much more long term process of social development and cultural values. In this way, as Garland notes, it counters the Foucauldian tendency 'to regard punishment as being shaped almost exclusively by strategic considerations of a political order' (1990: 229). In much the same way Spierenburg's (1991) *The Prison Experience* challenges the emphasis Foucault gives to imprisonment as a specifically modern phenomenon – one that suddenly replaces centuries of punishments to the human body. Instead, he agues that this transition, at least in relation to the Netherlands and Germany, actually began in the 16th century, with the two modalities of punishment existing alongside one another for another two centuries. Once again, the gradual shift from public 'spectacles of suffering' to privately inflicted punishment in the form of punitive labour in prison workhouses (*rasphuis*) came about because of changing sensibilities: the invisibility of prison life became more tolerable than the sight of labour gangs, parades of convicts going off to the galleys and so on. Elias, as well, of course, gave importance to the changing nature of state power. However, not only was the process of change different from that envisaged by Foucault – gradual and long term, rather than sharp and sudden – but at the same time the growth of state power in the modern age did not simply act as some sort of monolithic form of 'social control'. Instead, changes in state formation in the modern age took place in conjunction with cultural changes, social habitus and modes of knowledge. In terms of subsequent penal development and values underpinning it, the increasing authority of the state, for example, meant that, when disputes arose, citizens would look increasingly to it to resolve such matters for them, rather than attempt to do this for themselves. In this way, a gulf emerged between the penal process and the rest of society, leading to the kind of ignorance and misunderstandings that informs much of popular understandings about prisons and prisoners in the 21st century. However, the growth of European nation states and the formation of firm and defensible territorial boundaries were likely to bring a concomitant rise in feelings of responsibility towards and identification with fellow citizens. It would make possible the formation of 'interdependencies' that would become both wider and more firmly cemented with the heterogeneous divisions of labour in modern society and the attendant shift from rural to urban life. One's significant others, for whom some kind of reciprocity/obligation was owed became more extensive and necessitated restrictions on impulse behaviour and aggression while simultaneously fostering the converse: foresight and self-restraint. In such ways, limits began to be imposed on both the quantity and quality of punishment in modern society. If imprisonment suited its sensibilities, because it ensured that punishment was hidden from view, it also imposed limits on the degree of deprivation imposed on the prisoners – hence the carefully calibrated measurements regarding how much food those in English prisoners were entitled to in the 19th century. While imprisonment was intended to disadvantage them, they were not going to be allowed to starve to death (Pratt, 2002).

Nor is it the case that we only come to a have a different understanding of *the past* through Elias' work. It also sheds light on *the present*. In much of the Anglophone world today we find developments that have a resonance with *decivilizing* processes: a growing emphasis, for example, on special and enforceable conditions and regulations in parole licences and probation orders – imposing external restraints on offenders rather than trusting their self-restraint; an increasing expectation that victims of crime will not only have a role to play in sentencing and parole adjudications, but will also be able to use such occasions to proclaim the extent of their suffering for all to know, thereby undermining the order and carefully defined non-emotive etiquette of the court with uncontrolled and unpredictable outbursts of rage and anger; and a decline in any mutual identification between law abiding citizens and law breakers, with antagonism towards paedophiles one of the clearest examples of such hostilities.

It was the presence of such features in the contemporary penal arrangements of Anglophone societies that I tried to explain in *Punishment and Civilization* (Pratt, 2002). The argument was that for much of the modern period, penal development had followed the course of the civilizing process: the demise of public punishments to the human body; the eventual abolition of the death penalty; the 'disappearance of prison' as noted earlier; and the gradual amelioration of prison life. As with the use Elias made of his manners books, so it was possible to trace in, by reference to annual prison reports, what the penal authorities determined to be appropriate standards of health, personal hygiene, clothing and diet – what were thought to be, in effect, the necessary features of prison life itself. The pivotal role of the penal bureaucracies in both the determination of prison life and the control of knowledge about it also points to adaptations to the Elias thesis. Because he left the civilizing process at a point in the early 19th century it does not capture the significance of bureaucratic governance in modern society. From the 1980s, however, the emergence of new punishment possibilities noted above were seen as decivilizing symptoms. The argument was not that civilizing and decivilizing processes of development are incompatible with each other (Vaughan, 2000); rather, it was that the concepts had to be understood as operating together with varying degrees of intensity and effects: a continuity of the bureaucratic rationalism associated with the former, running alongside the emotive penal sentiments associated with the latter. While *Punishment and Civilization* can be faulted because of its generality – it looked too much for points of similarity to sustain its argument rather than differences to illustrate the effects of 'local centrifugal forces'- what it also shows is that Elias' work is important not as a means to understanding the past, but also the present.

THE CIVILIZING PROCESS AND MODERN PENAL DEVELOPMENT

Let us now examine in more detail the development of punishment in modern society through the theoretical grid of the civilizing process. By 'modern', I am referring to penal development from the early 19th century onwards, which means that we leave behind the premodern world of gallows and gibbets, stocks and whips. We begin instead at the point when prison is becoming the central response to crime. It will be illustrated by reference to developments in each of the layers of the civilizing process. The focus will primarily be on the Anglophone world but, to illustrate the differing pace of the civilizing process, there will also be a discussion of its effects and consequences in the Scandinavian countries.[6]

Structural processes

After the phasing out of public punishments in the first half of the 19th century prison for the first time became a central feature of penal development.[7] In the UK, prior to the establishment of a central prison administration in 1877, there had been competing accounts from prison governors about the preferred prison 'model': how much religious instruction there should be; to what extent should the prisoners be kept in solitary confinement and to what extent should they be allowed to work with others in silence (Pratt, 2002). At the same time, prison chaplains enjoyed equal status with governors (Griffiths, 1875: 46), notwithstanding the potential for conflict and uncertainty this might create. Furthermore, prison doctors could use their discretionary power to prescribe 'invalid diets' to prisoners as they saw fit, and were free to comment on dietary and health conditions in the prison. After centralization, however, the competing claims and counter claims, authority conflicts and discretionary powers came to an abrupt end. Thereafter, official commentaries on prison development were largely made in the annual report of the Prison Commission, which had Sir Edmund Du Cane as its first chairman. The individual reports of prison governors were now appended to the general summary of the commissioners and became increasingly anodyne and routine.[8] The autonomy of the other prison professionals was restricted and their status downgraded. Chaplains, for example, were often overseers of rudimentary teaching arrangements that were provided towards the end of the 19th century for some prisoners, or served a merely ornamental purpose: sitting with the governor on adjudications to provide dignity to what was taking place, but effectively powerless to intervene, as one cleric revealed to a prisoner after witnessing prison officers inflicting a beating: 'its no good … there's nothing we can do' (Balfour, 1901: 224). Attendance at chapel was even made optional in the UK in 1915.

The increasingly monopolistic power of the penal bureaucracy that these developments were characteristic of had two important consequences in relation to the course of the civilizing process. First, it ensured that there would be longer chains and denser interdependencies *within* the penal bureaucracy itself. If, at one level, this brought about greater consistency in training, regulations and so on, it also meant, at another, that it would be increasingly difficult for those in the particular institutions to act as individuals, rather than bureaucratic representatives: to express their own views rather than those of the bureaucracy. Indeed, the way in which the British state later made all its prison employees sign the 1920 Official Secrets Act cemented this reality and added to the increasing secrecy and regimentation associated with imprisonment. Second, the penal bureaucracy was able to shape, develop and report on prison policy as this suited its own interests and largely free from any public involvement. Du Cane, a former officer in the Royal Engineers, had ruthlessly implemented the 'hard bed, hard fare, hard labour' regime in British prisons, after complaints that the first early modern prisons were too luxurious (Pratt, 2002). Following his forced retirement in 1895, however, the prison authorities came to act and speak more in the manner of a Weberesque bureaucracy, carefully promoting and protecting their interests, rather than allowing these to be determined by the whims of charismatic individuals within them.

The Prison Commission thus tended to take a more liberal approach to prison administration, fending off periodic complaints about 'pampered prisoners'. As Chair of the Prison Commission Sir Lionel Fox later elliptically and characteristically explained, 'one cannot be unaware that the body of assumptions underlying the common talk of common people and directing their praise and praise alone are not, in these matters, the assumptions on which contemporary prison administration is based' (1952: 137). The interests of the penal bureaucracies superseded those of the general public. The *Report of the Director of Penal Services* thus condescendingly stated that 'the public should accept something less than one hundred per cent security ... if the public wants to develop the positive and redemptive side of prison work, it must face the fact that the occasional prisoner may escape and do damage' (1957: 8).

There had been great excitement and curiosity with the beginning of new prison building in the 1840s: architects vied with one another to design them; foreign dignitaries were escorted around them (Ignatieff, 1978). Not only this, but up to the mid-19th century they had been open to the public at large to wander around (Dixon, 1850). However, public interest began to decline as the penal bureaucracies made entry increasingly restrictive. Indeed, other than public interest being provoked by scandals that emerged from time to time (whether this was in relation to prisoners being treated too leniently or too brutally) public knowledge and understanding of prison life had largely come to an end. Thus, while the bureaucratic structure of prison management had created longer and denser interdependencies within it, creating uniformity and standardization, the chains between it and the general public had actually become much shorter. The penal bureaucracy controlled most of the publicly available knowledge about prison: members of the public, for the most part, lost interest in these institutions that were now outside their own experience.

Changes in manners/culture

However, in addition to the administrative veil that had been drawn across the punishment process, prison design and location increased the physical distance between punishment and the general public. The gothic architecture that characterized prison building in the first half of the 19th century was replaced by an outward appearance that denoted 'functional austerity' rather than extravagance (Pratt, 2002). And from the late 19th century, new prisons were more likely to be built away from city centres rather than at the heart of them. While there had previously been no need to separate prisons from public life (Evans, 1982; Brodie et al., 2002), growing public distaste for them, as in the Wellington example noted earlier, led to a more general relocation of prisons: out of city centres and into isolated suburbs or remote rural areas. Nor did the public want to see to prisoners working outside the prison. This led to them being removed from public works beyond its walls. Thereafter the prison authorities steadily 'anonymized' prisoner transport from prison to court. By the early 20th century, when moving between prisons, they travelled in reserved railway carriages with blinds drawn in the UK. They were also allowed to wear civilian clothing to ease their shame during these increasingly fleeting public appearances. These sensibilities were later incorporated within the 1948 prison rules: '[prisoners] shall be exposed to public view as little as possible, and proper safeguards shall be adopted to protect them from insult and injury' (Fox, 1952: 164–5).

This distaste for the presence of prisons and prisoners occurred in conjunction with *diminishing contrasts* within the punishment spectrum. As the death penalty rapidly declined in use during the first half of the 20th century, the choice of punishment was, in effect, between custodial and community sanctions, with increasing variations between them, rather than the more stark options of life or death, as in the premodern world. Thus, at the beginning of the 20th century, special institutions began to be opened for 'inebriates', 'habitual offenders' and the mentally deficient, with borstals for young offenders. By the 1950s this differentiation had come to include open and closed prisons and psychiatric prisons. There were also variations in the conditions that could be imposed in probation orders. From the 1960s, more varied community penalties became available, such as suspended sentences, community service and deferred sentences.

Within the prison figuration we find growing mutual identification between the prison authorities and the prisoners themselves (or at least on behalf of the management elites – prison officer culture seems to have been much more resistant to such sensibilities). By the early 20th century in the UK, prisoners were being addressed by their name rather than their number. The language of punishment reflected these changes in prison culture from the late 19th century. The term 'convict' was falling into disuse, to be replaced by 'prisoner', which in turn by the 1960s had been replaced by the less stigmatic 'inmate' or even 'trainee'. In conjunction with this growing mutual identification and reduced social distance, prisoners were now to be pitied more than feared. As the prominent British psychiatrist Edwin Glover explained, 'they have certainly injured their fellows but perhaps society has unwittingly injured them' (1956: 267). Indeed, for the prison authorities, it was as if there was little innate difference between those in prison and the public beyond it: 'between a hundred prisoners and a hundred persons chosen at random from the street outside, the resemblances are more noticeable than the differences' (Fox, 1952: 111).

Changes in social habitus

Du Cane had written that prisoners had characteristics that were 'entirely those of the inferior races of mankind – wandering habits, utter laziness, absence of thought or provision [and] want of moral sense' (1875: 302–3). However, this moralizing that was characteristic of the late Victorian era steadily gave way to more objective, scientific understandings. Ruggles-Brise argued for the need for 'criminal laboratories' as in the 'United States where science and humanity march hand in hand exploring prisons as places of punishment' (1921: 194). At the same time, the sight of cowed and broken prisoners had become repugnant as thresholds of shame and embarrassment advanced. On a visit to Dartmoor Prison, Prison Commissioner Sir Alexander Paterson noted with distaste that 'as [the prisoners] saw us coming, each man ran to the nearest wall and put his face against it, remaining in this servile position, till we had passed behind him … the men looked hard in body and in spirit, healthy enough in physique and colour, but cowed and listless in demeanour and response' (Ruck, 1951: 26).

Thereafter, it was recognized that 'the deterrent effect of imprisonment must finally be in the loss of personal liberty and all that this involves … that effect is not reinforced of the period of loss of liberty is used in a mere repressive and punitive way' (Home Office, 1959: 13, emphasis added). Instead, 'we have found that the study of art, music and drama has for those in prison a particular appeal, and that these arts may bring for the first time to the lives of depressed and distorted men and women perceptions of beauty, goodness and truth' (*Report of the Commissioners of Prisons for the Year 1951*, 1952: 52). Now the prison authorities expected that prison officers would share in these new ways of understanding prisoners. It was thus claimed that 'group counselling [enables] closer relationships with inmates and allows guards to have an even greater impact in terms of changing inmate behaviour' (*Report of the Director of Penal Services*, 1963–4: 2).

Changes in modes of knowledge

Expert knowledge and research became increasingly influential on penal development, particularly in the post-1945 era. In the

UK the Advisory Council on the Treatment of Offenders was established in 1944. A new section titled 'Research' appears in the English prison reports from 1956. As Home Secretary Butler later explained, 'research may sound academic, but I am quite certain that in this field of crime it is the absolutely vital basis without which we cannot work' (Hansard, 1958, vol. 59, 31 October: 505). For the elite groups undertaking research or developing policy, prisoners had become detached from the irredeemable moral culpability previously and incorrigibility that been associated with them in the development of 19th-century prison policy. Instead, they were understood as inadequates, living unfulfilled lives. They no longer constituted a menace to the rest of the community. Taylor, in his study of preventive detention prisoners, found that 'they were lonely men who had become inept in handling personal contacts and from their experiences had developed paranoid attitudes towards other people. In their view, the world was a threatening and frightening place' (1960: 35). The punishment that they had received was not only out of proportion to their wrongdoing but also magnified their sense of isolation from the rest of society. In these respects, to avoid such destructive excesses, prison was increasingly relegated to a 'last resort' penal option, to be reserved for those for whom there seemed to be no viable alternative. From the 1960s to the 1980s increasing resources were used in the development of what were thought to be more humane community based alternative sanctions.

While the UK has been used as the main example to illustrate these trends, a similar pattern emerges across the other Anglophone societies (Pratt, 2002). However, it is important to note that, notwithstanding the significant changes to prison life that took place from the 1870s to the 1970s, the purpose of this kind of analysis is to provide a sociological explanation of them, rather than use them to teleologically demonstrate the increasing 'civilization' of these societies. Indeed, they provide no guarantee that this was occurring. Official discourse had become more sanitized but, as around a century of prisoner biographies testified (Pratt, 2002), the pains and deprivations of imprisonment persisted. At the same time, the civilizing process can be said to have allowed the prison bureaucracy to grow stronger and become more deeply entrenched, automatically giving its own accounts more credibility than those of prisoners. It had become one of those organizations that took care of 'disturbing events', with control over knowledge and information that was available to the public. At the same time, the physical and administrative distance that had come to exist between between the public and prisoners meant that the former thought of the latter as 'outsiders' or 'different'.[9]

Furthermore, these aspects of the civilizing process should be understood as a spectrum of possibilities rather than some uniform standard. There were thus variations as well as similarities within the Anglophone societies. The civilizing process had come much later to the Southern USA, for example, as was reflected, up to the 1950s, in their high rates of imprisonment, chain gang and vigilante traditions, fondness for the death penalty and slowness in instituting prison reform (Pratt, 2002):[10] features which were indicative of the weak central state authority in this region and low thresholds of shame, embarrassment and self-restraint. In the first half of the 20th century, it was as if penal practices here were remnants of much longer cultural traditions bound up in racism, slavery and prebellum plantation practices, where owners imposed and implemented their own penal arrangements in these fiefdoms. Elsewhere in Western society, the Scandinavian countries stood at the opposite end of this civilizing continuum. Here, the death penalty in peacetime had effectively ceased (if not *de jure* then at least *de facto*) in the mid-19th century, as opposed to the mid-20th century in the most of the Anglophone world. These countries not only had some of the lowest levels of imprisonment in the West[11] but (particularly Sweden) had also become renowned for humane, 'civilized' prison conditions. In an article titled 'Almost the best of everything', Tom Wicker wrote that 'Sweden's prisons are models of decency and humanity ... Although debate continues among socially aware Swedes as to whether prisons here are not still too harsh, most American inmates would regard ... Sweden's maximum security penitentiary – as a country club' (1975: 10). At this time, these countries were regarded by the liberal elites in control of policy development in the Anglophone world as 'the leaders' of the civilized world, setting the example for the rest to follow.

Why had the civilizing process become more advanced and intensified in this region? In these countries, there was a long tradition of egalitarianism that reduced social distance and made interdependencies much longer throughout society (the extreme homogeneity of the region also contributed to this, in contrast to Elias' assumptions that dependencies grew stronger as societies became more complex and heterogeneous).[12] Norway, for example, abolished its nobility in 1817. Furthermore, inherited land was divided between descendants rather than the first born, thus preventing the build up of a landed gentry. By the early 20th century, its egalitarianism had become one of its identifying characteristics: 'among civilised states, there is scarcely any that is so fortunate with regard to the equality of its social conditions as Norway. There is no nobility with political or economic privileges, no large estates, no capitalist class ... The highest and lowest strata of society are on the whole no farther removed from one another than that there is constant reciprocal action between them, and transition from one to the other' (Hansen, 1900: 202). Accordingly, in these countries, there were much shorter social distances between prisoners and the rest of society in the 19th century. They were thus initially re-educated and remoralized by priests and teachers (the reason why the separate system of confinement lasted until the 1940s and beyond in Scandinavia); and later 'treated' by psy-professionals with a view to reintegrating them into society (Pratt and Eriksson, 2011). In contrast, in the Anglophone world, prisoners belonged to the 'dangerous classes', to be feared and shut out of society. They were right at the bottom of a long series of divisions that extended throughout British society: divisions which separated the social classes and then further divided them, all the way down to the very lowest strata of society where we find the respectable poor, followed by workhouse paupers, the mentally ill and finally prisoners.

Again, in the Scandinavian countries, penal institutions are characteristically small (usually housing between 50 to 100 prisoners) and remain in the centre of local community development. Post 1945, prisoners were more likely to be working outside the prison, or at least able to move more easily between prison and community, emphasising the way in which those in prison were not thought to be fundamentally 'different' from those outside it. This relatively short social distance between the two groups meant that the way in which 'prison' was imagined in Scandinavia was likely to have far less fantasy content and much higher levels of tolerance. In Sweden, the literal translation of their term for 'prison officer' is 'prison carer' (*fångvårdare*). Furthermore, because virtually the whole population materially benefited from the generous universalism of the Scandinavian welfare state, there seems to have been less stigma attached to welfare beneficiaries than in the Anglophone world. As such, prisoners were usually regarded as just another group of claimants, no different from any others and of no particular interest.

In addition, the Scandinavians place a high value on education. In Norway and Finland, for example, the study of language and literature became a means of solidifying their 19th-century struggles for independence from Sweden and Russia, respectively. The importance of education to the well-being and identity of the nation became another feature of the local culture of these societies, and perhaps is another reason for the high levels of trust and status accorded to experts in these societies. This then allowed them to develop their aspirations for penal reform further than it was possible for their Anglophone counterparts to do. At the same time, the functional democratisation of penal governance, whereby debate was conducted much more in public, between representatives of all 'stakeholders' ensured that the public at large had a better and more realistic understanding of penal affairs. In this region, these matters were not allowed to become the exclusive property of bureaucratic elites, as had happened in the Anglophone world. There are thus annual meetings between all stakeholders in the Norwegian prison system – judges, politicians, prisoners and so on (Christie, 2000). Similarly in Sweden, where these debates and discussions are televised. Furthermore, lay people sit with judges in lower courts and (unlike British juries) decide sentencing as well as guilt or innocence.

However, even in this region, the civilizing process can provide no guarantees against uncivilized outcomes. The high levels of trust in the Scandinavian 'protective state' allowed abuses of state power to develop: for example, an emphasis on indeterminate prison sentences (in Sweden especially), in the belief that crime was a form of mental illness – the time for release would be when each individual prisoner was cured; and the maintenance of a eugenics programme for deviants of various kinds from the 1930s to the 1970s, in the belief that the state could 'humanely' control those who could not control themselves (Hagelund, 2003).

DECIVILIZING SYMPTOMS

Overall, though, the more general penal arrangements across Western society were dependent upon a particular configuration of the civilizing process. That is, a strong central state authority with monopolistic control of the power to punish; high levels of shame and embarrassment; high levels of trust in the penal authorities that then allowed them to develop research driven policy. From the 1970s, economic and social reconstruction across much of the Anglophone world in particular has meant that it has been impossible to sustain the unity of this configuration. The ascendancy of neo-liberal polities has meant that the authority of the central state has fragmented. It now assumes a more residual role in everyday governance that is no longer privileged around the idea of a strong central state working as one with its bureaucracies. Recourse has been made to alternative modes of governance in the private and voluntary sectors. As this has happened, interdependencies have become much shorter. Many of the longstanding institutions and cultural expectations that had become deeply embedded in these societies have declined: job security, the stability of family life, membership of trade unions, churches and other organizations (Beck, 1992; Fukuyama, 1995; Putnam, 2000). Shorter interdependencies are likely to reduce tolerance and increase insecurity.

In addition, the deregulation of the news media and the introduction of new print technology since the 1980s has been conducive to modes of knowledge that have high levels of fantasy content rather than detached, objective analysis. Newsmaking and reporting become more sensationalized as each paper or television channel competes with its rivals. It also becomes more simplified to attract and secure advertising revenue. This has meant that crime and punishment issues are likely to receive greater coverage than used to be the case because of their innate interest to audiences. The media also have a vested interest in sensationalizing these matters, creating a public interest and providing opportunities for more public 'say', rather than leaving such matters to be determined 'behind the scenes' by elite experts.

As a result of this array of concentrated change, we can now discern decivilizing symptoms in each sector of the civilizing process, with significant effects on penal development.

Structural processes

Private prisons, which had disappeared from most of the Anglophone world during the course of the 19th century have now been reintroduced and dilute the state's monopoly of the power to punish. Civil service restructuring has considerably undermined its capacity to obstruct more punitive political agendas and impose its own liberal imprint on policy (Loader, 2006). As this has happened, so single issue law and order lobby groups, variously claiming to represent crime victims in particular and 'ordinary people' in general, become key players in policy development (Pratt, 2007), campaigning for more punitive sentences and more victim input to the punishment process. In some jurisdictions, these groups have taken advantage of the provision for plebiscites and referenda in the electoral process to provide the momentum for the introduction of particularly punitive legislation.[13] Governments have also indicated a readiness to acquiesce to the agendas of these groups while distancing themselves from the criminal justice establishment that had previously enjoyed almost exclusive control of policy development. For example, when introducing the Labour government's Crime and Disorder Bill (which made provision for anti-social behaviour orders), the then Home Secretary Jack Straw proclaimed that '[it] represents a triumph of community politics over detached metropolitan elites' (The Times, 8 April 1998: 16).

These social structural changes have led to a reinvigoration of prison use and a resurrection of a variety of other penal strategies and symbols from the past: stigmatic and highly visible public punishments such as 'community payback' orders in Britain (formerly community service) and chain gangs in some of the Southern states in the USA. We also find a deterioration in prison conditions, often the product of overcrowding but sometimes deliberately engineered by governments. Prison austerity, it is thought, symbolizes the new unity between government and the general public in relation to the punishment of crime. It not only manifests public outrage and anger towards criminals but will also commonsensically ensure that those who experience such conditions will not choose to return to prison in the future (in contrast to the overwhelming body of research evidence which demonstrates exactly the opposite). In so doing, it jettisons much of the humanizing ethos of post war administrations for prison conditions that are stripped down to the bare minimum for existence and where any improvements to this have to be earned (which has resonances with the 19th century 'progressive stage' system of prison management). At the same time, some of the restrictions that had been steadily put in place since the late 19th century to prevent the incarceration of particular groups (juveniles, some first time offenders, young adults and so on) have been removed. Thus, in 2009, in England, there were 400 children aged between 12 and 14 in prison, something that had largely disappeared in the early 20th century in that country.

Changes in manners/culture

As the influence of criminal justice elites on policy has declined, so too has the culture of tolerance and forbearance that they were associated with. Instead of the restraints and moderation that this 'established group' were able to impose on penal policy, the public representations of anger and intolerance of the former 'outsiders' – the general public – have become more dominant influences. Governments have been eager to position themselves alongside these sentiments. Tony Blair, when prime minister, thus made the point that 'crime, anti-social behaviour, racial intolerance, drug abuse, destroy families and communities. They destroy the very respect on which society is founded … Fail to confront this evil and we will never build a Britain where everyone can succeed ... by acknowledging the duty to care, we earn the right to be tough on crime ... it is time for zero tolerance of yob culture' (*Guardian*, 27 September 2006: 6). Now, the difference between law breakers and the rest of society is re-emphasised. Law breakers, much like the 'dangerous classes' of the 19th century, are seen as irredeemable enemies of society, rather than victims of it. The only politically acceptable response to them is one of punishment and exclusion, rather than welfare and integration. This speech is also a reflection of the new language of punishment that now informs penal debate. Other examples include phrases such as 'Three Strikes and You're Out' and 'Life Means Life – No Parole.' These phrases all originated in the USA – the Western society which punishes the most and the most inhumanely, illustrative of the turnaround in the leadership of punishment in the civilized world. Instead of the steady shift towards mutual identification with offenders that was characteristic of the civilizing process, what we are now more likely to find is a growing mutual identification with their victims – and antagonism and hostility towards their offenders. This has led to policies designed to 'bridge the justice gap' and to 'rebalance the criminal justice system'. Victims have thus been given a range of representational rights that can include opportunities to be heard at sentencing and parole adjudications through victim impact statements and so on.

This rebalancing simultaneously involves a reduction in the rights of offenders. For example, the state's control over prisoners *after* their sentence has finished can be extended. Electronic monitoring, introduced as a liberal and cost efficient way to reduce the prison population in the 1980s, is used in some jurisdictions to regulate sex offenders for upwards of ten years on their release from prison. Opportunities they might have to 'profit' from their crimes are removed. In New Zealand, the Prisoners and Victims Claims Act 2005 was backdated to cover a payout to six prisoners (around US$100,000 in total) in 2004 after their ill-treatment by the Department of Corrections – they had been kept in conditions close to those in an American supermax prison,[14] for which there was no lawful authority. The legislation made provision for victims to be able to sue their offenders for any windfall they might receive (whether this be a lotto ticket or damages from the government for mistreatment) for up to six years on leaving prison. In explaining the Bill, the Minister of Justice rejected the notion that criminals 'pay their debt to society' while in prison: 'it costs us $50,000 a year to keep someone in prison ... that is the cost to society, not the repayment of a debt ... you don't repay your debt to the victim by being in prison' (*Dominion Post*, 25 January, 2005: A3). In this new penal culture, redemption is not automatically granted at the end of one's sentence. For some, the stigma of conviction and punishment may have to be permanently borne, much like the physical stigmata from punishment in the premodern world.

Changes in social habitus

Because of its weakened authority, the central state is now more likely to acquiesce to citizen's demands for greater involvement in the exercise of penal power. Community consultation regarding released sex offenders, in varying degrees depending on the jurisdiction,[15] is one example of this. Even so, such gestures are frequently not enough to restrain waves of public anger and frustration – at particular offenders, at the criminal justice system and the elites who administer it, and at a much broader panoply of anxieties and insecurities that regularly intrude on everyday life. As such, we are likely to find sporadic outbursts of aggression and vindictiveness and the return of vigilante activities (Johnston, 1996; Girling et al., 1998). These have no reliable pattern or predictability, other than that they are likely to occur among those sectors of society where the state's authority is weakest. As evidence of its decline, just a rumour or newspaper headline may be enough to ignite them. One of the most well-known and wide-ranging outbursts came in the aftermath of the rape and murder of a young child in England in 2000. The leaders of one local group of vigilantes claimed to possess a self-constructed self-styled 'list of power' – the names and addresses of local people whom they suspected of paedophile activities and whom they were intent on hunting down. One woman who was later interviewed about her participation in these activities explained that she had 'enjoyed walking up the street with a gang of women, all shouting to get the paedophiles out. 'I can't help it but this is how I felt. Walking the streets will all the noise, I got a buzz out of it. I know it sounds really childish. But when I came back [home] I thought, what have I done' (*Observer*, 13 August 2000: 4). Again, though, participation in such activities seems more 'natural', more taken for granted, when thresholds of shame and embarrassment are lowered.

Within this reconfigured habitus, policy making seems to have become more impulsive. Rather than the product of long term planning and research, it is increasingly likely to be developed in immediate response to exceptional cases that are then seen as 'the norm', indicative of a habitus that now demands instant, commonsensical responses to social problems. In Britain, there were 54 new criminal justice bills between 1997 and 2006 (Garside, 2006). The Home Office White Paper *Justice for All* states that 'the people are sick and tired of a sentencing system that does not make sense' (2002: 86). It argues for the need to 'rebalance the [criminal justice] system in favour of victims, witnesses and communities', on the basis that 'the people of this country want a criminal justice system that works in the interests of justice'. Not only are such statements illustrative of the new configuration of penal power that directs policy, but they also reflect the taken for granted assumption that the interests of justice necessitate an enhanced role for victims with, again, a reduced focus on the well-being of offenders.

Changes in modes of knowledge

The spokesperson for the Sensible Sentencing Trust, a particularly influential law and order/victims' rights (the two concerns seem to be merging) lobby group in New Zealand, proclaimed in 2007 that 'We do not need academics, criminologists or psychologists to tell us the simple truth that if you reward bad behaviour you will get more of it!'[16] Again, policy is more likely to be directed by commonsense imperatives that come from these newly influential pressure groups. The almost total absence of any interdependencies that previously existed between criminal justice elites and 'ordinary people' under the previous configuration of penal power has helped to produce these dramatic changes in modes of knowledge. The social distance that existed between these two sectors of society only built up resentment and distrust. Criminal justice elites are thus seen as responsible for rising crime because of their apparent ineptitude (even though all the indications are that it has been falling right across Western society since the early 1990s); and are associated with punishments that are too liberal (even though prison populations have been increasing). Hence the claims, regularly made in the popular press and by law and order lobbyists that they are 'out of touch', 'living on another planet' and so on (Hough, 1996).

The restructuring of the news media has contributed to these changes in modes of knowledge because of its preoccupation with crime and punishment issues. The perceptions it has created that crime is increasing give added legitimacy to those law and order lobbyists who vividly draw attention to this menace, while reducing the credibility of academic commentators who discuss crime in a more detached, analytical fashion. They seem to play down its threat even though in the media, the main source of information about it for most people, it is ever-present and in need of immediate, more punitive responses.

THE END OF CIVILIZATION?

At various points then we can see that the contours of the civilizing process have been interrupted by these decivilizing symptoms. However, their presence does not then act as some sort of time machine, reversing the entire course of penal development. Some of the reversals that have taken place tend to be peripheral – indicative of new horizons and possibilities for punishment to suit the changing values of these societies, perhaps, but not cornerstones of a new penal apparatus. Other than this, the most striking feature of contemporary penal arrangements – the enlarged presence of the prison – something that would have been unthinkable in the 1970s – may reflect a reversal of those earlier political priorities aimed at reducing prison numbers, but this has not been accompanied by a renaissance of punishments to the human body (outside the USA). Indeed, such punishments seem to have slipped off the penal agenda altogether in these societies. It can also be argued that much of this reconfiguration can be attributed to the civilizing process itself and is another indicator of the way in which it can produce 'uncivilized' consequences. The use of electronic monitoring, introduced as an efficient and humane way of reducing the prison population, can actually expand it. It leads to increasing numbers being sent back to prison not because of further crimes but because of parole violations that this technology more carefully monitors and detects. The bureaucratic veil that has been drawn across the prison has allowed the authorities in the USA to devise 'supermax' prisons: these are the products of penal bureaucrats rather than state governments.

It should also be noted that the reduction in the threshold of shame and embarrassment and the more emotive content that has been brought into criminal justice proceedings – decivilizing symptoms – has also given rise to the restorative justice movement. Here, outpourings of emotion – from both victim and offender – are actively encouraged but are designed to be used productively and reintegratively, leading to apologies, forgiveness and reconciliation (Braithwaite, 1989). It is possible that, in just the same way that the civilizing process can lead to uncivilized consequences, so the decivilizing tendencies may have the potential to bring more civilized outcomes.

These themes are now common across much of the Anglophone world. They are, though, greatly exaggerated in the USA. Why should this be so? As Mennell (2007) has demonstrated, despite recent declines, incidents of violent crime, carrying the most severe penalties, are still higher in the USA than corresponding societies. One of the reasons for such high levels may relate to the way in which the central state was never really able to gain the monopolistic control of violence that was the case in Europe. As we have seen, its authority, particularly in the South, was always fragile. It may also be that, because the free market has been given greater license here than in corresponding societies in the aftermath of social and economic reconstruction, interdependencies have been weakened. With individuals having to rely on themselves rather than the state to take care of difficulties in life, this variously generates deep feelings of anxiety, fear and intolerance. These find then outlets in the opportunities provided by the constitutional structure of that country for more direct citizen involvement in the policy making process – plebiscites, citizens' 'propositions' and so on. Much of its groundbreaking punitive legislation – three strikes, sexual predator and community notification laws – have come about through these mechanisms rather than originating at the level of state governments and their bureaucracies (Zimring, 1996; Domanick, 2004).

SCANDINAVIAN EXCEPTIONALISM

In contrast, the Scandinavian societies have remained largely untroubled by these decivilizing trends. While there have been some increases in imprisonment in this region, Finland, the previous exception to the Scandinavian penal model,[17] has actually seen a dramatic decline in imprisonment from the 1970s, to the level where it is now on a par with the other Scandinavian societies. One of the reasons why its prison population remained the highest in Western Europe for much of the 20th century seems attributable to the authoritarian and repressive culture that gripped this country in the aftermath of its 1918 civil war (Kekkonen, 1999). This began to change in the 1960s as civil war scores and memories faded, and allowed more liberal sentiments to have influence. At the same time, despite some tightening of maximum security arrangements, prison conditions, if anything, have improved still further (Pratt, 2008). In these respects, there is now a massive gulf between Anglophone and Scandinavian societies in relation to prison levels and conditions.

Yet, on the face of it, the foundations of the civilizing process have been shaken in this region as well. The high levels of mutual identification that its extreme homogeneity had provided have been eroded as immigration (to Sweden particularly) has increased.[18] There have been stirrings from right wing populist parties across these societies (indeed the Norwegian Progress Party has the second highest number of seats in parliament). Its message is based around division and exclusion: anti-immigration, secure borders, welfare for Norwegians and no-one else, longer prison sentences. In Sweden, expert opinion regarding drug use and drug control – with its connotations of Eastern menace to this most advanced Western society – has been largely ignored in favour of a more commonsensical 'zero-tolerance' policy (Tham, 2001). We also find other modifications to everyday life that are indicative of changes in manners and culture. Stockholm bus drivers do not carry cash for fear of being robbed – passengers must buy tickets in advance to board; and there were massive public outpourings of grief in relation to the funeral of ten year old Engla Hoglund, which was televised in full on state television – she had been murdered by a man with a history of violent crime.[19] One is also likely to see skinhead gangs wandering around Stockholm city centre, often threatening and harassing ethnic minorities, again indicative of previously high levels of restraint and tolerance breaking down.

It is not the case, then, that there are no discernible signs of decivilizing symptoms in such societies. As yet, however, these have made comparatively minor impact on penal development. For the most part, the strong Scandinavian central state authorities remain very much in place – there has been no recourse to private prisons, for example. Furthermore, the extensive Scandinavian welfare state remains largely intact. It is under no threat from mainstream parties of both Left and Right. Its guarantees of security reduce danger levels and incalculable risk. We find this exemplified in the Norwegian Labour Party's *Crime Policy* (2006), which also stands in stark contrast to the comments made by former British Prime Minister Tony Blair on the need for the state to expel its troublemakers because of their menace. Here, the emphasis is on reintegration and solidarity: 'with good welfare services for everyone, crime can be prevented and many of the initial incentives for a life of crime can be removed. Given that 60 per cent of violent crime is committed under the influence of alcohol, it is important to adhere to a restrictive drug and alcohol policy. Good psychiatric health care services and an active labour market policy are important for comprehensive crime fighting' (2006: 1).

Not only, then, does the Scandinavian welfare state allow these societies to remain largely inclusive, but it is also likely to develop high levels of trust between individuals and state authorities (Rothstein and Uslander, 2005) – including the criminal justice establishment, thereby allowing it to remain in control of much of policy development. Again, there was never the wide division between experts and the public that was allowed to develop in the Anglophone world (vs). Furthermore, victims of crime have not been shut out of criminal justice proceedings, then allowed to proclaim the injustice of their exclusion to the popular media as in the Anglophone world. Instead, they receive compensation from the state as soon as guilt is pronounced, which then tries to recover this from their offender. This also means that there are no emotive 'victim impact statements' read to the court. As such, most of the new initiatives we see in the Anglophone penal arrangements – community payback orders, naming and shaming practices and so on – would be quite out of the question in the Scandinavian penal world. And in just the same way, because of the different experience and pace of the civilizing process in these two clusters of societies, Scandinavian penal practices would be equally out of the question in the Anglophone penal world. It remains to be seen whether their respective penal routes now drift further apart, or whether they move closer together. The civilizing process itself contains no predictive capabilities, nor has it any endpoint in sight.

CONCLUSION

This chapter has attempted to provide an explanation of both long term changes in penal development *and* contemporary penal practices. Through the lens provided by Norbert Elias' *magnum opus* we can see the interconnections and subtleties between cultural values, structural processes, social habitus and modes of knowledge that underlie such developments. Furthermore, while *The Civilizing Process* is probably best known for the way in which it refers to changing sensibilities to pain and suffering over time, we have seen that this is only one dimension of the overall process that has occurred. The nature of these sensibilities is intricately linked to other social, political and economic forces – state formation, modes of knowledge and so on. In these respects, Elias is able to shed light on aspects of the history of penal development in modern society and current trends that would seem to be beyond the purview of other major social theorists. As regards Foucault, the emotive and expressive sanctions in many modern societies in the early 21st century, particularly the Anglophone countries, that deliberately provoke and arouse human sensibilities rather than suppress them seem to run counter to the kernel of 'rationality' that is epistemologically embedded in his later work (Foucault, 1991). Equally, the way in which these developments are being driven by these cultural rather than economic forces that reflects a political and public tolerance of high imprisonment levels irrespective of their financial burden, seems to undermine the economistic explanations so central to Marx and neo-Marxists. And the teleology of Durkheim, so confident of the prowess of the modernizing forces of the late 19th century that would have the effect of keeping such sentiments firmly in check as respected civil servants charted and planned the development of modern penal arrangements, would be nonplussed by these trends that can now prioritize expressions of public sentiments leading to, in some cases, the complete exclusion of scientific expertise (Zimring, 1996).

Having said this, then it must be acknowledged that Elias' work has been variously criticized on the grounds that it prioritizes culture while ignoring politics. For example, in the early 19th century, the role played by fears of class conflict in Britain in debates about public executions (McGowan, 1983); and that the shift from body punishments to incarceration came about more through system failure than sensitivities – as if early modern society simply could not cope with the 'overload' that execution and other punishments to the body (we can include, for the sake of argument, transportation in this category) were placed on it in the first half of the 19th century (Gatrell, 1994; Deveraux, 1996): sending offenders into prison instead would be administratively more convenient and at the same time minimize the chaotic drama and disruption to everyday life that was associated with 'the spectacle of suffering' – in this way, the authority of the criminal justice system could be upheld. Equally, it seems evident that in some Western societies in the 19th century (and beyond) there was actually a high rather than declining tolerance of public executions in, for example, of Aborigines in parts of Australia (McGuire, 1998) and of African Americans in parts of the USA. Do such criticisms weaken the viability of *The Civilizing Process* as a mode of explanation? Perhaps. But then it can be argued in defence that the role of class conflict in penal development can probably be incorporated in changes in state formation. And that the importance of technological efficiency over the emotive extravaganza that public punishments to the human body represented would seem to fit within changes in social habitus and state formation – the increasing emphasis given to rationalization in the midst of changing conditions of labour and urban development. In addition, as we have noted, the pace of the civilizing process will vary from society to society, depending on local centrifugal forces.

More important, however, than in trying to present *The Civilizing Process* as a theory of individual and social development that is beyond criticism (which, of course, it is not), is recognition of what it does to help us to understand in the relationship between punishment and modern society. In particular, the multi-layered forces underpinning this long-term developmental process rather than sweeping and abrupt patterns of penal change. It demonstrates both the progression of penal development in modern society in a historical and a humanitarian sense (the normative tension that is in Elias' work never really disappears); yet it simultaneously illustrates the uncertain and unpredictable nature of this process. If the rise of the prison from the early 19th century meant, for the most part, that offenders would no longer be subjected to physical torture, then the new configuration of penal power around the prison would be replete with its own tensions and continuing shifts and realignments – at every level of its existence. We can thus examine the nature of interdependencies within it, the formation of the particular habitus that was necessary for this; we can see how social distances within this figuration are drawn and redrawn, variously demarcating the changing positions and power relations of its established and outsider groups. This chapter has attempted to illustrate some of these features in its portrayal of the shifting relationship between punishment and modern society, as the civilizing process itself meanders on.

FURTHER READING

David Garland's (1990: ch. 10) *Punishment and Modern Society* almost certainly made Elias' work, in terms of its relationship to penal development, accessible to an Anglophone audience for the first time. Studies that are specifically informed by *The Civilizing Process* include Pieter Spierenburg's (1984) *The Spectacle of Suffering* and his 1991 *The Prison Experience*. There is Herman Franke's (1995) *The Emancipation of Prisoners* and my own *Punishment and Civilization* (Pratt, 2002). However, Elias' influence is also implicit in a range of other research, including Louis Masur's (1989) *Rites of Execution* and Victor Gatrell's (1994) *The Hanging Tree*.

NOTES

1 See, for example, Pratt (1991, 1992).

2 Similarly, van Krieken (1999) provides an Eliasian explanation of Australia's stolen children: that is, the way in which the post war Australian state simply removed lighter skinned aboriginal children from

their families and placed them with whites in the belief that this was the best way to 'civilize' these offspring.

3 On this point, see Doob and Webster (2007) in relation to Canada's relatively low rate of imprisonment (105 per 100,000 of population) by the standards of Anglophone societies.

4 See, for example, Dickens (1846) and Thackeray (1840).

5 Whitman (2003) makes a similar point in relation to the way in which Continental Europe assimilated premodern aristocratic values within their democracies, leading to a much stronger emphasis on 'dignity' in the penal systems of those countries than in the Anglophone world.

6 In 2009, the Anglophone countries (with the exception of Canada – see note 2 above) are at the top end of the Western imprisonment spectrum. In 2009, The USA, the highest, has a rate of imprisonment of 760 per 100,000 of population; New Zealand, third highest after Mexico, has a rate of 191; the UK, fifth highest after Spain, has a rate of 152. In contrast, the rates of imprisonment in the Scandinavian countries are: Denmark 63, Finland 67, Norway 70, and Sweden 74. Prison rates are taken from the World Prison Brief website of the International Centre for Prison Studies, Kings College, London University, www.kcl.ac.uk.

7 Prior to this, prisons had been used mainly in a holding capacity prior to trial transportation or execution.

8 For example, *Eighteenth Report of the Commissioners of Prisons* (1895, Appendix 23, 51), in relation to Liverpool Prison: 'the secular instruction of prisoners has been duly carried on'; and at Leeds: 'the [separate] stage system and educational system continue to give satisfactory results.'

9 See also Gatrell (1994) on the way in which the bureaucratization and 'civilizing' of public executions is likely to have increased the suffering of the condemned.

10 The rate of imprisonment in Georgia in 1970 was 258 per 100,000 of population (the rate for the USA as a whole was then 110).

11 For example, the rate of imprisonment in Norway in 1970 was 37 per 100,000 of population.

12 Durkheim (1893) as well seemed to associate homogenous societies with higher levels of repression and greater penal severity.

13 See Zimring (1996) in relation to California; Pratt and Clark (2005) in relation to New Zealand.

14 Lynch provides the following description of a supermax prison: 'inmates are generally subjected to solitary lockdown for approximately 23 hours per day in windowless cells that allow for very little visual stimuli, where possessions are restricted and activities nearly completely eliminated, and where, by design, contact with other human beings is almost non-existent' (2005: 68). In these respects supermax provides an important illustration of what the running together of civilizing and decivilizing processes can lead to. For example, it reflects the civilizing process in that it replaces direct confrontation between prison officers and recalcitrant inmates by providing a technological interface between them. In contrast, it also leads to both the mental and physical deterioration of inmates.

15 In some jurisdictions, such as the UK, the police may inform teachers and other child welfare professionals. In the USA, under the provisions of Megan's Law, these capabilities tend to be much wider. Individual states decide what information will be made available and how it should be disseminated. Commonly included information includes the offender's name, picture, address, incarceration date, and nature of crime. The information is often displayed on free public websites, but can be published in newspapers, distributed in pamphlets, or through various other means.

16 'Sensible Sentencing Rally for Safe NZ', www.nzcpr.com/forum/viewtopic.php?f=3&t=562&st=0&sk=t&sd=a).

17 On the decline of the Finnish prison population, see Lappi-Seppälä (2001).

18 Immigration has been at such a level that one in ten Swedes have now been born outside Sweden.

19 In contrast, Fleisher wrote that in Sweden, 'the appreciation of restraint, a certain aloofness, and the disapproval of displays of emotion play a vital part in forming the general outlook toward violence' (1967: 170).

REFERENCES

Balfour, J. (1901) *My Prison Life.* London: Chapman and Hall.

Beck, U. (1992) *Risk Society.* London: Sage.

Braithwaite, J. (1989) *Crime, Shame and Reintegration.* Cambridge: Cambridge University Press.

Braithwaite, J. (1993) 'Shame and modernity', *The British Journal of Criminology*, 33 (1): 1–18.

Brodie, A., Croom, J. and Davies, J. (2002) *English Prisons: An Architectural History.* Swindon: English Heritage.

Chambers Dictionary (2002) Edinburgh: Chambers.

Christie, N. (2000) *Crime Control as Industry.* London: Routledge.

Cyclopedia Company Limited (1897) *The Cyclopedia of New Zealand: Wellington Provisional District.* Wellington, NZ: The Cyclopedia Company Limited.

Deveraux, S. (1996) 'Transportation, penal practices and the English state', in C. Strange (ed.), *Qualities of Mercy*. Vancouver: UBC Press. pp. 53–76.

Dickens, C. (1846) 'Letter', *The Daily News*, 23 February: 6.

Dixon, W. H. (1850) *The London Prisons*. London: Jackson & Walford.

Domanick, J. (2004) *Cruel Justice: Three Strikes and the Politics of Crime in America's Golden State*. Berkeley, CA: University of California Press.

Doob, A. and Webster, C. (2007) 'Punitive trends and stable imprisonment rates in Canada', *Crime and Justice: An Annual Review of Research*, 36: 143–195.

Du Cane, E. F. (1875) 'Address on the repression of crime', in C. Wager Ryalls (ed.), *Transactions of the National Association for the Promotion of Social Science*. London: Longmans, Green and Co. pp. 271–308.

Durkheim, E. (1893[1964]) *De la Division du Travail Social*, trans. G. Simpson *The Division of Labor in Society*. New York: Free Press.

Eighteenth Report of the Commissioners of Prisons (1895) Cmnd 7880. London: HMSO.

Elias, N. (1939 [1969]) *The Civilizing Process: Vol. I. The History of Manners*. London: Blackwells.

Elias, N. (1982) *The Civilizing Process: Vol. II. State Formation and Civilization*. London: Blackwells.

Elias, N. (1994) 'Notes on a Lifetime', in N. Elias, *Reflections on a Life*, Cambridge: Polity Press.

Elias, N. (1996) *The Germans*. Cambridge: Polity Press.

Elias, N. and Scotson, J. (1965) *The Established and the Outsiders*. London: SAGE Publications.

Evans, R. (1982) *The Fabrication of Virtue: English Prison Architecture, 1750–1840*. Cambridge: Cambridge University Press.

Fleisher, F. (1967) *The New Sweden*. New York: David McKay Company Inc.

Fletcher, J. (1997) *Violence and Civilization: An Introduction to the work of Norbert Elias*. Cambridge: Polity Press.

Foucault, M. (1991) 'Governmentality', in G. Burchell, C. Gordon and P. Miller (eds), *The Foucault Effect*. Chicago: Chicago University Press. pp. 87–104.

Fox, L. (1952) *The English Prison and Borstal Systems: An Account of the English Prison and Borstal Systems After the Criminal Justice Act 1948, with a Historical Introduction and an Examination of the Principles of Imprisonments as a Legal Punishment*. London: Routledge and Kegan Paul.

Franke, H. (1995) *The Emancipation of Prisoners*. Edinburgh: Edinburgh University Press.

Fukuyama, F. (1995) *Trust: The Social Virtues and the Creation of Prosperity*. New York: Free Press.

Garland, D. (1990) *Punishment and Modern Society: A Study in Social Theory*. Oxford: Oxford University Press.

Garside, R. (2006) *Right for the Wrong Reasons: Making Sense of Criminal Justice Failure*. London: Crime and Society Foundation.

Gatrell, V. (1994) *The Hanging Tree: Execution and the English People, 1770–1868*. Oxford: Oxford University Press.

Girling, E., Loader, I. and Sparks, R. (1998) 'A telling tale: a case of vigilantism and its aftermath in an English town', *British Journal of Sociology*, 49 (3): 474–490.

Glover, E. (1956) *Probation and Re-education*. London: Routledge & Paul.

Griffiths, A. (1875) *Memorials of Millbank, and Chapters in Prison History*, London: Chapman and Hall.

Guardian, 27 September 2006, Tough on Crime.

Hagelund, A. (2003) 'A matter of decency? The Progress Party in Norwegian immigration politics', *Journal of Ethnic and Migration Studies*, 29 (1): 47–65.

Hansard (New Zealand) (1900, vol. 113), Wellington: Government Printer.

Hansard (UK) (1910, vol. 16), London: HMSO.

Hansard (UK) (1958, vol. 59), London: HMSO.

Hansen, H. M. (1900) *Norway: Official Publication of the Paris Exhibition 1900*. Kristiania: Aktie-bogtrykkeriet.

Home Office (1959) *Penal Practice in a Changing Society. Aspects of Future Development*. Cmnd 645. London: HMSO.

Home Office (2002) *Justice for All*. London: HMSO. CM. 5563.

Hough, M. (1996) 'People talking about punishment', *Howard Journal of Criminal Justice*, 35: 191–214.

Ignatieff, M. (1978) *Just a Measure of Pain: The Penitentiary in the Industrial Revolution*. London: Macmillan.

Johnston, L. (1996) 'What is vigilantism?', *British Journal of Criminology*, 36: 220–36.

Kekkonen, J. (1999) 'Judicial Repression after the civil wars in Finland (1918) and Spain (1936–1939)', in M. Lappalainen and P. Hirvonen (eds), *Crime and Control in Europe from the past to the present*. Helsinki: Academy of Finland. pp. 35–48.

Lappi-Seppälä, T. (2001) 'The decline of the Finnish prison population', *Scandinavian Journal of Criminology and Crime Prevention*, 1: 27–40.

Loader, I. (2006) 'Fall of the 'platonic guardians': liberalism, criminology and political responses to crime in England and Wales', *British Journal of Criminology*, 46: 561–86.

Lynch, M. (2005) 'Supermax meets death row: legal struggles around the new punitiveness in the US', in J. Pratt, D., Brown, M. Brown, S., et al. (eds), *The New Punitiveness: Trends, Theories, Perspectives*. Devon: Willan Publishing. pp. 66–84.

Masur, L. (1989) *Rites of Execution*. New York: Oxford University Press.

McGowan, R. (1983) 'The image of justice and reform of the criminal law in early 19th century England', *Buffalo Law Review*, 32: 89–125.

McGuire, J. (1998) 'Judicial violence and the civilizing process', *Australian Historical Studies*, 111: 187–209.

Mennell, S. (1990) 'Decivilizing processes: theoretical significance and some lines of research', *International Sociology*, 5: 205–13.

Mennell, S. (1992) *Norbert Elias: An Introduction*. Oxford: Blackwells.

Mennell, S. (2007) *The American Civilizing Process*. Cambridge: Polity.

Norwegian Labour Party (2006) *Crime Policy*. Oslo: Norwegian Labour Party.

Observer, 13 August 2000, Vigilantes Attack Paedophiles.

Pratt, J. (1991) 'Punishment, History and Empire', *Australia and New Zealand Journal of Criminology*, 24: 118–138.

Pratt, J. (1992) 'Punishment and the lessons from history', *Australian and New Zealand Journal of Criminology*, 25: 97–114.

Pratt, J. (2002) *Punishment and Civilization: Penal Tolerance and Intolerance in Modern Society*. London: SAGE Publications.

Pratt, J. (2007) *Penal Populism*. London: Routledge.

Pratt, J. (2008) 'Scandinavian exceptionalism in an era of penal excess, part I: The nature and roots of Scandinavian exceptionalism', *British Journal of Criminology*, 48: 119–37.

Pratt, J. and Clark, M. (2005) 'Penal populism in New Zealand', *Punishment & Society*, 7: 303–22.

Pratt, J. and Eriksson, A. (2011) 'Mr Larsson is walking out again. The origins and development of Scandinavian prison systems', *Australian and New Zealand Society of Criminology*, 44: 7–23.

Putnam, R. (2000) *Bowling Alone: The Collapse and Revival of American Community*. New York: Simon and Schuster.

Report of the Commissioners of Prisons for the Year 1951 (1952) Cmnd 8692. London: HMSO.

Report of the Director of Penal Services (1957) (1958–9) Melbourne: Victoria Penal Department.

Report of the Director of Penal Services (1961) (1963–4) Melbourne: Victoria Penal Department.

Rothstein, B. and Uslander, J. (2005) 'All for all. Equality, corruption and social trust', *World Politics*, 58: 41–72.

Ruck, S. (ed.) (1951) *Paterson on Prisons*. London: F. Muller.

Ruggles-Brise, E. (1921 [1985]) *The English Prison System*. New York: Garland.

Smith, G. (1996) 'Civilized people don't want to see that kind of thing: the decline of physical punishment in England 1760–1820', in C. Strange (ed.), *Qualities of Mercy*. Vancouver: UBC Press. pp. 21–51.

Spierenburg, P. (1984) *The Spectacle of Suffering*. Cambridge: Cambridge University Press.

Spierenburg, P. (1991) *The Prison Experience: Disciplinary Institutions and their Inmates in Early Modern Europe*. New Brunswick, NJ: Rutgers University Press.

Taylor, R. S. (1960) 'The Habitual Criminal', *British Journal of Criminology*, 1: 21–36.

Thackeray, W. (1840) 'Going to see a man hanged', *Fraser's Magazine for Town and Country*, 22(128): 150–8.

Tham, H. (2001) 'Law and order as a leftist project? The case of Sweden', *Punishment and Society*, 3: 409–26.

Times (1998), Anti-Social Behaviour Orders, 8 April.

Van Krieken, R. (1999) 'The barbarism of civilization', *British Journal of Sociology*, 50(2): 297–316.

Vaughan, B. (2000) 'The civilizing process and the janus-face of modern punishment', *Theoretical Criminology*, 4 (1): 71–91.

Whitman, J. (2003) *Harsh Justice: Criminal Punishment and the Widening Divide between America and Europe*. New York: Oxford University Press.

Wicker, T. (1975) 'Sweden: Almost the best of everything', *New York Times*, 28 September: 10.

Zimring, F. (1996) 'Populism, democratic government, and the decline of expert authority', *Pacific Law Journal*, 28: 243–56.

5

Punishment and Meaning: The Cultural Sociological Approach

Philip Smith

The purpose of a collection on 'punishment and society' is to suggest that the connections between these two nouns are more complex, multifarious and problematic than we might otherwise suppose. Put another way the ambition is to show that there is more going on than can be captured by a jurisprudential eye on the law and its violation. In pursuit of this end most explorations by social scientists focus on what we might think of as the 'hard' connections of the social system. These are institutional and organizational environments and objective patterns of inequality. Generally speaking punishment is said to reflect the social structures into which it is embedded and to reproduce these in turn. The coinage of such analyses are power, resources and interests – or in less radical accounts the mildly compromised quest for rationality and efficiency. These approaches rarely take meaning to be central to the task of explanation. When it appears it is often understood as an ideology to be exposed and debunked. Sometimes it shows up as the situated folk traditions, stereotypes and pragmatic know-how of agents in workplaces. Almost invariably these ideologies and know-hows work to reproduce those 'hard' connections of the social system.

Like a growing body of scholarship (Lynch, 2004; Garland, 2006; Smith, 2008; Brown, 2009) this chapter starts from a different perspective. Motivated by cultural sociology rather than a sociology of culture (and more particularly by the Yale Strong Program, see Alexander and Smith, 2001, 2010) it suggests that we should pay more attention to the invisible 'soft' connections at work in social life. Every institution and procedure, no matter how pragmatic, sensible or instrumental it might at first appear to be, is also the carrier of meaning. Hence the world of punishment is bound to the social through culture as well as more material channels. Technologies, procedures, policies and initiatives all reflect and reproduce collective codes, narratives and symbolic processes. They are thought of as sacred and profane, as legitimate or disturbing, as progressive or atavistic (Smith, 2008). Through opinion formation, public sphere deliberation and sometimes scandal these wider non-technical understandings come to exert pressures on the narrow business of the punishment sphere. They can also inspire thinking within that realm – as we often find when innovations emerge. Of course power, interests, legal and administrative concerns still play a role. Yet a truly comprehensive analysis of 'punishment and society' must come to terms with the need to interpret formal social control as a realm of meaningful human activity.

THE CASE FOR CULTURAL SOCIOLOGY

Just how to meet this challenge remains to be decided. When it comes to successfully connecting culture with punishment a familiar strategy has been to invoke contending but intellectually brilliant accounts of long-term penal evolution (Garland, 1991). More specifically the task has been to look at explanations of the end of public displays and the emergence of confinement in modernity. The Foucauldian narrative of penal change is perhaps the best known of these. In the Early Modern period, Michel Foucault (1975) says, there were cruel punishments directed at the body. These were often allegorical or didactic. They symbolized or dramatized the power of the sovereign to an on-looking public. One might think here of the public execution, the pillory or a flogging. Such interventions came to be replaced by what he terms 'disciplinary power'. Driven by the quest for efficiency this sought to retrain the body of the criminal in microscopic detail, converting the deviant it into a pliant source of productive labor. Through drill, the scientific use of space, and uncompromising observation, new techniques propagated by experts in enclosed institutions extended the reach and intensity of power, although now without any clear communicative intent. The image that comes to mind here is of the Victorian model prison with its solitary confinement and 'pointless' but arduous work tasks. In the language of jurisprudence the logic was of reform and rehabilitation rather than general deterrence. Foucault's account is generally seen as the analysis of new blueprints of power. That is to say it maps out patterns of understanding that are somewhat dry and cognitive even if arbitrary when viewed with the ironic gaze of hindsight. They are 'cultural' in the sense that they involve meanings, but only those related to beliefs and theories about efficient control held by educated experts. They are also 'cultural' in that the prison and its associated techniques of have to 'fit' with diffuse expectations about the institutional appearance and activity in an age of dispersed disciplinary thinking. Still Foucault never fully explores the role of emotion, passions or public debate in his account of penal modernity. We have inherited, he suggests, a cold, grim, technocratically driven world.

To date the most significant and lively challenge to this claustrophobic Foucauldian narrative, at least when it comes to empirical research, has been from advocates of a 'civilizing process' thesis. Drawing on the work of Norbert Elias this points for the most part to changes in sensibility that have taken place within the wider population over the centuries. In the transition from a medieval society organized around spontaneous violence to a court society and next to a bourgeois one where relationships were altogether more subtle, people became increasingly discomforted by reminders of the more primal dimensions of human existence. Death, sex and sleep came to be hidden. Likewise rotting bodies, dismembered corpses or even laboring chain gangs generated sentiments of unease and disgust (Spierenburg, 1984). Aversive behaviors and more 'clinical' procedures resulted. Punishment came to leave bodies intact, but as it generated feelings of public discomfort it was nevertheless increasingly sequestered. Nobody wanted to see what was really going on (Pratt, 2002).

The conventional Durkheimian vision of penal evolution offers a third major alternative. For Emile Durkheim (1984) in

The Division of Labor in Society increasing cultural complexity arising from evolution and differentiation functionally requires and generates a particular value pattern: tolerance for difference. New forms of inclusive and flexible social solidarity arise. These are refracted into the world of punishment, where the urge for retribution is replaced with more restitutive sanctions. A recent variant of this thesis points more vigorously to the parallel emergence of what Durkheim called the 'cult of the individual' in the transition to modernity. This involves the sacralization of the person with the concomitant emergence of concepts of human dignity and rights (Joas, 2008). A softening of punishment reflects the growing power of the understanding that each individual, no matter how evil, is entitled to elemental respect.

These three canonical traditions, the Foucauldian, Eliasian and Durkheimian, vary radically in their theoretical logics, their causal attributions, and their normative commitments. Yet they share a common flaw. Each is painted with too broad a brush. Precisely because they identify and capture epochal shifts in striking and elegant ways they are of less use than we might suppose for explaining local and contingent outcomes. Yet specific policies, innovations, crusades, crack downs, fads and agendas are the stuff of routine social science of the middle range. We want to explain the 'war on drugs', 'zero tolerance', 'three strikes', 'the electric chair', 'electronic monitoring' and 'boot camps'. Just how well we can explain the specifics of each of these with flexible and polyvalent abstractions like 'disciplinary society' or 'the sacred self' is open to question.

The theories that have dominated the study of punishment and culture struggle especially when it comes to dealing with those points of detail that look to be reversals to the long-term historical trends they identify. Grand social theory on penal evolution treads on a thumb-tack when it encounters periodic and surprisingly common efforts to revive those harsh, public and communicative punishments that are supposed to have fallen by the wayside of history. Much hopping about results by way of explanation. Anachronisms must be dismissed as relics or survivals or as atavistic and accidental returns to pre-modern cultural patterns. We often find that residual categories and ad hoc out-of-paradigm theory (for example ideas of 'penal nostalgia') come to the rescue. The imprecise and variously understood Eliasian concept of the 'decivilizing process' is a noted rabbit from the hat here. Work admits that that the rolling back of civilizing norms is found during contingencies such as war, disaster and civil disorder (Pratt, 2000: 422). Yet it is unclear if the 'decivilizing process' at play is a causal origin of, a dependent output from, or simply a shorthand descriptor for brutality and human rights abuses. Further this focus on disordered Hobbesian scenarios leaves the model unable to explain the emergence of what John Pratt (2000: 417) calls 'emotive and ostentations punishment' in stable and strong state situations such as Nazi Germany or the Jim Crow Deep South. Those attempting to use Elias's model inevitably have to bring in other variables to do the explanatory heavy lifting, such as the need or desire to dramatize power. With social life as messy and unpredictable as this, perhaps a more flexible, meaning centered mode of cultural sociological analysis will be more useful to us than grand theories of historical and cultural change.

We can of course understand the history of the social sciences as one that enacts a tension between lumping and splitting. Lumping has its place. It creates major paradigms and enables thought to transcend the tyranny of detail. Yet the fact remains that most scholarship in the routine social science mode that we find in journals is caught up in explaining particularities in outcomes in defined cases rather than broad similarities of taxonomy. We might very well be living in an era where the forces of 'neoliberalism' or 'postmodernity' or 'surveillance society' are at work in shaping penal activity. Indeed we see signs of these all around. Yet each trend plays out in a different way in a different context. There might be leads and lags, the incomplete or hybrid import of ideas, variations in intensity and duration, controversy or consensus. When it comes to explaining such particularities our big concepts look increasingly like blanket generalities. They capture something of what is going on, but an adequate 'causal' account requires attention to institutional, legal and historical contexts using the comparative method in a more Weberian way to leverage analytical claims. It also necessitates a turn to culture and an understanding of how meanings play out in particular settings. Cultural sociology provides the vocabulary and tool kit for this activity.

An embrace of the cultural sociology approach might also allow penal theory to take properly on board the neglected lessons of the cultural turn that has shaken the social sciences and humanities to the core since the 1960s. This last point needs explanation: Are not Foucault, Durkheim and Elias cultural theorists par excellence? Appearances to the contrary our three major traditions have never quite come to terms with the revolutionary idea that social life is linguistically, symbolically and communicatively mediated and patterned, preferring to point to power, emotion or social structure as the drivers of human organization. Commonly invoked as explorations of 'culture and punishment' none is really, I believe, cultural enough. Foucault's *Discipline and Punish* has done more than any other book to institutionalize the approach of discourse analysis. Yet it was an attempt to roll back the theoretical advances of his own earlier texts – advances that ironically enough had contributed in significant ways to the cultural turn itself. Influenced by phenomenology, hermeneutics and structuralism the early and middle-period Foucault had indicated that arbitrary meanings shaped expert practices in spheres like health and psychiatry. Like Lévi-Strauss before him Foucault also pointed to the radical contingency of classification systems, their freedom from empirical or pragmatic determination. With the later 'genealogical project' that drove his work on punishment, however, Foucault tried to sidestep a serious consideration of meaning and symbol by looking instead to the visible process and material effects engendered by discourses. Punishment could be explored for how it worked (or was intended to work) rather than subjected to hermeneutical reconstruction. This effort to move beyond hermeneutics was compounded and confused by Foucault's Weber-like vision of history. This was one in which spectacle and charismatic authority are replaced by routine and bureaucracy. The corollary: If meaning might be an explicans in historical inquiry, it has no place in the explanation of the present. Foucault in effect takes a bet each way, trying to sideline deep meanings empirically and epistemologically, and replacing them with a 'shallow meaning' of instrumental know-how and expert common sense.

Elias's (1978) project looks more promising, yet it understands meaning largely in terms of psychological process and affect. Emerging in the 1930s and strongly influenced by Freud and early Frankfurt School psychology it weights the personal and immediate interpretation of experience over the linguistic mediation at a distance of social life. We might argue against Elias that the interpretation of events depends not only on sense-datum or sensibility, but also on the coding of that which is witnessed against a circulating symbolic repertoire. Books on etiquette, for example, are rather brilliantly taken by Elias as indicators of shifting norms on interpersonal behavior. Yet we might also understand them in a more obvious way – as the ossification of a cultural system. They were a tool through which the concrete behaviors of actors at the time could be judged, or with which individuals could engage in the reflexive construction of the self with reference to arbitrary codes of civility and profanity. This, after all, is why they were written. We might also object that Elias understands civility as a realm of face-to-face interaction, but does not seem to have an understanding of a civil sphere. That is to say of a mediated and understood as abstract space for a more discursive or communicative, text-like contestation or deliberation on experience itself. These flaws, of course, reflect the more general limitations of interactionist social theory, which privileges ontology over epistemology, the body over code.

Emile Durkheim's major contributions to the sociology of punishment come from before his own cultural turn, an event that culminated in his late masterwork *The Elementary Forms of Religious Life*. In that book Durkheim (1968) talks about symbolic and ritual process in detail. In his earlier writing on punishment such themes exist but their ubiquity as a limited pool of sound bite quotations in the punishment literature says more about contemporary concerns than Durkheim's own. Close attention to his texts shows a far greater emphasis given to structural functionalism with its focus on the mirroring of culture and social structure. Culture responds to social needs, but is not set free to more actively shape social life. As Geertz (1973) put it, this is a 'strain theory' of culture, in which meaning does the job of holding society together in the face of threats to stability and order. It does not really drive social life forward. Durkheim's legacy is further muddled by a psychologistic understanding of shared meanings. These are derived from *fin de siècle* crowd psychology. There are elaborate but overly abstract metaphorical references to the workings of the supra-individual collective conscience, to electrical currents, vibrations and sympathetic resonances in the nervous system of shared morality. A somewhat contrived labor of theoretical reconstruction is required in order to bring the later and more cultural Durkheim of *The Elementary Forms* to bear on his earlier, functionalist writings on punishment (for an attempt at this see Joas [2008]; or my own more extended effort Smith [2008]).

In developing and illustrating a flexible, cultural-turn inspired alternative to these grand traditions we might do well to look to the methodological tool-kit developed by the Yale Strong Program in Cultural Sociology (for an overview see Alexander and Smith [2001, 2010]). Briefly: Drawing on a diverse range of theoretical resources this intellectual movement has tried to bring the cultural turn into the social sciences, but without the baggage of critical theory that insists that meanings are largely shaped by power. The argument is a radical one for the autonomy of culture from power, but not a relativistic one that gives up on the effort to produce generalizable knowledge or to explain real world outcomes. Strong Program approaches point to binary oppositions, narratives and iconic representations as core components of culture-structures. The meanings these carry are not merely administrative or cognitive but rather have something of the sacred and profane about them. Meanings drive activity because people care. A model of cultural pragmatics developed by the Strong Program points to the significance of performance and public sphere debate. No matter how powerful the agency or how routinized the implementation of policy, a shift in meaning or performative failure can bring doubt and the call for reform.

Such challenges driven by culture are common, perhaps inevitable, in civil discourse about criminal justice. Although we (and especially critical theory) tend to think of the punishment nexus as a robust and powerful set of dominant institutions and taken-for-granted meanings it also appears curiously vulnerable to scandal, to readings that run 'against the grain' and to narrative inflation that converts the banal into the abominable. In part this is due to a broad semiotic web of background referents that key into the signs of the body, to pain, to suffering and to death and connect them to the sacred (Smith, 2008). There are especially strong attractors here for artistic and religious commentary. Think for example of the crucifixion of Jesus and its various impacts. A second vulnerability is, as Jonathan Simon notes at the end of Chapter 3 in this book, public expectations for penal efficacy – whether as inmate reform or risk mitigation – are unrealistically high.

Because outcomes invariably fall short there is an open invitation for accounting activity diagnosing failure. Third, as Durkheim explains punishment is a moral issue that generates a huge emotional charge. The ever-present storms over generic societal morality (e.g. 'culture wars') find a ready lightening rod in struggles over appropriate and illegitimate penal activity, just as they do in one or two other fields such as sexuality and drugs.

HARSH AND HUMILIATING PUNISHMENT

Climate is what you expect, weather is what you get. Grand theories of culture and punishment do a great job of explaining the long-term penal climate. I have suggested already that they stumble in confronting local and short-term variation. We might illustrate this theme with reference to the problem of harsh and humiliating punishments. Looking to the history of the past one hundred years it is surprising how easy it is to detect reversals and exceptions to the trend towards reduced physical suffering and increased privacy and dignity in confinement. Calls for and experiments with boot camps, for chain gangs and public shaming emerge with regularity. For example, in the USA in recent years we have seen judges handing out sentences whose logic mimics that of Hawthorne's Scarlet Letter. In 2009, two adult Pennsylvania offenders were ordered to stand outside the courthouse holding a sign saying 'I stole from a 9-year old on her birthday! Don't steal or this could happen to you.' In 2002, teens that broke into a church were sentenced by Judge Michael Cicconetti to lead a donkey through town with a sign: 'Sorry for the Jackass Offense.' A Texas judge had another convicted felon sleep in a doghouse for 30 days, the alternative to this coupling of physical discomfort and humiliation by metaphor being 30 days in jail (Turley, 2009).

These are scattered and inconsistent if troubling events. At the more extreme end of the scale the Holocaust suggests that some familiar thematic alignments need to be closely reconsidered. This act of genocide was organizationally as 'modern' as Adolf Eichmann's railway timetables. Yet it came without any Durkheimian 'sacralization of the individual' or Foucauldian efforts at the disciplined rebuilding of the self. In concentration camps the SS guards engaged in elaborate rituals of Prussian military etiquette with each other. They famously enjoyed in cultured artistic pursuits such as chamber music concerts even as they systematically humiliated, tortured and denied human status to inmates. The Eliasian 'civilizing process' seems to have existed only in a restricted socio-spatial domain. The Holocaust is especially instructive as it suggests that generalities about cultural change do less explanatory work than we would wish. The 'sacralization of the individual', the 'civilizing process' and the 'disciplinary imperative' are fragile in their application and seem contingent in their alignment. In the case of the Holocaust these depend upon the boundaries that were established between insiders and outsiders, and beyond these upon embedded narratives of *Volk* and nation. Cultural theory, I think, can help us explain the local and embedded process through which such local meanings (weather) can intersect with more general templates (climate) and often produce unexpected results.

Sociology often does well to look to extreme cases where trends and patterns are displayed in a form of heightened reality. The Holocaust, however, is a methodologically risky singularity with no relationship to judicial punishment. Indeed to make this claim would be insulting. Scattered instances of caprice such as we have also noted, conversely, might be plausibly interpreted as Weber's kadi justice. What is needed is a modern location where the march of history appears to have been reversed in an ongoing or institutionalized form. So we turn to Maricopa County, Arizona, USA. This offers an especially perspicuous location for our inquiries. Here we see an elaborate and coordinated array of seemingly retrograde penal strategies. These cause suffering, humiliate and communicate.

With a population of four million including Phoenix, Maricopa County, Arizona, is sprawling, hot, fast growing and suburban. It is also the unlikely site of penal innovation. A search of any media database will reveal worldwide interest in these reforms. Yet the volume of public concern has not been reflected in academic research (for an excellent exception see Lynch [2004]). This neglect is all the more disappointing given that Maricopa County's strategies and choices are hugely anomalous when set against the standard picture of penal modernity. The changes have been spearheaded by the attention seeking Sheriff Joe Arpaio. Elected to his job in 1992 and holding onto it ever since, he is a now elderly man who likes to style himself 'the toughest sheriff in America'. Notable features of his longstanding initiatives include deliberate efforts at making punishment visible, placing offenders in the public eye, and making jail less comfortable. Critics also complain that there is intent to make the experience more humiliating. Each dimension flies in the face of history.

Let us make this concrete. Arpaio introduced a live jail cam that was accessible from the Internet. Inmates were given pink underwear. Un-macho pink handcuffs and flip-flops are also used. Retro-style striped prison uniforms were reintroduced. Food was priced down to a minimum of 15 cents per meal and included a green bologna. Arpaio boasted that the dogs guarding his jails cost more to feed than the inmates. Salt, pepper, tea, coffee and hot lunches went. To avoid either raising taxes or releasing inmates Arpaio built a Tent City Jail under the Arizona sun using army surplus tents. It is situated between a waste treatment plant, a dog pound and a rubbish dump. Fitted out with mobile latrines the smell in the camp can be appalling. Dust is everywhere and temperatures routinely rise above 100°F during summer, dropping below freezing at night in winter. Above the camp a neon sign proclaims 'Vacancy'. Arpaio introduced chain gangs for men and women and had them dig graves to bury the city's indigent. Chain gangs of juveniles had to pick up trash. Various 'luxuries' were denied to inmates, such as pornographic magazines, tobacco, movies and television other than The Weather Channel, C-SPAN and Newt Gingrich's conservative talk show. Abuse seems to be rife even if it is not officially condoned. Thousands of lawsuits have exposed a shadow regime of beatings and mistreatment, many of these involving a notorious 'restraint chair' where one inmate choked (or was choked) to death (Schwartz, 1998). Health accreditation has been withdrawn. A judge has ruled that conditions are unconstitutional (Finnegan, 2009). Yet for all this unpleasantness, Arpaio welcomes the publicity. In an age where punishment has been hidden and where elaborate permissions are required to visit or film, journalists have found it easy to tour Tent City Jail, to interview inmates and to report on what they see.

In attempting to explain Arpaio's initiatives and similar ones elsewhere, commentators such as Simon, O'Malley and Garland often refer to the psychological variable 'nostalgia' and make use of various articulations of the concepts 'modernity', 'late-modernity' 'postmodernity' and 'postmodern' (Lynch, 2004: 258–9). The material is used to engage in broader theoretical disputes aimed at labeling and diagnosing our current stage in penal evolution and predicting its future direction. An alternative approach is to step aside from upward translations into abstract theory and instead to account for policy in a more immanent way. For cultural sociology this means that we have first to reconstruct the local worldview that underpins Arpaio's reasoning. Far from being a crazed egomaniac, the sheriff can be understood as articulating and acting out a system of beliefs that is shared by many of his fellow Arizonans. This is why he is continually re-elected to his job with a strong majority and indeed is arguably the most popular politician in his state with approval ratings of around 80 percent. It has been said that Arpaio could walk into the State governor's job. Certainly 'he has paid almost no political price' for any of the controversy surrounding his jails (Finnegan, 2009). His innovations must be understood as meaningful penal strategies formed within a wider cultural system. They are intended to deal with crime, yes, but they also express shared beliefs within a community about the limits of appropriate punishment and about the nature of criminals. Further, Arpaio's system makes use of meaning as a way of punishing and preventing – meaning is not surplus to the real business of crime control but rather is implicated in the very core of it. Using the resources of cultural sociology and cultural theory we can start to interpret what is going on here.

One of the most fundamental structures in any cultural system is the binary opposition. Theorists from Durkheim to Lévi-Strauss and Roland Barthes have argued that binaries are the raw material from which societies build more complex and subtle myths and narratives. More recently sociological research from Michele Lamont (2000) and others has highlighted the role of moral boundaries. Working in a binary way these separate out the deserving from the undeserving, the right thinking from the problematic. Such moral binaries provide the basis for classification and with this hierarchies of inclusion and exclusion often emerge.

Criminological research generally points to a substantial grey area between the law abiding and the criminal. Most people break the law at some point in their lives, but not all deviance is detected and only a few of the guilty are labeled criminal. Fewer still go to jail. Most cultural and organizational systems work by recognizing in one way or another the inadequacy of the legal/illegal binary. That is why there is discretion in sentencing – a process that can take into account wider contexts and levels of blameworthiness (Wheeler et al., 1992). In the Arpaio universe we find a much firmer line separating the law-abiding from the law-breaking, the binary feeding into a narrative suggesting that the latter are taking over and that a golden age of safety and family life has gone. As Arpaio puts it:

> We've got to get back to how we were ... before drugs and gangs and decent law-abiding citizens locked up inside their own homes while the criminals roam the streets. It should be the other way around. Lock up all the bad guys, punish them severely, and let decent people walk the streets in peace. (Quoted in Grant, 1995: 8).

Arpaio's jails contain a diverse set of petty offenders. Many are imprisoned on minor misdemeanors, such as the non-payment of fines. Yet it is the image of the predatory drug dealer he invokes. This amplification of deviance through the generalization of a worst-case scenario category allows for a weaker application of norms about the sacred self. The law breaking have terrorized the law abiding. They are to be accorded only minimal rights. So we find little attention given to the reality that those in jail are formally in a kind of legal limbo. They have been arrested and retained, but they have not yet been found guilty by a court of law. The narrative of righteous society under siege also has a race dimension. Having snuck across the desert, illegal Hispanic migrants are said to have imported crime and disease and to be responsible for tax hikes by placing a burden on public services. The regime of harsh imprisonment is rolled up with the support of a white majority for a range of anti-immigration strategies, most notably campaign of heavy-handed raids on Latino neighborhoods. These have led to a small number of arrests, but more importantly work as another visible signal that something is 'being done' to turn back the tide.

The radical distinction of the law abiding and the criminal, the citizen and the 'illegal,' feeds through into a complex moral accounting that sustains tough prison conditions. Historians of punishment have noted that in Victorian times institutions of confinement were often subject to critique. The argument was that they were too luxurious, not too harsh. So called 'palace prisons' with modern plumbing, running water, mattresses and leak-free roofs could be easily contrasted with the conditions of the laboring poor (Pratt, 2002; Smith, 2008). Such institutions, it was held, would not effectively deter crime. More importantly they were viewed as an insult to the honest, industrious but poorly remunerated worker. The so-called 'less eligibility principle' needed to be applied to redress this injustice. Under this rubric prison conditions should always be less attractive than those on the outside. For Arpaio and his supporters this stands as an axiomatic trope with which to justify harsh conditions. Only here there is a twist. As Arpaio put it: 'If tents were good enough for our boys during Desert Storm, then why isn't it good enough for criminals?' (quoted in Freedland, 1995: 3). Or 'Why should some murdering, drug-dealing criminal get special treatment over a patriotic American soldier? You tell me' (quoted in Grant, 1995: 8). By drawing on the image of the soldier rather than the working poor, and the drug dealer over the routine tax evader, Arpaio aligns his policy with a sacred symbol. Although wars and militarism are controversial in America, the soldier is sacrosanct. These are the people prepared to die to protect the freedom of others. It will not stand for criminals to profane this noble identity by having better living conditions than heroes.

A further element of this cultural cocktail is a dream of civic empowerment. Arpaio's rhetoric taps into popular myths of frontier justice and harkens back to an era when the administration of criminal justice was swift, uncomplicated and involved community participation. In this vision the complex bureaucracies and laws thrown up by modernity have served to protect rather than hunt down the criminal. Bringing the community back in is a way to mobilize the latent crime fighting energy of citizens. Pivotal to this strategy are a 'posse volunteer corps', this consisting mostly of middle-aged men with gun collections. With around 3000 members by 1995 who were prepared to patrol streets all night this might be described as a successful social movement. As Arpaio puts it 'they're the kind of people that built this nation' (in Grant, 1995: 8). Engaged in activities such as monitoring prostitution hot spots, arresting graffiti artists and so forth, this group enacts a long-gone past in which direct and forceful actions could reduce crime.

Arpaio's world, then, is one that is as meaningful as the Balinese cockfight so famously interpreted by Clifford Geertz (1973). The seemingly bizarre or whimsical makes sense once it is seen as the expression not of the mental life of the subject but rather of an underlying and visible, shared cultural pattern. This can be decoded using the cultural sociological toolkit whose components include words like binary opposition, narrative, discourse, symbol, the sacred and profane.

Of course there is more to the story than just culture. Demographics play a role too. High levels of illegal immigration, a substantial Latino community, and a large number of conservative white retirees from snow belt states make Maricopa County a more propitious spot for penal revanchism than most other places in North America. Even so demography does not explain everything. There are other places in America that have similar demographics but more orthodox penal regimes or higher levels of tolerance. We must instead think of the 'demographic' as the carrier of a cultural pattern, this being concentrated by processes such as selective migration. The snow belt retirees of San Francisco are probably a different bunch. Attention must also be given to America's decentralized justice system and the possibility for the direct election of criminal justice officials such as Sheriff Arpaio. Local politics allows what would be a minority view in most places to become dominant. Durkheim (1984) wrote in *The Division of Labor* of the buffering role of the state. It stands between the sentiments of the community and the body of the criminal. In most nations highly educated administrators and professionals enact laws and run criminal justice systems. Educated in metropolitan centers and trained to be dispassionate, they operate with a bureaucratic mentality. Yet in a context of decentralized justice with elected officials this constituency often lacks the legal-rational authority required to oppose populist agendas (Garland, 2010).

If a combination of nostalgia, resentment and populism has found its expression in Maricopa County, this has not been without a measure of contestation. An understanding of penal policies as engaged in a struggle for symbolic authority within an autonomous public sphere might help here. As might be expected, for liberal and international critics the Sheriff's expressive innovations can be re-described as a 'theatre of cruelty' which inflicts indignities on ordinary citizens. There is a sense that the Durkheimian imperative to respect the sacred self has not been obeyed. More surprising from the point of view of orthodox social theory is how often and centrally critique turns to issues of motivation and personality. Here again the resources of cultural sociology can help. Maricopa County is the sight of a social drama, not just a group of penal techniques. Arpaio is himself understood as a demagogue and populist who bends the law, by his harshest critics as a racist. Put simply he is often referred to in terms of the negative code within the wider discourse of American civil society. Existing in America for hundreds of years this contrasts rational, egalitarian, transparent and autonomous actors and institutions with irrational, hierarchical and dependent alternatives. US President Nixon, for example, was eventually understood by the majority as addicted to power, as secretive and as paranoid (Alexander and Smith, 1993). Precisely because public affairs are 'storied' in this way, efforts to discredit penal techniques in this case have hinged on showing a defective personality is behind them.

According to some critics Arpaio is a simplistic person with a 'comic book mentality of fighting crime' engaged in 'immature sadism' (Deutsche Presse Agentur, 1997). The Sheriff is a defective and dangerous individual suffering from a kind of arrested development. As Louis Rhodes the director of the Arizona Civil Liberties Union puts it:

> 'He's very creative. He dreams up these cute, catchy stunts that achieve nothing at all but let people believe they are living in a Hollywood Western. Joe grew up watching Tom Mix. Fifty years later he is living out his childhood fantasies. He's a comic book figure, with a distorted, simplistic picture of modern America' (quoted in Grant, 1995: 8).

Aside from being a man-child, Arpaio is also the 'tyrant of the desert' (Economist, 1999). He is often described as egocentric. Here is 'the self-anointed toughest Sheriff in America' who engages in 'tough on crime stunts' (Economist, 1999: 28) rather than a cool and detached professional. So to outsiders such as the journalist or most academics the Maricopa County regime seems like an anachronism or throwback. They are able to read cruelty and humiliation into the actions that are taking place – they seem to be deviant not simply mean spirited. Still there do seem to be limits to all that is going on. When it comes to justifications rather than activity, Arpaio is surprisingly 'modern' in his views. Arpaio does not speak of the wish to humiliate or to inflict pain. Nor does he bring up the theocratic language of repentance. Rather his policies are accounted for as rational, reasonable and proportional. The pink underwear prevents theft. The low cost meals prevent tax hikes. Grim conditions in Tent City Jail discourage recidivism. Visible chain gangs, the neon 'Vacancy' neon sign and Jail Cam can be easily described as pandering to a voyeuristic 'penal spectatorship' (Brown, 2009). Yet Arpaio insists that visibility enables punishment to act as a useful deterrent among those spectators. In this regard his arguments are remarkably Benthamite, remarkably 'rational'. As with Bentham's Panopticon the aim is to extract the maximum public benefit for the lowest cost, and without transgressing norms of decency.

So the public language of justification produces statements that are accountably 'modern'.

By the same token the need for this plausible accountability operates as a constraint on penal conditions. As evidence of enduring modernity we might also point to the continuing existence of elaborate bureaucratic and legal systems outside of the sheriff's direct control that buffer inmates from direct expressions of popular justice. Legal appeals and scrutiny by NGOs work to check many impulses. In many ways, then, Arpaio's regime is a cowboy one in style more than substance. It consists of a series of expressive gestures, albeit ones that have consequences for the thousands caught up in its now peculiar theatre. We might also point to another limit to what has taken place, namely the relatively weak diffusion of Arpaio's innovations. This provides evidence that really less is going on than meets the eye. Rather than signaling any broader shifts towards the 'late-modern', 'pre-modern' or 'postmodern' the case really signals the importance of the local and the conjunctural in American criminal justice as well as the stickiness of mainstream practices. Beyond Maricopa County there has been little uptake of the ideas so visibly trialed there. What diffusion has taken place has been in the realm of the global mass media. Arpaio has successfully produced circulating signs, symbols, iconographies and narratives rather than technologies and practices. Ironically these circulating discourses generate useful debate about appropriate penal regimes, about human dignity and privacy. Despite moments of voyeurism (Lynch, 2004) the public gaze has fallen not so much on the shamed criminals as on the Maricopa County regime itself. For the most part the verdict has been negative. Even in the tabloid media we find expressions of indignation rather than just desserts thinking. When all is said and done we have been exploring an instructive curiosity.

THE LETHAL INJECTION

Sheriff Arpaio's techniques have endured but also failed to catch on: Still they are colorful and deliberately demonstrative. Perhaps as an eccentric outlier they make a soft target for cultural analysis. At the other end of the scale we have established and widely shared penal methods that try to reduce communicative content to a minimum. The lethal injection stands out as a challenge for a cultural sociological approach precisely because it is a conventionalized protocol that is designed to signify nothing. It is an attempt at pure denotation without connotation that as David Garland (2010) points out indicates a deep ambivalence in the USA about the death penalty itself. The event is conducted behind closed doors before a small group of witnesses. There is little to see. A person lies on a gurney. Some tubes are connected. At some point that cannot be determined by the spectator the poison flows and the inmate dies. We might reasonably consider this event to be a culmination of the processes described by Durkheim, Elias and Foucault. The self is respected, the death is hidden, the body is regulated. But again this kind of gloss does not allow us to explore the detailed cultural processes through which abstract understandings of a need for respect, regulation and the rest come to be aligned with concrete practices at any particular juncture. This process of identification and alignment involves ongoing cultural work.

One can begin by noting the growing pollution of prior death technologies. Other methods slowly came to be seen as problematic. The predecessor of the lethal injection, the electric chair, stands out as an exhibit. Touted as a scientific means to bring instant death this became the dominant method of execution in the USA in the 20th century. In more recent decades, however, its narration has shifted. Botched executions were more widely reported. Even where things went well greater attention was given to its capacity to generate more material forms of pollution such as burning flesh and perforated bodily boundaries. What had been seen but not noticed was increasingly on the agenda. Meanwhile prison museums, waxworks and motion pictures pointed to sinister and supernatural possibilities, thus casting doubt on authorized understandings of how the technology worked. With Supreme Court intervention around the corner the switch to a new method of death seemed prudent (Sarat, 2001; Smith, 2008). The cultural history of the electric chair suggests that long term shifts in norms and modes of control are mediated by a more local and colorful symbolic and narrative landscape. Vague shifts in sensibility and common sense are anchored in repeated, local, concrete discursive and iconic practices.

Although it was intended to signify as little as possible, the cultural history of the poison injection looks set to repeat this pattern of proliferating and unruly meanings. Yet the challenge to theory is different from that of the seemingly retrograde Maricopa regime. Maricopa County bucks the trend. Here the trend is wildly accelerated. Legitimacy is shaky just two or three decades after innovation. With the lethal injection we see the new technology assailed by a number of rapidly indentified and mobilized legal problems that have unusually sympathetic iconic or metaphoric resonance. These work in more proximate ways to problematize and question. We might think here of cultural externalities to standard procedure – a surplus of meanings that seeps unintended into the circulating talk about punishment.

Attacks on the process of the lethal injection have come to replace efforts to overturn convictions or sentences or to contest the blanket constitutionality of the death penalty itself. By 2006 there was a situation where process related concerns could be described as 'the hottest trend in death penalty litigation' (Richey, 2006: 2). Even when narrowly or legalistically defined in court, such assaults on the lethal injection have fallen around powerful tropes or motifs. First there has been the effort to conjure the image of a kind of living death. This has been a longstanding vulnerability for all would-be humane execution protocols. The quest for an efficient, quick, aesthetically dignified and painless dispatch of life generally requires an immobilized body and the rapid application of lethal force, kinetic or otherwise. Yet the process of immobilization and force application makes the communication of suffering impossible. The image often persists of a sort of grey zone. The dying person experiences pain but is unable to let anyone know. In the case of the guillotine, for example, expert debates emerged in Revolutionary France over whether consciousness could survive for a while in a severed head. As such heads could not speak, macabre speculation and psychological identification was inevitable (Smith, 2008).

With the lethal injection we find exactly the same theme at the core of legal challenges and newspaper reporting. Because the first two drugs of the three-drug cocktail are intended to induce unconsciousness and then paralysis, there is a chance that pain could be experienced but not signaled once the third lethal dose of potassium chloride enters the blood stream. The case of *Baze* v. *Rees*, decided by the Supreme Court in 2008, was based upon such a scenario. As the Christian Science Monitor reported:

> The concern is that if the first drug fails to work properly the inmate will remain mentally aware as the other drugs are injected. Medical experts agree that a condemned inmate will endure unbearable pain and suffering from the injection of the potassium chloride. But because he has just been paralyzed by the second drug, the inmate will be unable to show any sign of distress. To an observer, the inmate may appear to have gone peacefully to sleep. But some experts say the inmate may, in fact, be fully conscious and in agony during his final moments of life. (Richey, 2008: 1)

This could be described in more gothic terms as a 'scenario with all the horror of an episode of The Twilight Zone' (Richey, 2006: 2). What makes things worse is the availability of a second powerful rhetorical move. Rightly or wrongly the three-drug protocol can be argued to be less humane than that given to animals. Such an inversion of the standard hierarchy of species seems to imply disrespect for human life and keys quite forcefully with the Durkheimian theme of the sacralization of the (human) individual in modernity. The 'not fit for animals' theme is repeatedly invoked by critics and repeated in mass media commentary whenever this chooses to relay expert testimony during appeal cases. When pets are euthanized, it is pointed out, they are given just a large dose of barbiturates. When we try to imagine it, this is a seemingly relaxing way to die. The use of a paralyzing agent, it has also been argued, is banned in 42 states because vets need to observe whether animals were in pain (Sherman, 2008). Humans, however, are not treated so well. A further problem is that the condemned is separated from the person administering the drugs by a wall and several feet of surgical tubing. They cannot be directly and closely observed the way a vet looks at an animal to assess whether it is sedated. Further, needles can fall out or the tubing can kink. Efforts to create an impersonal and clinical death without obvious human agency, a death that respects the individual can be read as demonstrating a lack of appropriate compassion. They have fallen 'below the standard for euthanizing household pets' (Milicia, 2008): unintended consequences indeed.

A third cultural problem confronting the lethal injection relates to the confounded boundary separating medicine and punishment. As with the living death motif, the theme here is of boundaries transgressed rather than boundaries inverted. The technology and setting of the injection make all too easily available the idea that a medical procedure is being carried out. Once this impression is anchored there follow a series of dissatisfactions. First, there was the sense that the process had been made fundamentally dishonest. The medicalization of death inappropriately masks a brutal act, one that should be transparently conducted by the state. As Christopher Hitchens (1998: 19) put it there seemed to be a 'nasty parody of a medical or surgical procedure' which he further interpreted as a 'furtive and phony attempt at a non-event'. The confounded boundary with medicine had engendered other problems too. The Hippocratic Oath – itself a cultural construct – was interpreted by the American Medical Association as preventing qualified doctors from participating in executions. Skilled practitioners had to be replaced by semi-trained prison staff. Chances of botched executions increased. Further the execution was responsible for 'degrading the tools and methods of medicine' (Hitchens, 1998). In short, cultural and ethical pollutions attendant to the medicalization of death have undercut the lethal injection's intent to spring clean a troubled institution. The seemingly communication-light lethal injection could not help but signify heavily.

CONCLUSION

To explain Maricopa County's unusual penal regime or the fragile legitimacy of the lethal injection one needs more than just a general theory of penal-cultural evolution, a model of the state or an account of legal institutions. In each case both policy and its contestation are underpinned by specific systems of circulating symbols, images and narratives. These struggle for interpretative authority, aiming to legitimate and de-legitimate activity in both the narrow and wider senses of that term. The resources of cultural sociology can help us to understand the ways in which such local, contingent and emergent meanings influence process.

The case studies provided here illustrate how culture makes a difference, but only in brief and imperfect ways. They focus largely on the broader circulations of meaning in the public sphere, using this to reconstruct motivations for action and opinion. However it is also important for cultural sociology to look closely at the semi-private meanings that inform intra-institutional life. We need stronger analyses of how symbolically rich, emotive and non-technical meaning systems that are in wider public circulation influence decision-making and policy within criminal justice bureaucracies or the legal sphere. This would require, perhaps, some form of institutional ethnography exploring how civil sphere pressures are translated and responded to within organizations. Such investigations could offer in particular new ways to approach intriguing questions surrounding the global diffusion of penal ideas and technologies. We can explore how nationally specific civil and institutional meanings shape the contexts of policy reception as ideas and technologies travel from one nation to another and are *interpreted*. The differential uptake 'zero tolerance', the 'no frills prison' and 'mandatory sentencing' becomes now a possible program for semantic research (splitting – see Melossi et al., 2011), as opposed to assertions on the hypodermic triumph of a cloned pattern of neoliberal ideology and the retreat of penal-welfarist thinking (lumping – see Wacquant, 1999).

Another challenge and opportunity for cultural sociology is to test its toolkit against more obdurate materials even than the lethal injection. During the 1960s symbolic interactionism and ethnomethodology gained enormous credibility from their demonstration that they could offer insight into even the most banal human activities. Riding the elevator, waiting, treading the sidewalk and even 'just doing nothing' were the topics of famous essays showing that everyday life had to be performed or accomplished. For the most part the cultural sociology approach has looked at more spectacular and colorful phenomena or the sort likely to generate symbolic resonance and public sphere controversy. The scope conditions of theoretical claims are unclear. It remains to be seen whether the most banal and routinized of punishments, such as probation, fines and traffic tickets, are amenable to a cultural analysis of deep meanings or whether there is really very little left to say. As Pat O'Malley points out in this volume (Chapter 18), fiscal penalties look especially slippery. They signal little, have no ritual enactment and somehow evade critical discourse or discussion through banality and ubiquity. Yet his chapter also hints that a hermeneutic approach might pay dividends. He shows that fines are seen as appropriate for 'respectable' people engaged in 'minor' misdemeanors. Clearly some classifications are at work. The historical record suggests popular resistance to the imposition of fines and charges as legislative responses to new 'victimless' crimes like speeding or parking. Particular technologies like the speed camera have also been interpreted as invasions of privacy or as surrogate and illegitimate revenue raising. It would seem that fines are read in many contexts as an index of the frontier between state and civil society. I add that the justice or reasonableness of any new ticket is certain to be the subject of ardent kitchen table or water cooler conversation. Fines are deeply, if often briefly, significant in everyday life. So it would seem that wherever there is punishment, there will be meaning. An analysis of the origins, form, logic, distribution and consequences of such meanings is the task of cultural sociology.

ACKNOWLEDGEMENT

Jonathan Simon commented helpfully on an earlier draft of this chapter.

REFERENCES

Alexander, Jeffrey C. and Smith, Philip (1993) 'The discourse of American civil society', *Theory and Society*, 22 (2): 151–207.

Alexander, Jeffrey C. and Smith, Philip (2001) 'The strong program in cultural theory: elements of a structural hermeneutics', in J. Turner (ed.), *Handbook of Social Theory*. New York: Kluwer Academic Publishers. pp. 135–50.

Alexander, Jeffrey C. and Smith, Philip (2010) 'The strong program: origins, achievements, prospects', in J. Hall, L. Grindstaff and M-C. Lo (eds), *Handbook of Cultural Sociology*. London: Routledge. pp. 13–24.

Brown, Michelle (2009) *The Culture of Punishment*. New York: NYU Press.

Deutsche Presse Agentur (1997) 'America's meanest sheriff makes life hard for his prisoners', 30 August.

Durkheim, Emile (1968) *The Elementary Forms of Religious Life*. London: Allen and Unwin (1st edn, 1912).

Durkheim, Emile (1984) *The Division of Labor in Society*. New York: Free Press (1st edn, 1893).

Economist, The (1999) 'Joe Arpaio: tyrant of the desert', 31 July: p. 28.

Elias, Norbert (1978) *The Civilizing Process Vol. 1: The History of Manners*. Oxford: Basil Blackwell.

Finnegan, William (2009) 'Sheriff Joe: Joe Arpaio is tough on prisoners and undocumented immigrants. What about crime?', *The New Yorker*, 85 (21): 42.

Foucault, Michel (1975) *Discipline and Punish*. London: Penguin.

Freedland, Jonathan (1995) 'Law and order: cruel and unusual: Sheriff Joe strikes home', *The Ottawa Citizen*, 10 June, Observer Section: B3.

Garland, David (1991) *Punishment and Modern Society*. Oxford: Oxford University Press.

Garland, David (2006) 'Concepts of culture in the sociology of punishment', *Theoretical Criminology*, 10: 419–47.

Garland, David (2010) *Peculiar Institution*. Cambridge, MA: Belknap.

Geertz, Clifford (1973) *The Interpretation of Cultures*. London: Hutchinson.

Grant, Richard (1995) 'The mean machine – meet America's toughest cop', *Sydney Morning Herald*, 10 June, Spectrum Section: 8.

Hitchens, Christopher (1998) 'At 12:01 AM the prisoner gave a splutter and made a slight heave upwards ... ', *The Evening Standard*, 3 February: 19.

Joas, Hans (2008) 'Punishment and respect: the sacralization of the person and its endangerment', *Journal of Classical Sociology*, 8: 159–77.

Lamont, Michele (2000) *The Dignity of Working Men: Morality and the Boundaries of Race, Class and Immigration*. Cambridge, MA: Harvard University Press.

Lynch, Mona (2004) 'Jail cam and the changing penal enterprise', *Punishment and Society*, 6 (3): 255–70.

Melossi, Dario, Sozzo, Maximo and Sparks, Richard (2011) 'Introduction. Criminal questions: cultural embeddedness and global mobilities', in Dario Melossi, Maximo Sozzo and Richard Sparks (eds), *Travels of the Criminal Question*. Oxford: Hart Publishing. pp. 1–14.

Milicia, Joe (2008) 'Doctor testified in challenge to Ohio's lethal injection, calls procedure unfit for animals', *Associated Press*, 7 April.

Pratt, John (2000) 'Emotive and ostentatious punishment: its decline and resurgence in modern society', *Punishment and Society*, 2: 417–39.

Pratt, John (2002) *Punishment and Civilization*. London: SAGE Publications.

Richey, Warren (2006) 'Judges re-examine lethal injection for convicts', *Christian Science Monitor*, 26 April: 2.

Richey, Warren (2008) 'Court upholds lethal injection', *Christian Science Monitor*, 17 April: 1.

Sarat, Austin (2001) *When the State Kills*. Princeton, NJ: Princeton University Press.

Schwartz, David (1998) 'Amnesty group takes aim at Arizona sheriff's jails', *Dallas Morning News*, 18 January.

Sherman, Mark (2008) 'Study says most US states bar veterinarians from using common lethal-injection drug in animals', *Associated Press*, 4 April.

Smith, Philip (2008) *Punishment and Culture*. Chicago: University of Chicago Press.

Spierenburg, Pieter (1984) *The Spectacle of Suffering*. New York: Cambridge University Press.

Turley, Jonathan (2009) 'Shaming undermines justice', *USA Today*, 17 November: 13A.

Wacquant, Loic (1999) 'How penal common sense comes to Europeans', *European Societies*, 1–3: 319–52.

Wheeler, Stanton, Mann, Kenneth and Sarat, Austin (1992) *Sitting in Judgment: The Sentencing of White Collar Criminals*. New Haven, CT: Yale University Press.

6

Punishment and Risk

Kelly Hannah-Moffat

International research has revealed recent shifts in how systems of crime control and punishment are managed. The pervasiveness of high crime rates along with the well-recognized limits of criminal justice agencies are forcing governments to create new strategies to cope with the social and political demands of crime control (Garland, 2001). A primary trend in new crime control and punishment systems is the use of risk management. This trend reflects a broader social phenomenon in which risk information is being used by public authorities to govern social problems more generally (Beck, 1992; Baker and Simon, 2002; Ericson and Doyle, 2003). Some researchers have suggested that we are becoming a 'risk society'; many aspects of social life (medical, financial, environmental, legal and economic) are governed through risk predictions and institutional and organizational structures are becoming more accountable for risk management (Baker and Simon, 2002). As with other social problems, crime is now being viewed as a calculable, avoidable and governable risk. Criminals are now characterized as a risky population to be managed efficiently and prudently – not only by the state, but by other citizens and a host of non-state agencies (Rose, 1996, 1998, 2000, 2002; Ericson and Haggerty, 1997; O'Malley, 1996, 1998, 2000; Stenson and Sullivan, 2001; Ericson and Doyle, 2003; Hornqvist, 2007). Offender populations are routinely subdivided, categorized and classified according to level of risk (high, edium, or low) and certain offender groups are perceived as exceptionally risky and thus as requiring special legislative control (i.e. sex offenders, mentally ill, recidivists, 'squeegee kids' and the homeless), which is also linked to expressions of punitive penal populism.

In general, the analysis of risk in punishment maps a range of eclectic the shifts in law and punishment , which accompanied what David Garland termed the 'collapse of the grand narrative'(Garland, 2001) of the modernist penal agenda – the widespread recognition of the failure of 'experts' the change offenders. The resultant disillusionment with the state and penal experts contributed to a problem of governmental legitimacy that prompted the decline of welfare-based penal strategies and the rise of neoliberal strategies that deemphasize individuals, state responsibilities and projects of normalization in favor of individual responsibilization, de-evolution of state authority and the efficient management of populations. For most punishment scholars risk is, a central feature of neoliberalism and its emphasis on prudentialism and characterization of individuals as rational subjects who ought to be responsible for their own welfare. By extension, current analyses show that risk is now a central feature of punishment (Garland, 2001; O'Malley, 2004; Hannah-Moffat, 2004). The calculation and application of actuarial risk in law and punishment increased dramatically with major advances in probability models during the 20th century. This expansion was mirrored by applications within the field of insurance and other industries. The move toward risk-based punishment was identified by American scholars Feeley and Simon in the early 1990s, and is still salient today. They argued that modern penal policies were shifting away from individualized rehabilitative models ('welfare' models) toward more strategic, administrative population management approaches that relied on actuarial techniques of quantifying and assessing the 'risk' of certain prisoners (Feeley and Simon, 1992). The authors claimed that the 'new penology' did not seek to 'change' offenders through 'targeted interventions'; rather that policies were concerned with efficiently identifying and managing a person at risk of reoffending, while minimizing potential risk to the community (Feeley and Simon, 1992; Simon, 1993). They claimed that the new penology was characterized by new discourses (e.g. the language of risk and systems analysis), new objectives (e.g. efficient control and risk management) and new techniques (e.g. actuarial profiles and audits) (Feeley and Simon, 1992, 1994). According to Feeley and Simon, the movement toward the new penology was the result of three important shifts within criminal justice. First, new kinds of discourse about the language of probability and risk replaced the reliance on strict clinical judgement. Second, the criminal justice system shifted its focus toward efficient control rather than rehabilitation and crime control. Third, offenders were no longer treated as distinct individuals who could be changed through rehabilitation, but were considered in terms of their membership in certain populations (i.e. recidivist, youth, violent and sex offenders). As part of the new penology, which still characterizes current penal systems in many jurisdictions, punishment has been repurposed from diagnosing and rehabilitating individuals to managing offending populations so as to reduce recidivism (Feeley and Simon, 1992).

In *The Culture of Control* (2001), David Garland argued that the welfare penal mode has been muted in favor of a punitive, expressive, risk-conscious penal mode. Accordingly, offenders are 'seen as risks that must be managed rather than rehabilitated. Instead of emphasizing rehabilitative methods that meet the offender's needs, the system emphasizes effective controls that minimize costs and maximize security' (2001: 175). Prior to his book was published and Feely and Simon (1992) coined the notion of the new penology, these risk logics and techniques have evolved and have been used to inform a wider range of penal practices. Concerns about risk are now shaping penal policy and offender management and are becoming increasingly important in sentencing reforms that advocate the adoption of 'smart sentencing' and 'evidence-based' sentences, best practices of correctional intervention, assessment and parole decision-making. Along with these trends has been the proliferation of actuarial risk assessment instruments including the well-known Level of Service Inventory – Revised (LSI-R),[1] Rapid Risk Assessment for Sex Offense Recidivism (RRASOR), Violent Offender Risk Appraisal Guide (VRAG) and Psychopathy Checklist (PCL-R). There are a multitude of offender and offence (female, youth, violent) 'risk instruments' that exist or are being developed. Most risk instruments share a common structure and focus on comparable 'risk' factors because they draw on the similar empirical literatures. What varies among these tools is the degree of emphasis placed on a particular set of factors; cut-off scores for the categorization of risk, or need; and the targeted offender population (youth, domestic violence, violent or sexual offenders). Consequently, the risk-assessment industry is influential and extensive, and has produced a variety of assessment tools. In the context of sentencing, risk instruments are being built into sentencing guidelines (i.e. Virginia), and used in the preparation of pre-sentence reports (Hannah-Moffat, 2011). As Harcourt notes 'prediction of criminality has become de rigueur in our highly administrative law enforcement and prison sectors – seen as necessary, no longer a mere convenience' (2007: 16).

A quick survey of how risk instruments are used in Canada, the UK, Australia and the USA reveals a general lack of consensus on the suitability, use, and actual role played by these instruments in sentencing, correctional management and parole. Some jurisdictions provide judges and parole boards with risk instruments and explicitly require the use of risk scores to determine appropriate sanctions (Simon, 2005; Harcourt, 2007; Maurutto and Hannah-Moffat, 2007, 2010). In other jurisdictions, the use of risk instruments is most pronounced in sexual or violent-offender cases where time and severity of offence allow for, and require, a detailed analysis of the offender's probable future conduct (Monahan, 2006). Risk instruments are commonly used by probation officers when they produce pre-sentence reports and make sentence recommendations, and to facilitate post-sentence management of offenders. Parole and correctional officials have a long history of using actuarial tools for classification and decision making (Simon, 1993).

This chapter outlines the emergence and entrenchment of risk thinking in punishment and how actuarial risk logic affects contemporary penal practices. It shows how risk, which is contested, negotiated, and tied to political programs, has changed our perception of 'just punishment'. It begins with a review of the various risk logics and discourses circulating in penal policy, followed by an investigation of theoretical and empirical research about risk-based practices, a discussion of the ongoing debate about the gendered and racialized nature of risk, and finally by emerging issues.

THE LOGICS OF RISK

The history of criminal punishment is characterized by cycles of retributive and rehabilitative punishment philosophies. Following profound dissatisfaction with the rehabilitative model that developed in the postwar period, a turn toward incapacitation based punishment regime has led to a massive expansion of correctional populations and has placed a heavy economic burden on the state (Andrews and Bonta, 2010). Importantly, the penal changes described here do not characterize all countries or reflect a consistent timeline. The adoptions of risk logics and practices vary temporarily and have differential geographical and socio-political effects. While the 'nothing works' dictum helped to justify this punitive turn within some criminal justice systems, rising prison populations have also more recently prompted researchers and policymakers to consider ways to reduce incarceration.[2] Various forms of risk are playing an important role in defining who is, and is not, a candidate for particular forms of punishment (diversion versus incarceration versus treatment). Inspired by the move toward evidence-based practices in medicine, many criminal justice systems have also tried to devise policies based on empirical evidence about what will and will not reduce recidivism (Naughton, 2005; Warren, 2008). As noted, the traditional rehabilitative model was focused on changing the individual, but the evidence-based practices now used in criminal justice are concerned with managing the population (see below for a discussion of the neo-rehabilitation claims of the what works movement). Because they are based on 'scientific evidence' and are informed by actuarial tools, these new practices are characterized as morally neutral and apolitical.

This portrayal is often juxtaposed with the difficulties associated with past welfarist regimes that relied on clinical judgement to make assessments about individual criminals. Supporters argue that these 'objective' actuarial tools can improve efficiency and make better use of scarce resources. Supporters argue that actuarial tools are objective and evidence based, and that they can improve efficiency and make better use of scarce resources.

Risk assessments and evidence-based interventions are now incorporated into the penal apparatus as a means of separating those who are more risky to public safety and more likely to commit additional criminal offences (Layton MacKenzie, 2000; Warren, 2008) from low-risk offenders. In this context, risk assessments or scores are used to determine the most suitable interventions and treatment programs for offenders. Both the risk instrument and the intervention are defined as evidence based because they are derived from correctional research on 'what works'. According to Warren, evidence-based interventions in corrections are based on three important questions: (1) 'who are the most appropriate offenders to assign to these programs; (2) what characteristics or needs of the offender should these programs address; and (3) how should the programs go about addressing the needs of these offenders' (2008: 598). Identification of low- versus high-risk offenders is now considered a necessary first step in correctional management.

Risk assessment involves a heterogeneous array of practices and *specificity* about types of risk. The instruments used are critical to clarifying how risk can shape policy and affect the penal population being studied. While the use of actuarially based risk assessment instruments to inform decision making is characterized as an 'empirical' or 'evidence-based' approach, 'empirical' assessment can involve different kinds of actuarial risk or risk/need assessments for various purposes. Risk assessment and risk tools have changed significantly over the past 40 years. Although current practices are influenced by local jurisdictional needs and laws, four main types of risk assessment[3] have evolved within this time frame, roughly corresponding to shifts in penal philosophies and practices. The following section outlines the shift away from clinical judgement and discusses the evolution of static risk-based models that inform incapacitation. Next, it explores the emergence of risk-based rehabilitation logic and demonstrates how risk came to be associated with effective correctional intervention practices. The following discussion heuristically divides risk into four types. However, multiple techniques of assessing risk co-exist in most jurisdictions. Further the development of actuarial risk instruments has not 'replaced' discretionary judgements about risk (Hannah-Moffat et al., 2010, Hannah-Moffat, 2011). Alternatively, scholars have argued that risk instruments simply create an appearance of objectivity, while 'black-boxing' subjective assessments, and at times racial, class and gender biases (Rose, 2002; Harcourt, 2007; Hannah-Moffat, 2004; Hannah-Moffat and O'Malley, 2007; Hannah-Moffat et al., 2010).

Discredited clinical judgements and static risk models

The first form of risk assessment was based on clinical prediction: unstructured clinical judgements by skilled practitioners such as social workers, psychologist and sometimes forensic psychiatrists who used their professional knowledge to make risk determinations. This widespread clinical method, which relied mainly on experience and judgement, continues to be used in most modern penal systems. However, the development and proliferation of statistically based risk assessment has discredited the clinical assessment method as subjective and unempirical, and criticized it for its poor predictive accuracy. Advocates of 'objective assessment asserted that risk-based decisions (such minimum, medium or maximum security classification or risk of violent recidivism) should rely on evidence-based research that identified the most reliable and valid criteria for making determinations about future risk. Research supporting the use of actuarial instruments consistently reports that actuarial risk scoring yields more accurate assessments of risk than clinical judgments based on professional training and experience (Monahan, 1984; Doyle and Dolan, 2002; Andrews et al., 2006; Andrews and Bonta, 2010). Clinical risk assessment were not replaced entirely, instead clinicians have incorporated the statistically based instruments discussed below into their professional assessments.

Although actuarial risk does not flourish until the 1970s, its antecedents can be traced back to the early work of Ernest Burgess, a Chicago School Sociologist who advocated the merits of prediction (Harcourt, 2007). During the 1970s, the second type of risk assessment, 'evidence-based' risk technologies, rose to prominence because they are easily aligned with the dominant political and administrative priorities of the time (O'Malley, 2004). Risk instruments are premised on the assumption that criminal recidivism is predictable and can be classified and sorted on the basis of numbers. These tools were developed based on research conducted on large population samples to categorize offenders according to their risk levels and likelihood of reoffending. The assignment of a risk score is a probabilistic calculation tested on aggregate groups. This means that large offender data sets are used to determine different levels of offending and the characteristics associated with groups of offenders. The risk score of high, medium or low represents statistical prediction. Our present risk knowledge allows us to provide a probalistic statement about an offender's likelihood of recidivism or the timing of potential recidivism. Risk scores cannot tell us with certainty *how* an offender will recidivate; whether violently, sexually or simply by violating a condition. This second type of risk tool assigns a quantitative risk score to an offender by assessing individual factors (e.g. history of substance abuse, age at first offence) that have been statistically linked to the risk of recidivism in correctional populations.

Actuarial risk assessment is often temporally associated with the decline of rehabilitative practices, but it actually has a much longer lineage dating back to 1920s (see Hart, 1923; Burgess, 1928). The Gluek's 1946 study was an important precursor to more contemporary statistically based risk prediction instruments. The Glueks and others (e.g. Burgess, 1928, 1936; Mannheim and Wilkins, 1955; Glaser, 1962) had already demonstrated the predictive superiority of these techniques over professional discretion and attempted, with minimal success, to have this type of risk assessment integrated into judicial, correctional and parole decision making (O'Malley, 2006). This kind of risk assessment, which is still used in many jurisdictions, uses static historic factors such as an offender's age, gender and number and type of convictions to make predictions about his or her risk of recidivism. Examples of these tools currently being used are the Salient Factor Score (in the USA), Static 99 (USA, Canada), the Statistical Inventory on Recidivism (SIR) (in Canada), and the Risk of Reconviction (in the UK). These static risk tools are still considered to be better predictors of recidivism than clinical judgments (Ægisdóttier et al., 2006; Andrews et al., 2006).

This second type of risk assessment has garnered considerable attention in American literature because it marks a significant shift in penality from rehabilitative treatment to management (Simon, 1993). Feeley and Simon (1994) used the term 'actuarial justice' to describe this focus on the management of aggregates within criminal justice. 'Actuarial justice' focuses on profiling, incapacitating, and monitoring high-risk and dangerous populations and repeat offenders. Within this framework, the offender is classified according to an approximate level of risk; because the factors used to determine this level of risk are historic and largely 'static' or unalterable (i.e. offense and criminal history), the scope of correctional intervention is largely limited to incapacitation. The tacit understanding of incapacitation as a preferable penal strategy for those designated as 'high risk' contributes to what penal scholars have dubbed the post-welfare era of 'hyper' or 'mass' incarceration. Actuarial tools (i.e. Salient Factor Score) are used to identify the subset of offenders that are believed to commit a disproportionate amount of crime and then selectively incapacitate them in the interest of public safety. In this context, parole and probation take on a different role, acting as cost-effective ways to manage groups of offenders considered a danger to public security, rather than focusing on reintegrating individual offenders back into society (Feeley and Simon, 1992: 456); determinations of fault are replaced by predictions of dangerousness (1992: 457). Here, risk logic is designed to differentiate levels of detention based upon an assessment of risk. In theory, lower risk offenders are to receive less severe penalties and diverting low-risk offenders into more treatment-based programs in the community will reduce recidivism better than incarceration.

Within this framework, incapacitation is used as a means to delay offenders from committing further acts. The key is to identify who is, and is not, a high-risk offender. A premised of incapacitation is that the vast majority of crime is committed by a select few offenders, thus selectively incapacitating high-risk offenders is expected to enhance public safety and reduce the overall recidivism rate. The connection between static risk logics and efficient management of offender populations means that evaluating and organizing groups according to risk is a priority for correctional sanctions, instead of therapeutically intervening in the lives of individual offenders. While continuing to inform decision making, in some jurisdictions the second type of risk tool is supplemented with or replaced by the third type of risk-need based rehabilitation tools discussed below.

Risk-need based rehabilitation and correctional management

Although the shifts in punishment outlined by Garland (2001), Feeley and Simon (1992, 1994), and others are exemplified in many international penal histories, recent research suggests that risk-based actuarial models have not simply replaced welfare strategies (Simon, 1996; Kemshall et al., 1997; Kemshall, 1998, 2002; Lynch, 1998; Robinson, 1999, 2001, 2002; Hannah-Moffat and Shaw, 2001a; Kemshall and Maguire, 2001; Miller, 2001; Leacock and Sparks, 2002; Harcourt, 2007). O'Malley (1999) convincingly demonstrated the existence of 'mixed models of governance' in which risk has been melded with other policy orientations, such as rehabilitation and restorative justice. Recent scholarship has revealed how risk strategies have evolved – and in cases such as RNR, have merged with new forms of rehabilitation (Hornvqvist, 2007; Feeley and Simon, 1992; Maurutto and Hannah-Moffat, 2007) and rely on the same subjective criteria as past forms of clinical assessments of risk (Hannah-Moffat et al., 2010).

In the 1980s, proponents of correctional treatment and corrections practitioners raised a host of concerns about the use of static risk models in correctional research about assessment and classification. This approach to risk research rejects the popularized *nothing works* claim, seeks to determine *what works* and strategically deploys *effective, targeted correctional interventions.* This approach endorses the use of science to resolve crime-related problems (Cullen and Gilbert, 2001). These criticisms resulted in new ways of understanding risk and the offender, and reaffirmed the rehabilitative theory that offenders can change if knowledge about their *needs* is incorporated into risk assessments. Although this approach was initially more prevalent in Canada, the UK and Australia, risk is now commonly associated with offender need and is used to help determine what type of correctional treatment an offender requires to reduce his/her risk level. The following section outlines the emergence of risk-need based rehabilitation logic and demonstrates how risk came to be associated with need and effective correctional intervention practices in a growing number of criminal justice systems.

As noted, criminal justice researchers and practitioners criticized static risk models for being too rigid and for their over-reliance on static offence-based risk criteria. These criteria yielded a 'fixed' prediction of risk, based on accumulated historic and immutable factors. Static risk logic implies that an offender's risk level cannot be reduced because the variables used to predict it do not change. This conceptualization of risk and the offender limited the scope of correctional management and provided little guidance for correctional professionals about possible interventions (other than incapacitation), because it offers no information on how to intervene or 'treat' the offender. Nonetheless, many static risk instruments are still being developed and used to inform decision making.

While the static risk logic was being mobilized in many jurisdictions to legitimate and inform penal policies, practitioners and correctional researchers were challenging this seemingly dominant understanding of risk, reasserting the importance of rehabilitative programming. Don Andrews, a leading Canadian proponent of the 'what works' movement (see below) and author of many well-known assessment tools, wrote that 'past (type 2) assessments of risk fail to prescribe interventions, and ignore the fact that, once in the correctional system, offenders are subject to events and experiences that may produce shifts in their chances of recidivism' (1989: 5). That is, lower-risk offenders may remain low-risk throughout their period of supervision, or they may move into higher-risk categories. Conversely, higher-risk offenders may remain high-risk or they may move into lower-risk categories. Andrews argued that improving the accuracy of prediction risk assessments requires assessing the characteristics of offenders and their circumstances, which may change during a sentence, and establishing which changes actually indicate an increased or reduced chance of recidivism. This assessment requires researchers and practitioners to look beyond risk factors that cannot be changed, such as criminal history, to include changeable factors (Andrews, 1989: 5–6). This reasoning led to the development of two additional types of risk tools (i.e. the LSI series of assessment tools) that aimed to provide an alternative to both clinical judgement and static models of risk assessment with the objective of reducing not just predicting risk.

Andrews (1989) pioneered the third type of risk tool, which is based on the hypothesis that some correctional treatment actually works to reduce offending. These treatments reportedly work because they target specific area of an individual's life that co-relate with offending. It is expected that targeted treatment if appropriately applied will reduce chances of recidivism (Andrews et al., 1990; Bonta and Wormith, 2007). 'What works' rehabilitation is central to the design of third generation risk tools: although they include some static factors (such as criminal history), they also include factors that can change over time, such as resent employment, criminal friends, and family relationships (Bonta and Andrews, 2007: 4). These changeable factors are known as 'dynamic risk factors' or 'criminogenic needs'. Some tools, such as the Youth Level of Service Inventory, include 'protective factors' (e.g. stable employment or housing, access to social services, positive self-esteem and positive attitudes, values, or beliefs),[4] which are positive influences that can improve the lives of individuals and diminish the likelihood of recidivism.

This third type of risk instrument is commonly referred to as 'risk-need' instruments, because offenders' needs are predetermined as factors shown to be statistically co-related with recidivism in aggregate offender populations; needs assessments in these tools are not 'individualized' or self-reported. Examples of these tools include the LSI-R, SARA (Spousal Abuse Risk Assessment), SAVRY (Structured Assessment for Violence Risk among Youth), HCR-20, PCL-R (Psychopathy Checklist Revised) and SONAR (Sex Offender Need Assessment Rating). These tools are designed to align risk prediction with the management of offender needs that are empirically shown to be 'treatable'; by default this means some needs are disqualified as targets for intervention. In other words, they distinguish between criminogenic and non-criminogenic needs. While non-criminogenic needs (e.g. poor health) may be important, they have not been empirically shown to be related to recidivism and are consequently considered low priority for intervention except for 'humane' reasons (Andrews, 1989).

The concept of dynamic risk is derived from the Risk-Needs Responsivity (RNR) Model (Andrews and Bonta, 2006). This model is considered central to the delivery of 'effective' correctional treatment programs (Andrews et al., 1990: 19), where 'effective treatment' refers to a measureable reduction in recidivism. Within the RNR model, the *risk principle* supports the theory that criminal behavior is predictable and that treatment services (often cognitive behavioral interventions that claim to 'teach' and not 'treat' as proposed by previous rehabilitative techniques) need to be matched to an offender's level of risk. 'High-risk' offenders are targeted for the greatest number of interventions. The *needs principle* targets for treatment an offender's *dynamic risk factors*, or *criminogenic needs*. Correctional researchers have established a set of criminogenic needs, some of which were discussed above, by identifying variables that had previously been empirically correlated with recidivism and thus are likely to be amenable to intervention.

Proponents of the RNR model argue that 'evidence of dynamic validity, that is, changes in risk scores signal changes in the likelihood of committing a new offence, is immensely important for correctional programs and the staff charged with managing offender risk. Maurutto and Hannah-Moffat (2006: 450) argue that 'the emphasis on "evidence-based principles" of risk/need assessment and program delivery is part of an extensive organizational restructuring that attempts to efficiently and effectively allocate scarce treatment resources to suitable and responsive offenders'. The what works framework embodied in contemporary risk assessments, like the LSI/CMI, inform not only the criteria contained in assessment tool, but also the types and delivery of correction treatment programs as well as the mission and purpose of correctional agencies. Knowledge of dynamic needs allows correctional officials to target interventions and prioritize scarce correctional resources. This targeting of interventions is linked to the *responsivity principle*, which refers to the matching of styles and modes of intervention to the learning styles and abilities of offenders (Andrews et al., 1990: 20). It requires the assessement of how: (1) diverse populations respond to various treatment options; and (2) 'specific' responsivity factors (e.g. self-esteem, motivation, personality traits, life circumstances and therapeutic relationships) may facilitate or impede an individual's response to intervention (Ogloff and Davis, 2004: 233). As discussed in detail below, responsivity is also related to how non-white and female offenders are managed. Risk instruments rarely distinguish between racialized or ethno-cultural groups of men and women; gender, culture, ethnicity, and race are only considered within the context of responsivity (i.e. how an offender from a particular ethno-racial group and/or gender may respond to an intervention based on population-level data).[5]

The responsivity principle features more prominently in fourth type of risk assessment and classification, which apply strategies and tools that systematically collate knowledge about an offender's history and needs to design a treatment plan and levels of monitoring. These tools (i.e. LSI–CMI) adopt the same basic approach as the third type of tools, but refine assessments of risk and need to ensure that they align more directly with case management. These risk assessments are not yet in wide use (Andrews et al., 2006), but many researchers are currently working to determine, measure, and categorize responsivity factors given their importance to this newest risk logic.

This risk and need logic has been accepted at a policy level in a number of jurisdictions, resulting in the integration of the LSI-R (or variations) into the preparation of pre-sentence reports and sentencing guidelines that explicitly stress risk–need assessment as an evidence-based technology (Cole and Angus, 2003; Cole, 2008; Hannah-Moffat and Maurutto, 2010). Hannah-Moffat (2004: 30) demonstrated that in the Canadian context, conceptions of risk have shifted from 'static' to 'dynamic' and have become fused with 'need', thereby necessitating particular types of interventions and treatments for offenders. These interventions are markedly different from older treatments that sought to 'cure'; instead, new interventions make offenders responsible for their own reform (2004: 30). However, only those aspects of an offender's life that are 'empirically' shown to contribute to recidivism are subject to assessment and intervention.

Proponents of the RNR model support evidence-based penal strategies that can reduce the risk of recidivism and enable lower-risk offenders to be efficiently, economically, and effectively managed in community settings (Cullen and Gilbert, 2001; Andrews and Bonta, 2006). They argue that penal resources should be redirected into correctional programs that are 'proven' to work and that all interventions should be accredited and evaluated to ensure that they help reduce recidivism. For example, Warren (2008) suggested that incarcerating low-risk offenders actually may increase recidivism due to the peer influence that higher-risk offenders may have on low-risk offenders. He argued that incarceration is not only an unjustified punishment for low-risk offenders, but that even community correctional programs should strictly separate low- and high-risk offenders to ensure maximum benefit from 'treatment' (Warren, 2008). For Warren, scarce criminal justice resources are better used to treat higher-risk offenders, as a 'low-risk' designation implies that an offender is unlikely to reoffend (2008: 600). Andrews and Bonta concurred, claiming that treatment resources are better used for high-risk offenders. They also argued that more negative outcomes could arise if low- and high-risk offenders are treated together (2010: 45).

These risk–need perspectives have been highly influential in correctional policy sectors. The increased use of formal actuarial risk assessment sentencing builds on past efforts to limit and structure discretion by directly linking sanctions to risk scores and/or tailoring conditions of probation or treatment to the outcomes of actuarial risk/needs instruments. Under the rehabilitative risk model, sanctions should support the reduction of recidivism. For example, probation is aligned with the results of the third and fourth types of risk assessments (such as the Level of Supervision Inventory [LSI-R])[6] and enable probation officers to stream an offender into a program that targets his or her areas of risk–need. The LSI was originally developed in Ontario, Canada in the late 1970s, is currently, the tool is used in jurisdictions throughout Canada, the USA, the UK, Europe, Hong Kong and Australia. In this way, sanctions reinforce the principle of effective correctional interventions by using risk–need assessment results to target treatment regimes that are empirically demonstrated to reduce criminogenic need, and the probability of recidivism. This approach to risk differs importantly from the correctional use of static risk (the second type of risk tools) for preventive or selective incapacitation or to deter recidivism through the administration of harsh penalties, which is another possible outcome of risk-based sentencing. Nonetheless, offenders who score high on rehabilitative-oriented risk–need scales will continue to endure incapacitation, especially if they are classified as non-responsive to treatment and/or unwilling to participate in treatment. The current conception of rehabilitation (or correctional treatment) is closely linked to statistical understanding of risk. Examples of risk/rehabilitation such as those discussed above help clarify how penal control gets restructured and what possibilities exist for new forms of risk governance.

PRACTITIONER ENGAGEMENT WITH RISK

There is significant disjuncture between the science of risk prediction and emerging practices. The risk assessment tools applied in many jurisdictions are developed 'in house' and/or poorly validated. Not all assessment tools are equally robust or empirically tested and even well validated tools have limitations for the prediction of recidivism that are sometimes overlooked in applied settings (Baird, 2009; Skeem, 2010). Moreover, legal and correctional professionals who use risk information in decision making are unlikely to have considered the documented limitations about the science of risk, and often have only a limited understanding of the actuarial technologies they are using.

Generally, the practitioners both favor using actuarial risk assessments to improve decision making and to limit discretionary powers; the appeal of these assessments stems from their perceived ability to deliver reliable, valid and objective determinations of future risks and to enhance managerial accountability. Canadian and British researchers have demonstrated omnipresence of standardized risk tools designed 'officially to promote consistency of assessments and deliver interventions according to the risk principle and interventions have sought to address factors shown statistically to be associated with re-offending' (Bullock, 2011: 121; see also Maurutto and Hannah-Moffat, 2006). With the evolution of RNR-based risk instruments, some authors claim that there is 'little justification for the continued use of professional judgment to make decisions related to risk' (Bonta, 2008: 1) and that 'any correctional agency that has the goal to reduce recidivism should use, at a minimum, third generation risk-needs assessment instruments' (Bonta and Wormith, 2008: 1).

Castel identified two major practical and political implications of risk. First, when the role of the practitioner is distanced from the subject, professional expertise operates differently. We have moved beyond treatment, in the traditional sense, to 'administrative assignation' and management of groups with certain risk profiles. The practitioner's expert knowledge remains critical for diagnosis and evaluation, but is no longer necessary for modern disciplinary purposes. Castel wrote, 'In a growing number of situations, medico-psychological assessment functions as an *activity of expertise* which serves to *label* an individual, to constitute for him or her a *profile* which will place him or her on a *career*' (1991: 290, emphasis added). In addition, Castel argued that practitioners have actually been reduced to executants or technicians who are subordinate to administrators. With management strategies taking over preventive technologies, penal administrators enjoy a newfound, near total autonomy. In terms of practical consequences, this means that practitioners no longer have a strong voice in preventive policy development.

Institutionally, adopting the new managerial logic of risk and 'effective' correctional intervention and risk has affected policy in terms of (1) how probation officers interact with courts and clients, (2) practices of case management, (3) resource allocation and (4) program design, delivery and availability (Hannah-Moffat et al., 2010). Few researchers have examined how the shift to risk-based penal management is received by, and affects, individuals working in various penal systems. The available international research reveals complex and nuanced interactions between the adoption of risk policies and how practitioners use and interpret these policies. Kemshall (2003) noted that although actuarial tools are increasingly used in probation services to categorize offenders (especially sexual and violent offenders) on the basis of risk, subjective and professional judgments still play an important role, sometimes even overriding actuarially derived risk classifications. She demonstrated that discrepancies between rhetoric and practice occur for a number of reasons, including ingrained occupational cultures and professional values, and ill-defined concepts. Other researchers have found that practitioners actively resist and embrace risk technologies and temper the impact these tools have on their discretionary decision-making, so introducing risk tools may shape, but does not eliminate, discretion (Hannah-Moffat and Shaw, 2001b; Hannah-Moffat et al., 2010; Bullock, 2011).

Actuarial risk instruments systematically organize a diverse range of information about an offender to guide practitioners through a logical and simple process to itemize and score that information. Theoretically, risk templates ensure that nothing is overlooked or missed when reviewing an offender or a case history; they are structured to produce a managerial form of defensible, consistent decision making. Practitioners report that they like using risk instruments because the tools standardize decision-making criteria, enhance the defensibility of decisions, and ensure that all the players in the system are working with the 'same information', making case files easier to transfer (Hannah-Moffat et al., 2009). Practitioners in discretionary decision-making contexts consistently reported that they believed actuarial risk scores can neutralize politics; institutionalization of risk can insulate practitioners who follow policy guidelines, scapegoat those who do not, and create new forms of organizational accountability. Regardless of their flaws, risk instruments foster confidence in the system because they appear to be objective, rational, and empirical. Uncritical acceptance of science and related risk technologies can jeopardize due process (Cole and Angus, 2003; Harcourt, 2007; Cole, 2008), generate disparities and discrimination (Morash et al., 1998; Bloom et al., 2003; Hudson and Bramshall, 2005; Belknap and Holsinger, 2006; Morash, 2009; Maurutto and Hannah-Moffat, 2010; Van Voorhis et al., 2010), undercut proportionality and escalate the severity of sentences (Harcourt, 2007; Netter, 2007). However, application of risk (and some evidence-based practices) may also facilitate a reduction in penal populations, and over time lead to the application of different and perhaps more constructive interventions.

Researchers have also shown that despite receiving training on these tools and their interpretation, practitioners tended to struggle with the meaning of the risk score and the importance of the items contained in the assessment tools (Hannah-Moffat and Maurutto, 2003; Hannah-Moffat, 2011). (Rather than understanding that an individual who obtains a high risk score *shares characteristics* of an aggregate group of high-risk offenders, the individual is likely to become *known as* a high-risk offender.) Instead of being understood as correlations, risk scores are misconstrued in court submissions, presentence reports and the range of institutional files that ascribe the characteristics of a risk category to the individual. Significantly, these reports follow the offender through the system and can stick with them for the entirety of their institutional careers. This is especially important since risk-based characterizations can have significant effects on outcomes for offenders (e.g. classification levels, institutional placement, treatment access, parole release, number and type of conditions, etc.). In practical terms, *correlation becomes causation* and potential risk is translated into an administrative certainty.

Some scholars maintain that the transition to risk-based penality has led to the 'deskilling', 'scientification' and 'erosion' of professional discretion (Robinson, 2003: 33; see also Schneider et al., 1996; Baker, 2005; Fitzgibbon, 2008), or that it has even eliminated discretion among criminal justice practitioners. Simon's (1993) analysis of the California parole system's upper management convincingly argued that actuarial techniques of identifying and managing populations appear to be replacing alternative strategies of parole supervision that rely on a subjective case by case 'moral diagnosis' of the causes of criminal behavior. However, Lynch (1998) found that while some elements of the actuarial model are flourishing at the state and regional management levels of parole, the model has not trickled down to frontline decision makers.

Hannah-Moffat et al. (2010) reported that probation officers see risk assessment technologies as serving their own professional interests and equate their use with 'best practices', which in turn enhance and professionalize their role. Robinson's (2003) assessment of the implementation of a risk instrument (Offender Assessment System [OASys]) in various parts of the UK and Kemshall's (1998, 2003) research about risk in probation support these findings; practitioners appear to equate the adoption of risk tools with a sense of reassurance or security. However, risk logics are obviously channeling and shaping practitioner recommendations, sometimes in problematic ways that disadvantage segments of the correctional populations. It is important to consider practitioner engagement with risk in any discussion of risk logics. Although risk assessment is empirically proven to be superior to clinical judgement or discretion, *both* figure prominently in the preparation of risk actuarial assessments. Assessments of risk routinely use criteria that are legally prohibited or problematic, and are often produced using an investigative and interpretive process that is largely concealed within the process of assessment (Monahan, 2006). Further, the statistical calculations that make up risk scores tend to 'black box' a number of evaluative and moral judgments (Rose, 1996; Kemshall, 1998, 2003; Maurutto and Hannah-Moffat, 2006).

THE LIMITS AND POSSIBILITIES OF RISK

Risk imparts a moral certainty and legitimacy to classifications, 'allowing people to accept them as normative obligations and therefore scripts for action' (Ericson and Haggerty, 1997: 7). However, most scholars agree that our present level of risk knowledge does not allow us to provide an absolute statement about an offender's likelihood of recidivism, type or the timing of potential recidivism. The possibility of making a prediction error (false positive or false negative) using a risk tool is probable, but not easily determined; this problem is generating considerable empirical research (Netter, 2007).

Several scholars have also questioned the ethics of punishing someone for *potential* future behavior. The danger is the possibility of shifting to what Silver and Miller (2002) and Reichman (1986) label 'statistical justice', wherein dispositions are determined on the basis of how closely an offender matches an actuarial profile, with less significance being given to other relevant legal criteria (Harcourt, 2007). In this way, actuarial risk (both rehabilitative and incapacitation oriented) de-individualizes the assessment of risk by categorizing offenders on the basis of unalterable group characteristics. This means that decisions about community or custodial punishments, the conditions of probation, and levels of supervision, are determined based not on what offenders did, but rather on how closely who they 'are' approximates subgroups of an offender population. There is a disjuncture between the logic of risk that underpins the assessment practices discussed above, and legal notions of proportionality that focuses, not on the individual, but on the offence committed.

Categorizing individuals as risky in comparison with an aggregate group contradicts the jurisprudential value of individualism (Simon, 1988: 776), and the use of aggregate statistics to apply individualized punishments has been criticized on theoretical, methodological, and ethical grounds (Cole and Angus, 2003; Hannah-Moffat and Maurutto, 2003; Simon, 2005; Monahan, 2006; Harcourt, 2007; Cole, 2008). The fact that actuarial risk assessments are typically created from the case files of a subpopulation of incarcerated offenders, and not general population data, raises concerns about the ability of any instrument to make an unbiased prediction of risk. Prison populations are not random; they are the products of past sentencing policies and patterns and disproportionately represent blacks, Aboriginals and other socially disadvantaged groups (Blumstein, 1982; Bushway and Morrison Piehl, 2007).

RISK AND DIVERSE POPULATIONS

Risk scholars and researchers have largely ignored the specific gendered and racialized character of risk governance and how institutional understandings of risk and their effects influence more global theorizations of risk. Without critical consideration, a disjuncture between theory and how risk is practiced in local institutional contexts seems inevitable. O'Malley noted that most analyses 'assume risk's unity, as if risk centered government can only be imagined as one thing, rather than a heterogeneous array of practices with diverse implications' (2004: 6). He and others have warned of the implications of seeing risk as a neutral statistical category and of using white male normative criteria to assess risk (Hannah-Moffat and O'Malley, 2007). Arguably, gendered norms, experiences and knowledges also shape what become risks and our responses to risks. A growing body of interdisciplinary research is focusing on how the emergence of risk-based policies is gendered or racialized in terms of conceptualization, legitimacy and effects. Risk differentially affects women, youth and ethno-racial groups. Debates about gender, race and risk have two dimensions: concern about the 'accuracy' of risk instruments when used for women and minority populations; and concern about the effects of using risk to manage women and racialized populations.

Gender and risk

Feminist scholarship over the past 40 years has contributed to measurable changes in how we think about and respond to social problems such as crime, mental illness, poverty and child welfare. Research has demonstrated not only that law and crime are gendered, but that gender shapes criminal justice responses to women and results in differential effects of policies for women and men. A number of scholars (Morash et al., 1998; Bloom et al., 2003; Belknap and Holsinger, 2006; Morash, 2009; Van Voorhis et al., 2010) have fault risk instruments for over-classifying women, ignoring the risk factors and needs most relevant to women offenders, and for not focusing on the validity of specific risk instruments for women.[7] The predictive reliability of existing instruments for women and racialized populations is unclear because the criminogenic factors included in generic risk tools are derived from statistical analyses of aggregate male correctional population data and are based on male-derived theories of crime; a gender/race problem is therefore built into the tools (Van Voorhis and Presser, 2001).

Feminist researchers have theoretically and empirically contested the use of risk instruments and policies that characterize men and women as having essentially the same risks and needs factors (Hannah-Moffat, 2009). These tools and their supporters demonstrate little regard for, or understanding of, the intellectual breadth and depth of feminist theory, the sophisticated feminist critiques of methodology, or the ample empirical and theoretical academic literature that documents how women's crime is qualitatively and quantitatively different from men's, even if they commit the same type of crime.[8] Research has empirically demonstrated differences in the motivational factors that lead to women's use of violence, involvement in drug and property crimes, and patterns of substance abuse, as well as how factors such as drug use are connected in gender-specific ways to initial and continued prostitution and other crimes (Hannah-Moffat and Shaw, 2001b; Bloom et al., 2003; Moretti et al., 2004; Blanchette and Brown, 2006; Heimer and Kruttschnitt, 2006). International data show clearly that women commit few violent crimes, are infrequently repeat offenders, and when they do reoffend, their crimes tend not to escalate in severity (Kong and AuCoin, 2008).

Empirical analyses of risk tools reveal that the criteria for establishing levels of risk routinely ignore gender, racial or ethnic differences and the differing social, economic and political contexts in which these tools are deployed (Maurutto and Hannah-Moffat, 2005). Such analyses also highlight that men and women have different needs and represent different kinds of risk, and note the importance of considering 'gender-specific needs' and the specific needs of minority women (Nesbitt and Argento, 1984; Brennan, 1998; Van Voorhis and Presser, 2001; Holtfreter and Morash, 2003; Holsinger and Holsinger, 2005; Belknap and Holsinger, 2006; Blanchette and Brown, 2006; Hollin and Palmer, 2006, 2007; Reisig et al., 2006; Wright et al., 2007). Empirical analysis of the use of LSI-R on women reveals 'a number of differences across areas of criminogenic need, although there was no difference in overall level of risk of reconviction' (Palmer and Hollin, 2007: 971). Risk tools can generically categorize women's risk, but these predictions are not solidly based in an empirically based understanding of female crime patterns, feminist theorization of etiology or gendered understandings of reintegration and desistance. This is at the heart of the gender and risk debate.

Recently, some conventional risk-assessment scholars have moved beyond concerns about predictive reliability and validity, focusing on the validity of non-gender-specific needs for female populations, or using feminist-inspired research to build risk tools (Brown and Blanchette, 2006). However, the emphasis is still overwhelmingly on 'validating' pre-existing risk tools that are based on theories and research about men's crime; their application to female offenders is conceptually incomplete and misses important nuances.

The development of gender-relevant classification schemes is a key issue for feminist-inspired scholars, prisoners-rights advocates and policymakers. Recent studies about 'what works' for women have led to the development of 'gender-responsive' guiding principles for women offenders (Bloom et al., 2003), new gender-based penal norms, and a plethora of feminist research about female offenders' risk, need and responsivity factors (Blanchette and Brown, 2006; Morash, 2009; Van Voorhis et al., 2010). Many feminist researchers focusing on corrections (e.g. on the National Institute of Corrections and Correctional Service of Canada) have supported and initiated the development of risk–need classification/assessment instruments that can identify and program for women's needs. These efforts to build tools from the ground up differ fundamentally from making gender 'fit' into a pre-existing template derived from knowledge about men's crime, but conceptual and operational problems remain (Hannah-Moffat, 2010).

Theoretical literature is beginning to show that when gender is used to inform the development of risk instruments and penal policies, women's needs are translated into risk factors. Hannah-Moffat (2004, 2009, 2010) examined Canadian correctional policy and found that narrow understandings of women's 'risks and needs' are integrated into correctional practices in a way that positions them as targets for correctional intervention. Advocates of gender-based classification are promoting and researching ways to include information about histories of domestic violence, sexual abuse, mental illness, self esteem, and parental responsibilities in assessment instruments and ensuring that correctional programs meet these needs (UN, 2008: 31–2). Theoretically and empirically it is possible to include 'gender-informed' variables in risk classification tools (Brown and Blanchette, 2006; VanVoorhis et al., 2010), but these variables may neutralize gender politics and decontextualize women's experiences.

Race and risk

Many researchers have argued that race disparities with the justice system are exacerbated once risk-based thinking is introduced (Petersilia and Turner, 1987; Feeley and Simon, 1992; Harcourt, 2007; Tonry, 2009; Hannah-Moffat and Maurutto, 2010). Uncritical adoption of risk instruments is also problematic from the standpoint of race and social inequality. As early as 1992, Feeley and Simon predicted that one outcome of actuarialism and the focus on aggregate populations would be a change in the understanding of poverty. They argued that the underclass, a predominantly marginalized group that is under-educated and lacking skills, would be reconstituted as a risky population that must be managed to protect society (1992: 467). Studies of risk that focus on race tend to emphasize the experiences of racialized men; studies of women often include too few participants to allow for an examination of subgroups of racialized women. Scholars have raised concerns about the racialized nature of women's crime and the stereotypical and discriminatory foundation of penality (Richie, 1991; Sudbury, 2005; Phillips, 2008; Christian and Thomas, 2009; Phillips and Earle, 2010), but policy or risk assessment/classification practices have yet to meaningfully address these criticisms.

Current research is beginning to reveal that racialized social economic structures and contexts are relevant to the production and composition of the offender population, and how risk-based practices may exacerbate inequalities and generate systemic discrimination (Hudson and Bramhall, 2005; Hannah-Moffat and Maurutto, 2010). Proponents of risk instruments often overlook the fact that both static and criminogenic risk variables cannot be easily abstracted from the socio-political, economic and cultural specificity of individuals. Examinations of race and risk have reported that risk tools such as the 'LSI-R yields mixed predictive validity when used with different ethnic and racial populations' and that 'different groups may be influenced by different risk and needs factors that lead to recidivism' (Fass et al., 2008: 1106). Racial minority females and males have been shown to require different needs (Gavazzi et al., 2005), and the race and ethnicity of offenders can influence the attribution of risk factors by practitioners (Hudson and Bramhall, 2005). Collectively, the literature reveals that, regardless of whether some generic factors (i.e. substance abuse, marital family difficulties and employment) are relevant or even predictive for men and women (Vose et al., 2008), these nonspecific factors are *experienced* differently and have different effects.

Petersilia and Turner (1987) noted that many of the factors assumed to be correlated with recidivism (prior record, unemployment) are also correlated with race. Using data collected in California, they found that black offenders were often convicted of more serious crimes and had more extensive prior criminal records, but that the ability of risk assessments to predict recidivism without racially correlated variables was much lower than when they included racially correlated variables (3–9 versus 20 percent predictive accuracy over chance). They argued that the rationale for punishment may dictate whether removing racially charged variables is appropriate, and that when the emphasis of sentencing is concerned with predicting recidivism, risk assessment tools could remove racially correlated variables without sacrificing too much by way of predictive accuracy. However, when 'just deserts' is the focus, predicting recidivism is a moot point: those with the most serious convictions should be incarcerated regardless of whether this variable happens to be correlated with race.

Crow (2008) explored the complex relationship between prior criminal record and race. He found that the effects of a prior record often depend on the race of the offender, but that the effects of race may vary across different types of offenses. Interestingly, the profiles of drug offenders provided even more evidence of interactions between race, prior record and type of offence. Crow found that while Black and Hispanic drug offenders with no prior criminal record were much more likely to be incarcerated than white drug offenders, some measures of prior record affected White offenders differently than blacks and Hispanics.

Wakefield and Uggen (2010) argued that the rising racialized population in prisons exacerbates the social stratification already experienced by minority populations outside the justice system. They maintained that the ethnic and class disparities in the prison population is partly due to a huge influx of low-level and low-rate delinquents entering the prison system, rather than dangerous or high-rate offenders. Specifically, the growth of the prison population is a result of the disproportionate number of African Americans and Hispanics who have been incarcerated for drug-related offences. They argued that the prison system generates social inequality in a myriad of ways (economics, health, disruption of family bonds) that are not directly related to a criminal act. For example, mass incarceration increases inequalities in the labor market by removing a large number of young men who already have limited skills and education; the net result is a lower number of available workers in the workforce and stigmatization of the cohorts once they return to society. A criminal record not only hampers wage mobility (Western, 2002), but it may complicate the ability to secure a job at all. According to Pager (2003), the role of race in shaping employment opportunities is equal to or greater than the impact of a criminal record. The effect of a criminal record appears be to more pronounced for blacks than whites. She reported that employers who are already wary of hiring blacks are even more concerned if the black person has a criminal record. Blacks are more likely to be asked up-front if they have a criminal record; although race has been specifically excluded as an item on many risk assessment tools (Harcourt, 2007), items such as prior criminal record are racially loaded.

The science behind risk tools has been contested and is insufficiently advanced to prove that these tools do not replicate or produce forms of systemic discrimination. Harcourt hypothesized that they make generate a 'ratchet effect' wherein 'profiled populations become an even larger portion of the carceral population' with highly determined consequences for their employment, educational, family and social outcomes (2007: 3). It is impossible to treat individuals fairly if they are treated as abstractions, unshaped by the particular contexts of social life.

FUTURE DIRECTIONS

Scholars have characterized actuarial technologies as a negative development that can result in racial targeting, de-individualization, social exclusion, a prioritization of recidivism and future conduct, and the devaluing of social context. However, O'Malley (2008) argued that focusing on the negative side of risk fails to account for how risk embodies a heterogeneous array of practices with diverse effects and implications. Following François Ewald (1991), he maintained that risk is an abstract technology, which is always shaped and given effect by specific social and political rationalities and environments (O'Malley, 2008: 453). By extension, law and criminal justice contexts play a pivotal role in shaping understandings of risk and how it should or should not be incorporated into penal practices. Risk technologies are malleable and 'constantly being reinvented, retrofitted and reassembled in response to institutional agendas' (Maurutto and Hannah-Moffat, 2006: 40). This fluidity enables multiple penal logics and forms of governance to operate alongside each other. Consequently, future examination of risk and punishment ought to consider the impact, ethics and limits of using risk in criminal justice context (Birdgen and Ward, 2003; Nelson and Cowburn, 2010).

Risk has influenced penality in diverse, uneven, and formative ways. Actuarial risk can be a viewed as a progressive or exclusionary penal practice that operates in accordance with the institutional conditions in which it is realized. Despite its conceptual and methodological deficiencies, it is unlikely that the emphasis on risk will dissipate. Appeals to actuarial sentencing simultaneously support two distinct utilitarian goals of sentencing: incapacitation and reformist intervention. Actuarial methods can accentuate, but may also minimize prejudices and biases that are built into law and criminal law enforcement because the structure of assessment instruments is opaque, making broader discriminatory practices less visible and contestable.

Future examinations of risk will need to explore how risk technologies affect various populations and begin to develop a more refined understanding of how risk criteria obscure and perpetuate a range of social inequalities. Research is also needed to produce a wider range of possibilities for penal intervention. The structural integration of risk into punishment realigns managerial priorities and shifts discretion to the organizations and individuals producing risk templates and providing risk scores and redirects debates about the subjective and normative dimensions of punishment. As risk technologies develop and expand into sentencing, bail courts and scholars will need to pay greater attention to how, why and on what 'evidence' we can justify the deprivation of liberty and penal practices in general (both punitive and therapeutic), based on probabilistic risk scores (Slobogin, 2005; Simon 2005; Harcourt, 2007; Hannah-Moffat, forthcoming).

NOTES

1 One of the most common risk instruments for the prediction of general criminality is the Level of Service Inventory – Revised (LSI-R). LSI-R is currently being utilized within Canada and the USA to guide sentencing decisions, placement in correctional programs, institutional assignments, and release from institutional custody. This instrument's widespread use and modification makes it a useful exemplar for this discussion. The LSI was originally developed in Ontario, Canada, in the late 1970s and quickly developed international notoriety. Currently, the tool is used in jurisdictions throughout Canada, the USA, the UK and Australia, among others. The tool, originally written in English, is available in Spanish, Croatian and French (French European and French Canadian), and it is in the process of being translated into Dutch and Icelandic. Multi Health Systems – the company that markets the LSI-R – indicates that more than 600 agencies in the USA currently use this risk-need tool (Lowenkamp et al., 2004). It is one of the most extensively researched offender classification instruments; consequently, it is less vulnerable to some of the methodological critiques of less rigorously tested local risk instruments. Nonetheless the LSI-R, similar to all risk tools, has limits, and its current use in sentencing generates a complicated debate, as well as a need for further empirical research.

2 It is important to note the penal changes described here does not characterise all countries or a consistent timeline. Risk logics vary temporarily and have had differential geographical and political impacts.

3 Andrews and Bonta (1998) provide a detailed description of the development of risk instruments.

4 Additional factors for youth include parental supervision and strong parenting skills, social support, and positive role models and peer groups.

5 See Ward and Maruna (2007) for a fuller critique of RNR. The critical literature on punishment includes a lively debate about the 'what works' analyses of the logic of RNR and cognitive behavioralism (Ward, 2002; Ward and Stewart, 2003; Ward and Brown, 2004).

6 The LSI-R, originally written in English, is available in Spanish, Croatian and French (French European and French Canadian), and it is in the process of being translated into Dutch and Icelandic.

7 For a more comprehensive discussion of this debate and present developments, see Van Voorhis et al. (2010).

8 For a more detailed discussion of the concerns surrounding gender and risk, see Hannah-Moffat (2009), Hannah-Moffat and O'Malley (2007) and Blanchette and Brown (2006).

REFERENCES

Ægisdóttier, S., White, M.J., Spengler, P.M. Maugherman, A.S. and Anderson, L.A. (2006) 'The meta-analysis of clinical judgment project: fifty-six years of accumulated research on clinical versus statistical prediction', *Counseling Psychologist*, 34: 341–82.

Andrews, D.A. (1989) 'Recidivism is predictable and can be influenced: using risk assessments to reduce recidivism', *Forum on Corrections Research,* 1 (2): 11–17.

Andrews, D.A. and Bonta, J. (1998) *The Psychology of Criminal Conduct,* 2nd edn. Cincinnati, OH: Anderson.

Andrews, D.A. and Bonta, J. (2003) *The Psychology of Criminal Conduct,* 3rd edn. Cincinnati, OH: Anderson.

Andrews, D.A., and Bonta, J. (2006). *The Psychology of Criminal Conduct* 4th edn. Newark, NJ: LexisNexis.

Andrews, D.A. and Bonta, J. (2010) 'Rehabilitating criminal justice policy and practice', *Psychology, Public Policy, and Law,* 16 (1): 39–55.

Andrews, D.A. and Bonta, J. (2010a). *The Psychology of Criminal Conduct,* 5th edn. Cincinnati, OH: Anderson Publishing Company.

Andrews, D.A., Bonta, J. and Hoge, R.D. (1990) 'Classification for effective rehabilitation: rediscovering psychology', *Criminal Justice and Behavior,* 17: 19–52.

Andrews, D.A., Bonta, J. and Wormith, S.J. (2004) *The Level of Service/Case Management Inventory (LS/CMI).* Toronto: Multi-Health Systems.

Andrews, D.A., Bonta, J., and Wormith, S.J. (2006). 'The recent past and near future of risk and/or need assessment', *Crime and Delinquency,* 52, 7–27.

Andrews, D.A. and Dowden, C. (2008) 'The risk-need-responsivity model of assessment and human service in prevention and corrections: crime-prevention jurisprudence', *Canadian Journal of Criminology and Criminal Justice,* 49 (4): 439–464.

Baker, K. (2005). 'Assessment in youth justice: professional discretion and the use of ASSET', *Youth Justice,* 5: 106.

Baker, T. and Simon, J. (2002) *Embracing Risk: The Changing Culture of Insurance and Responsibility.* Chicago, IL: University Of Chicago Press.

Baird, C. (2009) A question of evidence: A critique of risk Models used in the Justice System. Madison: National Council on Crime and Delinquency. Accessed January 13, 2011 from: http://faculty.uml.edu/jbyrne/44.203/NCCD%20Baird%20on%20Risk.pdf

Beck, U. (1992) *Risk Society.* London: SAGE Publications.

Belknap, J. and Holsinger, K. (2006) 'The gendered nature of risk factors for delinquency', *Feminist Criminology,* 1: 48–71.

Birgden, A. and Ward, T. (2003) 'Jurisprudential considerations: pragmatic psychology through a therapeutic jurisprudence lens: psycholegal soft spots in the criminal justice system', *Psychology, Public Policy and Law,* 9: 334–60.

Blanchette, K. and Brown, S.L. (2006) *The Assessment and Treatment of Women Offenders: An Integrative Perspective.* Chichester: Wiley.

Bloom, B. (1996) 'Triple jeopardy: race, class, and gender as factors in women's imprisonment'. PhD dissertation, University of California, Riverside.

Bloom, B. (2003) *Gendered Justice: Addressing Female Offenders.* Durham, NC: Carolina Academic Press.

Bloom, B., Owen, B. and Covington, S. (2003) *Gender Responsive Strategies: Research, Practice and Guiding Principles for Women Offenders.* Washington, DC: National Institute of Corrections, US Department of Justice.

Bloom, B., Owen, B. and Covington, S. (2004) 'Women offenders and the gendered effects of public policy', *Review of Policy Research,* 21 (1): 31–48.

Bloom, B., Owen, B. and Covington, S. (2006) *A Summary of Research, Practice, and Guiding Principles for Women Offenders'. The Gender-Responsive Strategies Project: Approach and Findings.* National Institute of Corrections: Washington, DC. Available at: http://nicic.org/Library/020418 (accessed 19 September 2006).

Blumstein, A. (1982) 'On racial disproportionality of the United Sates prison populations', *Journal of Criminal Law and Criminology,* 73 (4): 1259.

Bonta, J. (2008) 'Offender risk assessment and sentencing', *Canadian Journal of Criminology and Criminal Justice,* 49 (4): 519–529.

Bonta, J. and Andrews, D.A. (2007) *Risk-Need-Responsivity Model for Offender Assessment and Rehabilitation.* Ottawa: Public Safety. Available at: http://www.publicsafety.gc.ca/res/cor/rep/_fl/Risk_Need_2007–06_e.pdf

Bonta, J. and Wormith, J.S. (2007) 'Risk and need assessment', in G. McIvor and P. Raynor (eds), *Developments in Social Work with Offenders.* London and Philadelphia: Jessica Kingsley Publishers. pp. 131–152.

Brennan, T. (1998) 'Institutional classification of female offenders', in R. Zaplan (ed.), *Female Offenders: Critical Perspectives and Effective Interventions.* Gaithersberg, MD: Aspen Publishers. pp. 179–204.

Brown, M. and Bloom. B. (2009) 'Re-entry and renegotiating motherhood: maternal identity and success on parole', *Crime & Delinquency,* 55: 313–336.

Bullock, K. (2011) 'The construction and interpretation of risk management technologies in contemporary probation practice', *British Journal of Criminology,* 55: 120–35.

Burgess, E. (1928) 'Factors making for success or failure on parole', *Journal of Criminal Law and Criminology,* 19: 239–306.

Burgess, E. (1936) 'Protecting the public by parole prediction', *Journal of Criminal Law and Criminology,* 27: 491–502.

Bushway, S.D. and Morrison P.A. (2007) 'The inextricable link between age and criminal history in sentencing', *Crime & Delinquency,* 53 (1): 156–183.

Canadian Human Rights Commission (CHRC) (2003) Protecting their Rights: A Systematic Review of Human Rights in Correctional Services for Federally Sentenced Women. Available at: http://www.chrc-ccdp.ca/legislation_policies/consultation_report-eng.aspx (accessed 26 February 2011).

Castel, R. (1991) 'From dangerousness to risk', in G. Burchell, C. Gordon and P. Miller (eds.), *The Foucault Effect: Studies in Governmentality.* Chicago: University of Chicago Press. pp. 281–98.

Christian, J. and Thomas, S.S. (2009) 'Examining the intersections of race, gender and mass imprisonment', *Journal of Ethnicity in Criminal Justice,* 7 (1): 69–84.

Cole, D. (2008) 'The umpires strike back: Canadian judicial experience with risk assessment instruments', *Canadian Journal of Criminology,* 49 (4): 493–519.

Cole, D. and Angus, G. (2003) 'Using pre-sentence reports to evaluate and respond to risk', *Criminal Law Quarterly,* 47 (3): 302–64.

Crow, M.S. (2008) 'The complexity of prior record, race, ethnicity, and policy: interactive effects in sentencing', *Criminal Justice Review,* 33 (4): 502–23.

Cullen, F. and Gilbert, K. (2001) 'From nothing works to what works: changing professional ideology in the 21st century', *Prison Journal,* 81: 313.

Daly, K. (1989) 'Criminal justice ideologies and practices in different voices: some feminist questions about justice', *International Journal of the Sociology of Law,* 17 (1): 1–18.

Daly, K. (1997) 'Different ways of conceptualizing sex/gender in feminist theory and their implications for criminology', *Theoretical Criminology,* 1 (1): 25–51.

Doyle, M. and Dolan, M. (2002). 'Violence risk assessment: combining actuarial and clinical information to structure clinical judgments for the formulation and management of risk', *Journal of Psychiatric and Mental Health Nursing,* 9: 649–57.

Ericson, R. and Doyle, A. (2003) *Risk and Morality.* Toronto: University Of Toronto Press.

Ericson, R. and Haggerty, K. (1997) *Policing the Risk Society.* Toronto: University of Toronto Press.

Fass, T., Heilbrun, K., DeMatteo, D., et al. (2008) 'The LSI-R and the compass: validation data on two risk-needs tools', *Criminal Justice and Behavior,* 35: 1095–1108.

Feeley, M. and Simon, J. (1992) 'The new penology: notes on the emerging strategy of corrections and its implications', *Criminology,* 30 (4): 449–474.

Feeley, M. and Simon, J. (1994) 'Actuarial justice: the emerging new criminal law', in D. Nelken (ed.), *The Futures of Criminology.* London: SAGE Publication. pp. 173–201.

Fitzgibbon, W. (2008) 'Fit for purpose? OASys assessments and parole decisions', *The Probation Journal,* 55 (1): 55–69.

Ewald, F. (1991) 'Insurance and Risk', in G. Burchell (ed.), *The Foucault Effect: Studies in Governmental Rationality.* Hempstead: Harvester Wheatsheaf.

Garland, D. (2001) *The Culture of Control.* Chicago: University of Chicago Press.

Gavazzi, S.M., Yarcheck, C.M. and Lim, J.Y. (2005) 'Ethnicity, gender, and global risk indicators in the lives of status offenders coming to the attention of the juvenile court', *International Journal of Offender Therapy and Comparative Criminology,* 49 (6): 696–710.

Glaser, D. (1962) 'Prediction tables as accounting devices for judges and parole boards', *Crime and Delinquency,* 8: 239–58.

Guleck, S. and Gluek, E. (1946) *After Conduct of Discharged Offenders.* New York: Macmillan.

Hannah-Moffat, K. (1999) 'Moral agent or actuarial subject: risk and Canadian women's imprisonment,' *Theoretical Criminology,* 3: 71–94.

Hannah-Moffat, K. (2004) 'Criminogenic need and the transformative risk subject: hybridizations of risk/need in penality', *Punishment and Society,* 7: 29–51.

Hannah-Moffat, K. (2007). Gendering dynamic risk: assessing and managing the maternal identities of women prisoners', in K. Hannah-Moffat and P. O'Malley (eds), *Gendered Risks.* London: Routledge Cavendish Publishing.

Hannah-Moffat, K. (2009) 'Gridlock or mutability: reconsidering 'gender' and risk assessment', *Criminology and Public Policy,* 8 (1): 221–229.

Hannah-Moffat, K. (forthcoming) 'Actuarial Sentencing: An 'Unsettled' Proposition', *Justice Quarterly.*

Hannah-Moffat, K. and Maurutto, P. (2003) *Youth Risk/Needs Assessment: An Overview of Issues and Practices.* Ottawa: Department of Justice.

Hannah-Moffat, K. and Maurutto, P. (2010) 'Re-contextualizing pre-sentence reports: race and risk', *Punishment & Society,* 12 (3): 262–86.

Hannah-Moffat, K. and Shaw, M. (2001a) 'Situation risqué: le risqué et les services correctionnels au Canada', *Criminologie – Special Issue on Risk,* 34(1): 47–72.

Hannah-Moffat, K. and Shaw, M. (2001b) *Taking Risks: Gender, Diversity, Risk Assessment and Security Classifications for Federally Sentenced Women.* Ottawa: Status of Women Canada.

Hannah-Moffat, K. and Shaw, M. (2003) 'What is a risk: rethinking categories and meanings', in B. Bloom and S. Covington (eds), *Gendered Justice: Programming for Women and Girls in Correctional Settings.* Durham, NC: Carolina Academic Press.

Hannah-Moffat, K. and O'Malley, P. (eds), (2007) *Gendered Risks.* London: Routledge Cavendish Publishing.

Hannah-Moffat, K., Maurutto, P. and Turnbull, S. (2010) 'Negotiated Risk: Actuarial Assessment and Discretion in Probation', *Canadian Journal of Law and Society,* 24 (3).

Harcourt, B. (2007) *Against Prediction: Profiling, Policing and Punishing in the Actuarial Age.* Chicago: University of Chicago Press.

Hart, H. (1923) 'Predicting parole success', *Journal of Criminal Law and Criminology,* 14: 405–13.

Heimer, K. and Kruttschnitt, C. (2006) *Gender and Crime: Patterns in Victimization and Offending.* New York: New York University Press.

Hollin, C.R. and Palmer, E.J. (2006) 'Criminogenic need and women offenders: a critique of the literature', *Legal and Criminological Psychology,* 11: 179–95.

Holsinger, K. and Holsinger, A.M. (2005) 'Differential pathways to violence and self-injurious behavior: African American and white girls in the juvenile justice system', *Journal of Research in Crime and Delinquency,* 42: 211–42.

Holtfreter, Kristi and Morash, Merry (2003) 'The needs of women offenders: Implications for correctional programming', *Women & Criminal Justice,* 14: 137–160.

Hood, R. and Shute, S. (2000) T*he Parole System At Work: A Study Of Risk Based Decision Making.* London: Home Office Research Study – Research, Development and Statistics Branch.

Hornqvist, M. (2007) 'The organized nature of power: on productive and repressive interventions based on considerations of risk'. Doctoral thesis in Criminology at Stockholm University, Sweden.

Hudson, B. (2003) *Justice in the Risk Society.* London: SAGE Publications.

Hudson, B. and Bramhall, G. (2005) 'Assessing the other: Constructions of Asianness in risk assessment by probation officers', *British Journal of Criminology,* 45(5): 721–740.

Kemshall, H. (1998) *Risk in Probation Practice.* Aldershot: Ashgate Publishing.

Kemshall, H. (2002) 'Effective practice in probation: an example of advanced liberal responsibilization?', *The Howard Journal of Criminal Justice,* 41 (1): 41–58.

Kemshall, H. (2003) *Understanding Risk in Criminal Justice.* Maidenhead: Open University Press.

Kemshall, H. and McGuire, M. (2001) 'Public protection, partnership and risk penality: the multi-agency risk management of sexual and violent offenders', *Punishment and Society,* 3: 237–264.

Kemshall, H., Parton, N., Walsh, M., et al. (1997) 'Concepts of risk in relation to organizational structure and functioning within personal social services and probation', *Social Policy and Administration,* 30 (3): 213–32.

Kong, R. and AuCoin, K. (2008) 'Female offenders in Canada', *Juristat: Canadian Centre for Justice Statistics,* Catalog 85–002-XIE, 28 (1): 1–23. Accessed April 4, 2012 http://www.statcan.gc.ca/pub/85-002-x/85-002-x2008001-eng.pdf

Layton MacKenzie, D. (2000) 'Evidence-based corrections: identifying what works', *Crime & Delinquency,* 46 (4): 457–471.

Layton MacKenzie, D. (2001) 'Corrections and sentencing in the 21st century: evidence-based corrections and sentencing', *The Prison Journal,* 81 (3): 299–312.

Leacock, V. and Sparks, R. (2002) 'Riskiness and at-risk-ness: some ambiguous features of the current penal landscape', in N. Gray, J. Laing and L. Noaks (eds), *Criminal justice, mental health and the politics of risk.* London: Cavendish Publishing. pp. 199–218.

Lowenkamp, C.T., Latessa, E.J. and Holsinger, A.M. (2004) 'Empirical evidence on the importance of training and experience in using the Level of Service Inventory–Revised'. Retrieved from: http://www.nicic.org/Misc/URLShell.aspx?SRC=Catalog&REFF=http://nicic.org/Library/period274&ID=period274&TYE=PDF&URL=http://www.nicic.org/pubs/2004/period274.pdf

Lynch, M. (1998) 'Waste managers? The new penology, crime fighting and parole agent identity', *Law and Society Review,* 32 (4): 839–870.

Mannheim, H. and Wilkins, L. (1955) *Prediction Methods in Relation to Borstal Training.* London: HMSO.

Manson, A. (1995) 'Accountability and the national parole board', in P. Stenning (ed.), *Accountability for Criminal Justice.* Toronto: University of Toronto Press. pp. 422–449.

Maurutto, P. and Hannah-Moffat, K. (2005) 'Assembling risk and the restructuring of penal control', *British Journal of Criminology,* 45: 1–17.

Maurutto, P. and Hannah-Moffat, K. (2006) 'Assembling risk and the restructuring of penal control', *British Journal of Criminology,* 46 (3): 438–54.

Maurutto, P. and Hannah-Moffat, K. (2007) 'Understanding risk in the context of the Youth Criminal Justice Act', *Canadian Journal of Criminology,* 49 (4): 465–91.

Miller, L. (2001) 'Looking for post modernism in all the wrong places', *British Journal of Criminology,* 41: 168–84.

Monahan, J. (1984) 'The prediction of violent behavior: toward a second generation of theory and policy', *American Journal of Psychiatry,* 141: 10–15.

Monahan, J. (2006) 'A jurisprudence of risk assessment: forecasting harm among prisoners, predators, and patients', *Virginia Law Review,* 92: 391.

Morash, M. (2009) 'A great debate over using the Level of Service Inventory–Revised (LSI-R) with women offenders', *Criminology & Public Policy,* 8: 173–81.

Morash, M., Bynum, T.S. and Koons, B.A. (1998) *Women Offenders: Programming Needs and Promising Approaches.* Washington, DC: USDOJ, National Institute of Justice.

Moretti, M.M., Odgers, C.L. and Jackson, M.A. (2004) *Girls and Aggression: Contributing Factors and Intervention Principles. Vol. 19.* New York: Kluwer Academic/Plenum.

Naughton, M. (2005) 'Evidence-based policy' and the government of the criminal justice system – only if the evidence fits', *Critical Social Policy,* 25 (1): 47–69.

Nelson, P. and Cowburn, M. (2010) 'Social work admissions: applicants with criminal convictions: the challenge of ethical risk assessment', *British Journal of Social Work,* 40 (4): 1081–1099.

Nesbitt, C.A. and Argento, A.R. (1984) *Female Classification: An Examination of the Issues.* College Park, MD: American Correctional Association.

Netter, B. (2007) 'Using groups statistics to sentence individual criminals: an ethical and statistical critique of the Virginia risk assessment program', *Journal of Criminal Law and Criminology,* 97 (3): 699–730.

Ogloff, J.R.P. and Davis, M.R. (2004) 'Advances in offender assessment and rehabilitation: contributions of the risk-needs-responsivity approach', *Psychology, Crime and Law,* 10: 229–42.

O'Malley, P. (1996) 'Risk and responsibility', in A. Barry, T. Osbourne and N. Rose (eds), *Foucault and Political Reason: Liberalism, Neoliberalism and Rationalities of Government.* Chicago, IL: University of Chicago Press. pp. 189–208.

O'Malley, P. (1998) *Crime and the risk society.* Aldershot: Dartmouth.

O'Malley, P (1999) *The Risk Society Implications for Justice and Beyond.* Report Commissioned for the Department of Justice, Victoria, Australia.

O'Malley, P. (2000) 'Risk societies and the government of crime', in M. Brown and J. Pratt (eds), *Dangerous Offenders: Punishment and Social Order.* London: Routledge. pp. 189–208.

O'Malley, P. (2004) *Risk, Uncertainty and Government.* London: Gladstone Press.

O'Malley, P. (2006) 'Criminology and risk', in G. Mythen and S. Walklate (eds), *Beyond the Risk Society: Critical Reflections of Risk and Human Security.* Berkshire: Open University Press.

O'Malley, P. (2008) 'Experiments in risk and criminal justice', *Theoretical Criminology,* 12 (4): 451–469.

O'Malley, P. (2010) *Crime and Risk.* Thousand Oaks: SAGE Publications.

Pager, D. (2003) 'The mark of a criminal record', *American Journal of Sociology,* 108: 937–975.

Palmer, E.J. and Hollin, C.R. (2007) 'The level of service inventory-revised with English women prisoners: a needs and reconviction analysis', *Criminal Justice and Behavior,* 34: 971–984.

Petersilia, J. and Turner, S. (1987) 'Guideline-based justice: prediction and racial minorities', *Crime & Justice,* 9: 151–82.

Phillips, C. (2008) 'Negotiating identities: ethnicity and social relations in a young offenders' institution', *Theoretical Criminology,* 12 (3): 313–331.

Phillips, C. and Earle, R. (2010) '*Reading difference differently? Identity, epistemology and prison ethnography', British Journal of Criminology,* 50 (2): 360–78.

Power, M. (2004) *The Risk Management of Everything: Rethinking the Politics of Uncertainty.* London: Demos.

Pratt, J. (1999) 'Governmentality, neo-liberalism and dangerousness', in R. Smandych (ed.), *Governable Places: Readings on Governmentality and Crime Control.* Sydney: Ashgate Dartmouth. pp. 133–162.

Reichman, N. (1986) 'Managing crime risks: towards an insurance based model of social control', *Research in Law Deviance and Social Control,* 8: 151–172.

Reisig, Michael Holtfreter, Kristy and Morash, Merry (2006) 'Assessing recidivism risk across female pathways to crime', *Justice Quarterly,* 23: 384–405.

Richie, B. (1991) 'Challenges incarcerated women face as they return to their communities: findings from life history interviews', *Crime and Delinquency,* 47: 368–389.

Richie, B. (1996) *Compelled to Crime: The Gender Entrapment of Battered Black Women.* New York: Routledge.

Robinson, G. (1999) 'Risk management and rehabilitation in the probation service: Collision and collusion', *The Howard Journal,* 38 (4): 421–33.

Robinson, G. (2001) 'Power, knowledge and 'what works' in probation', *The Howard Journal,* 40 (3): 235–54.

Robinson, G. (2002) 'Exploring risk management in probation practice: Contemporary developments in England and Wales', *Punishment & Society* 4 (1): 5–25.

Robinson, G. (2003) 'Implementing OASys: Lessons from Research into LSI-R and ACE', *The Probation Journal,* 50 (1): 3–40.

Rose, N. (1996) 'Governing 'advanced' liberal democracies', in A. Barry, T. Osbourne and N. Rose (eds), *Foucault and Political Reason: Liberalism, Neoliberalism and Rationalities of Government.* Chicago: University of Chicago Press. pp. 37–64.

Rose, N. (1998) 'Governing risky individuals: the role of psychiatry in new regimes of control', *Psychiatry, Psychology and the Law,* 5 (2): 177–95.

Rose, N. (2000) 'Government and control', *British Journal of Criminology,* 40 (2): 321–39.

Rose, N. (2002) 'At risk of madness', in T. Baker and J. Simon (eds), *Embracing Risk: The Changing Culture of Insurance and Responsibility.* Chicago: University of Chicago Press. pp. 209–237.

Schneider, A.L., Ervin, L. and Snyder-Joy, Z. (1996) 'Further exploration of the flight from discretion: the role of risk/need instruments in probation supervision decisions', *Journal of Criminal Justice,* 24 (2): 109–121.

Shearing, C. (2001) 'Punishment and the changing face of governance', *Punishment & Society,* 2 (2): 203–220.

Silver, E. and Miller, L. (2002) 'A cautionary note on the use of actuarial risk assessment tools for social control', *Crime and Delinquency,* 48 (1): 138–161.

Simon, J. (1988) 'The ideological effects of actuarial practices', *Law & Society Review,* 22 (4): 771–800.

Simon, J. (1993) *Poor Discipline: Parole and the Social Control of the Underclass 1980–1990.* Chicago: University of Chicago Press.

Simon, J. (1996) 'Criminology and the recidivist', in D. Schichor and D. Schrest (eds), *Three Strikes and You're Out: Vengeance as Public Policy.* London: SAGE Publications. pp. 24–50.

Simon, J. (2005) 'Reversal of fortune: the resurgence of individual risk assessment in criminal justice', *Annual Review of Law and Social Science,* 1: 397–421.

Simon, J. and Baker, T. (2002) *Embracing Risk: The Changing Culture of Insurance and Responsibility.* Chicago: University of Chicago Press.

Skeem, J. (2010) 'Risk Technology in Sentencing: Testing the Promises and Perils (Commentary on Hannah-Moffat, 2010)', Symposium on Sentencing, SUNY Albany (Albany, NY). Available at: http://www.albany.edu/scj/symposium_home.php

Slobogin, C. (2005) 'A jurisprudence of dangerousness', *Northwestern University Law Review,* 98 (1): 1–62.

Stenson, K. and Sullivan, R. (2001) *Crime Risk And Justice: The Politics of Crime Control in Liberal Democracies.* Cullompton: Willan.

Sudbury, J. (ed.) (2005) *Global Lockdown: Race, Gender and the Prison-Industrial Complex.* New York: Routledge.

Taylor, G. (1998) 'Offender needs – providing the focus for our correctional interventions', *Forum On Corrections Research,* 10 (3): 3–8.

Tonry, M. (2009) 'Explanations of American punishment policies: a national history', *Punishment & Society,* 11 (3): 377–94.

Turpin-Petreosino, C. (1999) 'Are limiting enactments effective? An experimental test of decision making in a presumptive parole state', *Journal of Criminal Justice,* 27 (4): 321–32.

United Nations (UN) (2008) *Draft United Nations Rules for the Treatment of Women Prisoners and Non-Custodial Measures for Women Offenders.* Vienna: Commission on Crime Prevention and Criminal Justice, Eighteenth Session. Available at: http://zh.unrol.org/files/ECN152009_CRP8.pdf (accessed 26 February 2011).

Van Voorhis, P. and Presser, L. (2001) *Classification of Women Offenders: A National Assessment of Current Practices.* Washington, DC: USDOJ, National Institute of Corrections.

Van Voorhis, P., Wright, E.M., Salisbury, E., et al. (2010) 'Women's risk factors and their contributions to existing risk/needs assessment: the current status of a gender-responsive supplement', *Criminal Justice and Behavior,* 37 (3): 261–288.

Vose, B., Cullen, F.T. and Smith, P. (2008) 'The empirical status of the level of service inventory', *Federal Probation,* 72: 22–29.

Wakefield, S. and Uggen, C. (2010) 'Incarceration and stratification', *Annual Review of Sociology,* 36: 381–406.

Ward, T. (2002) 'Good lives and the rehabilitation of offenders: promises and problems', *Aggression and Violent Behaviour*, 7: 513–528.

Ward, T. and Brown, M. (2004) 'The good lives model and conceptual issues in offender rehabilitation', *Psychology, Crime & Law,* 10(3): 243–257.

Ward, T. and Stewart, C. (2003) 'Criminogenic needs and human needs: a theoretical critique', *Psychology, Crime and Law*, 9, 3, 125–143.

Ward, T. and Maruna, S. (2007) *Rehabilitation: Beyond the Risk Paradigm.* London: Routledge.

Warren, R.K. (2008) 'Evidence-based sentencing: the application of principles of evidence-based practice to state sentencing practice and policy', *University of San Francisco Law Review*, 43: 585–634.

Western, B. (2002) 'The impact of incarceration on wage mobility and inequality', *American Sociological Review*, 67: 477–98.

Wright, E., Salisbury, E. and van Voorhis, P. (2007) 'Predicting the prison misconducts of women offenders: the importance of gender-responsive needs', *Journal of Contemporary Criminal Justice*, 23: 310–340.

7

Punishment and the Penal Field

Joshua Page

Something is missing. Theoretical explanations of penal change and reproduction are powerful, yet they do not sufficiently explicate how macro-level, social-structural phenomena produce particular criminal punishment outcomes in particular places. The intervening mechanism or mechanisms that translate these large-scale phenomena into actual outcomes are missing. Why is it that states or countries exposed to similar economic developments, levels of crime, political trends, socioeconomic and ethnic-racial inequality, and shifts in sensibilities have variable sentencing laws, imprisonment rates, prison conditions and routines, and the like? The answer clearly has to do with actors. People make decisions that translate into concrete penal policies, programs and priorities. Although people make penal history, 'they do not make it under circumstances chosen by themselves' (to borrow from Karl Marx, 1963: 15). There is a context that structures the decisions that actors make. It links the micro with the macro, helping us understand how large-scale phenomena do or do not translate into penal outcomes. This context – this field – is the subject of this essay.

BOURDIEU AND THE SHAPE OF STRUGGLE

The late sociologist Pierre Bourdieu spent much of his career developing and using the concept of field. Along with the kindred notions of habitus and capital, Bourdieu employed field to understand action – or, as he called it, 'practice' – in various social worlds, including those of education (Bourdieu and Passeron, 1990), politics (Bourdieu, 1999), art (Bourdieu, 1996), economics (Bourdieu, 2005), law (Bourdieu, 1987) and sport (Bourdieu, 1988). He viewed practice as the product of both internal and external factors. People make conscious decisions and act spontaneously or habitually because of their objective position in a social field or fields and their habitus.

A product of socialization and ongoing practice, habitus is an internal set of dispositions that shape perception, appreciation, and action (Bourdieu, 1980: 52; Bourdieu, 1997: 138). These dispositions 'orient individuals at a subconscious level towards the world around them' (Sayer, 2005: 24). Each individual possesses a relatively unique general habitus, for he or she has a particular biography.

An actor also develops a field-specific habitus, particularly after participating in the field for significant time.[1] For example, a skilled academic (i.e. one who successfully plays the scholarly game) has a well-developed academic habitus developed during graduate school (and possibly even before graduate school, as in the case of the academic who has professors for parents) and while earning his or her scholarly stripes as a researcher or professor. Likewise, skilled politicians have a well-tuned political habitus that allows them to effectively navigate the political game. Individuals who lack the dispositions of the effective academic or politician would need to develop them to compete with their more experienced (i.e. better socialized) competitors.

Whereas habitus affects actors from within, fields affect them from without. Bourdieu argued that numerous fields and sub-fields (e.g. the religious field, economic field, academic field, journalistic field, political field, and legal field) constitute contemporary western societies (Bourdieu and Wacquant, 1992: 16–17). A field is a semi-autonomous, relatively bounded sphere of action in which people, groups, and organizations struggle with and against each other. A social field is not a visible, physical entity. It is a theoretical device that helps us understand the relational character of social action. Although not 'real' in the material sense, it is real in its consequences.

Each field has a particular form of capital, a specific resource that actors strive to obtain and use to improve or conserve their position in the field. For example, academics work to gain academic capital by earning doctoral degrees from prestigious universities, publishing articles in top-flight journals or books with high-status presses, winning teaching awards and getting grants (particularly large external grants). With this academic capital, actors get plum jobs at desirable universities and esteemed positions within professional associations. As they become dominant actors within the academic field (or an academic sub-field like criminology), they can help determine the nature of legitimate academic work in their area of expertise – that is, they can influence the nature and conversion rates of academic capital within their disciplines.

Each field also has rules or regularities and taken-for-granted assumptions and values – a field-specific common sense that Bourdieu calls *doxa* (Bourdieu and Wacquant, 1992: 98). All actors in a field believe that the game is worth playing – that is, it is worth the effort to strive to advance in the field. For example, academics believe that publishing articles in scholarly journals is a worthy and necessary activity. Those outside of the field do not comprehend academics' deep desire to publish articles in journals that few people outside of academia read or even know exist. Experienced agents in a field intuitively grasp the mores, expectations and acceptable actions of that field (Bourdieu, 1980: 67). Habitus is what gives them a distinct 'feel for the game' (Bourdieu and Wacquant, 1992: 128).

Bourdieu used two metaphors to describe fields. First, he likened a social field to a *magnetic field*. A field, he explained, is a 'patterned system of objective forces … *a relational configuration endowed with a specific gravity* which it imposes on all the objects and agents which enter it' (Bourdieu and Wacquant, 1992: 17, my emphasis).[2] This gravity has two, interrelated sources. The first is the composition or structure of the field. Each agent (individual, group, or institution) occupies a specific position within the hierarchy of positions in a field. Position is determined by the agent's amount and composition of capital. Each position offers certain (and not other) paths of actions (or 'position takings'). Agents tend to describe their behavior in terms of 'free will' or principle (it was the 'right thing to do') without recognizing that their possible actions are limited because of their position in the field.

The other source of gravity is doxa, the basic, taken-for-granted assumptions and categories that determine what is thinkable and unthinkable (or orthodox and heterodox) in a given field. Although rarely discussed or even recognized by agents in a field, doxa is a deep, enduring cultural phenomenon that circumscribes possible moves actors may make, giving the game a certain logic and order. In this regard, Martin remarks, 'Every particular field has a coherence based on a working consensus as to the nature of the game, and people take predictable sides due to the more general structuring of social space' (2003: 23). Actors who breech the consensus on acceptable behavior within the field (e.g. a criminologist who tries to get tenure by writing novels rather than publishing in academic journals) are viewed as strange (and possibly demented), and, if they maintain their taboo activities, are eventually eliminated from the game altogether.

Bourdieu also drew parallels between a social field and a *battlefield*. The field is a 'locus of struggle to determine the conditions and the criteria of legitimate membership and legitimate hierarchy, that is, to determine which properties are pertinent, effective and liable to function as capital so as to generate specific profits guaranteed by the field' (Bourdieu, 1984: 11). The dominant actors in the field struggle to conserve the game's shape, orienting principles, and criteria for membership (i.e. who is and is not a legitimate player). Competitors, meanwhile, grapple to alter the distribution of capital so as to improve their position in the field. They also attempt to alter the nature and conversion rates of the field-specific capital. For example, academics routinely struggle to define acceptable, status-generating research and publications (e.g. public-oriented accessible books versus academic-oriented technical journal articles). In other words, agents in the academic field (and its sub-fields) countries over the question: What types of research and manuscripts are worthy of publication, credit toward promotion, and recognition within the field? Similar questions about teaching and service are also routinely struggled over. Because a field's architecture (including the boundaries), orienting principles, and even forms of capital are sources of continual, often-fierce struggle, the potential for transformation (or 'social change') always exists within fields.

A third metaphor – that of a *sporting field* – is also useful for understanding Bourdieu's notion of a social field. Like a football, baseball, or basketball field, a social field has rules, positions, and superior and subordinate players (those with more capital – i.e. skill, talent, experience). Moreover, players make moves based on their relation to other players in the game (or expected moves other players will make) and because of ingrained, taken for granted assumptions on how best to score, defend and win. In both sporting and social fields, the most skilled players perform intuitively – they have a refined, deep 'feel for the game'. That feel is due to their sporting habitus, honed through years of practice and competition. The critical difference between sporting and social fields is that the rules, boundaries, positions and stakes in sporting fields are fixed, but those of social fields are continually contested and mutable.

As conceptualized thus far, practice derives from an actor's habitus and position in the field. Where then do macro-level, social structural factors such as economic shifts, political transformation and demographic expansion fit into this theoretical perspective? Bourdieu argues that fields act like prisms and refract external trends (Bourdieu and Wacquant, 1992: 17). In other words, 'external influences are always retranslated into the internal logic of fields. External sources are always mediated through the structure and dynamic of fields' (Swartz, 1997: 128). The extent to which a field refracts external forces according to its specific logic depends on the field's degree of autonomy. So, macro-level, structural trends affect practice (what agents do and what decisions are made). However, they do not do so automatically and without mediation. The composition of actors, taken for granted assumptions and categories, and predominant orientation channel these trends in particular directions, helping us understand why they have variable outcomes in different fields (e.g. academic versus religious) or the same field in different locales (e.g. the academic field in the USA versus the academic field in France).

PUTTING FIELD TO WORK

As noted above, Bourdieu employed the concept of field (and the kindred notions of habitus and capital) to understand practice in a variety of areas. And though he wrote and lectured about the law (or more precisely, the legal field), his focus was not the criminal law or sentencing practices. As Loïc Wacquant (2009: 289) notes, Bourdieu did not analyze the 'right hand of the state' – i.e. the actors, institutions, and practices used to sanction lawbreakers. However, other scholars have drawn on his concept of field to understand penal phenomena in Asia, Australia, Europe, North America and South America. This section describes three general (and somewhat overlapping) ways that scholars have put the concept of field to work.

Comparing crime control fields

Within the sociology of punishment, scholars have used the concept of field mostly for descriptive and comparative purposes – to describe changes in penality over time and between countries. The concept is useful for these purposes because it pushes analysts to examine not only changes in policies, rhetoric, and trends (e.g. imprisonment rates), but also transformations in the principles that orient penal practice, the nature of penal authority and status, the composition of positions in the field, and the relationship between the penal and neighboring fields (e.g. political field).

In *The Culture of Control*, David Garland (2001) describes and explains the reconfiguration of the 'crime control field' in the USA and UK from the 1970s to the present. This field 'is characterized by two interlocking and mutually conditioning patterns of action: the formal controls exercised by the state's criminal justice agencies and the informal social controls that are embedded in everyday activities and interactions in civil society' (Garland, 2001: 5). His conception of the field is expansive because he is concerned with crime control *in toto*, from capital punishment to surveillance techniques in suburban shopping centers.

Garland delineates major changes in the field, including the decline of the rehabilitative ideal; ascent of punitive sanctions, expressive justice, and managerial practices and priorities; centrality of crime victims in penal policymaking; intensive politicization of punishment; growth of penal populations; commercialization of social control; and shifts in criminological discourse. These developments are not simply due to changes in public opinion or high crime rates. Rather, they are associated with 'late modern' developments such as shifts in the economy (e.g., decline of manufacturing and expansion of service and informational sectors), growing and hardening of ethnic-racial and class inequality, changes in family organization and gender relations, enhanced mobility due to technological advances, transformation and increased importance of mass media, and demographic change (e.g., the baby boom and immigration). These social structural developments led to increased crime and intensified middle class insecurity. They also made voters receptive to political claims from the likes of Ronald Reagan, Richard Nixon and Margaret Thatcher that government (particularly social welfare, including rehabilitation) was ineffective and even dangerous, and insufficient 'law and order' was a major problem.

The late modern trends and their consequences (i.e. high crime, middle-class insecurity and disillusionment with government) did not automatically or naturally translate into particular penal outcomes. Rather, they were filtered through the crime control field.

> The field of crime control and criminal justice is a relatively differentiated domain with its own dynamics and its own norms and expectations to which penal agents orient their conduct. The social and economic determinants of 'the outside world' certainly affect the conduct of penal agents (police officers, judges, prison officials, etc.) but they do so indirectly, through the gradual reshaping of the rules of thought and action within a field that has what sociologists call a 'relative autonomy.' Social trends – such as rising rates of crime and feelings of insecurity, economic crises, political shifts from welfarism to neo-liberalism, changing class, race or gender relations, and so on – have to be translated into the folkways of the field before they have an effect there. (Garland, 2001: 24)

Because the field mediates social trends, shifts in policy and rhetoric have not neatly or quickly taken hold on the ground or re-shaped the habitus of penal agents. Rather,

> change has been a matter of *assimilating new elements* (the victim, crime prevention, restorative justice); *altering balances and relations* (between punishment and welfare, state provision, and commercial provision, instrumental means and expressive ends, the rights of offenders and the protection of the public); and *changing the field's relation to its environment* (above all its relation to the political process, to public opinion, and to crime-control activities of civil society. (Garland, 2001: 174, original emphases)

This last point is very important. The crime control field changed in relationship to neighboring fields. For example, as politicians increasing became involved in the crime and punishment game, they decreased the autonomy of the crime control field and shaped penal policies and priorities according to political considerations. As such, traditional experts in the field (e.g. penologists, criminologists, judges and leaders of penal agencies) lost the authority to shape penal outcomes.

Since the publication of *The Culture of Control*, other scholars have used the notion of crime control field to describe reconfigurations of penality in various parts of the world, including Latin American, Spain and Japan (Medina-Ariza, 2006; Johnson, 2007; Iturralde, 2008, 2010). For example, David Johnson (2007) analyzes claims that Japan, a country known for low crime and a generally lenient criminal justice system, has become less safe and increasingly punitive. He documents changes in the 'orthodoxy' of the crime control field. The old orthodoxy proudly emphasized Japan's relative safeness, reliance on informal social controls to deal with deviance and crime, and restraint of its penal arm. On the contrary, the new orthodoxy 'holds that since citizens of the country are at much greater risk of victimization than they used to be, they are right to feel insecure, and they are justified in demanding that their elected representatives do more to protect them from the dangers lurking around them' (Johnson, 2007: 375).

Johnson finds little empirical support for the new orthodoxy. Nevertheless, the changing orientation within the field has contributed to parallel shifts in penal law, practices and policies. For example, Japan has increased its use of the death penalty; implemented laws that lengthen prison terms; criminalized conduct that previously was not subject to formal punishment; and instituted more aggressive policing practices. Japan's imprisonment rate nearly doubled between 1990 and 2005 (from 32 per 100,000 to 60 per 100,000) and the country's prisons became overcrowded (Johnson, 2007: 382–3). As in the USA and UK, increased punitiveness in Japan has been accompanied by other changes in the field, such as the decline of the rehabilitative ideal, growing importance of crime victims in the penal process, commercialization of crime control, and spreading of management styles and ideologies indicative of the new penology (Johnson, 2007: 395). Taken together, Johnson argues that Japan 'does seem to be taking steps in the Anglo-American direction' (2007: 395).

Penality in Japan may have more in common with Anglo-American countries than it previously did, however, it is still far less punitive than places like the USA and UK. For example, Japan's imprisonment rate is small compared to that of the USA and UK. At 60 prisoners per 100,000 residents,

Japan's rate is not even half as large as the state of Maine, which has the smallest imprisonment rate (130 per 100,000) of the American states (Sabol and Couture, 2008: 17). It is also less than half the rate in England and Wales of 159 per 100,000 (Adams, 2010).

Johnson shows that Japan faces many of the same 'late modern' trends that Garland sees as fueling penal changes in the USA and UK. He also shows that penality has become increasingly politicized in Japan. However, Japan's crime control field seems to refract those trends in ways that make penality in the island country both similar to *and* different from that in Anglo-American countries. Japan's comparative restraint (at least in terms of imprisonment), I would hypothesize, is due principally to the uniqueness of its crime control field. It its likely that the crime control field's old orthodoxy, which privileged informal over formal social control of deviance and crime, continues to hold sway within the field – even in the face of an encroaching 'culture of control.' Moreover, it is likely that agents who promote the old orthodoxy remain relatively influential in the field.

In general, scholars have used the concept of crime control field to *describe* reconfigurations of criminal punishment in particular regions of the world. However, they suggest that social analysts can use the concept to help *explain* such changes. As Garland argues, the field directs social-structural 'determinants' in particular directions. Although countries such as the USA, UK and Japan have experienced similar trends in criminal punishment in recent decades, penality is considerably different in all three nations. Close analyses of the composition of orientation of the penal fields in these countries, would help us understand this variation – and connect the macro-level trends Garland describes so well to the micro-level decisions that produce penal outcomes on the ground. To move from description to explanation would require scholars to systematically articulate the relationships between positions in the field, detail which actors occupy those positions, and delineate the dispositional orientations of those actors.

The context of penal culture and practice

Scholarship on crime control fields focuses on large-scale shifts in sentiments, rationalities, practices and policies. Scholars, such as Garland and Johnson, suggest that the shape and culture of these fields influences penal actors' habitus and behavior at both the individual and group levels. However, they do not investigate how contemporary crime control fields (or their sub-fields) affect agents' subjective orientation to penal practice. In other words, they do not concretely show if or how reconfigurations of crime control fields play out in practice.

Other scholars have begun to fill this void.[3] Fergus McNeill and his colleagues, for instance, use the concept of field to understand the orientation and behavior of contemporary criminal justice social workers in Scotland. These workers prepare pre-sentencing reports for judges in the Scottish courts. (Although Scotland is part of the UK, it has its own legal and criminal justice system.) In particular, the authors seek to 'elucidate how discourses and practices of risk (a key feature of the new penology) are constructed in the production of pre-sentence reports' (McNeill et al., 2009: 420). As expected, they find that criminal justice social workers face formal and informal pressures to focus on risk assessment and protection of the public (rather than on offenders' moral character, needs and potential for rehabilitation) in their interviews and reports. These pressures, however, do not dictate the workers' practice:

> Despite the increasing emphasis on risk assessment in policy documents, inspection regimes and (to a lesser extent) in workers' practice discourses, even where risk assessments were included in reports, risk assessment remained a fairly peripheral concern in most cases – or at least it was

> not an explicit concern of most of the reports. Rather ... the principal focus of social enquiry seemed to be on assessing the offenders' responsibility, character, attitudes, motivation to change and likely compliance with community sanctions. (McNeill et al., 2009: 428)

The pre-sentence reports are like quilts, layered with elements of the new penology (managerialism) and old penology (penal-welfarism).

To understand criminal justice social workers' practice, McNeill et al. examine the employees' social position. As their job title indicates, criminal justice social workers occupy a position at the intersection of the social work and penal fields. Hence, they are subject to pressures from both fields. On the one hand, 'penal policy and public debates lead social workers to believe that their welfare affiliations are a liability that must be offset by adapting to a risk management and protection ethos' (McNeill et al., 2009: 434). Using managerial rhetoric and techniques, the workers receive recognition and capital within the penal field (because of their marginal position in the penal field, they have to prove their worth to more dominant actors, particularly judges). On the other hand, social work training, policies and practices promote welfarism – in this case, penal-welfarism. Focusing solely, or even principally, on risk and public protection is taboo in the social work field. The criminal justice social workers' habitus and practice reflect the tension between the penal and social work fields. (In making this argument, the authors highlight an important point: there is struggle *between* fields, not just within them.)

This study skillfully shows that penal trends affect individual and collective agents differently depending on their habitus and position in the field (or fields, as is the case with the criminal justice social workers). On this topic, the authors argue, 'For different penal actors with different histories in the field and different sources of capital, transformations are differently paced, configured and experienced, and differently accommodated, resisted and subverted' (McNeill et al., 2009: 436). McNeill et al. affirm one of Bourdieu's central theoretical claims: the structural location of actors affects agents' subjective orientations and actions – regardless of the agents' personal characteristics.

Like the study of criminal justice social workers, other research on ground level penal practice reveals evidence of both the old and new penologies, of penal modernism and postmodernism. For example, parole agents and staff in female prisons use rhetoric and engage in conduct that is simultaneously rehabilitative, managerial and punitive (Lynch, 2000; Kruttschnitt and Gartner, 2005). Field analysis, as McNeill et al. suggest, helps us understand what, on the surface, may seem contradictory. As discussed above, agents in a field share principles, assumptions and beliefs, which take time to develop and uproot. And while the dispositions that constitute habitus are flexible and capable of change, they are also quite durable. They do not change rapidly or easily (nor do the institutions, rationalities and practices that developed during earlier penal areas in accordance with a particular penal orientation, the rehabilitative ideal). So, although the field of crime control has changed dramatically in recent decades, neither the 'culture of control' nor the 'new penology' have fully taken root in the heads and habits of penal agents – the people responsible for implementing the 'new crime control arrangements' (Garland, 2001: 204). It is not surprising, therefore, that agents in the field can, and often do, simultaneously promote helping (even rehabilitating) individuals *and* managing and punishing groups of offenders defined in terms of dangerousness. These agents are not disingenuous. They are part of a field in transition.

Interest groups and the penal field

In my analysis of the California Correctional Peace Officers Association (CCPOA), the extremely successful and powerful labor union that represents prison officers and other correctional employees in California, I employ the concept of penal field to understand the ascent of the CCPOA and related organizations and delineate their effects on penal policies and priorities. My larger aim was to extend understandings of interest groups and penal change and stability (Page, 2011).

I define the penal field as the social space in which agents struggle to accumulate and employ penal capital – the legitimate authority to determine penal policies and priorities. The penal field intersects the bureaucratic, political and legal fields, and it neighbors the economic, academic and journalistic fields. It includes agents (people, groups and organizations) that participate in and affect these struggles and the rhetoric, signs and symbols that are both weapons in and products of the struggles that take place in this social microcosm. The penal field contains various sub-fields, such as the fields of imprisonment, policing, probation and parole. As with all sub-fields, those in the penal field have their 'own logic, rules and regularities' (Bourdieu and Wacquant, 1992: 104).

My conception of the penal field is different from Garland's notion of the crime control field because Garland and I focus on distinct problems. Whereas Garland seeks to understand changes in formal and informal social control, I focus specifically on the relationships between organizations and state-level penal policies and priorities. This distinction in our conceptions of field highlights a key analytical point: analysts construct fields to answer concrete empirical questions (Bourdieu and Wacquant, 1992: 31). Conceptions of the penal field will vary depending on scholars' object(s) of analysis, as well as level of analysis (e.g. nation versus state). Hence, there is not *a* definition of penal field (or crime control field) that is universally applicable.

The concepts of penal field and imprisonment field (or sub-field) were very helpful to understanding the CCPOA's social trajectory and character. Prison officers started the CCPOA to obtain higher wages, better benefits and respect. They also sought to improve their lowly positions in the imprisonment and penal fields. (Officers' low wages, shoddy benefits and lack of respect were due in large part to their subordinate positions in these fields.)

During the 'Era of Treatment' in California (roughly 1944–76), legitimate authority in the imprisonment field was based primarily on penological expertise developed through training in colleges and professional schools (e.g. social work) or administrative experience in prisons and other penal institutions. 'Correctional experts' (as defined by credentials and other indicators of penological expertise) had extensive authority over imprisonment and related practices like parole (McGee, 1981; Simon, 1993; McCarty, 2004). Consequently, these actors occupied a relatively dominant position in the imprisonment field. They helped shield carceral policy from actors inside and outside of the field who criticized the practice and philosophy of rehabilitation and attempted to shape penal policy according to non-penological criteria – for example, politics. These experts provided 'scientific' evidence that bolstered the prevailing ideas of crime and punishment and helped fend off threats from actors who did not possess penological expertise.

At the same time, the government hired large numbers of 'treatment staff' – including social workers, psychiatrists, psychologists, educators and sociologists – to work alongside prison officers in the state's penal facilities (Irwin, 1980). Because of their ostensible penological expertise (or willingness to develop that expertise through work experience) and their responsibility for implementing rehabilitative practices, treatment staff occupied a position in the imprisonment field slightly higher than custody staff, who typically lacked penological credentials.

During the 1960s, the federal courts made several landmark decisions regarding prisoners' rights and prison conditions and practices, which firmly placed them within the imprisonment field. These decisions opened the floodgates to prison litigation, making prisoner rights' attorneys important actors in the field. Toward the late 1960s, as the 'radical prison movement' gained steam in California, activist organizations also became actors within this social arena (Cummins, 1994).

In the decades following the Second World War, prison officers were subordinate actors in California's imprisonment field. Although 'prison guards' were renamed 'correctional officers,' rank-and-file staff generally were not viewed as having penological expertise, were not included in policy discussions, and had little authority inside the prisons and no authority in the state capitol. Officers became very resentful of their lack of status behind the walls – especially vis-à-vis treatment staff and the new breed of professional managers – and their inability to affect prison routines, practices and conditions, which became increasingly violent, hectic and unpredictable during the late 1960s and 1970s. Officers were also angered because they believed that prison officials, state bureaucrats and federal judges cared more about prisoners and their rights than officers and their needs.

It was in this particular context in which the CCPOA was forged. From the start, the union was pugilistic, militant and independent (it was a union *of* and *for* prison officers with no connections to the American Federation of Labor and Congress of Industrial Organizations or 'labor movement'). It was also fiercely anti-management, anti-federal courts, anti-prisoner rights and anti-rehabilitation. The CCPOA sought to return authority inside the prisons to line staff and old-time administrators (those who rose up through the ranks), toughen prison conditions, and harden sentencing and other penal policies. It wanted to re-masculine criminal punishment, which its leaders felt had become problematically feminine. The union, therefore, was not simply (or even mainly) motivated by material considerations. It was also driven by ideological commitments, which were shaped in a particular structural environment. We cannot understand the CCPOA's characteristics and trajectory without situating prison officers within the 'network of relations' – the field – in which they toiled from the mid-1940s to the 1970s.

The CCPOA became a powerful and very successful union during the 1990s, due in large part to changes in the penal field. In the 1970s and 1980s, the penal field became increasingly politicized as legislators made 'law and order' a central political issue and showed they were 'tough on crime' by hardening penal policy. The politicization of crime and punishment in general and imprisonment in particular increased the status of law enforcement groups like the CCPOA. As the union gained symbolic capital, legislators and electoral candidates sought the union's endorsement. More importantly, politicization of the penal field led to a massive prison boom as legislators passed laws that lengthened prison terms and mandated imprisonment for numerous types of offenses (many of which previously earned prisoners probation or other non-custodial sanctions). As the prison population climbed and the state built numerous new penitentiaries, California hired thousands of new officers who became members of the CCPOA. Hence, the prison explosion both increased the union's membership roles and padded its financial coffers. The CCPOA, then, converted its economic windfall into political capital. In short, changes in the penal field – especially the incredible prison growth – produced ripe conditions for the CCPOA's ascent.

Since becoming a dominant agent in the imprisonment and penal fields, the CCPOA has greatly affected these fields' shape and orientation. For example, the union has encouraged some and discouraged other politicians (for example, those who support private imprisonment or oppose 'Three Strikes and You're Out') from participating in the field. Since the 1980s, the CCPOA has rewarded lawmakers who advance its positions on criminal punishment issues with lavish campaign contributions and endorsements. The union's support has been an incentive for politicians to participate in the penal game – on the side of CCPOA, of course. In emboldening politicians to take positions on imprisonment issues, the CCPOA has contributed to the politicization of the penal field.

The CCPOA has also altered the composition of the penal field by helping to create politicized, punitive crime victims' groups. CCPOA-allied organizations are indisputably the most influential crime victims' groups in California, if not all of the USA. It is extremely difficult to overestimate the effect of these groups in the penal and imprisonment fields, for they help determine what is and is not even *possible* in terms of reform. Politicians, state officials, and other actors in the fields orient their actions in relation to CCPOA-related victims' groups. Because of the organizations' moral authority and resources (which are provided mainly by the CCPOA and other law enforcement groups), lawmakers deem certain reforms (e.g., decreasing prison sentences for violent criminals) simply 'unthinkable'.

In addition to affecting the composition of the imprisonment and penal fields, the CCPOA has shaped dominant conceptions about crime and punishment that orient action in these fields. For example, the union has contributed to the view that offenders are rational actors who simply make bad choices or, worse yet, are 'natural born criminals'. Based on these conceptions of criminal action, the union has added to the general perception that 'prison works' – that is, that hyper-imprisonment drastically reduces crime through deterrence and incapacitation (hence the CCPOA's unflagging commitment to 'Three Strikes' and similar mandatory-minimum policies).

The CCPOA also has promoted the perception that adult and youth prisons are perpetually chaotic, violent and dangerous facilities filled with incorrigible, predatory offenders that are more animal than human. The CCPOA claims that prison officers work the 'toughest beat' because, unlike officers on the street, prison officers must deal with dangerous convicted felons 24 hours a day, 7 days a week. Put differently, the 'toughest beat' is reportedly *so* tough because of prisoners' allegedly depraved nature. A street officer's beat, according to this logic, is 'soft' because street officers deal primarily with people who are not felons (this is particularly true of highway patrol officers, the CCPOA claims). The CCPOA's strategy to enhance its officers' professional image, status and compensation depends on the public, press and politicians believing that California prisoners are the 'worst of the worst'. This vision of prisoners inspires and justifies mandatory-minimum sentencing laws; initiatives to decrease prisoners' rights, amenities and opportunities; and funding for super-maximum-security prisons.

The CCPOA also projects and reinforces the notion that prisoners and victims are enemies locked in a fierce, eternal grudge match in which one side must win and the other must lose. This division underpins policies that allegedly help victims and their families while hurting prisoners. This zero-sum view is inherently punitive: to help victims is to hurt offenders and vice versa. Proponents automatically reject non-punitive or less punitive conceptions of justice such as restorative justice, which focuses on repairing the harm prisoners cause to victims, communities and themselves. Seen within this narrow, zero-sum vision, advocates of restorative justice not only appear quixotic, but deranged. It is, after all, impossible to imagine prisoners (and ex-prisoners) and victims (not just individual victims, but also family members and communities affected by crime) coming together to repair the harm that lawbreakers cause if offenders and victims are perpetual enemies.

The CCPOA and its allies have also helped re-define penal expertise. They criticize psychologists, criminologists, social workers, sociologists, treatment professionals, legal scholars and (most) judges as counterfeit experts. These groups, the union contends, lack direct insight into crime; they do not have *real life experiences of crime*. Instead, it is argued, victimization provides crime victims and their family members with real life expertise, representing crime victims in court makes prosecutors experts, and routinely viewing the consequences of crime gives street and prison officers special insight into crime and public policy. Thus, the CCPOA and related groups have helped establish a new variant of capital – one based on 'real life expertise' – that has become extremely valuable within the penal field.

The division between traditional experts and 'real life' experts has serious consequences in the 'real world'. Because of their alleged penal expertise, punitive crime victims and former law enforcement workers fill the ranks of consequential boards and commissions (e.g. the Board of Prison Terms). Politicians, journalists and state officials solicit their opinions about penal matters. 'Real life experts' now have extensive authority to shape penal thinking and policies in California. Traditional experts, conversely, who largely guided penal thinking in the rehabilitative era, have been remarkably absent from policy debates for much of the last several decades.[4] The CCPOA has supported and, at times, orchestrated this shift of power from traditional experts to 'real life experts'.

The CCPOA by no means created the categories, discourses and images about crime and punishment that pervade the penal field. Nor is the union the only agent that promotes them. Along with its allies, however, the CCPOA has pushed them consistently and with gusto. Because of the union and its counterparts' dominant positions in the penal and related fields, the visions they champion are efficacious.

The fact that interest groups like the CCPOA shape the penal field (and its sub-fields) is analytically important because the field ultimately determines what is possible and impossible as concerns criminal punishment. As previously discussed, fields are like prisms – they refract macro-level trends in areas such as economics, politics, demographics and crime. The set of relations and principles that constitute the penal field, then, determines how jurisdictions respond to these trends. Because states have varying penal fields, they may not react to these social trends in the same ways. In order to understand why one state (or county or federal government) responds to structural trends in a particular manner, we must comprehend the composition and orientation of its own penal field.

A THEORETICAL STANCE TOWARD PUNISHMENT

Bourdieu insisted time and again that he developed concepts out of practical necessity, to understand concrete questions about the social world. In this regard, Bourdieu's longtime collaborator Loïc Wacquant writes of the late sociologist, 'His own relation to concepts is a pragmatic one: he treats them as "tool kits" (Wittgenstein) designed to help him solve problems' (Bourdieu and Wacquant, 1992: 31). Bourdieu did not strive to develop grand theory that explains everything; he sought to advance a theoretical stance, a middle-range perspective that emphasizes the fundamentally *relational* nature of practice (Merton, 1968). This stance or perspective assumes certain things about the social world (such as *everything is relational*) and pushes researchers to ask certain types of questions as they make sense of that world.

The concept of field is useful to scholars who study criminal punishment precisely because it forces us to ask certain questions when analyzing penal phenomena. For example, when examining policy outcomes such as sentencing laws, implementation and make-up of a sentencing commission, or authorization of private prisons, it is necessary to ask which actors are involved (and, importantly, not involved) in the struggle over the policy matter and what is the relation between these actors' positions in the field. To situate the competitors in relation to each other, we need empirical indicators of the actors' respective composition and volume of capital. And, it is necessary to identify alliances on the various sides of the issue, seeing how agents combine (or do not combine) resources.

The composition of the fight over a penal policy is key to the outcome of the struggle. Not only does the shape of struggle help us understand the results of the battle, it helps us understand why the actors take certain positions in that fight (for, as previously stated, players in a field orient their actions to other relevant actors in that social space). How agents frame their positions depends, in part, on the composition of the fight. Framing also depends on the prevailing principles and beliefs in the field, which determine what is currently thinkable or unthinkable, realistic or unrealistic. (Since relations of power and prevailing assumptions shape outcomes, whether a policy is feasible, will 'work,' save money, or achieve other practical ends may be immaterial to the policy's fate. Moreover, the policy's potential effectiveness is itself a source of struggle in the field.)

Similar types of questions need to be posed to understand the dispositions and behavior of penal agents. An agent's demographic characteristics and biography do not tell the whole story. We must also understand their position in the field or fields in which they ply their trade (as seen with the criminal justice social workers, agents may occupy positions in multiple fields, which may lead to conflicts for the agents). What are the knowledge, practical purposes, assumptions, and typical moves associated with that position or positions? What is the relationship between this position and others in the field (subordinate, dominant, level)? As discussed in the example of the CCPOA, an agent's past position in a field affects its current dispositions and behavior. Therefore, we must examine possible changes in the player's position over time. Field analysis, in short, insists that we cannot understand practice solely as the product of individual attributes. Like policy outcomes, agents' rhetoric, beliefs, taken-for-granted assumptions and behavior are forged in a 'network of relations that assign its most distinctive properties' (Bourdieu and Wacquant, 1992: 228).

Put simply, penal decisions are the outcomes of struggle within a relatively bounded social space, the penal field. However, these struggles occur *in relation* to 'the social and economic determinants of the "outside world"', to quote Garland (2001: 24). For instance, economic decline and budget shortfalls may lead to calls for shrinking penal systems (as is currently the case in many American states), initiating struggles within the penal field over if and how to achieve shrinkage. Ethnic and racial divisions also permeate the penal field, as actors in the field tap into racial prejudice and fear to advance their agendas. Demographic and crime trends also affect the nature and outcome of struggle within the field – for example, players use upticks in crime to justify demands for harsher sentences or intensified preventative measures. 'Critical events' such as heinous crimes, acts of terrorism and war also factor into the field – such as when a sensational murder provides a 'window of opportunity' for players to gather support for radical sentencing reforms (Tonry, 2004). In brief, macro-level trends and critical events undoubtedly affect practice in the penal field (it is also true that practice in the field affects broader trends, such as ethnic and racial division). However, the architecture and orientation of the penal field ultimately determine if and how these trends and events produce particular outcomes.

Practice in the penal field also occurs in relation to developments in neighboring fields. For example, the ascent of 'law and order' and tendency to 'govern through crime' in the political field greatly affects practice in the penal field (Beckett, 1999; Simon, 2007; Wacquant, 2009).[5] Criminal justice practitioners increasingly must justify and mold their practices in terms of punishment and risk management (rather than rehabilitation). Political capital is now more important than penological or criminological expertise.

Politicians and interest groups such as the CCPOA tend to dominate struggles in the penal field over sentencing, prison operations, community sanctions and the like. It is important to note that players in the field also use institutions in the political field (e.g., the ballot initiative in some American states) in their struggles to determine the nature and scope of criminal punishment (Barker, 2009).

The theoretical stance I propose complements (or extends) leading sociological perspectives on penal change – whether Durkheimian, Eliasian, Foucauldian or Marxian. Structural factors such as forms of social organization and solidarity, sentiments and sensibilities, power regimes and economic trends (e.g. shifts in the labor market) both shape and are shaped by punishment (Garland, 1990). These factors do not directly affect penality. They are first processed through particular penal fields. Hence, because the field mediates structural developments, it makes sense that countries or states that experience the same macro-level trends (e.g. neoliberal economics or major shifts in social sensibilities) do not have the same penal outcomes.

Classical theories of penal transformation operate at a high level of abstraction, with little, if any, attention to struggles between actual people, organizations or institutions. The middle-range concept of penal field forces us to take relations of actors seriously, to examine how the structure and basic rules and assumptions of the penal game affect penal outcomes. It also pushes us to examine how macro-level trends, critical events, and developments in neighboring fields play out in particular penal fields and their sub-fields. Because penal fields vary, we would expect these trends, events, and developments to produce variable outcomes across time and place. Of course, only systematic comparative research can determine the validity of this prediction. Such research can assess my central thesis: The penal field is the 'something missing' described at the beginning of this paper, an analytical construct capable of linking macro to micro phenomena and social structure to practice.

ACKNOWLEDGEMENTS

I would like to thank Jonathan Simon and Richard Sparks for their insightful suggestions and encouragement, Gretchen Purser for reading several drafts and providing pointed feedback, Letta Page for editing the manuscript, and Loïc Wacquant for introducing me to field theory and challenging me to put it to work. I am grateful to the late Pierre Bourdieu for developing useful conceptual and methodological tools.

NOTES

1 An actor may develop more than one field-specific habitus if he or she participates fully in multiple fields. For example, Loïc Wacquant (2004) exhibits both an academic habitus and a pugilistic habitus after years as a practicing sociologist and boxer. However, his academic habitus is far more developed than his pugilistic habitus because he was immersed in the academic field longer and prior to becoming a boxer.

2 Bourdieu's insistence that fields are objective structures with *magnetic force* distinguishes field from similar concepts like 'policy domain' or 'policy environment'. For an overview of these related concepts see Baumgartner and Leech (1998).

3 For example, Janet Chan argues that the 'policing field' shapes contemporary policing culture in New South Wales, Australia: 'police cultural practice results from the interaction between the socio-political context of police work and various dimensions of police organizational knowledge' (1996: 110). Amy Lerman and I argue that prison officers in California have more punitive views about imprisonment than prison officers in Minnesota because California's penal field is more ideologically polarized and politicized than Minnesota's (Lerman and Page, 2011). Factors internal *and* external to prisons affect prison officers' attitudes about imprisonment and related topics.

4 There is some evidence that traditional experts are slowly regaining some clout within California's penal field. Because of judicial interventions and the state's dire fiscal situation, public officials are searching for ways to decrease prison overcrowding and

the bloated correctional budget. Out of necessity, they have turned to professional criminologists to find ways to cut the prison population without jeopardizing public safety. For example, criminologists have been brought in to implement risk assessment tools for parole release and to develop 'evidence based' in-prison and post-release programs (see, for example, Petersilia, 2008).

5 Of course, trends in other fields affect practice in the penal field. Obsessive coverage of crime by actors in the journalistic field, development of private prisons companies in the economic field, the dominance of certain criminological perspectives in the academic field, the refusal of judges to enforce mandatory-minimum sentences in the juridical field, and budgetary crises in the bureaucratic field all potentially affect the character and outcome of struggles within the penal field.

REFERENCES

Adams, William Lee (2010) 'Britain's prisons: will spending cuts cause crime?', *Time*, 1 July. Available at: http://www.time.com/time/world/article/0,8599,2000666,00.html (accessed 20 September 2010).

Barker, Vanessa (2009) *The Politics of Imprisonment: How the Democratic Process Shapes the Way America Punishes Offenders*. New York: Oxford University Press.

Baumgartner, Frank and Leech, Beth (1998) *Basic Interests: The Importance of Groups in Politics and in Political Sciences*. Princeton, NJ: Princeton University Press.

Beckett, Katherine (1999) *Making Crime Pay: Law and Order in Contemporary American Politics*. New York: Oxford University Press.

Bourdieu, Pierre (1980) *The Logic of Practice*. Palo Alto, CA: Stanford University Press.

Bourdieu, Pierre (1984) *Home Academicus*. Palo Alto, CA: Stanford University Press.

Bourdieu, Pierre (1987) 'The force of law: toward a sociology of the juridical field', *Hastings Law Journal*, 38: 209–48.

Bourdieu, Pierre (1988) 'Program for a sociology of sport', *Sociology of Sport Journal*, 5 (2): 153–61.

Bourdieu, Pierre (1996) *The Rules of Art: Genesis and Structure of the Literary Field*. Palo Alto, CA: Stanford University Press.

Bourdieu, Pierre (1997) *Pascalian Meditations*. Palo Alto, CA: Stanford University Press.

Bourdieu, Pierre (1999) *Language and Symbolic Power*. Cambridge, MA: Harvard University Press.

Bourdieu, Pierre (2005) *Social Structures of the Economy*. Cambridge: Polity.

Bourdieu, Pierre and Passeron, Jean-Claude (1990) *Reproduction in Education, Society and Culture*. Newbury Park, CA: SAGE Publications.

Bourdieu, Pierre and Wacquant, Loïc (1992) *An Invitation to Reflexive Sociology*. Chicago: University of Chicago Press.

Chan, Janet (1996) 'Changing Police Culture', *British Journal of Criminology*, 36 (1): 109–34.

Cummins, Eric (1994) *The Rise and Fall of California's Radical Prison Movement*. Palo Alto, CA: Stanford University Press.

Garland, David (1990) *Punishment and Modern Society: A Study in Social Theory*. Chicago: University of Chicago Press.

Garland, David (2001) *The Culture of Control: Crime and Social Order in Contemporary Society*. Chicago: University of Chicago Press.

Irwin, John (1980) *Prisons in Turmoil*. Boston, MA: Little, Brown and Company.

Iturralde, Manuel (2008) 'Emergency penality and authoritarian liberalism: recent trends in Colombian criminal policy', *Theoretical Criminology*, 12 (3): 377–97.

Iturralde, Manuel (2010) 'Democracies without citizenship: crime and punishment in Latin America', *New Criminal Law Review*, 13 (2): 309–32.

Johnson, David (2007) 'Crime and punishment in contemporary Japan', *Crime and Justice: A Review of Research*, 36: 371–423.

Kruttschnitt, Candace and Gartner, Rosemary (2005) *Marking Time in the Golden State: Women's Imprisonment in California*. New York: Cambridge University Press.

Lerman, Amy and Page, Joshua (2011) 'The state of the job: an embedded work role perspective on prison officer attitudes'. Working paper.

Lynch, Mona (2000) 'Rehabilitation as rhetoric: the ideal of reformation in contemporary discourse and practice', *Punishment & Society*, 2 (1): 40–65.

Martin, John Levi (2003) 'What is field theory?', *American Journal of Sociology*, 109: 1–49.

Marx, Karl (1963) *The Eighteenth Brumaire of Louis Bonaparte*. New York: International Publishers.

McCarty, Heather Jane (2004) 'From con-boss to gang lord: the transformation of social relations in California prisons, 1943–1983'. PhD dissertation, University of California, Berkeley.

McGee, Richard (1981) *Prisons and Politics*. Lexington, MA: Lexington Books.

McNeill, Fergus, Burns, Nicola, Halliday, Simon, Hutton, Neil and Tata, Cyrus (2009) 'Risk, responsibility and reconfiguration: penal adaptation and misadaptation', *Punishment & Society,* 11 (14): 419–42.

Medina-Ariza, Juanjo (2006) 'Politics of crime in Spain, 1978–2004', *Punishment & Society,* 8 (2): 183–201.

Merton, Robert (1968) *Social Theory and Social Structure.* New York: The Free Press.

Page, Joshua (2011) *The Toughest Beat: Politics, Punishment, and the Prison Officers Union in California.* New York: Oxford University Press.

Petersilia, Joan (2008) 'Influencing public policy: an embedded criminologist reflects on California prison reform', *Journal of Experimental Criminology,* 4 (4): 335–56.

Sabol, William and Couture, Heather (2008) *Prison Inmates at Midyear 2007.* Washington, DC: USA Department of Justice, Bureau of Justice Statistics.

Sayer, Andrew (2005) *The Moral Significance of Class.* Cambridge: Cambridge University Press.

Simon, Jonathan (1993) *Poor Discipline: Parole and the Social Control of the Underclass, 1890–1990.* Chicago: University of Chicago Press.

Simon, Jonathan (2007) *Governing Through Crime: How the War on Crime Transformed American Democracy and Created a Culture of Fear.* New York: Oxford University Press.

Swartz, David (1997) *Culture & Power: The Sociology of Pierre Bourdieu.* Chicago: University of Chicago Press.

Tonry, Michael (2004) *Thinking about Crime: Sense and Sensibility in American Penal Culture.* New York: Oxford University Press.

Wacquant, Loïc (2004) *Body & Soul: Notebooks of an Apprentice Boxer.* New York: Oxford University Press.

Wacquant, Loïc (2009) *Punishing the Poor: The Neoliberal Government of Social Insecurity.* Durham, NC: Duke University Press.

PART II

Mass Imprisonment and Inequality

8

Punishment and Inequality

Christopher Muller and
Christopher Wildeman

INTRODUCTION

The study of punishment and inequality is hardly new. Since the dawn of social scientific research on punishment, scholars have rehearsed the point that to enter a nation's prisons is to dwell among its poorest, least educated, most socially isolated and dishonored. As early as 1939, sociologists Rusche and Kirchheimer (1939 [2005]: 6) could conclude with little controversy that, 'the mere statement that specific forms of punishment correspond to a given state of economic development is a truism'. In the 70 years since their seminal *Punishment and Social Structure*, social scientists have time and again empirically confirmed their conclusion that social inequality in the world outside the prison strongly predicts the distribution of inmates inside it.

Formally speaking, studies of punishment and inequality until recently have been studies of the effects of inequality in socioeconomic and marital status on inequality in criminal punishment. Almost exclusively they have focused on a single link, depicted in Figure 8.1, that between inequality at T_1 and punishment at T_2.

In the last 15 years, however, largely in response to changes in the penal system itself, research on punishment and inequality has taken a turn in a new direction. Rather than focus on how social inequalities express themselves in the prison population, it has instead examined how punishment itself might exacerbate those inequalities. The new generation of research on punishment and inequality, in other words, concerns itself primarily with the link between punishment at T_2 and inequality at T_3.

The new path of prison research promises its own opportunities and pitfalls. Empirical researchers steeped in counterfactual thinking conceive of incarceration as a quasi-experimental treatment – one that affects its recipients in two ways (Pager, 2007).[1] Compared to many other types of treatment evaluated in the social sciences, a prison dosage is strong. Prison subjects inmates to confinement and isolation (Haney, 2006; Gawande, 2009), on the one hand, and contact with others similarly disadvantaged (Pettit and Western, 2004) or criminally inclined (Sykes, 1958), on the other. With a median sentence of 36 months, it takes place over a substantial duration. Moreover, it

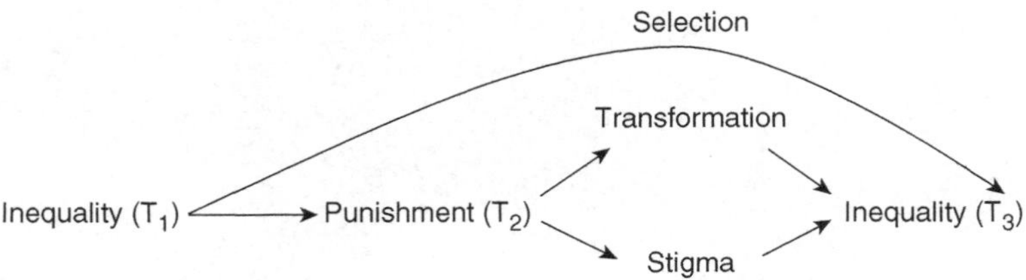

Figure 8.1 Previous studies of punishment and inequality focused on the link between inequality in socioeconomic and marital status at T_1 and inequality in punishment at T_2. The new literature focuses on the link between inequality in punishment at T_2 and its effect on inequality in socioeconomic and marital status at T_3. This literature identifies two primary mechanisms by which inequality in punishment might exacerbate inequality in socioeconomic and marital status: the transformation and the stigmatization of inmates. However, because the distribution of inmates is affected by the distributions of socioeconomic and marital status in the population, inequality might have widened between T_1 and T_3 even absent large increases in the prison population

deprives prisoners of economic, educational, familial and civic resources available outside prison walls (Braman, 2004; Page, 2004; Manza and Uggen, 2006; Western, 2006). Given the severity of the treatment, it requires little stretch of the imagination to expect the prison experience to transform inmates themselves.

However, incarceration can negatively affect inmates even if they remain personally unchanged by the experience. As Pager (2007) notes, it can do so by distributing a negative credential – a mark of infamy – in attaching to them a criminal record difficult to conceal or shake, even if legally permitted to do so. A former inmate whose poor economic prospects might have influenced his path to prison may therefore find himself with even worse prospects upon release. Legal bans on voting and the receipt of welfare, public housing and financial aid might further impede his chances of success following a spell of incarceration (Travis, 2002). The stigma of incarceration, moreover, might partially explain his comparatively high risk of divorce (Lopoo and Western, 2005; Apel et al., 2010).

Even with two theoretical means by which punishment could widen inequalities in socio-economic and marital status, health and civic participation, the new literature on punishment and inequality faces significant methodological obstacles. The major challenge, somewhat paradoxically, is advanced by previous research on inequality in punishment. If social inequalities so strongly determine the distribution of prison inmates, how can one distinguish the effects of prison from the effects of being the type of person *likely to go to prison*? Concerns about selection bias suffuse social science, but they are particularly acute in research on punishment, where there are strong theoretical and empirical reasons to believe that any effect of incarceration is simply attributable to the negative endowments that landed a person in prison in the first place. In an era when rehabilitation guided correctional philosophy (Garland, 2001), one might have expected a prison term to improve the life chances of inmates. Since the onset of 'mass imprisonment' and, with it, the curtailment of correctional programming, however, the belief that imprisonment further undercuts the resources available to the already disadvantaged appears more plausible.

Methodological challenges to the new literature on punishment and inequality have encouraged scholars to adopt more sophisticated causal identification strategies such as field experimentation (Pager, 2003) and instrumental variables estimation (Kling, 2006; Green and Winik, 2010). If research on punishment and inequality is to advance, it must supplement the descriptive and demographic studies that have placed it on solid empirical footing with methods to identify imprisonment's causal effects.

Recent research on punishment and inequality has taken one additional step forward. Rather than consider the effects of imprisonment solely on the offender, it has asked how the increasing severity of punishment might affect the families and communities of the imprisoned and formerly imprisoned (Comfort, 2007). As the scope of incarceration has grown, so has the length of its shadow. If the claims of this research are borne out empirically, the families, friends, and neighbors of the incarcerated may bear additional burdens without having committed any crime of their own.

This chapter proceeds in six parts. First, we summarize broad changes in imprisonment in the USA over the last 130 years. We focus on prison and jail incarceration in the USA alone because the current scope of penal confinement in the USA makes it the most likely case to reveal an aggregate relationship between punishment and inequality. Next, we review evidence on four indices of inequality – socio-economic status (SES), marriage, health and civic participation – regarding both their effects (on imprisonment) and causes (by imprisonment). We consider imprisonment's effects not only on offenders, but also on their families and communities. We conclude by highlighting areas of research that will enable us more precisely to understand American imprisonment so that we might imagine a better future for all those whom it affects.

THE GROWTH OF IMPRISONMENT

Over the century between 1870 and 1970 the American incarceration rate hovered between 100 and 200 persons per 100,000. Before the 1970s, incarceration in the USA remained so stable that criminologists Blumstein and Cohen (1973) predicted it would deviate little from its largely trendless course. As depicted in Figure 8.2, the year these predictions were published the incarceration rate began an upward ascent from which it has only recently departed. Today the US imprisonment rate (not including jails) exceeds 500 per 100,000 people. America's rate of incarceration falls closer to those of South Africa and the former Soviet Union than to those of the UK, Canada and other comparable democracies. As Figure 8.3 demonstrates, the American rate of imprisonment is an extreme outlier among other wealthy democracies. The scale of imprisonment in the USA makes Spain's incarceration rate, which experienced the most dramatic increase in imprisonment in the EU between 1983 and 2006, appear nearly flat.

Although the ascent of the American incarceration rate is a historically recent phenomenon, inequalities in an individual's chance of being incarcerated are much older. Despite a rising risk of imprisonment for women during the prison boom years (Bonczar, 2003), men are still eight times as likely ever to experience imprisonment. Racial and educational differentials are nearly as drastic. As depicted in Table 8.1, black men born between 1965 and 1969 were seven times more likely to have been imprisoned by 1999 than comparable white men (Western and Wildeman, 2009; see also Pettit and Western, 2004), although racial disparity in imprisonment remained roughly constant over the course of the prison boom. Black men without a high school diploma born just 10 years later (in the late 1970s) faced nearly a 70 percent chance of ever going to prison. The risk for comparable whites is about 15 percent (Western and Wildeman, 2009). Prisoners are more likely than the average citizen to have been abused as children, to suffer some form of mental illness, to have been homeless, or to be addicted to drugs and alcohol (Mumola, 2000). Coupled with histories of criminal

Table 8.1 Cumulative risk of imprisonment by age 30–34 for men born 1945–9 to 1975–9, by race and education

	Birth year						
	1945–9	*1950–4*	*1955–9*	*1960–4*	*1965–9*	*1970–4*	*1975–9*
White men							
High school dropouts	4.2	7.2	8.0	8.0	10.5	14.8	15.3
High school only	0.7	2.0	2.1	2.5	4.0	3.8	4.1
All noncollege	1.8	2.9	3.2	3.7	5.1	5.1	6.3
Some college	0.7	0.7	0.6	0.8	0.7	0.9	1.2
All men	1.2	1.9	2.0	2.2	2.8	2.8	3.3
African American men							
High school dropouts	14.7	19.6	27.6	41.6	57.0	62.5	69.0
High school only	10.2	11.3	9.4	12.4	16.8	20.3	18.0
All noncollege	12.1	14.1	14.7	19.9	26.7	30.9	35.7
Some college	4.9	3.5	4.3	5.5	6.8	8.5	7.6
All men	9.0	10.6	11.5	15.2	20.3	22.8	20.7

Source: Western and Wildeman (2009: 231)

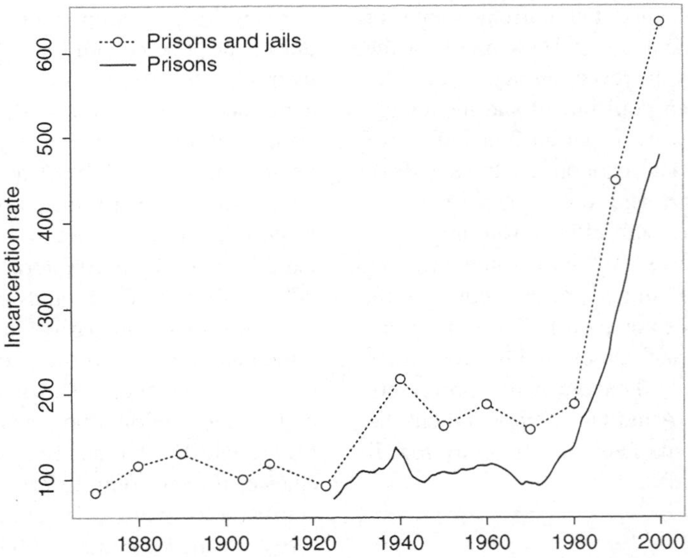

Figure 8.2 Beginning in 1973, the US incarceration rate began a historically unprecedented ascent
Source: Authors' calculations using data from historical Censuses of the United States and the Sourcebook of Criminal Justice Statistics

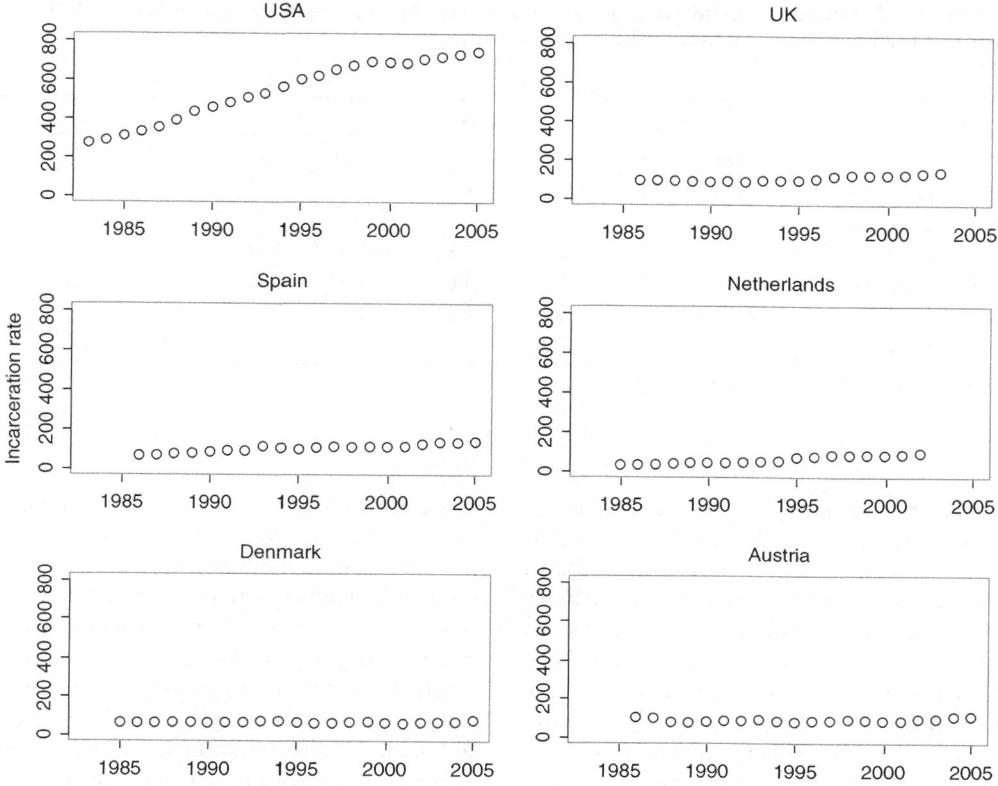

Figure 8.3 The American rate of imprisonment is an extreme outlier among other wealthy democracies

Source: Authors' calculations using data from the United Nations Survey on Crime Trends and the Operations of Criminal Justice Systems, the Council of Europe, the European Sourcebook of Criminal Justice, Eurostat, and the United States Bureau of Justice Statistics

activity, unemployment, and residency in poor neighborhoods, most prisoners began life at a significant disadvantage to the general population.

As imprisonment became common among adults, so also did parental imprisonment become common among children. Wildeman (2009) estimates that one in four black children born in 1990 had a parent imprisoned by his or her 14th birthday. For black children of high school dropouts, parental imprisonment was modal. These risks are about twice the risk of those for children born 12 years earlier – and significantly higher than the risks for comparable white children (Table 8.2).

THE EFFECTS OF IMPRISONMENT ON INDIVIDUALS, FAMILIES AND COMMUNITIES

The massive increase in the American imprisonment rate over the last 35 years will affect social inequality if it has negative consequences and if those consequences are unequally distributed. The magnitude of these

Table 8.2 Cumulative risk of paternal and maternal imprisonment by age 14 for children born in 1978 and 1990, by race and parental education

	White children				*African American children*			
	Paternal		*Maternal*		*Paternal*		*Maternal*	
	1978	*1990*	*1978*	*1990*	*1978*	*1990*	*1978*	*1990*
All children	2.2	3.6	0.2	0.6	13.8	25.1	1.4	3.3
By parental education								
All noncollege	2.9	5.6	0.2	0.8	15.6	30.2	1.5	3.6
High school dropout	4.1	7.2	0.2	1.0	22.0	50.5	1.9	5.0
High school only	2.0	4.8	0.2	0.7	10.2	20.4	0.9	2.6
Some college	1.4	1.7	0.2	0.3	7.1	13.4	1.2	2.6

Source: Wildeman 2009: 271, 273

effects on inequality will depend both on how large the micro-level effects of incarceration are and on how unevenly distributed the experience of incarceration is. We know imprisonment is commonest among men of color with low levels of schooling who have histories of mental illness and physical and drug abuse. Any universally negative effects of imprisonment therefore will fall disproportionately on them. This very fact, however, may undermine claims about incarceration's aggregate effects on inequality. Given the poor pre-incarceration employment prospects of those most likely to receive a prison sentence, even a relatively large effect of incarceration on their likelihood of employment may have only a modest aggregate effect on racial inequality in employment. Throughout the chapter this fact should be borne in mind. In the following section, we consider the potential consequences of imprisonment for prisoners, their families and the broader social units to which they belong.

Rather than provide an exhaustive review (for this, see Wakefield and Uggen, 2010), we focus instead on a few of the most active areas of research: imprisonment's effect on SES, family structure and integrity, health and mortality and civic participation. We do so for three reasons. First, limiting the scope of the literature creates space for a deeper discussion of its implications. Second, since obstacles to causal inference here are especially pervasive, we use the additional space to differentiate between the mechanisms leading individuals into prison and the mechanisms that transform or stigmatize them once they get out. We also discuss how imprisonment itself might affect the partners, families and communities to which prisoners are tied. Finally, limiting our focus gives us more space to consider gaps in the literature and suggest directions for future research.

PUNISHMENT AND SES

Since the seminal contribution of Rusche and Kirchheimer (1939), social scientists have amassed a wealth of studies considering the influence of SES – generally measured as race, class, education and income – on individual point-in-time (Blumstein and Beck, 1999) and cumulative risks of imprisonment (Pettit and Western, 2004). This literature trades in statistical associations, perhaps at the expense of a thorough consideration of precisely what mechanisms drive the relationship between SES and incarceration. Are people, as in a Marxian framework, impelled to crime by economic necessity, forced to steal or participate in illicit economies due to a lack of viable options in legitimate labor markets (Linebaugh, 2003)? Does growing up in a poor neighborhood dull the normative sanction on crime such that it carries a weaker stigma among the dispossessed than it does among the wealthy (Venkatesh, 2006)? How much of the racial disparity in incarceration can be traced to perceptions of racial dishonor among the officials of criminal justice (Wacquant, 2001)? Sampson and Wilson advance a theory combining these three hypotheses. '[M]acrosocial patterns of residential inequality,' they argue, 'give rise to the social isolation and ecological concentration of the truly disadvantaged, which in turn leads to structural barriers and cultural adaptations that undermine social organization and hence the control of crime' (1995: 38). Despite the literature's long pedigree, it could benefit greatly from increased analytical specificity and elaboration of precisely how a person's economic and social status influences his likelihood of engaging in crime or – independently – his chances of being incarcerated. Recent work on how family SES increases the risk of parental imprisonment (Wildeman, 2009), how joblessness biases the decisions of criminal justice officials (Spohn and Holleran, 2000) and how spatially concentrated imprisonment might be self-perpetuating (Clear, 2007; Sampson and Loeffler, 2010) points in promising new directions.

The new literature on punishment and inequality considers the reverse relationship. It asks whether the experience or negative credentialing of imprisonment might reduce the SES of former prisoners. The direct effects of incarceration on one's economic status hardly need to be elaborated: confinement prevents one from earning a wage comparable to those outside of prison, if one at all; following incarceration, it inserts a large gap into one's résumé. Although prisons once provided avenues for educational attainment, outside of a few successful demonstration projects tied to universities, federal funding for such programs has largely been cut (Page, 2004). The modal former prisoner, moreover, accrues substantial legal debt as a result of his crime, trial, and incarceration (Harris et al., 2010).

On any given day in America, one out of nine young black men are absent from their communities due to incarceration. By incapacitating prisoners, incarceration prevents these men from committing crimes in the outside world. It also, however, separates them from civic life, the lives of their families, children and romantic partners, and the world of work. The possible tradeoffs entailed by the complexity of incapacitation have only recently begun to be considered in any detail.

There are additional reasons incarceration might diminish an individual's SES. Comparatively little research considers how prison, in changing individuals, might thereby undercut their social and economic standing. Long before the onset of the prison boom, Sykes (1958) noted the potential negative behavioral effects of prolonged institutionalization. Imprisonment, for instance, could reduce the skills inmates already possess or would have developed absent confinement. Prisoners likewise might adopt survival techniques inside prison that work at cross-purposes to their desire to find work upon release (Kaminski, 2004; Nurse, 2002). Goffman (2009), for example, demonstrates how wanted young men cultivate unpredictability inconsistent with the sort of routine necessary to maintain stable work. Better understanding what prison does to transform those who experience it would enable us to assess what its broader effects will be once prisoners are released.

If scholarship on the effects of incarceration on human capital is relatively scant, research on the stigma or negative credential incarceration confers is substantially larger. The leading conclusions in this area stem from the research program of Pager (2003, 2007; Pager and Quillian, 2005; Pager et al., 2009). Pager (2003) and Pager et al. (2009) report the results of audit studies in which matched pairs of testers present employers with résumés identical but for a randomly assigned line signaling a low-level felony drug conviction. The presence of such a line substantially decreases an applicant's chance of receiving a call for an interview. The experimental design of these studies permits the effect of negative credentialing to be distinguished from other discernible characteristics of applicants. Pager and Quillian (2005) elucidate possible mechanisms behind these causal estimates with qualitative evidence suggesting that employers respond strongly to the negative status of ex-offenders. Using observational data, Western (2002, 2006) concludes that having ever been incarcerated diminishes one's future earnings by approximately 30 percent.

Kling (2006), using the random assignment of defendants to judges who mete out shorter or longer average sentences, conversely finds that longer prison sentences have no measurable effect on the post-incarceration wages of former prisoners. There are many possible explanations for these null findings. One possibility is that prison's effect on wages works primarily through stigma, a treatment that should take effect irrespective of the strength of the treatment, rather than by diminishing human capital, the extent of which should vary with sentence length. Another is that the counterfactual comparison group may already have experienced imprisonment before the study began (or experienced it soon after the treatment window), a possibility that would bias the estimates toward zero. Although the design used by Kling (2006) points to a promising new line of quasi-experimental research on the effects of incarceration, the approach is not without its limitations. Clean causal identification may come at the expense of producing estimates that are not of the greatest scientific interest.

Incarceration's negative credentialing, it should be noted, is not restricted to the labor market. Prisoners with a felony drug conviction are legally forbidden from receiving welfare or public housing (Rubinstein and Mukamal, 2002). As Gowan (2002) demonstrates, making such funds available to recently released prisoners can be the decisive factor in determining whether they remain homeless. Perhaps most remarkable is the relationship of imprisonment to one's perception of one's own identity. In an innovative study, Saperstein and Penner (2010) show that having been imprisoned increases the probability that individuals will self-identify as African American and that others will likewise identify them.

As we suggest in the introduction, the direct effects of imprisonment on SES may extend beyond the individual offender. Through ethnographic observation, Comfort (2008) uncovers hidden financial costs associated with having a partner go to prison. In a parallel work, Braman (2004) shows that an incarcerated father's absence reduces a mother's income by forcing her to cut back on work hours or increase her expenditures on childcare. Geller et al. (2011) find that ever-incarcerated men contribute nearly 15 percent less income to their families than comparable men (conditional on contributing at all). The relationship between parental imprisonment and childhood SES, however, is less well understood. Foster and Hagan (2007, 2009) suggest that paternal incarceration reduces children's educational attainment. Cho (2009a, 2009b), in contrast, finds that maternal imprisonment weakly diminishes or has no effect on children's educational attainment.

Despite substantial progress since Western and Beckett (1999) initiated research on the economic consequences of incarceration, considerable work remains to be done. Future studies should exploit the random assignment of judges and prosecutors to defendants to test Kling's (2006) and other results in other states (Green and Winik, 2010), bearing in mind the limitations of this research design. Moreover, future work should consider the consequences of imprisonment for inequalities in the SES of families, communities, states and nations. Here the greatest challenge will be to identify the microfoundations underlying aggregate statistical relationships.

PUNISHMENT AND FAMILY LIFE

Criminologists have long acknowledged the connections between family life and crime. With little disagreement, they have concluded that a stable marriage discourages men who have ever been criminally active from further criminal activity (Sampson and Laub, 1993; Laub et al., 1998). Sampson and Laub, who have made the greatest contributions to this literature, claim that 'it is the *social investment* … in the institutional relationship, whether it be in a family, work, or community setting, that dictates the salience of informal social control at the individual level' (1993: 611–12). Given the deterrent effect of a stable family life, it is unsurprising that the average prisoner has weaker family ties than the average member of society (Lopoo and Western, 2005; Goffman, 2009).

Because ever-imprisoned men have more tenuous family connections than the average man even prior to imprisonment, and because quasi-experimental evidence has yet to be introduced to this literature, efforts to estimate the effect of imprisonment on family structure should be interpreted with caution. For example, although qualitative research (Edin et al., 2004) argues that women avoid the stigma of incarceration when choosing a marital partner, quantitative research finds that having been imprisoned has no relation to a man's chance of marrying (Lopoo and Western, 2005). Future research should attempt to reconcile these discrepant findings. If the stigma of going to prison weakens the average prisoner's familial bonds, then any spell of imprisonment, no matter how short, should disrupt his family life. However, if prison affects prisoners' families primarily through its effects on prisoners themselves, longer sentences should be more disruptive. Quasi-experimental evidence could help resolve these competing claims.

Research on divorce is more conclusive. Qualitative and quantitative studies agree that imprisonment is positively related to one's risk of divorce and separation (Nurse, 2002; Braman, 2004; Lopoo and Western, 2005; Apel et al., 2010). Although none of these studies has determined what drives the association, Nurse (2002) provides ethnographic evidence that some combination of time apart, behavioral changes in fathers and the disapproval of the wife's family drives a wedge into the martial unions of prisoners (Nurse, 2002).

The largest body of research on the collateral effects of incarceration concerns the partners men leave behind when they enter prison. Here the evidence is almost entirely ethnographic (Nurse, 2002; Braman, 2004; Goffman, 2009). Comfort's (2008) work on the partners of incarcerated men deserves special attention, although her findings are limited to women who stay romantically attached to their partners while those partners serve time. A quarter of the women Comfort (2008) interviewed felt they derived short-term benefits from their partner's imprisonment. For some of these women, imprisonment gave them respite from a partner's addiction; others enjoyed the increased attention they received from their confined partners. Other studies report that women suffer from their partner's incarceration (Nurse, 2002; Braman, 2004; Goffman, 2009). Although the findings of these studies may differ because of differences in their respective samples, the discrepancies should motivate future research. Quantitative evidence especially could determine whether any associations observed in small, biased samples hold in large, unbiased samples (Wildeman and Western, 2010).

The stability of marital unions, of course, affects not only the partners involved, but also any children born to those unions. Given the impressive amount of research that has accumulated on this topic and the number of high-quality reviews of it we focus on just two empirical articles (Hagan and Dinovitzer, 1999; Murray and Farrington, 2008; Wakefield and Uggen, 2010; Wildeman and Western, 2010).

The first of these articles considers the consequences of increases in the female imprisonment rate on the number of foster care caseloads between 1985 and 2000. Swann and Sylvester (2006) find that increases in the female imprisonment rate explain around 30 percent of the massive increase in the number of foster care caseloads over this period. Although some of this effect is doubtless due to changes in children's living arrangements in their mother's absence, the authors attribute the remaining share to legal changes in how long children can be in foster care before their parents lose custody – a duration shortened in 1997 to well below the length of the median prison sentence (Swann and Sylvester, 2006; see also Travis, 2002).

Legal barriers to family formation have in times past compromised the integrity of the African American family. In his comparative treatise on slavery, for example, Patterson (1982) argues that one of the institution's defining features is its denial of slaves' claim on blood relations. Given racial disparities in admission to prison, today incarceration – even for short periods of time – has the legal capacity to impose its own variant of 'natal alienation'. Although one's losing parental rights is not a formal component of any criminal sentence, an unintended consequence of racial disparity in incarceration may be a large relative disruption in the legal status of African American families.

A second article examines the consequences of paternal incarceration for children's physically aggressive behaviors. It finds that paternal incarceration substantially increases the physically aggressive behaviors of boys (Wildeman, 2010). These effects hold only if the father in question was neither abusive to the child's mother nor incarcerated for a violent offense. This suggests that the effects of incarceration on children depend substantially on the prior characteristics of the incarcerated father. Since the children considered in this study were relatively young – most were only about five years' old – it cannot speak to the question of whether parental imprisonment increases boys' likelihood of committing crimes. If aggression in childhood provides any indication of later criminality, however, this study might reveal paths through which mass imprisonment increases crime in the long run and contact with the penal system is consequently passed down from fathers to sons.

A final, more difficult, task is to identify the relationship between incarceration and community-level patterns of marriage, family formation and child-wellbeing. Research on social stratification in America (Wilson, 1987; Anderson, 1999) reveals that declines in marriage and family stability coincided with increases in community-level rates of incarceration (Clear, 2007), but the relationship could easily be spurious. Future research should dedicate more energy to understanding how imprisonment has direct effects on the family lives of the ever-imprisoned and indirect effects on the communities from which they hail.

PUNISHMENT AND HEALTH

As with SES and family stability, imprisonment could affect individual and population health directly or indirectly. Most directly, it could alter the disease environment to which prisoners are exposed and facilitate the diffusion of illnesses that spread best in environments of close human contact (Farmer, 2002). Diseases contracted in prison, in addition, migrate with prisoners when they return to their home communities. Less directly, former prisoners might experience discrimination by health care providers and institutions. The stigma of a criminal record, in other words, may extend beyond the labor market and civic institutions, impeding a former prisoner's chance not only of finding work, but also of maintaining good health. Some speculate that it is incarceration's indirect effects that most threaten the health of former prisoners (Schnittker and John, 2007).

Evidence from state- and cohort-data (Massoglia, 2008a,b; Johnson and Raphael, 2009) reveals that imprisonment is associated with substantial increases in HIV/AIDS infection rates. The relationship, moreover, is strongest among African American women. Although macro-level data cannot adjudicate between mechanisms potentially responsible for this association, because men have a much greater likelihood of imprisonment than women, and African American men a much greater likelihood than white men, a non-spurious relationship could indicate that African American women face greater risks of infection by becoming romantically involved with a formerly imprisoned man. In communities where incarceration is fairly common (Clear, 2007), this risk will spread beyond those directly involved with former prisoners (Bearman et al., 2004).

The rise of the prison population in the last four decades coincided with precipitous declines in mental institutionalization (Harcourt, 2006). Over this period prisons came to house a greater share of the nation's mentally ill (James and Glaze, 2006). For those without histories of mental illness, the experience of confinement can compromise cognitive functioning (Gawande, 2009) and encourage the onset of stress-related diseases (Massoglia, 2008a,b; Wang et al., 2009). The negative effects of the experience of prison are stronger still among those already at risk. Long before the US incarceration rate began its ascent, observers voiced concern over the mental health consequences of living in a crowded prison environment (Clemmer, 1940; Sykes, 1958). As prison overcrowding has worsened in recent years, its effects on mental illness may have grown more acute (Haney, 2006).

Incarceration's effect on other measures of health tells a different story. Since those at risk of imprisonment also have high risks of homicide and low rates of medical coverage, it is possible that imprisonment actually decreases the mortality rate of those protected by its walls and legally mandated services. For all their deficits, prisons provide minimal health care and protection from violence compared to the environments from which many inmates hail. Mumola (2007), which compares prisoners to matched non-incarcerated individuals, comes to just such a conclusion, although the short-term health benefits of imprisonment are limited to African American men. These findings have been independently replicated twice using different samples (Patterson, 2010; Spaulding et al., 2011). Again, the precise mechanisms explaining this association are unclear. It could be, for example, that prison only improves the health of those who would otherwise live in the nation's most dangerous and underserved communities.

For recently released prisoners, on the other hand, the mortality costs of having ever been imprisoned appear to be quite high. Binswanger et al. (2007), for instance, finds that recently released prisoners face especially high death rates in the two weeks following release, although Spaulding et al. (2011) suggests that in some settings these rates may be exaggerated. Homicide and drug overdose are the most common reasons for early death upon release. A study by Goffman (2009), moreover, indicates that men with warrants out for their arrest may avoid hospitals and emergency rooms for fear of being apprehended by law enforcement. Untreated infections and broken bones can compromise the health of these men for the rest of their lives. Weighing short-term mortality gains against the long-term health losses caused by imprisonment will be necessary if we hope to estimate the total effect of punishment on health.

As our discussion of HIV/AIDS indicates, the health consequences of imprisonment can extend beyond the individual offender. Green et al. (2006), for example, finds that the mothers of incarcerated men suffer more mental health problems than otherwise comparable women. In an age when corrections spending and Medicaid vie for dominance in state budgets (Jacobson, 2005), imprisonment may undermine population health mechanically by reducing the amount a state spends on health care. Ellwood and Guetzkow (2009; see also Beckfield and Krieger, 2009), for instance, demonstrate that increases in the imprisonment rate are negatively associated with spending on public goods that might promote population health and wellbeing.

PUNISHMENT AND CIVIC PARTICIPATION

The mechanisms relating punishment to inequality in the political process hardly need to be spelled out. In most cases they are direct: all but two states legally bar prisoners from voting; 35 prevent them from voting for life if they have been convicted of a felony offense (Wood, 2009). In states where voting rights can be restored upon release, the procedure for doing so often lacks transparency. It follows that inequality in admission to prison will spill over into inequality in political access.

Research in this area is centered around the work of Manza and Uggen (2006), whose most provocative finding is that felon disfranchisement swung the historically close 2000 presidential election in favor of the Republican candidate. Given the strong relationship between Republican governance and increasing national economic inequality (Bartels, 2008), the import of this outcome is potentially immense. To our knowledge, only one study considers the effects of imprisonment on the civic participation of those connected to prisoners. Foster and Hagan (2007) show that the children of ever-incarcerated fathers have weaker connections to the political process than otherwise similar adolescents and adults.

One additional and often overlooked aspect of mass imprisonment is its effect on the drawing of state legislative districts. As the number of inmates grew over the last quarter of the 20th century, states began building prisons farther from the communities where most prisoners are arrested and sentenced. Because prisoners in all but two states cannot vote, districts drawn to include prison populations comprise fewer voting citizens than other districts. The vote of a person in a district with a prison is consequently worth more than the vote of a person in an adjacent district without a prison (Lotke and Wagner, 2004). These voting inequalities result solely from a community's chance of building a prison; they harm rural and urban districts alike. As this chapter goes to print, four states – California, Delaware, Maryland and New York – have passed laws to correct the distortions caused by prison-based gerrymandering. This changing legal environment forms a quasi-experiment through which the effects of incarceration on inequalities in political access and civic participation might be estimated.

CONCLUSION

Prisons have always housed those on the margins of society. In this sense, imprisonment has with few exceptions moved in lockstep with social inequality. In the last 35 years, however, and almost exclusively in the USA, the prevalence of incarceration in the population became common enough that it might not only reflect but actively produce inequality in American society at large. This dramatic shift in the penal system led many researchers of social stratification to shift their attention from the predictors to the consequences of imprisonment. It also inspired them to consider the effects of the institution on the children, families and communities of those who reside in it (Bonczar, 2003; Pettit and Western, 2004; Western and Wildeman, 2009; Wildeman, 2009).

This new area of research has yielded a number of disquieting findings, many of which we have reviewed here. The current state of research allows us to conclude that having ever been incarcerated is associated with lower SES, disruptions of family life, poor health (with important short-term exceptions) and higher levels of political and social exclusion than would be expected based on the observed characteristics of adult men. These associations appear to extend to the families, communities, and states of the incarcerated, although our confidence in them dissipates as the level of aggregation grows. These findings have led many scholars to conclude that mass imprisonment has exacerbated social inequality in America.

Yet the relationship may not be so straightforward. A small but growing literature suggests that imprisonment in some situations may enhance the wellbeing of prisoners and those tied to them. Three studies illustrate, for instance, that imprisonment is associated with lower mortality risks for African American men while they are in prison (Mumola, 2007; Patterson, 2010; Spaulding et al., 2011). Likewise, other research suggests that some women express relief when their romantic partners go to prison – even if this relief is only short-lived (Comfort, 2007, 2008). Still others note that paternal incarceration negatively affects the behavioral problems of children only if the father in question is not violent or abusive (Wildeman, 2010). In most cases, these findings speak as loudly about the poor conditions of life prisoners would otherwise experience as they do about any potential benefits the institution might confer. More difficult to assess is when the negative effects of imprisonment outweigh its short-term benefits for victims of domestic violence or other physical abuse. Imprisonment, as we note in the introduction, is a multifaceted treatment. Scholars looking to devise less harmful ways of promoting public safety would do well to distinguish the incapacitative effect of incarceration from its rehabilitative and deterrent capacities. There may be ways to give an individual necessary time away from a corrosive social setting without inducing long-term harm to mental health in the way prisons usually do (Kleiman, 2009).

The most significant threat to stating confidently that incarceration increases social inequality is selection bias. The inequality it appears prisons breed, in other words, may simply result from prior inequality. Only a small portion of the studies we review here rests on experimental or quasi-experimental evidence. Even these studies, moreover, may not be informative about the aggregate effects of incarceration on inequality. Where experimentation is impossible, researchers must search for robust relationships that hold across various statistical models.

For obvious ethical reasons, randomly assigning individuals to prison is impossible. Pager (2003) circumvents this problem by using actors in one of the most celebrated studies this literature has to offer. But randomization in criminal sentencing does exist – albeit in unexpected places. In one recent study, for instance, Green and Winik (2010; see also Kling, 2006) use exogenous judge-level variation in sentencing to isolate the effects of sentence length on recidivism. Since sentence length is related to the characteristics of judges rather than defendants, these estimates approximate the ideal experiment. Some states randomly assign prosecutors, whose sway over sentence length should be even greater than that of a judge (Davis, 2002). Using quasi-experimental evidence such as this to test imprisonment's effect on additional outcomes points research in a promising new direction. The use of these studies, however, introduces a separate concern: that the treatment and control groups are so similar in their eventual likelihood of experiencing imprisonment that any treatment effect will be small.

As research on punishment and inequality makes better efforts to estimate the effects of imprisonment, however, it should not lose sight of its origins. The solutions to America's incarceration problem, after all, may reside outside the criminal justice system. Mass imprisonment is of vital importance for social inequality even if it does nothing itself to exacerbate that inequality. Scholars should bear in mind that understanding how the relative balance of welfare and penal state intervention in the lives of the poor shapes the distribution of the nation's inmates is at least as important as estimating any effects of the institution itself.

ACKNOWLEDGEMENTS

We thank Jonathan Simon, Richard Sparks, and Bruce Western for helpful comments.

NOTE

1 Incarceration also, as we explain, has direct effects simply in its ability to incapacitate. Although we discuss the fact that prison, for example, forcibly removes one from the labor market and one's family, and therefore mechanically affects one's SES and family stability, we place our emphasis on the ways prison transforms or stigmatizes the ever-incarcerated.

REFERENCES

Anderson, E. (1999) *Code of the Street: Decency, Violence, and the Moral Life of the Inner City.* New York: Norton.

Apel, R., Arjan A.J., Blokland, P., et al. (2010) 'The impact of imprisonment on marriage and divorce: a risk set matching approach', *Journal of Quantitative Criminology,* 26 (2): 269–300.

Bartels, Larry M. (2008) *Unequal Democracy: The Political Economy of the New Gilded Age.* Princeton: Princeton University Press.

Bearman, Peter, Mood, James and Stovel, Katherine (2004) 'Chains of affection: the structure of adolescent romantic and sexual networks', *American Journal of Sociology,* 110 (1): 44–91.

Beckfield, Jason and Krieger, Nancy (2009) 'Epi + demos + cracy: linking political systems and priorities to the magnitude of health inequities – evidence, gaps, and a research agenda', *Epidemiologic Reviews,* 31 (1) :152–77.

Blumstein, Alfred and Beck, Allen J. (1999) 'Population growth in U.S. prisons, 1980–1996', *Crime and Justice,* 26 (1): 17–61.

Blumstein, Alfred and Cohen, Jacqueline (1973) 'A theory of the stability of punishment', *Journal of Criminal Law and Criminology,* 64 (2): 198–207.

Binswanger, Ingrid A., Stern, Marc F., Deyo, Richard A., et al. (2007) 'Release from prison – a high risk of death for former inmates', *The New England Journal of Medicine,* 356 (2): 157–65.

Bonczar, Thomas P. (2003) *The Prevalence of Imprisonment in the U.S. Population, 1974–2001.* Washington, DC: US Department of Justice.

Braman, Donald (2004) *Doing Time on the Outside: Incarceration and Family Life in Urban America.* Ann Arbor, MI: University of Michigan Press.

Cho, Rosa Minhyo (2009a) 'Impact of maternal imprisonment on children's probability of grade retention', *Journal of Urban Economics,* 65 (1): 11–23.

Cho, Rosa Minhyo (2009b) 'The impact of maternal imprisonment on children's educational achievement: results from children in Chicago public schools', *Journal of Human Resources,* 44 (3): 772–797.

Clear, Todd R. (2007) *Imprisoning Communities: How Mass Incarceration Makes Disadvantaged Neighborhoods Worse.* New York: Oxford University Press.

Clemmer, Donald (1940) *The Prison Community.* New York: Harcourt and Brace.

Comfort, Megan (2007) 'Punishment beyond the legal offender', *Annual Review of Law and Social Science,* 3 (1): 271–96.

Comfort, Megan (2008) *Doing Time Together: Love and Family in the Shadow of the Prison.* Chicago: University of Chicago Press.

Davis, Angela J. (2002) 'Incarceration and the imbalance of power', in Marc Mauer and Meda Chesney-Lind (eds), *Invisible Punishment: The Collateral Consequences of Mass Imprisonment.* New York: New Press. pp. 61–78

Edin, Kathryn, Nelson Timothy J. and Paranal, Rachelle (2004) 'Fatherhood and incarceration as potential turning points in the criminal careers of unskilled men', in Mary Patillo, David F. Weiman, and Bruce Western (eds), *Imprisoning America: The Social Effects of Mass Incarceration.* New York: Russell Sage. pp. 46–75

Ellwood, John W. and Guetzkow, Joshua (2009) 'Footing the bill: causes and budgetary consequences of state spending on corrections', in Steven Raphael and Michael A. Stoll (eds), *Do Prisons Make Us Safer? The Benefits and Costs of the Prison Boom.* New York: Russell Sage Press. pp. 207–38.

Farmer, Paul (2002) 'The house of the dead: Tuberculosis and incarceration', in Marc Mauer and Meda Chesney-Lind (eds), *Invisible Punishment: The Collateral Consequences of Mass Imprisonment.* New York: New Press. pp. 238–57.

Foster, Holly and Hagan, John (2007) 'Incarceration and intergenerational social exclusion', *Social Problems,* 54 (4): 399–433.

Foster, Holly and Hagan, John (2009) 'The mass incarceration of parents in America: issues of race/ ethnicity, collateral damage to children, and prisoner reentry', *Annals of the American Academy of Political and Social Science,* 623 (1): 179–94.

Garland, David (2001) *The Culture of Control: Crime and Social Order in Contemporary Society.* Chicago: University of Chicago Press.

Gawande, Atul (2009) 'Hellhole', *New Yorker,* 30 March.

Geller, Amanda, Garfinkel, Irwin and Western, Bruce (2011) 'Paternal incarceration and support for children in fragile families', *Demography,* 48 (1): 25–47.

Goffman, Alice (2009) 'On the run: wanted men in a Philadelphia ghetto', *American Sociological Review,* 74 (3): 339–57.

Gowan, Teresa (2002) 'The nexus: homelessness and incarceration in two American cities', *Ethnography,* 3 (3): 500–34.

Green, Kerry, Ensminger, Margaret E., Robertson, Judith and Juon, H-S. (2006) 'Impact of adult sons' incarceration on African American mothers' psychological distress', *Journal of Marriage and Family,* 68 (2): 430–41.

Green, Donald and Winik, Daniel (2010) 'Using random judge assignments to estimate the effects of incarceration and probation on recidivism among drug offenders', *Criminology,* 48 (2): 357–87.

Hagan, John and Dinovitzer, Ronit (1999) 'Collateral consequences of imprisonment for children, communities, and prisoners', *Crime and Justice,* 26 (1): 121–62.

Haney, Craig (2006) *Reforming Punishment: Psychological Limits to the Pains of Imprisonment.* Washington, DC: American Psychological Association.

Harcourt, Bernard (2006) 'From the asylum to the prison: rethinking the incarceration Revolution', *Texas Law Review,* 84 (7): 1751–86.

Harris, Alexes, Evans, Heather and Beckett, Katherine (2010) 'Drawing blood from stones: legal debt and social inequality in the contemporary United States', *American Journal of Sociology,* 115 (6): 1753–99.

Jacobson, Michael (2005). *Downsizing Prisoners: How to Reduce Crime and End Mass Incarceration.* New York: New York University Press.

James, Doris J.J. and Glaze, Lauren E. (2006) *Mental Health Problems of Prison and Jail Inmates.* Washington DC: U.S. Department of Justice.

Johnson, Rucker and Raphael, Steven (2009) 'The effects of male incarceration dynamics on Acquired Immune Deficiency Syndrome infection rates among African American women and men', *Journal of Law and Economics,* 52 (2): 251–93.

Kaminski, Marek M. (2004) *Games Prisoners Play: The Tragicomic Worlds of Polish Prison.* Princeton, NJ: Princeton University Press.

Kleiman, Mark A.R. (2009) *When Brute Force Fails: How to Have Less Crime and Less Punishment.* Princeton, NJ: Princeton University Press.

Kling, Jeffrey R. (2006) 'Incarceration length, employment, and earnings', *American Economic Review,* 96 (3): 863–76.

Laub, John H., Nagin, Daniel S. and Sampson, Robert J. (1998) 'Trajectories of change in criminal offending: good marriages and the desistance process', *American Sociological Review,* 63 (2): 225–38.

Linebaugh, Peter (2003) *The London Hanged: Crime and Civil Society in the Eighteenth Century.* New York: Verso.

Lopoo, Leonard and Western, Bruce (2005) 'Incarceration and the formation and stability of marital unions', *Journal of Marriage and Family,* 67 (3): 721–34.

Lotke, Eric and Wagner, Peter (2004) 'Prisoners of the Census: electoral and financial consequences of counting prisoners where they go, not where they come from', *Pace Law Review,* 24 (2): 587–607.

Manza, Jeff and Uggen, Christopher (2006) *Locked Out: Felon Disenfranchisement and American Democracy.* New York: Oxford University Press.

Massoglia, Michael (2008a) 'Incarceration as exposure: the prison, infectious disease, and other stress-related illnesses', *Journal of Health and Social Behavior,* 49 (1): 56–71.

Massoglia, Michael (2008b) 'Incarceration, health, and racial disparities in health', *Law & Society Review,* 42 (2): 275–306.

Mumola, Christopher J. (2000) *Incarcerated Parents and Their Children.* Washington, DC: US Department of Justice.

Mumola, Christopher J. (2007) *Medical Causes of Death in State Prisons, 2001–2004.* Washington, DC: US Department of Justice.

Murray, Joseph and Farrington, David P. (2005) 'Parental imprisonment: effects on boys' antisocial behaviour and delinquency through the life course', *Journal of Child Psychology and Psychiatry,* 46 (12): 1269–78.

Murray, Joseph and Farrington, David P. (2008) 'Effects of parental imprisonment on children', *Crime and Punishment,* 37 (1): 133–206.

Nurse, Anne (2002) *Fatherhood Arrested: Parenting from Within the Juvenile Justice System*. Nashville, TN: Vanderbilt University Press.

Page, Joshua (2004) 'Eliminating the enemy: the import of denying prisoners access to higher education in Clinton's America', *Punishment and Society*, 6 (4): 357–78.

Pager, Devah (2003) 'The mark of a criminal record', *American Journal of Sociology*, 108 (5): 937–75.

Pager, Devah (2007) *Marked: Race, Crime, and Finding Work in an Era of Mass Incarceration*. Chicago: University of Chicago Press.

Pager, Devah and Quillian, Lincoln (2005) 'Walking the talk? What employers say versus what they do', *American Sociological Review*, 70 (3): 355–80.

Pager, Devah, Western, Bruce and Bonikowski, Bar (2009) 'Discrimination in a low-wage labor market', *American Sociological Review*, 74 (5): 777–99.

Patterson, Evelyn J. (2010) 'Incarcerating death: mortality in U.S. state correctional facilities, 1985–1998', *Demography*, 47 (3): 587–607.

Patterson, Orlando (1982) *Slavery and Social Death: A Comparative Study*. Cambridge, MA: Harvard University Press.

Pettit, Becky and Western, Bruce (2004) 'Mass imprisonment and the life course: race and class inequality in U.S. incarceration', *American Sociological Review*, 69 (2): 151–69.

Rubinstein, Gwen and Mukamal, Debbie (2002) 'Welfare and housing – denial of benefits to drug offenders', in Marc Mauer and Meda Chesney-Lind (eds), *Invisible Punishment: The Collateral Consequences of Mass Imprisonment*. New York: The Free Press. pp. 37–49.

Rusche, Georg and Kirchheimer, Otto (1939 [2005]) *Punishment and Social Structure*. New York: Columbia University Press.

Sampson, Robert J. and Laub, John H. (1993) *Crime in the Making: Pathways and Turning Points Through Life*. Cambridge, MA: Harvard University Press.

Sampson, Robert J. and Loeffler, Charles (2010) 'Punishment's place: the local concentration of mass incarceration', *Daedalus*, 139 (3): 20–31.

Sampson, Robert J. and Wilson, William Julius (1995) 'Toward a theory of race, crime, and urban inequality', in John Hagan and Ruth Peterson (eds), *Crime and Inequality*. Stanford, CA: Stanford University Press. pp. 177–89.

Saperstein, Aliya and Penner, Andrew M. (2010) 'The race of a criminal record: how incarceration colors racial perceptions', *Social Problems*, 57 (1): 92–113.

Schnittker, Jason and John, Andrea (2007) 'Enduring stigma: the long-term effects of incarceration on health', *Journal of Health and Social Behavior*, 48 (2): 115–30.

Spaulding, A.C., Seals, R.M., McCallum, V.A., Perez, S.D., Brzozowski, A.K. and Steenland, N.K. (2011) 'Prisoner survival inside and outside of the institution: implications for healthcare planning', *American Journal of Epidemiology*, 173 (5): 479–87.

Spohn, C. and Holleran, D. (2000) 'The imprisonment penalty paid by young, unemployed black and Hispanic male offenders', *Criminology*, 38 (1): 281–306.

Swann, Christopher and Sylvester, Michelle Sharan (2006) 'The foster care crisis: what caused caseloads to grow?', *Demography*, 43 (2): 309–35.

Sykes, Gresham (1958) *The Society of Captives: A Study of a Maximum Security Prison*. Princeton, NJ: Princeton University Press.

Travis, Jeremy (2002) 'Invisible punishment: an instrument of social exclusion', in Marc Mauer and Meda Chesney-Lind (eds), *Invisible Punishment: The Collateral Consequences of Mass Imprisonment*. New York: New Press. pp. 15–36.

Venkatesh, Sudhir (2006) *Off the Books: The Underground Economy of the Urban Poor*. Cambridge, MA: Harvard University Press.

Wacquant, Loïc (2001) 'Deadly symbiosis: when ghetto and prison meet and mesh', *Punishment and Society*, 3 (1): 95–134.

Wakefield, Sera and Uggen, Christopher (2010) 'Incarceration and stratification', *Annual Review of Sociology*, 36 (1): 387–406.

Wang, Emily A., Pletcher, Mark, Lin, Fong, et al. (2009) 'Incarceration, incident hypertension, and access to health care', *Archives of Internal Medicine*, 169 (7): 687–93.

Western, Bruce (2002) 'The impact of incarceration on wage mobility and inequality', *American Sociological Review*, 67 (4): 477–98.

Western, Bruce (2006) *Punishment and Inequality in America*. New York: Russell Sage.

Western, Bruce and Beckett, Katherine (1999) 'How unregulated is the U.S. labor market? The penal system as a labor market institution', *American Journal of Sociology*, 104 (4): 1030–60.

Western, Bruce and Wildeman, Christopher (2009) 'The black family and mass incarceration', *Annals of the American Academy of Political and Social Science*, 621 (1): 221–42.

Wildeman, Christopher (2009) 'Parental imprisonment, the prison boom, and the concentration of childhood disadvantage', *Demography*, 46 (2): 265–80.

Wildeman, Christopher (2010) 'Paternal incarceration and children's physically aggressive behaviors: evidence from the Fragile Families and Child Wellbeing Study', *Social Forces*, 89 (1): 285–310.

Wildeman, Christopher and Western, Bruce (2010) 'Incarceration in fragile families', *The Future of Children*, 20 (2): 157–77.

Wilson, William J. (1987) *The Truly Disadvantaged: The Inner City, the Underclass, and Public Policy.* Chicago: University of Chicago Press.

Wood, Erika (2009) *Restoring the Right to Vote.* New York: Brennan Center for Justice.

9

Gender and Punishment

Mary Bosworth and Emma Kaufman

INTRODUCTION

Gender is strangely missing from studies of punishment and society. Outside the work of a few scholars (Daly, 1994; Bosworth, 1996, 1999; Howe, 1996; Hannah-Moffat, 2001), all of whom are women writing about women, gender is usually ignored or relegated to the footnotes of this field of scholarship (Garland, 1990; Liebling, 2004). To be sure there are some exceptions – Ben Crewe's (2009) recent account of prison life in HMP Wellingborough contains a number of references to masculinity, as does Eamonn Carrabine's (2006) genealogy of the Strangeways' prison riot. Fifteen years ago, Joe Sim (1995) warned of the dangers of the 'hypermasculinity' that, he said, was endemic in prisons. In general, however, those authors most associated with the study of punishment and society – David Garland, Jonathan Simon, Dario Melossi, Loïc Wacquant – have apparently seen little explanatory or analytic value in gender.

This article sets out to explain why gender matters and how gender theory, in particular, might inform critical accounts of punishment. To do this, we begin by mapping the themes of contemporary gender studies, a diverse and evolving field. We first examine the emergence of women's studies, its divergence from gender studies and queer theory, and the connections between feminist work and questions about race, class and sexuality. We then trace the presence and absences of those ideas in contemporary studies of punishment and society. This brief genealogy reveals notable gaps in criminological writing on gender and punishment, particularly around key concepts in feminist and queer theory. We explore those overlooked concepts in the context of wider debates about criminological methodology, asking how the study of punishment would shift if gender were a more prominent site of enquiry. This concluding turn to methodology aims to bring questions about gender into the compelling debate about how and why scholars examine the wider social context of punishment practices (Braithwaite, 2002; Zedner, 2002). This enquiry has been described as 'the sociology of punishment', the study of 'penality' and in this volume, as a key part of the field known as 'punishment and society'. Our task is to situate gender within that sociological line of thought. Our aim, in short, is to explore what happens when gender is placed at the centre rather than at the periphery of criminological analysis.

GENDER STUDIES

Contemporary gender studies is a highly varied field. Less a discipline than a set of organizing questions, gender studies spans academic boundaries and methodologies, in many cases challenging both. Its central concerns include the meaning and making of gender differences, the connections between gender, sex and sexuality, and the relationships between gender and inequalities in the social world. As a body of scholarship, gender studies emerged from the French and Anglo-American feminist movements of the 1950s and 1960s. Pioneering works of that period (de Beauvoir, 1949; Friedan, 1963) reignited a century of feminist social activism, precipitating significant advances toward women's equality and raising new theoretical questions about the treatment of 'the second sex' (de Beauvoir, 1949).

During the 1970s, black and radical feminist critiques expanded the reach of the largely white, middle-class women's movement, pushing feminists to consider the experiences of working-class women, lesbians and women of colour (Cade Bambara, 1970; Davis, 1971; Firestone, 1970; Ladner, 1971; Rowbotham, 1973; Rich, 1980; hooks, 1973; Carby, 1982). A decade later, the 'second wave' was transformed again by the HIV/AIDS epidemic, and with it, by the wave of critical scholarship on sexuality, cultural construction and identity politics (Fuss, 1989; Irigaray, 1985; Kristeva, 1981). This scholarship brought the notion of 'discourse' (Foucault, 1977) and the experiences of gay, lesbian, bisexual and transgender people into the feminist field of focus. Michel Foucault's three-volume *History of Sexuality* (1976–84) proved as formative to this critical moment as his *Discipline and Punish* (1977) did to the analogous period in criminology. Propelled by Foucault's insights into the link between knowledge and disciplinary power, scholars interested in gender began producing queer theory, a corpus of writing concerned with the production and transgression of social norms surrounding sexuality (Sedgwick, 1990; Warner, 1993; Corber and Valocchi, 2003; Halberstam, 2005).

Within academic circles, the turn toward queer theory was at once defining and divisive. Long committed to questions about women as a social group (and the related fight for women's equality and the establishment of women's studies departments), many feminist scholars of the early 1990s began to look anew at the categories – women, men, male, female – which had shaped the feminist enterprise for over a century (Butler, 1990; Laqueur, 1992; Schor and Weed, 1994). Scholars also revisited black feminist critiques during this period, examining the intersections between these gender categories and other facets of identity such as race, class and sexuality (Williams, 1988; Crenshaw, 1989, 1993). In *Gender Trouble*, Judith Butler (1990) famously challenged the assumptions that constitute gender norms, arguing that masculinity and femininity are idealized tropes through which conceptions of gender difference are produced. Butler (1990) also critiqued the connection between gender and the biological notion of sex, arguing that both are cultural constructions created by the repeated performance of gender norms.

This critical writing on gender, sexuality and identity politics brought women's studies into conversation with the emerging fields of gay and lesbian studies, performance studies, cultural studies and critical race theory. It also entailed an implicit (and sometimes more direct) critique of 'traditional' women's studies, which in this new frame seemed to emphasize gender at the expense of other aspects of identity, and to reify the distinctions between genders that queer theorists were working to unfold. This complex debate persists today in combined 'women's and gender studies' departments and centres across the USA and UK where, roughly speaking, women's studies encapsulates a body of writing that takes women and women's experiences as its object of inquiry, while gender studies (and queer theory) are concerned with sexuality and gender's structural role in organizing the social world. Though sometimes divisive, such intellectual disputes over the terms of reference within feminism, gender theory and women's studies (for example, Benhabib et al., 1996), have also been highly productive, propelling academic inquiry forward and producing an extensive and influential body of interdisciplinary research and theory.

Notwithstanding the vigour and passion of some of their internal debates, contemporary scholars of 'women's and gender studies' – among whom we count ourselves – are also united and motivated by shared ideas and themes. Authors working on gender and sexuality are generally interested in the difference between gender as a set of expectations about behaviour and sex as a biological idea.[1] They (we) are also largely committed to the anti-essentialist project of breaking down assumptions about what is 'natural' to human identity. This critical project is linked to the broader activist legacies of feminism and queer theory, which have long sought to produce social change.

Building on the activist lessons of the women's movement, most applied feminist research adopts a reflexive, qualitative methodology. The impact of this approach has been two-fold. On the one hand, feminist researchers across a range of fields have spent considerable time discussing and seeking to redress the power imbalances inherent in the research process (Oakley, 1981; Reinharz, 1992). On the other hand, feminists' qualitative approach has shed light on many subjects previously effaced from academic analysis (Williams, 1988; Spivak, 1989). In both strategies, feminist literature underscores how the questions scholars ask relate to the types of knowledge that get counted as legitimate and true (Smith, 1987). Knowledge is productive in this view, both in a Foucauldian sense and in its potential for social activism. Therefore, while feminist writing spans from empiricism to high theory (and in some cases can appear distant from the messiness of daily life), all feminist research begins from a commitment to connect academic inquiry to change in the social world. Such a close and purposeful link between the politics and the practice of feminist research holds out considerable promise for critical accounts of punishment.

A GENEALOGY OF GENDER IN THE SOCIOLOGY OF PUNISHMENT

Feminist ideas about the subjects of research – and the way research should be done – have surfaced in criminology more and more over the past 30 years. In particular, criminologists have heeded the call of women's studies to write 'by, on and for' women, producing a small but steady stream of work on women in prison (Rafter, 1985; Carlen, 1983; Padel and Stephenson, 1988), policing (Chan, 1997; Westmarland, 2001), courts, (Daly, 1994); gangs (Campbell, 1984; Miller, 2001), offending (Chesney-Lind, 1986; Steffensmeier and Allan, 1996) and, above all, on women's experiences of victimisation (for example, Stanko, 1992; Hoyle, 1998; Walklate, 2006). Alongside such empirical studies, there has been a limited amount of theoretical writing about the relationship between feminism, gender and criminology more broadly (for example, Smart, 1976; Gelsthorpe and Morris, 1990; Daly and Chesney-Lind, 1988; Naffine, 1995; Flavin, 2001). The past decade has also witnessed a handful of feminist theoretical texts on punishment (Howe, 1996), justice (Hudson, 2003) and the law (Valverde, 2003; Wells, 2004).

These publications are not all products of an explicitly feminist turn in criminological writing. Studies of women's imprisonment existed before the modern women's movement; first-hand accounts by serving or former prisoners, female wardens, prison governors and penal reformers date back at least to the 19th-century work of Elizabeth Fry (Fry, 1827; see also Henry, 1973; Padel and Stephenson, 1988). Sociological accounts of women's imprisonment have also been around for some time. The early prison sociologists in the USA, with their strict typologies of inmate subculture and their concerns about importation and deprivation, often included women's prisons in their analysis (Ward and Kassebaum, 1965; Giallombardo, 1966; Heffernan, 1974). More critical accounts of women's imprisonment followed in the UK, starting with Pat Carlen's ethnography of the Scottish women's prison at Cornton Vale (Carlen, 1983) and Alexandra Mandaraka-Sheppard's (1986) analysis of the relationship between women's self-image and their behaviour in prison.

For many years, scholars of women's imprisonment sought to fill in the knowledge gap about prison, giving details about women's establishments to complete a broader understanding of the impact of incarceration. Though often critical – both of regimes and of the pains of imprisonment – few, if any, of these studies were explicitly feminist in orientation. Until Carlen, prison sociologists were heavily influenced by sex role theory that explained women's behaviour and experiences behind bars as the result of their universal, fixed, subject positions as mothers, daughters and wives. Such accounts often merely reaffirmed the views of penal managers, who held that one of the key tasks of the woman's prison was to (re)socialise female offenders into appropriate heterosexual, feminine behaviour and aspiration.[2]

Pat Carlen's work did much to open the sociology of imprisonment to the insights of gender theory. Describing her book as an attempt to 'theorize about the relationships between the biographies of women prisoners, the discourses which constitute them and the politics which render them the "female" subject (albeit denied) of penology', Carlen made it clear that women's experiences of imprisonment were heavily dependent on (largely negative) and socially constructed notions of gender (Carlen, 1983: 3). Famously critical of the prison's 'regimes of femininity', she argued that women prisoners were routinely infantilized, denied agency and choice and required to follow outmoded and unrealistic forms of feminine behaviour. Rather than being taught 'general survival skills which would enable them to live without a man', female prisoners were given lessons to help them 'fill their ideal place in the ideal family' (Carlen, 1983: 73).

Carlen's writing on women in prison moved criminology beyond its rigidly gendered categories, initiating a new discussion about the ways that prisons create and operate through gender roles. In the decades since Carlen's work was first published, sociological accounts of women's imprisonment have tended to be more explicitly feminist in orientation and, in some cases at least, have engaged more directly with gender studies and critical social theory (for example, Owen, 1998; Bosworth, 1999; Cook and Davies, 1999; Hannah-Moffat, 1995, 2001; Gardner and Kruttschnitt, 2005; Sudbury, 2005). While most of this literature follows the logic of women's studies in its primary focus on women as a category of analysis, some feminist criminology has branched out to engage more directly with gender theory, exploring in some detail the self-constitutive relationship between imprisonment and gender. According to the latter body of work, prison regimes do not simply reflect and reward gendered notions of appropriate feminine behaviour; rather, the prison solidifies and propagates particular (binary) constructions of gender throughout society.

Much of this theoretical literature on women's imprisonment draws heavily on the work of Michel Foucault, particularly on *Discipline and Punish* and his later essays on governmentality (Foucault, 1977, 1978). Such accounts examine gender both as a mode of discipline in prison and as a potential site of – and resource for – resistance (Bosworth, 1999; Bosworth and Carrabine, 2001). In this view, prison rules and 'penal governance' are understood as more than just repressive tools of control; instead, they are also 'a form of productive power that has the intention of producing individuals who meet certain normative expectations' (Hannah-Moffat, 2001: 7). Here the structure of the penal institution operates *through* gender, and in doing so creates 'appropriately' gendered human behaviour and socialized (docile) subjects. The power to punish, in other words, simultaneously depends on and produces notions of gender. At the same time, however, gender is not foreclosed or fixed, but is itself subject to change and reinterpretation. Likewise, prisoners are not inert, nor do they wholly lack agency. Penal regimes and expectations about feminine behaviour can thus create a resource – however limited – for transgression and resistance (Bosworth, 1999; Bosworth and Carrabine, 2001).

The counterpoint to the range of work on women in prison is the more-or-less absence of research on gender in men's penal institutions. In contrast to the attention paid to 'regimes of femininity' in women's imprisonment, and notwithstanding a body of work that sprang up in the mid-1990s about masculinities and crime (Campbell, 1993; Messerschmidt, 1993; Newburn and Stanko, 1995; Collier, 1998), few criminologists have focused on masculinity in prison. Such silence is both regrettable and confounding, for ideas about masculinity and normative, heterosexual male behaviour flow throughout the prison. Those texts which do exist depict masculinity as a structural factor underpinning men's behaviour behind bars, both as prison officers and as inmates (Sim, 1995; Carrabine and Longhurst, 1998). Gender identity, in such accounts, is primarily a practical accomplishment and one that must be constantly reasserted.

Perhaps one of the reasons for the relative paucity of research into gender in men's prisons is that masculinity exists as a somewhat paradoxical resource for men behind bars. On the one hand, masculinity is heavily equated with power and control within the prison, particularly for those who acquire a dominant position in the social and institutional hierarchy. Yet, unless there is a total breakdown of order, a prisoner's ability to reap the full benefits of masculinity is always held in check by the authority of the prison staff. As in women's prisons, then, only a certain form of gender is encouraged in men's prisons; while elements of hegemonic masculinity may be championed – for instance, by encouraging prisoners to engage in paid work – the fact remains that men in prison are, like imprisoned women, entirely dependent on the institution for all their needs. This state of dependency is clearly at odds with the primary tenets of masculinity and, as Ben Crewe makes clear, has a potent effect on relationships among prisoners, and also between them and prison officers (Crewe, 2006, 2009).

Though there is some criminological discussion of the negative implications of hegemonic masculinity (or what Sim (1995) labels hypermasculinity), particularly in terms of its links to violence (Bowker, 1997), the literature on men in prison is not nearly as engaged in constructing a broader critique of gender in society as much of the work on women's prison has been. To some extent, this distinction reflects the differing intellectual origins of both bodies of work. Whereas feminist criminology draws (at least to some extent) on wider debates and theoretical literature in women and gender studies, much of the extant literature on masculinity in criminology is heavily dependent on a fairly small body of writing, primarily the notion of hegemonic masculinity first articulated in R.W. Connell's 1987 book *Gender and Power* (Connell, 1987; see also Connell, 1995, 2010).[3] While Connell emphasizes the negative impact of certain attributes of and assumptions about men, the studies of masculinity that draw on her work have yet to yield an effective social movement – nor, save for the writings on self-help by figures such as Robert Bly (1991), do they seem very concerned with doing so.

Indeed, most accounts of imprisonment simply do not consider gender at all, referring instead to 'the prison' without qualification. Much of this work – which constitutes the centre of gravity in studies of punishment and society – presents imprisonment in conceptual terms, as a metaphor for the state of democracy (Barker, 2009), neoliberalism

(Wacquant, 1999, 2009) or the culture of control (Garland, 2001). While admirable in its reach, this approach to imprisonment can suppress the material reality of incarceration – the fact, in other words, that prisons are actual places composed of real (gendered) people living in real time. Even in those prison studies which do examine institutional life, prisoners are often disembodied and disconnected from the gendered practices that shape penal expectations and daily life within the prison (for example, Sparks et al., 1996; Liebling, 2004). In this latter body of work, power flows among prisoners, restraining some and encouraging others according to notions of 'justice', 'legitimacy' and 'order'. Skilfully revisiting Weber's theories of social order (Weber, 1968; Beetham, 1991) and Foucauldian (1977) notions of 'the carceral', this writing underexplores the feminist research on justice and identity that grew from both authors' work (Hudson, 2003; Butler, 2004; Sedgwick, 2004). As a result, theoretical accounts of power within the prison tend to overlook how concepts like justice and legitimacy are refracted through ideas about gender. From a feminist perspective, this means that many accounts of punishment miss a significant point about the way power gets expressed.

TURNING TO FEMINIST THEORY

Feminist writing on power is one of many avenues for further research on the relationship between gender and justice. There is no question that contemporary scholars of punishment are more attuned to questions about gender than at previous times. The experiences of women, the forces of femininity and masculinity, and the production of gender norms play a much more prominent part in criminological work than they have in the past. Yet there remain significant gaps in the criminological engagement with gender, especially in terms of gender theory. While a limited number of criminologists have (at least to some degree) acknowledged women's experiences as an important object of sociological inquiry, much less consideration has been given to how feminist and queer critiques of identity might affect the understanding of punishment (though see, Howe, 1996; Bosworth, 1999). This is a significant oversight, for many of the terms of gender theory have straightforward relevance to the study of punishment and penality.

In particular, criminologists might turn to three of the most significant theoretical contributions to emerge from feminist writing in the past 20 years: intersectionality (Crenshaw, 1989, 1993); performativity (Butler, 1990); and embodiment (Scarry, 1985; Butler, 1993). Coined by legal scholar Kimberlé Crenshaw in 1989, 'intersectionality' is the sociological theory that identity – and with it, discrimination and marginalization based on identity – emerges from the complex interaction of constructed categories such as race, ethnicity, class, gender and sexuality. This view, which grew from black feminist critiques of the second wave feminist movement (hooks, 1984; Hill Collins, 1991), emphasizes the overlapping, mutually constitutive nature of identity. In doing so, it resists reductionist tendencies that had characterised much 'mainstream' feminist, Marxist, and critical race scholarship. As Crenshaw explains:

> Feminist efforts to politicize experiences of women and antiracist efforts to politicize experiences of people of color have frequently proceeded as though the issues and experiences they each detail occur on mutually exclusive terrains. Although racism and sexism readily intersect in the lives of real people, they seldom do in feminist and antiracist practices. And so, when the practices expound identity as 'woman' or 'person of color' as an either/or proposition, they relegate the identity of women of color to a location that resists telling. My objective here is to advance the telling of that location. (1993: 1)

Crenshaw analyses violence against women of colour, arguing that neither a 'feminist' nor a 'critical race' lens alone can explain the amplified marginalization women of colour experience within the criminal justice system. In her other work, Crenshaw (1989) examines the intersection of race, class and gender in employment practices and workplace discrimination. In both cases she argues that scholars, including those explicitly concerned with structural inequality, often fail to recognize the problems with myopic accounts of identity. As a result, much of the scholarship on issues like crime, poverty and punishment – that is, topics dealing with social stratification – effaces the complexities of its subject matter. Such writing often fails to recognize how social injustice emerges at and from the intersection of people's identities – say, as working-class women of colour, single ex-felon fathers or 'undocumented' foreign workers.

Crenshaw's argument resonates strongly with literature on punishment and society, a field often defined by its concern with the disproportionate exercise and effects of state power. Sociologists of punishment since Foucault (and arguably since Durkheim) have examined the use of punishment against particular groups and toward particular ends, mapping how disciplinary strategies demarcate the boundaries of the state and the social community through categories such as 'the delinquent' and 'the dangerous' (Durkheim, 1961; Foucault, 1977). So, too, Stan Cohen (1972) famously asked why certain classes of people become 'folk devils' and sites of 'moral panics'. More recently, Loïc Wacquant (1999, 2009) has examined how African American men and the poor become disproportionately subject to mass imprisonment, while Jonathan Simon (2000) has explored the marginalization of sex offenders in a 'victim culture'. Each of these inquiries, and the many more they have inspired, explore how particular groups of people are targeted and affected by the state's punitive apparatus. In this sense, the study of punishment can be conceived as an inquiry into how identity interacts with disciplinary power.

Feminist writing on intersectionality – on the complexity of identity, and on its irreducible connection to race, class, gender and other social phenomena – could enrich this work. The theory of intersectionality demands and propels a dynamic, contextual understanding of social inequality, one attuned both to the force and to the complexity of identity categories. With its focus on the contextual nature of inequality, intersectionality theory might push criminologists to reconsider how and why poor, young, African American and Latino men and poor, young, British Muslims have different experiences of punishment than their white, Christian or middle-class counterparts – why, for instance, some people of colour and members of religious groups report racism within prisons, or why racialized and classed sentencing disparities persist in systems with and without judicial discretion.

Scholars are already interested in these issues and have done much to map them out (for example, Bourgois, 2003; Bhui, 2007, 2009, on the first issue; Philips, 2008; Philips and Earle, 2010, on the second; and Tonry, 1996; Mauer, 1999, on the sentencing disparities). However, such accounts do not take the intersection of identity categories as their starting point. Instead, as the scholars of women's imprisonment did before them, these authors tend to fill gaps in our understanding of ethnic minorities in the criminal justice system. This work is vital to criminology, and our consideration of it is not intended as criticism. Rather, we want to suggest that the existing work on race and ethnic minorities might serve as a catalyst for more critical work on how the intersectionality of identity affects the exercise and meaning of punishment. The question, in other words, is how current conversations about punishment might be pushed forward if criminologists explored the links across marginalised groups and mapped how power flows between them.

Anthropologist Asale Angel-Ajani (2003) provides a compelling example of the potential of such an approach in her account of border control in Italy. Directing attention to the border – then a new site for criminological analysis – Angel-Ajani examines how populist racist discourses intersect with gendered conventions to shape African women's experiences of Italian migration control. According to Angel-Ajani, race and gender are interwoven in border control and policing practices that frame female migrants as undeserving, deviant offenders. This analysis illustrates that race and gender are inseparable, and indeed, amplify one another in the experience of migration. It also demonstrates how a feminist understanding of identity might enrich writing on social control.

Performativity, a theory crafted by feminist philosopher Judith Butler (1990, 1993) in the early 1990s, also holds much promise for the sociology of punishment beyond the areas in which it has already been applied (Bosworth, 1999; Valverde, 2003). Building from British philosopher J.L. Austin's (1975) work on performative speech, Butler argued that notions of gender are produced through the repeated performance of social norms. Gender, in other words, is an act – a part played out and made real in the contours of daily life. Performativity is at once a thesis on the construction of identity and, at least in some readings, a roadmap for its transgression; if gender is performed, then it can – and some would argue should – be performed otherwise as a means to contest the constraints which shape power relations in an unequal world.

The performativity thesis, which has been consistently reconfigured and reiterated in the last two decades of feminist scholarship (Butler, 1997; Muñoz, 1999; Sedgwick, 2004), has a great deal to offer scholars concerned with the link between punishment and society. At its base, performativity is a theory about how norms are produced and simultaneously productive. Butler's central point – that identity norms are performed, and duly attached to power within a social system – applies smoothly to the analysis of punishment. This insight, for instance, might inform criminologists' questions about how 'expressive' policymaking works to reconstitute the faltering nation-state (Garland, 2001) and how 'the flow of power' functions in penal institutions (Liebling, 2004). Governments that 'act out' (Garland, 2001), the disproportionate sentencing of 'deviant' female offenders (Daly, 1994), and prison hierarchies revolving around the performance of masculinity (Crewe, 2009) make new sense in Butler's frame. So, too, do prisoners' expressions of resistance (Bosworth, 1996; Bosworth and Carrabine, 2001), the rituals of violence in gang culture (Miller, 2001) and even methodological concerns about presenting our work as 'practical' enough to gain access to closed institutions (Hannah-Moffat, 2011).

Criminologists have begun to examine each of these topics, but few have seen their work through the lens of performativity. Garland's writing on the 'culture of control' (2001), for instance, does not consider the ways in which a punitive culture is performed through penal policy; nor do most methodological debates see social science as a performance of 'proper' research. While the masculinities literature has (to some extent) considered performativity, this work typically situates performance as an explanatory factor for behaviour in penal institutions. From Butler's perspective, performativity is a productive enterprise connected to the broader social world. In the case of the prison, then, performativity studies might push criminologists to consider how masculine practices within the penal institution shape the expression of gender *outside* prison walls, particularly in those communities most subject to the penal apparatus, such as low-income urban areas and minority ethnic communities. This kind of analysis would connect questions about the 'interior life' of the prison (Liebling, 2004) to concerns about the prison's effect on marginalized communities (Clear, 2007). In the case of Garland's influential work on culture, the theory of performativity could foreground questions about why and how passing punitive legislation works to create communities and make them feel safe. In both instances, performativity encourages further consideration of the mechanisms through which state power is realized.

The writing on performativity can also draw feminist concerns about *embodiment* into conversation with criminology. In *Bodies That Matter* (1993), Butler makes clear that performativity is a theory that begins from the material body – from the actual acting out of gender norms, and from the often deeply repressive ways that gender difference gets expressed in society. She explains:

> It will be as important to think about how and to what end bodies are constructed as it will be to think about how and to what end bodies are *not* constructed and, further, to ask after how bodies which fail to materialize provide the necessary 'outside,' if not the necessary support, for the bodies which, in materializing the norm, qualify as bodies that matter. (1993: 16)

In her own work, Butler brings the theory of performativity to bear on the question of social justice by asking which kinds of performances get counted in the social world. The performance of masculine and feminine genders registers as meaningful, for instance, and in doing so works to construct gender norms and legitimate 'normally' gendered bodies. But what happens to bodies whose performances diverge from this script? What happens to transgender bodies, to butch bodies, to femme bodies in this economy of gender? The underside to performativity, it seems, is that some people – those who conform – end up mattering more than others.

The question of how certain bodies come to be considered socially important – worth reforming, worth punishing, worth paroling, worth researching – shapes the sociology of punishment. Indeed, it was this question that motivated Foucault's (1977) writing on 'the birth of the prison', a text which has had such an influence on the field. As Foucault explained it:

> In our society the systems of punishment are to be situated in a certain 'political economy' of the body: even if they do not make use of violent or bloody punishment, even when they use 'lenient' methods involving confinement or correction, it is always the body that is at issue – the body and its forces, their utility and their docility, their distribution and their submission. (1997: 25)

For Foucault, the state's power to punish gets expressed on and through the physical body, whether it is tarred and feathered, incarcerated, or electronically tagged. The sociology of punishment is in this sense *about bodies* – about their treatment, their confinement, their constitutive part in the realization of 'criminal justice'. And as gender theorists have long noted, the bodies at the centre of the justice system come in genders and races, ethnicities and sexualities, all attached to class structures and the histories of particular political systems.

Following Foucault and Butler, sociologists of punishment might then look back to the body as a starting point for critical questions about the expression of power in the late modern state. Gender theorists have been doing this kind of questioning for some time: one-quarter of a century ago, Elaine Scarry (1985) argued that the vulnerability of men's bodies becomes the basis for torture, and for waging war. More recently, Judith Butler (2004) has written about the relationship between embodiment and state violence, while feminist accounts of the conditions in both state and military prisons (Howe, 1996; Britton, 2003; Bosworth, 2010) have explored the embodied politics of imprisonment. This writing paves the way for further criminological work on the link between current practices of punishment and the 'political economy of the body' (Foucault, 1977).

Like intersectionality and performativity, then, feminist theory on embodiment could provide the basis for a new vantage point on the study of punishment. Where intersectionality directs our attention to the complexities of social inequality, performativity motivates a fresh account of power within and around state institutions. The notion of embodiment, on the other hand, becomes a way to reconsider how and why particular punishments express particular social meanings. Building from a focus on the actual physical body, for instance, sociologists of punishment might ask what we as societies mean to do when we constantly videotape residents (Goold, 2004) and electronically tag deviants, levy ASBOS against the 'anti-social' (Donoghue, 2010) and imprison 'the dangerous' for public protection (Zedner, 2005, 2007). What becomes of the deviant bodies in these transactions, and how does their embodiment allow for – and perhaps resist – this realization of state-sponsored punishment? Where, moreover, are the bodies that we do not see: those in the war prisons, for example, or those which wash ashore after failed attempts to reach the relative safety of Europe (Pickering and Weber, 2011)? Such questions foreground the link between embodiment and the ethical nature of criminological enquiry. In doing so, they raise one final challenge to research on punishment and society.

THE POLITICS OF STUDYING 'PUNISHMENT AND SOCIETY'

Gender theorists' emphasis on the material body aims to underscore the part that gender (and other facets of identity) play in determining power relations. This is an epistemological and methodological point: gender matters to the way the world works, and so we should look at gender when we are writing about the social world. It is also, however, a political – and ethical – claim, for feminists' focus on bodies aims to acknowledge the people that inhabit them, and in doing so, to *make those people matter*. Judith Butler wants to 'challenge … the symbolic hegemony' in a way that 'force[s] a radical rearticulation' of what qualifies a life 'worth protecting' (1993: 16); Kimberlé Crenshaw (1993) works to 'locate' women of colour in a discussion about criminal justice from which they have been effaced; and so many other feminist authors write with similar motivations. In sum, gender scholars' emphasis on embodiment connects their academic and activist goals.

Criminologists concerned with the sociological aspects of punishment – with the interpreted meanings of punishment, and with the stratifying effects of punitive regimes – might take a page from this methodological book. Scholars of punishment and society are defined by our interest in the wider world in which penality takes root. The political tone of this 'sociological' focus is barely beneath the surface, particularly in contrast with alternate traditions in mainstream criminological scholarship. As a group, we are interested in how and why we punish, in acknowledging state power and the exercise of state force as sociological phenomena. This interpretive frame not only provides a critical commentary on the practices of contemporary society. It also, as Lucia Zedner and John Braithwaite have noted, becomes a way to imagine the world otherwise arranged, a more moderate and perhaps less punitive society (Zedner, 2002; Braithwaite, 2002; see also, O'Malley, 1999; Loader, 2010; Simon, 2010).

Zedner lays out this positive vision of sociological criminology in her 'appreciative critique' of David Garland's (2001) *The Culture of Control* (Zedner, 2002). Taking Garland's influential book as a metonym for broader changes in the field, Zedner (2002) argues that the trend toward 'grand narratives' and deconstruction in 'sociological' criminology divorces scholars from the normative implications and the potential of our work. As she explains it, Garland's writing positions the criminologist as 'vigilant watch, the witness to the multiple, shifting dangers that attach to late modernity' (2002: 364). This descriptive vantage point, she warns, delivers a 'dystopic' approach to state power, one which is pessimistic about the possibility of political change and 'self-consciously indifferent to its own political or normative import' (2002: 364).

Through its deconstructionist method, the sociology of punishment thus becomes a fatalistic enterprise, one which entails 'the abandonment of a larger political vision and smack[s] of capitulation to the "hyper-modern, flexible, neo-conservative, economic politics" that are the very subject of Garland's analysis' (Zedner, 2002: 364–5; see also van Swaaningen, 1997: 194; Braithwaite, 2002; Bosworth and Loader, 2010). There is, in other words, a latent and paradoxical politics to the 'apoliticism' of much contemporary writing on punishment and society. This, of course, marks a stark divergence from the politically explicit writing on punishment that emerged from National Deviancy Conference in the 1960s and 1970s. Today, scholarly accounts of punishment often seem to chart the trajectory of state power from a distance, sidestepping normative claims to the way things *ought* to be – who ought to be in prison, for instance, or what we as a society ought to be doing to and for those most affected by criminal justice policies.[4] Engaging with such normative claims, which spring directly from a sociological perspective on punishment, is then one way to counter the fatalism of contemporary sociologies of punishment. Zedner's critique thus becomes the grounds for newly normative criminological work.

Zedner does not, however, spell out how such normative work begins. Here we might return to gender theory – and in particular, to the writing of the late queer theorist and literary critic Eve Sedgwick. In her last book (2004), Sedgwick launched a methodological critique that reads much like Zedner's account of *The Culture of Control*. In Sedgwick's case, the troubling academic trend is toward 'paranoid reading', a deconstructionist model of enquiry in which the literary critic aims to *unveil* or *reveal* some knowledge that lies beneath the novel (Sedgwick, 2004: 126). For Sedgwick, the paranoid impulse – which, she notes, is 'now nearly synonymous with criticism itself' – is a pervasive outgrowth of Paul Ricoeur's hermeneutic of suspicion, one that makes a full-blown methodology of suspecting, demystifying and tracking what knowledge does (Sedgwick, 2004: 124; Ricoeur, 1969). Extending this analysis to criminology, we might say that sociologists of punishment often adopt a 'paranoid' hermeneutic, engaging in a kind of deconstructionist detective work whose aim is to eke out the repressive workings of state power wherever they exist. The problem, just as Zedner pointed out, is that this hermeneutic quickly becomes a normative epistemology in which the *right* kind of knowledge is that which is found and exposed through paranoia, deconstruction, and the practice of 'ever-vigilant watch' (Zedner, 2002). Here again, the critic remains at a distance from the society under critique – and in doing so, makes a political decision and advances an implicitly normative claim about what academic enquiry ought to be doing.

Sedgwick argues that we can counteract this tendency by shifting critical inquiry away from deconstruction, and indeed, away from epistemology altogether. In their place, she suggests that critics turn to the normative and explicitly political ideas of feminist and queer theory, and to the lines of enquiry that flow from those ideas (Butler, 1993). From this perspective, criminologists ought to be concerned less with determining *where* state power is at work than with asking *what* the effort to expose state power is doing to the study of punishment. As Sedgwick puts it, 'what does knowledge *do* – the pursuit of it, the having and exposing of it, the receiving again of knowledge of what one already knows?' (2004: 124). What, for instance, are the effects of endlessly retelling the story of how the state disciplines, and in doing so creates, its subjects? What is the result of a 'dystopic' sociology of punishment? (Zedner, 2002).

One answer, it seems, is that new avenues of thought – like those emerging from feminist and queer studies – get obscured. As the contributors to a recent special issue of *Theoretical Criminology* argued (Bosworth and Loader, 2010), the sociology of punishment, at least in some readings, has become rather intellectually stuck. According to Ian Loader:

> For some time now analysts of punishment have been drawn – like bystanders to a car crash – to what has become known, perhaps a little complacently, as the 'punitive turn'. Article after article, and book after book, has sought to document and explain the rise and consequences of the penal state in the USA and UK – as registered by such indicators as record levels of imprisonment, the decline of rehabilitation, the return of expressive, ostentatious punishment, crackdowns on sex offenders, the flurry of anti-crime legislation and the generally shrill tone of political and popular debate about crime. (2010: 350)

As a result, sites or modes of punishment other than prisons (such as the fine, see O'Malley, 2010) are often ignored, while other lines of thought and intellectual approaches are either overlooked altogether or struggle for recognition. So, too, the relationship between epistemology and methodology gets suppressed.

While it may be contentious – or simply premature – to speak of a 'canon' of writing on punishment and society, this handbook demonstrates that a set of authors and texts have indeed emerged to mark out and constitute this disciplinary sub-field. Accordingly, there must also be ideas that, as yet, have not. Gender theories can be counted among them. Since its origins, the sociological study of punishment has championed theoretically informed, critical criminological scholarship, often in the face of narrower, empiricist, policy-driven research (Garland, 1990). But scholars' obeisance to only particular writings by Foucault,[5] Durkheim and Marx has restricted the sociological imagination, leaving other ideas and theories in ever-smaller and marginalised sub-fields. Notwithstanding the considerable work of individual feminist scholars, gender theory remains an area of scholarship that is drawn on only rarely, and still almost exclusively in studies of women's imprisonment.

Such positioning of gender theory has an effect not only on the intellectual development of sociological theory about punishment, but also on how research on punishment is done. As we argued above, feminist accounts of embodiment, performativity, and intersectionality work to connect the objects of academic inquiry to marginalized subjects in the social world. To return to its terminology, gender theory provides a critical model for 'making bodies matter' (Butler, 1993). This theoretical paradigm illuminates the political and ethical dimensions of criminological scholarship on the many subjects of criminal justice who 'don't count', such as those 'forgotten behind bars' (Kaufman, 2012; PRT, 2004), in immigration detention centres (Bosworth and Kaufman, 2011), and at secret military prisons abroad (Cole, 2003; Brown, 2005; Bosworth, 2010). Within a feminist frame, this writing on 'forgotten prisoners' – and so much of the sociological writing about punishment – becomes a form of academic activism. It also becomes one way to encourage more empirical work.

ENGENDERING EMPIRICAL CRITIQUE

Battles over method are familiar territory for social scientists across a range of disciplines. Criminologists are no different (see for example, Bosworth and Hoyle, 2011). Among scholars concerned with the links between punishment and society, there is a rough internal bifurcation between those who conduct fieldwork in prisons (Bosworth, 1999; Liebling, 2004; Phillips, 2008) and those who write primarily theoretical analyses of punishment and penality (Garland, 1990; Simon, 2007). Many of the most influential books in the field (Garland, 1990, 2001; Simon, 2001) fall into the latter category, pushing the conversation toward this theoretical pole. This division of labour means that sociological accounts of punishment are often divorced from actual prisons and those confined within them, while the wider emphasis on prisons obscures the far greater number of people subject to other forms of punishment. In sum, there has, to return to Lucia Zedner's diction, been a general trend toward 'grand narratives' (Zedner, 2002) that has pulled the field away from empirical analysis.

In addition to promoting a fatalist view of scholarship – the methodological problem we just explored – such 'grand' theories gloss over the real people whose lives they describe. Thus we find that theoretical writing in this field often refers to the general category of 'punishment' rather than to specific criminal justice practices. This tendency not only discounts the nuances between different practices of punishment; it also suppresses the experiences of the people subject to such practices. In doing so, 'grand' theory can, however unintentionally, efface its own subjects, rendering them disempowered objects of analysis. Theorizing without reference to the lived experience of punishment is not only a methodological choice; it also becomes an *ethical* oversight.

Scholars of punishment and society also tend to generalize about widespread societal belief systems, such as those in 'the culture of control' (Garland, 2001), the 'risk society' (Garland, 2003) or the 'neoliberal nation-state' (Wacquant, 2009; De Giorgi, 2010). Though attractive, these broad terms obscure forms of dissent and equate beliefs across diverse segments of the community and varied parts of the country. As a result, differences between parts of the world may be elided, particularly when the USA is used as the comparator (Tonry, 2007). 'Theory', in other words, all too easily proceeds with scant attention to the complexity of lived reality. It is no wonder then that issues of gender, and their intersections with race and economic deprivation, rarely surface in 'grand' sociological writing. Nor is it surprising that such scholarship receives little feedback from the communities it describes (see, in contrast, Gilmore, 2007).

In its emphasis on activism, gender theory has long resisted these trends – and with them, the chasm between theoretical and empirical work. Like Marxist sociology before it, and in conjunction with research in ethnic studies and critical theory, gender theory explicitly urges criminologists to integrate theory with practice (praxis) by turning to 'lived experience'[6] within the social world. In criminology, this normative view of research was evident in the early work of feminist criminologists and sociologists, some of whom were instrumental in mapping the boundaries of domestic violence and rape research and establishing the first domestic violence shelters (Stanko, 1992). These days, however, criminologists are rarely so bold. The problem is not that criminologists are not engaged; examples can easily be conjured of scholarship that shapes penal policy (Liebling, 2004), while elsewhere considerable effort is being expended to influence British and American criminal justice practice (Sherman et al., 2002). But the normative questions in such accounts rarely move beyond matters of efficacy or efficiency. Rarely if ever do these scholars ask how the system – as a whole – might be reconceived. Given the discipline's dependency on the state agencies for research access, we all too often become advocates for an improved version of the logic and rationale already underpinning penal practice.

This is not to say that activist criminology no longer exists. Indeed, within prison studies, there is an ongoing body of work arguing for the closure of penal institutions and an end to the 'prison industrial complex' (for example, Davis, 2001; Sudbury, 2005). Some of these accounts, particularly those associated with the work of the US organization Critical Resistance, begin from those marginalized communities who are most adversely affected by penal policies; they are, in other words, closely attuned to issues of race, gender and class (Sudbury, 2005). The point, however, is that these accounts, like their subject matter, are at best considered to be at the margins of the field of scholarship known as 'the sociology of punishment'. 'Activist' accounts of punishment are usually labelled as just that – somehow separate from 'academic' work and rather less well regarded within an intellectual framework that prioritises ideas over action.

Accounts of punishment which take the activism of gender theory as its model eschews such intellectual divisions, instead using the words and experiences of prisoners, prison officers, advocates and victims as the grounds for a theoretical account of punishment. This kind of scholarship does not merely 'flesh out' our understanding of punishment; it also aims to build a more persuasive critique of penality, one that champions a politics of recognition of our shared humanity (see for example, Bosworth et al., 2005). Such work serves as a reminder, above all, that punishment is not merely applied to others, but is inextricably connected to 'our' way of life. Within this frame, the experience of the individual can illuminate – and instigate – wider social transformation. This was the notion of social change from which the feminist movement grew in the 1960s, and the theory from which feminist academic work has developed since. Today, it is the methodological and ethical principle to which criminologists might turn to construct a simultaneously empirical and theoretically rich account of late modern penality.

CONCLUSION

All too often, paying attention to gender continues to be viewed simply as a call to include women in the conversation. In a field like criminology, which examines a system that primarily processes men, this understanding means that gender is rarely taken seriously as a starting point for critical analysis. Mainstream scholarship over the years has ignored gender, while all of the disciplinary subfields (including studies of punishment and imprisonment) have witnessed the publication of specific texts and accounts of women's experiences. However, as we have argued throughout this chapter, taking gender seriously involves much more than writing about women. While this remains an important part of any critical scholarship – since, notwithstanding their smaller numbers, women are also part of the criminal justice system – it is not the sole, nor even the primary aim of gender analysis. Instead, turning to gender may offer radical and far-reaching alternatives to our understanding punishment and to the practice of sociological criminology.

A feminist understanding of the sociological project has a number of elements – epistemological, methodological, and as we have suggested, ethical as well. The 'vantage point' of a gendered analysis begins from the view that the intersections between gender, race, class and sexuality are constitutive of our selves and of our experiences of the social world. These points of intersection are simultaneously productive subject positions and meaningful boundaries of individual identity. Through our complex identities, we thus become both subjects and subjected to the hierarchies and histories of power. This interplay between subjectivity and power relations recasts assumptions about the impact and experiences of punishment. As a result, there are both new sites for optimism and activism, and new causes for despair.

The feminist lens on identity compels criminologists to look differently at the relationship between the purposes and the experiences of punishment. This lens prompts new methodological work; it also shifts some of the sociological focus to the points of penality in which identity is most clearly at issue – points like the border, for instance, where national identity can determine a person's prison term (Kaufman, 2012; Zedner, 2010; Bosworth, 2011; Bosworth and Kaufman, 2011), or the expansion of surveillance and 'biometric monitoring' during the 'war on terror' (Cole, 2003; Goold, 2004). In sum, the turn to feminist theory pushes criminologists not only to include more women's voices – and more subjects in general – but also to look anew at the boundaries of our research.

Perhaps above all, a feminist vantage point also prompts normative discussions of these topics. The world is not as it should be, and it is our duty as researchers not only to understand it, but to try to change it. A gendered perspective, rather like criminology itself, is not bound by disciplinary borders. It can draw on work from subjects far afield and from a range of authors. Such an approach can free up our criminological imagination to broaden out from the same texts and sites of analysis to more distant topics, to more far-reaching and newly normative ideas. In so doing, doubtless, there will be conflict, but such debate may be just what the field needs to reenergise and re-imagine itself.

NOTES

1 Many scholars, like Butler (1990) and Laqueur (1992), contest the distinction between these two notions. Butler argues that 'sex' is only ever intelligible through gendered discourse, and as such, is equally constructed. Laqueur invokes the history of medical science, arguing that the modern dualist conception of sex (as male and female) emerged with the Enlightenment as a means to legitimate and maintain the patriarchal order. The phrase 'sex as a biological idea' aims to incorporate these critiques – and our own – into the term 'sex'.

2 See especially Ward and Kassebaum's (1965) prurient concern about women's 'homosexual' proclivities behind bars.

3 There are of course exceptions. For instance, both Tony Jefferson (2002) and John Hood Williams (2001) draw on psychoanalytic theory in their complex discussions of masculinity and crime, with Jefferson mounting a staunch critique of much criminological and sociological discussion of 'hegemonic masculinity'.

4 The body of writing on restorative justice (for an overview, see Hoyle and Zedner, 2007; Johnstone and Van Ness, 2007) is a notable exception to this claim about the relative dearth of normative discussion within criminology. That corpus imagines a different system of justice, though, and as Carolyn Hoyle points out, there often appears to be more academic discussion of restorative justice than actual examples of it in practice (Hoyle and Cuneen, 2010). Here, we explore how critical writing on the existing prison system could become similarly engaged with normative questions – namely, by beginning from the gendered bodies within penal institutions.

5 Criminologists, for instance, rarely engage with Foucault's work on sexuality, preferring instead to go over and over his writings on the prison, governmentality and security (Foucault, 1977, 1991). Queer theory, in contrast, derives many of its key ideas from his study of sexuality (Foucault, 1978).

6 Experience, in this view, should not be equated with authenticity. A gendered account of the prison would not seek to determine the 'real' (singular, static, authentic) 'experience' of imprisonment. Rather, experience is 'the complex and changing discursive processes by which identities are ascribed, resisted, or embraced' (Scott, 1992: 33). As gender is a key marker of social identity, so it is central to 'experience' and thus a starting point, not just a sociological quality, for understanding and analysis.

REFERENCES

Angel-Ajani, Asale (2003) 'A Question of Dangerous Races?', *Punishment & Society*, 5 (4): 433–48.

Austin, John L (1975) *How to Do Things with Words*. Oxford: Oxford University Press.

Barker, Vanessa (2009) *The Politics of Imprisonment*. New York: Oxford University Press.

Beetham, David (1991) *The Legitimation of Power*. London: Macmillan.

Benhabib, Seyla, Butler, Judith, Cornell, Drusilla and Fraser, Nancy (1996) *Feminist Contentions: A Philosophical Exchange*. New York: Routledge.

Bhui, Hindpal Singh (2007) 'Alien Experience: foreign national prisoners after the deportation crisis,' *Probation Journal*, 54 (4): 368–82.

Bhui, Hindpal (2009) 'Foreign National Prisoners: issues and Debates', in H. Bhui (ed.), *Race & Criminal Justice*. London: SAGE Publications. pp. 154–69.

Bly, Robert (1991) *Iron John: A Book about Men*. Shaftesbury: Element.

Bosworth, Mary (1996), 'Resistance and Compliance in Women's prisons: towards a Critique of legitimacy,' *Critical Criminology: An International Journal*, 7 (2): 5–19.

Bosworth, Mary (1999) *Engendering Resistance: Agency and Power in Women's Prisons*. Aldershot: Ashgate.

Bosworth, Mary (2010) *Explaining US Imprisonment*. London: SAGE Publications.

Bosworth, Mary (2011) 'Deporting foreign national prisoners in England and Wales,' *Citizenship Studies*, 15(5): 583–95.

Bosworth, Mary and Carrabine, Eamonn (2001) 'Reassessing resistance: gender, race and sexuality in prison,' *Punishment and Society*, 3 (4): 501–15.

Bosworth, Mary, Campbell, Debbie, Demby, Bonita, Ferranti, Seth, and Santos, Michael (2005) 'Doing Prison Research: Views from Inside,' *Qualitative Inquiry* 11(2): 249–264.

Bosworth, Mary and Loader, Ian (eds.) (2010) 'Reinventing Penal Parsimony,' Theoretical Criminology, 14(3) Special issue.

Bosworth, Mary and Hoyle, Caroline (eds.) (2011) *What is Criminology?* Oxford: Oxford University Press.

Bosworth, Mary and Kaufman, Emma (2011) 'Foreigners in a carceral age: immigration and imprisonment in the US,' *Stanford Law & Policy Review*, 22 (2): 101–27.

Bourgois, Philippe (2003) *In Search of Respect: Selling Crack in El Barrio*, 2nd edn. New York: Cambridge University Press.

Bowker, Lee (ed.) (1997) *Masculinities and Violence*. London: SAGE Publications.

Braithwaite, John (2002) *'What's wrong with the sociology of punishment?'*, *Theoretical Criminology*, 7: 5–28.

Britton, Dana (2003) *At Work in the Iron Cage: The Prison as Gendered Organization*. New York: New York University Press.

Brown, Michelle (2005) 'Setting the conditions for Abu Ghraib: the prison nation abroad,' *American Quarterly*, 57(3): 973–97.

Butler, Judith (1990) *Gender Trouble: Feminism and the Subversion of Identity*. New York: Routledge.

Butler, Judith (1993) *Bodies That Matter: On the Discursive Limits of "Sex"*. New York: Routledge.

Butler, Judith (1997) *Excitable Speech: A Politics of the Performative*. New York: Routledge.

Butler, Judith (2004) *Undoing Gender*. New York: Routledge.

Cade Bambara, Toni (1970) *The Black Woman: An Anthology*. New York: New American Library.

Campbell, Anne (1984) *The Girls in the Gang*. Oxford: Basil Blackwell.

Campbell, Bea (1993) *Goliath: Britain's Dangerous Places*. London: Virago.

Carby, Helen (1982) 'White women listen! Black feminism and the boundaries of sisterhood', in The Centre for Contemporary Cultural Studies (eds), *The Empire Strikes Back: Race and Racism in 70s Britain*. London: Routledge. pp. 67–92.

Carlen, Pat (1983) *Women's Imprisonment: A Study in Social Control*. London: Routledge & Kegan Paul.

Carrabine, Eamonn (2006) *Power, Discourse and Resistance: A Genealogy of the Strangeways Prison Riot*. Aldershot: Ashgate.

Carrabine, Eamonn and Longhurst, Brian (1998) 'Gender and prison organization: some comments on masculinities and prison management,' *The Howard Journal*, 37 (2): 161–76.

Chan, Janet (1997) *Changing Police Culture: Policing in a Multicultural Society*. Cambridge: Cambridge University Press.

Chesney-Lind, Meda (1986) 'Women and crime: the female offender,' *Signs: Journal of Women in Society*, 12: 78–96.

Clear, Todd (2007) *Imprisoning Communities*. New York: Oxford University Press.

Cohen, Stanley (1972) *Folk Devils and Moral Panics: The Creation of the Mods and Rockers*. Oxford: Blackwell.

Cole, David (2003) *Enemy Aliens: Double Standards and Constitutional Freedoms in the War on Terror*. New York: New Press.

Collier, Richard (1998) *Masculinities, Crime and Criminology*. London: SAGE Publications.

Connell, Raewyn (1987) *Gender and Power*. Cambridge: Polity Press.

Connell, Raewyn (1995) *Masculinities*. Cambridge: Polity Press.

Connell, Raewyn (2010) *Gender*. Cambridge: Polity Press.

Cook, Sandy and Davies, Susanne (1999) *Harsh Punishment: International Experiences of Women's Imprisonment*. Hanover, NH: University Press of New England.

Corber, Robert and Valocchi, Stephen (2003) *Queer Studies: An Interdisciplinary Reader*. New York: Wiley-Blackwell.

Crenshaw, Kimberlé (1989) 'Demarginalizing the intersection of race and sex: a black feminist critique of antidiscrimination doctrine, feminist theory and antiracist politics', *University of Chicago Legal Forum*, 1989: 139–167.

Crenshaw, Kimberlé (1993) 'Mapping the margins: intersectionality, identity politics, and violence against women of color', *Stanford Law Review*, 43 (6): 1241–99.

Crewe, Ben (2006) 'Male prisoners' orientations towards female officers in an English prison', *Punishment & Society*, 8 (4): 395–421.

Crewe, Ben (2009) *The Prisoner Society: Power, Adaptation, and Social Life in an English Prison*. Oxford: Oxford University Press.

Daly, Kathy (1994) *Gender, Crime and Punishment*. New Haven, CT: Yale University Press.

Daly, Kathy and Chesney-Lind, Meda (1988) 'Feminism and criminology', *Justice Quarterly*, 5: 497–538.

Davis, Angela Y. (1971) 'Reflections on the black woman's role in the community of slaves,' *Black Scholar*, 3: 2–15.

Davis, Angela Y. (2001) *The Prison Industrial Complex*. Oakland, CA: AK Press.

de Beauvoir, Simone (1949) *The Second Sex*. London: Penguin.

De Giorgi, Alessandro (2010) 'Immigration control, post-Fordism, and less eligibility: A materialist critique of the criminalisation of immigration across Europe', *Punishment & Society*, 12(2): 147–67.

Donoghue, Jane (2010) *Anti-Social Behaviour Orders: A Culture of Control?* London: Palgrave Macmillan.

Durkheim, Emile (1961) *Moral Education*. New York: Free Press.

Firestone, Shulamit (1970) *The Dialectic of Sex: The Case for Feminist Revolution*. London: Bantam Books.

Flavin, Jeanne (2001) 'Feminism for the mainstream criminologist: an invitation', *Journal of Criminal Justice*, 29: 271–85.

Foucault, Michel (1977) *Discipline and Punish: The Birth of the Prison*, A. Sheridan (trans.). New York: Vintage.

Foucault, Michel (1978) *The History of Sexuality, Volume I: An Introduction*, R. Hurley (trans.). New York: Vintage.

Foucault, Michel (1991) 'Governmentality,' in R. Braidotti (trans.), C. Gordon and P. Miller (eds.), *The Foucault Effect: Studies in Governmentality*, Chicago: University of Chicago Press, pp. 27–104.

Friedan, Betty (1963) *The Feminine Mystique*. New York: Norton.

Fry, Elizabeth (1827) *Observations on the Visiting, Superintendence, and Government of Female Prisoners*. London: Hatchard & Son.

Fuss, Diana (1989) *Essentially Speaking: Feminism, Nature and Difference*. New York: Routledge.

Gardner, Rosemary and Kruttschnitt, Candace (2005) *Marking Time in the Golden State: Women's Imprisonment in California*, Cambridge: Cambridge University Press.

Garland, David (1990) *Punishment and Modern Society: A Study in Social Theory*. Chicago: University of Chicago Press.

Garland, David (2001) *The Culture of Control*. Oxford: Oxford University Press.

Garland, David (2003) 'The rise of risk,' in R. Ericson and A. Doyle (eds.), *Risk and Morality*, Toronto: University of Toronto Press.

Gelsthorpe, Lorraine and Morris, Allison (eds.) (1990) *Feminist Perspectives in Criminology*. Milton Keynes: Open University Press.

Giallombardo, Rose (1966) *Society of Women: A Study of a Women's Prison*. New York: John Wiley & Sons.

Gilmore, Ruth (2007) *Golden Gulag: Prisons, Surplus, Crisis, and Opposition in a Globalizing California*. Berkeley, CA: University of California Press.

Goold, Ben (2004) *CCTV and Policing: Public Area Surveillance and Police Practices in Britain*. Oxford: Oxford University Press.

Halberstam, Judith (2005) *In a Queer Time and Place: Transgender Bodies, Subcultural Lives*. New York: New York University Press.

Hannah-Moffat, Kelly (1995) 'Feminine fortresses: women-centered prisons?', *The Prison Journal*, 75: 135–64.

Hannah-Moffat, Kelly (2001) *Punishment in Disguise? Penal Governance and Federal Imprisonment of Women in Canada*. London: University of Toronto Press.

Hannah-Moffat, Kelly (2011) 'Criminological cliques: narrowing dialogues, institutional protectionism, and the next generation', in M. Bosworth and C. Hoyle (eds), *What is Criminology?* Oxford: Oxford University Press. pp. 439–54.

Heffernan, Esther (1974) *The Cool, the Square and the Life*. New York: John Wiley & Sons.

Henry, Joan (1973) *Women in Prison*. London: White Lion Publishers.

Hill Collins, Patricia (1991) *Black Feminist Thought: Knowledge, Consciousness and the Politics of Empowerment*. New York: Routledge.

Hood Williams, John (2001) 'Gender, masculinities and crime: from structures to psyches,' *Theoretical Criminology*, 5 (1): 37–60.

hooks, bell (1973) *Ain't I A Woman*? Boston: South End Press.

hooks, bell (1984) *Feminist Theory: From Margin to Center*. Boston: South End Press.

Howe, Adrian (1996) *Punish and Critique: Towards a Feminist Analysis of Penality*. New York: Routledge.

Hoyle, Carolyn (1998) *Negotiating Domestic Violence: Police, Criminal Justice and Victims*. Oxford: Clarendon Press.

Hoyle, Carolyn and Zedner, Lucia (2007) 'Victims, victimization and criminal justice', in M. Maguire, R. Morgan and R. Reiner (eds), *The Oxford Handbook of Criminology*, 4th edn. Oxford: Oxford University Press. pp. 461–95.

Hoyle, Carolyn and Cuneen, Chris (2010). *Debating Restorative Justice*. Oxford: Hart Publishing.

Hudson, Barbara (2003) *Justice and the Risk Society*. London: SAGE Publications.

Irigaray, Luce (1985) *Speculum of the Other Woman*. Ithaca, NY: Cornell University Press.

Jefferson, Tony (2002) 'Subordinating hegemonic masculinity,' *Theoretical Criminology*, 6 (1): 63–88.

Johnstone, Gerry and Van Ness, Daniel (2007) 'The meaning of restorative justice', in G. Johnstone and D. Van Ness (eds), *Handbook of Restorative Justice*. Cullompton: Willan. pp. 5–23.

Kaufman, Emma (2012) 'Finding foreigners: race and the politics of memory in British prisons', *Population, Space and Place,* forthcoming.

Kristeva, Julia (1981) 'Women's time', *Signs: Journal of Women in Culture and Society*, 7: 13–35.

Ladner, Joyce (1971) *Tomorrow's Tomorrow: The Black Woman*. New York: Doubleday.

Laqueur, Thomas (1992) *Making Sex: Body and Gender from the Greeks to Freud.* Cambridge, MA: Harvard University Press.

Liebling, Alison (2004) *Prisons and Their Moral Performance*. Oxford: Clarendon Press.

Loader, Ian (2010) 'For Penal Moderation: Notes Toward a Public Philosophy of Punishment', *Theoretical Criminology*, 14(3): 349–367.

Mandaraka-Sheppard, Alexandra (1986) *The Dynamics of Aggression in Women's Prisons in England.* Aldershot: Gower.

Mauer, Marc (1999) *The Race to Incarcerate*. New York: Free Press.

Messerschmidt, James (1993) *Masculinities and Crime: Critique and Reconceptualisation of Theory*. Totowa, NJ: Rowman & Littlefield.

Miller, Jody (2001) *One of the Guys: Girls, Gangs, and Gender*. Oxford: Oxford University Press.

Muñoz, Jose E. (1999) *Disidentifications: Queers of Color and the Performance of Politics*. Minneapolis, MN: University of Minnesota Press.

Naffine, Ngaire (1995) *Feminism and Criminology*. Philadelphia, PA: Temple University Press.

Newburn, Tim and Stanko, Betsy (eds) (1995) *Just Boys Doing Business?* London: Routledge.

Oakley, Ann (1981) 'Interviewing women: a contradiction in terms,' in Helen Roberts (ed.), *Doing Feminist Research*. London: Routledge & Kegan Paul. pp. 30–62.

O'Malley, Pat (1999) 'Volatile and contradictory punishments,' *Theoretical Criminology*, 3 (2): 175–96.

O'Malley, Pat (2010) *Crime and Risk*. London: SAGE Publications.

Owen, Barbara (1998) *'In the Mix': Struggle and Survival in a Women's Prison*. New York: CUNY Press.

Padel, Una and Stevenson, Prue (1988) *Insiders: Women's Experience of Prison*. London: Virago Press.

Phillips, Coretta (2008) 'Negotiating identities: ethnicity and social relations in a young offenders institution', *Theoretical Criminology*, 12: 313–31.

Phillips, Coretta and Earle, Rod (2010) 'Reading difference differently? Identity, epistemology and prison ethnography,' *British Journal of Criminology*, 50 (5): 360–78.

Pickering, Sharon and Weber, Leanne (2011) *Globalization and Borders: Death at the Global Frontier*. London: Palgrave.

Prison Reform Trust (PRT) (2004) *The Forgotten Prisoners: The Plight of Foreign Prisoners in England and Wales*. London: PRT.

Rafter, Nicole (1985) *Partial Justice: Women in State Prisons, 1800–1935*. Boston: Northeastern University Press.

Reinharz, Sheila (1992) *Feminist Methods in Social Research*. New York: Oxford University Press.

Rich, Adrienne (1980) 'Compulsory heterosexuality and lesbian existence', *Signs: Journal of Women and Culture in Society*, 5 (4): 631–90.

Ricoeur, Paul (1969) *The Conflict of Interpretations: Essays in Hermeneutics*. Chicago: Northwestern University Press.

Rowbotham, Sheila (1973) *Woman's Consciousness: Man's World*. London: Penguin Books.

Scarry, Elaine (1985) *The Body in Pain: The Making and Unmaking of the World*. New York: Oxford University Press.

Schor, Naomi and Weed, Elizabeth (eds) (1994) *The Essential Difference*. Bloomington, IN: Indiana University Press.

Scott, Joan (1992) 'Experience', in Butler, Judith and Scott, Joan (eds), *Feminists Theorize the Political*. New York: Routledge. pp. 22–40.

Sedgwick, Eve (1990) *Epistemology of the Closet*. Berkeley, CA: University of California Press.

Sedgwick, Eve (2004) *Touching Feeling: Affect, Pedagogy, Performativity*. Durham, NC: Duke University Press.

Sherman, Lawrence, Farrington, David, Welsh, Brandon and MacKenzie, Doris (eds) (2002) *Evidence-Based Crime Prevention*. London: Routledge.

Sim, Joe (1995) 'Tougher than the rest? Men in prison', in T. Newburn and B. Stanko (eds), *Just Boys Doing Business?* London: Routledge. pp. 100–17.

Simon, Jonathan (2000) 'Megan's law: crime and democracy in America', *Law & Social Inquiry*, 25 (4): 1111–50.

Simon, Jonathan (2007) *Governing Through Crime*. Oxford: Oxford University Press.

Simon, Jonathan (2010) 'Do these prisons make me look fat? Moderating the USA's consumption of punishment', *Theoretical Criminology*, 14(3): 257–72.

Smart, C. (1976) *Women, Crime and Criminology: A Feminist Critique*. London: Routledge & Kegan Paul.

Smith, Dorothy (1987) *The Everyday World as Problematic: A Feminist Sociology.* Milton Keynes: Open University Press.

Sparks, Richard, Bottoms, Anthony and Hay, Will (1996) *Prisons and the Problem of Order.* Oxford: Clarendon Press.

Spivak, Gayatri (1989) 'Can the subaltern speak', in Cary Nelson and Lawrence Grossberg (eds), *Marxism & The Interpretation of Culture.* London: Macmillan. pp. 271–313.

Stanko, Betsy (1992) 'The Case of Fearful Women: Gender, Personal Safety and Fear of Crime,' *Women and Criminal Justice,* 4: 117–35.

Steffensmeier, Darren and Allan, Emilie (1996) 'Gender and crime: towards a gendered theory of female offending', *American Review of Sociology,* 22: 459–87.

Sudbury, Julia (2005) *Global Lockdown: Race, Gender, and the Prison Industrial Complex.* New York: Routledge.

Tonry, Michael (1996) *Malign Neglect: Race, Crime and Punishment in America.* New York: Oxford University Press.

Tonry, Michael (ed.) (2007) *Crime, Punishment, and Politics in Comparative Perspective.* Chicago: University of Chicago Press.

Valverde, Marianne (2003) *Law's Dream of a Common Knowledge.* Princeton, NJ: Princeton University Press.

Van Swaaningen, René (1997) *Critical Criminology: Visions from Europe.* London: Sage.

Wacquant, Loïc (1999) 'Suitable enemies: foreigners and immigrants in the prisons of europe,' *Punishment and Society,* 1(2): 215–22.

Wacquant, Loïc (2009) *Punishing the Poor: The Neoliberal Government of Social Insecurity.* Durham, NC: Duke University Press.

Walklate, Sandra (2006) *Imagining the Victim of Crime.* Milton Keynes: Open University Press.

Ward, David and Kassebaum, Gene (1965) *Women's Prison: Sex and Social Structure.* Chicago: Aldine.

Warner, Marina (1993) 'Fear of a queer planet: queer politics and social theory', *Journal of Homosexuality,* 45: 339–43.

Weber, Max (1968) *Economy and Society: An Outline of Interpretive Sociology,* Vols 1 and 2. Berkeley, CA: University of California Press.

Wells, Ida (2004) 'The impact of feminist thinking on criminal law and justice: contradiction, complexity, conviction, and connection', *Criminal Law Review,* 503–15.

Westmarland, Louise (2001) *Gender and Policing: Sex, Power and Police Culture.* Collumpton: Willan.

Williams, Patricia (1988) 'On being the object of property', *Signs,* 14 (1): 5–24.

Zedner, Lucia (2002) 'The dangers of Dystopias', *Oxford Journal of Legal Studies,* 22 (2): 341–66.

Zedner, Lucia (2005) 'Securing liberty in the face of terror: reflections from criminal justice', *Journal of Law and Society,* 32 (4): 507–33.

Zedner, Lucia (2007) 'Preventive justice or pre-punishment? The case of control orders', in C. O'Cinneide and J. Holder (eds), *Current Legal Problems.* Oxford: Oxford University Press. pp. 174–203.

Zedner, Lucia (2010) Security, the state, and the citizen: the changing architecture of crime control,' *New Criminal Law Review,* 13(2): 379–403.

10

The Carceral State and the Politics of Punishment

Marie Gottschalk

Throughout American history, politicians and public officials have exploited public anxieties about crime and disorder for political gain. Over the past four decades or so, these political strategies and public anxieties have come together in the perfect storm. They have radically transformed US penal policies, spurring an unprecedented prison boom. Since the early 1970s, the US prisoner population has increased by more than six-fold (Manza and Uggen, 2006). Today the USA is the world's warden, incarcerating a higher proportion of its people than any other country. A staggering 7.2 million people – or 1 in every 31 adults – are either incarcerated, on parole or probation, or under some other form of state supervision (Glaze et al., 2010). These figures understate the enormous and disproportionate impact that this bold and unprecedented social experiment has had on certain groups in the USA. If current trends continue, one in three black males and one in six Hispanic males born in 2001 are expected to spend some time in prison during their lives (Bonczar, 2003).

The emergence and consolidation of the US carceral state is a major milestone in American political development that arguably rivals in significance the expansion and contraction of the welfare state in the post-war period. The carceral state now exercises vast new controls over millions of people, resulting in a remarkable change in the distribution of authority in favor of law enforcement and corrections at the local, state and federal levels. This explosion in the size of the prison population and the retributive turn in US penal policy are well documented. But the underlying political causes and wider political consequences of this massive expansion have not been well understood.

This is beginning to change. Since the late 1990s, the phenomenon of mass imprisonment has been a growing source of scholarly interest. Today the carceral state is a subject of increasing public interest. Indeed, *Wired* magazine included emptying the country's prisons on its 2009 'Smart List' of '12 Shocking Ideas that Could Change the World', and *Parade* magazine featured Sen. Jim Webb's (D-Va.) call to end mass incarceration on its front page (Webb, 2009).

In their attempts to identify the political factors that help explain why the USA has the world's highest incarceration rate and locks up more people than any other country, scholars initially focused on political developments at the national level since the 1960s. More recently they have underscored the significance of political and institutional factors that pre-date the 1960s. Some of the most promising new research, which is discussed in more detail below, closely examines penal developments at the state and local levels.

The construction of such an expansive and unforgiving carceral state in the USA is a national phenomenon that has left no state untouched. All 50 states have seen their incarceration rates explode since the 1970s. But the state-level variation in incarceration rates is still enormous, far greater than what exists across the countries of Western Europe. Incarceration rates (including both the jail and prison populations) range from a high of over 1100 per 100,000 people in Louisiana to a low of about 300 per 100,000 in Maine (Pew Center on the States, 2009: 33). This great variation and the fact that crime control in the USA is primarily a local and state function, not a federal one, suggest that local, state and perhaps regional factors might help explain US penal policies.

Trying to unravel why the carceral state has been more extensive, abusive and degrading in some states than others is a blossoming area of research. The prison population edged downward in 24 states in 2009, but continued to grow in 26 others. That year the total state prison population declined for the first time in nearly four decades but the federal prison population increased by 3.4 percent (Pew Center on the States, 2010). Scholars have shown that differences in socioeconomic variables, demographic factors and/or crime rates help explain some of the state-by-state variation in incarceration and criminal justice policies (Hawkins and Hardy, 1989; Jacobs and Helms, 1996; Beckett and Western, 2001; Greenberg and West, 2001). Trying to account for the remaining variation, scholars have zeroed in on differences in the institutional and political context at the state level (Davey, 1998; Zimring et al., 2001; Domanick, 2004; Jacobson, 2005; Barker, 2009).

Some of the most promising new scholarship on the states has focused on the South and the Southwest. This work is upending the conventional narrative of the rise of the US penal system, with its emphasis on the northeast, notably New York and Pennsylvania. In the standard account, the foreboding penitentiaries of the 19th century, meant to restore wayward citizens to virtue through penitent solitude, evolved by fits and starts into the modern correctional bureaucracies of the 20th century that, at least for a time, viewed rehabilitating prisoners as a central part of their mission (Perkinson, 2010: 7). Lynch (2010), Schoenfeld (2009), Perkinson (2010), Campbell (2011) and others suggest that the history of punishment in the USA is more a Southern story than has been generally recognized. Notably, in much of the South and Southwest, the commitment to the 'rehabilitative ideal' appears to have been fragile and fleeting (Lynch, 2010).

The Great Recession has raised expectations that the USA will begin to empty its jails and prisons because it can no longer afford to be the world's warden.[1] The new state-level studies are a sober reminder that gaping budget deficits will not necessarily reverse the prison boom because a penal system is not only deeply embedded in a state's budget but also in its political, cultural, institutional and social fabric. These more fine-grained state-level case studies suggest that some states may be better able than others to reduce their prison populations in the future.

The wider political consequences of the carceral state are another new and expanding area of scholarly and public interest. Evidence suggests that having such a large penal system embedded in a democratic polity has enormous repercussions that reverberate throughout the political system and beyond. The carceral state has grown so huge in the USA that it has begun to metastasize and warp fundamental democratic institutions, everything from free and fair elections to an accurate and representative census. Furthermore, the emergence of the carceral state has helped to legitimize a new mode of 'governing through crime' that has spread well beyond the criminal justice system to other key institutions, including the executive branch, schools and the workplace (Simon, 2007).

Mass imprisonment within a democratic polity and the hyper-incarceration (Wacquant, 2008) of certain groups are unprecedented developments. The consolidation of this new model in the USA raises the question: Is this country exceptionally vulnerable to get-tough polices, or will other countries follow the USA down the same punitive path? Two decades ago there was next to no comparative literature on crime control and penal policy (Tonry, 2007). Since then scholars have begun to identify certain distinctive cultural, historical, constitutional, institutional and political factors that may render some countries more susceptible to get-tough policies.

The growing recognition that the enormous carceral state is a pressing economic, political and social problem has spurred interest in the politics of reversing the prison boom. Understanding what brought about major decarcerations in the past is a new frontier in research. So is understanding the constellation of interest groups and social movements that might successfully push to reverse the prison boom.

This essay first surveys work on the deeper political, institutional, and historical origins of the carceral state. It then turns to the new state-level scholarship on mass incarceration. After that, it examines some of the wider political consequences of the carceral state, including its impact on elections and political participation, the emergence of new conceptions of citizenship, the criminalization of immigration policy, the relationship between the carceral state and the welfare state and the phenomenon of 'governing through crime'. It concludes with a brief survey of new work on political resistance to mass incarceration and a discussion of the comparative politics of penal policy.

THE DEEPER ORIGINS OF THE CARCERAL STATE

Until recently, scholars of the carceral state generally adopted a truncated timeframe as they sought to identify what changed in the USA beginning in the 1960s to disrupt its generally stable and unexceptional incarceration rate and to bring back capital punishment with a vengeance. The main political explanations included: an escalating crime rate and related shifts in public opinion (Wilson, 1975: xvi; DiIulio, 1997; Ruth and Reitz, 2003); the war on drugs (Caplow and Simon, 1999: 92–3; Gordon, 1994; Tonry, 1995; Provine, 2007); the emergence of the profitable prison-industrial complex (Abramsky, 2007: ch. 6; Burton-Rose et al., 1998; Dyer, 2000; Sarabi and Bender, 2000; Hallinan, 2001); structural changes in American culture and society with the coming of late modernity (Garland, 2001); politicians playing the 'race card' by invoking the law-and-order issue for electoral gain (Edsall and Edsall, 1991; Beckett, 1997; Davey, 1998; Zimring et al., 2001; Flamm, 2005; Western, 2006: 58–62, 67–73); and the collapse of the urban labor market for unskilled men due to deindustrialization and globalization (Parenti, 1999; Western, 2006).

These contemporary factors are critical to understanding the origins of the carceral state. But accounts that stress recent developments seem to suggest that this major expansion of the state and radical shift in public policy have shallow roots. Yet contemporary penal policy actually has deep historical and institutional roots. Both state capacity to incarcerate and the legitimacy of the federal government to handle more criminal matters were built up slowly but surely well before the incarceration boom that began in the 1970s.

A number of historically embedded institutional developments laid the foundation for the construction of the carceral state (Gottschalk, 2006). These include, to list some of the most important ones, the historical underdevelopment of the US welfare state; the early establishment of an extensive network of rights-based and other public interest groups stretching back to the 1920s that helped lodge capital punishment in the courts, not the legislature; the exceptional nature of the origins and development of the public prosecutor in the USA; and the country's long history of morally charged crusades that helped build up the law enforcement apparatus by fits and starts.

In addition to these early institutional developments, a variety of other factors with deep historical roots need to be understood in order to trace the origins of the carceral state (Tonry, 2011). For example, the much-heralded 'liberal' features of American political culture may have contributed to making the US penal system harsher, more degrading, and less forgiving (Whitman, 2003). In the absence or rejection of an aristocratic political culture and society, prisons in the USA historically have been rooted in extending a brute egalitarianism that subjects all prisoners, regardless of their social or political status, to 'low status,' dehumanizing treatment, Whitman suggests. By contrast, waves of penal reform in Germany and France often entailed 'leveling up', or extending the penal and legal privileges enjoyed by political prisoners and incarcerated aristocrats to other offenders.

The conventional characterization of the last four decades as the country's first real 'law-and-order' era, when issues of crime and punishment were nationalized and politicized for the first time in US history, is incorrect. Law and order was a recurrent and major theme in American politics long before the 1960s and long before the modern Republican Party strategically wielded this issue to achieve national political domination. The USA had an early identity as a convict nation (Christianson, 1998: 13). Penal concerns informed broader debates about republicanism, utilitarianism, and law and order during the founding decades (Dumm, 1987; Masur, 1989; Rothman, 1990; Hirsch, 1992; Meranze, 1996; Pestritto, 2000). Disagreements over the establishment of the penitentiary were deeply entangled with disputes over slavery and abolition in the antebellum years (Hindus, 1980; Ayers, 1984; Hirsch, 1992). After the Civil War, the convict-lease system was pivotal in the politics of Populism, Progressivism, race relations and the economic development of the South (Carleton, 1971; Fierce, 1994; Walker, 1988; Lichtenstein, 1996; Mancini, 1996; Oshinsky, 1996; Myers, 1998; Shapiro, 1998; Curtin, 2000; Blackmon, 2008; Perkinson, 2010). Penal labor was a leading issue for organized labor and a central feature in electoral politics in the mid-to-late 19th century and early 20th century (McLennan, 2008). During the 1930s, Franklin D. Roosevelt and his attorney general Homer Cummings shrewdly and quite successfully exploited sensational crimes, most notably the Lindbergh kidnapping, to advance their broader agenda of extending federal jurisdiction into crime control (Cummings and McFarland, 1937: 482; Alix, 1978: 90–1; O'Reilly, 1982: 640–5; Simon, 2007: 47–9).

The construction of the carceral state also complicates our understanding of the role of race in American political development. The creation of the carceral state was not merely the latest chapter in a book that began with slavery and moved on to convict leasing, Jim Crow, and the ghetto to control African-Americans and other 'dangerous classes'. While there are similarities between these social control institutions, it is important not to flatten out their differences and the differences in the political, institutional, and economic context that created and sustained them. Treating these institutions as one and the same minimizes the unprecedented nature of the incarceration boom in the USA since the 1970s. For all the horrors of the convict-lease system, relatively few blacks were subjected to it in the decades following the Civil War, though many more feared it. Today's incarceration rate of approximately 5000 per 100,000 African-American males dwarfs by far the number of blacks imprisoned in the South under convict leasing (Gottschalk, 2006: 269, n. 42;

West and Sabol, 2009: 18). An African-American man with a felony conviction today scarcely has 'more rights, and arguably less respect, than a black man living in Alabama at the height of Jim Crow', according to Michelle Alexander. 'Once you're labeled a felon, the old forms of discrimination – employment discrimination, housing discrimination, denial of food stamps and other public benefits, and exclusion from jury service – are suddenly legal', she explains (2010: 2).

The country's racial divide both thwarted and facilitated the establishment of the carceral state. For much of US history, racial, ethnic and regional divisions periodically acted as a check on the development of criminal justice institutions, especially at the federal level, even as they fueled popular passions to criminalize certain behaviors and certain groups. The moral crusades over issues like 'white slavery', Prohibition and juvenile delinquency that regularly convulsed the country were a backhanded way of building up the criminal justice apparatus by fits and starts (Morone, 2003; Gottschalk, 2006: ch. 3). Once Jim Crow came tumbling down in the postwar decades, the path was clearer for the rapid development of the criminal justice system, which today disproportionately incarcerates African-Americans.

Recent scholarship on the carceral state and the civil rights movement underscores this point. The conventional view of the origins of the contemporary law-and-order era is that rising crime rates in the 1960s prompted national leaders, most notably presidential candidates, to address the issue of street crime. This provided an opening for the Republican Party, beginning with Barry Goldwater in 1964, to undermine the New Deal liberal coalition by making appeals to law and order that were really thinly veiled racialized appeals to white voters. But new research provides a much more nuanced account of how racial politics got funneled through criminal justice policies. Politicians so readily identified today as penal hardliners, such as Richard Nixon, Ronald Reagan and even segregationist Lester Maddox of Georgia, did not immediately march in lock step toward the prison and the execution chamber after Goldwater denounced the 'growing menace' to personal safety in his electrifying speech before the Republican convention in 1964 (Gottschalk, 2006: 10, 213–24, 234). Nor did these public officials single-handedly impose the carceral state.

It now appears that the construction of the carceral state was a deeply bipartisan project from early on. Conservative congressional Democrats began strategically wielding the street crime issue in the 1950s, well before crime rates began to escalate and leading Republicans took up the charge (Murakawa, 2005: 81–2). Southern conservatives initially cast their opposition to major civil rights legislation in criminological terms, arguing that 'integration breeds crime' (Murakawa, 2005: 82). As riots broke out in major cities across the country in the mid-to-late 1960s, they reformulated the connection between civil rights and crime, working 'vociferously to conflate crime and disobedience, with its obvious extensions to civil rights' (Weaver, 2006: 29).

This was a doctrine not just of words but also of deeds. Conservative southern Democrats shrewdly used civil rights bills as vehicles to stiffen and broaden criminal penalties. These add-ons to civil rights legislation experimented with certain sanctions that later became the central features of the major federal and state-level crime bills of the 1980s and 1990s, including stiff mandatory minimums, denial of federal benefits to people convicted of certain felonies, and sentencing enhancements for vaguely and capaciously defined violations, like rioting (Weaver, 2006: 27–8). Many urban white voters in the North initially maintained a delicate balancing act on the civil rights issue. While they opposed racial integration at the local level, they supported national candidates who were pro-civil rights. This split political personality became less tenable as crime and disorder 'became the fulcrum points at which the local and national intersected' (Flamm, 2005: 10), thus weakening the New Deal coalition.

The significance of race in unsettling the New Deal coalition and building the carceral state has long been recognized, if not always well understood. By contrast, gender is just beginning to be recognized as an important contributing factor to more punitive policies and mass imprisonment. New scholarship reveals that politicians of all stripes, including Goldwater, George Wallace, Lyndon Johnson, Richard Nixon, George H.W. Bush and Bill Clinton, strategically used highly gendered appeals related to crime and punishment to further their political and electoral agendas (Flamm, 2005: 42, 45, 51, 178; Bosworth, 2010). They promulgated the politically potent – but highly misleading – image of white women, preyed on by strangers, as the most likely victims of violent crime. But leading politicians were not the only culprits in feminizing the crime issue.

Women's groups and feminists in the USA have a long and conflicted history on issues related to crime, punishment, and law and order. Periodically, they have played central roles in defining violence as a threat to the social order and pushing for more enhanced policing powers to address law-and-order concerns (Gottschalk, 2006: chs 5 and 6). The women's reform movements and waves of feminist agitation that have appeared off and on since the 19th century in the USA helped to construct institutions and establish practices that bolstered stridently conservative tendencies in penal policy. For example, because of stark differences in the historical and institutional context, demands by women's groups in the 1970s and 1980s to address the issues of rape and domestic violence had more far-reaching penal consequences in the USA than other countries where burgeoning women's movements also identified these two issues as central concerns.[2] As a consequence, the women's movement helped facilitate conservative law-and-order politics in the USA but not Europe.

To sum up, the carceral state has become a key governing institution in the USA. Its construction has deep historical and institutional roots. Contrary to the popular view, law and order has been a central, not incidental, issue in national and local politics for much of US history. Struggles over penal policy and punishment have had 'important and lasting consequences' for 'the structure and legitimating fictions of American social order more generally' (McLennan, 2008: 3). Political elites in the USA have a long history of raising law-and-order concerns in an attempt to further their own political fortunes. And Americans have a long history of periodic intense anxiety about crime and disorder. Yet only recently have these concerns and anxieties resulted in such a dramatic and unprecedented transformation of penal policies in such a punitive direction. By understanding the deeper institutional and political context, we can begin to grasp why elite political preferences for a war on crime premised on a massive expansion of the penal system triumphed beginning in the 1960s despite public opinion polls persistently showing that public sentiment on crime and punishment was quite fluid.

THE CARCERAL STATE AT THE STATE AND LOCAL LEVELS

Among the many political questions about what propelled the turn to mass incarceration, one in particular remains central: why were law-and-order conservatives able to launch an expensive prison-building spree that spanned decades even though the burgeoning conservative movement they spearheaded was premised on fiscal conservatism and rolling back the public sector? New case studies of the development of penal policy at the state level are beginning to unravel this puzzle. This research identifies some common factors that help explain what propelled the prison boom at the state level, as well as some differences that account for variations in the timing, extent and nature of the punitive turn among the states.

One of the most puzzling cases is California, which was a trailblazer for the 'rehabilitative ideal' in the 1940s and 1950s and ground zero for the taxpayer revolt of the 1970s and 1980s. With passage of Proposition 13 in 1978, which capped property taxes and deprived municipal governments of key revenues, California faced growing opposition to tax increases and expansion of the public sector. Nonetheless the Golden State has been able to build approximately two-dozen prisons (at a cost of about US$280–350 million each) since 1982. This is twice as many as it constructed in the first century after statehood. California also added about two-dozen smaller penal facilities (Gilmore, 2007: 7–8). Over the last quarter century, spending on corrections has quadrupled in California, jumping from 2 to 8 percent of the general fund (Gilmore, 2007: 8–10). Even in the face of fiscal Armageddon and a federal court decision declaring that the state's overcrowded, underfunded penal system is unconstitutional (which was upheld in May 2011 by a divided US Supreme Court in *Brown* v. *Plata*), California has been unable to agree on a plan to shrink its penal population significantly.

In California and other Western (Edgerton, 2004) and Southern states, the postwar establishment of statewide departments of corrections to oversee their penal facilities, which had been run largely as independent, patronage-ridden fiefdoms, was a critical development. This gave states the capacity for the first time to develop integrated penal systems, pursue large-scale prison construction schemes, and respond to national trends in penal policy, if lawmakers chose to do so. When legislators sought to build up their penal capacity, they often enacted measures that exempted their departments of corrections from key oversight, budgeting and financial rules that applied to other state agencies.

In the case of California, the legislature reorganized its statutory relationship with the California Department of Corrections (CDC) in 1982 by forming the Joint Legislative Committee on Prison Construction and Operations (JLCPCO). This reorganization plan inured the CDC from the longstanding bidding and budget practices required of other state agencies. The creation of the JLCPCO also ensured that elected officials vulnerable to the powerful sway of law-and-order politics would be closely and publicly monitoring the CDC's activities. Moreover, the JLCPCO was required to hold public hearings, which provided the CDC with a highly visible platform to promulgate dire projections about an imminent prison-overcrowding crisis and to promote a vast expansion in the state's penal system. A dramatic increase in the CDC's planning capacity allowed the agency, beginning in 1984, to produce alarmist five-year master plans (Gilmore, 2007: 96).

These predictions, however dire, would not be enough to neutralize rising public reluctance to pay for more state services, especially prisons. With the shadow of Proposition 13 looming over them, legislators and other state officials were increasingly doubtful that taxpayers would support new prison bond packages at the polls. With the help of the state's financial sector, California turned to lease-revenue bonds (LRB's) as a backdoor way to fund new prison construction that allowed legislators and corrections administrators to maneuver around anti-tax sentiment.

LRB's skirted states' balanced budget rules, as well as requirements that voters must ratify new government bond projects. They originally were designed to provide financing for projects that could generate enough revenue over time to pay for themselves. LRB's typically had been used to finance items like mortgages for veterans and farmers and construction loans for hospitals, colleges and universities. In a creative sleight of public financing, money that corrections departments would use to 'pay back' the LRB's was considered 'revenue' even though it came from general fund appropriations authorized to the corrections department by the legislature in the annual operating budget.

These revenue bonds became a popular way to finance new prison construction in California and elsewhere beginning in the mid-1980s. Prior to that, new prisons had to be funded either on a pay-as-you-go basis out of general revenue funds or by borrowing money through the sale of government bonds sanctioned by taxpayers through bond referendums (Pranis, 2007: 37). By 1996, more than half of all new prison debt was in the form of LRB's, which tend to be more expensive than straightforward state bond sales (Pranis, 2007: 38). The new-fangled LRB's allowed the huge costs of the prison build-up and the budgetary trade-offs they necessitated (notably the conspicuous drop in public funding for higher education) to stay obscured from public view. And LRB's could be quickly organized and issued. In less than a decade, California's state debt for prison construction exploded from about 4 percent to over 16 percent of the state's total debt for all purposes (Gilmore, 2007: 101).

The CDC has been extremely inept at managing what goes on inside its prisons and the other facilities of its vast penal empire, in part because of organized resistance from the powerful prison guards' union and contract provisions that give the guards enormous latitude on the job (Page, 2011b: ch. 7). However, the department has been highly capable when it comes to building more prisons. Like corrections departments in many other states, the CDC pushed prison construction as a key tool of rural economic development. The CDC's Prison Siting Office was extremely effective at persuading economically distressed communities that a new prison in their midst would bring them an economic windfall. The office strategically targeted rural communities, figuring they would be an easier sell than urban areas after the CDC became embroiled in a nasty fight with community and religious groups who opposed building a new lockup in an East Los Angeles neighborhood (Gilmore, 2007).

California's massive prison expansion entailed a massive expansion of the corrections workforce at just the time that the scrappy prison officers' association, which originally resembled a social club or fraternal organization, was transforming itself into a powerful, militant and fiercely independent union (Page, 2011b). Under forceful and savvy leadership, the California Correctional Peace Officers Association (CCPOA) set out in the 1980s to capitalize politically and financially on the prison boom already underway to assure that the boom did not lose its momentum. Wielding its financial largesse, the union rewarded allies with generous campaign contributions and punished foes with well-funded primary challengers and disparaging and mean-spirited public attacks. It almost single-handedly created the powerful victims' rights movement in the Golden State that has pushed so hard for more punitive legislation, including the toughest three-strikes law in the country. The union deployed its political resources to create the 'specter of the CCPOA' – an image of a 'ruthless, unpredictable and powerful labor organization' (Page, 2011b: 65). It successfully framed the union's interests in terms of the public good and reached out to minority groups by celebrating diversity (but only once the union had more Hispanic, black and female members) and by funding ethnic- and gender-based criminal justice organizations and political action committees.

The CCPOA also framed its actions in highly charged moral terms. It portrayed prison guards as the frontline in an epic battle between good and evil, hence the union's longstanding motto, 'The Toughest Beat in the State'. Subtly and not so subtly, the union exploited negative racial stereotypes. It charged that inmates in the state's prisons were the worst of the worst and beyond redemption. One of its public relations videos portrayed typical California inmates, in the words of Page, as 'big, black, brutish gang members armed with homemade shanks' who hunt 'their prey: prison officers' (2011b: 81).

The CCPOA's political savvy and the financial sector's underwriting savvy do not on their own explain why California succeeded in launching a massive expansion of the public sector despite rising fiscal conservatism and anti-tax sentiment. Drawing on key insights from Vanessa Barker's (2009) comparative study of the development of penal policy in California, New York and Washington State, Page argues that the Golden State's political culture and institutions have rendered it especially vulnerable to the siren call of law-and-order politics. California's 'neopopulist political culture and institutions', most notably its ballot initiatives and its relatively low levels of civic engagement, helped foster the CCPOA's disproportionate influence, according to Page (2011a).

Like California, Arizona is another Sunbelt state that has been a main cauldron of the ascendant conservative movement premised on fiscal conservatism and disdain for the public sector. Nonetheless it, too, embarked on a huge, costly penal expansion. Home to Barry Goldwater, fiscal frugality has long been the 'guiding principle of all government endeavors in Arizona' (Lynch, 2010: 25). For its entire history until the late 1970s, Arizona had doggedly resisted making a big investment in new penal facilities (Lynch, 2010: 111). Yet between 1971 and 2000, the state's incarceration rate increased nearly sevenfold, going from a stable and minuscule 75 per 100,000 (a rate comparable to that of the Scandinavian countries today) to more than 500 per 100,000. Spending on corrections skyrocketed, escalating from 4 percent of the general fund in 1979 to nearly 11 percent in 2003 (Lynch, 2010: 171). As the prison population grew, the department of corrections solidified its position 'as one of the largest and most politically influential state agencies in Arizona' (Lynch, 2010: 172).

Lynch portrays the embrace of the carceral state in Arizona as largely a top-down phenomenon. Until the 1950s, Arizona looked like a traditional one-party Southern state dominated by conservative Democrats. Beginning in the 1960s, the state became more politically competitive as right-leaning Republicans made serious electoral inroads and pockets of progressive Democrats challenged the party's old guard, especially in more urbanized areas. This new political competition set the stage for the hyper-politicization of penal policy, as the 'practical, collaborative' style of lawmaking yielded to more 'symbolic, partisan-based' legislating (Lynch, 2010: 113). Legislators and state officials generally did not retreat from their hard line even in the face of reports from the department of corrections and elsewhere predicting that the proposed harsh sentencing regime would necessitate a massive increase in spending on corrections or that the vast prison expansion had had no measurable impact on the state's crime rate (Lynch, 2010: 95, 149).

As in the case of California, legislators and governors instigated the prison boom but other groups mobilized subsequently to spur it on. Unlike in California, victims' rights groups and unionized prison guards did not propel the boom. Law enforcement officers, notably prosecutors and sheriffs who shrewdly used the media, played a key role in Arizona. They mobilized to defend and extend the harsh sentencing regime imposed in the 1970s and helped scuttle major prison reform proposals in the early 1990s to reduce the incarcerated population as severe economic distress gripped the state. Instead, the reform efforts of the early 1990s morphed into yet another round of get-tough legislation (Lynch, 2010: 155). At the time, leading state officials were so committed to punitive segregation that the governor and director of corrections even supported turning down a private grant awarded to develop alternatives to incarceration (Lynch, 2010: 165).

Several factors helped neutralize or deflect concerns about how the huge size and growing expense of the penal system were at odds with Arizona's historical commitment to frugality and a limited public sector. Administrators and state officials stressed how the state's penal system was 'cheap and mean' (Lynch, 2010: 213). At every opportunity they underscored their frugality. '[T]he commitment to frugality spilled over as an expressive value to administrative operations,' explains Lynch. 'So even when *actual* spending was profligate ... such expenditures were sold politically to the populace as both necessary and cost-efficient' (2010: 213, original emphasis).

In their public statements and in the annual reports of the department of corrections, state officials celebrated cost saving measures like reducing the use of heat and air-conditioning in prisons, leveling more fees on inmates and their families, purchasing 'seconds' of damaged or old food from wholesalers, and cutting off the electricity on cellblocks during the day. They even heralded the cost savings to be had by the conversion of the Death House to accommodate lethal injection (Lynch, 2010: 142). Joe Arpaio, sheriff of Maricopa County since 1993, boasted how he spent only 20 cents a day feeding inmates in his jails, thanks in part to his infamous 'green bologna' (Lynch, 2010: 164). State officials also stressed the exploitation of penal labor to save money, noting that farming industries were run almost entirely by prison labor, and that all prison construction projects were required by law to use inmate labor (Lynch, 2010: 129). To make the point that programming for inmates was useless, one director of corrections in Arizona noted that Minnesota spent twice as much per inmate yet had a recidivism rate comparable to Arizona's (Lynch, 2010: 173). In its annual reports, Arizona's department of corrections 'prided itself on spending significantly less than the national average on inmates' (Lynch, 2010: 172). This deflected attention from the fact that as of 1999 Arizona 'ranked among the top three states in the nation in terms of the proportion of the state budget allocated to corrections' (Lynch, 2010: 171).

Lynch chronicles the origins and development of get-tough policies in Arizona and suggests this state has become a national trendsetter in meting out harsh punishment. The rehabilitative ideal never really took root in Arizona, partly because of the state's historic reliance on the widespread use of corporal punishment, degrading rituals and paramilitary style discipline in its jails and prisons. Whenever outsiders were recruited to run Arizona's penal system, they generally faced fierce resistance to importing new ideas like rehabilitation and the more humane treatment of prisoners, as did outsiders selected to helm the penal systems of other states, notably Florida and Texas (Schoenfeld, 2009; Perkinson, 2010).

As spending for corrections skyrocketed in Arizona, state officials emphasized how they were toughening up life behind bars for inmates. Arizona became a leader in not only incarcerating its citizens but also in pioneering the widespread use of supermax prisons and humiliating and degrading punishments like chain gangs. Beginning in the mid-1990s, prison guards routinely deployed pepper gas and Israeli foggers on inmates. In 1997, the director of corrections authorized the use of attack dogs in cell extractions. The dogs were trained to bite and hold on as the inmate was pulled from his cell by an animal attached to a 30-foot leash (Lynch, 2010: 169). This increasingly punitive approach faced little resistance from any constituencies with political power in Arizona (Lynch, 2010: 170).

State officials in Arizona attacked the reputed 'good life' in prison by requiring inmates to do a stint of hard labor during their confinement and by imposing new restrictions on clothes, grooming, personal items, visitors and compassionate leave (Lynch, 2010: 128). Alleged luxuries like television, weight-lifting equipment, access to the courts, and even suntan lotion for inmates working in the blazing Arizona sun came under attack. As in the case of California, Arizona's legislators moved to exempt the state's department of corrections from key rules that applied to other state agencies, including a requirement that the state give notice and hold public hearings on all major changes in rules and practices. This change 'contributed to the acceleration of the flagrant punitiveness of Arizona prisons' (Lynch, 2010: 140).

Arizona's department of corrections and governor's office doggedly fought to dismantle the limited federal protections the courts had extended to prisoners beginning in the 1960s. State officials demonized federal judges and other officials and groups who attempted to intervene in the operation of the penal system. They kept the public focus on states' rights issues and on allegations of excessive federal intrusion. State officials raged that Arizona's prisons had become such a fiscal burden because of onerous and intrusive federal regulation and oversight of the state's penal system. They also blamed federal permissiveness to inmate lawsuits. Their withering attacks on Washington and the federal judiciary obscured the fact that the prison boom in Arizona had radically increased the power of the state government, the size of the public sector, and the fiscal burden of the penal system.

In the late 1970s and early 1980s, the state scrambled to comply with federal consent decrees concerning overcrowding and other violations. By the mid-1980s or so, the governor, the head of the department of corrections and other state officials took a 'new oppositional stance' to prisoner lawsuits and federal oversight (Lynch, 2010: 180). The department of corrections openly defied earlier decrees in the name of budgetary constraints and aggressively sought to overturn a landmark court decision extending prisoners' rights. Arizona's 1996 Supreme Court victory in *Lewis* v. *Casey*, which significantly curtailed the rights established in the 1977 *Bounds* v. *Smith* decision, emboldened state officials (Lynch, 2010: 186). The state refused to pay special master's fees in federal consent decrees and challenged them in the courts. It denied the federal Department of Justice access to state prisons to investigate charges of widespread employee sexual misconduct involving prisoners (Lynch, 2010: 197). State officials in Arizona provided the legislative blueprint and crucial political momentum to propel the Prison Litigation Reform Act through the US Congress in 1996. This measure greatly restricted inmates' access to the courts to challenge their conditions of confinement. In short, Arizona was a 'trailblazer that ultimately reshaped the national landscape of prisoner litigation' (Lynch, 2010: 203), as were Texas (Perkinson, 2010) and Florida (Schoenfeld, 2009).

The gains of prisoner litigation in Arizona and elsewhere were extremely limited. After some initial victories, a backlash was in full force by the late 1980s. State officials faced little resistance because of the absence of organized pressure from the grass-roots to behave differently (Lynch, 2010: 217). Few organizations in Arizona were willing and able to challenge the erosion of prisoners' rights. Most of the push to defend prisoners' rights came from outside the state, notably the US Department of Justice and the national office of the American Civil Liberties Union (ACLU).

Lynch (2010), Perkinson (2010) and others suggest that Arizona, Texas and other Sunbelt states are the forerunners of a leading alternative model of criminal justice premised on maximum control at minimum cost with little outside oversight. Never very attached to the rehabilitative model to begin with, they became the crucibles for get-tough innovations like three-strikes laws, boot camps, the widespread use of solitary confinement through supermax cells, the revival of chain gangs, the exploitation of penal labor and an uncompromising defiance of federal intervention and oversight.

Perkinson (2010) draws much needed attention to the case of Texas, which operates the country's largest state prison system, imprisoning today more people than Germany, France, Belgium and the Netherlands combined. Like Arizona, Texas stands out not just for the sheer number of people under state control but also for the persistently brutal and inhumane conditions of their confinement. In graphic and often disturbing detail, Perkinson chronicles the many ways punishment repeatedly has been used in Texas 'to assert supremacy and debase prisoners' since the state built its first penitentiary in 1848 (Perkinson, 2010: 129).

In Texas, as in Arizona, rehabilitation was largely treated as a fad. It took a backseat to maintaining maximum control of inmates through surveillance, censorship, fierce staff solidarity, widespread use of solitary confinement and relentless self-promotion of the Texas control model (Perkinson, 2010: 237). State officials also sought to exploit inmate labor to make prisons and penal farms as productive as possible because, as George J. Beto, the director of the Texas Department of Corrections, told the American Correctional Association in 1970, 'the tax-conscious constituent will demand it' (Perkinson, 2010: 235). Perkinson argues that Texas developed an alternative 'control model' of punishment that was unapologetically premised on officially sanctioned violence, strident exploitation of penal labor, a strong retributive urge and stark racial stratification. He identifies slavery as the progenitor of the state's control mode. For well over a century now, Texas has operated a vast archipelago of self-sustaining penal labor farms on the old plantation lands of East Texas. These farms are 'probably the best example of slavery remaining in the country,' according to a national corrections expert (quoted in Perkinson, 2010: 6).

Suspicious of large state projects, Texas, like much of the South, was initially slow to embrace the penitentiary in the 19th century. Fearful that these large public buildings would become 'vampire[s] upon the public treasury', government officials in Texas and elsewhere sought to make their penal enterprises not just self-sustaining but also highly profitable (Perkinson, 2010: 73). Over the years, state officials were obsessed with turning a profit out of penal labor. Texas's first penitentiary, a fortress erected in Huntsville that is still known as 'The Walls' today, was the state's premier public institution, consuming nearly 17 percent of the state's budget in its first year. In the 1850s, the state constructed a massive cotton mill run by penal labor inside 'The Walls' that became the state's largest factory by far. During the Civil War this mill was a main source of tents, uniforms and supply bags for the Confederacy. Imperial Sugar Co., today the largest sugar refinery in the USA, was established with slave capital after the Civil War. Convicts leased from the state built the refinery and supplied it with sugar grown at Sugar Land, a massive estate established outside of San Antonio after the war.

The evolution and growth of Texas's penal system 'has had surprisingly little to do with crime' and much to do with 'America's troubled history of racial conflict and social stratification', Perkinson (2010: 8) contends. As segregationist barriers like slavery and Jim Crow fell, new ones like for-profit convict leasing and later the Texas 'control model', with its stress on maximum discipline and maximum profit, took their place. Prisons have proliferated in Texas and elsewhere despite their breathtaking human costs and minimal effect on crime control because 'they excel in other, generally unspoken ways, at dispersing patronage, fortifying social hierarchies, enacting public vengeance, and symbolizing government resolve' (Perkinson, 2010: 10).

One notable difference between Arizona and Texas is that the failures and abuses of the Lone Star State's penal system have periodically spurred reform movements since the 19th century. The most successful penal reform movements in Texas over the last century and a half did not act in isolation but were buoyed by other social movements. Once these reform movements sputtered out, they often left behind different but arguably no less brutal systems of punishment and confinement. The Populists of the late 19th century were pivotal players in the push to end convict leasing in Texas and elsewhere in the South. After a half-century of public agitation over the corruption and horrors associated with leasing convicts to private, for-profit firms, Texas outlawed this practice. Brutal state-controlled chain gangs and penal labor farms took its place. Women's groups linked to the Progressive movement sought to end sexual abuse and other atrocities in Texan prisons and on its penal farms. They played a vital role in the election of Governor Dan Moody, who launched a far-reaching but short-lived penal reform agenda in the late 1920s that was inspired by experiments with rehabilitation in the North in places like Sing Sing, Auburn and Bedford Hills (Perkinson, 2010: 189–90, 197–8). A colossal bribery scandal in 1972 opened the way for an influx of progressive reformers into the Texas legislature who pursued a short-lived penal reform agenda in the late 1970s and early 1980s that helped stave off a penal expansion.

The prison boom was slower to take off in Texas than Arizona or California. It was not until the early 1990s that the Lone Star State's incarceration rate leapfrogged ahead of California's and the rest of the South's (Campbell, 2011). In a familiar story, as Republicans made electoral inroads in the state in the 1980s and as old guard Democrats vied with pockets of progressive Democrats, the stage was set for the hyper-politicization of penal policy in a retributive, law-and-order direction. Governor William P. Clements, who in 1978 became the first Republican to lead the state since Reconstruction, sought to solidify his political base by mobilizing law enforcement groups on behalf of a more punitive agenda (Campbell, 2011). His tools included targeted mailings, a media campaign, crafty lobbying and strategic appointments to powerful quasi-government anti-crime commissions and task forces that generally excluded representatives from high-crime communities, supporters of alternatives to incarceration, and even victims' rights groups (Campbell, 2011).

Clements's successor, Democrat Mark White, attempted to use early release programs to manage the state's overcrowding crisis. But the media and the newly mobilized law enforcement community, notably the professional associations for the sheriffs, the police and especially the state's district attorneys, vilified him for doing so. He received no credit for the drop in the state's incarceration rate, which coincided with the first decline in serious crime in Texas in years. When Clements returned to office in 1987, he pushed for a major prison expansion with the help of business leaders and law enforcement groups, notably the Texas District and County Attorneys Association (TDCAA) and the Criminal Justice Task Force, which the administration established to coordinate efforts to pass an anti-crime and prison expansion package (Campbell, 2011). Even though Texas was in dire economic straits and economic issues dominated the 1986 election, Clements successfully pushed through a major general obligation bond for prison expansion bundled within a larger set of bonds, jettisoning a longstanding commitment to pay-as-you-go fiscal management. The 1979 landmark *Ruiz* v. *Estelle* decision, which found Texas's overcrowded and unhealthy prisons to be unconstitutional, provided Clements and other hard-liners with an opportunity to expand the state's penal system and to bureaucratize and professionalize its control model. Penal hard-liners faced little resistance because they operated in a political culture characterized by low levels of political participation (including low voter turnout and the absence of statewide civic associations) by African-Americans, low-income people and Mexican-Americans, which were the groups most likely to be ensnared in the state's widening dragnet.[3]

Penal politics in Texas has not been exclusively a top-down process. Prisoners themselves have played a pivotal role in penal reform in Texas that has been overlooked. In his revisionist account of the demise of convict leasing, Perkinson contends that the escapes, strikes, mutinies and riots of leased convicts, and their angry and mournful letters and memoirs documenting their abusive living conditions helped bring about the end of this practice. When traditional avenues of protest were blocked, prisoners would increasingly turn to self-mutilation, such as cutting off a limb or packing a self-inflicted wound with lye or injecting themselves with kerosene, in order to get some relief from backbreaking field labor and to protest the horrid conditions of their confinement. Initially, these self-mutilations did not have a wider political impact. But as the number of self-mutilations rose into the hundreds each year in Texas in the early 1940s and the practice spread to other states, it became impossible for state officials and enterprising journalists to ignore the abhorrent conditions that provoked the bloody protests.

Coinciding with the rise of the civil rights movement, prisoners began looking to the courts for relief. But as Perkinson shows, state and prison officials in Texas were as determined as those in Arizona to maintain the core features of the control model. They eventually eviscerated many of the court-ordered reforms after wars of attrition played out in the legal arena. Perkinson devotes nearly two chapters to the case of David Resendez Ruíz, the lead plaintiff in a landmark federal lawsuit brought against Texas's prison system in the 1970s. Battered around in the courts for about two decades, *Ruíz* v. *Estelle* eventually brought about some significant changes in the state's penal system. But indirectly it also 'helped create an equally severe and infinitely larger prison system in its place' (Perkinson, 2010: 253). As for Ruíz, he was kept in solitary confinement in a cramped, dank dungeon-like cell for decades after the lawsuit was settled. Just months before he died in 2005, he was moved to a prison hospital after being denied medical parole. As Perkinson dryly notes, Ruíz fought the law but the law ultimately won.

If history is any guide, Texan prisons, already some of the toughest in the nation, could become even leaner and meaner in the future. Vexed with growing budget deficits and a virulent anti-tax fever, government and prison officials in Texas and elsewhere have been attempting to cut costs by privatizing more prisons and prison services, intensifying their efforts to exploit penal labor and slashing spending on inmates' medical care, food and other penal 'luxuries' like vocational, substance abuse and educational programs. Recently Texas enacted a slew of penal reforms aimed at shrinking its prison population, but its incarceration rate stubbornly remains the second highest in the country (Fabelo, 2010). If Perkinson's analysis is correct, the Lone Star State will not begin shuttering its prisons without enormous political pressure.

The control model pioneered by Texas and exported to other states has become a key tool to manage an increasingly diverse society ridden with many politically and economically marginalized groups in Texas, Arizona and elsewhere. But the Lone Star State ultimately may be more successful than Arizona in instituting penal reforms that make sizable cuts its incarceration rate. Unlike Arizona, Texas has a history of periodic bursts of penal protest movements linked to wider social movements. Moreover, the get-tough, anti-federal stance has been formative for the political identity of many state officials in Arizona. This helps explain why the pivotal 1977 overhaul of its criminal code and the 1993 modifications of the code that drove the prison boom remain largely untouchable as one economic crisis after another has buffeted the state (Lynch, 2010: 223–4).

THE WIDER POLITICAL CONSEQUENCES OF THE CARCERAL STATE

For a long time, the expansion of the carceral state was widely viewed as a peripheral problem in American politics and society that was largely confined to poor urban communities and minority groups. But the carceral state has grown so huge that it has begun to metastasize and directly impinge on fundamental democratic institutions. Scholars and penal reformers have begun focusing attention on the wider political consequences of mass imprisonment. The carceral state bears down on many central issues in contemporary

American politics, everything from broad questions about how we conceptualize the American state to more specific ones concerning voting rights, voter participation, public opinion and changing conceptions of citizenship.

The political development of the carceral state challenges the common understanding of the US state as weak and is cause to rethink our understanding of the US welfare state. The US state has developed an awesome power and an extensive apparatus to monitor, incarcerate and execute its citizens that is unprecedented in modern US history and among other Western countries. This development raises deeply troubling questions about the health of democratic institutions in the USA and the character of the liberal state. As Mary Bosworth notes in her analysis of the origins, development, and transformation of the US penal system from the colonial era to today, 'Imprisonment is, by nature, an articulation of state power' (2010: 22).

The emergence of the carceral state in the USA has revived interest in the ways in which punishment is a 'uniquely revealing lens into how political regimes work' (McBride, 2007: 3). Political theorists have focused in particular on how punishment is 'a central problem for political administration that requires careful negotiation of the stated ideals of a polity in the exercise of power' (McBride, 2007: 3). Some of them have been especially interested in the relationship between the contemporary death penalty, state sovereignty and the late liberal state (Sarat, 1999, 2001; Kaufman-Osborn, 2002).

Voting rights and the carceral state is another growing area of interest. The voting irregularities of the 2000 and 2004 presidential elections drew enormous public attention to the plight of the estimated 5 million Americans barred from voting by a maze of state laws that deny people with criminal records the right to vote, sometimes temporarily, sometimes permanently (Manza and Uggen, 2006: v). Many established democracies place few, if any, restrictions on the right to vote for people with criminal convictions, including those in prison. The USA not only disenfranchises most of its prisoners but also is the only democracy that routinely disenfranchises large numbers of nonincarcerated offenders and ex-offenders – people on parole or probation or who have completed their sentences (Manza and Uggen, 2006: 38–9). The political impact of felon disenfranchisement in the USA is so huge because the number of people with felony convictions on their records is so huge (more than 16 million Americans, according to Uggen et al., 2006) and because felon disenfranchisement laws have stark racial origins and racial consequences (Brown-Dean, 2004; Pettus, 2005: chs. 3 and 5; Hull, 2006: ch. 2; Manza and Uggen, 2006: ch. 2). More than one in seven black men in the USA is disenfranchised because of his criminal record (Manza and Uggen, 2006: 10).

Felon disenfranchisement raises fundamental questions about how we define (and redefine) citizenship (Ewald, 2002; Brown-Dean, 2004: ch. 2; Pettus, 2005). It also may be a decisive factor in close elections. Manza and Uggen (2006) calculate that if Florida had not banned an estimated 800,000 former felons from voting in the 2000 election, Al Gore would have handily carried the state and won the White House, a claim disputed by Burch (2008). Manza and Uggen (2006) also contend the Democratic Party might have controlled the US Senate for much of the 1990s had many former felons been permitted to vote (Manza and Uggen, 2006: 192–6). Their work implicitly challenges claims about the sources of and degree of political dominance of the Republican Party in the 1980s and 1990s. If felon disenfranchisement is factored in, the ascendancy of the Republican Party may have been as much a function of locking out wide swaths of the electorate as crafting a new, more conservative message that successfully appealed to Democrats disenchanted with the remnants of the New Deal coalition.

The felon disenfranchisement issue is cause to rethink another fundamental question in the study of American politics: is the American voter vanishing? Building on earlier work by McDonald and Popkin (2001),[4] Manza and Uggen (2006: 177) contend that much of the so-called drop in voter turnout may be a consequence of faulty calculations and assumptions used in official turnout statistics. The standard accounts fail to properly consider the large number of noncitizens, prisoners, people on parole or probation and ex-felons who have been disenfranchised by electoral laws and thus overstate the decline in voter turnout.

But the impact of mass imprisonment on voter turnout and citizenship ties cuts even deeper. Having a criminal conviction is a more significant factor in depressing voter turnout among offenders and ex-offenders than formal legal barriers to voting (Burch, 2007). Moreover, contact with the criminal justice system appears to have large negative effects not just on voting but also on civic involvement and trust in government, thus fostering weak citizenship ties. Since people with convictions are concentrated within certain racial groups and certain geographic areas, the carceral state appears to be creating a troubling phenomenon that Burch calls 'concentrated disenfranchisement' (2007: chs 5 and 6).

Research by Burch (2007), Cohen (2010), Weaver and Lerman (2010) and others on the impact of penal policies on political and civic participation and by Bobo and Thompson (2006) on criminal justice and public opinion indicate that the carceral state may be rapidly cleaving off wide swaths of people in the USA from the promise of the American Dream. The political consequences of this are potentially explosive because the American Dream has arguably been the country's central ideology and has served as a kind of societal glue holding together otherwise disparate groups (Hochschild, 1995).

Evidence is growing that many of today's crime control policies fundamentally impede the economic, political and social advancement of the most disadvantaged people in the USA. Prison leaves them less likely to vote and to participate in other civic activities, find gainful employment and maintain ties with their families and communities (Roberts, 2003/2004; Pattillo et al., 2004). The landmark work on the collateral consequences of imprisonment is Bruce Western's (2006) *Punishment and Inequality in America*. Western soberly concludes, after a careful analysis of wage, employment, education and other socioeconomic data, that mass imprisonment has erased many of the 'gains to African-American citizenship hard won by the civil rights movement' (2006: 191). Incarceration significantly reduces the wages, employment, and annual income of former inmates (ch. 5). Incarceration also decreases the likelihood that they will get married or stay married and increases the risk of domestic violence for their partners (ch. 6). The hyper-incarceration of African-Americans also may help explain enduring racial disparities in morbidity and mortality (Pettit and Sykes, 2008: 7–8). These negative effects are concentrated among poor, uneducated, black men, drawing a sharp demarcation between poor and middle-class blacks and between poor blacks and the rest of society. 'By cleaving off poor black communities from the mainstream, the prison boom left America more divided,' Western concludes (2006: 7).

The carceral state raises other troubling and largely unexplored issues about political participation and citizenship. Mass imprisonment is helping to create and legitimate a whole new understanding of citizenship and belonging (Roberts, 2003/2004). Fixated on the staggering increase in the number of people behind bars, analysts have paid less attention to the political and social implications of the stunning rise in the number of people consigned to legal and civil purgatory who are not fully in prison or fully a part of society. On any given day, in addition to the more than two million people sitting in jail or prison, another five million people are on probation or parole or under some form of community supervision (Glaze et al., 2010). Parole and probation officers are permitted to regulate major and mundane aspects of offenders' lives – everything from where they live and whom they associate with to whether they have a beer in their refrigerator and whether they are permitted to carry a cell phone (Beckett and Herbert, 2009). Many people on parole or probation are subject to random drug tests. Law enforcement officers also are permitted to conduct warrantless searches of parolees and probationers that are not subject to the standard Fourth Amendment protections. Goffman's (2009) ethnographic study of 'life on the run' in a poor neighborhood in Philadelphia is a chilling account of how the expansive systems of policing and supervision that have accompanied the rise of the carceral state have fostered a pernicious climate of fear and suspicion that penetrates all aspects of daily life, including intimate and family relations, labor force participation and access to medical care. Men on parole or probation and those with outstanding warrants, even for trivial offenses, avoid the police and the courts at all costs, even when they are the victims of violent attacks and other serious crimes, out of a justified fear they will be sent back to prison or jail (Goffman, 2009: 353).

For many former offenders, their time in purgatory never ends, even after they have served their prison sentence or successfully completed their parole or probation. Former felons (and some former misdemeanants) risk losing the right to vote and also are subject to other acts of 'civil death' that push them further and further to the political, social and economic margins. Former felons often must forfeit their pensions, disability benefits and veterans' benefits. Many of them are ineligible for public housing (Simon, 2007: 194–8), student loans or food stamps. Dozens of states and the federal government ban former felons from jury service for life. As a result, nearly one-third of African-American men are permanently ineligible to serve as jurors (Kalt, 2003: 67).[5] States prohibit former offenders from working in scores of professions, including plumbing, palm reading, food catering, and even haircutting, a popular trade in many prisons (Hull, 2006: 33; Gottschalk, 2006: 22 n. 45). A recent American Bar Association study funded by the National Institute of Justice counted 38,000 statutes that impose consequences on people convicted of crimes (*Crime and Justice News*, 2011). In April 2011, Attorney General Eric Holder urged states to eliminate the legal burdens on former offenders that do not imperil public safety, such as certain restrictions on housing and employment (*Crime and Justice News*, 2011). Many jurisdictions forbid employers to discriminate against job applicants solely because of their criminal record unless their offense is directly relevant to the job. But applicants with criminal records are disproportionately denied jobs (Pager, 2003, 2007), and rejected job seekers have great difficulty getting redress in the courts (Hull, 2006: 32–4). In some major cities, 80 percent of young African-American men now have criminal records (Street, 2002) and thus are subject to a 'hidden underworld of legalized discrimination and permanent social exclusion' (Alexander, 2010: 13). Wacquant characterizes this underworld as 'a closed circuit' of perpetual social and legal marginality (Wacquant, 2000: 384). Alexander contends that the criminal justice system should not be thought of as an independent system but 'rather as a *gateway* into a much larger system of racial stigmatization and permanent marginalization' (Alexander, 2010: 12, original emphasis).

In a remarkable development, elaborate gradations of citizenship are on their way to becoming a new norm in the USA. The carceral state has helped to legitimize the idea of creating a very separate political and legal universe for whole categories of people. These 'partial citizens' (Manza and Uggen, 2006: 9) or 'internal exiles' (Simon, 2007: 175), be they felons, ex-felons, convicted sex offenders, legal resident aliens, undocumented immigrants or people burdened with banishment orders, are now routinely denied a range of rights and access to state resources.[6] Some ex-felons succeed in having their political rights restored, but it often involves elaborate, capricious, intrusive and daunting procedures that establish a new standard of 'worthiness' for political participation (Goodnough, 2004). This is a modern-day reincarnation of earlier standards of worthiness, such as the infamous literacy test.

Another growing and related area of scholarly and public interest is the criminalization of immigration policy (De Giorgi, 2006: ch. 5). In the case of immigrants, documented and undocumented, a whole new penal apparatus has been quietly under construction for decades. It operates under the auspices of the US Immigration and Customs Enforcement (formerly the Immigration and Naturalization Service) but has been largely shielded from public and legal scrutiny. Changes in immigration policy over the past 30 years or so have become new drivers of the carceral state (Bohrman and Murakawa, 2005). In the early 1980s, the Reagan administration ended the prevailing practice of releasing undocumented immigrants pending administrative proceedings. Two landmark pieces of legislation in 1996 - the Antiterrorism and Effective Death Penalty Act and the Illegal Immigration Reform and Immigrant Responsibility Act - dramatically expanded the categories of crimes for which legal residents could be deported and eliminated many opportunities for waivers. A conviction for simple battery or shoplifting with a one-year suspended sentence could be cause to trigger mandatory detention and deportation (Dow, 2004: 173–4). During the debate over the immigration reform bill that imploded in mid-2007, an amendment was even proposed that called for the mandatory detention of anyone who overstayed his or her visa (*New York Times*, 2007: A22).

The number of people held in special detention centers and elsewhere on any given day has increased more than eleven-fold since the early 1970s (calculated from Dow, 2004: 7–9; Kolodner, 2006: C1) as the immigration service has become a mini-Bureau of Prisons. A notable recognition of this shift is the increasingly detailed accounting of trends in immigration detention included in the Bureau of Justice Statistics biannual reports on the incarcerated population in the USA (for example, Sabol et al., 2009: 10). In a remarkable development, Latinos now represent the largest ethnic group in the federal prison system. This is a consequence of the dramatic rise in immigration raids and prosecutions for immigration violations, and the drop in federal prosecutions of other crimes, including gun trafficking, corruption, organized crime and white-collar crime (Gorman, 2009).

Ironically, since people who cross the border illegally are not technically considered 'criminals', they have fewer legal protections and rights and often are subjected to more capricious and brutal conditions of confinement than citizens charged with crimes (Dow, 2004). Secret detentions, physical abuse, closed court proceedings, denial of contact with family members, attorneys and the media, notoriously arbitrary administrative reviews, 'institutionalized anti-Arab bias' (Dow, 2004: 211), indefinite detentions and state resistance to habeas corpus reviews have long been the standard operating procedures of the parallel universe of immigrant detention. Recent scholarship on immigrant detention and the carceral state is cause to rethink and reexamine the conventional view that the 9/11 attacks were the catalyst for a drastic shift in immigration policy. In fact, there appears to be a remarkable continuum between the pre-9/11 and post-9/11 treatment of immigrants, with the differences being primarily in degree, not kind.

'GOVERNING THROUGH CRIME'

The criminalization of immigration policy is just one example of how the 'technologies, discourses, and metaphors of crime and criminal justice' have been migrating to all kinds of institutions and public policies that seem far afield from crime fighting (Simon, 2007: 4). A new civil and political order based on 'governing through crime' has been in the making for decades. The war on crime has created imbalances in the political system. The US Department of Justice and the office of the attorney general have swollen at the expense of other parts of the federal government. The power of the prosecutor has expanded at the expense of judges, defense attorneys and other actors in the criminal justice system. Perhaps even more significantly, the all-powerful, largely unaccountable prosecutor has become the new model for exercising executive authority in the USA. In word and deed, mayors, governors and presidents increasingly fashion themselves as 'prosecutors-in-chief'. They 'define their objectives in prosecutorial terms', frame 'political issues in the language shaped by public insecurity and outrage about crime' and push for vast expansions of executive power (Simon, 2007: 35).

The war on crime has fundamentally recast both governmental and nongovernmental institutions in the USA, according to Simon (2007). In the new regime, criminal analogies are wielded in many diverse settings, from homes to schools to the workplace. Principals, teachers, parents and employers all gain authority and are viewed as acting legitimately if they can redefine family, education or workplace issues as criminal matters.

Decades ago 'racial inequality was the pivot around which the federal government mandated a vast reworking in the way schools were governed at the state and local levels' (Simon, 2007: 9). Now, Simon contends, it is crime. The federal Safe Schools Act 1994 and the state-level Safe Schools Acts it spawned singled out crime control as the main vehicle for improving public education. In introducing his No Child Left Behind Act 2001, President George W. Bush cast educational failure and crime in the schools as parallel problems. As a result of these and other measures, educational policy has been criminalized. Schools have been prisonized with the proliferation of school-based police officers, drug sweeps, uniforms, metal detectors, zero-tolerance rules and the greater use of sanctions like detention and expulsion (Simon, 2007: 222–6).

Governing through crime has transformed the everyday lives of not just the poor and disadvantaged but also of the middle class. Lyons and Drew (2006) describe in chilling detail how paramilitary police and a menacing K-9 unit of drug-sniffing dogs carry out 'lockdowns' and random drug searches at an affluent suburban high school. In their tale of two schools in Ohio – a suburban high school and an inner-city one – they show how politicians and lawmakers strategically cultivate an excessive fear of crime and violence 'to divest from any notion of public education as a democratic social good' (Lyons and Drew, 2006: 4). Students, teachers and communities internalize the 'zero-tolerance culture' foisted on them, making it difficult to resist the 'transformation of schools from sites of democratic education to sites of social control and punishment' (2006: 90).

The suburbs and suburban life have been fortified; so has the workplace. With the decline of organized labor and collective bargaining and the retreat of the state in regulating the workplace, employers increasingly are using the crime issue to establish their dominance on the job (Simon, 2007: 246). Their tools include the widespread use of drug testing and other forms of intensive surveillance and the dismissal of employees for off-the-job infractions like domestic violence and drug abuse.

THE CARCERAL STATE AND THE WELFARE STATE

The emergence of the carceral state is cause to reconsider how we think about the US welfare state. Western's portrait in *Punishment and Inequality* of the deteriorating labor-market position of poor, unskilled blacks is at odds with the conventional view that the US labor market outperforms the labor markets of Western Europe. His account undermines the widespread claim that the USA, with its relatively unregulated labor market, weak unions and stingy welfare benefits, is better at reducing unemployment, especially for low-skilled workers, than 'nanny states', such as France, Italy and Germany. 'The invisible disadvantage produced by mass imprisonment challenges this account of how meager social protections benefit the least-skilled workers', according to Western (2006: 104). Moreover, state regulation of the poor did not recede in the USA in the 1990s, it merely shifted course. The government significantly increased its role in regulating the lives of poor, uneducated men and women by sweeping more and more of them up into the criminal justice system's growing dragnet (Western, 2006: 105).

As Wacquant (2009), Beckett and Western (2001), and others have documented, the carceral state has expanded at the expense of the welfare state. By a number of measures – expenditures, personnel, congressional hearings and legislation – the law enforcement apparatus has been growing while social welfare provision has been contracting. Some states have experienced a direct dollar-for-dollar trade-off as budgets for higher education shrank and corrections budgets grew. States and countries that spend more on social welfare tend to have relatively lower incarceration rates (Sutton, 2004; Downes and Hansen, 2006). Communities that are not ridden with economic and racial stratifications also appear to have lower crime rates, especially for violent crime (Peterson and Krivo, 2010).

Examined more closely, what we may be seeing is not so much the contraction of the welfare state as its absorption by the carceral state, which has become the primary regulator of the poor and a main conduit of social services for the poor and disadvantaged. Jails and prisons in the USA are now responsible for the largest number of mentally ill people in the country. Drug courts and domestic violence courts and parole and probation officers not only monitor the behavior of offenders but also often provide key links to dwindling social services and employment and educational opportunities. Wacquant suggests that it is untenable to analyze social and penal policy in isolation from one another because they are so enmeshed today and have been for a long time (Wacquant, 2009: 13).

Wacquant provocatively suggests that the USA (and perhaps other developed countries) is groping toward a new kind of state, one he calls the 'centaur state', which is 'guided by a liberal head mounted on an authoritarian body'. What he really means is a neoliberal head – where the doctrine of laissez faire rules with respect to the social inequalities produced by largely unregulated capital and labor markets – that is attached to a body that is 'brutally paternalistic and punitive' (Wacquant, 2009: 43).

The disadvantages that mass imprisonment confers on the most disadvantaged members of American society has remained largely invisible for many reasons, some political, some analytical, and some, a combination of the two. For example, the US census veils and distorts the wider impact of the carceral state (Gottschalk, 2007). How to tabulate prisoners was one of the most vexing issues for the US Census Bureau as it prepared for the 2010 census. The bureau chose to enumerate prisoners as residents of the towns and counties where they are incarcerated. But most inmates have no personal or civic ties to these communities and almost always return to their home neighborhoods upon release.

The way prisoners currently are counted has enormous and unsettling political and economic consequences. In every state except Maine and Vermont, imprisoned felons are barred from voting. Yet these disenfranchised prisoners are included in the population tallies used for Congressional reapportionment and for redistricting state House and Senate seats, city councils and other government bodies. This practice dilutes the votes of urban areas and of rural areas without prisons. For example, nearly 40 percent of the inmates in Pennsylvania's state prisons come from Philadelphia, which has no state prisons in its city limits. For census and redistricting purposes, these Philadelphia citizens are considered residents of the counties far from their homes where they are imprisoned. These tend to be predominantly white, rural districts that are Republican strongholds.

The evidence of political inequities in redistricting arising from how the Census Bureau counts prisoners is 'compelling', according to a report by the National Research Council of the National Academies (2006: 9). A provocative analysis by the Prison Policy Initiative suggests that several Republican Senate seats in New York State would be in jeopardy if prisoners in upstate correctional institutions were counted in their home neighborhoods in New York City (Wagner, 2002: 1–6). A recalibration of New York's prison population would likely put the Republican Party's decades-old domination in the state Senate at risk.

The current census practice grossly distorts demographic and socioeconomic data, leading to misleading conclusions in vital areas like economic growth, migration, household income and racial composition (Lotke and Wagner, 2004; Wagner, 2004). For example, in the 2000 census, 56 counties nationwide – or 1 in 50 – with declining populations were misleadingly reported to be growing, thanks to the inclusion of their captive populations (Heyer and Wagner, 2004). Pennsylvania's Union County, which has an archipelago of federal penitentiaries, is 90 percent white, according to the 2000 census. But without its 5000 prisoners, Union would be 97 percent white (Prisoners of the Census, 2006).

Mass imprisonment also distorts labor market, economic and demographic data. Official statistics mask an invisible inequality generated by mass imprisonment. Large surveys run by the Census Bureau to determine the poverty rate, unemployment rate and wage levels exclude people who are incarcerated (Western, 2006: 87). Other major demographic and health surveys also exclude prisoners, skewing the results (Pettit and Sykes, 2008: 9). Western's work challenges claims about the achievements of the 1992–2000 economic expansion, hailed as the largest peacetime expansion in US history. If prison and jail inmates were counted, the US unemployment rate for males would have been at least 2 percentage points higher by the mid-1990s (Western and Beckett, 1999: 1052), and the true jobless rate for young black males in 2000 would have been 32 percent, not the official 24 percent (Western, 2006: 90).

RESISTANCE TO THE CARCERAL STATE

The carceral state raises many important issues about power and resistance. Some scholars suggest that a new social movement may be coalescing around opposition to the carceral state (Katzenstein, 2005; Gilmore, 2007). This embryonic movement raises a question central to the study of politics: how do marginalized and stigmatized groups organize and effectively assert political power?

Mainstream African-American organizations and leaders have been slow to enlist in a battle against the carceral state (Alexander, 2010). Historically, black leaders have had a persistent unease about focusing on criminal justice issues (DuBois, 1970; Curtin, 2000: 9–10, ch. 10; Muhammad, 2010). Some of the same factors that prompted African-Americans to distance themselves from the HIV/AIDS crisis in the black community in the 1980s and 1990s (Cohen, 1999, 2010) may be causing them to turn a blind eye to the crisis of blacks and the carceral state today. The reluctance to embrace and publicize the plight of the disproportionate number of incarcerated African-Americans may be the result of fears that this will reflect unfavorably on blacks as a whole and impede black leaders' efforts to identify with what they perceive to be the middle-class moral values of the mainstream. For example, some civil rights groups were reluctant to use the federal Voting Rights Act to challenge felon disenfranchisement laws 'for fear of a backlash that might jeopardize the rights of the more privileged members of the black community' (Warren, 2000). Many black legislators and other black leaders initially were enthusiastic recruits in the war on drugs and even supported the enormous sentencing disparity between crack and powder cocaine, which disproportionately hurts African-Americans (Kennedy, 1997: 370–2; Barker, 2009: 149–52). Cohen contends that the black media and black elites, including Oprah Winfrey, Bill Cosby and Barack Obama, have contributed to a 'moral panic' based on 'an exaggerated fear of black youth' (Cohen, 2010: 39). At the same time, they have remained relatively silent about the enormous structural barriers, including racism, that ensnare black Americans. This 'secondary marginalization' – or public policing by black elites – denies 'community recognition and resources to those labeled deviant in the black community by indigenous organizations, institutions, and leaders' and legitimizes the 'heightened policing and criminalization' of young black Americans (Cohen, 2010: 42).

Mainstream African-American leaders and groups have sporadically challenged the war on drugs and the carceral state (Clemetson, 2004). In 1993–4, the Congressional Black Caucus (CBC) was a major factor in getting crime prevention programs included in the federal crime bill. The CBC also waged a valiant but ultimately losing battle to enact the Racial Justice Act, which would have permitted introducing statistical evidence of racial discrimination in capital punishment cases. The NAACP, ACLU and some other civil rights organizations initially were at the forefront of the push begun in the mid-1990s to challenge laws that disenfranchise former offenders. At its start, the campaign focused on the discriminatory nature of these laws, their stark racial consequences and their deeper historical origins in the Jim Crow era's efforts to undo Reconstruction and push blacks out of the electorate. But as the felon disenfranchisement issue attracted a broader array of supporters, including People for the American Way, DEMOS, the AFL-CIO and the Brennan Center, 'the discourse surrounding reform de-emphasized race' (Brown-Dean, 2010: 202). The new deracialized strategy emphasized the importance of universal suffrage 'for preserving the legitimacy of the democratic process' (Brown-Dean, 2010: 202).

For decades, the NAACP, the country's most prominent civil rights organization, was politically somnambulant as the carceral state and the gap between black and white incarceration rates continued to grow. That appears to be changing since Benjamin Jealous became head of the NAACP in 2008. Jealous has characterized mass incarceration as the leading civil rights issue of the 21st century (Serwer, 2009). In early 2011, the NAACP released a major report on the schools-to-prison pipeline that documented how corrections budgets have grown at the expense of funding for education. Shortly thereafter, the NAACP unveiled a major national billboard campaign to draw attention to the problem of mass incarceration (NAACP, 2011). At its annual convention in July 2011, the NAACP enacted a historical resolution calling for an end to the war on drugs (Smith, 2011).

Penal reformers are enlisting not only civil rights but also international human rights laws and norms to challenge the carceral state. The accelerated political and economic integration of Europe over the past couple of decades has increased pressure on European countries to be more aware of how their penal policies and prison conditions compare with those of their neighbors. This has helped neutralize some of the growing internal political pressures to be more punitive in the UK, which has one of the highest incarceration rates in Western Europe. The USA is likewise highly vulnerable to unfavorable cross-national comparisons of penal policies and penal conditions. Through their detailed reports on capital punishment, the widespread use of life sentences, supermax prisons, abuse of female prisoners, prison rape and other disturbing conditions in US prisons, human rights organizations, such as Amnesty International, Human Rights Watch and the ACLU, and leading penal reform groups, such as The Sentencing Project, have been drawing increased national and international attention to how US penal practices are exceptionally punitive when compared to other Western countries.

The carceral state has the potential to reconfigure the politics of feminism and women's issues. With more than two million people behind bars, the overwhelming majority of them men, millions of women are the mothers, daughters, wives, partners and sisters of men entombed in the carceral state. Moreover, since 1995, women have been the fastest growing segment of the US prison population (Harrison and Beck, 2006: 4). The enormous expansion of the carceral state may finally bring about a day of reckoning for feminism and women's groups on the issue of law enforcement and the state. Over the past decade or so, the chorus of doubts about relying on penal solutions to address violence against women has grown louder across a broad range of feminists, crime experts, academics and social workers.

Concerns have been growing about mandatory arrest, presumptive arrest and no-drop policies in the case of domestic violence and about community notification and civil commitment laws for sexual offenders. These legal remedies do not necessarily reduce violence against women and children and may have contributed to greater state control of women, especially poor women. They also have fostered gross public understandings of the causes of sexual and other violence against women and children and how to prevent it (Zorza and Woods, 1994; Minow, 1998; Coker, 2001: 807; Lombardi, 2002; Sontag, 2002; Miller, 2005; Janus, 2006; Gruber, 2007; Bumiller, 2008; Whittier, 2009). The rising number of women behind bars for minor drug violations or for being the unwitting or reluctant accomplices to abusive partners has highlighted the persistent problems with the drug war, as has the growing number of imprisoned mothers with young children (Talvi, 2007; Kruttschnitt, 2010). A number of critics suggest that the women's movement needs to address the problem of violence against women not by strengthening its ties with law enforcement and victims' groups but by connecting up with other progressive reform movements calling for social justice, an expanded welfare state and a retreat of the carceral state (Harris, 1987; Snider, 1994: 110; Bumiller, 2008).

The most significant political challenges to the carceral state appear to be occurring at the subnational level. Today many states are attempting to slow their incarceration rates, with varied degrees of success. Barker (2009) demonstrates how differences in the structure of state governance and in the practice of civic engagement help explain why California has pursued far more punitive policies than New York or Washington State. Although many national civil rights organizations and leaders have been slow to challenge the carceral state, poor neighborhoods in urban areas have been 'hotbeds of mobilization' around criminal justice issues (Miller, 2007: 313). Some urban neighborhoods have been intensely engaged in developing policing and other criminal justice policies at the local level (Skogan, 2006). Local community groups in urban areas appear to take a less punitive approach to penal matters. They situate menaces like criminal violence and the illegal drug market within a wider social context that highlights how racial discrimination, high employment, inadequate housing and health care, and failing schools are all part of the 'crime problem' (Miller, 2007: 311). For a variety of institutional and political reasons that analysts are just beginning to excavate, these local groups in high-crime areas have been persistently locked out of the crime and punishment debate at the state and national levels (Miller, 2008).

African-American and Hispanic women have been establishing important grass-roots and statewide organizations to challenge the carceral state on a number of fronts, from three-strikes laws to the siting of new prisons. Gilmore traces how the organization Mothers Reclaiming Our Children (ROC), founded in California in the early 1990s, evolved from being a self-help group 'into a pair of political organizations trying to build a powerful movement' to challenge what she calls 'domestic militarism' (2007: 239). Mothers ROC 'critically deploys the ideological power of motherhood to challenge the legitimacy' of the carceral state by emphasizing how each prisoner is someone's child (Gilmore, 1999: 27). Mothers ROC and other reform organizations also stress the devastating impact that incarceration is having on the children and communities that offenders leave behind. As Gilmore poignantly explains, prisons 'wear out places by wearing out people, irrespective of whether they have done time' (1999: 17). Scholars and activists are drawing increased attention to how US penal policies constitute a 'war on the family' that leaves the millions of children of imprisoned and formerly imprisoned parents shattered and traumatized (Bernstein, 2005; Golden, 2005).

The political economy of the carceral state is emerging as another point of attack for opponents of the carceral state. We are beginning to get a much more sophisticated understanding of who benefits economically and who does not from the carceral state. This work challenges the narrowly economistic view, popular for a long time among many anti-prison activists, that attributes the origins of the carceral state to the private interests that profit from building prisons, running prisons and exploiting prison labor. Gilmore develops a more subtle political economy argument to explain the creation of a 'golden gulag' in California. She singles out the specific contours of the state's wrenching economic and political restructuring beginning in the 1970s that created surplus finance, surplus land, surplus labor and surplus state capacity (2007: 88).

Anti-prison activists are using new economic and political arguments and forging new rural-urban coalitions and alliances with environmental groups to unhinge the carceral state (Braz and Gilmore, 2006; Gilmore, 2007). For example, a coalition of family ranchers and farmworker families in Farmersville, California, successfully fought the construction of a new prison in their community. They based their strategy on showing how prisons do not solve the economic problems of rural areas but do create new ones as they endanger the water supply, aggravate class and racial inequalities and raise rates of domestic violence (Gilmore, 2007: 177).

THE COMPARATIVE POLITICS OF PENAL POLICY

Mass imprisonment within a democratic polity and the hyper-incarceration (Wacquant, 2008) of certain groups are unprecedented developments. The consolidation of this new model in the USA has spurred interest in comparative penal policy and raises the question: Is this country exceptionally vulnerable to get-tough policies, or will other countries emulate the USA?

Deep-seated cultural differences have been a consistent theme in recent scholarship on US exceptionalism in criminal justice policy. Cultural factors singled out include an abiding mistrust of the government (Zimring et al., 2001; Whitman, 2003; Zimring, 2003), a history of vigilantism (Zimring, 2003), an enduring attachment to liberal egalitarianism (Whitman, 2003) and the impact of centuries of white supremacy on American political development (Kaplan, 2006). Some scholars have focused on more recent cultural and social changes to explain American exceptionalism, most notably the arrival of late modernity in the postwar era and the onset of a new 'culture of control' (Garland, 2001).

Institutional and political factors are not incidental to these accounts of American exceptionalism in penal policy but they do not predominate.

The issue of American exceptionalism in penal policy has spurred greater interest in comparative work on crime control and penal policy and in how exceptional institutional, political, and economic factors create exceptional penal policies (Cavadino and Dignan, 2006; Lacey, 2008; Garland, 2010). In the introduction to a pathbreaking volume surveying penal developments in several advanced industrialized countries, Tonry (2007) concedes a role – though a circumscribed one – for specific national characteristics in explaining variations in punitiveness. But he resists the contention that transnational forces associated with globalization and with the economic and social dislocations of late modernity, including rising existential angst, individualism and alienation, are the main engines propelling more punitive policies.

Most of the contributors to the Tonry volume agree that crime patterns generally explain little about why some countries are more punitive than others. From the 1960s to the early to-mid 1990s, crime rates generally increased in the USA and most other industrialized countries (with some fluctuations over this period). But only the USA, the Netherlands, the UK and New Zealand experienced sharp increases in their incarceration rates (Tonry, 2007), though the US incarceration rate remains in a league all its own. Tonry and many of his contributors single out a combination of institutional, political, socioeconomic and cultural factors to explain such wide variations in punitiveness.

Several institutional factors are pivotal. 'Conflict' political systems based on two dominant parties, first-past-the-post electoral systems, and single-member electoral districts are more likely to enact harsher measures than consensual, multiparty systems with proportional representation, coalition governments and greater policy continuity. Not surprisingly, conflict-style political systems (like those in the USA and the UK) tend to produce conflict-style political cultures with lower levels of public trust and lower levels of government legitimacy – two important contributors to law-and-order politics. Other important institutional variables include the level of party discipline and whether the political economy leans more toward neoliberalism, corporatism or social democracy. Another key variable appears to be the varied ways that industrialized countries have responded to the decline of the Fordist model of production and the emergence of a more contingent workforce and a less regulated global market (De Giorgi, 2006).

Another important institutional factor is sharp differences in the organization and selection of judges and prosecutors. The USA is the only major Western country in which judges and prosecutors are either elected or selected according to partisan criteria, making these officials highly susceptible to public opinion and emotions (Tonry, 2007). In most civil-law countries, judges and prosecutors are career civil servants 'who have spent a professional lifetime absorbing norms of professionalism, political nonpartisanship and impartiality', which helps insulate them from 'public emotion and vigilantism' in individual cases (Tonry, 2007: 35).

Institutional factors also have acted as a check on law-and-order politics in Canada. Legislative power over sentencing is the exclusive domain of Canada's federal government. Provincial governments, which are more susceptible to populist pressures to get tough, have no real legislative authority to alter criminal laws. Local, grass-roots citizens' groups lack viable structural mechanisms (such as referendum) to directly push punitive measures, such as three-strikes laws, and the Canadian government has sharply limited their influence in public bodies dealing with crime policy (Webster and Doob, 2007). The majority of bills passed by

Parliament originate with the government, not individual legislators. This tends to make the government more sensitive to the broader financial and other ramifications of criminal justice legislation. It also permits a wide range of other government departments to weigh in on proposed legislation. Criminal justice policy has remained largely the domain of nonpartisan career civil servants who soldier on despite shifts in which party heads the government. Divided responsibilities between the federal government, which handles all criminal justice legislation, and the provinces, which administer the justice system, ensure that any change in criminal law 'requires extensive consultation between the two "partners"' (Webster and Doob, 2007: 340). This is a time-consuming process that reduces the likelihood of the knee-jerk style of criminal justice policymaking that vexes the USA. Furthermore, judges are selected in a nonpartisan process, which insulates the judiciary from public pressures and political interference. The Canadian judiciary has served as an important safety valve, minimizing the impact of especially punitive legislation enacted for blatantly political reasons (Brodeur, 2007; Webster and Doob, 2007).

Differences in the organization of the media are also an important institutional factor. All countries experience horrific sensationalistic crimes. But the mark that headline-grabbing crimes leave on penal policy varies enormously. In a fascinating essay, Green (2007) compares the infamous case of Jamie Bulger, the toddler abducted and killed in 1993 by two 10-year-old boys outside Liverpool, UK, with the 1994 death of five-year-old Silje Marie Redergard, who was attacked by three six-year-olds in a suburb of Trondheim, Norway. Bulger's death propelled English politicians on a law-and-order campaign that pushed England in a sharply punitive direction, while Redergard's homicide left no lasting mark on Norwegian penal policy. In England, 'the highly adversarial, zero-sum-game-style political culture' interacted with 'a highly competitive and sensationalistic media culture to create incentives for politicians and journalists to politicize events such as the Bulger homicide to score political points and sell newspapers' (Green, 2007: 593). These differences in the organization of the media help explain why Tony Blair and 'New' Labour were so successful at exploiting the Bulger case to express their unapologetically populist and tough new stance on penal policy. This is another example of how US-style punitiveness has made its greatest inroads in the UK, where political pressure to talk – and act – tough on crime and punishment remains strong despite drops in the crime rate (Newburn, 2007).

An underlying theme of much of the work on comparative penal policy is that stable incarceration rates and penal policies cannot be taken for granted. Even countries such as Canada, best known for its persistent 'penal blandness,' are 'extremely vulnerable to a burst for the worst' (Brodeur, 2007: 84; Johnson, 2007; Webster and Doob, 2007). A panoply of historical, cultural and institutional factors have shielded Canada from wider punitive forces – thus far. But the country's decades-old stance of punitive restraint may be in jeopardy due to a series of political scandals that robbed the federal government of its moral authority, a succession of unstable minority governments and a dramatic spike in gun-related homicides in Toronto, the country's media capital. These developments provided an opening for politicians across the board to adopt 'get tough' platforms for electoral gain beginning around 2005. Confidence in nonpartisan expert opinion is eroding, and personal attacks on civil servants are on the rise. Canada could go the way of the Netherlands and Japan, where several somewhat independent events rapidly eroded the protective factors that had made them two of the most lenient countries in the world (Downes, 2007; Johnson, 2007; Webster and Doob, 2007).

Differences in country-specific institutional, socioeconomic and cultural factors dominate explanations for variations in punitiveness.

However, transnational factors are not incidental. As Downes pithily remarks, '[T]he prison system may be an archipelago, but it is not an island' (2007: 118). Transnational factors are exerting contradictory pulls on penal policy. On the one hand, the USA has become 'an aggressive exporter of its penal ideas and management systems' as 'American correctional industries trawl the world for markets, finding ready buyers in England for a twentieth-century version of the prison hulks' (Downes, 2007: 118). Some contend that the growing transnational pressures of migration and neoliberalism are likely to exert significant upward pressure on the incarceration rates of other developed countries (De Giorgi, 2006; Wacquant, 2009). Others are more optimistic that domestic institutions and conditions are capable in many cases of moderating these outside pressures so that many developed countries will maintain 'relatively moderate and modest penal systems in the decades to come' (Lacey, 2008: 167).

The accelerated political and economic integration of Europe over the past couple of decades has increased pressure on European countries to be more aware of how their penal policies and prison conditions compare with those of their neighbors. This has helped neutralize some of the growing internal political pressures to be more punitive in the UK (Newburn, 2007; Snacken, 2007; Tonry, 2007). However, European integration may be a mixed blessing for penal policy over the long term. It may force get-tough countries such as Britain to lighten up. But it may also push the more lenient ones to toughen up and match some evolving European mean of punitiveness. Some analysts have been quite critical of multilateral attempts to harmonize criminal law. They fear this will result in stiffer sentences 'without any real debate as to the efficacy and justice of such sentences' (Padfield, 2004: 89, cited in Lappi-Seppälä, 2007: 286, n. 36). The time-consuming deliberations that have been the hallmark of Europe's more lenient countries, notably in Scandinavia, are at risk. This increases the likelihood that political arguments and symbolic messages will trump arguments based on principles and professional expertise (Lappi-Seppälä, 2007).

Despite some new developments that suggest industrialized countries in Europe and elsewhere may be becoming more punitive, the USA remains in a league all its own. As Franklin Zimring once remarked, comparing increases in incarceration rates over the last three decades in Europe to those in the USA is like comparing a haircut to a beheading (quoted in Downes, 2007: 103). But it does raise the question, '[I]s the United States an outlier or a harbinger of things to come elsewhere?' Or, in other words, '[I]s a haircut the prelude to a beheading' (Downes, 2007: 103)?

FUTURE RESEARCH

Interest in examining the political factors that have propelled a country or state to drastically cut its incarceration rate or otherwise pursue less punitive policies is growing. The recent analysis of the factors behind a major decarceration in California in the 1960s when conservative Ronald Reagan was governor is a remarkable story (Gartner et al., 2011). So is the account of why California repealed its felon disenfranchisement laws in 1974, defying the trend toward greater punitiveness at the ballot box as the nonwhite population of a state increases (Campbell, 2007).

The experience of other industrialized countries may shed some light on how to dampen the enthusiasm in the USA for putting so many of its people under lock and key and the watchful eye of the state (Roberts and Gabor, 2004). If the experience of other countries is any guide, the so-called root causes approach to progressive penal reform, however well intentioned, may be shortsighted (Brodeur, 2007: 77). This approach seeks to solve the crime and punishment dilemma by focusing on ameliorating structural problems, such as rampant poverty, high unemployment, dysfunctional schools, an abysmal health-care system and entrenched racism. Long-term fixes are problematic not just because they take a long time. As Brodeur (2007) notes, they are nettlesome because they are harder to sustain from one change of administration to the next. In the US case, the absence of a respected, expert, insular, nonpartisan civil service that maintains policy continuity despite political shifts compounds the problem. The focus on structural problems overshadows the fact that many of the people in US prisons are serving time for nonviolent offenses, many of which are property or petty drug offenses that would not warrant a prison sentence in many other countries. It also deflects attention away from the fact that prisons exacerbate many social ills that contribute to crime and poverty and are unlikely to significantly rehabilitate anyone. Finland made changing penal policy in the short term – not social and economic policy over the long term – its top priority as it consciously sought in the 1960s to slash its incarceration rate. It reduced its prison population significantly over a relatively short period of time without a sustained attack on deeper structural problems (Brodeur, 2007: 75; Lappi-Seppälä, 2007: 234). Germany did the same in the 1980s (Graham, 1990).

Many other critical areas remain to be explored. The need is great for more sophisticated studies of public opinion on a range of criminal justice issues and also on the impact of public opinion on criminal justice policy (Zimring and Johnson, 2006). A number of public opinion surveys offer compelling evidence that public attitudes in the USA have hardened on criminal justice matters even though they have liberalized on a range of other issues, such as sexual behavior, abortion and civil liberties (Sharp, 1999: 53, 52, Figs 2–3; Gaubatz, 1995). Although public attitudes about crime and criminals appear to have hardened, it is misleading to portray the public as overwhelmingly punitive. The role of public opinion in penal policy is extremely complex.

For all the talk about a more punitive public mood, the public's anxiety about crime is 'subject to sudden, dramatic shifts, unrelated to any objective measure of crime' (Frase, 2001: 268). The widespread impression that public concern about crime skyrocketed in the 1960s with the jump in the crime rate and the general uneasiness associated with the riots and demonstrations of these years is not solidly supported by public opinion data (Beckett, 1997: 23–5; Chambliss, 1999: Table 1.1, 20; Loo and Grimes, 2004). The public certainly 'accepts, if not prefers' a range of hard-line policies like the death penalty, three-strikes laws, and increased use of incarceration. But support for these more punitive policies is 'mushy', partly because public knowledge of criminal justice is so sketchy (Roberts and Stalans, 1998: 37–8; Cullen et al., 2000: 1). The public consistently overestimates the proportion of violent crime and the recidivism rate (Gest, 2001: 267). Possessing limited knowledge of how the criminal justice system actually works, people in the USA and elsewhere generally believe the system is more forgiving of offenders than it really is (Roberts, 1997: 250–5; Roberts and Stalans, 1998: 50; Roberts et al., 2003). Overly simplistic public opinion surveys reinforce the 'assumption of an unflinching punitive "law and order" tilt of US public opinion on crime' and mask 'large and recurrent' differences between the views of blacks and whites on the criminal justice system (Bobo and Johnson, 2004; see also Unnever and Cullen, 2010).

Moreover, policymaking elites tend to misperceive public opinion on crime, viewing the public as more punitive and obsessed with its own safety than is in fact the case (Gottfredson and Taylor, 1987). Some of the more sophisticated surveys and focus groups reveal a potentially more forgiving public supportive of rehabilitation but increasingly opposed to spending more on prisons (Doob, 1995: 210, fn 23; Roberts, 1997: 250–4; Roberts and Stalans, 1998; Cullen et al., 2000: 28–33; Justice Policy Institute, 2001;

Hart Research Associates, 2002; Cohen et al., 2006).

Another key area for analysts to investigate is whether a radically new penal model is taking root in the USA and, if so, what are the political implications of this development. The breathtaking and unprecedented increase in the number of people under state supervision in the USA has overshadowed a 'profound qualitative transformation' in penal policy over the past two to three decades (McLennan, 2001: 408). Important changes include: the growing exploitation of prison labor; the proliferation of private prisons and the privatization of food, medical, and other prison services; the widespread use of paramilitary technologies and techniques in penal and police operations; the blurring of the distinction between police and military forces; the escalating number of incarcerated women; and the proliferation of supermax cells and other degrading and inhumane conditions of confinement, like boot camps, chain gangs, and prison rodeos (Kraska, 2001; McLennan, 2001; Rhodes, 2004; Sudbury, 2005; Gómez, 2006; Abramsky, 2007). More work needs to be done on whether these changes herald the ascent of a new penal model. McLennan (2001) and others contend that the new penal model is not exclusively a domestic phenomenon but is also a product of important transnational forces, including globalization, the 'war on terror,' growing militarization and the ascendancy of the neoliberal political and economic model (McLennan, 2001: 416; Strange, 2006; Gilmore, 2007; Wacquant, 2009; Bosworth, 2010).

CONCLUSION

For all the recent advances in our understanding of the contemporary politics of crime and punishment, this remains an emerging field. Almost four decades have passed since David Bazelon, the chief judge of the US Court of Appeals in Washington, DC, told the American Society of Criminology, '[P]olitics is at the heart of American criminology' (1978: 3). Yet the discipline of political science is just beginning to recognize crime and punishment as a critical area in the study of politics in the USA and elsewhere, and that crime control strategies are profoundly political because they both reflect and direct the distribution of power in society (Scheingold, 1998: 857). Alarmed by the pernicious consequences of the hyper-politicization of criminal justice policymaking since the 1970s, criminologists generally have recoiled from paying serious attention to the how the political context influences all aspects of crime and punishment (Loader and Sparks, 2011). Many criminologists have sought refuge in producing state-of-the-art, ostensibly apolitical, evidence-based research centered largely on how to reduce crime or on how to help government agencies or other groups reduce crime. But such a 'narrowly instrumental focus appears to forget that in a liberal democracy it matters not only that crime is prevented and detected, but also *how* that happens' (Loader and Sparks, 2011; 107, original emphasis). Loader and Sparks rightfully beseech criminologists to recognize that all aspects of crime and punishment are inherently political for they lie at the 'heart of matters of state, authority, and sovereignty' and are central to how we think about what constitutes a good and fair society (2011: 60, 108).

NOTES

1 For a skeptical view of whether the economic crisis marks the beginning of the end of mass incarceration, see Gottschalk (2011).

2 Ironically, some of the very historical and institutional factors that made the US women's movement relatively more successful in gaining public acceptance and achieving its goals for women (Gelb, 1987) were important building blocks for the carceral state that emerged simultaneously in the 1970s. Several key institutional variables include: the greater permeability of the US Department of Justice to outside political forces compared to, for example, the Home

Office in Britain; the relative weakness of the welfare state in the USA; the greater presence of diverse mass membership organizations like the National Organization for Women (NOW); the expansive role of the courts in the USA; and the decentralized and fragmented nature of the US political system (Gottschalk, 2006: chs 5 and 6).

3 Campbell (2011) attributes the low level of civic involvement to several institutional factors, including Texas's frequent elections, its off-year gubernatorial contests, numerous constitutional amendments related to trivial aspects of government, and a deep-seated patriarchal political culture.

4 An updated version of the time series is available from the authors at http://elections.gmu.edu/Voter_Turnout_2004.htm

5 In one county in Georgia about 70 percent of the African-American men are ineligible for jury service due to a felony conviction (Wheelock, 2006, in Wheelock and Uggen, 2008: 278).

6 On how the proliferation of banishment orders, which often are invoked against people who have committed trivial infractions, are creating their own special kind of legal and civil purgatory, see Beckett and Herbert (2009). On the 'escalating strategies of surveillance and containment' of sex offenders, see Simon and Leon (2008) and Janus (2006).

REFERENCES

Abramsky, Sasha (2007) *American Furies: Crime, Punishment, and Vengeance in the Age of Mass Imprisonment.* Boston, MA: Beacon Press.

Alexander, Michelle (2010) *The New Jim Crow: Mass Incarceration in the Age of Colorblindness.* New York: The New Press.

Alix, Ernest (1978) *Ransom Kidnapping in America, 1874–1974: The Creation of a Capital Crime.* Carbondale and Edwardsville, IL: Southern Illinois University Press.

Ayers, Edward (1984) *Vengeance and Justice: Crime and Punishment in the 19th-Century American South.* New York: Oxford University Press.

Barker, Vanessa (2009) *The Politics of Imprisonment: How the Democratic Process Shapes the Way America Punishes Offenders.* New York: Oxford University Press.

Bazelon, David (1978) 'The hidden politics of criminology', *Federal Probation,* 42: 3–9.

Beckett, Katherine (1997) *Making Crime Pay: Law and Order in Contemporary American Politics.* New York: Oxford University Press.

Beckett, Katherine and Herbert, Steve (2009) *Banished: The New Social Control in Urban America.* New York: Oxford University Press.

Beckett, Katherine and Western, Bruce (2001) 'Governing social marginality: welfare, incarceration, and the transformation of state policy', *Punishment & Society,* 3 (1): 43–59.

Bernstein, Nell (2005) *All Alone in the World: Children of the Incarcerated.* New York: The New Press.

Blackmon, Douglas (2008) *Slavery by Another Name: The Re-Enslavement of Black Americans from the Civil War to World War II.* New York: Doubleday.

Bobo, Lawrence and Johnson, Devon (2004) 'A taste for punishment: black and white Americans' Views on the death penalty and the war on drugs', *Du Bois Review,* 1: 151–80.

Bobo, Lawrence and Thompson, Victor (2006) 'Unfair by design: the war on drugs, race, and the legitimacy of the criminal justice system', *Social Research,* 73 (2): 445–72.

Bohrman, Rebecca and Murakawa, Naomi (2005) 'Remaking big government: immigration and crime control in the United States', in Julia Sudbury (ed.), *Global Lockdown: Race, Gender, and the Prison-Industrial Complex.* New York: Routledge. pp. 109–26.

Bonczar, Thomas (2003) *Prevalence of Imprisonment in the US Population, 1974–2001.* US Department of Justice, Bureau of Justice Statistics.

Bosworth, Mary (2010) *Explaining US Imprisonment.* Thousand Oaks, CA: SAGE Publications.

Braz, Rose and Gilmore, Craig (2006) 'Joining forces: prisons and environmental justice in recent California organizing', *Radical History Review,* 96: 95–111.

Brodeur, Jean-Paul (2007) 'Comparative penology in perspective', in Michael Tonry (ed.), *Crime, Punishment, and Politics in a Comparative Perspective—Crime and Justice: A Review of Research,* vol. 36. Chicago: University of Chicago Press. pp. 49–91.

Brown-Dean, Khalilah (2004) 'One lens, multiple views: felon disenfranchisement laws and American political inequality'. PhD dissertation, Ohio State University.

Brown-Dean, Khalilah (2010) 'Once convicted, forever doomed: race, ex-felon disenfranchisement, and fractured citizenship'. Unpublished manuscript.

Bumiller, Kristin (2008) *In an Abusive State: How Neoliberalism Appropriated the Feminist Movement against Domestic Violence.* Durham, NC: Duke University Press.

Burch, Traci (2007) 'Punishment and participation: how criminal convictions threaten American democracy'. PhD dissertation, Harvard University.

Burch, Traci (2008) 'Did disenfranchisement laws help elect President Bush? a closer look at the characteristics and preferences of Florida's ex-felons.' Northwestern University School of Law, Law and Political Economy Colloquium, November 3.

Burton-Rose, Daniel Pens, Dan and Wright, Paul (eds) (1998) *The Celling of America: An Inside Look at the US Prison Industry.* Monroe, ME: Common Courage Press.

Campbell, Michael (2007) 'Criminal disenfranchisement reform in California: a deviant case study', *Punishment & Society*, 9 (2): 177–99.

Campbell, Michael (2011) 'Politics, prisons, and law enforcement: an examination of "Law and Order" politics in Texas', *Law & Society Review,* 45(3): 631–65.

Caplow, Theodore and Simon, Jonathan (1999) 'Understanding prison policy and population trends', in Michael Tonry and Joan Petersilia (eds), *Prisons – Crime and Justice: A Review of Research.* Chicago: University of Chicago Press. pp. 63–120.

Carleton, Mark T. (1971) *Politics and Punishment: The History of the Louisiana Penal System.* Baton Rouge, LO: Louisiana State University Press.

Cavadino, Michael and Dignan, James (2006) *Penal Systems: A Comparative Approach,* 4th edn. London: SAGE Publications.

Chambliss, William (1999) *Power, Politics, and Crime.* Boulder, CO: Westview Press.

Christianson, Scott (1998) *With Liberty For Some: 500 Years of Imprisonment in America.* Boston, MA: Northeastern University Press.

Clemetson, Lynette (2004) 'NAACP Legal Defense Fund Chief Retires'. *New York Times,* January: A10.

Cohen, Cathy (1999) *The Boundaries of Blackness: AIDS and the Breakdown of Black Politics.* Chicago: University of Chicago Press.

Cohen, Cathy (2010) *Democracy Remixed: Black Youth and the Future of American Politics.* New York: Oxford University Press.

Cohen, Mark, Rust, Roland and Steen, Sara (2006) 'Prevention, crime control or cash? Public preferences towards criminal justice spending priorities', *Justice Quarterly,* 23: 317–35.

Coker, Donna (2001) 'Crime control and feminist law reform in domestic violence law: a critical review', *Buffalo Criminal Law Review,* 4: 801–60.

Criminology & Public Policy (2011) 'Special issue on mass incarceration', 10 (3).

Cullen, Francis, Fisher, Bonnie and Applegate, Brandon (2000) 'Public opinion about punishment and corrections', *Crime and Justice,* 27: 1–79.

Cummings, Homer and McFarland, Carl (1937) *Federal Justice: Chapters in the History of Justice and the Federal Executive.* New York: The Macmillan Company.

Curtin, Mary (2000) *Black Prisoners and Their World, Alabama, 1865–1900.* Charlottesville, VA: University of Virginia Press.

Davey, Joseph Dillon (1998) *The Politics of Prison Expansion: Winning Elections By Waging War on Crime.* Westport, CT: Praeger.

De Giorgi, Alessandro (2006) *Re-Thinking the Political Economy of Punishment: Perspectives on Post-Fordism and Penal Politics.* Aldershot: Ashgate.

Dilulio John, Jr (1997) 'Are voters fools? Crime, public opinion, and representative democracy', *Corrections Management,* 1: 1–5.

Domanick, Joe (2004) *Cruel Justice: Three Strikes and the Politics of Crime in America's Golden State.* Berkeley, CA: University of California Press.

Doob, Anthony (1995) 'The United States sentencing commission guidelines: if you don't know where you are going, you might not get there', in Chris Clarkson and Rod Morgan (eds), *The Politics of Sentencing Reform.* Oxford: Oxford University Press. pp. 226–33.

Dow, Mark (2004) *American Gulag: Inside US Immigration Prisons.* Berkeley, CA: University of California Press.

Downes, David (2007) 'Visions of penal control in the Netherlands', in Michael Tonry (ed.), *Crime, Punishment, and Politics in a Comparative Perspective—Crime and Justice: A Review of Research 36.* Chicago: University of Chicago Press. pp. 93–125.

Downes, David and Hansen, Kirstine (2006) 'Welfare and punishment in comparative context', in Sarah Armstrong and Lesley McAra (eds), *Perspectives on Punishment: The Contours of Control.* Oxford: Oxford University Press. pp. 33–54.

DuBois, W.E.B. (1970) 'Courts and jails', in Walter Wilson (ed.), *The Selected Writings of W.E.B. DuBois.* New York: Signet Classics. pp. 126–7.

Dumm, Thomas (1987) *Democracy and Punishment: Disciplinary Origins of the United States.* Madison, WI: University of Wisconsin Press.

Dyer, Joel (2000) *The Perpetual Prisoner Machine: How America Profits from Crime.* Boulder, CO: Westview.

Edgerton, Keith (2004) *Montana Justice: Power, Punishment, and the Penitentiary.* Seattle, WA: University of Washington Press.

Edsall, Thomas Byrne and Edsall, Mary (1991) *Chain Reaction: The Impact of Race, Rights, and Taxes on American Politics.* New York: Norton.

Ewald, Alec (2002) '"Civil Death": the ideological paradox of criminal disenfranchisement law in the United States', *Wisconsin Law Review,* 5: 1045–138.

Fabelo, Tony (2010) 'Texas justice reinvestment: be more like Texas?', *Justice Research and Policy,* 12(1): 113–31.

Fierce, Mildred (1994) *Slavery Revisited: Blacks and the Southern Convict Lease System, 1865–1933.* New York: Africana Studies Research Center, Brooklyn College, CUNY.

Flamm, Michael (2005) *Law and Order: Street Crime, Civil Unrest, and the Crisis of Liberalism in the 1960s.* New York: Columbia University Press.

Frase, Richard (2001) 'Comparative perspectives on sentencing and research', in Michael Tonry and Richard S. Frase (eds), *Sentencing and Sanctions in Western Countries.* Oxford: Oxford University Press. pp. 259–92.

Garland, David (2001) *The Culture of Control: Crime and Social Order in Contemporary Society.* Chicago: University of Chicago Press.

Garland, David (2010) *Peculiar Institution: America's Death Penalty in an Age of Abolition.* Cambridge, MA: Belknap Press of Harvard University Press.

Gartner, Rosemary, Doob, Anthony and Zimring, Franklin (2011) 'The past as prologue? Decarceration in California then and now', *Criminology & Public Policy,* 10 (2): 291–325.

Gaubatz, Kathlyn Taylor (1995) *Crime in the Public Mind.* Ann Arbor, MI: University of Michigan Press.

Gelb, Joyce (1987) 'Social movement "success": a comparative analysis of feminism in the United States and United Kingdom', in Mary Fainsod Katzenstein, Carol McClung Mueller (eds), *The Women's Movements of the United States and Western Europe.* Philadelphia: Temple University Press. pp. 267–89.

Gest, Ted (2001) *Crime & Politics: Big Government's Erratic Campaign for Law and Order.* Oxford: Oxford University Press.

Gilmore, Ruth Wilson (1999) 'You have dislodged a boulder: mothers and prisoners in the post Keynesian Californian landscape', *Transforming Anthropology,* 8: 12–38.

Gilmore, Ruth Wilson (2007) *The Golden Gulag: Prisons, Surplus, Crisis, and Opposition in Globalizing California.* Berkeley, CA: University of California Press.

Glaze, Lauren, Bonczar, Thomas and Zhang, Fan (2010) 'Probation and parole in the United States, 2009', *Bureau of Justice Statistics Bulletin,* December.

Goffman, Alice (2009) 'On the run: wanted men in a Philadelphia ghetto', *American Sociological Review,* 74 (June): 339–57.

Golden, Renny (2005) *War on the Family: Mothers in Prison and the Families They Leave Behind.* New York: Routledge.

Gómez, Alan (2006) 'Resisting living death at Marion federal penitentiary, 1972', *Radical History Review,* 96: 58–86.

Goodnough, Amy (2004) 'Disenfranchised Florida felons struggle to regain their rights', *New York Times,* 28 March: 1.

Gordon, Diana (1994) *The Return of the Dangerous Classes: Drug Prohibition and Policy Politics.* New York: W.W. Norton & Co.

Gorman, Anna (2009) 'Latinos make up a growing bloc of federal offenders', *Los Angeles Times,* 19 February: A10.

Gottfredson, Stephen and Taylor, Ralph (1987) 'Attitudes of correctional policymakers and the public', in Stephen D. Gottfredson and Sean McConville (eds), *America's Correctional Crisis: Prison Populations and Public Policy.* New York: Greenwood Press. pp. 57–75.

Gottschalk, Marie (2006) *The Prison and the Gallows: The Politics of Mass Incarceration in America.* Cambridge: Cambridge University Press.

Gottschalk, Marie (2007) 'Prisoners of the Census Bureau', *LA Times,* 19 February: A9.

Gottschalk, Marie (2011) 'The great recession and the great confinement: the economic crisis and the future of penal reform', in Richard Rosenfeld, Kenna Quinet, and Crystal Garcia (eds), *Contemporary Issues in Criminological Theory and Research: The Role of Social Institutions,* 2nd edn. Belmont, CA: Wadsworth/Cengage. pp. 343–70.

Graham, John (1990) 'Decarceration in the federal republic of Germany: how practitioners are succeeding where policy-makers failed', *British Journal of Criminology,* 30 (3): 150–70.

Green, David (2007) 'Comparing penal cultures: child-on-child homicide in England and Norway', in Michael Tonry (ed.), *Crime, Punishment, and Politics in a Comparative Perspective – Crime and Justice: A Review of Research 36.* Chicago: University of Chicago Press. pp. 591–643.

Greenberg, David and West, Valerie (2001) 'State prison populations and their growth, 1971–1991', *Criminology,* 39 (3): 615–53.

Gruber, Aya (2007) 'The feminist war on crime', *Iowa Law Review,* 92 (March): 741–833.

Hallinan, Joseph (2001) *Going Up the River: Travels in a Prison Nation.* New York: Random House.

Harris, M. Kay (1987) 'Moving into the new millennium: toward a feminist vision of justice', *Prison Journal*, 67: 27–38.

Harrison, Paige and Beck, Allen (2006) 'Prisoners in 2005', *Bureau of Justice Statistics Bulletin*, rev. 18 January 2007.

Hart, P.D. Research Associates (2002) *Changing Public Attitudes Toward the Criminal Justice System*. New York: The Open Society Institute.

Hawkins, Darnell and Hardy, Kenneth A. (1989) 'Black-white imprisonment rates: a state-by-state analysis', *Social Justice*, 16 (4): 75–94.

Heyer, Rose and Wagner, Peter (2004) 'Too big to ignore: how counting people in prisons distorted 2000 census', April. Available at: www.prisonersofthecensus.org/toobig/ (accessed 5 May 2011).

Hindus, Michael (1980) *Prison and Plantation: Crime, Justice, and Authority in Massachusetts and South Carolina, 1767–1978*. Chapel Hill, NC: University of North Carolina Press.

Hirsch, Adam (1992) *The Rise of the Penitentiary: Prisons and Punishment in Early America*. New Haven, CT: Yale University Press.

Hochschild, Jennifer (1995) *Facing Up to the American Dream: Race, Class, and the Soul of the Nation*. Princeton, NJ: Princeton University Press.

Hull, Elizabeth (2006) *The Disenfranchisement of Ex-Felons*. Philadelphia, PA: Temple University Press.

Jacobs, David and Helms, Ronald (1996) 'Toward a political model of incarceration: a time-series examination of multiple explanations for prison admission rates', *American Journal of Sociology*, 102 (6): 322–57.

Jacobson, Michael (2005) *Downsizing Prisons: How to Reduce Crime and End Mass Incarceration*. New York: New York University Press.

Janus, Eric (2006) *Failure to Protect: America's Sexual Predator Laws and the Rise of the Preventive State*. Ithaca, NY: Cornell University Press.

Johnson, David (2007) 'Crime and punishment in contemporary Japan', in Michael Tonry (ed.), *Crime, Punishment, and Politics in a Comparative Perspective – Crime and Justice: A Review of Research 36*. Chicago: University of Chicago Press. pp. 371–423.

Justice Policy Institute (2001) *Cutting Correctly: New Prison Policies for Times of Fiscal Crisis*. Washington, DC: Justice Policy Institute.

Kalt, Brian (2003) 'The exclusion of felons from jury service', *American University Law Review*, 53 (1): 65–189.

Kaplan, Paul (2006) 'American exceptionalism and racialized inequality in American capital punishment: the contradictions of American capital punishment', *Law & Social Inquiry*, 31 (Winter): 149–75.

Katzenstein, Mary Fainsod (2005) 'Rights without citizenship: activist politics and prison reform in the United States', in David Meyer, Valerie Jenness and Helen Ingram (eds), *Routing the Opposition: Social Movements, Public Policy, and Democracy*. Minneapolis, MN: University of Minnesota Press. pp. 236–58.

Kaufman-Osborn, Timothy (2002) *From Noose to Needle: Capital Punishment and the Late Liberal State*. Ann Arbor, MI: University of Michigan Press.

Kennedy, Randall (1997) *Race, Crime, and the Law*. New York: Pantheon.

Kolodner, Meredith (2006) 'Private prisons expect a boom: immigration enforcement to benefit detention companies', *New York Times*, 19 July: C1.

Kraska, Peter (ed.) (2001) *Militarizing the American Criminal Justice System: The Changing Role of the Armed Forces and the Police*. Boston, MA: Northeastern University Press.

Kruttschnitt, Candace (2010) 'The paradox of women's imprisonment', *Daedalus*, Summer: 32–42.

Lacey, Nicola (2008) *The Prisoners' Dilemma: Political Economy and Punishment in Contemporary Democracies*. Cambridge: Cambridge University Press.

Lappi-Seppälä, Tapio (2007) 'Penal policy in Scandinavia', in Michael Tonry (ed.), *Crime, Punishment, and Politics in a Comparative Perspective – Crime and Justice: A Review of Research 36*. Chicago: University of Chicago Press. pp. 217–95.

Lichtenstein, Alex (1996) *Twice the Work of Free Labor: The Political Economy of Convict Labor in the New South*. London: Verso.

Loader, Ian and Sparks, Richard (2011) *Public Criminology?* London and New York: Routledge.

Lombardi, Chris (2002) 'Justice for battered women', *The Nation*, 15 July: 24–7.

Loo, Dennis and Grimes, Ruth (2004) 'Polls, politics, and crime: the "Law and Order" issue of the 1960s', *Western Criminology Review*, 5 (1): 50–67.

Lotke, Eric and Wagner, Peter (2004) 'Prisoners of the census: electoral and financial consequences of counting prisoners where they go, not where they come from', *Pace Law Review*, 24: 587–608.

Lynch, Mona (2010) *Sunbelt Justice: Arizona and the Transformation of American Punishment*. Stanford, CA: Stanford University Press.

Lyons, William and Drew, Julie (2006) *Punishing Schools: Fear and Citizenship in American Education*. Ann Arbor, MI: University of Michigan Press.

Mancini, Matthew (1996) *One Dies, Get Another: Convict Leasing in the American South, 1866–1928.* Columbia, SC: University of South Carolina Press.

Manza, Jeff and Uggen, Christopher (2006) *Locked Out: Felon Disenfranchisement and American Democracy.* New York: Oxford University Press.

Masur, Louis (1989) *Rites of Execution: Capital Punishment and the Transformation of American Culture, 1776–1865.* New York: Oxford University Press.

McBride, Keally (2007) *Punishment and Political Order.* Ann Arbor, MI: University of Michigan Press.

McDonald, Michael and Popkin, Samuel (2001) 'The myth of the vanishing voter', *American Political Science Review*, 95: 963–74.

McLennan, Rebecca (2001) 'The new penal state: globalization, history, and American criminal justice, c. 2000', *Inter-Asia Cultural Studies*, 2: 407–19.

McLennan, Rebecca (2008) *The Crisis of Imprisonment: Protest, Politics, and the Making of the American Penal State, 1818–1938.* New York: Cambridge University Press.

Meranze, Michael (1996) *Laboratories of Virtue: Punishment, Revolution, and Authority in Philadelphia, 1760–1835.* Chapel Hill, NC: University of North Carolina Press.

Miller, Lisa (2007) 'The representational bias of federalism: scope and bias in the political process revisited', *Perspectives on Politics*, 5: 305–21.

Miller, Lisa (2008) *The Perils of Federalism: Race, Poverty and the Politics of Crime Control.* New York: Oxford University Press.

Miller, Susan (2005) *Victims as Offenders: The Paradox of Women's Violence in Relationships.* New Brunswick, NJ: Rutgers University Press.

Minow, Martha (1998) 'Between vengeance and forgiveness: feminist response to violent injustice', *New England Law Review*, 32: 967–81.

Morone, James (2003) *Hellfire Nation: The Politics of Sin in American History.* New Haven, CT: Yale University Press.

Muhammad, Khalil Gibran (2010) *The Condemnation of Blackness: Race, Crime, and the Making of Modern America.* Cambridge, MA: Harvard University Press.

Murakawa, Naomi (2005) 'Electing to punish: congress, race, and the American criminal justice state'. PhD dissertation, Yale University.

Myers, Martha (1998) *Race, Labor and Punishment in the New South.* Columbus, OH: Ohio State University Press.

National Association for the Advancement of Colored People (NAACP) (2011) *Misplaced Priorities: Over Incarcerate, Under Educate.* Baltimore, MD: NAACP.

National Research Council, Panel on Residence Rules in the Decennial Census (2006) 'Once, only once, and in the right place: residence rules in the decennial census'. Available at: http://newton.nap.edu/exec-summ_pdf/11727 (accessed September 2006).

Newburn, Tim (2007) '"Tough on Crime": penal policy in England and Wales', in Michael Tonry (ed.), *Crime, Punishment, and Politics in a Comparative Perspective – Crime and Justice: A Review of Research 36.* Chicago: University of Chicago Press. pp. 425–70.

O'Reilly, Kenneth (1982) 'A new deal for the FBI: the Roosevelt administration, crime control, and national security', *Journal of American History*, 69: 638–58.

Oshinsky, David (1996) *'Worse Than Slavery': Parchman Farm and the Ordeal of Jim Crow Justice.* New York: The Free Press.

Padfield, Nicola (2004) 'Harmonising of sentencing: will it encourage a principled approach?', in Kauko Aromaa and Sami Nevala (eds), *Crime and Crime Control in an Integrated Europe.* Helsinki: Heuni. pp. 85–91.

Page, Joshua (2011a) 'Fear of change: prison officer unions and the perpetuation of the penal status quo', *Criminology & Public Policy*, 10 (3): 735–70.

Page, Joshua (2011b) *The Toughest Beat: Politics, Punishment, and the Prison Officers Union in California.* New York: Oxford University Press.

Pager, Devah (2003) 'The mark of a criminal record', *American Journal of Sociology*, 108: 937–75.

Pager, Devah (2007) *Marked: Race, Crime, and Finding Work in an Era of Mass Incarceration.* Chicago: University of Chicago Press.

Parenti, Christian (1999) *Lockdown America: Police and Prisons in the Age of Crisis.* London: Verso.

Pattillo, Mary, Weiman, David and Western, Bruce (eds) (2004) *Imprisoning America: The Social Effects of Mass Incarceration.* New York: Russell Sage Foundation.

Perkinson, Robert (2010) *Texas Tough: The Rise of America's Prison Empire.* New York: Metropolitan Books.

Pestritto, Ronald J. (2000) *Founding the Criminal Law: Punishment and Political Thought in the Origins of America.* DeKalb, IL: Northern Illinois University Press.

Peterson, Ruth and Krivo, Lauren (2010) *Divergent Social Worlds: Neighborhood Crime and the Racial-Spatial Divide.* New York: Russell Sage Foundation.

Pettit, Becky and Sykes, Bryan (2008) 'The demographic implications of the prison boom: evidence of a "third demographic transition"?', unpublished manuscript.

Pettus, Katherine (2005) *Felony Disenfranchisement in America: Historical Origins, Institutional Racism, and Modern Consequences*. New York: LFB Scholarly Publishing.

Pew Center on the States (2009) *One in 31: Behind Bars in America 2008*. Washington, DC: Pew Center on the States.

Pew Center on the States (2010) *Prison Count 2010*. Washington, DC: Pew Center on the States.

Pranis, Kevin (2007) 'Doing borrowed time: the high cost of backdoor prison finance', in Tara Herivel and Paul Wright (eds), *Prison Profiteers: Who Makes Money from Mass Incarceration*. New York: The New Press. pp. 36–51.

Prisoners of the Census (2006) Too big to ignore interactive tables: Union County. Available at: http://www.prisonersofthecensus.org/toobig/countydetail.php?geo_id=05000US42119 (accessed 26 March, 2012).

Provine, Doris (2007) *Unequal Under Law: Race in the War on Drugs*. Chicago: University of Chicago Press.

Rhodes, Lorna (2004) *Total Confinement: Madness and Reason in the Maximum Security Prison*. Berkeley, CA: University of California Press.

Roberts, Dorothy (2003/2004) 'The social and moral cost of mass incarceration in African-American communities', *Stanford Law Review*, 56: 1271–305.

Roberts, Julian (1997) 'American attitudes about punishment: myth and reality', in Michael Tonry (ed.), *Sentencing Reform in Overcrowded Times: A Comparative Perspective*. New York: Oxford University Press. pp. 250–55.

Roberts, Julian and Gabor, Thomas (2004) 'Living in the shadow of the prison: lessons from the Canadian experience in decarceration', *British Journal of Criminology*, 44: 92–112.

Roberts, Julian and Stalans, Loretta (1998) 'Crime, criminal justice, and public opinion', in Michael Tonry (ed.), *The Handbook of Crime and Punishment*. Oxford: Oxford University Press. pp. 31–57.

Roberts, Julian, Stalans, Loretta, Indermauer, David, and Hough, Mike (2003) *Penal Populism and Public Opinion: Lessons from Five Countries*. Oxford: Oxford University Press.

Rothman, David (1990) *The Discovery of the Asylum: Social Order and Disorder in the New Republic*, rev. ed. Boston, MA: Little, Brown and Company.

Ruth, Henry, and Reitz, Kevin (2003) *The Challenge of Crime: Rethinking Our Response*. Cambridge, MA: Harvard University Press.

Sabol, William, West, Heather and Cooper, Matthew (2009) 'Prisoners in 2008', *Bureau of Justice Statistics Bulletin*, December. [Revised edition published June 30, 2010]

Sarabi, Brigette and Bender, Edwin (2000) *The Prison Payoff: The Role of Politics and Private Prisons in the Incarceration Boom*. Portland, OR: Western States Center and Western Prison Project.

Sarat, Austin (ed.) (1999) *The Killing State: Capital Punishment in Law, Politics, and Culture*. New York: Oxford University Press.

Sarat, Austin (2001) *When the State Kills: Capital Punishment and the American Condition*. Princeton, NJ: Princeton University Press.

Scheingold, Stuart (1998) 'Constructing the new political criminology: power, authority, and the post-liberal state', *Law and Social Inquiry*, 23: 857–95.

Schneider, Anne Larason (2006) 'An integration of path dependence, punctuated equilibrium and policy design approaches', *Political Research Quarterly*, 59: 457–70.

Schoenfeld, Heather (2009) 'The politics of prison growth: from chain gangs to work release centers and supermax prisons, Florida, 1955–2000'. PhD dissertation, Northwestern University.

Serwer, Adam (2009) 'The other black president: the NAACP confronts a new political – and racial – era', *The American Prospect*, 25 February. http://prospect.org/article/other-black-president (accessed 26 March, 2012).

Shapiro, Karen (1998) *A New South Rebellion: The Battle Against Convict Labor in the Tennessee Coalfields, 1871–1896*. Chapel Hill, NC: University of North Carolina Press.

Sharp, Elaine (1999) *The Sometime Connection: Public Opinion and Social Policy*. Albany: S.U.N.Y. Press.

Simon, Jonathan (2007) *Governing Through Crime: How the War on Crime Transformed American Democracy and Created a Culture of Fear*. New York: Oxford University Press.

Simon, Jonathan and Leon, Chrysanthi (2008) 'The third wave: American sex offender policies since the 1990s', in Shlomo Giora Shoham, Ori Beck and Martin Kett (eds), *The International Handbook of Penology and Criminal Justice*. Boca Raton, FL: CRC Press. pp. 733–54.

Skogan, Wesley (2006) *Police and Community in Chicago: A Tale of Three Cities*. New York: Oxford University Press.

Smith, P. (2011) 'NAACP calls for the end to the war on drugs'. Available at: http://stopthedrugwar.org/print/28244 (accessed 29 July 2011).

Snacken, Sonja (2007) 'Penal policy and practice in Belgium', in Michael Tonry (ed), *Crime, Punishment, and Politics in a Comparative Perspective – Crime and Justice: A Review of Research 36*. Chicago: University of Chicago Press. pp. 127–215.

Snider, Laureen (1994) 'Criminalization: panacea for men who assault women but anathema for corporate criminals', in Dawn H. Currie and Brian D. MacLean (eds), *Social Inequality, Social Justice*. Vancouver: Collective Press. pp. 101–24.

Sontag, Deborah (2002) 'Fierce entanglements', *New York Times Magazine*, 17 November: 52.

Stark, Evan (2004) 'Insults, injury, and injustice', *Violence Against Women*, 10: 1302–30.

Strange, Carolyn (2006) 'Pain and death: transnational perspective', *Radical History Review*, 96: 137–50.

Street, Paul (2002) *The Vicious Circle: Race, Prison, Jobs, and Community in Chicago, Illinois, and the Nation*. Chicago: Chicago Urban League, Department of Research and Planning.

Sudbury, Julia (ed.) (2005) *Global Lockdown: Race, Gender, and the Prison-Industrial Complex*. New York: Routledge.

Sutton, John (2004) 'The political economy of imprisonment in affluent Western democracies, 1960–1990', *American Sociological Review*, 69 (2): 170–89.

Talvi, Silja (2007) *Women Behind Bars: The Crisis of Women in the US Prison System*. Emeryville, CA: Seal Press.

Tonry, Michael (1995) *Malign Neglect: Race, Crime and Punishment in America*. New York: Oxford University Press.

Tonry, Michael (2007) 'Determinants of penal policy', in Michael Tonry (ed.), *Crime, Punishment, and Politics in a Comparative Perspective – Crime and Justice: A Review of Research 36*. Chicago: University of Chicago Press. pp. 1–48.

Tonry, Michael (2011) *Punishing Race: A Continuing American Dilemma*. New York: Oxford University Press.

Uggen, Christopher, Manza, Jeff and Thompson, Melissa (2006) 'Citizenship, democracy, and the civic reintegration of criminal offenders', *The Annals of the American Academy of Political & Social Sciences*, 605: 281–310.

Unnever, James and Cullen, Francis (2010) 'The social sources of Americans' punitiveness: a test of three competing models', *Criminology*, 48.1: 99–129.

Wacquant, Loïc (2000) 'The new "peculiar institution": on the prison as surrogate ghetto', *Theoretical Criminology*, 4 (3): 377–89.

Wacquant, Loïc (2008) 'Forum', in Glenn C. Loury (ed.), *Race, Incarceration, and American Values* Cambridge: MIT Press. pp. 57–72.

Wacquant, Loïc (2009) *Punishing the Poor: The Neoliberal Government of Social Insecurity*. Durham, NC: Duke University Press.

Wagner, Peter (2002) 'Importing constituents: prisoners and political clout in New York', *Prison Legal News*, 13 (10): 1–6.

Wagner, Peter (2004) 'Prison expansion made 56 counties with declining populations appear to be growing in census 2000'. Available at: http://www.prisonersofthecensus.org/news/fact-26-4-2004.html (accessed 23 May, 2008).

Walker, Donald (1988) *Penology for Profit: A History of the Texas Prison System, 1867–1912*. College Station, TX: Texas A&M University Press.

Warren, Dorian (2000) 'The intersection between voting rights and criminal justice: the national black organizational response to felon disenfranchisement', unpublished paper.

Weaver, Vesla (2006) 'Dark prison: race, rights, and the politics of punishment', paper presented at Annual Meeting of the American Political Science Association, Philadelphia. 31 Aug–3 Sept.

Weaver, Vesla (2007) 'Frontlash: race and the development of punitive crime policy', *Studies in American Political Development*, 21: 230–65.

Weaver, Vesla and Lerman, Amy (2010) 'Political consequences of the carceral state', *American Political Science Review*, 104 (4): 817–33.

Webb, Jim (2009) 'Why we must fix our prisons', *Parade*, 26 March. Available at: http://www.parade.com/news/2009/03/why-we-must-fix-our-prisons.html (accessed 26 March, 2012).

Webster, Cheryl Marie and Doob, Anthony (2007) 'Punitive trends and stable imprisonment rates in Canada', in Michael Tonry (ed.), *Crime, Punishment, and Politics in a Comparative Perspective – Crime and Justice: A Review of Research 36*. Chicago: University of Chicago Press. pp. 297–369.

West, Heather and Sabol, William (2009) 'Prison inmates at midyear 2008 – statistical tables', Washington, DC: US Department of Justice, Office of Justice Programs. March. Rev. 8 April.

Western, Bruce (2006) *Punishment and Inequality in America*. New York: Russell Sage Foundation.

Western, Bruce and Beckett, Katherine (1999) 'How unregulated is the U.S. labor market? the penal system as a labor market institution', *American Journal of Sociology*, 104: 1030–60.

Wheelock, Darren (2006) 'A jury of "peers": felon jury exclusion, racial threat, and racial inequality in United States criminal courts'. PhD dissertation, University of Minnesota.

Wheelock, Darren and Uggen, Christopher (2008) 'Punishment, crime, and poverty', in Ann Chih Lin and David R. Harris (eds), *The Colors of Poverty: Why Racial and Ethnic Disparities Persist*. New York: Russell Sage Foundation. pp. 261–92.

Whitman, James (2003) *Harsh Justice: Criminal Punishment and the Widening Divide between America and Europe*. Oxford: Oxford University Press.

Whittier, Nancy (2009) *The Politics of Child Sexual Abuse: Emotion, Social Movements, and the State*. New York: Oxford University Press.

Wilson, James Q. (1975). *Thinking About Crime*. New York: Basic Books.

Zimring, Franklin (2003) *The Contradictions of American Capital Punishment*. New York: Oxford University Press.

Zimring, Franklin, Hawkins, Gordon and Kamin, Sam (2001) *Punishment and Democracy: Three Strikes and You're Out in California*. Oxford: Oxford University Press.

Zimring, Franklin and Johnson, David (2006) 'Public opinion and the governance of punishment in democratic political systems', *Annals of the American Academy of Political and Social Science*, 605 (May): 266–80.

Zorza, Joan and Woods, Laurie (1994) *Analysis and Policy Implications of the New Domestic Violence Police Studies*. New York: National Organization for Women Legal Defense and Education Fund.

11

The Social Psychology of Mass Imprisonment

Mona Lynch

INTRODUCTION

The concept of mass imprisonment emerged at the turn of the 21st century in recognition of the intractable nature of the late modern penal explosion, especially in the USA (Lynch, 2011). What had been perceived in the previous two decades to be a dynamic yet alarming phenomenon – the rapid growth and expansion in the use of incarceration – had now taken on a sense of permanence and immutability. Theorists and empirical researchers expanded their inquiries that aimed to understand how and why the explosion happened and what its parameters were, to include assessments of the human impacts of mass incarceration. Thus, a growing body of work over the last decade has grappled with the social and psychological damage done by the imprisonment binge (Haney, 2006a; Western, 2006; Clear, 2007).

The USA is generally seen as 'ground zero' for contemporary mass incarceration, for several reasons. First is the sheer size and scale of growth in imprisonment use across the USA. Our rates of incarceration, particularly in the southern and western states, are many times higher than our democratic peers; and the steep incline in those rates over a relatively short period of time is globally unprecedented. Second is the relatively sharp and dramatic turn away from the rehabilitative ideal and toward a more punitive model of imprisonment that accompanied this growth. As a nation, the USA was a leading innovator of penal rehabilitation in the early to mid 20th century, and so its relative abandonment beginning in the 1970s was striking. Finally, the influential role that the USA plays in shaping international criminal justice policies and practices has meant that American-style penality has been exported to jurisdictions around the world (Godoy, 2008; Wacquant, 2009). Because the USA offers the paradigmatic case of mass incarceration, this chapter will primarily focus upon the American transformations in punishment and their social psychological consequences. Nonetheless, I will also look to research on contemporary imprisonment in contexts outside of the USA in order to explore whether and to what degree the American case is exceptional.

I have several specific goals with this chapter: By attending to a diverse body of literature, I aim to tease out what is different about the social psychological impact of 'mass' incarceration, and what is more universal about the incarceration experience. I first trace the insights offered by psychological and sociological research on imprisonment, then I consider several key issues specific to contemporary conditions of mass confinement. Finally, I look to the broader social psychological impacts of mass incarceration, since the contemporary practices have directly touched so many more people than in any time in our history. While the literature on 'collateral' consequences of mass incarceration is large and varied, I focus on its impact on offenders' families and social networks.

While I will attend to a range of social science research on the prison and its social effects, my analysis will primarily be social psychological in approach. By that I mean that I will consider the micro-level social processes inherent to mass incarceration. This includes group dynamics and interpersonal relations, as well as the more individual level psychological and behavioral effects of the social contexts of interest.

Social psychological insights into american imprisonment, generally

The negative psychological impacts of imprisonment have been recognized since the earliest penitentiaries in Pennsylvania and New York, most notably by Gustave Beaumont and Alexis de Tocqueville (1835 [1964]) who reported on the damaging effects of solitary confinement in the first of such institutions. Yet until the mid-20th century, the prevailing ethos underlying critiques of the prison (and driving reform efforts) was that the institution had yet to be perfected, and that it was only a matter of advancing techniques to achieve a functional system of incarceration. A disparate body of scholarly and activist work, beginning mid-century and peaking in the 1970s, began to question whether the very nature of the practice itself – locking people up in isolated institutions – caused or contributed to ill-effects among those so confined. Sociologist Donald Clemmer (1940) was an early pioneer in this regard, introducing the concept of prisonization, which referred to how inmates adopt and identify with an 'inmate subculture'. Gresham Sykes (1958) significantly advanced Clemmer's conceptual framework by specifying the deprivations, indignities and pains of imprisonment that give rise to the inmate culture.

This critical body of work expanded in the 1960s to include not only prisons, but also other 'total institutions' (Goffman, 1961), particularly locked mental hospitals that held long-term involuntarily committed patients. Thus, sociologist Erving Goffman's *Asylums* provided an intimate micro-level examination of how institutions and their agents understand and impact 'inmates', and how inmates, in turn, responded to the degradations of the institution. His work used a dramaturgical, symbolic interactionist approach, and led to novel insights about the detrimental process of institutionalization across types of total institutions.

Subsequently, a number of social scientists began to explore how penal and other repressive institutions were at odds with their reformative mission, due in part to the inherently harmful aspects of institutional life. Among the most well known of these studies was the famous Stanford Prison Experiment conducted in 1971, which assigned 'psychologically healthy' college students to the role of either prisoner or guard in a simulated prison built in the basement of the Stanford University psychology building (Haney et al., 1973; Haney and Zimbardo, 1998). This study clearly revealed the power of roles, and of immediate situational contexts, in shaping institutional behavior. The simulated prison very quickly became a dysfunctional and even dangerous place, and the experiment was shut down after only 6 days (instead of the 2 weeks it was scheduled to run).

Some of those assigned to the prisoner role experienced acute psychological trauma and even full-blown mental breakdowns; others became obedient and dependent. The 'guards' were also dramatically influenced by their role, some actively engaging in cruelty against the prisoners; others standing by and letting abuses occur. The experimenters concluded that:

> The negative, anti-social reactions observed were not the product of an environment created by combining a collection of deviant personalities, but rather the result of an intrinsically pathological situation which could distort and rechannel the behaviour of essentially normal individuals. The abnormality here resided in the psychological nature of the situation and not in those who passed through it. (Haney et al., 1973: 90)

During this era of penal flux, psychologist Hans Toch (1977) characterized the experience of imprisonment as an issue of survival, rather than as reformation, and laid out a number of specific ways that penal institutions needed to change in order to mitigate their damaging effects. Thus, the chorus of scholars who, during this period, illuminated these kinds of pathologies of the prison provided an empirical backbone for the activist movement that aimed to decarcerate and otherwise radically alter the structures and practices of such institutions. The larger prison reform movement, which included academics, activists, prisoners, and even some policymakers and practitioners, spoke explicitly about the context of the institution as a target for change (Blomberg and Lucken, 2009). Consequently, by the 1970s, there appeared to be a burgeoning transformation in corrections – represented by expansive new community corrections programs, smaller and more socially integrated correctional facilities, and novel alternative sanctions – that was even supported by mainstream policymakers and practitioners (Scull, 1977; 1983; Cohen, 1979; Blomberg and Lucken, 2009; Lynch, 2010).

Yet this reconfiguration of American penality was short-lived. Despite a now solid body of psychological and sociological research indicating that incarceration not only had exceptionally limited rehabilitative value in and of itself, but that it was also an impediment to success for many offenders, the USA made the other turn – toward mass incarceration. This story has been well told by others (Garland, 2001a; Gottschalk, 2006; Simon, 2007), however, it is important to note that one feature of the move to mass incarceration was that penal policy became even more decoupled from social research.

The 1980s was a turning point in this regard, as prisons came to be seen simply as incapacitators (Feeley and Simon, 1992) and there was little pressure on corrections administrators to do much but house the huge influx of offenders as economically as possible. Consequently, the psychological well-being and rehabilitative improvement of those confined fell out as a primary goal precisely at a time when institutions were being overwhelmed by the surge of admissions, and conditions inside quickly deteriorated due to overcrowding. As Toch observed, just as the dramatic ascent in mass incarceration first became clear:

> In recent prison history two disasters converged to cancel each other. The advent of (1) unprecedented overcrowding coincided with (2) the loss of faith in correctional rehabilitation. The latter made the former more viable, because to have rehabilitative goals for overcrowded prisons would be a particular travesty. Today's prison administrators at least lose no sleep pretending programmatic concerns as they bend over blueprints and spend their time juggling cells and human bodies. (Toch, 1985: 59)

Indeed, the field of *social* psychology, which directly addresses the impact of contexts and situations on human behavior, was summarily shut out of the new 'warehouse' prison that emerged in the 1980s and has prevailed ever since (Toch, 1985; Haney, 1998, 2006a).[1] Its subsequent return, in the late 1990s, has generally been an adversarial endeavor, as social psychologists have gained some limited access to prisons and inmates as a result of court challenges to the declining conditions behind bars.

SOCIAL PSYCHOLOGY AND MASS INCARCERATION

Mass incarceration can be distinguished from incarceration more generally through several characteristics, some of which have direct social psychological implications. Although mass incarceration does not have a single set definition, David Garland has put forth the following working framework for the concept:[2]

> What are the defining features of mass imprisonment? There are, I think, two that are essential. One is sheer numbers. Mass imprisonment implies a rate of imprisonment and a size of prison population that is markedly above the historical and comparative norm for societies of this type. The US prison system clearly meets these criteria. The other is the social concentration of imprisonment's effects. Imprisonment becomes *mass imprisonment* when it ceases to be the incarceration of individual offenders and becomes the systematic imprisonment of whole groups of the population. In the case of the USA, the group concerned is, of course, young black males in large urban centres. (Garland, 2001b: 5–6)

Garland's delineation provides a good starting point for distinguishing the features and effects of mass incarceration, in that it suggests dramatic changes have occurred both within penal institutions, and outside those institutions in the communities from which prisoners disproportionately come. Subsequent scholarship has explored the specific ways that these changes have impacted prisoners and their extended networks.

In this section, I will detail the internal, institutional transformations inherent to mass incarceration that have significant psychological implications for prisoners. Specifically, these are: (1) unprecedented and unrelenting overcrowding; (2) very limited constructive activities and programmatic opportunities for mass incarcerated prisoners; (3) a novel twist on solitary confinement – the 'supermax'; (4) a new (or renewed) strain of cruelty that accompanies the normal deprivations of imprisonment; (5) the more general deindividualization of prisoners; and (6) a dramatic increase of mentally ill and other special needs prisoners within regular housing units. The effect of these changes has been intensified in most jurisdictions because those sent to prison are there for significantly longer stretches under the more punitive sentencing policies enacted in the 1980s and 1990s. Moreover, these features of mass incarceration interact in a way to exacerbate their negative impacts, as I will discuss further below.

Overcrowding

As noted at the start of this chapter, prisons have perennially been crowded places that afford little privacy or space to inmates. But the contemporary levels of overcrowding are qualitatively distinct in scale, density and temporal dimensions. Moreover, as Craig Haney (2006b) points out, overcrowding does not merely refer to the density of the prisoner population or the percentage of population above rated capacity, it also encompasses the degree to which those so housed have access to basic life necessities including health care, sanitation facilities and outlets for meaningful activity.

California stands out as a particularly large and paradigmatic example in this regard. By 2007, the state's penal system housed almost two adult inmates for every permanent bed (occupancy was 196 percent of design capacity [CDCR, 2008]). The 81,000 men and women who comprised the state's overflow inmate population were double- and triple-celled on fold-down metal cots inside the tiny cells designed for half the capacity, or were living in hallways, recreation rooms and gyms in tight rows of double or triple bunks. Many of those so housed had lived like that for years. At the start of the mass incarceration era, both double-celling and the reliance on temporary bunks were viewed by corrections administrators as highly problematic and to be used only as emergency stop-gap measures. Today they are an unquestioned necessity in the view of prison managers, and even with these measures, some systems still come up short on the bedspace needed for the population (Haney, 2006b).

As Toch (1985) and others have described, this kind of large-scale, system-wide overcrowding has a number of negative correlates that increase the likelihood of harm. One direct consequence of overburdened facilities is that institutions may be unable to keep prisoners of different security levels within appropriate housing, thereby endangering lower security inmates in less controlled environments (Toch, 1985). Overcrowding also forces administrators to relocate prisoners within and between institutions much more frequently as they juggle the few open beds within the system, thereby disrupting relations and routines within units and increasing the likelihood of strife. It is difficult to establish stability, much less a sense of community, within the micro-level world of housing units when those who reside in them are constantly being moved in or out. Positive relationships between staff and prisoners are also exceptionally difficult to establish given these conditions. At the system level, the unprecedented levels of growth and accompanying capacity shortfall has engendered organizational instability (Haney, 2006b). Short- and long-term planning has given way to crisis management as an operational norm (Haney, 2006b; Lynch, 2009).

The more direct effects of overcrowding in prison are well documented in research – it can cause high levels of stress that then may lead to physical illness, mental distress and mental illness, and behavioral problems (Cox et al., 1984). Cox et al. reported on a large scale, multi-year program of research on the effects of overcrowding on prisoners, and found that as prison populations increased without requisite increases in appropriate facilities in the 1970s and early 1980s, *rates* of inmate 'death, suicide, disciplinary infraction, and psychiatric commitment' also increased (1984: 1156). Double-celling and dormitory housing, especially in large institutions, exacerbated the negative effects.

Ultimately, facilities that are chronically over-capacity are hard pressed to do anything but try to mitigate the harm they inflict on the occupants. As I explore below, this has become exceptionally difficult due to the co-effects of overcrowding.

Programming deficits

There are several contributing factors to the severe shortfall of meaningful programmatic and recreational opportunities in contemporary prisons. The first is directly tied to overcrowding – there are simply many, many more people locked up than there are established program slots or programmatic facility capacity. Furthermore, in many overcrowded systems, those spaces that were originally designated for recreation and other activities – such as gyms and day rooms – have been converted into tightly packed dorm rooms. Such housing is often classified as 'temporary' but in many institutions they have been in place and fully occupied for decades. As a result there is literally no place for prisoners to do things other than sit or lie on their bunks, especially when the weather is inclement. The population growth has also impacted the ability of prisoners to work during their period of incarceration. The inmate unemployment rate in some systems (such as California) is nearly 50 percent, and even the most menial and unrewarding jobs, such as janitorial positions, are in high demand as outlets for activity.

There is a spiral effect at work with mass incarceration and the ability to meet the programmatic needs of prisoners. The population explosion is a hugely expensive endeavor, in large part due to custodial costs (correctional officer salaries in particular), so even where there is an institutional and political will to provide constructive outlets for prisoners, administrators have had to raid the allocations for programming in order to pay for expanding custodial costs. Such was the case in California in the 2009/10 budget year. The California Department of

Corrections and Rehabilitation took a US$1.8 billion budget cut, and consequently slashed the educational, vocational and other rehabilitative programs budget from US$600 million to US$350 million (CDCR, 2010). Thus, the recent financial crisis has served as an added drain on programmatic resources, so that there are even fewer opportunities than ever in most US penal facilities.

More fundamentally, in many systems, programming became a low priority in the emerging 'law and order' political environment of the 1980s and 1990s. Because the mass incarceration era is very much tied to a rise in public and political punitiveness, correctional expenditures that could be conceived of as having benefits for inmates were targeted for elimination by elected officials, administrators and increasingly powerful victims' rights groups (Haney, 1998; Lynch, 2001; Simon, 2007). For example, Arizona's correctional administrators prided themselves on spending less and less on inmate rehabilitation and other such programs, even quantifying the spending reductions on inmate needs in annual reports from about 1985 on (Lynch, 2010). At the national level, in 1994, the US Congress cut Pell Grant funding for prisoners taking college classes as part of the ongoing 'war on prisoners' (Haney, 2008), which impacted inmates in every state system that offered access to such opportunities (Page, 2004).

The impact of widespread programming deficits on prisoners' daily lives, in the context of overcrowded and chaotic living situations, is significant. Programming has intrinsic psychological, social and practical benefits for prisoners, thereby mitigating the harm done by penal confinement, and it has been demonstrated to be a valuable management tool for administrators. Wooldredge (1999), for instance, has found that inmates who spend less time in structured activities and programs are more depressed, anxious and more likely to suffer from stress. Educational attainment by prisoners is especially valuable for raising self-esteem, developing practical skills and is highly correlated with success upon release from prison (Chase and Dickover, 1983; Fabelo, 2002). More generally, program participation reduces the likelihood and degree of negative institutionalization and prisonization, thereby decreasing behavioral problems inside and increasing successful adaptation at re-entry into the community. As such, it contributes to stability and a greater sense of order within institutions, making the frontline management less stressful and dangerous.

Deindividualization

There is an irony of timing in the exploding popularity of Foucault's (1977) *Discipline and Punish,* in which he described the rise of the penal institution, which aims to know and reshape the mind and soul of the imprisoned offender. His articulation of this individualized disciplinary process transformed the sociology of punishment just as the disciplinary prison was on its way out. Most famously, at about the same time, the conservative American political scientist, James Q. Wilson (1975), suggested that it was time to stop looking for the root causes of criminal behavior and simply accept that 'wicked people exist'. As such, he urged policymakers to assume that criminal behavior is simply a product of individual rational, albeit evil choices 'disembodied from all social context' (Cohen, 1996: 5). Flowing from this assertion was a policy recommendation that was quite prescient – that the criminal justice system should simply aim to incapacitate those 'wicked' criminals, and abandon its efforts to understand and change them.

Thus, as Feeley and Simon (1992) have suggested, the incapacitation model is not concerned with understanding or reforming individual offenders; rather, it is concerned with the efficient management of the risk posed by (predominantly underclass) offender subgroups. To the extent that incapacitation became hegemonic in American criminal justice policy in the 1980s and 1990s, it also reshaped institutional life inside prisons. I have argued elsewhere (Lynch, 2008, 2009) that the contemporary prisoner is relatively dehumanized, and is administratively treated as one of a stereotyped problematic population that is nearly interchangeable with any other prisoner within a broad classification category. This change is evidenced in how administrators characterize institutional needs and goals (such as the contemporary emphasis on creating system-wide 'bedspace' rather than holistic, purposeful institutions).

The kind of deindividualization that exists in mass incarcerative prisons is not totally new; the stark distinctions between prisoners and staff have traditionally catalyzed the development of group-level division and conflict (Clemmer, 1940; Sykes, 1958; Bright, 1996), and institutional efforts to know and act upon individual prisoners were impeded by this division. But its current incarnation is of a scale and level of acceptance that renders individualization obsolete even as an ideal. This gives rise to new kinds and levels of dysfunctionality within the prison context. As Zimbardo (2007) has pointed out, 'deindividuation' occurs when people's sense of individuality and uniqueness is submerged, which decreases self-regulation and sense of responsibility and leads to a range of problematic behavior, especially aggression. In the prison, deindividuated prisoners may become more aggressive and violent (Haney, 2006a). Correctional officers who view prisoners not as individuals but as members of an antagonistic group, and who are themselves deindividuated by their role, are also more likely to use violence and cruelty against prisoners (Zimbardo, 2007).

Mentally ill and special needs incarcerated populations

Despite the deindividualization process that has co-occurred with mass incarceration, the diversity of those incarcerated – and especially the diversity of need among incarcerated populations – has increased. In particular, because of the diminution of specialized institutions within and outside of correctional systems, general population prisons have increasingly become catch-all facilities that house those with a variety of mental health issues, cognitive disabilities, physical health challenges, language barriers and basic skill deficits.

As Craig Haney (2006a) has detailed, this is in part the product of decreased availability of therapeutic and rehabilitative services to populations in need in society at large. In essence, the criminal justice system – and its penal institutions – have filled the void left by the steady cuts to mental health, education and social services. And while the numbers of special needs prisoners has dramatically risen inside prisons, there has not been a corollary growth in specialized units designed for such populations. Thus, they are housed in general population units where their issues are not addressed, and where they are especially vulnerable to victimization, harassment and other pains of imprisonment (Kupers, 1999).

Such a situation would have been challenging even for the 'rehabilitative' prison, yet in the incapacitative, mass incarcerative institution, the high numbers of special needs inmates pose a whole new level of chaos and disorder. Mentally ill prisoners in particular are likely to fall into a downward spiral in which their symptoms are aggravated by the conditions of confinement, which in turn triggers disruptive and maladaptive behavior that then leads to a punitive administrative response, including punitive segregation, which can then cause more decomposition (Haney, 2006a).

Furthermore, the level of psychological intervention for all state prisoners has dramatically declined since the hey-day of the 'medical model' (Scharf, 1983), so psychiatric problems among inmates are often left untreated until they manifest in full-blown and highly symptomatic episodes. Only at that point will some type of intervention occur, and it is not always in the form of appropriate mental health care (Haney, 2006a). The one form of psychological intervention that now predominates inside some penal institutions exemplifies the abandonment of a context-sensitive therapeutic approach. That is, those therapies – some self-administered through workbooks, and others offered in group settings, that aim to correct the deviant and otherwise problematic cognitions of offenders (Fox, 1999; van Voorhis et al., 2004). This therapeutic approach assumes an internal, yet universal, one-size-fits-all source of deviance – 'pro-criminal thinking errors' (van Voorhis et al., 2004: 284) – that can be corrected through lessons about proper cognitions.

Punitiveness and cruelty as institutional policy

In some mass incarcerative penal systems, the harm-producing and dysfunctional conditions have not just been a product of overwhelmed facilities and benign neglect. Rather, there are some states that have waged a proactive 'war on prisoners' (Haney, 2008) through the institution of policies designed to cause prisoners discomfort, humiliation and even pain. The 1990s in particular witnessed grandstanding elected politicians and (in some states) penal administrators publicly announcing an array of such policies. Many of them did nothing to enhance the safety of the institution or the general public, much less contribute to improvements in offenders' lives (Haney, 1998; Lynch, 2001, 2010). Such policies included the removal of physical fitness equipment inside prisons; drastic new restrictions on prisoners' access to television, reading materials and other property; cutting higher education opportunities; imposing charges on medical care, electricity and other necessities; restricting access to legal materials; instituting visiting policies that made access to family even more difficult; cuts to the quality and quantity of daily meals; and the reinstitution of chain gangs, hard labor and other tough and nostalgic measures.

Many of these policies have served to further degrade prisoners, and deepen the antagonistic divide between inmates and correctional staff. Specifically, Blevins et al. (2010) apply Agnew's general strain theory to the contemporary prison context, and suggest that the level of deprivation in overcrowded and punitive prisons, and the lack of positive social support due to current conditions, is a source of strain for prisoners. Depending upon the prisoners' own individual coping skills and orientations, adaptation to strain can include violence and misconduct, as well as general negative feelings toward staff, depression and stress related disorders. Furthermore, to the extent that the deprivations and punitive policies are viewed by prisoners as unjust and arbitrary, negative effects will be amplified.

Reactance theory (Brehm and Brehm, 1981) also predicts that the trend of scaling back privileges and freedoms and piling on rules and restrictions may catalyze maladaptive behavior and rule violations (Pritikin, 2008). Put simply, when people have freedoms taken away and perceive a loss of control over their lives, they fight back (at least figuratively) to re-establish that control, which in a prison setting may escalate to considerable conflict between staff and prisoners. Indeed, the perception of personal control over one's day-to-day life appears to be crucial to prison adjustment. MacKenzie et al. (1987) looked at perceptions and expectations of control among prisoners in four different prisons and found that:

> Inmates who have low expectancies for control and perceive that they have little opportunity to exert control do not simply direct their coping difficulties inward by experiencing stress, depression and low self-esteem. Rather their difficulties in functioning appear to manifest themselves in problems in all areas of their lives, from depression and psychosomatic symptoms to a lack of prosocial activities, to hostility toward institutional staff and administration. (MacKenzie et al., 1987: 63).

Their research also adds further support to the finding that with increased flexibility and inmate autonomy, as offered by the institution (in terms of custody level), prisoners are less stressed and more positive toward the staff and the institution. Similarly, Kruttschnitt and Gartner (2005) found that California women prisoners' institutional assignment mattered much for how women adapted to prison. In this case, women assigned to the institution with a more open campus setting that allowed for a relatively significant amount of personal control over day-to-day routines were better adapted to being incarcerated and healthier psychologically. The institution that was more controlling in its policies, and that was physically more restrictive (it was a generic, non-gender-sensitive 1980s prison designed primarily for custodial control), seemed to catalyze oppositional and/or withdrawn behavior on the part of the women assigned to it.

My own research on Arizona's implementation of punitive policies in the 1990s indirectly indicates that levels of frustration, anxiety and distress rose significantly among prisoner populations as draconian new policies were put into place (Lynch, 2010). Prisoners and their advocates were particularly angry at the arbitrary and openly cruel nature of reforms, and consequently mounted legal action against the state as well as protest and disobedience within institutions.

The supermax as the ultimate mass incarcerative management tool

One of the intra-institutional consequences of American mass incarceration has been the birth of the distinctly American penal phenomenon, the 'supermax' housing unit. In many ways, the supermax is the ultimate physical embodiment of the changes inherent to mass incarceration. 'Supermax' or 'SHU' units, which have grown hugely popular with corrections officials across the nation since the 1990s, are a form of highly restrictive housing where inmates are generally subjected to solitary lockdown for approximately 23 hours a day in windowless cells that allow for very little visual stimuli, where possessions are restricted and activities nearly completely eliminated, and where by design, contact with other human beings is almost made nonexistent (King, 1999).

Penal administrators argue that the use of supermax is necessary to maintain internal security, in that inmates who are defined as 'the worst of the worst' can be isolated and contained within these units. Thus, they are said to provide the state corrections machinery with an effective tool to manage unruly populations within the system (Leary, 1994; Hermann, 1996; King, 1999). The harshly punitive nature of these settings is generally downplayed or denied by prison officials; they argue that the extreme deprivation to which inmates such housing units is necessary for security and that they are not used for punitive motives (Leary, 1994). Nonetheless, their proliferation has generally been most pronounced in Western states that have weaker ties to rehabilitation, and that have been leaders in penal cruelty (Lynch, 2010).

The use of supermax for prolonged confinement of inmates has been controversial, for the most part due to the effect of the harsh conditions on inmates' mental and physical health. SHUs are routinely used for indefinite periods of confinement, and some inmates may spend years upon years in this housing. This feature in particular causes psychological harm to inmates (Haney and Lynch, 1997; Haney, 2003; Rhodes, 2004). The kinds of documented effects that isolated SHU prisoners experience include attempted and completed suicides, self-mutilation, psychotic breaks, extreme feelings of anger, rage and hopelessness, eating and sleeping disturbances, and physical ailments, among others (Haney and Lynch, 1997). Haney (2003) examined the psychological and emotional trauma experienced among a randomly selected sample of 100 men confined to California's SHU at Pelican Bay State Prison, and found that 9 out of 10 experienced at least one indicator of psychological distress. Over one-half of the sample experienced 11 of the 12 symptoms of trauma. These kinds of symptoms are directly linked to the unremitting, long-term social isolation that is inherent to such confinement. Thus, while the SHU unit at Pelican Bay was also rife with violence against and neglect of inmates by staff, a wealth of research spanning decades and contexts has established that the use of long-term isolation leads to severe psychological distress, even among psychologically healthy people (Haney and Lynch, 1997). The risk of psychological damage is even greater for inmates who come to such units with preexisting psychological conditions, who, ironically, are often disproportionately represented in the SHU due to their propensity to be management 'problems' in the general population (Rhodes, 2004; Cloyes et al., 2006).

The supermax differs from its carceral predecessor – solitary confinement – in some important ways. Ever since its fall as a universal mode of confinement in the very earliest penitentiaries, solitary confinement has been used as a very individualized punishment (or 'correction') for those who violate rules in general population. Its use has generally been in response to specific infractions and at least on the books, stints in solitary were prescribed and determinant In other words, those so punished knew when they would be released from solitary, assuming no further violations, which made it more psychologically manageable. In contrast, in many systems that currently utilize supermax facilities, the majority of those confined to them are in for indeterminate periods – for some prisoners this can be decades – for status characteristics, particularly for being identified as a gang member (Haney, 2003).

Ironically, the gang problem is a direct consequence of the transformation of the prison since the 1980s. Haney (2006a) points out that prison gangs have proliferated as a mode of collective action to guard against the threats to safety and general dangers wrought by the deteriorating conditions inside. He also suggests that they further serve to provide some order in an otherwise socially disorganized setting, and provide a means of identity where those confined are dehumanized and deindividualized. While cliques and affiliations have long been an organizing force among prisoners, the gangs of today have a particularly hard edge. So while many new prisoners feel compelled to join a gang for their own personal protection against violence and crime inside, their membership may entangle them in serious rule-violating activities, and generally marks them as problem inmates who may be subject to supermax assignments. Once sent to supermax for gang affiliation, the only way out is to snitch on other gang members, which can in itself be a life-threatening endeavor (Shalev, 2007; Reiter, 2010). Thus, as Shalev (2007) has illustrated, there are multiple ways to get 'classified' into a supermax unit, but it is exceptionally difficult to reverse that process and get classified out.

Moreover, the supermax has become the iron-fisted, and very expensive, solution to the chaos and dysfunctionality of the contemporary mass incarcerative prison where problem inmates – acting-out mentally ill prisoners; those identified as gang members; those unable to abide life in the general population without misbehaving – are stored indefinitely. There is no pretense in its logic or design that it serves a rehabilitative purpose for those inside, which distinguishes it from its predecessors (at least in the ideal, if not in practice). As such, the message to inmates is that the purpose of their confinement is not meant to be beneficial or even benign. The 'perceived intent' (Grassian, 2006: 347) of the solitary confinement plays a significant role in how well those subject to it are able to adapt, with the least debilitation when the intent is thought to be benign. In the end, the supermax functions as the ultimate incapacitator within the large system of incapacitation, while doing nothing to alleviate the conditions within the institution (much less within the prisoners' lives) that gave rise to the problems in the first place (see Shalev, 2007, 2009, for more on this).

IMPACTS BEYOND INSTITUTIONAL WALLS

Mass incarceration has also reshaped familial relations, neighborhoods and communities if for no other reason than it has directly touched so many more people than in any point in history. Its extended effects begin when offenders are sent away. Approximately 2.2 million American children have parents in prison (Wildeman, 2010). Those prisoners who were primary caregivers for those children, or for other dependant family members, typically left a void in care that was difficult to fill. Psychologically, children with incarcerated parents suffer a range of harms, from the psychic trauma of losing a parent in their daily lives, to the added insecurity wrought by the loss of emotional and economic support, to the stigma of having a loved one in prison (Travis and Waul, 2003). The manifestations of these harms in children include increased rates of aggression and delinquency (Wildeman, 2010), lower levels of educational attainment (Foster and Hagan, 2007) and social isolation (Wakefield, 2009).

Owing to the racial and class disproportionality among those sentenced to prison in the USA, minority children are especially likely to experience parental loss to incarceration: Approximately one in every four black children born in 1990 had a parent go to prison by the age of 14; for white children, that ratio was 1 in 25 (Wildeman, 2009). As such, the harmful effects of parental incarceration help perpetuate the stratification brought on by mass incarceration (Wakefield and Uggen, 2010), as well as deepen the cycle of disadvantage (Braman, 2004; Foster and Hagan, 2007) and increase the risk of criminal justice involvement intergenerationally, especially among boys (Murray and Farrington, 2008).

More broadly, Megan Comfort (2007) has reviewed the growing body of scholarship on she calls 'legal bystanders' who are impacted by mass incarceration, including spouses and partners, neighborhoods and communities. She has also delved deeply into the impacts of men's incarceration on their women partners in her own qualitative research, illustrating the ongoing psychological and economic turmoil that comes with it (Comfort, 2008).

Comfort's (2007) review of the work that deals specifically with the reverberations of mass incarceration in families and communities highlights the way in which the criminal justice intervention that is tied to mass incarceration directly impinges upon those connected to offenders. The surveillance and state intrusion that accompanies the arrests leading to the prison sentence, and the correctional supervision that follows, is also experienced by those who live with or near offenders. During the prison sentence, family and friends who visit at the institution are subject to invasive and sometimes humiliating procedures (Comfort, 2007; Lynch, 2010). Comfort suggests this results in a now-widespread 'secondary prisonization' of prisoners' kin (2007: 279).

Mass incarcerated prisoners' return to their communities can also be disruptive and emotionally taxing for themselves and their loved ones. Haney (2001) suggests that the institutionalization process that happens to all prisoners contributes to problems in adjustments upon release. He highlights an array of specific effects that are common among those who have been incarcerated, particularly those who served long sentences: an over-dependence on the institutional structure that is created by lack of autonomy and control while inside; hypervigilance and distrust of others brought about by the dangerous living situations inside today's prisons; emotional suppression and distancing to mask vulnerability; social withdrawal; the internalization of the prison subculture; low self-esteem and self-worth; and post-traumatic stress disorders.

These responses to imprisonment are functional within the prison, and indeed are forms of survival mechanisms, but they are impediments to successful re-entry. Relationships with family members and friends are likely to be strained and distant; healthy and nurturing parenting will be difficult; and the interpersonal skills needed to obtain work and re-establish oneself in society may be lacking. To the extent that some communities have a steady in- and out-migration of their members going into or coming home from prison, these adjustment issues have profound impacts on the entire social fabric, particularly in poor urban locales. So while the negative impact of prison institutionalization on the chances of successful return to the community is not unique to mass incarceration, the sheer scale of contemporary American imprisonment has greatly expanded its impacts into communities. Moreover, the co-occurring transformation within parole agencies that shifted significant resources and attention from reintegration efforts to surveillance and crime control activities (Simon, 1993; Petersilia, 2004) has resulted in dramatically fewer forms of support for many times more released prisoners.

IS THE AMERICAN PRISON EXPERIENCE AN EXCEPTION?

As I suggested in the beginning of this chapter, the USA is widely accepted as an aberrational incarcerator, in that it imprisons at drastically higher rates, and with a much more punitive edge, than do its Western peers. It has also been suggested that the USA has been something of punitive innovator and leader, and has enthusiastically exported its penal paradigm to other places. As such, mass incarceration is characterized as a more mega-structural, global phenomenon. Thus, there is a bit of debate in sociological and political science literature about whether contemporary US penal practices are fundamentally different as a function of a series of historical and structural factors (Whitman, 2003; Gottschalk, 2006; Tonry, 2006; Snacken, 2010), or whether they are just an extreme example of the more global paradigm shift (Garland, 2001a; Wacquant, 2009). This body of work has less to say about the micro-level processes that are experienced by those subject to mass incarceration. There is, nonetheless, scholarship that sheds light on the overlaps and distinctions between American practices, and, particularly, European ones.

The first point to be made is that no Western democratic nation incarcerates at even near the same rate as the USA as a whole, thereby eliding many of the negative consequences that are a product of huge proportions of the population under correctional control. Among Western European jurisdictions, Spain incarcerates at the highest level; its rate in the late 2000s (159/100,000) was just above Maine's state imprisonment rate (150/100,000), which stood as the lowest rate of all American states (World Prison Brief, 2009; West et al., 2010). And while a number of European jurisdictions have increased their rates of imprisonment, especially since the 1990s, there is no sense that the kind of explosion that occurred in the USA is likely to happen across the Atlantic.

As to conditions of confinement, the strength of other states' commitment (relative to the USA) to human rights law and policy in relation to domestic incarceration conditions provides for a higher baseline than does the US Constitution, at least under current standards. Specifically, a varied body of international human rights law places 'positive obligations on government officials to take all reasonable precautions to insure prisoner safety' (Nilsen, 2007: 167) as well as a negative obligation to refrain from action that undermines rights. The ICCPR in particular provides substantial positive rights to prisoners in participating states, in that Article 10 mandates 'all persons deprived of their liberties shall be treated with humanity and with respect for the inherent dignity of the human person', and that 'the penitentiary system shall comprise treatment of prisoners the essential aim of which shall be their social rehabilitation' (ICCPR, Article 10, quoted in van Zyl Smit, 2010: 511). While the USA did ratify the ICCPR, it did so with the expressed intent that the prohibitions against cruel, inhuman and degrading punishment be binding only to the extent that the 5th, 8th and 14th amendments of the US Constitution apply, and that the purpose of the prison not be limited to rehabilitation (van Zyl Smit, 2010). Consequently, the limited case law that has considered international human rights violation claims by American prisoners has generally not given much weight to the mandates of international law (Dubinsky, 2010).

In the EU, the regional European Court of Human Rights also regularly considers alleged violations of the European Convention on Human Rights (ECHR) that occur within prisons (Livingstone, 2000; van Zyl Smit and Snacken, 2009). The human rights afforded prisoners under the ECHR are the same ones that exist for those outside – aside from the legally imposed loss of liberty inherent in a prison sentence – so prisoners are entitled, at least on paper, to a number of freedoms that would be unheard of in most American prisons, including the right to vote (*Hirst* v. *The United Kingdom*, 2005).[3]

Finally, most western European nations have developed their own regulatory systems that oversee the operation of, and conditions within, prison facilities. While these mechanisms vary in force, they have ensured that prisons in these jurisdictions have not been completely closed to both scrutiny and intervention from independent outsiders (van Zyl Smit, 2010). In contrast, the USA has no mandatory regulatory system for ensuring minimal standards of care within state and federal prisons, and the single most potent avenue to remediation is via individual legal petitions alleging constitutional rights violations to the federal courts.[4]

While scholars have highlighted the constraints of human rights laws in regulating prison conditions even in places where they are taken seriously (at least rhetorically; see van Zyl Smit and Snacken [2009] for a sustained discussion), the very fact that prisoners are considered within the scope of human rights protections has an ameliorative effect on punitive conditions. In the USA, the principles of human rights discourse in regard to civilian prisoners' right to dignity and humane treatment has not, at least yet, penetrated the legal, political, or general public realms in any meaningful way (Nilsen, 2007). As a result, prisoners' rights are not conceived of, in the American context, as a positive obligation of the state, and constitutional conditions of confinement jurisprudence works at the very cellar of acceptability, mainly policing utterly abusive and physically harmful conditions.

As a practical matter, the divergent legal and regulatory structures (and commitments implied by these structures) mean that the American prison experience differs in a number of important dimensions from its western peers. The use of solitary confinement is more extraordinary and highly regulated in western Europe, and the American-style supermax is generally considered to fundamentally violate human rights (Snacken, 2010). The kind of 'life-trashing' sentences (Simon, 2001) that have fueled the American mass incarceration binge and that are regularly imposed in American criminal courts are the great exception in peer jurisdictions. Indeed, there are bright-line proscriptions against life without parole sentences for juveniles and adults in Europe, whereas they are considered legally valid (and are meted across the country) in the USA (Snacken, 2010). Finally, prisons in Europe and other Western democracies hold 'rehabilitation' as a primary goal of prison – as expected under human rights doctrine – so institutions necessarily invest in education, therapy, skills training and other such programmatic resources.

Perhaps the clearest illustration of the differences in punitive style comes from anthropologist Lorna Rhodes (2010), who has extensively studied American supermax prisons, and who has recently done field work in England's Grendon prison. Her observations highlight just how keen the contrast is between the American mass incarcerative penal experience and the British one.

Grendon houses inmates with violent criminal histories, many of whom – in the USA – would likely be assigned to a supermax unit. Yet, the prisoners who end up at Grendon are provided extensive autonomy over their lives, including how they decorate the facility, what clothes they where and how they manage their daily schedules. Modeled as a therapeutic community, the Grendon regime includes extensive group therapy and fosters an environment where exploring and expressing emotions is safe, encouraged and actually done. While challenges exist to its ability to thrive in the changing British penal landscape, Grendon stands as a model embodiment of human rights ideals. As Genders and Player suggest: 'there is an inherent optimism in its functioning: there is a fundamental belief that individual change is possible and this sets an agenda that looks for the best in people rather than one that anticipates and looks out for the worst' (2010: 443).

CONCLUSION

In some sense I have tried to make clean and discrete what are really complexly interrelated social psychological processes that are inherent to mass incarceration. The combined and cumulative effects of the array of changes to American penology are now a huge, singular policy problem that cannot simply be fixed through addressing one or another aspect. This behemoth is well illustrated in the legal challenges in the state of California regarding the conditions of confinement throughout the prison system, which is the third largest in the world (Specter, 2010), and in particular the atrocious deficiencies in the institutional medical and mental health care. The plaintiffs' allegations underlying the now settled case, *Coleman/ Plata v. Schwarzenegger* (*Brown v. Plata* (2011) as decided by the US Supreme Court), poignantly illustrate how all of the above-described elements of mass incarceration converge to create an inhumane system of punishment that seems to be irremediable.

Coleman's case was originally filed in federal court two decades ago, and alleged at that time that the state did not provide adequate mental health care. In 1995, after a lengthy evidentiary hearing, the federal district court found the state's mental health system was inadequate, leaving 'thousands' of prisoners who needed treatment without any mental health care, and in violation of the 8th Amendment of the US Constitution. The second suit was filed by prisoner Marciano Plata in 2001, and the next year, state settled the case and agreed to fix the medical health care system. Nonetheless, few fixes were made in the ensuing years, and the entire medical system was put into receivership by the court. In the written order, Judge Thelton Henderson justified the court's action as follows:

> The harm already done in this case to California's prison inmate population could not be more grave, and the threat of future injury and death is virtually guaranteed in the absence of drastic action … Indeed, it is an uncontested fact that, on average, an inmate in one of California's prisons needlessly dies every six to seven days due to constitutional deficiencies in the CDCR's medical delivery system. This statistic, awful as it is, barely provides a window into the waste of human life occurring behind California's prison walls due to the gross failures of the medical delivery system.

Four years later, when the Department had still not been able to improve heath care to a minimally constitutional level, a three judge panel declared that the primary cause of the quite serious, even deadly, deficiencies in care was overcrowding. It thereby ordered the state to reduce its prisoner population to 137.5 percent capacity. Rather than complying, the state appealed the order to the US Supreme Court, which issued its decision in May 2011. By a 5–4 decision, the Court ruled against the state and upheld the decision of the three-judge panel.[5] As other commentators have noted, the federal courts' intervention into this situation is remarkable, because prisoner conditions of confinement cases are more difficult to mount in the USA than they have been in decades.[6] Yet, even with the plaintiffs' legal victories, California's prison system remains overcrowded, continues to prioritize security functions rather than programs and treatment in its budget, and continues to be largely unsuccessful in returning prisoners to our communities with the psychological and practical resources needed to make the transition back to society. Moreover, while the state has since complied in reducing the prisoner population through the use of early release mechanisms, and via new legislation that keeps low-level felons in local jails for up to three years (rather than one year), there is a sense that in many local jurisdictions, particularly those that overindulged in the use of state prison, mass incarceration has just gone local (ACLU, 2012).

Nonetheless, this case may mark a first step away from the dehumanizing and failed practices that have characterized American mass incarceration. As Jonathan Simon recently commented: "The road from *Brown v. Plata* to a humane and dignified prison system for the US will be a long one. But this opinion represents a turning point. The system of mass incarceration depends deeply and irretrievably on a simple condition, the denial of the humanity of prisoners. In *Brown*, the Supreme Court overturned that denial." (Simon, 2011: 255).

NOTES

1 See Jonathan Simon (2000) for a more general discussion of the decline of social science (especially sociology) interest and intervention into American prisons in the mass incarceration era.

2 Scholars have used the terms 'mass incarceration' and 'mass imprisonment' somewhat interchangeably to characterize these phenomena. In this chapter I will generally use 'mass incarceration'.

3 Six years later, the UK has still not complied with this ruling, though. The right to vote is also considered a basic human right in Canada and in South Africa, and the European Court on Human Rights cited Canada's and South Africa's policies in the *Hirst* decision – *Hirst v. The United Kingdom (No. 2)* [2005] ECHR 681, 42 EHRR 41, (2006) 42 EHRR 41.

4 The American Correctional Association does offer a voluntary institutional accreditation process, and publishes detailed guidelines of recommended minimum standards, but this organization has no regulatory power. See van Zyl Smit (2010) for more on this.

5 While it did not reference international human rights standards at all in the decision, the majority opinion was written by Justice Kennedy who has been among the most vocal in terms of applying international norms and standards to challenges involving various aspects of American criminal justice.

6 The US Congress passed the Prisoner Litigation Reform Act 1995 (PLRA), which severely constrained prison inmates' access to federal courts and imposed substantial limits on the ability of federal courts to intervene in prison conditions cases.

REFERENCES

American Civil Liberties Union of California (ACLU) (2012) *Public Safety Realignment: California at a Crossroads*. (March). Available at: http://www.aclunc.org/docs/criminal_justice/public_safety_realignment_california_at_a_crossroads.pdf (Last accessed March 21, 2012).

Beaumont, Gustave de and de Tocqueville, Alexis (1835 [1964]) *On the Penitentiary System of the United States*. Reprint. Carbondale, IL: Southern Illinois University Press. Originally published 1835.

Blevins, Kristie, Listwan, Shelley Johnson, Cullen, Francis and Lero Jonson, Cheryl (2010) 'A general strain theory of prison violence and misconduct: an integrated model of inmate behavior', *Journal of Contemporary Criminal Justice*, 26: 148–66.

Blomberg, Thomas and Lucken, Kristin (2009) *American Penology: A History of Control*. New Brunswick, NJ: Transaction Publishers.

Braman, Donald (2004) *Doing Time on the Outside: Incarceration and Family Life in Urban America*. Ann Arbor, MI: University of Michigan Press.

Brehm, Sharon and Brehm, Jack (1981) *Psychological Reactance: A Theory of Freedom and Control*. New York: Academic Press.

Bright, Charles (1996) *The Powers That Punish: Prison and Politics in the Era of the 'Big House,' 1920–1955*. Ann Arbor, MI: University of Michigan Press.

California Department of Corrections and Rehabilitation (CDCR) (2008) 'Historical trends: 1987–2007', Sacramento: State of California, Department of Corrections and Rehabilitation. Available at: http://www.cdcr.ca.

gov/reports_research/offender_information_services_branch/Annual/HIST2/HIST2d2007.pdf (accessed March 21, 2012).

California Department of Corrections and Rehabilitation (CDCR) (2010) 'Master plan annual report for 2009', Sacramento: State of California, Department of Corrections and Rehabilitation. Available at: http://www.cdcr.ca.gov/fpcm/docs/masterplan2009_pages_1-249.pdf (Last accessed March 21, 2012).

Chase, Lawrence and Dickover, Robert (1983) 'University education at Folsom Prison: an evaluation', *Journal of Correctional Education*, 34: 92–5.

Clear, Todd (2007). *Imprisoning Communities: How Mass Incarceration Makes Disadvantaged Neighborhoods Worse.* New York: Oxford University Press.

Clemmer, Donald (1940) *The Prison Community.* New York: Holt, Rinehart & Winston.

Cloyes, Kristin, Lovell, David, Allen, David and Rhodes, Lorna (2006) 'Assessment of psychosocial impairment in a supermaximum security unit sample', *Criminal Justice and Behavior,* 33: 760–81.

Cohen, Stanley (1979) 'The punitive city: notes on the dispersal of social control', *Contemporary Crises,* 3: 339–63.

Cohen, Stanley (1996) 'Crime and politics: spot the difference', *The British Journal of Sociology,* 47: 1–21.

Comfort, Megan (2007) 'Punishment beyond the legal offender', *Annual Review of Law and Social Science*, 3: 271–96.

Comfort, Megan (2008) *Doing Time Together: Love and Family in the Shadow of the Prison.* Chicago: University of Chicago Press.

Cox, Verne, Paulus, Paul and McCain, Gervin (1984) 'Prison crowding research: the relevance for prison housing standards and a general approach regarding crowding phenomena', *American Psychologist*, 39: 1148–60.

Dubinsky, Paul (2010) 'International law in the legal system of the United States', *American Journal of Comparative Law*, 58: 455–78.

Fabelo, Tony (2002) 'The impact of prison education on community reintegration of inmates: the Texas case', *Journal of Correctional Education*, 53: 106–10.

Feeley, Malcolm and Simon, Jonathan (1992) 'The new penology: notes on the emerging strategy of corrections and its implications', *Criminology*, 30: 449–74.

Foster, Holly and Hagan, John (2007) 'Incarceration and intergenerational social exclusion', *Social Problems*, 54: 399–433.

Foucault, Michel (1977[1975]). *Discipline and Punish: The Birth of the Prison.* New York: Pantheon.

Fox, Kathryn (1999) 'Changing violent minds: discursive correction and resistance in the cognitive treatment of violent offenders in prison', *Social Problems*, 46: 88–103.

Garland, David (2001a) *The Culture of Control: Crime and Social Order in Contemporary Society.* Chicago: University of Chicago Press.

Garland, David (2001b) 'Introduction: the meaning of mass imprisonment', *Punishment and Society*, 3: 5–7.

Genders, Elaine and Player, Elaine (2010) 'Therapy in prison: revisiting Grendon 20 years on', *The Howard Journal,* 49: 431–50.

Godoy, Angelina Snodgrass (2008) 'America doesn't stop at the Rio Grande: democracy and the war on crime', in Mary Louise Frampton, Ian Haney Lopez and Jonathan Simon (eds), *After the War on Crime: Race, Democracy and a New Reconstruction.* New York: NYU Press. pp. 37–48.

Goffman, Erving (1961) *Asylums: Essays on the Social Situation of Mental Patients and Other Inmates.* Garden City, NY: Anchor Books.

Gottschalk, Marie (2006) *The Prison and the Gallows: The Politics of Mass Incarceration in America.* Cambridge: Cambridge University Press.

Grassian, Stuart (2006) 'Psychiatric effects of solitary confinement', *Journal of Law and Policy*, 22: 325–383.

Haney, Craig (1998) 'Riding the punishment wave: on the origins of our devolving standards of decency', *Hastings Women's Law Journal*, 9: 27–78.

Haney, Craig (2001) 'The psychological impact of incarceration: Implications for post-prison adjustment. Commissioned paper for *From Prison to Home: The Effect of Incarceration and Reentry on Children, Families, and Communities. National Policy Conference by the US Department of Health and Human Services*. Available at: http://aspe.hhs.gov/hsp/prison2home02/Haney.htm. Last accessed May 22, 2012. Originally accessed November 9, 2010.

Haney, Craig (2003) 'Mental health issues in long-term solitary and 'supermax' confinement', *Crime and Delinquency*, 49: 124–56.

Haney, Craig (2006a) *Reforming Punishment: Psychological Limits to the Pains of Imprisonment.* Washington, DC: APA Books.

Haney, Craig (2006b) 'The wages of prison overcrowding: harmful psychological consequences and dysfunctional correctional reactions', *Journal of Law and Policy*, 22: 265–93.

Haney, Craig (2008) 'Counting casualties in the war on prisoners', *University of San Francisco Law Review*, 43: 87–138.

Haney, Craig and Lynch, Mona (1997) 'Regulating prisons of the future: a psychological analysis of supermax and solitary confinement', *New York University Review of Law and Social Change*, 23: 477–570.

Haney, Craig and Zimbardo, Philip (1998) 'The past and future of US prison policy: twenty-five years after the Stanford Prison experiment', *American Psychologist*, 53: 709–27.

Haney, Craig, Banks, Curtis and Zimbardo, Philip (1973) 'Interpersonal dynamics in a simulated prison', *International Journal of Criminology and Penology*, 1: 69–97.

Hermann, William (1996) 'Escape unlikely at new high-security unit; best prison for worst inmates', *Arizona Republic*, 22 June: A1.

King, Roy (1999) 'The rise and rise of supermax: an American solution in search of a problem?', *Punishment and Society*, 1: 163–86.

Kruttschnitt, Candace and Gartner, Rosemary (2005) *Marking Time in the Golden State: Women's Imprisonment in California*. New York: Cambridge University Press.

Kupers, Terry (1999) *Prison Madness: The Mental Health Crisis Behind Bars and What we Must do About it*. Hoboken, NJ: Jossey-Bass.

Leary, Kevin (1994) 'Pelican Bay as prison of the future', *San Francisco Chronicle*, 18 April: A7.

Livingstone, Stephen (2000) 'Prisoners' rights in the context of the European Convention on Human Rights', *Punishment & Society*, 2(3): 309–24.

Lynch, Mona (2001) 'From the punitive city to the gated community: security and segregation across the social and penal landscape', *Miami Law Review*, 56: 89–112.

Lynch, Mona (2008) 'The contemporary penal subject(s)', in Jonathan Simon, Ian Haney López and Mary Louise Frampton (eds), *After the War on Crime: Race, Democracy, and a New Reconstruction*. New York: NYU Press. pp. 89–105.

Lynch, Mona (2009) 'Punishment, purpose and place: a case study of Arizona's prison siting decisions', *Studies in Law, Politics, and Society*, 50: 105–37.

Lynch, Mona (2010) *Sunbelt Justice: Arizona and the Transformation of American Punishment*. Stanford, CA: Stanford University Press.

Lynch, Mona (2011) 'Mass incarceration, legal change and locale: understanding and remediating American penal overindulgence', *Criminology and Public Policy*, 10: 673–98.

MacKenzie, Doris Layton, Goodstein, Lynne and Blouin, David (1987) 'Personal control and prisoner adjustment: an empirical test of a proposed model', *Journal of Research in Crime and Delinquency*, 24: 49–68.

Murray, Joseph and Farrington, David (2008) 'Parental imprisonment: effects on boys' anti-social behavior and delinquency through the life-course', *Journal of Child Psychology and Psychiatry*, 46: 1269–78.

Nilsen, Eva (2007) 'Decency, dignity, and desert: restoring ideals of humane punishment to constitutional discourse', *UC Davis Law Review*, 41: 111–75.

Page, Joshua (2004) 'Eliminating the enemy: the import of denying prisoners access to higher education in Clinton's America', *Punishment and Society*, 6: 357–78.

Petersilia, Joan (2004) *When Prisoners Come Home: Parole and Prisoner Reentry*. New York: Oxford University Press.

Pritikin, Martin (2008) 'Is prison increasing crime?', *Wisconsin Law Review*, 1049–108.

Reiter, Keramet (2010) 'Parole, snitch, or die: California's supermax prisons and prisoners, 1987–2007'. ISSC Fellows Working Papers, Institute for the Study of Social Change, UC Berkeley. Available at: http://escholarship.org/uc/item/04w6556f (accessed June 10, 2011).

Rhodes, Lorna (2004) *Total Confinement: Madness and Reason in the Maximum Security Prison*. Berkeley, CA: University of California Press.

Rhodes, Lorna (2010) 'This can't be real: continuity at Grendon Prison', in E. Sullivan and R. Shuker (eds), *Grendon and the Emergence of Forensic Therapeutic Communities: Developments in Research and Practice*. New York: Wiley. pp. 203–216.

Scharf, Peter (1983) 'Empty bars: violence and the crisis of meaning in the prison', *The Prison Journal*, 63: 114–24.

Scull, Andrew (1977) *Decarceration: Community Treatment and the Deviant*. London: Prentice Hall.

Scull, Andrew (1983) 'Community corrections: panacea, progress or pretence?', in D. Garland and P. Young (eds), *The Power to Punish*. London: Heinemann. pp. 146–165.

Shalev, Sharon (2007) 'The power to classify: avenues into a supermax prison', in D. Downes, P. Rock, C. Chinkin and C. Gearty (eds), *Crime, Social Control and Human Rights: From Moral Panics to States of Denial: Essays in Honour of Stanley Cohen*. Cullompton: Willan. pp. 107–119.

Shalev, Sharon (2009) *Supermax: Controlling Risk Through Solitary Confinement*. Cullompton: Willan.

Simon, Jonathan (1993) *Poor Discipline: Parole and the Social Underclass, 1890–1990*. Chicago: University of Chicago Press.

Simon, Jonathan (2000) 'The 'society of captives' in the era of hyper-incarceration', *Theoretical Criminology,* 4: 285–309.

Simon, Jonathan (2001) 'Entitlement to cruelty: neo-liberalism and the punitive mentality in the United States', in K. Stenson and R. Sullivan (eds), *Crime Risk and Justice.* Cullompton: Willan. pp. 125–43.

Simon, Jonathan (2007) *Governing Through Crime: How the War on Crime Transformed American Democracy and Created a Culture of Fear.* New York: Oxford University Press.

Simon, Jonathan (2011) 'Editorial: mass incarceration on trial,' *Punishment and Society,* 13: 251–55.

Snacken, Sonja (2010) 'Resisting punitiveness in Europe?', *Theoretical Criminology,* 14: 273–92.

Specter, Donald (2010) 'Everything revolves around overcrowding: the state of California's prisons', *Federal Sentencing Reporter,* 22: 194–99.

Sykes, Gresham (1958) *Society of Captives: A Study of a Maximum Security Prison.* Princeton, NJ: Princeton University Press.

Toch, Hans (1977) *Living in Prison: The Ecology of Survival.* New York: The Free Press.

Toch, Hans (1985) 'Warehouses for people?', *Annals of the American Academy of Political and Social Science,* 478: 58–72.

Tonry, Michael (2006) *Thinking About Crime: Sense and Sensibility in American Penal Culture.* New York: Oxford University Press.

Travis, Jeremy and Waul, Michelle (eds) (2003) *Prisoners Once Removed: The Impact of Incarceration and Reentry on Children, Families, and Communities.* Washington, DC: Urban Institute Press.

Wacquant, Loic (2009) *Punishing the Poor: The Neoliberal Government of Social Insecurity.* Durham, NC: Duke University Press.

Wakefield, Sara (2009) 'Parental loss of another sort? Parental incarceration and children's mental health'. Working Paper, University of California, Irvine.

Wakefield, Sara and Uggen, Christopher (2010) 'Incarceration and stratification', *Annual Review of Sociology,* 36: 387–406.

West, Heather, Sabol, William and Greenman, Sarah (2010) *Prisoners in 2009.* Washington, DC: Bureau of Justice Statistics.

Western, Bruce (2006) *Punishment and Inequality in America.* New York: Russell Sage Foundation.

Whitman, James (2003) *Harsh Justice: Criminal Policy and the Widening Divide Between America and Europe.* NewYrok: Oxford University Press.

Wildeman, Christopher (2009) 'Parental imprisonment, the prison boom, and the concentration of childhood disadvantage', *Demography,* 46: 265–80.

Wildeman, Christopher (2010) 'Paternal incarceration and children's physically aggressive behaviors: evidence from the Fragile Families and Child Wellbeing Study', *Social Forces,* 89(1): 285–309.

Wilson, James (1975) 'Lock 'em up and other thoughts on crime', *New York Times,* 9 March: 44–8.

Wooldredge, John (1999) 'Inmate experiences and psychological well-being', *Criminal Justice & Behavior,* 26: 235–50.

World Prison Brief, International Centre for Prison Studies (2009) Available at: http://www.prisonstudies.org/info/worldbrief/wpb_stats.php?area=all&category=wb_poprate (accessed June 10, 2011)

Van Voorhis, Patricia, Spruance, Lisa, Ritchey, Neal, Listwan, Shelley and Seabrook, Renita (2004) 'The Georgia cognitive skills experiment: a replication of reasoning and rehabilitation', *Criminal Justice and Behavior,* 31: 282–305.

Van Zyl Smit, Dirk (2010) 'Regulation of prison conditions', *Crime and Justice,* 39: 503–63.

Van Zyl Smit, Dirk and Snacken, Sonja (2009) *Principles of European Prison Law and Policy.* Oxford: Oxford University Press.

Zimbardo, Philip (2007) *The Lucifer Effect: Understanding How Good People Turn Evil.* New York: Random House.

12

Punishment, (Neo)Liberalism and Social Democracy

Nicola Lacey

Introducing this volume, Simon and Sparks argue that a key feature of punishment and society scholarship is to 'distance punishment from the legal and moral apparatus which normally encapsulates it, and instead view the discourses and practices of punishment in relation to a myriad of other institutions and social forces' (p. 8). Punishment and society scholarship has, accordingly, to determine which institutions and social forces are of relevance, and why. This is no easy matter. Economic, cultural, technological, demographic and political factors – to mention only the most obvious – jostle for space amid variously particularistic, pluralistic or synthetic accounts. And even within each of these forces or clusters of institutions, questions arise about how the student of punishment and society should conceptualize and characterize the relevant phenomena and understand the precise nature of their 'relation to' punishment.

In this chapter, I address recent attempts to understand the relevance of broadly political forces and institutions in shaping the practice and the social meaning of punishment. A focus on politics is amply justified by the fact that penal practices are the outcomes of political decision making, and by the salience of the 'politicization' of penal policy – its prominence, for example, in election campaigns – in a number of countries over recent decades. Political structures and institutions (parties, electoral systems, the organization of political representation, the constitutional allocation of power); political interests and how they are conceived and organized, institutionally; political mentalities and climates of political opinion; all these seem to claim our attention. And each of these factors calls for consideration in both historical and comparative perspectives, and in relation to other social phenomena. How, for example, has the climate of political opinion in relation to punishment changed in the UK or the USA over the last half century? How far are such changes driving, or driven by, political action? And how are they related to other features of social structure? How far can the distribution of political interests, itself shaped by distinctive political institutions, explain trends in punishment? Can we arrive at broad conceptualizations of families of political system which shed light on the distinctive trajectory of penal policies in different countries?

Making a selection, therefore, I will focus on one argument about the relevance of the political which has been especially influential in the punishment and society field during the last decade. This is the argument that politics (in some countries? – a point to which we will return) can usefully be characterized as broadly liberal or neoliberal, or as social democratic: and that the decline or attenuation of social democracy, and the concomitant rise of (neo)liberalism has been associated with an intensification of penality. I will call this the 'neoliberal penality thesis' (for key examples, see Reiner [2007], Wacquant [2009], at least one further book-length contribution has recently appeared: Bell [2011]). In what follows, I set out what I take to be the key arguments for that thesis, before presenting a critical analysis of the utility of such a broad conceptualization of political systems.

In making my argument, I distinguish between three components of the neoliberal penality thesis. First, we have a set of claims about what we might call the 'ontology' of (neo)liberalism and social democracy – the sorts of assumptions that these doctrines make about human motivation and about the relationship between individuals and social formations such as political systems. Second, we can distinguish a set of claims about what we might call the political philosophy and substantive politics of (neo)liberalism and social democracy – the values and the sorts of policies with which each form of politics is associated. And third, we can identify a set of claims about the conditions of existence of (neo)liberalism and social democracy: causal claims, for example, about the relationship between the emergence of a particular form of politics and certain social, economic or technological conditions.

Examining this differentiated account of the neoliberal penality thesis, I argue that it has been of value in re-establishing a focus in punishment and society scholarship on nation states and their politics, and in emphasizing the links between national politics and local and global economic forces. The neoliberal penality thesis has provided a suggestive characterization of a cluster of economic, political and penal phenomena in certain countries. If tracing patterns or associations is what is meant by understanding punishment 'in relation to' other social phenomena, the neoliberal penality thesis has undoubtedly made a significant contribution. We might think, however, that punishment and society scholarship should aspire to a more ambitious conception of what it is to understand punishment 'in relation to' other phenomena: a conception which seeks to understand the logic of these patterns, including the causal linkages between their components. And ultimately, though exponents of the neoliberal penality thesis often present it as an ambitious, general theory, I shall argue that it fails the key test to be applied to any such account: viz, does it have the capacity to shed *explanatory* light on the relationship between punishment and society?

The shortcomings of the neoliberal penality thesis at an explanatory level derive, I shall argue, from a failure to explicate just which political, economic and social institutions constitute neoliberalism; how, systematically, they relate to one another; and precisely how they are implicated in producing neoliberal penality. Particularly in the most incautious statements of the neoliberal penality thesis, notably that of Loïc Wacquant (2009), this institutional deficit and conceptual vagueness, implying causal indeterminacy, leads to over-generalization; and to an unfortunate tendency to 'reify', 'neoliberalism', 'neoliberal politics' or 'neoliberal penality' without really disaggregating their components or coming to a full understanding of their significance and indeed their conditions of existence. These problems may best be illuminated by asking not only what neoliberalism *is* but also analytic, historical and comparative questions about *how* it has emerged and what sorts of institutional structures are needed to sustain the policies, practices and arrangements which have come to be associated with neoliberalism; *when* they emerged; and *where* they hold sway. Such comparative and historical scrutiny reveals that the purportedly distinctive defining features of neoliberalism may be found in a number of times and places beyond the contemporary era of neoliberalism, while, conversely, many of its purported conditions of existence apply in times and places which have *not* produced neoliberal penality. Under conceptual, historical and comparative scrutiny, the neoliberal penality thesis melts into air. In conclusion, and in consequence, this essay makes the case for a more differentiated and a more specifically institutional account of the defining features of political systems for the purposes of understanding punishment.

(NEO)LIBERALISM AND SOCIAL DEMOCRACY IN RECENT SCHOLARSHIP

Notwithstanding the obvious status of punishment as a product of political action, interdisciplinary work on punishment in society has tended to focus far more closely on cultural, demographic and economic variables than on political ones. Shaped by the prevailing concerns of sociology, on the one hand, and of Marxist-inspired political economy, on the other, the influence on punishment of factors such as cultural norms oriented to solidarity and altruism, or of the structure of labour markets, unemployment rates and the distribution of wealth, has dominated the effort to understand punishment in its full social context (Rusche and Kirchheimer, 1969; Garland, 1990). And though Foucault's (1977) famous distinction between sovereign and disciplinary power lends itself to being mapped onto differently constituted political orders, relatively little has been done by way of applying his work to an analysis of the institutional structure of contemporary political systems (for partial exceptions, see, Rose, 1999; Harcourt, 2011).

In much scholarship of the 1980s onwards, however, this began to change. A new intensification of the electoral salience of 'law and order politics' in countries such as the UK and the USA has been at the root of an newly emerging interest in the ways in which the political system, culture or environment shapes penality. And over the last decade, one theme has had particular prominence amid this resurgent interest in the politics of punishment: the diagnosis of a distinctive neoliberal political culture and mode of governance; and of a concomitant 'neoliberal penality'.

What is neoliberalism, and how did it emerge?

While the diagnosis of a neoliberal politics with distinctive implications for punishment is sometimes represented as having virtually global reach, it is easiest to grasp the details of the argument by tracing its application to a particular country (for a more comprehensive account, see Harvey, 2005). Taking the UK as our initial example, the story goes something like this. The right-wing agenda pursued by the Thatcher administration in spheres such as industrial relations and welfare state reform was nested within an unusually strongly articulated vision of a more individualistic society of self-reliant citizens. This amounted to a new vision of the old 'nightwatchman' state providing a minimal support and disciplinary framework rather than an extensive safety blanket, let alone a framework for realizing the duties of solidarity and reciprocity inherent in a social democratic conception of citizenship. Like Ronald Reagan in the USA, the Thatcher government in the UK pursued a deregulatory agenda geared to making the economy more flexible and hence more competitive in the wake of the collapse of Fordism and the restructuring of the world economy after the oil crisis of the 1970s. This was both an economic and a political agenda. Breaking the power of the unions was seen as a necessary condition for the government's securing the capacity to impose flexibility necessary for competition in world markets. And though an assault on unions might seem an obvious policy for a right-wing government, in this instance it had implications across the political spectrum. For once the 'Thatcherite' economic policy was in place, it became very hard for the Labour Party to reverse it by supporting trade barriers which would have excluded British consumers from access to cheap goods from countries such as Japan, China and Taiwan, because of the attendant electoral costs of doing so (note the conception of voter preferences as fundamentally driven by consumption – a key feature associated with neoliberalism). The accelerated development of an interdependent globalized economy bolstered the argument for increased flexibility and competitiveness at the level of national politics; the deregulation of financial markets gave a new spin to the sway of financial capital in the UK and the USA; and a celebration of consumption was presented rhetorically as, respectively, a radical assault on the class system and a confirmation of the American Dream.

Over the last two decades, the repositioning of politics attendant on these reforms of the economy and the welfare state in countries such as the UK and the USA has come to be conceptualized by a number of influential punishment and society scholars in terms of a decline of social democracy and a rise of neoliberalism (Reiner, 2006). As Robert Reiner, one of the most thoughtful and meticulous exponents of the neoliberal penality thesis, puts it:

> Neoliberalism is the most common label for the economic theory and practice which has swept the world since the early 1970s, displacing communism in Eastern Europe and China, as well as the Keynesian, mixed economy, welfare state consensus that had prevailed in Western liberal democracies since the Second World War. As an economic doctrine it postulates that free markets maximise efficiency and prosperity, by signalling consumer wants to producers, optimizing the allocation of resources and providing incentives for entrepreneurs and workers. Beyond economics, however, neoliberalism has become the hegemonic discourse of our times, so deeply embedded in all corners of our culture that its nostrums, once controversial and contested, have become the common sense, taken-for-granted orthodoxy underpinning most public policy debates. (2007: 1–2)

Penetrating the cultural and political realms, neoliberalism has come to be associated with a host of phenomena bearing on both crime and every aspect of punishment. In an irony particularly underscored in the work of Loïc Wacquant, the 'neoliberal' impetus to economic deregulation, welfare state retraction and individualization of responsibility has, paradoxically, gone hand in hand with the burgeoning of state powers, state pro-activity and state spending in the costly and intrusive business of punishment. The state has steered welfare entitlements towards a 'workfare' system in which benefits are closely related to effort within a contractual system, which is in itself punitive to those unable or unwilling to work; and increasingly relies on 'prisonfare' as the preferred mode of 'governing social marginality' in relation to those falling foul of the 'workfare' system (Wacquant, 2009; see also Beckett and Western, 2001).

Two purportedly novel features of penality are born of this 'neoliberal' impetus to economic deregulation, welfare state retraction and individualization of responsibility: the growth of the 'penal state' – that is, the penal power of state operations, at the same time as a 'rolling back of the state' is key to political rhetoric (and welfare policy); and an increasing pattern of exclusion, with the use of the penal state to discipline the poor and otherwise dangerous or dispossessed. The results are evident in increasing *anomie* and insecurity generating greater incentives to deviance; in increasing political resort to punishment as a tool of social ordering as the state comes to rely more heavily, both materially and symbolically, on penality as a form of social ordering; and in the precise shape of criminal justice interventions: rising imprisonment (Reiner, 2006, 2007; Wacquant, 1999, 2009); an accentuation of the demographic inequalities marking the distribution of punishment (Garland, 2001; Western, 2006); an array of criminal justice interventions premised on the 'responsibilization' of individuals as both risk- and crime-avoiders (Garland, 2001); and an insistent political rhetoric of 'toughness on crime'. Just as left parties such as Blair's 'New Labour' in the UK were induced to sign up to key aspects of the neoliberal economic agenda, so attendant insecurity about rising crime made a shift to their being 'tough on crime' an electoral imperative.

For the (many) punishment and society scholars who deplore this state of affairs, the key factors here are what Reiner identifies as the 'harms' of neoliberalism; economic harms which lead to a greater concentration of wealth in the hands of the few, and greater poverty and un-or under-employment for many (Hale, 1998, 1999), generating both greater inequality and greater insecurity in the wake of attenuated welfare safety nets and uncontrolled fluctuations in the deregulated economy; social and political harms in terms of health, social conflict and violence (Hillyard et al., 2004); ethical harms in terms of increased materialism, egoism and irresponsibility towards others (Reiner, 2007: 3–8). As Reiner puts it:

> [T]he advent of neoliberalism [is] the underlying factor in both the crime explosion and the shift to more authoritarian and exclusionary law and order crime control strategies ... [A] major difficulty is that neoliberalism has relinquished the tools that had been available to social democratic states to try to remedy inequality and exclusion. For example, greater mobility of capital flows, partly because of technological and cultural changes associated with globalization, but crucially because of liberalization of controls over financial movements, has weakened the regulatory and taxation capacity of individual governments in relation to corporations. (2007: 169).

Liberalism, neoliberalism and social democracy

Readers will note that my account so far has said a lot about 'neoliberalism' but little about 'social democracy'. The main reason for this has already been mentioned: it is that an understanding of punishment and society as fundamentally driven by a shift in politics (as opposed to economy or society) is a relatively recent development in scholarship, and one in which the focus is on 'neoliberalism' – with 'social democracy' standing for values such as reciprocity and solidarity which are lost in the shift to neoliberal governance. But what, more precisely, is the 'social democracy' in contrast to which 'neoliberalism' is conceived (Reiner 2006)? And how do neoliberalism and social democracy relate to liberalism – arguably the most influential doctrine in both politics and punishment in western countries over the last two centuries? In order to assess this question, we need to step back and say a little more about classical liberalism and the competing worldviews which informed the development of politics in the advanced economies during the last century.

This is far too large a topic for a survey such as this. We can, however, sketch a schematic historical story which may be seen as underlying the recent scholarship. One way of looking at the question is in terms of what we might call social ontology: what distinguishes classical liberal, neoliberal and social democratic worldviews is the underlying view of human nature and the relation of individuals to society which informs them. On the one hand, we have a socialist or social democratic, 'communitarian' view of the relationship between individuals in society. On this view, a recognition of interdependence and the centrality of identity and group membership to human identity and motivation gives rise to a robust conception of reciprocal responsibilities among individuals and a potential role for the state in providing the conditions for the realization of those social responsibilities. On the other hand, we have the vision of the atomistic, autonomous individual of classical liberalism, which finds its way back in to the contemporary politics of neoliberalism (Harcourt, 2010, 2011).

This contrast, which of course predates the neoliberal penality thesis, is a familiar one in penal theory (Duff, 1986, 2001; Lacey, 1988; Braithwaite and Pettit, 1990). On communitarian or republican theories of punishment, the apparent opposition between autonomy and welfare which bedevils classical liberalism is recast in less stark terms, moving from a conception of 'negative freedom' (freedom as being unregulated) towards a positive vision of freedom (freedom as consisting, at least in part, of being enabled to exercise one's autonomy not only by the guarantee of negative freedom but also by the provision of certain facilities such as money, security, education). This more expansive conception of freedom refuses a simple opposition between welfare and autonomy, and lends itself quite readily to a more ambitious conception of the role of the state, such as the one associated with the 'welfarist' tradition in punishment which, in David Garland's (1985) analysis, dominated penal policy for the first two thirds of the 20th century in the UK and the USA.

Social ontology, however, may affect but does not determine substantive values. While, in the hands of progressive penologists, the 'communitarian' ontology of mutual dependence provides the basis for norms of reciprocity and a more welfarist approach to social policy, it can be – and has been, for example in the Soviet bloc countries – used to underpin authoritarian and repressive arrangements. So it is perhaps more useful to think of the relevant intellectual history in terms of political doctrines. The great political doctrines of liberalism, and of liberal democracy, epitomised by thinkers such as John Stuart Mill and Alexis de Tocqueville, were well entrenched in the self-conception (if not fully realized in the political practice) of most of the advanced economies by the end of 19th century. However, under this broad umbrella of an attachment to individual freedom, representative democracy and – increasingly from the middle of the 20th century – individual rights, there was always substantial disagreement about the proper role and extent of government, with the classical liberal view of *laissez-faire* and a 'nightwatchman state' increasingly challenged by more ambitious conceptions of the role of the state, and by an attachment to ideas of equality most strongly associated with the socialist tradition. Already in 19th-century Britain, for example, government was in some sense attempting to steer social policy through institutions such as the criminal justice system, generating developments which would lead to the welfarist approach to punishment whose origins Garland (1985) has charted. In party political terms, both paternalistic, conservative parties and socialist/labour parties tended to subscribe to a basically liberal worldview, while a certain kind of communitarianism (generated, respectively, by paternalism and a commitment to solidarity) underpinned the continuing development of a steering role for government.

In the wake of the Second World War, a new, 'Keynesian' settlement generated a yet more social democratic equilibrium, in which a recognition of the moral imperatives of liberal freedom and democracy were tempered by a recognition of both social interdependence and proper limits on freedom at the level of social policy, and the need for regulation of the economy and the deployment of fiscal policy to stabilize and otherwise temper the dangers of unrestricted markets, particularly in generating inequality. In the wake of large economic disruptions in the 1970s, this consensus started to break down, with the conservative wing of politics realigning itself with the libertarian aspects of liberalism rather than with traditional paternalist authoritarianism, and the left – somewhat later – realigning itself around key aspects of the 'neoliberal' agenda in an effort to make itself electable (Downes and Morgan, 2007; Newburn, 2007; Reiner, 2007; Lacey, 2008). Economically, this led to greater insecurity and inequality; politically, it led to greater reliance on the harder edges of penal social control, particular in relation to what Marx called the 'reserve army of labour'.

So what is the key difference between a society based on classically liberal assumptions about human nature and about the proper role of the state, and the neoliberal order of, for example, late 20th-century Britain? Given the emerging importance of 'neoliberalism' as a conceptual tool in the field, a key question for punishment and society scholars must be whether neoliberalism is a genuinely distinctive political culture or formation and – if so – how widely its application can be generalized. Our analysis so far suggests that it is, conceptually, a form of *laissez-faire* liberalism in a new environment and under new technological conditions (in terms of governmental institutionalization, economic production, communication, mobility), leaving 'neoliberalism' in the balance between the characterization of a zeitgeist, and a coherent political doctrine. It is, certainly, a striking characterization; but it is one which operates at an extraordinarily high level of generality. To take the argument further, we need to know more about precisely how neoliberalism works not only as a form of governmental rationality (Rose, 1999: chs 1, 4, 7) but also at an institutional level to produce a particular form of penality, and about how generally that institutional formation is to be found.

Unfortunately, however, the literature is somewhat confusing on this key question. Some scholars more or less ignore the question, using 'neoliberal' as a convenient descriptive typology without addressing why the institutional features that characterize that typology hold together and persist over time in certain places (Cavadino and Dignan, 2006; see Lacey, 2008: 52–6). Scholars who do focus on the question take quite different views. For example, Reiner (2007) offers what is in effect an account based on a shift in incentives for actors in a whole variety of political and economic roles, though with a strong emphasis on underlying economic dynamics reminiscent of historical materialism, while building in a considerable space for agency. In his account of the upswing of 'law and order politics' in the UK, neoliberalism functions as a convenient label for a cluster of developments whose origins are to be explained in other, primarily economic, terms. Conversely, Wacquant offers an account based on the idea of a diffusion of neoliberal politics from the most powerful economic and political actors (global corporations and the USA) reminiscent of the 'class hegemony' version of Marxism:

> Neoliberalism is a *transnational political project* aiming to remake the nexus of market, state and citizenship from above. This project is carried by a new global ruling class in the making, composed of the heads and senior executives of transnational firms, high-ranking politicians, state managers and top officials of multinational organizations ... and cultural-technical experts in their employ. (2009: 306–7)

In this account, neoliberalism is reified as the consolidated ambition of an unidentified cluster of powerful interests associated with the USA and multinational corporations. Yet although the restructuring of the state, and the changing balance between its penal and its welfare functions are absolutely central to Wacquant's argument (2009: 285–91), he gives us a relatively thin account of just how, at the level of key institutions, the shift from welfare to 'workfare', and the creation of 'prisonfare', were brought about, even in his primary reference point, the USA. Moreover there is virtually no attempt to provide such an explanation for the European and Latin American countries which are plausible candidates for the denomination 'neoliberal'. And while the neoliberal penality thesis certainly has some purchase as a characterization of recent developments in some South American countries, the pathway to and conditions of existence of neoliberal penality in these countries cannot plausibly be assumed to be the same as in Europe (itself encompassing widely different national trajectories: Cheliotis and Xenakis, 2010), let alone the USA. Like theories of 'modernity' (Garland,

2001; Young, 2007), then, the neoliberal penality thesis risks imposing a framework shaped by one part of the world onto the analysis of other parts to which it does not apply or applies only in modified form. Wacquant's (2009) latest book gives many reports of penal practices and policy documents which illustrate 'neoliberal' developments. The difficulty lies in the fact that there is no systematic, mid-level institutional account to fill the explanatory space between the macro account ('neoliberalism' produces 'hyperincarceration' via a replacement of 'workfare' with 'prisonfare') and the micro examples, and to explain its distinctive dynamics in different countries. Without such an account, the analytic promise of 'neoliberalism' remains elusive.

The neoliberal penality thesis within punishment and society scholarship

Before moving on, let us note briefly the relationship between scholarship propounding the neoliberal penality thesis and other influential work in contemporary punishment and society scholarship. The briefest survey of the literature shows that many of the themes emphasized by scholars committed to the neoliberal penality thesis also feature in a wide array of scholarship which presents somewhat different arguments, many of them more closely tied to institutional specifics. These overlapping accounts give pause for thought about the level of abstraction at which the idea of neoliberal penality works. For example, Feeley and Simon's (1992) famous notion of actuarial justice, like Garland's (2001) notion of the managerial criminology of everyday life and Harcourt's (2007) analysis of predictive justice share with the 'neoliberal penality' thesis a vision of the responsibilized individual subject of penality, while drawing attention to variations in the levels of repression and punitiveness not only across social groups but also in terms of types of offending. Simon's (2007) notion of 'governing through crime, Pratt's (2007) 'penal populism', Tonry's (2004b) 'punishment and politics', De Giorgi's (2006) post-Fordist political economy of punishment, Garland's (2001) 'culture of control' with its hysterical criminology of 'acting out' in relation to some forms of crime and Young's (1999) 'exclusive society' all overlap with the neoliberal penality thesis in their insistence (mainly in relation specifically to the USA or the UK) on an intensified resort to penality and exclusionary punishments and an increased politicization of punishment. More broadly, the vast literature on governmentality, risk and criminal justice intersects with the neoliberal theme of responsibilization, identifying a distinctive rationality which cuts across a variety of institutions (see Rose, 1999; O'Malley, 2004, 2010).

Yet most of these approaches either present, or lend themselves to, a more differentiated picture of the canvas of penal politics in particular countries. All of these arguments unfold satisfactorily without any reliance on neoliberalism as a conceptual or explanatory tool. In addition, many of these works also offer a historical account of some of the institutional and conceptual conditions of existence of developments associated with neoliberalism, and make claims about detailed institutional developments which overlap with those analysed by proponents of the neoliberal penality thesis. What, precisely does the neoliberal penality thesis add to – or indeed subtract from – these more differentiated accounts?

To sum up

A diagnosis of neoliberalism has, over the last decade, come to be one of the most influential ways in which scholars of punishment in society have tried to understand their field. Whether seen as the form and means of a creeping Americanization of punishment (Wacquant, 2009); as the basis for characterizing developments in a single country and relating them to environments such as changing technology and the global economy (Reiner, 2007); or as the basis for typologies sorting countries into more and less punitive families (Cavadino and Dignan, 2006), 'neoliberalism' has become a familiar conceptual tool in punishment and society scholarship. But if we are to assess not merely its utility as a characterization but rather its potential as an explanatory theory, we need to know something more about the institutional linkages between 'neoliberalism' and punishment: about when and where those linkages emerge, and about the institutional conditions under which they emerge. In the following sections, I argue that the best way to get more purchase on these problems with the neoliberal penality thesis is to subject it to some questions prompted by a historical and a comparative perspective.

WHEN IS NEOLIBERALISM?

We have seen that the argument about the emergence of neoliberal politics and penality is, at least implicitly, a historical argument – one rooted in broader changes in the economic and social environment of modern nation states during the last three decades of the 20th century. There is, however, some difference of opinion among those who invoke the neoliberal penality thesis about just how far back in time the roots of neoliberalism reach, with Harcourt (2010, 2011), for example, rejecting the usual focus on the late 20th century in favour of a genealogical analysis of the roots of neoliberalism in the emergence of a notion of 'free' markets as natural orders in (false) opposition to 'regulation' from the mid 18th century on. Belief in a natural market order brought with it, Harcourt suggests, a perceived need for intense penal regulation of those disrupting 'free' market conditions. Questions remain to be answered about how such ideas travelled between and applied in different places: but this argument nonetheless helps to illustrate the point that if we are to test the claim that there is a link between emerging neoliberal politics and a distinctive form of penality, it is indeed helpful to look at a broader historical canvas.

Neoliberal penality is said to be marked by four key features: its distribution is ever more demographically unequal and trained on groups marginalized by poverty and/or by attitudes to factors such as their race or nationality, with the upshot that it contributes to a strongly polarizing and exclusionary social dynamic; particularly in relation to those marginalized groups, it is intensively punitive, and relatively undisciplined by norms of restraint (human rights, dignity), which would apply were punishment more equally distributed; it is legitimated in terms of a model of individual choice and responsibility; yet, conversely, it forms a key mode of state-building. Conceived in this way, how new is neoliberal penality?

It is surely a reason for entertaining a degree of caution about the distinctiveness of neoliberal penality and the power of 'neoliberalism' as an explanatory concept in the field of punishment and society scholarship that mechanisms for the selective and highly punitive demonization and exclusion of targeted low-status 'outsiders' have a depressingly long history, at least in Britain. As early as the mid fourteenth century, in a policy worthy of one of today's 'neoliberal' think-tanks:

> the royal council had alerted local officials not only to the excessive demands of wage labourers but to the accompanying prevalence of 'sturdy beggars', who refused work and took to crime. Following the biblical injunction that 'he who will not work neither shall he eat', it forbade giving them alms or charity. In the last quarter of the century petitions and legislation against vagrants and 'vagabonds' attempted to curb mobility, requiring all beggars to stay in their own vill and all vagabonds to return there. (Harriss, 2005: 244)

Think of the history of the Bridewell, used to mop up 'vagrants' from its inception (Beier, 1985). Think, too, of the poor laws, with the infamous distinction between the 'deserving' and 'undeserving' poor echoing down through the arrangements of the welfare state, even in its supposed golden age; the repeated Victorian attempts to purge London of the social 'residuum' (Stedman Jones, 1971); the regular resurgence of the 'respectable fears', projected onto particular excluded groups, charted in Geoffrey Pearson's (1983) *Hooligan*; or, more recently, the invention of the black mugger as emblem of the 'law and order crisis' of the 1970s, as documented by Stuart Hall and his colleagues (1978) in *Policing the Crisis*. All of these, of course, predate the supposed onset of 'neoliberalism'. Yet while they represent different forms of discipline and penality, their targets and their rationales are remarkably similar. If the primary impulse of 'neoliberalism' – indeed one of its defining features (Wacquant, 2009: 304–13) – is the move to the targeted exclusion of marginalized groups, 'neoliberal' punishment has been around in the UK for centuries, and it is rather the welfarist, inclusive, 'social democratic' penal policies of the first two-thirds of the 20th century, which begin to look like an historical exception calling for explanation.

But perhaps we should conceive neoliberalism not so much in terms of a distinctive substantive politics as in terms of its social ontology. Of course we must not exaggerate the shaping power of political doctrines or ontologies in shaping penal policy: as we have already noted, a communitarian worldview can lead to authoritarianism of either populist or paternalist kinds – the latter being, arguably, the best way of characterizing much Victorian penal policy in the UK. (This ambiguity indeed reminds us that the very distinction between exclusionary/neoliberal punishments and inclusionary/welfarist punishments can be overdrawn.) Nonetheless, governmental assumptions about human nature and motivation do influence the design of policy. And, notwithstanding the pervasive authoritarian paternalism of 19th-century Britain, we can find, underlying much Victorian penal and indeed social policy, strong strains of what is being cast as 'neoliberalism' today. The huge influence of Becarrian neo-classical penology and Bentham's utilitarianism, both of them focusing on individual agents who can be motivated by incentives created by social policy, further demonstrates that key features claimed to be definitional of neoliberalism are hardly new (Wiener, 1991; see also Garland, 1985). Prison reformers, for example, agonized over prison regimes precisely because they assumed that individual prisoners could be brought to 'work on their characters' through, variously, laborious work, religious contemplation and solitary reflection (Wiener, 1991). Conversely, the (in)famous classifications on which much late 19th-century social and criminal policy was based – 'inebriecy', 'feeble-mindedness' and so on – fit, albeit in a very different way, the allegedly neoliberal dynamic of exclusion. How useful is a conceptual frame which can readily embrace such very different phenomena?

If neither the substantive penal politics nor the underlying ontology of neoliberalism is peculiar to it, can we find its distinctive core in the importance neoliberalism attaches to penality or 'the penal state'? Once again, we find continuities. The Victorians, like the late 20th-century 'neoliberals', used the creation of a modern criminal justice system – notably the prison and the police – as a key part of their state-building agenda. The creation of the police, the invention of the modern prison, the rationalization of penal policy and the reform of the criminal trial stand as central pillars in the edifice of the Victorian state (Radzinowicz and Hood, 1999).

It seems clear that more argument would be needed to establish that neoliberalism is really distinctive as a constellation of ideas about either political philosophy or social ontology. The one genuinely unprecedented feature of contemporary penality – the phenomenon of mass imprisonment – characterizes one advanced capitalist country, the USA, to a qualitatively distinctive degree, while the broad developments associated with 'neoliberalism' are much more widely spread. Indeed, it looks as if it is not neoliberal politics, but rather a distinctive set of environments – institutions at the national and international levels; technologies; economic developments – which has given a new spin to exclusionary and vicious penal practices in some countries in the late 20th century. If we are to tease out the shaping force of the political in penality, we will need a more institutionally concrete understanding of what counts as a neoliberal system, and of why and how such systems come about. Without such an understanding, we have no way of distinguishing between a genuinely causal explanation and a simple characterization of dynamics which recur with some regularity through the course of British social history.

WHERE IS NEOLIBERALISM?

We now need to move beyond the example of the UK so as to assess the more general claims implicit in the diagnosis of 'neoliberal penality'. In trying to assess the distinctiveness and explanatory power of 'neoliberalism', a comparative approach offers a further possibility for analytic purchase. The historical path to neoliberalism sketched above is one which applies only to certain countries: this in itself gives some pause for the idea of a general theory. Focusing on the present day, how many countries follow this supposed pattern? How consistently does the neoliberal environment operate across nation states? How far do different political institutional structures – democratic versus non-democratic; different forms of democratic system – affect the adaptation to that shared environment? If we find significant regional variation, this tells us something important about the interaction between international environment and national politics. It suggests that to take further our understanding of the linkages between macro factors such as changes in the structure of the world economy and national politics, and between national politics and penality, we need a clearer understanding of how national political systems differ at an institutional level. Might it be that a move to what is called neoliberalism was a good way to compete and manage social conflicts for some countries and not for others? And hence that comparative institutional advantage will lead to divergence not convergence? Or that apparently neoliberal adjustments will turn out to be ephemeral in some countries and lasting in others?

States are, of course, complex entities at the institutional level. The constellation of state institutions, in turn, is made up of actors with distinctive interests and incentives, themselves shaped in significant part by those institutions. Focusing on this institutional level, recent work in both comparative criminology and comparative politics shows conclusively that different states – to put it crudely – work in different ways (Cavadino and Dignan, 2006; Tonry, 2007, 2004a; Lacey, 2008; Lappi-Seppälä, 2008; Pratt, 2008a, 2008b; Cheliotis and Xanakis, 2010). As many of the exponents of the 'neoliberal penality thesis' acknowledge, this has key implications for punishment. Let us take the example of Wacquant's argument about a shift from welfare to workfare, and an intensified reliance on 'prisonfare' as the means of governing the socially marginal under neoliberal conditions. Esping-Andersen's (1990, 1996) important work on welfare states shows that there are three rather different regimes of 'welfare capitalism' across the developed world. Each of them has distinctive structures of entitlement, and – a key point, which moves the analysis from description to explanation – each is articulated in strikingly different ways with other features of the political economy. The 'neoliberal' move to 'workfare' is typical of only one of these three regimes. And, notwithstanding some recent pressure on the more generous welfare regimes of the corporatist countries of northern Europe and the social democratic regimes of the Nordic countries, there is strong reason to think that these differences will persist over time (Martin, 2004a, 2004b; Pontusson, 2005). As research has shown (Beckett and Western, 2001; see also Downes and Hansen, 2006), this has important implications for punishment.

The influence of welfare states on crime and punishment is widely acknowledged in punishment and society scholarship. However, welfare state regimes are not the only systematic institutional differences among advanced political economies. As the 'varieties of capitalism' literature has shown (Hall and Soskice, 2001), production regimes are also systematically different in institutional terms, implying very different levels of vulnerability to the collapse of Fordism. Moreover – and of key importance to the neoliberal penality thesis – production regime variation and differences in the form of economic activity in which countries excel imply very different constraints on the sway of the market, and very different levels of influence for financial capitalism. To take just one key example, there has been significantly less pressure for flexibilization in the more highly co-ordinated market economies of northern Europe and Scandinavia. Notwithstanding a certain level of 'neoliberal' (and punitive) political rhetoric, it is clear that these co-ordinated countries have, so far, been decisively less influenced by a neoliberal political and economic agenda than have liberal market economies such as the USA or the UK. As Figure 12.1 shows, it is also the case that their penal regimes have remained significantly more stable than have those of the liberal market economies (Lacey, 2008: ch. 3; see also Cavadino and Dignan, 2006). Even restricting our analysis to countries with relatively similar political histories and levels of economic development, differences in penality are striking.

This is not to say that the moderate rates of imprisonment and relatively humane criminal justice policies currently enjoyed by the

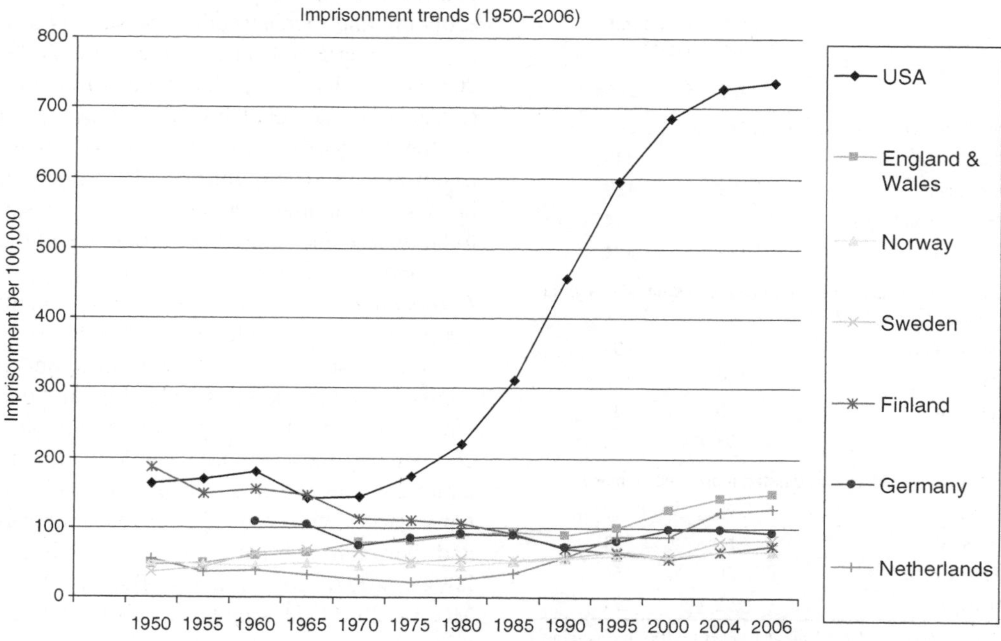

Figure 12.1 Imprisonment trends, 1950–2006
Source: International Centre for Prison Studies (2007); John Pratt, *British Journal of Criminology* (2008a, 2008b)

Nordic countries are immune to threats from the sorts of international developments on which the 'neoliberal penality' thesis focuses. Migration flows in particular seem likely to pose a challenge to penal moderation both because of the costs of extending generous welfare benefits to a significant new group, should attempts to incorporate them in the productive economy fail or proceed rather slowly; and because of attendant risks in terms of the attenuation of the solidaristic social culture on which political support for those welfare benefits has rested. However, 40 years after the emergence of the environmental conditions which arguably produced a 'neoliberal politics' in the UK, differences as significant as those persisting among European and Nordic countries (see Table 12.1) which are broadly similar in terms of levels of economic development and commitment to liberal values must be accounted very significant (Lappi-Seppälä, 2007; Tonry, 2007; Pratt, 2008a, 2008b).

Table 12.1 Political economy and imprisonment

	Imprisonment rate (per 100,000)	
	2002–3	*2008–9*
Neoliberal countries (liberal market economies)		
USA	701	748
New Zeland	155	199
England and Wales	141	154
Australia	115	134
Conservative corporatist countries (coordinated or hybrid market economies)		
Netherlands	100	94
Italy	100	112
Germany	98	88
France	93	96*
Social democracies (coordinated market economies)		
Sweden	73	78
Denmark	58	71
Finland	70	60
Norway	58	71

Source: Adapted from Hall and Soskice (2001); Cavadino and Dignan (2006); International Centre for Prison Studies (September 2010)

Note: *The figure for France has not been updated since 2008

On the face of it, these facts undermine any generalized neoliberal penality thesis. Yet proponents of that thesis have been curiously impervious to the test of difference. Notwithstanding the evident differences in terms of factors such as vulnerability to changes in the world economy, political/economic power to shape the development of 'globalization', and pressures on and incentives for countries to please the USA by bringing criminal justice policy into line with the 'Washington consensus', the USA, the UK, South America and Europe are all too often lumped together in an undifferentiated global order. Wacquant, for example, refers to a 'global firestorm of law and order' (1999: 162), and argues that the 'US carceral archipelago ... ' shows us the 'possible, nay probable, contours of the future landscape of the police, justice, and prison in European and Latin American countries that have embarked onto the path of "liberating" the economy and reconstructing the state blazed by the American leader' (Wacquant, 2009: 20). This, at least, introduces a qualification, recognizing that not all countries have moved in a 'neoliberal' direction. However, Wacquant is not always so circumspect. For example, he asks in another passage, 'who can say today where and when the ballooning of the jails and penitentiaries *visible in nearly all European countries* will stop?' (Wacquant, 2009: 26, emphasis added: see also 23–4).

Furthermore – a neglected question in punishment and society scholarship, and one which we might have hoped that the neoliberal penality thesis would have done more to address – the organization of political systems varies widely both between countries and between sub-national regions (Tonry, 2004a, 2007; Lacey, 2008; Barker, 2009; McAra, 2011). This makes a substantial difference to criminal justice in a number of ways. Of indirect but vast importance to punishment, the structure of the political system affects the capacity to build coalitions capable of providing stable support for long-term investment in institutions such as the welfare state, the education system and, crucially, the more welfarist versions of criminal justice intervention whose benefits are hard to quantify and are realised only in the long term. More directly, the shape of the political system affects the ways in which perceived anxiety about crime or insecurity register in the electoral process. In proportionately representative systems, to be brief, there are significant checks and balances, as well as more robust institutional arrangements facilitating co-ordination between settled interests, than in 'first past the post' systems. In the latter, a typically adversarial and individualistic political culture, along with declining partisanship, has fostered the volatility of law and order politics amid the unedifying scramble for the short-term support of the median voter. Given the extraordinary diffusion of electoral politics in the USA, this seems a potentially important factor in explaining the recent history of American penality (Lacey, 2010).

Note, finally, that even if we focus on what is undoubtedly a key example for proponents of the neoliberal penality thesis – the USA – the notion of an overarching, monolithic 'neoliberal penal state' is less than convincing. To take just one indicative factor, imprisonment rates across the USA vary hugely, encompassing a range which in the late 2000s spanned imprisonment rates less than double that of the most punitive of the other advanced economies through to rates many times higher. In 2007, the imprisonment rate ranged from a high of over 800 per 100,000 in Louisiana to a low of 159 in Maine, with a national average of 447; variations in the punitive quality and intensity of imprisonment also varied markedly across the country (Barker, 2009: 3–6). In 2001, average rates in the South were one and a half times those in the North East (Lacey, 2010). This variation also applies to racial patterns of incarceration: the rate of black imprisonment in the USA in 2006 ranged from staggering highs of 4710 and 4416 per 100,000 in, respectively, South Dakota and Wisconsin, to 'lows' of 851 in Hawaii, 1065 in Washington DC and 1579 in Maryland (Mauer and King, 2007). Even in the USA, therefore, the 'workfare' to 'prisonfare' nexus is working differently in different parts of the country – a fact which seems highly likely to be related to institutional differences in sub-national political systems such as those traced by Vanessa Barker (2009) and discussed in the next section. Yet, despite the obvious implications for their argument, scholars committed to the neoliberal penality thesis have given relatively little attention to these salient facts.

BEYOND (NEO)LIBERALISM AND SOCIAL DEMOCRACY: FOR AN INSTITUTIONAL ACCOUNT OF POLITICAL SYSTEMS

I hope to have done enough to convince the reader that, notwithstanding the welcome emphasis on the distinctive power of the political in shaping punishment in society that is represented by the emergence of an analysis of 'neoliberal penality', the neoliberal penality thesis suffers certain key defects: defects in terms of how clearly neoliberalism or neoliberal penality can be characterized as distinctive phenomena, either ideologically or institutionally; and – in part as a result of this conceptual indeterminacy – about where, when, how and why they prevail.

Concepts such as liberalism, neoliberalism and social democracy are, in short, insufficiently specified to be helpful analytic tools, though they can certainly be suggestive characterizations. If we want to understand the relationship between politics and punishment, we must turn to the task of trying to build up a more differentiated characterization of different kinds of system in terms of concrete institutional features which bear on variables which we know to be important to the shaping of penal policy: the distribution of veto points; the structure of electoral politics; the distribution of policymaking power across fora and among differently qualified, motivated and accountable actors. Electoral systems, party systems, local government, pressure groups and social movements are all a key part of this picture.

There are, of course, many ways in which an institutional account of the relationship between politics and punishment may be developed. I will offer a schematic account of some of the most obvious, each of them represented in punishment and society literature over the last decade. One approach is to work downwards, as it were, from a macro-model of political economy and society, in something of the way that the grand social theories of Marx, Weber and Durkheim attempted. In the field of contemporary political science, there are a number of such macro-models that present institutionally differentiated accounts of 'Varieties of Capitalism' (Hall and Soskice, 2001) or 'Families of Nations' (Castles, 1993) based on the methods of, variously, rational choice theory, historical institutionalism and the analysis of comparative institutional advantage. And in comparative legal and political history, James Whitman (2003) has produced a theory of penal difference grounded in a distinctive set of cultural norms in France and Germany as compared with the USA, refracted through time and reflected in the structure of the legal and penal order over the long term. Alternatively, one may work, as it were, upwards from studies of the impact of particular institutional structures and forces in particular cases, gradually developing generalizations from these ground level insights (Downes, 1988; Tonry, 2004a; Miller, 2008; Barker, 2009; McAra, 2011) or from long run historical interpretations, with closely textured case studies woven into the historical story (Gottschalk, 2006).

Of course, the contrast which I have drawn between these two approaches is exaggerated: models are answerable to institutional specifics, while case studies are designed around (explicit or implicit) assumptions about institutional structure and the role of collective and individual agency. Nevertheless, there is arguably a distinctive tone and focus to these genres of work, which may be helpful in organizing the field for survey purposes. In this final section, I will sketch some recent examples of each approach, in an attempt to map out a more productive way of thinking about the relation between politics and punishment, by demonstrating the complementary nature and importance of these genres of scholarship.

Comparativists and historians have tended to be more fully alive to the impact of political institutional structure on the development of punishment than have other scholars (Cavadino and Dignan, 2006; Nelken, 2009). In my own contribution to this field (Lacey, 2008), I drew on the 'varieties of capitalism' model and on comparative imprisonment rate data to suggest that economic differences are themselves reinforced by independently important features of political structure and organization. Certain sorts of political system, in other words, conduce to – or militate against – support for the economic and social policies which make it easier for governments to pursue inclusionary criminal justice policies. In liberal market economies with majoritarian electoral systems, particularly under conditions of relatively low trust in politicians, relatively low deference to the expertise of criminal justice professionals, and a weakening of the ideological divide between political parties focused on the median voter, the unmediated responsiveness of politics to popular opinion in the adversarial context of a two party system makes it harder for governments to resist a inflation of penal severity. These dynamics become particularly strong where both (main) parties take up a law and order agenda, and where – as in the UK and the USA over the last 30 years – economic inequality and insecurity has fed popular anxiety about crime so as to mark out penal policy as an especially suitable platform on which politicians from all points of the political spectrum may appeal to median voters. The result is, loosely speaking, a 'prisoners' dilemma' in which neither party can afford, electorally, to abandon its tough stance, while everyone (other than those with a financial interest in the prison build-up) loses from the increasing human and economic costs of an ever more punitive system.

By contrast, in the proportionally representative (PR) systems of the co-ordinated market economies of northern Europe and Scandinavia, where negotiation and consensus are central, and where incorporated groups can have greater confidence that their interests will be effectively represented by sectoral parties in the bargaining process which characterizes coalition politics (Iversen and Soskice, 2006), the dynamics of penal populism may be easier to resist. Due to the discipline of coalition politics in long-run PR systems, in which bargains have to be struck before elections, voters can be more confident about what policy slate they are voting for – a striking difference from majoritarian systems, where a party with a comfortable majority is more or less unconstrained by its own manifesto once elected. The result is that long-standing PR systems typically produce a significant buffer between a popular demand for punishment and the formation of penal policy.

Turning to historical and case-study based approaches, we also find that features of political institutional structure are beginning to attract some very fruitful criminological analysis. In a telling contribution to our understanding of the distinctively punitive practices of the USA, and one which offers a valuable institutionally focused supplement to cultural accounts such as that of Whitman (2003), Marie Gottschalk (2006) has traced the shifting role of criminal politics in American history, pointing up a gradual accretion of institutional capacity which ultimately underpinned the prison expansion of the late 20th century, and a political structure in which the preferences of a distinctively punitive victims' movement registered strongly. Vanessa Barker's (2009) recent study of state-level penal politics in California, New York and Washington focuses on different modes of governance emerging from distinctive political structures offering particular opportunities for collective action, which themselves become entrenched over time as a result of considerable path dependence and hence relative insulation from pressures at the national level. Barker shows the way in which the different structure and culture of state politics has fed into large regional disparities in patterns of punishment. In Washington, political structures invite and facilitate a form of deliberative democracy which has fostered a more moderate and inclusive approach to punishment; in New York, elite domination of politics has led to an expert-oriented managerialism that targets punitive strategies onto particular groups while maintaining moderate penal policies for others; in California – in stark contrast with Washington – the initiative system, under which citizens can invoke referenda, generally organized around polarizing yes or no questions, has generated a thin, populist form of political participation which has contributed significantly to a highly volatile and punitive penal culture. And Lisa Miller (2008) has illuminated the shaping force of the differently constituted policymaking environments at national, state and local levels, diagnosing a distortion of political representation at the national and state levels, and one which has been of great significance in the upswing in punishment as a result of the increasing federalization of criminal policy. Miller shows that local politics in Philadelphia evinced a markedly more complex, less straightforwardly punitive analysis of crime than that which pertained at national or state levels – a finding that meshes with Barker's (2009) findings about the moderating impact of richer forms of civic participation in Washington.

These examples, briefly though I have canvassed them, serve to demonstrate how institutionally focused work of different genres can generate specific hypotheses for further comparative and historical investigation. In the remainder of this section, I shall sketch two examples arising from the work cited so far.

First, an interesting difference of view emerges from my own argument about the moderating impact of a certain degree of political insulation – confirmed to some degree in Savelsberg's (1994, 1999) classic articles and in Downes' (1988) justly famous analysis of the Netherlands– and Miller's and Barker's findings that richer practices of civic participation are associated with a greater political capacity to sustain moderation in punishment (cf. Loader, 2006). Miller's argument, for example, is that the distance of state and national politicians from constituents' concerns, in which *both* criminal victimization *and* the deleterious social impact of imprisonment register rather strongly, and the influence of prosecutors and other pro-victim lobbies at state and national levels, have had a decisive impact on the acceleration of punitiveness at those levels. This is persuasive, and an excellent example of the ways in which both the size and the fragmentation of the US system have affected its penal policy. Yet a number of studies (for example, Dyke, 2007) nonetheless suggest that in the competition for office, law and order bidding wars also feature strongly at the local level (Lacey, 2011), while electoral competition affects decision making in a range of different institutions (for example, Shepherd, 2009). These contrasting findings are a useful provocation to further research designed to try to establish more precisely the ways in which different levels and qualities of political participation affect the development of penal policy and to identify the conditions under which participation works to moderate the demand for punishment. The USA in particular provides an extraordinary opportunity for this sort of institutional research, given that its federal structure assigns the majority of – though not all – criminal justice responsibilities to states. Hence the USA sets up, as it were, a natural comparative experiment in which some key environmental factors (i.e. those pertaining to the country as a whole) can be kept constant.

Second, and similarly, changes in political structure such as the introduction of referenda or the reform of the electoral system in different countries can provide excellent platforms for comparative investigation of the importance of particular features of institutional structure. For example, both Scotland and New Zealand have moved from first past the post to proportionally representative electoral systems during the last 15 years, while the unusual phenomenon of coalition politics in Britain following the 2010 general election provides an interesting, 'paler' version of co-ordinated policy making for comparative purposes. This sets up a potential case study to investigate both whether PR constitutes an institutional variable of independent importance, and to illuminate the conditions under which institutional arrangements inimical to adversarial politics and facilitating cooperation and bargaining shape the development of penal policy (Lacey, 2012).

To take just one example: in terms of the argument which I have sketched, New Zealand presents an obvious difficulty. The liberal/co-ordinated market economy model predicts that a proportionally representative political system will be associated with more stable levels of punishment, with a higher status professional bureaucracy, and with less highly politicized criminal justice. In New Zealand, by contrast, the adoption of proportional representation in 1996 has gone hand in hand with an acceleration of 'law and order' politics (Pratt and Clark, 2005; Pratt, 2007) and with an increase in levels of punishment: the imprisonment rate has risen substantially, from 128 per 100,000 of the population in 1995 to 197 in 2007. This is the case notwithstanding the fact that PR has been associated with stronger electoral performance by left of centre parties, and by consequently longer tenure for Labour governments. Is the fact that PR in New Zealand has been associated with penal populism an anomaly? A close look at the framework underpinning the original hypothesis, with its focus on interlocking institutions, should prompt us to look more closely at this case. If our overall account shows that proportionally representative electoral systems are, in a large number of systems, associated with a more moderate penal politics, what is it about the New Zealand case which is different? And what does this tell us about how the hypothesis should be refined?

The starting point for our reflections here should be the fact that, in systems in which it formed a part of the very transition to representative democracy in the 19th and early 20th centuries, PR is itself articulated with key economic and cultural features of co-ordinated market economies: with a tradition of bargaining in which a diversity of economic interests – within both unions and management – are incorporated; with a long-running multi-party system in which negotiated political compromises are the order of the day; and with production arrangements that depend on long term investments in education and training. This alone might give us reason to think that PR electoral arrangements, when grafted onto a substantially different set of economic, social and political institutions, would have a somewhat different impact on criminal justice. A closer look at the recent history of criminal justice politics in New Zealand confirms this surmise. While New Zealand conforms to the left-of-centre pattern of partisanship predicted by the model, the power which PR systems accord to small parties appears to have enhanced the political influence of groups advancing a 'law and order' agenda, by giving such groups bargaining power *vis-à-vis* larger parties unable to command sufficient support to form a government (Pratt, 2007). Single issue parties tend to be attractive coalition partners to larger parties, because their specific focus means that a bargain can be struck with them without the larger party having to tie its hands across a range of policy issues. The New Zealand case therefore suggests that the dynamics set up by the electoral system are rather different in a country in which PR is grafted onto a society otherwise organized on 'liberal market' lines than in one in which a long-standing PR system reflects established class interests articulated with the production regime and embedded social identities represented by political parties (Iversen and Soskice, 2009). This example further suggests that particular features such as electoral arrangements interact strongly with other institutional factors, rather than having an independent importance (see further, Lacey, 2012).

CONCLUSION

Over the last decade, an appeal to 'neoliberalism' – along with an explicit or implicit version of what I have called the neoliberal penality thesis – has established itself as the most prominent and influential account of the politics of punishment in contemporary societies. In doing so, it has succeeded in placing political dynamics at the centre of punishment and society scholarship. While this success is to be applauded, I have argued that the conceptual vagueness of neoliberalism, and the institutional deficit which characterizes the neoliberal penality thesis, dooms it to failure as an explanatory account of contemporary punishment. Historical and comparative examples – as well as regional examples from the USA, the country which so often forms the basis for production of neoliberal penality hypotheses – comprehensively undermine the idea that 'neoliberalism' is plausible as an explanation of current trends in punishment, striking though it may be as a characterization of a certain kind of political reaction to a constellation of current geo-political and economic conditions.

The neoliberal penality thesis should, therefore, be abandoned. But in its place, and learning from its failures and its insights, punishment and society scholarship has an exciting agenda to pursue: to build a systematic account of how political institutions shape penality, and to work towards an understanding of the linkages between those political institutions and other social forces. In pursuing this agenda, one second order lesson arising out of the failure of the neoliberal penality thesis should also be borne in mind. In our quest to understand punishment 'in relation to' other social forces and institutions, we can acknowledge that many different methods, and different understandings of what is implied by a 'relation' between social institutions, can make a contribution. 'Relations' consisting of associations or patterns are a useful place to start. However, if we want to understand the meaning of those patterns or associations, we need to move on to causal, genealogical or other more ambitious frameworks, deploying a range of qualitative and quantitative, comparative and historical, empirical and theoretical methods – and being self-conscious about which is being deployed, and why. Building up an institutionally concrete view of the relation of punishment to politics will be a laborious process. But it is a enterprise of the first intellectual and practical importance. It merits a central place in punishment and society scholarship.

ACKNOWLEDGEMENTS

My warm thanks go to the editors and to Manuel Iturralde, Robert Reiner and David Soskice for comments and discussion; and to the audience at an All Souls/Oxford Centre for Criminological Research Seminar for helpful feedback.

REFERENCES

Barker, V. (2009) *The Politics of Punishment: How the Democratic Process Shapes the Way America Punishes Offenders.* New York: Oxford University Press.

Beckett, K. and Western, B. (2001) 'Governing social marginality', in D. Garland (ed.), *Mass Imprisonment: Social Causes and Consequences.* London: SAGE Publications. pp. 35–51.

Beier, A.L. (1985) *Masterless Men.* London: Methuen.

Bell, E. (2011) *Criminal Justice and Neoliberalism.* London: Palgrave.

Braithwaite, J. and Pettit, P. (1990) *Not Just Deserts.* Oxford: Oxford University Press.

Castles, F.G. (ed.) (1993) *Families of Nations: Patterns of Public Policy in Western Democracies.* Aldershot: Dartmouth.

Cavadino, M. and Dignan, J. (2006) *Penal Systems: A Comparative Approach.* London: SAGE Publications.

Cheliotis, L.K. and Xenakis, S. (2010) 'What's neoliberalism got to do with it? Towards a political economy of punishment in Greece', *Criminology & Criminal Justice*, 10 (4): 353–73.

De Giorgi, A. (2006) *Rethinking the Political Economy of Punishment: Perspectives on Post-Fordism and Penal Politics.* Aldershot: Ashgate.

Downes, D. (1988) *Contrasts in Tolerance.* Oxford: Clarendon Press.

Downes, D. and Hansen, K. (2006) 'Welfare and punishment in comparative perspective', in S. Armstrong and L. McAra (eds), *Perspectives on Punishment.* Oxford: Oxford University Press, pp. 133–54.

Downes, D. and Morgan, R, (2007) 'No turning back: the politics of law and order into the millennium', in M. Maguire, R. Morgan and R. Reiner (eds), *The Oxford Handbook of Criminology*, 4th edn. Oxford: Oxford University Press. p. 201.

Duff, R.A. (1986) *Trials and Punishments.* Cambridge: Cambridge University Press.

Duff, R.A. (2001) *Punishment, Community and Communication.* Oxford: Oxford University Press.

Dyke, A. (2007) 'Electoral cycles in the administration of criminal justice', *Public Choice*, 133: 417–37.

Esping-Andersen, G. (1990) *The Three Worlds of Welfare Capitalism.* Cambridge: Polity Press.

Esping-Andersen, G. (1996) *Welfare States in Transition.* London: SAGE Publications.

Feeley, M. and Simon, J. (1992) 'The new penology: notes on the emerging strategy of corrections and its implications', *Criminology*, 39: 449–74.

Foucault, M. (1977) *Discipline and Punish: The Birth of the Prison*, trans. A. Sheridan. Harmondsworth: Penguin.

Garland, D. (1985) *Punishment and Welfare: A History of Penal Strategies.* Aldershot: Gower.

Garland, D. (1990) *Punishment and Modern Society.* New York: Oxford University Press.

Garland, D. (2001) *The Culture of Control.* Oxford: Oxford University Press.

Gottschalk, M. (2006) *The Prison and the Gallows.* Cambridge: Cambridge University Press.

Hale, C. (1998) 'Crime and the business cycle in post-war Britain revisited', *British Journal of Criminology,* 38: 681–98.

Hale, C. (1999) 'The labour market and post-war crime trends in England and Wales', in P. Carlen and R. Morgan (eds), *Crime Unlimited.* London: Macmillan, pp. 30–56.

Hall, Peter A. and. Soskice, D. (2001) 'An introduction to the varieties of capitalism', in P.A. Hall and D. Soskice (eds), *Varieties of Capitalism.* Oxford: Oxford University Press, pp. 1–68.

Hall, S., Critcher, C., Jefferson, T., and Clarke, J. (1978) *Policing the Crisis: Mugging, the State, and Law and Order.* London: Macmillan.

Harcourt, B. (2007) *Against Prediction: Profiling, Policing and Punishing in an Actuarial Age.* Chicago: University of Chicago Press.

Harcourt, B. (2010) 'Neoliberal penality: a brief genealogy', *Theoretical Criminology,* 14: 74–82.

Harcourt, B. (2011) *The Illusion of Free Markets: Punishment and the Myth of Natural Order.* Cambridge, MA: Harvard University Press.

Harriss, G. (2005) *Shaping the Nation: England 1360–1461.* Oxford: Clarendon Press.

Harvey, D. (2005) *A Brief History of Neoliberalism.* Oxford: Oxford University Press.

Hillyard, P., Pantazis, C., Tombs, S., and Gordon, D. (eds) (2004) *Beyond Criminology: Taking Harm Seriously.* London: Pluto Press.

Iversen, T. and Soskice, D. (2006) 'Electoral institutions and the politics of coalitions: why some democracies redistribute more than others', *American Political Science Review,* 100: 165–81.

Iversen, T. and Soskice, D. (2009) 'Distribution and Redistribution: The Shadow of the Nineteenth Century', *World Politics,* 61(3): 438–86.

Lacey, N. (1988) *State Punishment: Political Principles and Community Values.* London: Routledge.

Lacey, N. (2008) *The Prisoners' Dilemma: Political Economy and Punishment in Contemporary Democracies.* Cambridge: Cambridge University Press.

Lacey, N. (2010) 'American imprisonment in comparative perspective', *Daedalus,* Summer: 102–114.

Lacey, N. (2011) 'Why globalisation doesn't spell convergence: models of institutional variation and the comparative political economy of punishment', in A. Crawford (ed.), *International and Comparative Criminal Justice and Urban Governance.* Cambridge: Cambridge University Press. pp. 214–50.

Lacey, N. (2012) 'Political systems and criminal justice: the prisoners' dilemma after the coalition', *Current Legal Problems.* doi: 10.1093/clp/cus002 (online).

Lappi-Seppälä, T. (2007) 'Penal policy in Scandinavia', in M. Tonry (ed.), *2007 Crime, Punishment and Politics in Comparative Perspective, 36 Crime and Justice: A Review of Research.* Chicago: University of Chicago Press, pp. 1–81.

Lappi-Seppälä, T. (2008) 'Trust, welfare and political culture. Explaining difference in national penal policies', in M. Tonry (ed.), *Crime and Justice: A Review of Research.* Chicago: Chicago University Press, pp. 313–87.

Loader, I. (2006) 'Fall of the platonic guardians: liberalism, criminology and political responses to crime in England and Wales', *British Journal of Criminology,* 46: 561–86.

Martin, C.J. (2004a) 'Reinventing welfare regimes: employers and the implementation of active social policy', *World Politics,* 57(1): 36–69.

Martin, C.J. (2004b) 'Corporatism from the firm perspective', *British Journal of Political Science,* 35: 127–48.

Mauer, M. and King, R.S. (2007) *Uneven Justice: State Rates of Incarceration by Race and Ethnicity.* Washington, DC: The Sentencing Project.

McAra, L. (2011) 'The impact of multi-level governance on crime control and punishment', in A. Crawford (ed.), *International and Comparative Criminal Justice and Urban Governance.* Cambridge: Cambridge University Press, pp. 276–303.

Miller, L.L. (2008) *The Perils of Federalism: Race, Poverty, and the Politics of Crime Control.* Oxford: Oxford University Press.

Nelken, D. (2009) 'Comparative criminal justice: making sense of difference', *European Journal of Criminology,* 6(4): 291–311.

Newburn, T. (2007) '"Tough on crime"': penal policy in England and Wales', in M. Tonry (ed.), *Crime, Punishment and Politics in Comparative Perspective, 36 Crime and Justice: A Review of Research.* Chicago: University of Chicago Press, pp. 425–70.

O'Malley, P. (2004) 'The globalisation of risk? Distinguishing styles of neo-liberal criminal justice in Australia and the USA', in T. Newburn and R. Sparks (eds), *Criminal Justice and Political Cultures.* Willan Press: Devon. pp. 30–48.

O'Malley, P. (2010) *Crime and Risk.* London: SAGE Publications.

Pearson, G. (1983) *Hooligan: A History of Respectable Fears.* London: Macmillan.

Pontusson, J. (2005) *Inequality and Prosperity: Social Europe versus Liberal America.* Ithaca, NY: Cornell University Press.

Pratt, J. (2007) *Penal Populism.* London: Routledge.

Pratt, J. (2008a) 'Scandinavian exceptionalism in an era of penal excess', Part I: The nature and roots of Scandinavian exceptionalism', *British Journal of Criminology*, 47: 119–37.

Pratt, J. (2008b) 'Scandinavian exceptionalism in an era of penal excess', Part II: Does Scandinavian exceptionalism have a future?', *British Journal of Criminology*, 48: 275–92.

Pratt, J. and Clark, M.C. (2005) 'Penal populism in New Zealand', *Punishment and Society*, 7: 303.

Radzinowicz, L. and Hood, R. (1999) *The Emergence of Penal Policy in Victorian and Edwardian England.* Oxford: Clarendon Press.

Reiner, R. (2006) 'Beyond risk: a lament for social democratic criminology', in T. Newburn and P. Rock (eds), *The Politics of Crime Control.* Oxford: Clarendon Press, pp. 7–49.

Reiner, R. (2007) *Law and Order: An Honest Citizen's Guide to Crime and Control.* Cambridge: Polity Press.

Rose, N. (1999) *Powers of Freedom: Reframing Political Thought.* Cambridge: Cambridge University Press.

Rusche, G. and Kirchheimer, O. (1969) *Punishment and Social Structure, (first published, in German, 1939).* New York: Russell Sage.

Savelsberg, J. (1994) 'Knowledge, domination, and criminal punishment', *American Journal of Sociology*, 99: 911–43.

Savelsberg, J. (1999) 'Knowledge, domination and criminal punishment revisited', *Punishment and Society*, 1: 45.

Shepherd, J.M. (2009) 'The influence of retention politics on judges' voting', *Journal of Legal Studies*, 38: 169.

Simon, J. (2007) *Governing Through Crime: How the War on Crime Transformed American Democracy and Created a Culture of Fear.* New York: Oxford University Press.

Stedman Jones, G. (1971) *Outcast London: A Study in the Relationship Between Classes in Victorian Society.* Oxford: Clarendon Press.

Tonry, M. (2004a) 'Why aren't German penal policies harsher and imprisonment rates higher', *German Law Journal*, 10: 1187–206.

Tonry, M. (2004b) *Punishment and Politics.* Cullompton: Willan.

Tonry, M. (ed.) (2007) *Crime, Punishment and Politics in Comparative Perspective, 36 Crime and Justice: A Review of Research.* Chicago: University of Chicago Press.

Wacquant, L. (1999) *Les Prisons de la misère, Paris: Raisons d'agir Editions (translated as Prisons of Poverty Expanded Edition).* Minneapolis, MN: University of Minnesota Press.

Wacquant, L. (2009) *Punishing the Poor: The Neoliberal Government of Social Insecurity.* Durham, NC: Duke University Press.

Western, B. (2006) *Punishment and Inequality in America.* New York: Russell Sage Foundation.

Whitman, J.Q. (2003) *Harsh Justice.* Oxford: Oxford University Press.

Wiener, M. (1991) *Reconstructing the Criminal: Culture, Law and Policy in England, 1830–1914.* Cambridge: Cambridge University Press.

Young J. (1999) *The Exclusive Society.* London: SAGE Publications.

Young, J. (2007) *The Vertigo of Late Modernity.* London: SAGE Publications.

PART III

Modes of Punishment

13

Prisons beyond the New Penology: The Shifting Moral Foundations of Prison Management

Alison Liebling and Ben Crewe

> The present state of our prisons, blighted by age, severe overcrowding, insanitary conditions and painfully slow progress in modernization makes it necessary to consider urgent new ways of dealing with these problems which at present seem almost insoluble.
>
> (Home Affairs Committee, 1987: 1)

INTRODUCTION

The sociological study of prisons began with the prisoner community (Clemmer, 1940; Sykes, 1958), has unevenly included the study of prison officers (see, Toch, 1978; Liebling and Price, 2001; Crawley, 2004) but has rarely included senior managers (for the best exceptions, see Jacobs, 1977; also Riveland, 1999, on prison management trends in the USA).[1] In some respects, it is understandable that there has been so little close empirical study of prison managers – access is difficult, and as power-holders, senior managers appeal less to critical scholars than prisoners do. But it is unfortunate that we know so little about the professional orientations of senior prison practitioners. As translators and transmitters of penal policy, they shape what goes on in prison. They are also indicative of wider shifts in the terms of prison governance. Important transformations have taken place in the organization, management and purpose of prisons in the last few decades, and in the social and philosophical orientations of prison managers. These transformations can be detected in the experience of the prisoner and the prison officer.[2]

The version of managerialism seen to emerge in criminal justice during the late 1980s and onwards was described by Feeley and Simon (1992) as 'the new penology': an emerging strategy of corrections having negative ideological effects on practitioners via new techniques and languages emphasizing 'actuarial norms'. It was aggregate, risk-focused, distant, quantitative, rational, control-oriented and treated offenders as units to be managed rather than moral agents with futures (Feeley and Simon, 1992) and in this sense, formed part of a 'critical struggle over who we are' (Simon, 1988: 775). Surveillance, cost control and systems for the management of unruly groups were privileged over 'social or personal transformation' (Feeley and Simon, 1992: 465). The new penology 'neutralized' normative aspects of penality (Simon and Feeley, 1995: 172; Garland, 1990: 261) and had 'trouble with the concept of humanity' (Simon and Feeley, 1995: 173; also Simon, 1988). The prison was characterized as 'a space of pure custody, a human warehouse or even a kind of social waste management facility' (Simon, 2007: 142) aimed at containing 'toxic' populations 'at reasonable fiscal, political, and legal costs' (Simon, 2007: 153). Rehabilitation, it was claimed, had been discarded as the 'operant correctional philosophy' (Wacquant, 2009a: 150), with governors considerably more punitive than their predecessors and committed to neutralizing risk, minimizing prison incidents, and efficient systems management rather than wider social goals.

This critique is valid and powerful, but partial. While we agree to some extent with Simon and Feeley's account of the new penology and its corrosive effects on the moral life of criminal justice institutions, there are some important modifications to make to their account. In relation to the UK, it overstates the degree to which the 'old penology' was ever as humane and rehabilitative as its advocates may have wanted to claim, while overlooking the institutional chaos and abuse that help explain the shift towards a more managerialist era. Jacobs's (1977) account of transformations in management practices in Stateville penitentiary, Illinois, suggests that there are some parallels in the USA, in that the period prior to bureaucratization was hardly a halcyon time of penal-welfarism. Few other 'interior' accounts of penal management allow such comparisons, or explore the different forms that prison management can take. Since one of the defining characteristics of managerialism is its '*a*morality' – its capacity to be used as a means to very different ends – it is important to examine more closely the shape it has taken at different points during the new penology era. Defining several decades of penality using one characterization or term – while helpful for the sake of broader analysis – risks obscuring important fluctuations in the relative importance of financial, moral and other considerations and their effects. Finally, the new penology thesis has relatively little to say about criminal justice practitioners themselves, viewing them primarily as conduits of the wider managerial culture in which they find themselves. The *impact* of managerialism upon them, and their particular applications of it, are unclear (Liebling with Arnold, 2004; Cheliotis, 2006).

The main aims of this chapter are twofold. Drawing on evidence from England and Wales, the jursidication we know best and one that might reasonably be thought of as somewhat emblematic of certain forms of cultural and organizational change in prisons over the last several decades, we add in the largely unwritten history of prison life and management in the pre-managerialist period, in a manner that makes sense of, and to some degree defends, the reforms that followed. Second, we describe recent versions of the new penology in practice in this jurisdiction, differentiating between two distinct phases: early managerialism (which we call 'managerialism-plus'), and its current form ('managerialism-minus'). We outline some of the key differences between these phases, particularly the balance between moral and economic rationalities in each. To do so, we draw upon detailed accounts of the past and present provided by several generations of current and recently retired senior managers working in prisons, and reflect upon the professional ideologies of these practitioners during these different eras. Our account constitutes a case for taking senior managers and their orientations seriously in penology.

IN DEFENCE OF PENAL MANAGERIALISM

British prisons, 1970–1990

Life for prisoners in the 1970s and 1980s in British prisons was undoubtedly grim. Suicides, disturbances, industrial action, escapes and hostage-taking, were matters of public and media concern (Stern, 1987; Liebling, 1992: ch. 1; Rock, 1996). Regimes were poor, and levels of care even for vulnerable prisoners with mental health problems, were low. While there was a genuine commitment to rehabilitation in borstals (for young offenders) and some training prisons, many local prisons festered.[3] One then-budding governor (and future chief executive of the National Offender Management System) recalled that when he visited HMP Lincoln in 1981 and asked what the prison did in terms of rehabilitation, the governor 'almost split his sides'. Power flowed in unjustifiable ways, with undesirable consequences (including major disorders), at least in many prisons. Brutality was not uncommon, as we describe in more detail below (Fitzgerald, 1977; Fitzgerald and Sim, 1979; Sim, 1987, 2009; Scraton et al., 1991; Shaw, 2010). The culture among prison officers was macho, quasi-militaristic, and often racist (Sim, 1994).[4] Several inquiries, active campaigning by prisoners' rights organizations, and media exposés of (for example) controversial deaths in custody, had done little to precipitate improvement.

Many of the underlying problems in the Prison Service in England and Wales were exposed by King and McDermott, in their much-cited 1989 article, 'British prisons 1970–1987: The ever-deepening crisis'. King and McDermott reported a deterioration in regime conditions, including time out of cell, time spent in work, and access to facilities, in a range of adult male establishments over the course of two decades. Such deterioration had occurred despite the fact that levels of funding, and staff-prisoner ratios in particular, had increased over the period, suggesting that the penal crisis they described was an outcome of poor management of both resources and personnel. As King and McDermott noted, during the late 1960s and 1970s, the Prison Service had become 'dependent on the large-scale overtime of hourly paid officers'. Managers were 'bogged down' in 'perpetual disputes over manning levels, pay, and allowances' (King and McDermott, 1989: 109). Although a government committee led by Lord Justice May had been established in 1978 to inquire into these and other problems, according to King and McDermott, it could be considered only a partial success. While the recommendations which placed greater emphasis on efficiency and accountability in relation to both management and resources had been pursued 'with vigour' (King and McDermott, 1989: 109), those relating to specific standards of care and custody had not been fulfilled. To prevent further deterioration, King and McDermott argued for a 'commitment to specific minimum standards, which in turn must address questions of access and quality as well as mere provision of facilities' (1989: 127).

One of the weaknesses that King and McDermott highlighted was the lack of accountability for increasing spending – no-one knew 'where the money went' – and for staff resources. Their account of a crisis of management was supported by a range of other descriptions of British prisons in the 1970s and 1980s. Many governors were remote and uninformed about the reality of life on 'their' landings. Officers expressed contempt for a distant 'headquarters': 'we are run by governors who have never seen a prison' (Stern, 1987: 58). Many aspects of this uncomfortable relationship between prison officers and their managers were mediated by the Prison Officers Association (POA).

King and McDermott's call for clear criteria by which prison standards could be evaluated, and for greater management control, anticipated some of the terms of managerialism, framing it as a moral imperative. Towards the end of the 1980s, several developments coincided to help meet their call.

Prison regimes were facing considerable criticism, and collective action by prisoners was becoming widespread (Adams, 1992; Sparks et al., 1996). Inquiries into prison life and conditions, as well as a series of major disturbances, confirmed an emerging recognition that standards and cultures were poor.[5] At the same time, a general process of public sector transformation had started under the Conservative governments of the 1980s, which aimed to overcome the deficiencies of the bureaucratic machinery of government, paying close attention to budgets, targets, strategic plans, competition, performance measurement and the concept of 'value for money' (Hoggett, 1991; Pollitt, 1991, 1995; Pollitt and Bouckaert, 2000). Institutions were to be made more 'measurable' and transparent, in part through the use of targets, standards and technology. One motive for such a 're-making of the British State' was the breaking of unions – first the miners, and then the POA. As Windlesham (1993) notes, the then Prime Minister, Margaret Thatcher, certainly had a natural aversion to state monopolies and shared the view of influential free-market think-tanks of the time that the prison service, like other public sector institutions, was complacent, expensive, overstaffed and run in the interests of its employees.

The POA still has an unenviable reputation and was on the receiving end of considerable criticism throughout the period addressed in this chapter (Lewis, 1997; HMCIP, 2000; Laming, 2000; Ramsbotham, 2003).[6] Former Director General, Derek Lewis laid part of the blame for the 'poor record for security, humane treatment of prisoners and operating efficiency' in the Prison Service at the door of the POA:

> Its stubborn defence of restrictive practices, coupled with its belligerent and often threatening demeanour, resulted in deep public prejudice against prison officers, and an image of the service rooted in the past. (1997: 130)

Lewis described the POA as a malevolent force with the power to 'seduce' its leaders and members, spreading evil gossip about the future of prison employment, unsettling staff, and making sure the Prison Service was run the way the POA wanted it, marching into governors' offices and scaring them into submission. This is, of course, only part of the picture.[7] Yet the POA's part in the onset of managerialism and privatization, and the embracing of both by new generations of prison governors,[8] has been critical. Without attempting to describe or explain this aspect of Prison Service history in detail (except to note that it is a relatively common part of the narrative in many jurisdictions), part of the history, and much of the point, of managerialism in the Prison Service has been to determine more closely the ways that prison officers conduct themselves, to seek better and more effective management of a somewhat unwilling workforce, and to limit and control the unit cost of prison officer work.

To summarize, then, in this specific area of public services, there were three main and interrelated incentives for managerialist reforms: (1) the need to exert management 'grip' on organizational costs and resources; (2) the need to exercise control over prison staff and their union, and to regulate staff practices, particularly in the use of authority and (3) the need to drive up standards and conditions.

The next section provides further detail on the story so far, drawing on interviews with a large number of senior managers, who experienced these developments first hand. The interviews provide ground-level insight into the 'penal field': the institutional and organizational factors which shaped the emergence and subsequent development of new penological practices in England and Wales over several decades. The narrative accounts of operationally experienced senior 'players' add depth and insight which are generally absent from 'top-down' (Sim, 2009) or system-level analyses of penal practice. They also add an important empirical counterweight to those accounts that are largely negative about the onset of managerialism within this area of public services (Carlen, 2002; Cheliotis, 2006).

Prison governors on 'the past'

In a series of long, biographical career interviews carried out over a period of two years with 90 senior prison managers of several generations, supplemented by observations at Prison Service Headquarters in London, the authors collected a kind of oral history of prisons and prison work, relating to the period 1970 to the present.[9] This sense of the significance of history emerged spontaneously, as the sense of contrast – of an unacceptable status quo – was central to accounts of the present.[10] In recalling the 1970s and 1980s, the most consistent themes in these retrospective accounts were weak and ineffective senior management, corrupt and un-professional staffing practices and a general lack of accountability. One senior prison practitioner reflected that when he first became a 'governing governor', after 17 years in service, he had 'worked under only one good governor' along the way. Most had been 'idiosyncratic governors who behaved in an idiosyncratic way' (senior manager 12). Innovation was 'totally dependent on individuals' (senior manager 96). As other interviewees noted, many governors in the pre-managerialist era were almost peripheral figures in the management of their prisons, unaware of or unconcerned by the behaviour of their staff and the welfare of their prisoners, except in abstract ways.[11] Outstanding individual governor characters were recalled (as well as exceptional regimes), but these exceptional personalities operated without the benefits of coordinated senior management teams, or management systems and information that could direct their attention, values and skills in organized ways.

In this context, staff practices in many prisons were grossly under-regulated. Governors were regarded as weak, and without systems enabling them to hold staff to account. One senior manager described starting his prison career in the 1980s as an officer in HMP Leeds, an overcrowded Victorian local prison, where he found that staff who were meant to be working night-shifts would instead sleep in the prison's tea-room, and would be encouraged to do so by senior staff: ['That's] why I'm a zealot about compliance and things like that' (senior manager 23). He was aware that prisoners were regularly assaulted by officers, and that governors either knew that such acts were occurring but did little to prevent them, or had insufficient 'grip' over their prison to know that staff were colluding in a range of abusive or dishonest practices:

> I remember one senior officer saying to me: 'There's some things, lad, that Governors mustn't ever see', and I thought to myself well, actually, that's not what I want it to be like, that's not what it's going to be like if I'm going to continue in this role. ... So that was all around, and that experience has been a huge influence for me, because I think I learned an awful lot about what it was like on the frontline, and therefore I don't think I am blind to what officers do and can do, and what can happen, even when you've got the best managed systems ... I mean the classic bit about power, and where power is and how power's handled, [it's] massively important to me. (Senior manager 23)

Such experiences – including the feeling of being powerless to intervene, or feeling outraged that those who could intervene were allowing abuse to persist – were common among our interviewees. Some confessed to having played a role in the 'heavy' cultures they described, due to peer group pressure, the need for a social life, or their own 'age and stupidity'. More often, they reported having felt uncomfortable within traditional, regressive staff cultures, but being silenced or powerless to do anything about them. Here is a long (but significantly edited), illuminating and somewhat typical account of an early career in this period, illustrating how a generation of governors sought to make inroads into unacceptable staff cultures, but against the grain and with limited success:

> You get lots of young officers who come into a culturally bad prison where staff are trying to make people do things the wrong way or take short cuts, or try and stop them from doing things the right way ... After about two years I realized that that sort of thing went on and I thought,

I don't want anything to do with that, I can carve my own furrow here, and decide which way I want to do things ... Every time I've been promoted I've wanted to change things, but I've always found that you can't ... there's always somebody above you, telling you you can't.

It's quite hierarchical ... ? And what were the bad officers doing that you disapproved of?

The bad officers were the people who were involved in the gossip, they would run everybody down, deal with prisoners in a poor way, they weren't respectful to them, or to each other or to anybody really, and I just didn't want anything to do with that. The way I try to deal with it now is to manage people robustly and not allow them the leeway to move outside strict rules around how you will behave towards other people and to prisoners, and I make it very clear to them that if they do step outside that they will be dealt with in an appropriate way ... I couldn't actually affect it, you know, in those [early] days. ... I couldn't influence much of what was going on [in prison X, in the 1980s], in fact I was bullied there, pretty heavily bullied by a PO and another SO[12] who ... were running the show, they were in charge of overtime ... They were conspiring to run everything. It made me stronger actually ... I'm going to fight this stuff, I'm not going to let this happen in places where I work ...

Here we see a number of the rationalities of managerialism, expressed morally and within context: the need for greater management power to deal with inappropriate staff behaviour – towards prisoners, colleagues and managers – and the feeling that robust management was the best means of dealing with such problems. Many of our interviewees explicitly linked these issues to the power and culture of the POA.

Prison management, the Prison Officers Association and prison privatization

During the sixties, the mines started to close; steel workers started to be thrown out of work; fishermen, and the trawling industry started to decline; the building industry started to decline. And what did the Prison Service do? We rushed into those areas and we recruited like mad, all gleefully patting each other on the back and saying 'You know, we are getting in some very good people' — and we were. We were getting in people who enjoyed a masculine environment; we were getting in people who had a kind of discipline that they had constructed in their workplace. And they brought it to the Prison Service, and much of that was good. But what they also brought with them of course were very different trade union attitudes that prevailed in the industries they came from. And they murdered us, for about seven years. They took us by the tail and they swung us around. And when they'd finished with the governor, they started on the Directors. (Former governor and regional director Bill Driscoll, from 'Prison Britain III — Fresh Start', BBC Radio 4, 5 August 1997)

If you look at the early POA conference stuff, you will see that about 50% of it was about prisoners' rights ... I think the shift started when there was the expansion in prisons and the need for more prison officers, probably after the Blake escape[13], but equally as the ship building industry went and people from the ship building industry moved into the Prison Service, ... and then from the mining industry, and they brought the industrial muscle with them. (Senior manager 70)

Some of the 'resistances to change' of prison officer union behaviour may be linked to the special circumstances of prison officer work (for example, the constant risk of danger; see Liebling and Price, 2001). The risk of violence, periodic 'favouritism' shown by administrators to prisoners, low prestige and low pay make prisons 'ripe for unionization' (Jacobs and Crotty, 1978: 6). But older governors could recall a point at which the POA became more 'militant'. They linked this change of mood to the rise of prisoner disturbances (which followed student and public disturbances, with a 'typical 10 year time lag'), and a distant headquarters response that was liberal and in practice, and under new challenges, incompetent:

The student riots of the late 60s began to permeate prisons in the early 70s ... censorship was being challenged, human rights were arriving on the scene ... prisoners were challenging authority. The Trades Union movement was also perking up. What about prison officers' rights? The Prison Service did not know how to handle collective disobedience, from either prisoners or prison officers. Staff wanted to crack down. [X in a policy division of the PS] told us to 'back off'. That was the message from headquarters. That liberal

> reaction generated POA instransigence. Before that point there had been a genuine dialogue about the involvement of prison officers in rehabilitation. (Senior manager 91)

Prison officers lobbied, via their union, for increasing and minimum staffing levels (often a 'refraction of other discontents'; Rock, 1996: 267), so that, for example, 'if we don't have an SO and three on duty' (that is a senior officer and three main grade prisons officers) then 'we don't unlock prisoners on the landing'. 'Safe unlock' levels drove costs. Yet officers could unlock their landings in the morning, and then spend the rest of it in the tea room. The staffing levels agreed with unions did not differentiate between tasks, role, time of the day, or aspects of the operation of prison routines. Levels of sick leave among prison officers were high. Yet some earned more than governors by working endless hours of overtime. Officers felt a mixture of inferiority and resentment about the management of their work.[14]

In some establishments, 'alternative management structures' operated, with 'all the power' residing in the detail office, among particular chief officers (the then highest uniformed management role; see below), or in the staff club. As one interviewee explained, 'no governor grades understood the shift system, or resource management', which gave a huge amount of power to the uniformed staff who did. Prison governors were resisted, and sometimes bullied, by confident uniformed staff. It is important to note that prisons differed, here, and that separate systems of borstal (indeterminate training for young offenders), training prisons, local prisons (serving the courts) and a women's estate were managed in different ways (and to different ends). Within each 'model', considerable cultural variation was found.[15]

What matters in this account is the point that reforms to public sector prisons, such as 'Fresh Start',[16] and the introduction of private sector competition in 1991 cannot be understood outside this context. While motivated in part by ideological considerations (see Jones and Newburn, 2005), privatization was seen as a means of reducing costs, modernizing working practices and improving regimes by sidestepping and reducing union resistance (Harding, 1997). From the perspective of our interviewees, the inside story of prison privatization in the UK was principally the story of finally controlling or curbing union power. There was almost complete consensus that the public sector was 'in thrall to the POA' (senior manager 12) and could not have been reformed at the speed that it was without a competitive threat:

> If you read [former Home Secretary] Douglas Hurd's diaries you'll see how much the creation of the private sector was to do with the POA. If the POA had not been an awkward union with a track record of preventing change and driving up cost unnecessarily, then the conservatives in the mid-80s wouldn't have gone with the privatization legislation. (Senior manager 12)

> I don't think there's any way that we could've got some of the changes that we've got without the threat of private sector competition.
>
> *Is that mainly in relation to POA, staff resistance, those sorts of things?*
>
> Yeah ... absolutely about that. We couldn't have made the gains that we made in the prison service without huge external stimuli to get there. (Senior manager 23)

> I think there's no doubt that competition really shook the Service up and the thought that there is a different way of doing this, and just ... the possibility of competition, the threat of competition if you will, and I still think things like performance testing and the PIP (Performance Improvement Planning) programme were revolutionary in their impact on the Service. We were able to engage with extremely difficult and extremely militant trade unionists and get them to turn round horrible, horrible places like Dartmoor and say 'well, you know, unless you can do this effectively, we'll sack you, and we'll contract you out, we'll privatize you'. (Senior manager 44)

Again, it is worth emphasizing that anti-union views were expressed in terms of the treatment of prisoners as well as matters of efficiency and effectiveness. To quote one senior civil servant, the threat of privatization was required to 'convince staff that ... they couldn't with impunity assault [prisoners]' (senior manager 13). As the following section explains, most senior managers were acutely aware of the importance of managing staff power and the tendency for closed institutions of punishment to become abusive unless firmly led and tightly governed.

MANAGING OUT ABUSES OF POWER

> The day you think you've sorted violence, contempt … is a very dangerous day, because you can spend two years sorting a prison out and making it a genuinely decent place, and making [staff] treat prisoners in a positive and decent manner and they can take [no time] to regress. My experience of prisons is that you've never sorted that, you turn away for a few months and they're gone. … There's something deeply dangerous about prisons, and the default option in total institutions is abuse. (Senior manager 13)

> Well I think anybody who's running prisons has to be controlled for their worst excesses, because I think it's inevitable in prison that [the] worst excesses can occur, and if you think you can run a prison [by] just recruiting good people, and it will of itself be good without you being prepared to keep on looking to see where it's going wrong, you're naïve … And the things that go wrong can be brutality towards prisoners, it can also be … backing off from prisoners, effectively letting prisoners [get] away with things that you couldn't justify in public. So I think you should always be alert to the possibility of abuse of prisoners, abuse of power, or compromises in the running of prisons that are actually seedy and improper. (Senior manager 12)

In the extracts above, first-hand observations from practitioners converge with some of the most significant penological insight of the twentieth century: the prison is a *sui generis* institution, uniquely liable to abuses and distortions of power. On the one hand, as the Stanford prison experiment illustrated, power corrupts (Zimbardo, 2007). It can lead those who wield it to do terrible things to those who do not, almost regardless of personality attributes or decent moral convictions. The prison is inclined towards moral corrosion. Yet, at the same time, as prison sociologists have repeatedly noted, penal power is easily eroded, corrupted and compromised (Sykes, 1958), meaning that legally sanctioned authorities are under constant pressure to devolve power to those who have less legitimate claims to it.

In the period from the 1960s until the mid-1990s, prisons in England and Wales exhibited both of these inclinations, to a dangerous degree. In some high-security establishments, too much power was ceded to prisoners, resulting in prisons that were 'both riot-prone and escape-prone' (senior manager 12). In the early 1990s, for example, Long Lartin, the prison which embodied most closely the prevailing model for high-security establishments of a 'liberal regime within a secure perimeter' (Advisory Council on the Penal System, 1968; Liebling, 1992), experienced two prisoner-on-prisoner murders, considerable backstage violence (Sparks et al., 1996) and was characterized by our interviewees as a chaotic and dangerous environment, in which staff and managers had abdicated power to an indefensible degree:

> The place was definitely out of control … prisoners had a massive amount of inappropriate authority, and the staff were quite open and fairly positive in terms of trying to deal with prisoner issues but would never feel confident about challenging [prisoners]. [Prisoners] used to have mop handles with nails on them hung above the doors with cooking utensils hanging from the nails and whenever there was an incident the broom handle would come off. [They] didn't use them against staff but they actually would use them to scare staff. (Senior manager 42)

> Every light was painted out by the prisoners to make it not a proper light and there was a curtain across the end of the landing and it was full of furniture which effectively was barricade equipment, and it was frightening to walk along those landings. (Senior manager 67)

If the problem in these prisons was that staff authority was being under-used and the environment was under-controlled, the opposite was the case in many local establishments. Interviewees who had worked in prisons such as Feltham, Leeds, Manchester and Wormwood Scrubs during the 1980s and early 1990s spoke consistently of encountering malign indifference towards prisoners, outright racism and the widespread over-use by staff of control, restraint and illicit force. In such establishments, where prisoners were generally less organized and assertive than those in the high-security estate, the power vacuum left by weak senior managers was filled by uniformed staff and the POA.

The parallel hazards described here – the *under*-use and the *over*-use of staff authority – have forged the philosophy of contemporary senior managers working in the Prison Service and help explain why certain aspects of managerialism have enrooted themselves so firmly in its organizational soil. Senior practitioners working within the prison system accepted that 'management grip' was required because, unless closely regulated, power could so easily slip into an unwanted location. In the interests of safety and control, power should not lie with prisoners; in the interests of decency, it should not be wholly entrusted to staff:

> Looking at the job of running the prison, you can see where it can all slide away from you and therefore it is a case of making sure it doesn't slide. You can see by the prison officers not doing their jobs how prisons can get ... (Senior manager 68)

> Prisons fundamentally can be pretty abusive institutions if you don't control them. And even very good Prison Officers can go to the bad if they're not being managed properly and monitored properly and checked up on. ... Sometimes in some prisons you have to be transactional as well as transformational. It's not enough just to inspire and, sort of, enthuse and motivate people. Sometimes you have to use your authority. (Senior manager 2)

As suggested here, ensuring staff compliance required information systems, central direction and audit, and close management. 'Liberal' governing styles became associated with negligence, laxity and dangerous forms of indulgence (Liebling with Arnold, 2004; Crewe and Liebling, 2011). In one senior manager's terms, referring to the high security (or 'dispersals') estate:[17]

> We tried to build a culture of 'let's do this rigorously and properly', and that includes prisons where we've had control problems, like the dispersals, where behaviour towards prisoners was always pretty good, but [involved] staff backing off, doing deals, and not wanting to have to confront, and we've tried to say 'hey, if we do it, we'll do it properly, and we do it rigorously', and that's the culture we're trying to create, in which we care for prisoners, [but] we don't do it in a wet way, we do it in a systematic, rigorous way, and we're realistic about prisoners. (Senior manager 12)

Further, managers themselves would need to be overseen and regulated, since positive motivations were insufficient guarantees of institutional decency. Many interviewees recalled having worked under governors who were morally driven and intelligent but incapable of imposing their aims and ethics on their prisons. Several described well-meaning, value-driven and intellectually impressive managers who focused excessively on 'liberal projects' (which benefited only a hallowed minority of prisoners) rather than systematic decency (a less ambitious but more widespread concept of 'humanity'), who failed to tackle staff cultures that were abusive or corrupt, who were unable to 'connect' with frontline staff, or who were too disorganized to embed their visions in specific practices. Benign intentions did not produce benign institutions, particularly when governors were uncomfortable using their power or failed to establish the management systems required to maintain positive regimes.

Perceptions of this kind were so consistent that they suggest a kind of collective experience of prison work. This cannot, in itself, account for the introduction of new penal practices, not least because similar practices have been adopted throughout public services in many jurisdictions. However, they help explain why these practices have been embraced with some enthusiasm by the new generation of prison governors: clear management systems and processes, multiple targets and firm controls – what one interviewee described as a form of 'benign Stalinism' (senior manager 15) – were required both to prevent prisons from going wrong and to steer them towards going right.[18] The erosion of professional discretion was precisely the point of managerialist reforms (Carlen, 2002). In theory, managerialism could *manage out* abuse, neglect and disorder, and *manage in* decency, where governors had failed to do so. In the remainder of this chapter we argue that this development was partially successful during the early and explicitly values-driven phase of 'managerialism-plus', but has come to be replaced in a later period by a more dangerous phase of economic rationalism which resembles more closely some, though by no means all, of the terms of the 'new penology' (Feeley and Simon, 1992).

MANAGERIALISM-PLUS

> I am not prepared to continue to apologize for failing prison after failing prison. I've had enough of trying to explain the very immorality of our treatment of some prisoners ... We have to decide, as a Service, whether this litany of failure and moral neglect continues indefinitely ... It's a matter of caring, a matter of determination, and, I accept, not a little courage in taking on a culture in all too many places which we have allowed to decay ... The prize is ... a Prison Service of which we need no longer be ashamed. (Narey, 2001: 3)[19]

Accounts of managerialism in criminal justice tend to emphasize its lack of moral language and the associated dangers of this, as well as the shift in values from individual reformation to risk management, and from management to measurement (Bottoms, 1995; Nellis, 2001; Carlen, 2002). Employees can feel alienated by aggregate performance regimes that seem barely relevant to their work tasks accomplished on a day to day basis (Sennett, 2006). Information becomes a substitute for understanding. Much of this critique, and some healthy scepticism, was to accompany the introduction of managerialism into prisons. For example, in the Prison Service in England and Wales, individual prisons were placed in a league table rather than the more poorly performing prisons managed out of their impoverished states (Liebling with Arnold, 2004).

Conversely, in practice, the process (between 1983 and 2007) was driven by six director generals (eventually, chief executives), all of whom made strenuous efforts to tie improved management systems to moral ends.[20] What became known as 'the decency agenda' was the most obvious example of this effort, but there were many others, including a White Paper ('Custody, Care and Justice') and the Criminal Justice Act 1991 that led to reduced numbers in custody.[21] The political and policy atmosphere at the time reflected a broad liberal consensus among politicians, scholars and many publics that prisons were 'an expensive way of making bad people worse' (Home Office, 1991). The penal and criminal justice climate was moderate, and moral conversations about policy and practice were widespread. There were, for example, three biennial 'Lincoln conferences' throughout this period, hosted by the Bishop of Lincoln (Bishop to prisons) on the theme of 'Exploring Human Values in Prisons' ('against utility'). They were well attended, by a mixed and international audience of prison leadership, governors, probation staff, chaplains, academics and voluntary organizations. These meetings were highly reflective and scattered with references to the dangers and effects of detention, the significance of taking away liberty, the limits to punishment and 'a commitment to human beings as being, at least potentially, far more than they actually are'. The transcripts of each conference were published as, 'The Meaning of Imprisonment' (1989), 'Respect in Prison' (1991) and 'Relationships in Prison' (1993).

A comprehensive judicial inquiry about the widespread prison disturbances of 1990 (Home Office, 1991), the introduction of private prisons with explicitly 'cultural' targets (to outperform the public sector on staff attitudes towards and therefore 'service delivery' to prisoners) in 1991 (James et al., 1997), and the opening of new prisons, sent clear signals to the Service that 'decent' prisons were a basic requirement. A 'decency video' telling prison officers that abuse of prisoners would not be tolerated, and that 'if they could not sign up to the decency agenda, they should leave', was shown at full staff meetings, and its message reinforced at successive Prison Service Conferences (Liebling with Arnold, 2004: 39).

High levels of investment in prison programmes and education were achieved from government spending rounds throughout the late 1990s and early 2000s in the light of a rekindling of interest in 'what works' research findings (Liebling with Arnold, 2004: 34; Loesel, 2012). Prisons in England and Wales were shielded from a form of financial austerity that was to come later. A measure of the 'moral performance' of individual prisons, created by a team at Cambridge University, was enthusiastically adopted by the then Prison Service Standards Audit Unit for regular use in all prisons. The quality of staff-prisoner relationships, the level of respect and humanity experienced by prisoners, and the safety of prison regimes were by this stage (2002) a performance target. A major suicide prevention initiative branded as the 'safer custody project', and targeted at high risk local prisons with poor staff cultures, led to a reversal of long-standing increases in prison suicide rates, via newly built induction and first night centres, enhanced mental health in-reach provision, and increased use of Samaritan trained Listeners (Liebling et al., 2005). Staff initiatives were supported by a dedicated team at Prison Service Headquarters, and 'suicide prevention coordinators' established in all prisons. If this was managerialism in action, it had become overtly welded to better standards for prisoners and to greater control and encouragement of staff. Governors who had entered the Prison Service profession after 'toying with social work', finding it 'too disorganized', and then seeing an advert describing governing as 'management with a social purpose', were coming of age.

This sense of 'moral progression' and improved performance occurred throughout the first decade of the 21st century, despite increases in prison population size, the increased use of privatization and performance testing as 'threats' to the status quo, and some already savage budgets cuts (for a balanced account of such changes, see Shaw [2010]). Most prison governors, even those who had objected ideologically to the introduction of private sector management to prisons, accepted both that some private prisons outperformed their public sector counterparts, and that public sector prisons had improved enormously as a consequence of competition (Crewe and Liebling, 2012):

> I think [privatization has] been really helpful in raising our game, and it's been a wake-up call in terms of suddenly realising that ... this may not be a job for life, that we've actually got to deliver and if we don't there's people over there who will do it instead, and I think that's been generally good. (Senior manager 65)

Directors of newly operating private prisons – often disillusioned refugees from the public sector – talked with enthusiasm about the relief of managing cooperative staff, and the benefits this brought:

> In my first month here in (a private prison) I introduced a new shift system, and the staff went away and talked about it, came back, and said 'is it alright if we start on Monday, Governor?' I nearly fell off my chair! (Senior manager 26)

By 2010, the prison suicide rate was at its lowest, at 68 per 100,000 prisoners, since the mid-1980s (Spurr, 2011). In 2011, the incoming chief executive, previously the deputy, told prison governors that:

> We have significantly improved the experience for prisoners while reducing overall unit cost ... there are no "hell hole" prisons any longer. (Spurr, 2011)

Debates continued about whether the improvements were real, the broader risks to penal legitimacy (Sparks, 1994) and about the emergence during the process of a somewhat brutal attitude towards staff and senior mangers (Liebling, 2010). Dismissals, medical retirements and disciplinary hearings (of staff) increased over this period, many in the name of 'robust management'. The emphasis on 'performance' had some unintended consequences, such as the manipulation of performance figures, for example, prisoners being sent to workshops where no work was taking place so that the prison could still meet its target on 'purposeful activity'. Staff at establishments facing the threat of privatization experienced this process as demanding and deeply 'existentially troubling' (as Giddens [2001], Sennett [2006] and other critics of 'the new capitalism' would predict). When, for the first time, an existing public sector prison (HMP Birmingham) was awarded to the private sector, in March 2011, and an announcement made three months later to market test a further nine establishments, it marked out the new phase of managerialism that had dawned a few years before.

MANAGERIALISM-MINUS (2007–)

> Times are going to be tough ... the cuts might undermine our progress, and our values, but I am not going to be fatalistic about this. We need a 'doing things differently' agenda. (Spurr, 2011)

The roots of 'managerialism-minus' emerged before the onset of the financial crisis of 2008 but their effects have intensified since, and threaten to do so further under the new Conservative-Liberal Democratic coalition government. In the light of required savings by the Prison Service of 4 per cent, or £80 million over each of three years, from an annual budget of £2 billion (described as 'challenging'), a 'specification and benchmarking' exercise was launched, seeking to calculate the cost of all aspects of prison work, including exploring the extent to which prisons could be operated to a cheaper template, without losing too much 'quality'. Competition and prison size began to increase, and for the first time, existing public sector prisons had to compete against the private sector to continue to manage them 'in-house'. Some scepticism about the gains achieved from the investment in programmes during the previous decade began to creep back in, as research results from a large-scale roll out of accredited offending behaviour programmes became less clear (but see Loesel, 2012). The savings required (this time, 'austere cuts') increased to 10 percent from 2010. A 'public acceptability' test for regime activities was published in 2009 following negative media publicity about a Halloween party in a women's prison, and a comedy club in a maximum security prison (Liebling et al., 2011). Austere regimes were being defended on financial and moral grounds.

We use the term 'managerialism-minus' to describe this period because unlike in the earlier period described above, economy and efficiency are prioritized above any moral mission. The era is more in line with the original Feeley and Simon diagnosis, and shows more of the risks as well as the symptoms of the ideological shifts they described. 'Managerialism-minus' is an intensified and narrow version of what has come before, in that the emphasis on performance targets has become stronger while the resources allocated to meet these targets have reduced and the operational conception of the prisoner and his or her moral agency has also been diminished. Coupled with an 'era of [punitive] austerity', and in the current political context, it is harsh and pragmatic – a form of *punitive minimalism* which pledges no-frills, 'effective' punishment, while avoiding appearing in any way lenient or 'indulgent'.

First, and perhaps most strikingly, prison management has become permeated by a logic of *economic rationalism*. The term is used by Michael Pusey in an account of political and economic transformation in Australia during the 1980s. His account resonates powerfully with our observations and conversations with those at senior levels in the Prison Service and in the Ministry of Justice. It entails the pursuit of frugality and efficiency almost regardless of other goals or considerations, and reflects a changing demographic composition of Treasury civil servants and policy advisers towards a new generation of 'socially privileged, technocratic whizz kids' with no memory of harder economic times (Pusey, 1991; and see Liebling, 2011). Certainly, a new language of financial austerity predominates at senior levels of the Civil Service and it is assumed in such circles that private sector expertise is more valuable than public sector experience:

> The Permanent Secretary had all the MOJ[22] leaders round the table and he pointed out [X] and [Y] and somebody else as having come from the private sector and he would like them to share their insights with all their public sector colleagues. (Senior manager 81)

'Old penology' values of decency and relationships are being transformed into the 'new penology' language of cost-savings and effectiveness, as Simon predicted in 1998. A financial justification is required even for the provision of humane treatment: one senior manager within NOMS described the need to make a 'business case' for adding greater 'care' into the prison system and resisting more punitive, exclusionary practices:

> [In meetings, I have to say] I think [those practices] damage, and if you damage you pay the consequences for the damage you cause, and so actually that just doesn't make sense, in business case terms. (Senior manager 81)

This logic is applied to almost every area of service provision and treatment. For example, proposals were discussed for the Prison Service to make savings in their food supply chain by making all prisons work to a standardized menu, with the same dishes appearing on the same days each week. For those serving lengthy sentences especially, this form of bureaucracy can quickly becomes brutality (Bauman, 1990; Aly and Heim, 2002). Meanwhile, governors complain that cuts are relentless, are 'apportioned indiscriminately' (that is, regardless of the particular circumstances or financial track record of an establishment) and threaten the core principles of imprisonment:

> [My line manager said] 'The message [from the centre] is very clear: the things you must not compromise on are decency and security', and I felt insulted, that he's going to take three million out of [my prison] and say it doesn't affect decency ... because if you take all that out, the quality that is left for prisoners will not be decent. Here they will probably have no [offending behaviour] programmes, we're looking at locking them up every [evening] ... So I felt offended and insulted ... And it really is total lack of care, they just don't care if it's safe, they don't care ... it's just 'find the money', so there's a bit of it that makes me think, actually, the centre just doesn't care about people in prisons any more, ... and lots and lots of us feel like that, that they have lost any sense of what reality is, and what the difficulties are, and that perhaps they are going beyond what is possible, what they expect people to do. (Senior manager 84)

Referring to the UK's largest supermarket chain, senior managers talk of a 'Tesco prison' model – the standardization of relatively low-cost, large-scale, decent-but austere punishment provision.

A second characteristic of managerialism-minus, linked to this economic logic, is an intensified emphasis on performance targets. In the early part of the 2010s, almost all governors spoke positively about the impact of performance culture on the standards and moral quality of prison life. In contrast, by the latter half, even some of the most performance-oriented governors were expressing concern about a culture of hyper-managerialism:

> I don't think it is any coincidence that HMCIP reports are getting worse and worse, and I think it's because what people have been focusing on is the weighted scorecard, and how to look as if you are performing well. And you can play the weighted scorecard, and what we haven't been doing is bothering about the quality, and the decency, and I think we've now got too many targets, and I think some of them are totally unrealistic, the centre knows they're unrealistic. What was, I think, originally a good motivator, is in danger of becoming a serious de-motivator, I think. And the scorecard (and I know it's going to be replaced) ..., is now a tool that is so flawed it's almost meaningless, and yet it's still the tool

> people use to judge you by. So no, I think in terms of targets and all that, we've just gone over the top. (Senior manager 84)

Alongside these developments, the *language of retribution* and *less eligibility* has been revived in mainstream political discourse about prisons (see, the recent Green Paper: 'Breaking the Cycle' [Ministry of Justice, 2010]). It has become politically acceptable to shear away the distinction between the punitive aims of sentencing and the discrete aims of imprisonment. In a speech in June 2008, the British government's Secretary of State for Justice, Jack Straw, argued that the purpose of prison should be 'punishment and reform', and that prisons not only are but should be 'first and foremost places of punishment, primarily through the deprivation of liberty but also through a regime behind bars which is tough and fair'.[23]

The most recent incarnation of less eligibility has been given official expression in the 2010 government Green Paper, in particular its language of 'robust and demanding punishments' and 'hard work and discipline' (Ministry of Justice, 2010: 14, 16). At a time of economic stagnation and rising unemployment, these developments are not surprising (in that the conditions of punishment bear relation to labour markets, as Rusche and Kirchheimer (1939 [2008]) argued. In current circumstances, the driver of a less eligibility argument appears to be the legitimation of the prison system in the eyes of 'society and the taxpayer' (Ministry of Justice, 2010: 14) – an increasingly important political consideration – as much as the latent need to deter criminality among the unemployed.

Meanwhile, the increasing emphasis placed on work within prison is also better explained through a concept of 'poor discipline' (Simon, 1993) than via any vision of future human flourishing. In the current model, work is assumed to be the route to 'changing lives' and reducing reoffending less because of the skills it provides, or the value of the work, than the ethic it instils. Prisoners are to sign work compacts, wear corporate uniforms, and live according to expectations similar to those in the external workforce. The prison is to be seen 'as a work environment' ('so you can't smoke in the prison just like you can't in the workplace outside' (senior manager 90), and prisoners are to be made to feel 'like employees'. As one governor explained, 'the challenge is to help offenders change the way they see themselves' (senior manager 90).

This development is interesting in a number of respects. First, it marks a shift from a period when many governors preferred to regard the prison as a 'community' (however distorted), in recognition of the fact that these were 'total institutions' (Goffman, 1961), in which prisoners slept and socialized as well as worked.[24] Second, alongside cognitive behavioural programmes, it places emphasis on prisoners shedding 'anti-social' traits and developing certain kinds of habits which represent a partial form of citizenship that is more 'reminiscent of Marx's figure of the wage-labourer than of Marshall's notion of the citizen' (Hornqvist, 2010: 99). That is, its focus is on such things as the ability to follow the instructions of superiors, to pay bills and taxes, and to meet the demands of the new service economy. As Hornqvist (2010: 99) argues: 'At best, basic employability is achieved; the programme will not lead the inmates "to be accepted as full members of society, that is, as citizens" (Marshall 1997: 8)'. Third, there are good reasons to think that this optimism about the fruits of prison labour is misplaced. Prisons are not normal workplaces, providing meaningful wages or 'the broader aspects of gainful employment such as social status, social interaction, career progression, long-term financial reward or involvement in workplace development' (Crook, 2009: 44; and see van Zyl Smit and Snacken, 2009). Most prison work is monotonous and meaningless. The kinds of activities most likely to provide prisoners with alternative self-narratives are being excised from prisons precisely because they are seen as enjoyable.

The conjunction of discourses of less eligibility and 'workplace normalization', then, indicate a form of punitive minimalism, whose aims seem narrowly focused on imposing and inculcating discipline (Ministry of Justice, 2010), at minimal cost and without any semblance of indulgence. The language is starkly pragmatic – 'this is the real world' is a constant refrain, a justification for environmental and emotional austerity. The rhythms of work will help prisoners get into the 'rut' of life that awaits them on release. In response to new financial conditions, some senior governors talk of 'parking' long-term prisoners, and reserving opportunities for personal development for prisoners approaching release. While the ethos in some local prisons is more aspirational, transformative and permeated by external agencies than in the past, long-term, high-security prisons, where humanitarian principles used to be more visible, are becoming places of greater moral and emotional austerity. These are the prisons in which it was previously felt that a humane and relaxed environment could offset some of the privations of long-term incarceration and help 'train' prisoners for their eventual release. When 'reducing reoffending' becomes the main priority of the penal system, the positive mission of such establishments becomes harder to defend.

Proposals for a 'rehabilitation revolution' reflect similar underlying principles. Ostensibly, the idea runs counter to the aims of the 'new penology' which, in Feeley and Simon's (1992) characterization, comprise smooth administration and secure warehousing, with no external social goals such as rehabilitation or re-socialization. However, in England and Wales, rehabilitation outcomes are prominent but defined narrowly, according to small gains in reducing reconviction rates rather than a philosophy of re-socialization, and the rehabilitative impulse is directed by an economic logic, in the sense that imprisonment is presented as being essentially *expensive* (rather than, say, damaging). As one private sector executive acknowledged, 'finance is the driver' (senior manager 30). There is certainly clarity of focus, in terms of external goals, but of a kind that is experienced as somewhat brutal by practitioners. Prison governors (and now, private companies) are given clear aims, based around reducing reconviction rates, but are provided with diminishing resources with which to meet them (including cuts to offending behaviour programmes). Like other public sector workers, they are being asked to deliver 'more for less', as 'payment by results' shifts increasing responsibility onto their shoulders, and into the hands of private sector investors. Managers are to be less driven by processes and audits, and thus handed more autonomy, in some respects. However, the post-prison outcomes with which they must align themselves are not within their sphere of control. In reality, their freedom from central direction is extremely limited compared to governors of the pre-managerial era. Rather than being able to impose any personal vision, they are largely better or worse at steering the managerial ship. The expectations that they 'deliver' on well-defined targets mean that this autonomy effectively represents an intensification of neoliberal modes of governance. Any freedoms in relation to means must be used in the interests of highly circumscribed ends.

The emerging model of penal provision is consistent with a logic of organizational efficiency and streamlining. In what one senior executive described as the 'Apple model' of the near future, the state will continue to provide the material hardware (that is, prisons) while private and third sector organizations are invited to provides 'apps' – rehabilitative programmes, education and other interventions. Lower reconviction rates are the destination, but the state will leave it to non-state providers to provide their own route-maps. The risks of failure and the spoils of success are contracted out, diminishing state responsibility for the criminal justice processes as well as outcomes. Here, as elsewhere in public service provision, we are beginning to see a new phase and version of private sector involvement in punishment.

PRISON GOVERNORS AND THEIR VALUES

Prison governors enter prison work with complex motivations, and derive their satisfaction from 'making things work' – but what it is they are 'making work' shifts with changing directives, public sentiment, political imperatives, penal philosophies and financial constraints. Their criminology moves over time. Paul Rock (1996) showed how, at the level of a single establishment (for women, as it happens) this changing criminology helps determine the daily struggles, accomplishments and tragedies of prison life.

Although a disparate group (Crewe and Liebling, 2011), prison governors working in England and Wales exhibit some relatively common tendencies. When politicians have called for prisons to be explicitly punitive places, they have generated considerable disquiet among governors, most of whom have no wish to run such institutions and recognize the risks of politicians being rhetorically blasé:

> Bear in mind I've gone through ten months of troubled times because I'm trying to get the place decent and I've been driving home the decency message, 'right this is how I want you to behave and how you treat prisoners', and then [the Justice Minister] is telling us he wants prisons to be places where the regime is tough, well what does that mean? We've always been told that, you know, that punishment is the sentence and once you're inside ... The loss of liberty is your punishment.
>
> If I was a prison officer here I'd be sitting there thinking 'I can't wait for the next staff meeting because I'm going to tell the governor 'can he clarify what that means now?' I'd stick me hand up and say "Governor what does this mean 'prisons are places of punishment and the regime should be tough' and you're telling us to call them 'mister'? (Senior manager 41)

There is considerable frustration that 'prisoners are being constrained by leader writers of the *Daily Mail*' (senior manager 64) and deep cynicism about the system of party politics.

Yet the re-emergence within political discourse of ideas of '*less eligibility*' has generated less resistance among governors and other senior prison managers. Many support the view that prisons have become excessively generous in terms of material provision:

> I can sympathize with the 'Disgusted of Tunbridge Wells' letter which says, you know, 'why should these people be sitting in their cells playing PlayStations when my poor old granddad can't afford his electricity bill?[25] I really sympathize with that. (Senior manager 65)

> I'm absolutely clear, absolutely clear, that we've gone too far in terms of letting prisoners have too many things that are luxuries, and so in that way I'm not soft and I think that prison should be reasonably austere; I think it should be decent but reasonably austere. (Senior manager 37)

Most new generation prison governors define 'decency' (a term which still has organizational currency) in terms that are rather narrow: clean wings and 'respectful treatment', with respect comprising 'civility' rather than a deeper from of recognition of human dignity (Hulley et al., 2012). This version of decency is considerably thinner and more managerialist than some officially stated visions of its predecessor (see note 11). To some degree, decency has been embedded in systems – that is, in more regular access to facilities, in the provision of hours-out-of-cell and so on – but excessive faith has been placed in the capacity of targets and performance measures to achieve it. In assessing their establishments, many governors are too reliant on performance indicators such as time-out-of-cell and constructive activity, or cursory 'rounds' of their wings. Few governors elaborate to their staff what the interpersonal aspects of decency mean in practice, and many have little sense of the 'feel' of their establishment beyond the 'virtual prison' constituted by performance data. Some governors rarely leave the administrative corridors, and, when presented with non-performance data about their establishments – based on long-term qualitative research or well-validated quality of prison life data – some say they 'don't recognize the prison' these data describe.

Some governors are relishing the opportunity to 'deliver' in this environment. Many entered the Prison Service more because it offered interesting opportunities to manage than because of any wider social goal:

> I didn't come in to this job because I thought I would be doing a public service necessarily, so I don't know that that is why I do it, or why I would stay doing it.
>
> *Why do you do it, do you think?*
> Why do I do it? Because I do enjoy the challenge ... I like the challenge, because I think you can make a difference in the place that you're at. I do genuinely believe that you dictate the tone of your establishment, and so even if you're not stopping people from going out there and committing further crimes, if you're making sure they're safe while they're in here, that they're being educated if they can, they gain skills, that's no bad thing, is it? (Senior manager 84)

For the majority of governors, prison work is not 'labour of love type stuff' (senior manager 41). Most note that the skill-set required to run a prison differs very little from what would be needed to manage any large organization. Such views are consistent with Simon and Feeley's argument that, in the new penology: 'The problems of penality are no different than the problems of managing other types of large systems, whether they be transportation networks or military logistics' (1995: 172; see also Wacquant, 2009b). The task is essentially *managerial*, especially in increasingly large institutions. Prison governors in general focus more on the internal self-maintenance tasks of the prison (maintaining good order, or internal performance) than on any higher aspirations (see further Crewe and Liebling, 2011):

> I'm a mainstream prison governor and bringing order, control and security to the prison will be the legacy I'll leave. (Senior manager 26)

This is not quite the 'bare-bones managerialism' described in the USA (Wacquant 2010: 75). However, it suggests the same relatively apolitical culture, in which the focus is delivery, effectiveness and value for money. Most governors express little unease about privatization, evaluating it in terms of these goals:

> I'm not uncomfortable with it as a tax payer or as a member of society. As long as what is being delivered is appropriate, it shouldn't really matter too much whether it's public or it's in the private sector, it doesn't bother me too much. (Senior manager 1).

> If it is cheaper and does the job, what's the problem? If the taxpayer can get the same job done for less money, then great, does it matter who is providing it? (Senior manager 63).

Likewise, the language of governing is one of administration, business planning and systems management: 'investing' in staff and prisoners, and providing behavioural incentives to ensure compliance. It is insufficient, perhaps unnecessary or undesirable, to 'feel the offender experience' (senior manager 90). Indeed, many governors have little conception of prisoners as human beings, with complex needs and frustrations.[26] Instead, the vision of prisoners is as emotionally inert, disembodied beings, 'balls of actuarial risk' (Simon, 2011). 'Protecting the public', the dominant organizational motivation, requires little further vision of the prisoner. Although there is a strong and genuine commitment among practitioners to forms of social rehabilitation, there is limited support for prisoner voting rights and no lobby whatsoever for conjugal visits.[27] Compassion is limited in scope or depth, in part because of a neoliberal occupational 'criminology' emphasising choice, responsibility, and a just deserts notion of punishment:

> People are adults, and they have that choice [to offend or not]. So in that sense I am fairly hard-nosed I guess, but once they're in we have a duty of care for them. (Senior manager 71)

> *Do you feel sympathy and compassion for prisoners?*
> I feel some sympathy towards some people, not prisoners in general, and I don't feel compassion towards prisoners in general. I do with individuals, some individuals. (Senior manager 48)

> The vast majority have made the wrong choices along the way and that may be because they

> haven't had much choice, or because they haven't learnt to make those choices ... haven't learnt to assess risk, haven't learnt what is acceptable with everyone else. So I don't excuse the offending, I think one has to take personal responsibility. (Senior manager 65)

The internal critique of the governing context is less about the 'new austerity' than relentless operational demands. Even some governors who consider themselves unsentimental managerialists have begun to baulk at diminishing resources, increasing pressure to deliver and the reduction of complex work to endless audit. Told that they are being pushed 'to the absolute limits of what [is] possible' (senior manager 84), some argued that there is 'an absence of emotional intelligence in the organization': 'the lack of any kind of sensitivity or consideration is staggering' (senior manager 84). Many described a growing 'lack of trust' between governors and those above them:

> Questions are not being asked ... There are dangers in speaking out. There's loads of elephants sat in the room ... There's no warmth for others, it feels quite dismissive. Some of the scripts being played out in the organization are very unpleasant. What we are being told to do bears no relation to what the officer is experiencing ... it is all sound-bites and clichés. (Senior manager 64).

There is some sympathy among governors for the state of the officer, who under 'managerialism-minus' represents a workforce under threat. Governors who are not 'signed up' to the current agenda are drawing closer to those with whom they empathize.

Yet little of this dissatisfaction is being expressed openly. 'Romantic optimism' and humanitarian critique are rarely audible or visible, despite the existence within the Service of a number of governors – some in senior positions – who hold these views in private and have considerable appetite for discussions of values and morality in prison work (for a more detailed analysis of current governor 'types' see Crewe and Liebling [2011]). On the whole, new generation governors are highly compliant, with little appetite to take risks (and little room in any case to do so). Operational priorities are rarely questioned, in public at least. Most senior managers report the belief that 'if you speak up, you get a reputation for being difficult' (senior manager 40). Most have been socialized so successfully into a culture of managerial compliance that they would not consider challenging policy. Paradoxically, many of the most idealistic and liberal senior managers have left the public sector to work in private prisons, where they feel more able to speak out, innovate and apply their values.

The determination among most governors to achieve prescribed goals and to 'deliver', almost regardless of consequences, has become a cause for concern among some of their colleagues and line managers, who fear that, if told to do so, some would 'do anything, including locking prisoners up all day and poking them with sticks' (senior manager 12):

> Governors will think they're being successful if they manage to implement the core day, get the savings out, get the Unions to agree the profiles, not have too much prisoner kickback. They'll say 'there I've delivered it for you'. I don't think always we think [about] what it feels like to be told 'right you're going to be locked up on a Friday [evening] for the next thirty years'.
>
> *And you're saying modern Governors aren't worrying or don't have that on their conscience, they're thinking about delivering the goods?*
>
> Yeah. I think that's probably true of maybe all [my governors] at the moment. [Pause] I think it sounds a bit pejorative to say they don't care, but I don't think they care particularly. ... It's a bit like with suicides I think. ... We get quite dispassionate we sort of say 'yeah we have had a death in custody, it was very sad, we've done all the bits with the family, we've done all the other bits', and we move on. (Senior manager 75)

At its extremes, this culture of dispassionate compliance has led to some of the kinds of abuses that managerialism was meant to expunge. Operational management has overshadowed moral management. In the desire to receive positive audits, and in the name of 'performance', managers have corrupted figures and mistreated or neglected prisoners, albeit in ways that are different from the pre-managerial era. It is harder for governors to be lazy, brutal, or 'ineffective', because they are much more accountable. But there are new blind spots, and new problems of legitimacy for the organization.

THE CONTEMPORARY PRISONER EXPERIENCE

> 'As the penal system ballooned, state policy and funding decisions made prisons increasingly stark, depressing and punitive. Thousands of prisoners now serve long periods – sometimes decades – in austere, technologically sophisticated, super-maximum security housing units, which purposefully deprive inmates of sensory stimulation. Many literally go crazy. California's prisoners have few genuine opportunities to change their lives, as quality educational, vocational, chemical dependency treatment and counselling programmes are sparsely available (and those that do exist are always full, with very long wait lists). Because, for the most part, the penal facilities simply punish and incapacitate offenders, some critics refer to the state's prisons as human warehouses. Unlike their idealistic predecessors, prison officials in California today have little hope for "correcting" their charges ... Instead they obsessively focus on managing their enormous, gang-ridden, ethnically polarized, often violent, and packed institutions' (Page, 2011: 4–5).

Page's recent account of the state of Californian penality resonates with recent trends in England and Wales, although it reflects a particularly dystopian version. While the flawed liberal idealism of the past often failed to deliver decent standards or good outcomes for prisoners, its opposite – cynicism, distance and a climate of financial and moral austerity – poses serious dangers too. Prisoners in one recent study described the shock of being taken off programmes that were attracting negative media publicity, the difficulties of 'making progress', or finding meaning in bleak prison regimes, the increasing prospects of recall under stringent license conditions, and deteriorating relationships with probation officers and psychologists due to an overwhelming emphasis on 'risk' (Liebling et al., 2011; see also Crewe, 2009; Padfield, 2011). As we have noted elsewhere (Crewe, 2009; Crewe, 2011; Crewe and Liebling, 2011), most prisoners in England and Wales experience a 'deeper', 'tighter' and arguably less liberal form of imprisonment than their predecessors, *despite* unarguable improvements in levels of sanitation, food quality, access to exercise and association, and staff-prisoner relations. Prisoners complain much less than they once did about *conditions* or *treatment* (although chronic overcrowding is threatening improvements in these areas) and much more about the *administration of punishment*, the lack of empathy for their predicament and limited of opportunities for growth and development.

As individuals, prisoners are existentially less visible than they were 10 or 20 years ago – un-recognized and ignored in almost all of the ways that are essential for healthy human development. At the same time, as carriers of risk, they are *hyper*-visible to prison staff and subject to a debilitating regime of risk assessment and scrutiny. This regime is psychologically highly invasive, forcing prisoners to re-form their identities so as to meet the demands of the system, and making it virtually impossible to escape the reach of penal power (Crewe, 2009, 2011). Prisoners fear 'soft power' – that is, the cold hand of risk assessment – as much as its traditional, harder forms. It individualizes prisoners, while simultaneously pushing them to forge new identities and social groups based around faith and race – new sources of conflict among prisoners as well as between prisoners and staff. In high-security prisons especially, fears about new complexities of faith and ethnicity, and about conditioning, security threats, and violence, mean that staff have withdrawn somewhat from prisoners. Relationships with prisoners risk becoming superficial, emotionally barren and defined by the absence of trust (Liebling et al., 2011). Some governors describe with dismay the way that the 'relational' model of staff-prisoner relationships was jettisoned, or at least de-prioritized, after the high-profile prison escapes of the 1990s:[28]

> The escapes happened and everything was security and ... I didn't fit in again. I was much more into [the idea that] if you like me as a person you won't hit me. ... ... a relationship model: 'I know what makes these guys tick'. (Senior manager 59)

Prison staff are also forging less committed relationships to each other, and to their institutions. New generation prison staff are less optimistic about rehabilitation, somewhat more punitive, and less inclined to commit to prison work and relationships in the long term (Crewe et al., 2011). This can be dangerous, if officers feel they can no longer take the fast appearance of their colleagues at times of trouble for granted (Liebling et al., 2011). It is the unintended converse of the problem of the 1980s, where staff were bonded so tightly to each other that managers could be resisted and prisoners intimidated. It is particularly characteristic of private sector prisons, where deliberately high levels of staff turnover, poorer terms and conditions, and weaker unions have created a more flexible and transient workforce. As the private sector model is applied increasingly to the public sector, the public sector's hidden strength of staff loyalty and professionalism may be lost.

There is evidence of dissatisfaction among members of the POA (or the need for a change of role) as individual officers see 'the writing on the wall', realize that 'modernization' and changes to their working conditions are imminent, and breakaway unions are formed (and, in many privately managed establishments, gain recognition). The modern prison service employee, who like prisoners is kept somewhat anxious, needs to pursue rational self-interest, to survive the demands of a powerful and demanding economy. Unlike in Page's account, there is no necessary relationship between high levels of incarceration, a punitive turn and the ascent of a union. The prison officer's union has been a casualty of modernization and managerialism in England and Wales – a development some would see as its main triumph, but others would see as a tragic reflection of the failure of the union to reform itself.

CONCLUSION

This chapter seeks to insert prison managers into the field of prison sociology, by describing their experience in England and Wales and outlining some of the trends and transformations taking place in their professional values and orientations over recent decades. It reflects the beginning of such an exercise, and as such, we are hopeful that it opens up the field to further inquiry rather than constituting a fixed account.

We have tried to differentiate between the economic and moral dimensions of managerialism, a distinction which deserves greater consideration in relation to the recent management of prisons in England and Wales. Our argument is that it is a mistake to present managerialism as inherently lacking in values; its ethicality is an empirical issue. Weber makes a similar point about bureaucracy – it makes no sense to denounce it without knowing more about its conduct and direction. In its early years in England and Wales, managerialism was largely values-driven and was welcomed by values-driven managers. Many of the reforms made to public sector prisons were about 'putting prisoners back centre-stage' (senior manager 96), in a Service which had been stymied by staffing issues and shamed by the manner in which it held many prisoners. While some critics of managerialism express concern that it seeks to eliminate 'the variable human' and suppress the idiosyncratic values of practitioners (Cheliotis, 2006), our account from within makes such ambitions more understandable. A certain amount of bureaucratic rationalization might be helpful, especially if managers are weak or their charisma is insufficient to guarantee moral practice (or if their prisons are simply too large). At the same time, we are concerned about the recent phase of 'managerialism minus', which appears more emotionally barren, more morally denuded, and dominated by a logic of economic rationalism.

Sim (2009) argues that penal politics since the 1970s has demonstrated considerable continuity, despite various shifts in policy and practice. We concur that this is true at some level – not least, the ongoing love affair with imprisonment itself – and that there is a tendency for some scholars to overstate the disruptive nature of changes in punishment and penality. At another level, though, what look like relatively minor changes in penal aims and sensibilities percolate down through prison institutions and matter a great deal to those 'on the ground' (Liebling with Arnold, 2004). They can be detected quite quickly in the daily tone and experience of prison life, for prisoners and frontline staff. Prison governors, who have been neglected in prison scholarship, mediate the changing politics of law and order. Their profile, orientation and approach to staff and prisoners both illustrate and shape the contours of prison life. Our understanding of prison life is deepened by an appreciation of who they are and what it is that they do.

NOTES

1 Useful accounts can be found in DiIulio (1987), Barak-Glantz (1981) and Useem and Reisig (1999) in the USA; and Adler and Longhurst (1994), Vagg (1994), Bryans and Wilson (2000), Coyle (2002), McEvoy (2001) in the UK; on what effective senior management teams look like, see also Gadd (in progress).

2 Riveland (1999) argues that the *content* and complexity of prison work has also changed, as prison size has increased and populations have become less 'white' and more drug dependent. The job has become more politicized, and technological.

3 In England and Wales, 'local' prisons are those that hold prisoners sent from the courts on remand, those given short sentences, and prisoners on longer sentences awaiting allocation.

4 One of the present authors can recall her first research post in a prison in 1986, when a principal officer came into her office/cell on a landing to introduce himself: 'I just thought I'd tell you that I don't approve of women working in this prison', he said, politely, and left.

5 In 1976 there were 34 incidents of industrial action by POA branches. In 1977 there were 42 and in 1978 there were 119 (Stern, 1987: 63).

6 A scholarly history of the POA in England and Wales has yet to be written (see Page, [2011] on the Californian Correctional Peace Officers Association [CCPOA] ; also Jacobs [1977] and Jacobs and Crotty [1978] on the emergence of prison officer unionization in the USA). Partial accounts are also available in Rock (1996), Lewis (1997) and Evans, with Cohen (2009).

7 The POA plays an important role in providing 'insurance' for its members, in championing health and safety matters, and in negotiating for pay and conditions. The tendency for senior managers to come and go from their posts means that a residual knowledge and understanding of managing any particular establishment on a day-to-day basis is found in the prison officer group and its union. Some have argued that lack of management competence in handling and shaping the POA, and ensuring better levels of cooperation, has contributed to the ongoing difficulties. There has been for many decades, however, considerable evidence of POA 'intransigence' at particular establishments and nationally.

8 By 'new generations', we mean those currently governing or otherwise managing prisons, many of whom are in their early 40s, have done management (rather than social science) degrees or 'worked their way up through the ranks', and who are 'doing well' in the contemporary prison management world. Others have either left, moving on to other professions, retiring early, or joining the private sector, express private concern about current developments, or find ways of doing the 'old penology' in new ways.

9 Oral history in biographical career interviews is not 'history' but reflects much that is important about both past and present experience, and fills in some of the gaps left by official reports of the period.

10 All of the senior managers approached agreed to be interviewed, and most took place in Cambridge, over at least one (but sometimes several) long and uninterrupted session, with both authors present. The age range was 32–70, a small number were retired, and some had moved from the public to the private sector (and one or two, back again). 18 were women. We used a snowball sampling technique, exploiting existing contacts and research relationships. Many were governing governors or private prison directors, but some were area managers, NOMS board members, or policymakers. We have no reason to believe that our sample were selective or especially biased in favour of a particular account of the period. This chapter represents one of our first, early attempts to analyse this material.

11 That is, they were not particularly visible in their prisons. In the 1960s and 1970s, some governors did not even carry keys to their establishment. 'Prisons were anarchic – governors were in charge but not in control' (senior manager 96).

12 PO – principal officer; SO – senior officer. Until recently, senior managers sat above officers in the prison management chain, and principal officers above senior officers.

13 The escape of George Blake from HMP Wormwood Scrubs in 1966 led to significant changes in the security practices and organization of the Prison Service. Blake was serving the longest sentence ever imposed by a British court – 42 years – as a result of his activities spying for the Soviet Union.

14 There is also a built in rift between prison officers – recruited with no formal education, often out of military and other uniformed occupations – and prison governors – from 1968, at least, university educated, direct entrants, with more 'liberal' aspirations for the treatment of prisoners, and according to most staff, 'out of touch with reality'. A form of 'class war' between working class prison officers and 'gentleman governors' has been evident in the Prison Service throughout its history. Governors see staff as obstructing reform and modernization, resisting the humane and decent treatment of prisoners (despite occasional statements to the contrary), and acting in their own self-interest against management directives. Officers, on the other hand, see Governors undermining their safety, pay and conditions, taking their effective management of challenging prisoners for granted, and requiring them to 'fill in the gaps' between regimes designed on paper, and the real world of prison regimes in operation.

15 So, for example, some open Borstals were operated on a public school ethos, with highly motivated staff, highly constructive regimes, and visionary governors. Other (more often, closed borstals including Portland and Rochester) were self-consciously harsh, and aimed at more challenging and difficult offenders (see Hood, 1965; Bottoms and McClintock, 1973).

16 The ending of prison officer overtime, the unification of uniformed and non-uniformed grades, clearer line management, and enhanced pay; thus leading to the abolition of the role of the highest managerial uniformed role, the chief officer.

17 So-called because of the decisions (Advisory Council on the Penal System, 1968) to 'disperse' the highest-security prisoners among prisoners categorized at lower security levels rather than concentrate them within a single institution.

18 There are other less benign attractions too: a sense of control, the simplicity of clear systems, and the apparent identification of 'levers' as management tools. We shall say more about the contemporary senior management scene at the end of the chapter.

19 Martin Narey was at this time the Chief Executive of the Prison Service. This quotation is from his speech to Governing Governors at their annual conference.

20 Chris Train, Joe Pilling, Derek Lewis, Richard Tilt, Martin Narey and Phil Wheatley. Chris Train was instrumental in introducing Fresh Start, the first 'management objectives' in the Prison Service, and is regarded as a significant shaper of new prison management trends by some of our interviewees. He was the longest serving director general (1983–1991).

21 For example, a 'Back to basics' lecture (Pilling, 1992); the Lincoln conferences and proceedings (1989–93); 'Caring for the Suicidal' (Prison Service, 1994), 'Doing or Using Time' (HMCIP, 1993), the newly launched Statement of Purpose, declaring that 'looking after prisoners with humanity' was a key aim (1988), and so on. These developments were, as Rock (1995) describes in policymaking more generally, somewhat contested. There was at the time a powerful alliance between 'pressure groups', academics and liberal humanitarian prison governors, who were numerous, and publicly visible. We refer to them as 'value intellectuals' or 'thinker-speakers' in our typology (see Crewe and Liebling, 2011).

22 MOJ – Ministry of Justice.

23 http://www.hmprisonservice.gov.uk/news/index.asp?id=8569,22,6,22,0,0.

24 Wacquant (2009a) notes a similar shift in the USA, where there has been a marked move away from seeing the prison as a complex 'people changing' organization.

25 The proverbial phrase for a letter of complaint sent to a newspaper, written in a tone of conservative moral outrage.

26 In contrast, our older interviewees described a much closer relationship with their clients: one explained that he spent a week in the inner-city area from which most of his Borstal boys came, in order to understand them better; another worked in probation one day every week in order to develop a more rounded sense of his prisoners.

27 This stands in contrast to the ethos in some other countries, for example, in Nordic nations, where governors are more often oriented to liberal-humanitarian or human rights perspectives, and feel that it is their professional duty to be vocal – rather than mute – about matters of penal policy.

28 These included the escape of six prisoners from the Special Secure Unit of Whitemoor high-security prison in 1994, and of three prisoners from another high-security prison, HMP Parkhurst, only a few months later.

REFERENCES

Adams, K. (1992) 'Adjusting to prison life', *Crime and Justice*, 16: 275–359.

Adler, M. and Longhurst, B. (1994) *Discourse, Power and Justice: Towards a New Sociology of Imprisonment.* London: Routledge.

Advisory Council on the Penal System (1968) *The Regime For Long-Term Prisoners In Conditions Of Maximum Security* (Radzinowicz Report). London: HMSO.

Aly, G. and Heim, S. (2002) *Architects of Annihilation: Auschwitz and the Logic of Destruction.* London: Weidenfeld & Nicolson.

Barak-Glantz, I.L. (1981) 'Toward a conceptual schema of prison management styles', *The Prison Journal,* 61 (2): 42–60.

Bauman, Z. (1990) *Thinking Sociologically.* Oxford: Basil Blackwell.

Bottoms, A. (1995) 'The philosophy and politics of punishment and sentencing', in C. Clarkson and R. Morgan (eds), *The Politics of Sentencing Reform.* Oxford: Clarendon Press. pp. 17–49.

Bottoms, A.E. and McClintock, F.H. (1973) *Criminals Coming of Age: A Study of Institutional Adaptation in the Treatment of Adolescent Offenders.* London: Heinemann.

Bryans, S. and Wilson, D. (2000) *The Prison Governor: Theory and Practice,* 2nd edn. HMP Grendon: Prison Service Journal.

Carlen, P. (2002) 'Governing the governors', *Criminology and Criminal Justice,* 2 (1): 27–49.

Cheliotis, L. (2006) 'Penal managerialism from within: Implications for theory and research', *International Journal of Law and Psychiatry,* 29: 397–404.

Clemmer, D. (1940) *The Prison Community.* New York: Holt, Rinehart and Winston.

Coyle, A. (2002) *A Human Rights Approach to Prison Management: A Handbook for Prison Staff.* London: International Centre for Prison Studies.

Crawley, E. (2004) *Doing Prison Work: The Public and Private Lives of Prison Officers.* Cullompton: Willan.

Crewe, B. (2009) *The Prisoner Society.* Oxford: Clarendon.

Crewe, B. (2011) 'Soft power in prison: Implications for staff-prisoner relationships, liberty and legitimacy', *European Journal of Criminology,* 8: 455–468.

Crewe, B. and Liebling, A. (2011) 'Are liberal humanitarian penal values and practices exceptional?', in T. Ugelvik and J. Dullum (eds), *Nordic Prison Practice and Policy – Exceptional or Not? Exploring Penal Exceptionalism in the Nordic Context.* Cullompton: Willan, pp. 175–198.

Crewe, B. and Liebling, A. (2012) 'Insider views of private sector competition', in V. Helyar-Cardwell (eds.), *Delivering Justice: The role of the public, private and voluntary sectors in the prison system.* Criminal Justice Alliance publications.

Crewe, B., Liebling, A. and Hulley, S. (2011) 'Staff culture, use of authority and prisoner quality of life in public and private sector prisons', *Australia and New Zealand Journal of Criminology,* 44(1): 94–115.

Crook, F. (2009) 'Work in prisons', *Prison Service Journal,* 182: 43–47.

DiIulio, J. (1987) Governing Prisons: *A Comparative Study of Correctional Management.* New York: Free Press.

Evans, D. with Cohen, S. (2009) *The Everlasting Staircase.* London: Prison Officer's Association.

Feeley, M.M. and Simon, J. (1992) 'The new penology: notes on the emerging strategy of corrections and its implications', *Criminology,* 30 (4): 449–74.

Fitzgerald, M. (1977) *Prisoners in Revolt.* London: Penguin.

Fitzgerald, M. and Sim, G. (1979) *British Prisons.* Oxford: Blackwell.

Garland, D. (1990) *Punishment and Modern Society.* Oxford: Clarendon Press.

Garland, D (2003) 'Penal modernism and postmodernism', in T.G Blomberg and S. Cohen (eds), *Punishment and Social Control.* New York: Walter de Gruyter. pp. 45–74.

Giddens, A. (ed.) (2001) *The Global Third Way Debate.* Cambridge: Polity.

Goffman, E. (1961) *Asylums: Essays on the Social Situation of Mental Patients and Other Inmates.* Harmondsworth: Penguin.

Harding, R. (1997) *Private Prisons and Public Accountability.* Buckingham: Open University Press.

HM Chief Inspector of Prisons (HMCIP) (1993) *Doing Time or Using Time: Report of a Review by Her Majesty's Chief Inspector of Prisons for England and Wales of Regimes in Prison Service Establishments in England and Wales.* London: HMSO.

HM Chief Inspector of Prisons (HMCIP) (2000) *Unjust Deserts: A Thematic Review of the Treatment and Conditions for Unsentenced Prisoners in England and Wales.* London: The Stationery Office.

Hoggett, P. (1991) 'A new management in the public sector?', *Policy & Politics,* 19 (4): 243–56.

Hood, R. (1965) *Borstal Re-assessed.* London: Heinemann.

Home Affairs Committee (1987) Fourth Report from the Home Affairs Committee, Contract Provision of Prisons, 6 May 1987.

The Home Office (1991) *Custody, Care and Justice: The Way Ahead for the Prison Service in England and Wales*. London: HMSO

Hornqvist, M. (2010) *Risk, Power and the State: After Foucault*. Oxford: Routledge.

Hulley, S., Liebling, A. and Crewe, B. (2012) 'Respect in prisons: prisoners' experiences of respect', *Criminology and Criminal Justice*, 12 (1): 3–23.

Jacobs, J.B. (1977) *Stateville*. Chicago: University of Chicago Press.

Jacobs, J. and Crotty, N.M. (1978) *Guard Unions and the Future of the Prisons*. New York: Ithaca Regional Office.

James, A.K., Bottomley, K., Liebling, A. and Clare, E. (1997) *Privatizing Prisons: Rhetoric and Reality*. London: SAGE Publications.

Jones, T. and Newburn, T. (2005) 'Comparative criminal justice policy-making in the US and the UK: the case of private prisons', *British Journal of Criminology*, 45: 58–80.

King, R. and McDermott, K. (1989) 'British prisons 1970–1987: the ever-deepening crisis', *British Journal of Criminology*, 29 (2): 107–28.

Laming, Lord (2000) *Modernising the Management of the Prison Service*. London: Home Office.

Lewis, D. (1997) *Hidden Agendas: Politics, Law and Disorder*. London: Hamish Hamilton.

Liebling, A. (1992) *Suicides in Prison*. London: Routledge Press.

Liebling, A. (2010) '"Governmentality" and governing corrections: do senior managers resist?', in L.K. Cheliotis (ed.), *Roots, Rites and Sites of Resistance: The Banality of Good*. Basingstoke: Pallgrave Macmillan. pp. 220–45.

Liebling, A. (2011) 'Perrie lecture: the cost to prison legitimacy of cuts', *Prison Service Journal*, 198: 3–11.

Liebling, A. and Price, D. (2001) *The Prison Officer*. Winchester: Waterside Press.

Liebling, A. with Arnold, H. (2004) *Prisons and Their Moral Performance: A Study of Values, Quality, and Prison Life*. Oxford: Clarendon Press.

Liebling, A., Arnold, H. and Straub, C. (2011) *Staff-Prisoner Relationships at HMP Whitemoor: Twelve Years On*. London: Home Office.

Liebling, A., Tait, S., Stiles, A. and Harvey, J. (2005) 'An evaluation of the safer locals programme'. Report submitted to the Home Office.

Lincoln Conferences (1989) 'The Meaning of Imprisonment', Lincoln: Bishop of Lincoln's Office.

Lincoln Conferences (1991) 'Respect in Prison', Lincoln: Bishop of Lincoln's Office.

Lincoln Conferences (1993) 'Relationships in Prison', Lincoln: Bishop of Lincoln's Office.

Loesel, F. (2012) 'What works in correctional treatment and rehabilitation for young adults?', in F. Loesel, A. Bottoms and D. Farrington (eds), *Young Adult Offenders: Lost in Transition?* Cullompton: Willan.

Marshall, S. (1997) 'Control in category-c prisons', *Research Findings*, 54, Home Office, HMSO.

McEvoy, K. (2001) *Paramilitary Imprisonment in Northern Ireland*. Oxford: Clarendon Press.

Ministry of Justice (2010) *Breaking the Cycle: Effective Punishment, Rehabilitation and Sentencing of Offenders*. London: HMSO

Narey, M. (2001) 'Speech to the prison service conference 2001', paper given at Nottingham, February 2001.

Nellis, M. (2001) 'Community penalities in historical perspective', in A.E. Bottoms, L. Gelsthorpe, and S. Rex (eds), *Community Penalities: Change and Challenges*. Cullompton: Willan. pp. 16–40.

Padfield, N. (2011) 'Understanding recall', unpublished research report, University of Cambridge.

Page, J. (2011) *The Toughest Beat*. Oxford: Oxford University Press.

Pilling, J. (1992) *Back to Basics: Relationships in the Prison Service*. Eve Saville Memorial Lecture. London: HM Prison Service.

Pollitt, C. (1991) 'A public management for all seasons?', *Public Administration*, 69 (1): 3–19.

Pollitt, C. (1995) *Managerialism and the Public Services: Cuts or Cultural Change in the 1990s?* Oxford: Blackwell.

Pollitt, C. and G. Bouckaert (2000) *Public Management Reform: An International Comparison*. Oxford: Oxford University Press.

Prison Service (1994) Caring for the Suicidal: Training Manual London: Prison Service

Pusey, M. (1991) *Economic Rationalism in Canberra: A Nation-building State Changes its Mind*. Cambridge: Cambridge University Press.

Ramsbotham, D. (2003) *Prisongate: The Shocking State of Britain's Prisons and the Need for Visionary Change*. London: Simon & Schuster.

Riveland, C. (1999) 'Prison management trends 1975–2025', in M. Tonry and J. Petersilia (eds), *Prisons*. Chicagos: The University of Chicago Press. pp. 163–204.

Rock, P. (1995) 'The opening stages of criminal justice policymaking', *British Journal of Criminology*, 35(1): 1–16.

Rock, P.E. (1996) *Reconstructing a Women's Prison: The Holloway Redevelopment Project*. Oxford: Clarendon Press.

Rusche, G. and Kirchheimer, O. (1939 [2008]) *Punishment and Social Structure.* New York: Russell & Russell.

Scraton, P., Sim, J. and Skidmore, P. (1991) *Prisons under Protest. Crime, Justice and Social Policy Series.* Milton Keynes: Open University Press.

Sennett, Richard (2006) *The Culture of the New Capitalism (Castle Lectures in Ethics, Politics, & Economics).* New Haven, CT: Yale University Press.

Shaw, S. (2010) *Fifty Year Stretch: Prisons and Imprisonment 1980–2030.* Hook: Waterside Press.

Sim, J. (1987) 'Working for the clampdown: prisons and politics in England and Wales', in P. Scraton (ed.), *Law, Order and the Authoritarian State.* Maidenhead: Open University Press. pp. 190–211.

Sim, J. (1994) 'Reforming the penal wasteland: a critical reading of the Woolf report', in E. Player and M. Jenkins (eds), *Prisons After Woolf.* London: Routledge. pp. 31–45.

Sim, J. (2009) *Punishment and Prisons: Power and the Carceral State.* London: SAGE Publications.

Simon, J. (1988) 'The ideological effects of actuarial practices', *Law and Society Review,* 22 (4): 771–800.

Simon, J. (1993) *Poor Discipline: Parole and the Social Control of the Underclass, 1890–1990.* Chicago: University of Chicago Press.

Simon, J. (2007) *Governing through Crime: How the War on Crime Transformed American Democracy and Created a Culture of Fear.* Oxford: Oxford University Press.

Simon, J. (2011) 'The view from Castle Rock', paper presented at Punishment and Society conference, Edinburgh, May 2011.

Simon, J. and Feeley, M. (1995) 'True crime: the new penology and public discourse on crime', in T.G. Blomberg and S. Cohen (eds), *Punishment and Social Control.* New York: Aldine de Gruyter. pp. 147–80.

Sparks, R. (1994) 'Can prisons be legitimate?', in R.D. King and M. McGuire (eds), *Prisons in Context.* Oxford: Clarendon Press. pp. 14–28.

Sparks, R., Bottoms A.E. and Hay, W. (1996) *Prisons and the problem of Order.* Oxford: Oxford University Press.

Spurr, M. (2011) 'Perrie Lecture: Reducing costs and maintaining values', Conference paper, Perrie Lectures, Newbold Revel, June 2011

Stern, V (1987) *Bricks of Shame: Britain's Prisons.* London: Penguin.

Sykes, G. (1958) *The Society of Captives: A Study of a Maximum-Security Prison.* Princeton, NJ: Princeton University Press.

Toch, H. (1978) 'Is a 'correction officer', by any other name, a 'screw'?', *Criminal Justice Review,* 3: 19–36.

Useem, B. and Reisig, M.D. (1999) 'Collective action in prisons: protests, disturbances and riots', *Criminology,* 37 (4): 735–59.

Vagg, J. (1994) *Prison Systems: A Comparative Study of Accountability in England, France, Germany and the Netherlands.* Oxford: Clarendon Press.

Wacquant, L. (2009a) *Prisons of Poverty.* Minnesota, MN: University of Minnesota Press.

Wacquant, L. (2009b) *Punishing the Poor: The Neoliberal Government of Social Insecurity.* Durham, NC: Duke University Press.

Wacquant, L. (2010) 'Class, race & hyperincarceration in revanchist America', *Deadelus,* 139 (3):74–90.

Windlesham, D. (1993) *Responses to Crime Volume 2: Penal Policy in the Making.* Oxford: Clarendon Press.

Van Zyl Smit, D. and Snacken, S. (2009) *Principles of European Prison Law and Policy: Penology and Human Rights.* Oxford: Oxford University Press.

Zimbardo, Philip (2007) *Lucifer Effect: How Good People Turn Evil.* London: Random House Group; Rider and Co.

14

Capital Punishment in the USA: Prospects and Possibilities

Austin Sarat

In April 2005, then Massachusetts Governor Mitt Romney was gearing up for an effort to secure the Republican nomination for President of the USA. A Republican from Massachusetts with a progressive record on social issues he was looking for ways to reassure conservatives that he really was one of them. Thus it should not have been a surprise when he introduced a bill to reinstate the death penalty in this bluest of blue states (Lewis, 2005). As *The New York Times* put it at the time, 'Mr. Romney, who is widely believed to have national political ambitions, may intend his death penalty bill for a different audience as well: conservatives outside his state who are pivotal in Republican Party politics' (Belluck, 2005).

That bill, which would have reinstated the death penalty in a state that abolished it in 1984, restricted capital punishment to a very limited number of crimes, namely murders that involve terrorism, prolonged torture, multiple killings, or the killing of police officers, judges, witnesses or others involved in the criminal justice system. Defendants who had previously been convicted of first-degree murder or were serving life sentences without parole would also have been eligible for the death penalty under the Romney bill (Belluck, 2005).

Moreover the bill, which Romney called 'a model for the nation' and the 'gold standard' for capital punishment legislation, included several provisions that had never been tried in any other state (Belluck, 2005). The bill required that there be 'conclusive scientific evidence', such as DNA or fingerprints, to link a defendant to a crime (Jasanoff, 2006). And it would have allowed a death penalty to be imposed only if a sentencing jury found that there was 'no doubt' about a defendant's guilt, a standard that is even stricter than 'beyond a reasonable doubt' (Belluck, 2005).

Romney's bill also included a requirement that defendants get at least two and possibly three lawyers, that scientific evidence be examined by a review board, that every death sentence be reviewed by the state's highest court, and that a special panel be set up to handle complaints (Belluck, 2005).

The narrowness and caution of Romney's bill, a bill that nonetheless was easily defeated in the Massachusetts legislature (*New York Times*, 2005), provides one important sign that the tide has turned in America's conversation about capital punishment. The USA, long a bastion of attachment to state killing (Steiker, 2005), seems to have entered a period of national reconsideration of capital punishment, a period in which the prospects for abolition are very much on the upswing (Ogletree and Sarat, 2010). What is at stake in this national reconsideration is whether the USA will remain an outlier or join the long established trend of abolition in European nations and other constitutional democracies (Sarat and Martschukat, 2011).

As is well known, there is hardly any issue where Europe and the USA seem as far apart as they are on the death penalty. Whereas most American states authorize capital punishment, since the 1980s Europe has emerged as a bastion of abolitionism and its worldwide advance, with the European Union having made abolition a strict requirement for membership.

Yet, the divide between Europe and America is more complex than it seems (Sarat and Martschukat, 2011). First, while most American states authorize capital punishment, few use it on a regular basis. For at least the past 10 years, there have been no executions at all in 25 of the retentionist jurisdictions. Moreover, lately the perception and politics of the death penalty in the USA have been changing. This change has been driven in part by a large number of exonerations from death row. Americans are increasingly aware of judicial errors and wrongful convictions. This along with concerns about the high cost of capital prosecutions has changed the climate surrounding capital punishment in the USA. In Europe, the death penalty is not considered primarily to be an issue of the criminal justice system and its reliability, and but instead is seen an issue of human rights.

For several decades, the European position on capital punishment moved in the opposite direction from the American position, with the death penalty a significant influence in shaping a European identity (Sarat and Martschukat, 2011). In the press and to the public, European opposition to capital punishment is often presented as an offspring of the European Enlightenment and secularization since the 18th century, whereas American adherence to the death penalty is described as a vestige of a centuries old frontier mentality.

This version of a deeply rooted European-American dichotomy is overly simplistic because the reforms triggered by the Enlightenment initiated a reduction of the number of capital felonies and a 'modernization' of execution procedures. In the USA cultures and systems of punishment were and remain manifold and diverse. Often northern and mid-western states were pioneers in the transatlantic criminal justice reform movement, whereas southern states were most ardently retentionist. Until the post-Second World War period, Europe was not the abolitionist continent it is today. Indeed neither the Nazi regime nor the horrors of the Holocaust and the Second World War changed the dominant public attitude of many European countries that taking a life in the name of the state was acceptable and necessary in particular cases. Significantly, in the years immediately after the war, in addition to Finland only West Germany, Italy and Austria – former fascist states and Second World War aggressors – abandoned the death penalty. When the parliamentary assembly was set up in West Germany in 1948–9 to write a new democratic constitution, it finally abolished the death penalty. But, many members of the German parliament were not primarily motivated by humanistic reasons. For them, the first priority was to protect from the death penalty war criminals or those who had been loyal to the regime to the very end (Sarat and Martschukat, 2011).

The Council of Europe and the European Convention on Human Rights were established in 1949 and 1950 with the mission of defending humanity, yet their general commitment to the right to life explicitly excluded lawful death sentences. This ambivalent position on capital punishment was reflected in the policies of several influential European countries. Executions in the UK continued until 1964. The death penalty was struck down the following year, and abolition was made permanent in 1969. In Spain the era of the death penalty lasted until three years after the end of the Franco regime in 1975, and France continued to carry out executions until 1977. It did not formally abolish capital punishment until 1981.

Thus the much ballyhooed European position with regard to the death penalty is a relatively recent development. A milestone was the March 1985 enactment of Protocol No. 6 to the European Convention on Human Rights. It was the first international treaty to call for the abolition of the death penalty, and since 1994, adoption of the protocol has been a requirement for acceptance of new members to the Council of Europe. Since 1999 the same has been true for the European Union, which has made abolition of the death penalty obligatory for members and declared a worldwide execution moratorium one of the major pillars of its human rights policy. Thus it was not before the late 20th century that European penal policy was guided by the 'firm conviction that capital punishment ... has no place in civilized, democratic societies governed by the rule of law,' as the Council of Europe's Commissioner of Human Rights, Thomas Hammarberg, stated in 2007 (see Sarat and Martschukat, 2011).

Coinciding with the period from the mid-1960s, when the UK abolished capital punishment, to the early 1980s, when France followed the British example, the USA itself had a *de facto* moratorium, a moratorium which lasted from June 1967 to January 1977. Yet, whereas the death penalty was found constitutional by the Supreme Court in 1976, returned in a constantly increasing number of US states afterwards, and reached its heyday in the 1990s, in the very same decade European abolitionism gained momentum. The dynamics of regional and political integration spurred abolition in Eastern and South Eastern Europe.

Nonetheless, the European–American divide on the death penalty is more complex than it has often been thought to be, and the constellations of forces on both sides of the Atlantic are more ambivalent than they appear at first sight to be. Europe's firm abolitionism has a short history, has often been driven by tangible political and economic interests, and has no steadfast support among populations in several European countries. At the same time, the position of the death penalty in America is weakening, criticism is growing, and its popular support is still strong, but shrinking.

To get a sense of the prospects for, and possibilities of, abolition in the USA, we might move from the Romney bill in Massachusetts, to Trenton, New Jersey where on 18 December 2007, New Jersey Governor Jon Corzine signed a bill making his state the first in a generation to abolish capital punishment (Peters, 2007; Henry, 2008).

> 'Today,' Corzine said, 'New Jersey evolves. This is a day of progress for us and for the millions of people across our nation and around the globe who reject the death penalty as a moral or practical response to the grievous, even heinous, crime of murder. I have been moved by the passionate views on both sides of this issue, and I firmly believe that replacing the death penalty with life in prison without parole best captures our State's highest values and reflects our best efforts to search for true justice.'
>
> 'There were many reasons to ban the death penalty in New Jersey,' Corzine continued, 'It is difficult, if not impossible, to devise a humane technique of execution that is not cruel and unusual, and to develop a foolproof system that precludes the possibility of executing the innocent. New Jersey spent more than a quarter of a billion dollars to maintain its capital punishment system since 1982, even though it had not carried out a single execution for more than four decades, demonstrating little collective will or appetite to enforce this law. But for me, the question was more fundamental. State-endorsed violence begets violence and undermines our commitment to the sanctity of life. We in New Jersey are proud to be the first state to prohibit the death penalty since it was permitted by the U.S. Supreme Court in 1976, and we are proud to serve as leaders on this profound issue of conscience.' (Peters, 2007)

Abolition of capital punishment in New Jersey came despite the pleas of some high-profile victims, including Richard and Maureen Kanka, whose 7-year-old daughter, Megan, was killed by a repeat sex offender, Jesse K. Timmendequas, who was at the time Corzine signed the abolition bill on New Jersey's death row. Megan Kanka's 1994 killing gave rise to 'Megan's Law', requiring public notification when a convicted sex offender moves into a neighborhood. Moreover, at the time Corzine signed the bill the eight prisoners languishing on New Jersey's death row were straight from the headlines of some of the state's most sensational crimes (Johnston, 2009). And, at the time of abolition, New Jersey voters were opposed to ending the death penalty by a margin of 53 to 39 percent (Scherzer, 2009).

Another stop in this brief tour of the recent history of capital punishment, takes us to Sante Fe, New Mexico, 18 March 2009. There, 18 months after New Jersey abolished its death penalty, Governor Bill Richardson signed a bill abolishing that state's death penalty (CNN.com/crime, 2009b). Richardson, who formerly supported capital punishment, said replacing execution with life in prison without the possibility of parole was 'the most difficult decision of his political life'. However, noting that 130 death-row prisoners have been exonerated in the last decade, four of them in New Mexico, Richardson observed,

> Throughout my adult life, I have been a firm believer in the death penalty as a just punishment – in very rare instances, and only for the most heinous crimes. I still believe that. However, the issue became more real to me because I knew the day would come when one of two things might happen: I would either have to take action on legislation to repeal the death penalty, or more daunting, I might have to sign someone's death warrant.
>
> Regardless of my personal opinion about the death penalty, I do not have confidence in the criminal justice system as it currently operates to be the final arbiter when it comes to who lives and who dies for their crime. Faced with the reality that our system for imposing the death penalty can never be perfect, my conscience, Richardson said, compels me to replace the death penalty with a solution that keeps society safe. (New Mexico Governor Repeals Death Penalty in State, 2009)

In March of 2011, Illinois joined New Jersey, New Mexico in abolishing its death penalty. In explaining his decision to sign the legislation ending capital punishment, Illinois Governor Pat Quinn, a Democrat who had long been a penalty supporter, explained, 'If the system can't be guaranteed, 100-percent error-free, then we shouldn't have the system. It cannot stand.'

Massachusetts, New Jersey, New Mexico, Illinois and Connecticut which abolished its death penalty in 2012 hardly a tsunami of abolitionist activity. While no one can say with any confidence – 'As New Jersey goes so goes America', what happened there, in Massachusetts, New Mexico, Illinois and Connecticut would have seemed also unimaginable two decades ago when 80 percent of the American public supported the death penalty and no American politician wanted to risk being labeled soft on crime for expressing opposition to the death penalty.

A key moment in that era came during the 1988 Presidential campaign of Michael Dukakis when, at the start of his second debate with then Vice President Bush, then CNN anchor Bernard Shaw asked:

> SHAW: Governor, if Kitty Dukakis were raped and murdered, would you favor an irrevocable death penalty for the killer?
>
> DUKAKIS: No, I don't, Bernard. And I think you know that I've opposed the death penalty during all of my life. I don't see any evidence that it's a deterrent, and I think there are better and more effective ways to deal with violent crime. We've done so in my own state. And it's one of the reasons why we have had the biggest drop in crime of any industrial state in America; why we have the lowest murder rate of any industrial state in America. But we have work to do in this nation. We have work to do to fight a real war, not a phony war, against drugs. And that's something I want to lead, something we haven't had over the course of the past many years, even though the Vice President has been at least allegedly in charge of that war. We have much to do to step up that war, to double the number of drug enforcement

agents, to fight both here and abroad, to work with our neighbors in this hemisphere. And I want to call a hemispheric summit just as soon after the 20th of January as possible to fight that war. But we also have to deal with drug education prevention here at home. And that's one of the things that I hope I can lead personally as the President of the United States. We've had great success in my own state. And we've reached out to young people and their families and been able to help them by beginning drug education and prevention in the early elementary grades. So we can fight this war, and we can win this war. And we can do so in a way that marshals our forces, that provides real support for state and local law enforcement officers who have not been getting that support, and do it in a way which will bring down violence in this nation, will help our youngsters to stay away from drugs, will stop this avalanche of drugs that's pouring into the country, and will make it possible for our kids and our families to grow up in safe and secure and decent neighborhoods. (Presidential Debate at UCLA, 1988)

Twenty years after Dukakis's bloodless response, and the Willie Horton ads which painted him as just another soft-on-crime, out of the mainstream liberal, there is little doubt that something important is happening today that may foretell the end of America's love affair with capital punishment (Ogletree and Sarat, 2010). The USA is in a period of national reconsideration of capital punishment and, in this period, the tables have been turned with those who support capital punishment now on the defensive, trying to hold the line against a rising tide of doubts about its efficacy, workability and appropriateness.

In the remainder of this chapter I situate the current period of national reconsideration of capital punishment in the history of the death penalty in the USA and discuss data that indicate whether this reconsideration is likely to lead to the end of America's death penalty.

Since George Kendall was put to death for being a spy for Spain in Jamestown in 1608, more than 15,000 people have been legally executed in America—more than 7000 of them in the 20th century alone (Reggie, 1997; Boyer, 2001). Treason, murder, manslaughter, rape, robbery, counterfeiting, burglary, arson, theft, all were capital crimes in the American colonies (Boyer, 2001; Banner, 2003). While colonial American put crimes in roughly the same hierarchy that we do, there was scarcely any disagreement that death was the right penalty for all of them. Thus all 13 colonies mandated public hanging for crimes against the state, person or property (Banner, 2003). And, when the Bill of Rights was adopted in 1791, 'the Eighth Amendment's prohibition against "cruel and unusual" punishment was understood to outlaw torture and the intentional infliction of pain, not the death penalty itself' (Boyer, 2001).

Executions in the early history of the USA were dramatic, public events (see 'America's Tug of War over Sanctioned Death: The US History of Capital Punishment', 2007). Thus to take but one example, historian and law professor Stuart Banner (2003: 1) recounts the story of the 1821 execution of Stephen Clark in Salem, Massachusetts. Clark who had set fire to a barn, came from a respectable family, had no prior criminal record and was 16 years' old.

'The execution' Banner writes,

'began around noon, when Clark was taken from jail to the gallows in a carriage, escorted by a military guard, along with the sheriff and his deputies mounted and armed. The jailer rode with Clark as did a few ministers ... Hundreds, maybe thousands, of spectators walked alongside the procession. As the crowd watched, Clark emerged and climbed up the stairs of the scaffold. The ministers and the sheriff followed. Clark's last words were read by one of the ministers: 'May the youth who are present take warning from my sad fate, not to foresake the wholesome discipline of a parent's home. May you all pray to God to give you timely repentance, open your eyes, enlighten your understandings, that you may shun the paths of vice and follow God's Commandments all the rest of your days. And may God have mercy on you.'

After one of the ministers delivered a sermon from the gallows. The deputies tied Clark's hands behind his back, slipped the noose over his head and pulled a hood over his face. The sheriff gave a signal, a deputy sprang the trap door in the floor, and Clark dropped with a sudden jerk a few feet down 'dangling between heaven and earth' as the 19th-century cliché put it'.

By the middle of the 19th century the situation of capital punishment in the USA was changing in several ways (Bohm, 1999). First, the invention of the penitentiary provided a clear alternative to death as a punishment, an alternative thought severe enough that the criminal law gradually reduced the number of crimes punishable by death while introducing other reforms that lowered the number of executions (Rothman, 1972). As Boyer (2001) notes, 'Pennsylvania, for example, introduced a distinction between murder and manslaughter and limited the death penalty to offenders convicted of the former. And, in the 1840s states began to grant juries the discretion to impose life imprisonment in capital cases.'

Second, by the middle of the century five states (Pennsylvania, New York, New Jersey, Rhode Island and Massachusetts) had outlawed public executions. Others would soon follow suit, with the last public execution being held in Kentucky in 1935 ('The Last Public Execution in America', 2001).

Third, abolitionist activity began to dramatically increase. Abolitionists drew on diverse and sometimes incompatible sources including religious precepts and biblical injunctions as well as Enlightenment values, yet more immediate practical concerns were of equal, if not greater, importance. Among these were growing doubts about the efficacy of capital punishment as a means of deterring crime (Banner, 2003). Thus one of the earliest political leaders in this country to call for the abolition of the death penalty was New Hampshire Governor William Badger who was concerned as much to find a way to control crime as to serve humanitarian ends. In an 1834 message to the New Hampshire Legislature Badger said:

> A sense of duty impels me to invite your attention to one of the principles of our criminal code, and to recommend to your consideration and reflections ... whether in the present improved state of society, with well constructed and regulated Penitentiaries for solitary confinement and hard labor, the good of society or sound police requires Capital Punishment. As expressed in the Constitution, 'the true design of all punishment is to reform and not to exterminate mankind'. No one will attempt to controvert the principle that 'the prevention of crime is the sole end of punishment,' and 'every punishment which is not necessary for that purpose, is cruel and tyrannical.' If then the principle is admitted, that the sole end of punishment is the prevention of crime, two questions arise – How shall the offender be disposed of so as to prevent a repetition of the offence? And what punishment shall be most effectual in deterring others from its commission! The first question is readily answered. Perpetual solitary imprisonment is as effectual to prevent the repetition as death itself, and is attended with this desirable consideration, that it leaves the offender with all that space for repentance and time to make his peace with his God that He may see fit to extend it to him. The other is a more complicated one and not so readily answered: and, were the punishment of death as sure to follow the commission of crime as some other punishment, it would probably be the most effectual, as it is the heaviest punishment that the law inflicts; although many are of opinion that the apprehension of solitary imprisonment and hard labor is as impressive and more terrible than death itself. But it is the certainty and not the severity of the punishment that prevents crime. The humanity of mankind revolts at the idea of taking the life of a fellow human being. And the result at the criminal tribunal is, that none are convicted unless the criminality is established beyond all doubt, adopting probably the maxim that 'it is better ten guilty escape than one innocent suffer.' But when the punishment is imprisonment and hard labor, if the criminality is established beyond a reasonable doubt conviction follows, and few escape the merited punishment, confirming the correctness of the principles of certainty of punishment rather than its severity for the prevention of crimes, thereby destroying one of the principle sources of temptation, the hope of impunity. (Journals of the Honorable Senate and House of Representatives State of New Hampshire, 2009: 24).

The end of the 19th century and the start of the 20th century saw growing restrictions in capital statutes, as states eliminating horse thievery, cattle rustling, assaults and, finally, rape as capital crimes. By 1977, only murder could result in capital punishment (Boyer, 2001).

That time period also witnessed the invention of a new and improved technology for putting people to death: the electric chair (Brandon, 1999; Moran, 2002). As Blackwell (n.d.) notes,

> Under the old code of justice, every county had its own hangman, every county jail its gallows. But separate executions in each jurisdiction seemed too inefficient as government became more centralized. As for the method, it was, well, unpleasant. Dying men thrashed about, choking and wetting themselves. Execution by hanging had always been a grim, hands-on business in America. It took a strong stomach to wrap a noose around the condemned man, then let him drop through a gallows trapdoor to choke and gasp and swing until he died.

New York's legislature, revolted by several inefficient hangings, took the lead in looking for a new way to execute people. Their solution was inspired by Thomas Edison. Edison, inventor of the light bulb and pioneer of electricity, who was marketing an electric transmission system based on direct current. But another inventor, George Westinghouse, cut into Edison's business with a rival invention – alternating current. New York soon decided on alternating current as its humane substitute for hanging (Blackwell, n.d.; Moran, 2002).

The first electrocution, 6 August 1890, was anything but humane (Masur, 1989). The condemned man, axe murderer William Kemmler, lived through the first round of shocks (Long, 2008; also *In re Kemmler*, 1890). His executioners at Auburn prison in upstate New York had to do it all over again as the odor of Kemmler's burning flesh filled the death house. 'They would have done better with an axe', Westinghouse commented (Blackwell, n.d.).

Eventually, New York's executioners perfected the combination of amperes and voltage needed to kill a man without cooking him (Blackwell, n.d.). Other states 'began to replace the noose with the chair' (Blackwell, n.d.). From 1930–1980 electrocution was the most common method of execution in the USA (Banner, 2002; also 'The Death Penalty', n.d.).

Since the start of the last century the search for a reliable and humane technology of execution has led states to abandon electrocution, first in favor of lethal gas, and more recently in favor of lethal injection, which was used for the first time by Texas in 1982 (Sarat, 2001: ch. 3). Unlike the 19th century execution of Stephen Clark, today things are very different. Executions, when they occur, do not come within months of the crime, but generally after a decade or more of litigation. The crowds do not number in the hundreds or the thousands, but are limited to a dozen or to two witnesses at an execution carried out behind prison walls. Execution has been stripped of its close connection to religion and the pedagogy of the gallows sermon. Today we have a thoroughly bureaucratized, medicalized procedure for putting people to death (Masur, 1989).

Nonetheless, as it has been throughout our history, the death penalty remains the focus of some of America's most bitter debates. In today's America capital punishment remains 'a major front in culture war' (Sarat, 2001: 247). Traditionally those debates have proceeded through a series of abstract, moral and philosophical questions. Proponents of capital punishment have defended it as just and appropriate for those who commit the most heinous crimes (Berns, 1991). Thus in his book, *Devaluing of America: The Fight for Our Culture and Our Children* the conservative thinker William Bennett (1994: 116) describes a part of an interview he did on *Larry King Live* in which a caller pressed him as follows, 'Why build prisons? Get tough like (Saudi) Arabia. Behead the damned drug dealers. We're just too damned soft.' Bennett responded by saying,

> One of the things that I think is a problem is that we are not doing enough that is morally proportional to the nature of the offense. I mean, what the caller suggests is morally plausible, legally, it's difficult.

'Behead?' King asks.

> Yeah. Morally, I don't have anything wrong with it ... I mean ask most Americans if they saw

> somebody out on the streets selling drugs to their kid what they would feel morally justified in doing – tear them limb from limb ... What we need to do is find some constitutional and legally permissible way to do what the caller suggests, not literally to behead, but to make the punishment fit the crime. And the crime is horrible.

Or, as the law professor Robert Blecker argues (quoted in Lee, 2009), the death penalty is justified by 'an intuitive, if inexact, sense of justice, as well as a kind of Old Testament wrathfulness'.

Opposition to the death penalty has come in several guises. Some abolitionists have opposed the death penalty in the name of the sanctity of life. Even the most heinous criminals, they urge, are entitled to be treated with dignity. Or as former Supreme Court Justice William Brennan (*Furman* v. *Georgia*, 1972: 308) once wrote, there is nothing that anyone can do, no matter how terrible, that will lead him or her to forfeit the 'right to have rights'. Others have emphasized the moral horror, the 'evil', of the state's willfully taking the lives of any of its citizens (Kateb, 1992: 191–2). Still others contend that death as a punishment is always cruel and, as such, is incompatible with the Eighth Amendment's prohibition of cruel and unusual punishment (Bedau, 1987).

Each of these arguments has been associated with, and is an expression of, humanist liberalism or political radicalism. Each represents a frontal assault on Blecker's simple and appealing retributivist rationale for capital punishment. Each puts the opponents of the death penalty on the side of society's most despised and notorious criminals; to be against the death penalty one has had to defend the life of people like Oklahoma City bomber Timothy McVeigh or cop killers and child murderers. Thus it is not surprising that while traditional abolitionist arguments have been raised repeatedly in philosophical commentary, political debate and legal cases, none has ever carried the day in the debate about capital punishment in the USA (Zimring and Hawkins, 1986).

Recently the focus of the debate has changed in such a way as to help explain why death penalty supporters have lost their advantage. Now the conversation is less about the abstract justness or injustice of capital punishment and more about questions of fairness in its administration. It is less about who deserves to be executed and why they deserve that fate and more about whether we can retain the death penalty without doing damage to some of our most cherished legal and political values. Today the debate is mostly about the question of whether our system for deciding who deserves to die is administered in an arbitrary or discriminatory fashion and is reliable enough to prevent executing the innocent. The death penalty debate is being played out on the terrain of what might be called this 'new abolitionist rhetoric' (Sarat, 2001: ch. 9).

Crucial in this changing landscape has been the DNA revolution and the resulting well publicized exonerations from death row (Cole and Aronson, 2010). Since 1973, 140 people in 26 states have been released from death row with evidence of their innocence (Death Penalty Information Center, 2012a)

New abolitionists no longer make frontal assaults on the morality or constitutionality of state killing. Instead, arguments against the death penalty occur in the name of constitutional rights other than the Eighth Amendment, in particular due process and equal protection. Abolitionists now argue against the death penalty claiming that it has not been, and cannot be, administered in a manner that is compatible with the American legal system's fundamental commitments to fair and equal treatment.

However, the new abolitionism is perhaps less new than it might first appear. Glimpses of it can be found as far back as the 1972 Supreme Court decision in *Furman* v. *Georgia*, a case in which the Court temporarily stopped the death penalty in the USA. In *Furman* the Court invalidated the death penalty on the grounds that there was a risk that in its application it was arbitrary and discriminatory. But the real origin of the new abolitionism might be dated to a February 1994 opinion by former Supreme Court

Justice Harry Blackmun in which he announced that 'From this day forward I no longer shall tinker with the machinery of death' (*Callins* v. *Collins*, 1994: 1144). This dramatic proclamation capped his evolution from long time supporter of the death penalty to tinkerer with various procedural schemes and devices designed to rationalize death sentences to outright abolitionist.

Twenty-two years before his abolitionist announcement, he dissented in *Furman* v. *Georgia* (1972), refusing to join the majority of his colleagues in what he labeled the 'legislative' act of finding execution, as then administered, cruel and unusual punishment. Four years after *Furman* he joined the majority in *Gregg* v. *Georgia* (1976), in reinstating the death penalty in the USA.

However, by the time of his abolitionist conversion, Blackmun had left a trail of judicial opinions moving gradually, but inexorably, away from this early embrace of death as a constitutionally legitimate punishment. As a result, the denunciation of capital punishment which he offered in 1994 was as categorical as it was vivid – 'I no longer shall tinker with the machinery of death'. It was most significant as a moment in the transformation of abolitionist politics, as an example of abolition as a kind of legal and political conservatism, and as an indicator of the anxiety that abolitionists seek to cultivate about the way the death penalty is used in the USA.

Blackmun's abolitionism finds its locus in neither liberal humanism nor radicalism, nor in the defense of the most indefensible among us. He did not reject the death penalty because of its violence, argue against its appropriateness as a response to heinous criminals, or criticize its futility as a tool in the war against crime. Instead, he shifted the rhetorical grounds.

Harkening back to *Furman* v. *Georgia* (1972), as if re-writing his opinion in that case, Blackmun focused on the procedures through which death sentences were decided. '… [D]espite the efforts of the States and the courts', Blackmun noted, 'to devise legal formulas and procedural rules … , the death penalty remains fraught with arbitrariness, discrimination, caprice, and mistake … Experience has taught us that the constitutional goal of eliminating arbitrariness and discrimination from the administration of death … can never be achieved without compromising an equally essential component of fundamental fairness–individualized sentencing' (*Callins* v. *Collins*, 1994: 1145).

The new abolitionism that Blackmun championed presents itself as a reluctant abolitionism, one rooted in an argument about the damage that capital punishment does to central legal values and to the legitimacy of the law itself. It finds its home in an embrace, not a critique, of those values. Those who love the law, in Blackmun's view, must hate the death penalty for the damage that it does to the object of that love. 'Rather than continue to coddle the Court's delusion that the desired level of fairness has been achieved …', Blackmun stated, 'I feel morally and intellectually obligated simply to concede that the death penalty experiment has failed. It is virtually self-evident to me now that no combination of procedural rules or substantive regulations ever can save the death penalty from its inherent constitutional deficiencies' (*Callins* v. *Collins*, 1994: 1145). In this admonition we again see Blackmun's categorical conclusion that nothing can 'save' capital punishment, a conclusion spoken both from within history, as a report of the result of an 'experiment', but also from an Archimedean point in which the failure of the death penalty is 'self-evident' and permanent.

The new abolitionism provides an important contemporary avenue for engagement in the political struggle against capital punishment, providing abolitionists a position of political respectability while simultaneously allowing them to change the subject from the legitimacy of execution to the imperatives of due process, from the philosophical merits of killing the killers to the sociological question of the impact of state killing on our politics, law and culture (Sarat, 1998). Blackmun's rhetoric has enabled opponents of capital punishment to say that the most important issue in the debate about capital punishment is one of fairness not one of sympathy for murderers, concern for the law abiding not for the criminal. One can, abolitionists now are able to concede, believe in the retributive or deterrence based rationalizations for the death penalty and yet still be against the death penalty; one can be as tough on crime as the next person yet still reject state killing. All that is required to generate opposition to execution is a commitment to the rule of law.

Also fueling the new abolitionism is the issue of cost. Several states have legislation pending that would abolish the death penalty, many of them citing its costs (CNN.com/crime, 2009a). In Colorado, a bill would take money usually spent on capital cases and use it to help clear unsolved cases. In Kansas, a legislator wants to use money for capital cases to close a budget shortfall. 'In a way, we have life without parole, but we're paying more money to achieve it', said state Senator Carolyn McGinn-Sedgwick, noting that Kansas has not executed an inmate in decades (Mills, 2009). As Mills (2009) explains, 'Capital cases have had other unintended results. In Georgia, the public defender system is underfunded and in crisis after the death penalty trial of a man convicted of killing a judge and three other people during his 2005 escape from an Atlanta courthouse. The case cost more than $2 million. The man, Brian Nichols, received a life sentence.'

In California, legislators are wrestling with the cost of maintaining the nation's largest death row even though the state has executed only 13 inmates since 1976. At the same time, officials are debating construction of a new US$395 million death row prison many lawmakers say the state cannot afford. And in Louisiana, the Orleans Parish district attorney's office has considered filing for bankruptcy protection after it was ordered to pay US$15 million to John Thompson. He sued prosecutors after he was freed from death row; a jury found prosecutors had engaged in misconduct (Mills, 2009).

Mills (2009) notes that 'Many of the costs are built into the system and cannot be changed. They include the costs of specially trained defense lawyers, mental health and mitigation experts and a longer course of appeals. And there are the many added costs of housing Death Row prisoners.'

Two other things have played a key role in explaining the changing landscape of the death penalty debate in the USA. First is the fact that the rate of violent crime and the murder rate have remained relatively low by historical standards. The rate of violent crime fell from a high of 758 violent crimes per 100,000 people in 1991 to 466 per 100,000 in 2007 (Massachusetts Executive Office of Public Safety and Security, 2009: Fig. 4). The murder rate fell from 9.8 per 100,000 in 1991 to 5.6 in 2007 (United States Department of Justice, 2008).

Second, on a state level, changes in the law have also made a difference. Many states have made it easier for prosecutors to seek a life sentence instead of a death penalty (see *USA Today*, 2008). Across the nation, all of the 33 death penalty states now offer life without parole as a sentencing option (King and Nellis, 2009).

Today when asked to choose between the death penalty and life without parole as a punishment for murder, the public splits right down roughly the middle. A Field poll in California found that 'Given the option, 42 percent would prefer life in prison without parole for a murder, 41 percent would choose the death penalty, 13 percent say it depends on the situation and 4 percent had no opinion' (Gardner, 2010). Moreover, a recent Gallup poll of American opinion on the death penalty found that '65% of Americans support the death penalty, significantly lower than the 80% support recorded in 1994 and near the lowest support of 64% in the past 25 years recorded last year' (Newport, 2009).

As a result, at the end of 2011, new death sentences in the USA were at, or near, a three-decade low and the number of people executed was the lowest since 1994. There were 70 death sentences handed out in 2011.

This represents a more than 60 percent drop from 1998, reflecting a steady decline over the last decade (*USA Today*, 2008).

43 people were executed in 2011. That's down from the 98 people executed in 1999, the high point in the last 30 years (Death Penalty Information Center, 2012b). Moreover, today the death penalty in the USA has become predominantly a Texas phenomenon. Putting aside Texas (and the deep south and border states), very few executions are being carried out in the rest of the country.

What does all of this mean for the future of capital punishment in America? While scholarly opinion is deeply divided, many are now reasonably confident that the death penalty is dying (for a contrary view see McCann and Johnson, 2010). Although no one foresees a quick or painless end to capital punishment, many believe that the question is *when*, not *if*, the USA will join Europe in ending capital punishment (see, for example, Harcourt, 2010; Radelet, 2010; Steiker and Steiker, 2010) 'The empirical data', Harcourt observes, 'reflect a clear trend toward abolition: in all probability, the United States, like the larger international community, will experience greater abolition of the death penalty during the first half of the twenty-first century ... It may well take 20 more years for the momentum to reach the tipping point, but the direction of change favors abolition rather than retention' (2010: 91–2).

Abolition likely will occur gradually, with *de facto* abolition coming long before the death penalty is formally ended. America will stop sentencing people to death and executing them long before we formally change laws allowing for capital punishment. Today, it seems, the USA is well along the way toward that result. As former Supreme Court Justice John Paul Stevens (quoted in Greenhouse, 2008) put it,

> [D]ecisions by state legislatures, by the Congress of the United States, and by this Court to retain the death penalty as a part of our law are the product of habit and inattention rather than an acceptable deliberative process that weighs the costs and risks of administering that penalty against its identifiable benefits, and rest in part on a faulty assumption about the retributive force of the death penalty ... The time for a dispassionate, impartial comparison of the enormous costs that the death penalty imposes on society with the benefits that it produces has surely arrived.

REFERENCES

'America's tug of war over sanctioned death: the US history of capital punishment' (2007) Random History and Word Origins for the Curios Mind. Available at: http://www.randomhistory.com/2009/09/19_capital-punishment.html

Banner, Stuart (2003) *The Death Penalty: An American Story*. Cambridge, MA: Harvard University Press.

Bedau, Hugo Adam (1987) *Death Is Different: Studies in the Morality, Law and Politics of Capital Punishment*. Boston, MA: Northeastern University Press.

Belluck, Pam (2005) 'Massachusetts governor urges death penalty', *New York Times*, 29 April. Available at: http://query.nytimes.com/gst/fullpage.html?res=9801E6DC1131F93AA15757C0A9639C8B63&sec=&spon=&pagewanted=all

Bennett, William (1994) *De-Valuing Of America: The Fight For Our Culture And Our Children*. New York: Simon and Schuster.

Berns, Walter (1991) *For Capital Punishment*. New York: University Press of America.

'Bill to Restore Death Penalty Fails in Boston' (2005), *New York Times*, 16 November, Available at www.nytimes/2005/11/national/16 romney.html

Blackwell, Jon (n.d.) 'A comfortable seat in which to die', Available at: http://www.capitalcentury.com/1907.html

Bohm, Robert (1999) 'Deathquest: an introduction to the theory and practice of capital punishment in the United States', *Crime, Law and Social Change*, 31: 154.

Boyer, Paul (2001) *The Oxford Companion to United States History, Capital Punishment*. Available at: http://www.encyclopedia.com/doc/1O119-CapitalPunishment.html

Brandon, Craig (1999) *The Electric Chair: An Unnatural American History*. Jefferson, NC: McFarland.

Callins v. *Collins* (1994) 510 US 1141.

CNN.com/crime (2009a) 'Budget concerns force states to reconsider the death penalty', 2 March. Available at: http://www.cnn.com/2009/CRIME/03/02/economy.death.penalty/index.html

CNN. Com/Crime (2009b) 'New Mexico governor repeals death penalty in state', 18 March. Available at:

http://www.cnn.com/2009/CRIME/03/18/new.mexico.death.penalty/index.html

Cole, Simon and Aronson, Jay (2010) 'Blinded by science on the road to abolition?', in Charles Ogletree and Austin Sarat (eds), *The Road to Abolition?: The Future of Capital Punishment in the United States*. New York: NYU Press. pp. 46–71.

Death Penalty Information Center (2012a) 'The innocence list'. Available at: http://www.deathpenaltyinfo.org/innocence-list-those-freed-death-row

Death Penalty Information Center (2012b) 'Executions by year'. Available at: http://www.deathpenaltyinfo.org/executions-year

Furman v. *Georgia* (1972) 408 U.S. 238.

Gardner, Michael (2010) 'Death penalty still gets overwhelming support : 70% of voters favor it, split when given choice', *SignOn San Diego*. Available at: http://www.signonsandiego.com/news/2010/jul/21/death-penalty-still-gets-overwhelming-support/

Greenhouse, Linda (2008) 'Justice Stevens renounces capital punishment', *New York Times*, 18 April. Available at: http://www.nytimes.com/2008/04/18/washington/18memo.html

Gregg v. *Georgia* (1976) 428 US 153.

Harcourt, Bernard (2010) 'Abolition in the United States by 2050: on political capital and ordinary acts of resistance', in Charles Ogletree and Austin Sarat (eds), *The Road to Abolition?: The Future of Capital Punishment in the United States*. New York: NYU Press. pp. 72–96.

Henry, Jessica (2008) 'New Jersey's road to abolition', *Justice System Journal*, 29: 408–22.

In re Kemmler, 136 U.S. 436 (1890).

Jasanoff, Sheila (2006) 'Just evidence: the limits of science in the legal process', *The Journal of Law, Medicine & Ethics*, 34: 328–41.

Johnston, James (2009) 'Executing capital punishment via case study: a socratic chat about New Jersey's abolition of the death penalty and convincing other states to follow suit', *Journal of Legislation*, 34: 1–16.

Journals of the Honorable Senate and House of Representatives State of New Hampshire (2009) Ithaca, NY: Cornell University Library.

Kateb, George (1992) *The Inner Ocean: Individualism and Democratic Culture*. Ithaca, NY: Cornell University Press.

Lee, Nathan (2009) 'Film in review: "Robert Blecker wants me dead"', *New York Times*, 27 February. Available at: http://query.nytimes.com/gst/fullpage.html?res=9C05E1DB1F30F934A15751C0A96F9C8B63&sec=&spon=

Lewis, Raphael (2005) 'Romney files death penalty bill: measure sets tight restrictions', *Boston Globe*, 29 April. Available at: http://www.boston.com/news/local/articles/2005/04/29/romney_files_death_penalty_bill/

Long, Tony (2008) 'Aug. 6, 1890: Kemmler first to "ride the lightning"'. Available at: http://www.wired.com/science/discoveries/news/2008/08/dayintech_0806

Massachusetts Executive Office of Public Safety and Security (2009) 'Violent crime in Massachusetts'. Available at: http://www.mass.gov/Eeops/docs/eops/Publications/082009_violent_crime_v5_jul09.pdf

Masur, Louis (1989) *Rites of Execution: Capital Punishment and the Transformation of American Culture, 1776–1865*. New York: Oxford University Press.

McCann, Michael and Johnson, David (2010) 'Rocked but still rolling: the enduring institution of capital punishment in historical and comparative perspective', in Charles Ogletree and Austin Sarat (eds), *The Road to Abolition?: The Future of Capital Punishment in the United States*. New York: NYU Press. pp. 139–82.

Mills, Steve (2009) 'In many states, cost is slowly killing death penalty: price tag of trial and execution is driving many to repeal law', *Chicago Tribune*, 8 March. Available at: http://articles.chicagotribune.com/2009–03–08/news/0903070157_1_death-penalty-death-row-capital-cases

Moran, Richard (2002) *Executioner's Current: Thomas Edison, George Westinghouse, and the Invention of the Electric Chair*. New York: Vintage Books.

King, Ryan and Nellis, Ashley (2009) *No Exit: The Expanding Use of Life Sentences In America*. Washington, DC: The Sentencing Project.

Newport, Frank (2009) 'In U.S., two-thirds continue to support death penalty', Gallup Press Release, 13 October. Available at: http://www.gallup.com/poll/123638/in-u.s.-two-thirds-continue-support-death-penalty.aspx

Ogletree, Charles and Sarat, Austin (2010) *The Road to Abolition?: The Future of Capital Punishment in the United States*. New York: NYU Press.

Peters, Jeremy (2007) 'Death penalty repealed in New Jersey', *New York Times*, 17 December. Available at: http://www.nytimes.com/2007/12/17/nyregion/17cnd-jersey.html

Presidential Debate at UCLA (1988) The American Presidency Project. Available at: http://www.presidency.ucsb.edu/ws/index.php?pid=29412

Radelet, Michael (2010) 'The executioner's waning defenses', in Charles Ogletree and Austin Sarat (eds), *The Road to Abolition?: The Future of Capital*

Punishment in the United States. New York: NYU Press. pp. 19–45.

Reggie, Michael (1997) 'History of the death penalty', in Laura Randa (ed.), *Society's Final Solution: A History and Discussion of the Death Penalty.* New York: University Press of America. Available at: http://www.pbs.org/wgbh/pages/frontline/shows/execution/readings/history.html

Rothman, David (1972) 'Invention of the penitentiary', *Criminal Law Bulletin*, 8: 1.

Sarat, Austin (1998) 'Recapturing the spirit of *Furman*: the American Bar Association and the new abolitionist politics', *Law and Contemporary Problems*,61: 5.

Sarat, Austin (2001) *When the State Kills: Capital Punishment and the American Condition.* Princeton, NJ: Princeton University Press.

Sarat, Austin and Martschukat, Jurgen (2011) *Is the Death Penalty Dying: European and American Perspectives.* New York: Cambridge University Press.

Scherzer, Aaron (2009) 'Note: the abolition of the death penalty in New Jersey and its impact on our nation's "evolving standards of decency"', *Michigan Journal of Race and Law*, 15: 223.

Steiker, Carol (2005) 'Capital punishment and American exceptionalism', in Michael Ignatieff (ed.), *American Exceptionalism and Human Rights.* Princeton, NJ: Princeton University Press. pp. 38–53.

Steiker, Carol and Steiker, Jordan (2010) 'The beginning of the end?', in Charles Ogletree and Austin Sarat (eds), *The Road to Abolition?: The Future of Capital Punishment in the United States.* New York: NYU Press. pp. 19–45.

'The last public execution in America' (2001) NPR. Available at: http://www.npr.org/programs/morning/features/2001/apr/010430.execution.html

USA Today (2008) 'Report: US executions, death sentences on decline', 11 December. Available at: http://www.usatoday.com/news/washington/2008–12–11-death-penalty-executions_N.htm

United States Department of Justice (2008) *Crime in the United States.* Available at: http://www.fbi.gov/ucr/cius2008/data/table_01.html

Zimring, Franklin and Hawkins, Gordon (1986) *Capital Punishment and the American Agenda.* New York: Cambridge University.

15

Punishment *in* Society: The Improbable Persistence of Probation and Other Community Sanctions and Measures

Gwen Robinson, Fergus McNeill, and Shadd Maruna

INTRODUCTION

Things were looking awfully bleak for probation at the turn of the last century. Despite being around for nearly 100 years, probation in the UK, for instance, was said to be 'uncomfortable, threatened, unsure of its role, and not at all confident of its social or political credibility' in the 1990s (Garland, 1997: 3). Similar perceptions led to a series of high-profile conferences and reports on the state of probation in the USA at the end of the 1990s. According to one of the experts participating in the influential *Rethinking Probation* meeting, for instance: 'Public regard for probation is dangerously low … We have to realize that we don't have broad public legitimacy' (Dickey and Smith, 1998: 6). A subsequent, and equally prestigious report, titled *Reinventing Probation* followed only two years later, raising the alarm level even higher (Beto et al., 2000). The authors argued that community corrections were suffering from a 'crisis of legitimacy', arguing: 'Although low ratings [in public opinion polls] obviously are related to poor performance, they also signal a failure on probation's part to convey an image to citizens of a model of practice that embodies widely held values and serves overriding public safety concerns' (Beto et al., 2000: 1, 4). Things really hit bottom, though, the following year. In an article titled 'The end of probation?,' published in the in-house magazine of the American Probation and Parole Association, community corrections experts Maloney et al. (2001: 24) argued that the US model of probation had 'gone the way of the Edsel' in terms of performance and reputation. They argued that, like the Ford Motor Company's infamous failure, 'probation' as a brand needed to be retired. By that, they not only advocated the end of traditional US probation practice (which they saw as based on the 'rather bizarre assumption that surveillance and some guidance can steer the offender straight'), but also dispensing with the 'brand name' of probation in the USA.[1]

So, what happened next? Whatever became of that allegedly endangered species of penal sanction we used to call 'probation?' Actually, rumours of probation's imminent extinction had been rather exaggerated. Not only is probation still alive, it may be stronger than ever. Internationally, community-based sanctions have grown rapidly in number and significance since their inception and in most jurisdictions they now heavily outnumber custodial sentences. In the jurisdictions of the USA, there were more than twice as many people (over 5 million in total) on probation or parole as there were people in custody (around 2 million) at the end of 2007 (Glaze and Bonczar, 2009). European figures are harder to establish given the wide range of definitions and forms of community sanctions and differences in official recording of their use but Von Kalmthout and Durnescu's (2008) extensive recent survey suggests considerable expansion of the use of such sanctions in almost all European jurisdictions. Durnescu (2008) estimates that about 2 million people were incarcerated in Europe at the time of his survey, and about 3.5 million were subject to some form of community sanction. The fact that almost all prisoners are (eventually) released, often under some form of supervision, means of course that many 'custodial' sentences also involve community-based supervision, whereas the converse is not the case. The vast majority of the 'ordinary' (but barely visible) business of supervised punishment therefore plays out daily in probation or parole offices, and in supervisees' homes, rather than in custodial institutions.[2]

This chapter aims to explore and explain the conundrum represented by the durability and expansion of community sanctions despite the various diagnoses of their failing legitimacy and predictions of their demise. Specifically, we address the question: How have such sanctions adapted and survived in late-modern societies? To that end, we begin with a brief overview of some influential and important accounts of the history of community sanctions, before elaborating what we take to be the key 'adaptations' which have characterized community sanctions in their quest for legitimacy in late-modern societies and penal systems. As our analysis will reveal, we broadly concur with Hutchinson's (2006), and others', observation that developments in the penal field have been characterized by a braiding of 'old' and 'new' forms and functions: the old tends to survive (or adapt) alongside the new, rather than being supplanted by it. Our analysis seeks to draw out what we see as the key characteristics or dimensions of contemporary community sanctions that are more or less visible (albeit to different degrees and in variable combinations) across multiple jurisdictions. We thus seek not to describe empirical 'reality' in a fixed time and place, but rather to highlight some of the key dimensions against which community sanctions may be analysed, compared and contrasted *across* time and space. The characteristics of community sanctions on which we focus – 'managerial', 'punitive', 'rehabilitative' and 'reparative' – are, as shall become clear, overlapping rather than discrete categories which combine instrumental and expressive (or affective) elements. In our conclusion, we turn our attention to the future of community sanctions and ask whether and how these measures might achieve broad legitimacy.

A WORD ON WORD CHOICE

Before proceeding, however, we need to tackle some issues of definition and delineation of the subject. One of the leading commentators in the field has aptly described punishment in the community as a 'slippery fish' (Raynor, 2007: 1061). It is a sector of the penal field around which it is difficult to draw precise boundaries, which is described and labelled differently between jurisdictions, and which has been characterized by significant practical innovation/differentiation. Even naming the subject area is a contentious issue in itself. Raynor's preferred (and very Anglo-Welsh) term, 'community penalties', suffers (as he acknowledges) from its failure to include the large populations subject to some form of supervision following release from custody. Alternative labels, popular with North Americans, like 'community corrections', are broader in scope but arguably imply a particular form a practice (correctionalist), which is far from universal in its application, even in the jurisdictions in which the term is used. Given a range of problematic choices, we have opted for the more neutral but distinctly European label 'community sanctions and measures' (CSM), defined by the Council of Europe as:

> [those] which maintain the offender in the community and involve some restriction of his liberty through the imposition of conditions and/or obligations, and which are implemented by bodies designated in law for that purpose. The term designates any sanction imposed by a court or a judge, and any measure taken before or instead of a decision on a sanction as well as ways of enforcing a sentence of imprisonment outside a prison establishment. (Council of Europe, 1992: Appendix para.1)

Our choice of European terminology does not however indicate a restricted focus on Europe; indeed, we focus in particular on developments in the UK and in North America, which have arguably been the most influential jurisdictions internationally in terms of innovation and emulation elsewhere. Our choice of the Council of Europe definition principally reflects its inclusivity: it succeeds in capturing not just the wide array of penalties handed down by the courts (sometimes called 'front door' measures) which fall between non-supervisory penalties (such as fines) and custodial sentences, but also statutory post-custodial ('back-door') measures associated with early release schemes (such as parole). In the most general terms, what community sanctions and measures have in common is some form of oversight or supervision of individuals' activities while maintaining them in the community. What 'supervision' entails, the ends or purposes to which it is oriented and who assumes responsibility for it, are all dimensions of variation internationally and historically.

Adaptation and survival

There are a number of important historical accounts of community sanctions of various kinds, most of which, by necessity, concentrate on a single jurisdiction and a single type of sanction. A good example is Vanstone's (2004) account of the development of probation in England and Wales (although this does involve comparisons with the broad American experience of probation). Another is Jonathan Simon's (1993) now classic study of the development of parole in a single US jurisdiction (California). There are of course also broader accounts of the emergence of penal modernism, such as Garland's (1985) *Punishment and Welfare,* which (more indirectly) offer key contributions to the historical literature on community sanctions. All of these accounts locate the formal/legal origins of community sanctions in the context of the social, political and cultural shifts which coalesced around the turn of the 20th century to inaugurate a specifically 'modern' penality that brought the welfare or 'reform' of the individual into the domain of state responsibility.

The early community sanctions essentially formalized a range of practices that had previously been in the domain of what Garland refers to as 'penal philanthropy', giving them legal authority (for example, in England and Wales via the Probation of Offenders Act 1907; in California via the establishment of a system of parole in 1893), extending their reach, and creating specialist institutions and agencies charged with 'disciplining' (in the

Foucauldian sense) or 'normalizing' those individuals deemed eligible. So, just as Garland sees modern penality as the 'midwife' of the probation order in England and Wales, so Simon locates the origins of Californian parole in the modernist tradition and the quest for the 'normalization' of ex-prisoners. This 'normalization', Simon argues, progressed from a model based on participation in the labour market to a 'clinical' model of 'rehabilitation through personality adjustment'. Similarly, the early decades of the 20th century witnessed the transformation of probation practice as ideas about moral reformation gave way to a more 'scientific' discourse centred on diagnosis, treatment and 'rehabilitation' that, although profound, represented an important continuation of modernist narratives and 'transformative zeal' (Bottoms, 1980; Garland, 1985, 2001).

With their formal origins firmly embedded in the foundations of 'penal modernism', community sanctions have been deeply implicated in its 'crisis' (Garland, 1990, 2001), the elements of which we need not review again here. In this context, academic and policy debates have centred on strategies of adaptation, and the search for modes of exercising power and legitimate narratives for community sanctions in social contexts which have variously been characterized as 'post-industrial', 'post-modern', 'post-disciplinary' and so on (Bell, 1973; Lyotard, 1984; Simon, 1988; Bauman, 1991; Deleuze, 1995). Simon's (1993) California case study is a key contribution to this debate because it identifies a fundamental shift in modes of control that is explicitly tied to the collapse of penal modernism. At the heart of *Poor Discipline* is the decisive shift Simon observes, from the mid-1970s, from what he terms 'clinical' to 'managerial' parole – the latter characterized by significantly lowered expectations and functioning (in a manner redolent of Deleuze's 'societies of control') as a mechanism for securing the borders of communities by channelling its least stable members back to prison.

Simon's analysis of parole is part of a wider body of work which has utilized a Foucauldian framework to analyse shifts in the exercise of power, from the normalizing or 'disciplinary' mode of control characteristic of modern penality, toward an actuarial, managerial 'new penology' (Simon, 1987, 1988; Feeley and Simon, 1992, 1994). In the last two decades – as other chapters in this volume will attest – much academic attention has been devoted to assessing the extent to which the 'new penology' thesis represents an accurate characterization of developments in the field of community sanctions, and whether Simon's account of 'managerial parole' is a typical or an extreme case study of contemporary community sanctions. We take the view that it is too simplistic to identify any single 'replacement discourse' for community sanctions and measures generally. This is not only because of significant jurisdictional variations but also because the 'real story' is rather more complex.

Late-modern community sanctions are certainly characterized by the demise of the coherent meta-narrative or purpose that penal-welfarism (or more specifically the 'rehabilitative ideal') once provided (Simon, 1993); but the adaptations that have occurred in its wake have been multiple, various and fluid (Lynch, 1998). As the succeeding sections of this chapter will make clear, the adoption of managerial and actuarial discourses and practices has not been the only means of adaptation and survival open to probation. Indeed, as Stan Cohen (1985) predicted a quarter of a century ago, perhaps the most notable feature of community sanctions in the last 30–40 years has been the proliferation and diversification of their institutional forms, technologies and practices and (at least in some places) of their ideological foundations. We have therefore witnessed not only the re-storying and re-configuration of the traditional range of sanctions and measures (probation, parole) through new narratives and techniques, but also the emergence of new forms of community sanctions (e.g. unpaid work, community justice innovations, electronic monitoring). It is also notable that, whether old or new, the same community sanctions have been 'marketed' in very different ways internationally.

In the sections which follow, we identify some of the major adaptations in the CSM field which have been observable internationally in the last 30 years or so. We group these trends into four 'visions' of CSM which we characterize as 'managerial', 'punitive', 'rehabilitative' and 'reparative'. In the final section of the chapter we address the extent to which these various adaptations have enabled community sanctions – and the organizations and professionals associated with their administration – to present themselves as coherent and legitimate responses to crime in late-modern societies.

MANAGERIAL COMMUNITY SANCTIONS

If there is one point of consensus in the perennially contested field of penality, perhaps it is the idea that penal systems, alongside other public services such as education, health and so on, have come to be increasingly dominated by 'managerial' strategies and concerns (Peters, 1986; Feeley and Simon, 1992, 1994; Bottoms, 1995; Garland, 1996, 2001). We think this a key part of the story of efforts to bolster the legitimacy of community sanctions in late-modern societies, but by no means the whole story.

Although it is difficult to summarise the various dimensions of managerialism in criminal justice (or indeed other) contexts, at the heart of most accounts of managerialism in the penal realm has been the notion of '*systemization*': that is, the transformation of what was formerly a series of relatively independent bodies or agencies (courts, police, prisons, probation services, etc.) into a 'system'. For Bottoms (1995), this process of 'systemization' has, in most jurisdictions, tended to embrace characteristics such as an emphasis on inter-agency cooperation in order to fulfil the overall goals of the system; mission statements for individual criminal justice agencies that serve those general system goals; and the creation of 'key performance indicators' for individual agencies which tend to emphasize the efficiency of internal processes rather than 'effectiveness' in relation to any overarching objective. As Garland (1996) has observed, systemization has enabled the cooperative adoption of a variety of devices to deal with the problem of crime in a reconfigured field characterized by an acceptance of crime as a 'normal social fact': a risk to be managed rather than a social problem to be eliminated. The key imperatives of a 'managerial' penology are thus focused on the limited goals of 'managing a permanently dangerous population while maintaining the system at a minimum cost' (Feeley and Simon, 1992: 463).

It is not difficult to discern some of the ways in which community sanctions and the agencies responsible for implementing such sanctions have been re-cast along such lines, and how such developments have helped to bolster their 'systemic' legitimacy. For example, in many jurisdictions CSM have come to be appreciated more for what they can do for other parts of the 'system' than what they might accomplish for individual supervisees or communities. Arguably the key example of this is the adoption in many jurisdictions, in the 1980s, of a pragmatic rationale for community sanctions which emphasized the provision of credible 'alternatives to custody'. Here, the primary motivation for increasing the 'market share' of CSM was to relieve pressure on (and the expense of) prison places (Raynor, 1988; Vass, 1990). Another important example of the systemic functions of CSM in reducing prison costs, concerns the post-custodial supervision of ex-prisoners subject to conditional release from custody – a population which in many jurisdictions has been escalating (Padfield et al., 2010). Increases in rates of imprisonment and sentence lengths have encouraged the increased use of the 'safety valve' of early release mechanisms which, in turn, have brought greater numbers of individuals under the remit of post-custodial supervision (on licence or parole) (Cavadino and Dignan, 2007).

These developments have been underpinned by a shifting understanding of CSM agencies as 'partners' in offender management alongside other parts of the system, such as police and prison services, where previously ideological conflict would have made such partnerships problematic, if not unthinkable. This has been evident, for example, in England and Wales, where formal partnerships have emerged between police and probation services to manage various categories of 'high risk' individuals in the community (Kemshall and Maguire, 2001). Such partnerships, most notably Boston's famed Operation Nightlight (Corbett, 2002), are less unusual in the American context where probation and especially paroling authorities have long understood their role as partially a law enforcement one (Sigler and McGraw, 1984). Moreover, in many US states, probation and paroling authorities are administered within the same agency as prisons. This US-style 'correctional services' structure has also recently emerged in England and Wales with the emergence of the National Offender Management Service, combining prisons and probation in the pursuit of the common goal of 'public protection' (Raynor and Vanstone, 2007).

Alongside these developments we have also seen evidence of the redefinition and 'scaling down' of the criteria against which the performance of CSM agencies has been judged, with more emphasis on 'outputs' than 'outcomes'. For example, National Standards for CSM have emerged in a number of jurisdictions in the last 20 years, and the tendency of such standards to emphasize the timeliness of processes rather than their quality or effectiveness has been noted. Meanwhile, some of the features of 'actuarial justice' described by Feeley and Simon (1994) have become evident in the emergence and spread of new, actuarial technologies oriented to the assessment of risk, as well as new types of surveillant sanction oriented to what Feeley and Simon refer to as 'management in place'. Electronically monitored curfews and drug testing are arguably the best examples of this trend (Nellis, 2010). The emergence of a discourse of 'offender management' in UK jurisdictions is another example of this lowering of ambitions (Robinson, 2005).

The managerialist idea that 'systemic' goals are easily achievable or unproblematically generate legitimacy, however, has not necessarily been borne out (Wodahl et al., 2011). Taking the provision of 'alternatives to custody' as an example, this would certainly appear on the face of things to be a more achievable goal than transforming individuals or turning lives around. However, in practice, even this has proven to be a rather difficult goal to achieve: research studies have tended to show that community sanctions are in fact rarely used as genuine alternatives to custody. For example, research conducted in England and Wales in the late 1970s showed that only about half of those sentenced to community service orders were actually diverted from prison, even though this was supposed to be explicit in their imposition; the other half appeared to receive community service as an 'alternative' to probation or a fine (Pease, 1985). Tonry and Lynch (1996) argue that the evidence relating to 'intermediate sanctions' programmes which were developed in the USA in the 1980s and 1990s is similar: few such programmes have diverted large numbers of individuals from prison. Indeed, where the use of CSM has increased, this has almost always tended to be at the expense of lower-tariff penalties such as fines and discharges, leading to what Cohen (1985) has referred to as 'net widening' and 'mesh thinning'. That is, CSM frequently bring greater numbers of less serious offenders into the penal net than might otherwise have been the case, and impose upon them more rather than less severe sanctions (Bottoms et al., 2004).

A related problem is the so-called 'revolving door at the prison gate' (Padfield and

Maruna, 2006). Despite the penal reductionist aspirations alluded to above, more often than not more intensive and perhaps more risk-averse forms of post-release supervision have driven up recall rates and therefore prison populations (Munden et al., 1998). In recent years, as many as 40 per cent of parolees across the USA are reincarcerated either for committing a new offence or else a technical violation of their release conditions (for example, positive drug tests, failure to comply with treatment, missed appointments, and so forth) (Glaze and Bonczar, 2009). In fact, the number of parolees recalled to prison in the USA increased by more than 800 per cent in less than three decades (Sable and Couture, 2008). Such aggregate figures, moreover, hide disturbing variation between states. California has had particularly notorious experiences with recalls to imprisonment, for instance. In 2006, almost two-thirds of admissions to the state's prisons were parole violators, and one-third of those were based on technical violations of parole conditions (Grattet et al., 2009).

This 'waste management' approach to parole has been widely criticized (Simon, 1993), and indeed Wodahl et al. (2011) persuasively argue that the escalating rates of returns to prison represent the greatest threat to the perceived legitimacy of CSM today. The perception is that these 'alternatives' to custody are unable to do their job without resort to custody itself. Indeed, a distinct irony of the managerial turn in CSM is that, while the trend is motivated and animated by a distinct risk aversion and impression management, managerialism itself has been a near-constant target of criticism from politicians, practitioners and the wider public alike. On the one hand, 'managerial' performance indicators which bear little or no relation to the quality of supervision or service meet with criticism, for example in UK jurisdictions recently (National Audit Office, 2008; Chapman, 2010). On the other, despite the more intrusive and demanding nature (for those supervised) of joint risk management activities of police and probation services, little reassurance seems to be offered to an insecure public. It seems clear that instances of failure, whether systemic or not, tend to attract significant adverse publicity and thus to threaten the legitimacy of CSM (Robinson and McNeill, 2004; McCulloch and McNeill, 2007; McNeill, 2011; Fitzgibbon, 2011).

PUNITIVE COMMUNITY SANCTIONS

For many advocates of CSM, perhaps especially in European jurisdictions, the idea of punitive community sanctions is anathema. Traditionally, such sanctions have been associated not just with the provision of welfare, but also the avoidance of state punishment. For example, the probation order established in England and Wales by the Probation of Offenders Act 1907 enjoyed the legal status of an alternative to punishment. That said, such 'alternatives' have always involved the exercise of power and control over individuals, albeit a 'softer' form of power than the prison. Drawing on Foucault's (1975/1977) argument concerning the 'power of normalization', Garland (1985) for example noted that the new regime of probation established in the early 20th century represented both a more 'humane' response to crime and a more extensive and subtle 'network of control'. CSM have also tended to be backed up by the possibility of punitive sanctions in the face of non-compliance (Raynor and Vanstone, 2007).

In our view it would be naïve to suggest that contemporary CSM lack a punitive dimension. Rather than being implicit and concealed however, as was perhaps the case in earlier eras, in some jurisdictions the explicit display of punitive credentials has indeed become a key part of the quest for legitimacy in late-modern penal systems. This has to be understood in the context of at least three developments, which significantly impacted on CSM in the 1980s, 1990s and beyond.

The first two of these are linked with processes of 'managerialization' discussed in the previous section. The first is the systemic goal of 'penal reductionism' (Cavadino and Dignan, 2007): namely the idea that only punitive sanctions will be perceived by sentencers as 'credible' alternative sanctions. Perhaps the most obvious related development concerned the introduction in several jurisdictions of new orders requiring individuals to undertake unpaid work or 'community service', although (as we discuss below) the punitive identities of such orders were often blurred with their rehabilitative potential (McIvor, 2010). The second, related development is the adoption of desert-based sentencing frameworks that took hold across the USA in the 1970s with numerous international jurisdictions following suit in the decades that followed. As a number of commentators have observed, the turn to retributivism as the dominant rationale for sentencing is at least partly explicable with reference to the managerial pursuit of 'achievable' goals – in this case dispensing punishment in proportion to criminal behaviour – although there were other significant drivers behind it (Bottoms, 1995; Garland, 1996). The systemic pursuit of 'just deserts' for criminal acts necessitated thinking about penalties of all kinds in relation to their retributive content, or 'punitive weight'. CSM thus came, in this context, to be reconceptualized and calibrated along a new 'continuum of punishment' within which they were viewed as 'tough' and relatively inexpensive penalties for those guilty of less serious offences (Morris and Tonry, 1990). In this context, the constructive potential of CSM arguably became less important than their retributive qualities, which could be measured in length, intensity and intrusiveness.

The third, and most recent, driver of punitive community sanctions, has been the politicization of crime and criminal justice, and the increasing resort on the part of politicians and policy makers to 'populist punitiveness' or 'penal populism' (Bottoms, 1995; Pratt et al., 2005).[3] In this context traditional, rehabilitative CSM have met with criticism for being too 'soft' or aligned with the needs and/or interests of those convicted of crimes, rather than those of the 'law-abiding majority' or victims of crime (Home Office, 2006). In an important sense, since it was rehabilitation itself that was seen as being 'too soft', casting probationers as disadvantaged and in need of help or treatment, sanctions conventionally dressed in rehabilitative clothing were stripped of their legitimacy and left in need of new garb (Maruna and LeBel, 2003).

These drivers, on their own or in concert, make sense of a 'punitive turn' in the CSM context which has witnessed the creation and 'branding' of new types of 'intensive' CSM with a more explicit retributive or punitive orientation. The 'intermediate sanctions' movement in the USA, which saw the emergence in the 1980s and 1990s of community service, intensive supervision, house arrest, day reporting centres and boot camps is an example of this (Tonry and Lynch, 1996) as is the imposition of fees on probationers and parolees to pay for their own supervision (Diller et al., 2009). Another example is the tendency toward the 'creative mixing' of multiple conditions or requirements as part of a single sanction, as has been observed in England and Wales (Bottoms et al., 2004). Indeed, in England and Wales a plethora of separate community sanctions has recently been 'streamlined' into a single generic 'community order', which enables sentencers to select any combination of conditions from a 'menu' of twelve different requirements and restrictions (Mair et al., 2007).

As we noted above, many jurisdictions have also witnessed a lowering of tolerance in respect of 'failures to comply' with or 'violations' of CSM, which is arguably another correlate of the 'punitive turn' in CSM (Robinson and McNeill, 2008). Another (recent) example (discussed further below) is the 'punitivizing' of community service work (Maruna and King, 2008) through various forms of 'stigmatizing shaming' (Braithwaite, 1989). In the UK and many other jurisdictions, technological innovations have also been used to increase the 'punitive bite' of

CSM, or to increase the restrictions placed on probationers in the community. In the development of electronic monitoring (EM) it has been notable that little attention has been paid, despite some supporting research evidence, to the role that EM might play in more constructive or rehabilitative supervision practice (Nellis, 2010).

To a large extent, the 'punitive turn' in the CSM context has been driven by good 'liberal' intentions to reduce the use of custody (Morris and Tonry, 1990). However, an absence of punitive intent does not equate with an absence of 'penal bite' from the perspective of those subject to the more intensive community sanctions. Indeed, recent years have seen the emergence of interest among researchers in a variety of jurisdictions in the measurement of the relative punitiveness, deprivations or 'pains' of community sanctions of different types (Sykes, 1958). For example, researchers at the RAND corporation in the USA found that there are intermediate sanctions which surveyed prisoners equate with prison in terms of punitiveness. For some individuals, intensive forms of probation 'may actually be the more dreaded penalty' (Petersilia and Deschenes, 1994: 306; see also Petersilia, 1990; Payne and Gainey, 1998; May and Wood, 2010). More recently, Durnescu (2011) has specifically explored the 'pains of probation' as experienced in Romania.

It is clear then that the evolution of CSM in late-modern penal systems has been characterized by increasing attention to their 'punitive weight', and that this has been a significant part of the quest for legitimacy. Yet, some critics have argued that the narrative behind this 'get tough' approach to CSM is inherently self-defeating. Implicit in the premise of punitive CSM is that the individuals sentenced to these restrictive measures are too bad, too dangerous and too risky for ordinary CSM. Yet if they are so dangerous, sentencers and members of the public might rightly ask, why are they not in prison? CSM 'simply cannot compete with the iron bars, high walls and razor wire of the prison' when it comes to protecting the public from the dangerous (Maruna and King, 2008: 346).

In the next two sections, we examine two arguably more constructive strategies that have been used to bolster the legitimacy of CSM, essentially as a means of 'civilizing' punishment; namely, the revival of rehabilitation and the development of reparation.

REHABILITATIVE COMMUNITY SANCTIONS

Historically, probation practitioners in most jurisdictions have understood themselves and their practices as being aligned far more closely to social work and a welfare model than a criminal justice one. Yet, the rehabilitative ideal so central to this tradition famously fell out of favour in the 1970s (Allen, 1981), and CSM were rapidly reoriented – as we saw in the above sections – in more managerial and/or punitive terms. Rumours of the death of rehabilitation, however, turned out to be greatly exaggerated as a resurgent rehabilitative ideal emerged in the late 1980s in the form of the 'What Works' movement (see, especially, McGuire, 1995; Andrews and Bonta, 1998). Led by a collective of researchers associated with Correctional Services Canada and spread through a series of conferences and workshops with both academic and practitioner participants, 'What Works' has been a global success story. According to one of the scholars at the forefront of the movement:

> Three decades ago, it was widely believed by criminologists and policymakers that 'nothing works' to reform offenders and that 'rehabilitation is dead' as a guiding correctional philosophy. By contrast, today there is a vibrant movement to reaffirm rehabilitation and to implement programs based on the principles of effective intervention. How did this happen? I contend that the saving of rehabilitation was a contingent reality that emerged due to the efforts of a small group of loosely coupled research criminologists. (Cullen, 2005: 1)

Setting aside for a moment how one might best account for this success, proof of the redemption of the rehabilitative idea is provided, for example, by the state of California renaming its Department of Corrections with the rather redundant new title of Department of Corrections and Rehabilitation under the leadership of a Republican governor. Likewise, the current coalition government in the UK led by the Conservative Party (infamous in the mid-1990s for initiating a 'punitive turn' in penal policy around the argument that 'prison works') is promoting something they are calling a 'Rehabilitation Revolution' (Ministry of Justice, 2010). These are rather remarkable developments considering that for much of the past three decades 'rehabilitation' was viewed as something of a 'dirty word' (Ward and Maruna, 2007) not least among those on the political right (see Farabee, 2005).

Cullen (2005) is right to point out that the revival of rehabilitation in contemporary penal systems owes much to the efforts of criminological researchers who refused to accept that nothing could be done to change offenders' behaviour. However, there is rather more to the story in our view, and we should not overlook the ways in which rehabilitation has been transformed and re-marketed in the context of late-modern penality, such that far from going 'against the grain' of broader penal developments, it has been rendered compatible with them. As one of us has argued elsewhere, it is more accurate to talk of the 'evolution' of rehabilitation than of its survival or revival, the latter being terms that imply a somewhat static (and inaccurate) picture (Robinson, 2008). This evolutionary process has produced visions and modes of rehabilitation in the CSM context that have diverged from earlier incarnations in important ways, as we shall describe below.

First, the 'new' rehabilitation has had to adapt to social and political contexts that have become increasingly intolerant of approaches and interventions that appear to put the needs and interests of offenders above those of (actual and potential) victims. Proponents of rehabilitation in jurisdictions which have been subject to 'populist punitiveness' (see above) have thus had to de-emphasize its welfarist, humanitarian and essentially offender-centred justifications, in favour of rationales which emphasize the instrumental and more broadly 'utilitarian' value of rehabilitative sanctions. David Garland (1997: 6) was among the first to observe this realignment of rehabilitation in the USA and England and Wales when he observed that correctional staff 'now emphasize that "rehabilitation" is necessary for the protection of the public. It is future victims who are now "rescued" by rehabilitative work, rather than the offenders themselves'. This idea that the legitimacy of contemporary rehabilitation rests on a utilitarian justification (Robinson, 2008) helps to explain both the spread of 'programmes' under the banner of the 'What Works' movement, and the resurgence of interest and investment, in a number of jurisdictions, in the 'reentry' or 'resettlement' of ex-prisoners (Maruna and Immarigeon, 2004; Travis, 2005; Farrall and Sparks, 2006). What at first sight appears to indicate a heightened concern with the welfare and reintegration of ex-prisoners or a desire to undo the harmful consequences of imprisonment, however, is arguably more an expression of concern for the communities to which most prisoners ultimately return and resume their lives (Ward and Maruna, 2007; Wacquant, 2010). In the UK, for example, former prisoners are thought to account for around 1 million crimes a year, costing an estimated £11 billion annually (Social Exclusion Unit, 2001).

A second important adaptation is that rehabilitation has come to be understood less as an 'end' in itself than as a 'means' to the preferred 'ends' of late-modern penal systems (Garland, 1997, 2001). Specifically, rehabilitation has come to be understood as part of a 'toolkit' of measures oriented toward the protection of the public and the management of risk. A related development has been the repositioning of rehabilitative measures within managerial systems which have come to be dominated by the discourse of risk. In this regard, rehabilitation has not only come to be reconceived as a means toward the 'end' of risk reduction or management, but it is also increasingly rationed in line with assessments of risk which determine the eligibility of offenders for the new 'programmes'. Such an approach secures a space for rehabilitation among the range of legitimate responses to offending, but limits its reach and influence in new ways.

One of the best illustrations of this risk-driven, differentiated approach is a model of probation practice introduced in England and Wales in 2005 (National Probation Service, 2005). This so-called 'offender management model' uses the logic of risk to determine the level of resource appropriate to individual offenders; embedded within this model is a 'tiering framework' that specifies four, discrete intervention styles, to one of which all offenders under statutory supervision are assigned. These tiers are labelled 'punish', 'help', 'change' and 'control' and represent differential responses to increasingly serious risk profiles. Only the third tier, 'change', contains an explicitly disciplinary or rehabilitative element, and it is targeted at those posing a medium/high risk of reoffending. This explicitly actuarial model illustrates quite clearly that contemporary rehabilitative interventions are far from inimical to managerial systems.

However, the re-framing of rehabilitation in risk management terms and regimes has not simply entailed putting a new 'spin' on the same old product. Importantly, the product itself has adapted as part of the evolutionary process we have described. While it is probably unwise to characterize contemporary rehabilitative CSM as if they were a unified product, it is probably fair to say that among the range of contemporary CSM, the most explicitly 'rehabilitative' are those offending behaviour programmes which emerged under the banner of a 'What Works' movement initially led principally by Canadian and UK-based correctional researchers and practitioners. Based on cognitive-behavioural principles and methods, the new offending behaviour programmes proliferated and spread in the 1990s, particularly in Anglophone and Northern European jurisdictions, in the light of evidence (from experimental and 'demonstration' projects, for example, Ross et al. [1988]) of their technical effectiveness in reducing reoffending and contributing to public safety. Many governments convened expert 'accreditation panels' to ensure that programmes that were to receive public resources were 'evidence-based' and conformed to the design and delivery principles promoted by key 'what works?' researchers (Raynor and Robinson, 2009).

However, some have argued that we should not attribute the legitimacy of rehabilitative 'programmes' solely to their (putative) instrumental effectiveness. For some commentators, the dominance of cognitive-behavioural programmes in certain jurisdictions is at least in part attributable to their expressive and communicative qualities and their resonance with 'advanced liberal' forms of governance which emphasize personal responsibility for wrong-doing, and rely upon strategies of 'responsibilization' as the dominant response to anti-social behaviour (Garland, 1996; Rose, 2000; Kendall, 2004). The same has been said of the contemporary resurgence of 'restorative justice' approaches, which are a central part of CSM in at least some jurisdictions, in Africa, Europe and North America (Dignan, 2005; discussed further in the next section). Both modes of intervention seek to engage offenders in a 'moral discourse' that both communicates censure and seeks to instil in offenders both a measure of 'victim empathy' and a new 'moral compass' which, it is hoped, will dissuade them from future offending (Duff, 2001). The 'rehabilitated' offender, then, is presented as an individual capable of managing his or her own risks without recourse to externally imposed sanctions or controls, and without making any claims on the state in terms of its duties to create opportunities for reform and reintegration. Thus rehabilitation is cast as a personal project rather than a social project.

Despite some concerns about the overtly moralizing content of contemporary 'programmes', proponents of rehabilitative CSM have tended to view their proliferation and spread in a positive light. In jurisdictions such as England and Wales, the 'new rehabilitation' has attracted considerable financial investment from central governments eager to capitalize on the potential of such interventions to deliver public protection via measurable reductions in reoffending on the part of 'treated' subjects. However, to the extent that the legitimacy of rehabilitative CSM rests on a primarily instrumental justification, the future of CSM is far from assured. Given that a public protection focus does not privilege any particular approach or technology, failure to demonstrate the desired (crime reduction) outcomes invites reversion to other, potentially more 'effective' approaches in the penal toolkit; not least incapacitative ones (Robinson and McNeill, 2004). It is in this sense that Garland (1997) has rightly pointed to the contingent legitimacy of late-modern rehabilitation, and the same can be said of rehabilitative community sanctions more generally.

REPARATIVE COMMUNITY SANCTIONS

This vulnerability of rehabilitative CSM to their own instrumentalist logic suggests a need to look in other directions for more durable or secure sources of legitimacy. Writing in 1980, when the revival of rehabilitation still appeared an unlikely prospect, Anthony Bottoms (1980) suggested that penal systems might be about to turn towards a more reparative ideal. He noted that a reparative approach could retain the proportionality central to the justice model but eschew damaging forms of punishment in favour of more constructive options. Sometimes reparation might be directly focused on the particular victim; sometimes it might be directed at the community. Rehabilitation may be a by-product of reparative efforts, he argued, but it need not be sought directly.

The jurisdiction in which Bottoms was writing (England and Wales) had seen the inception of community service as a new standalone community sanction available across the UK in 1978, and the new sanction built on longstanding traditions of undertaking unpaid work as part of probation supervision. However, community service in many jurisdictions has not been 'marketed' solely or even principally as a reparative sanction. For example, reflecting on the development of the new sanction in neighbouring Scotland, McIvor explains its multifarious purposes thus:

> Community service in Scotland was intended to fulfil a number of sentencing aims including ***punishment*** (through the deprivation of the offender's free time), ***rehabilitation*** (through the positive effects of helping others) and ***reparation*** (by undertaking work of benefit to usually disadvantaged sections of the community). The ***reintegrative*** potential of community service was to be achieved through the offender being enabled to remain in the community, retaining employment and family ties, and, through coming into contact with others while carrying out unpaid work, avoiding social isolation. (2010: 42)

Alongside these multiple purposes and identities, community service or unpaid work at different places and at different times has had quite different legal meanings and functions – as a standalone sanction or as an adjunct to probation supervision, as an alternative to prosecution, as a direct alternative to custody, or as an autonomous sanction in its own right (McIvor et al., 2010).

Though these varied purposes and uses may have been useful in its popularization, in some jurisdictions at least they may also have deprived community service of the clear normative narrative that the decline of rehabilitation seemed to require. Indeed, the pragmatic popularization of community service as 'all things to all people' perhaps explains in part why the links between community service and ideals of restorative and community justice (more of which below) have tended to be more tenuous than they might have been. This is despite the fact that analyses like those offered by Bottoms (1980), Christie (1977) and Hulsman (1976) were arguing for a more victim-focused approach that blurred the distinction between criminal and civil wrongs, and sought victim-oriented solutions to harmful actions, rather than punishment. Bottoms (1980) expected such arguments and approaches to gather pace; partly because he accepted Durkheim's (1901 [1973]) analysis that more developed societies would increasingly tend towards seeking to 'redress the imbalance between the offender and the victim, rather than simply mete out sanctions against the offender' (Bottoms, 1980: 16–17).

Bottoms (1980) also pointed out that whereas rehabilitation, at least on a Foucauldian reading, represented (or was readily corralled into) a project of 'coercive soul-transformation', a different alternative to expressive pre-modern punishment had been identified in the work of the 18th-century Classicists (for example, Beccaria, 1764 [1963]) who argued for the use of punishment as a way of 'requalifying individuals as ... juridical subjects' (Foucault, 1975/1977: 130). Critically, reparation – and reparative work in particular – seems capable of fulfilling this function in ways in which rehabilitation[4] cannot, principally because rehabilitation offers no redress per se; it operates only on the individual, not on the conflict itself and not on the victim or the community (Zedner, 1994).

The problem of redress (or the lack of it) may lie behind recent attempts to bolster public and judicial confidence in CSM.[5] Both in Scotland and in England and Wales, these have centred, albeit in different ways, on the notion of reparation, or more specifically 'payback'. A recent Scottish Prisons Commission (2008), for example, argued that imprisonment should be de-centred from our conception of punishment by making paying back in the community the 'default option'. The Scottish Parliament subsequently passed legislation (the Criminal Justice and Licensing Act 2010) to rebrand almost all CSM as 'Community Payback Orders'. The Commission defined payback as 'finding constructive ways to compensate or repair harms caused by crime. It involves making good to the victim and/or the community. This might be through financial payment, unpaid work, engaging in rehabilitative work or some combination of these and other approaches' (Scottish Prisons Commission, 2008: para 3.28). The Criminal Justice and Licensing Act 2010 is notable in that it enshrines a reparative logic for almost *all* CSM, not just those involving unpaid work. As the Scottish Prisons Commission notes, 'one of the best ways for offenders to pay back is by turning their lives around' (2008: para 33; see also McNeill, 2011). Rehabilitative effort is thus cast as a form of reparation.

The likely success of this type of reparative legitimation strategy for CSM is difficult to judge. Around the time of the publication of the Scottish Prison Commission's report, the UK Cabinet Office published the Casey (2008) Report on 'Engaging Communities in Fighting Crime', which proposed building public confidence in 'unpaid work' by re-branding it as 'community payback'. Casey's 'payback' was quite different from the Scottish Prisons Commission's, however. She suggested that the work involved should not be something the general public would choose to do themselves (that is, it should be unfulfilling and unpleasant) and that individuals doing payback should wear high visibility vests identifying them as such (that is, it should be shaming) (Maruna and King, 2008).

Looking beyond community service or unpaid work, reparation has also been an important, if contested, discourse for CSM in other jurisdictions. Canton (2007) cites Austria, Belgium, Norway and parts of Germany as developing victim-offender mediation, as well as noting that some of the newer European probation services (for example, in the Czech Republic, Latvia and Turkey) have enshrined principles of reparation and mediation in their founding statements. Reparative work has also played a significant role in societies in transition in particular, often as an outgrowth of peace and reconciliation efforts on a community level (Eriksson, 2009). Northern Ireland, for instance, has one of the best developed, grassroots systems of community-based restorative justice in the world (McEvoy and Mika, 2001). In post-Apartheid South Africa, on the other hand, although probation services have developed rapidly, reparative justice remains more on the margins of this work (Roche, 2002; Ehlers, 2007). Elsewhere in Africa, however, community sentencing tends to focus almost entirely on community service, which Ehlers suggests 'fits well with cultural traditions of making amends as a response to wrong-doing' (2007: 229) (see Chapter 21 for more on punishment in post-conflict situations).

The 'community justice' movement that has spread from the USA (Clear and Karp, 1999; Karp and Clear, 2002) to the UK (Harding, 2000, 2003; Nellis, 2000, 2005) also assigns a central role to themes of reparation, based partially on a reading of the communitarian philosophy of Amitai Etzioni (1991). While there is no standard or agreed formula for what constitutes community justice (Clear and Karp, 1999), Winstone and Pakes suggest that community justice reflects three key principles:

> First, the community is the ultimate consumer of criminal justice. Rather than offenders, or even victims, it is communities that the system ought to serve. Second, community justice is achieved in partnership at the local level. Third, it is problem focussed: problems are addressed rather than cases processed. (2005: 2)

Most recently, the community justice movement has been perhaps most influential through the development of 'justice reinvestment' – an essentially problem-focused approach that aims to move spending from correctional budgets 'upstream' towards crime reduction initiatives in precisely those neighbourhoods from which incarcerated populations are most disproportionately drawn (Tucker and Cadora, 2003).

WHAT FUTURE FOR PUNISHMENT IN SOCIETY: LOOKING FOR LEGITIMACY

Criminal justice sanctions executed in open society represent a particularly interesting case study for students of 'punishment and society'; after all, as our title suggests, CSM represent a primary form of punishment *in* society, rather than removal from (mainstream) society as a form of punishment. A key contention of social analyses of penality is that we can, in the range of penal sanctions, institutions and practices, see reflections of wider social, political and cultural developments. Our account of adaptation strategies suggests that nowhere in the penal field is this more evident than in relation to community sanctions, which have proved remarkably 'elastic' in both form and function throughout their history. Because of probation's umbilical connection with the fading project of penal-welfarism (Garland, 1985), community sanctions have in the last 30–40 years been engaged in a particularly revealing struggle for legitimacy (Weber, 1922 [1946]; Suchman, 1995) – a struggle that has been much more profound for sanctions executed in the community than for the prison (albeit that prisons in many countries have experienced a variety of legitimation crises of their own: see further Liebling and Crewe, Chapter 13, this volume). Community sanctions have had to adapt to new social and political conditions, not from behind the 'safety' of the prison walls, but within and exposed to community and society.

As Joshua Page argues in this volume (see Chapter 7), accounts of penality and its transformations require careful analyses not just of the social forces that operate on the field (from 'outside', as it were), but of the relations and dynamics 'inside' the penal field itself, in its various subfields and in its interactions with other fields of social action. Drawing on the work of Pierre Bourdieu,

Page outlines the contours of the penal field, explaining the relationships between the habitus or dispositions of penal actors and their ownership of and struggles over various forms of capital within and across penality and its intersecting fields. Although we have not cast it principally as such, our analysis of the adaptation of CSM can be read as an account of a range of ways in which CSM's executives, practitioners and advocates have sought to secure such capital in an increasingly unsettled penal field – one in which CSM remain perennially marginal and insecure, despite their proliferation. Different forms of capital are being sought and struggled over in the different attempts to secure legitimacy that we have outlined.

As Wodahl et al. (2011) have recently noted (following Suchman, 1995),[6] different types of legitimacy are in play here: *pragmatic legitimacy* rests in the ability of CSM to meet the needs of its stakeholders; *moral legitimacy* relates to their commitment to achieving goals that conform to societal values; *cognitive legitimacy* arises only when an institution's actions and functions are so woven into the social fabric that they 'simply make sense' in such a way that 'alternatives become unthinkable' (Suchman, 1995: 583). Thus, as penal-welfarism came to be eclipsed, the rehabilitative ideal lost its moral legitimacy, undermining the progress of CSM towards a 'taken-for-granted' (that is, cognitively legitimate) position in the penal field. This occasioned a loss of cultural and symbolic capital as old forms of knowledge and distinction become devalued. The pursuit of new forms of capital required CSM to learn to 'play the (penal) game' by different rules; the managerial adaptation described above (ironically, sometimes called 'modernization') represents a pitch for pragmatic legitimacy in a changing field characterized by reconfigured stakeholder needs (for example, for low cost alternatives to custody). But the politicization of criminal justice changed the game again in at least two ways. First, pragmatic legitimacy became insufficient – CSM needed to respond to shifting societal and political penal values by offering the 'punitive bite' that it was hoped might secure some 'moral legitimacy'. In Bourdieu's terms this might be cast as a grab for symbolic capital that depended on being seen to be sufficiently 'tough' in delivering 'symbolic violence' for and by the punishing the state (in Bourdieu's terms). Second, broader social forces related to risk and insecurity impelled CSM towards a different form of pragmatic legitimacy rooted in the promise to meet stakeholder needs for protection. Here, the cultural and symbolic capital with which CSM sought to trade resided in new claims of expertise and effectiveness around risk and its management.

The reparative strategy is the outlier on this list. It is perhaps the most interesting contemporary development and, in our view, the brightest hope for the future of CSM. If today's proponents of CSM recognize the vulnerabilities of trading on the promise to protect (a promise on which they cannot ever adequately deliver), they might instead now look towards a reparative strategy which seems, in theory at least, potentially capable of delivering *both* pragmatic and moral legitimacy – both cost-effective sanctioning and constructive redress.[7] After all, reparation's pre-modern historical forms and precedents suggest deep and enduring cultural resources (Braithwaite and Pettit, 1990) that might somehow be mined to provide new forms of capital for CSM. Such forms of capital might even be secure enough (because of their deeper historical and cultural roots) to allow CSM to achieve the taken-for-grantedness that has eluded them and condemned them to live in the shadow of the prison; always the alternative, never the main attraction – or as our Edinburgh-based editors might say: 'Always the Fringe, never the Festival.'[8] That said, the Edinburgh Fringe is bigger, (some say) better and perhaps more profitable than the Festival, and neither its performers nor its audiences could be accommodated in the Festival. The same is true of CSM vis-à-vis prisons. In a very important sense, for all their travails, the position of CSM may be symbolically fragile but materially secure, expressively insufficient but instrumentally necessary. CSM will survive because they must; we could not afford to do (punishment) without them. The questions of adaptation we have raised probably speak more to the future forms and functions of CSM than to their longevity. In any event, we suggest that penologists must pay more attention to watching this space, and not just the one inside the prison walls.

NOTES

1 These recent travails of probation may have been most dramatic in Anglophone jurisdictions around the world, but elsewhere, for example in many mainland European countries, probation services seemed to face their own struggles to secure or sustain credibility and legitimacy within criminal justice systems and penal political discourses. For an analysis of one particularly interesting continental example – the reconfiguration of Belgian criminal justice social work in the wake of the Dutroux case – see Bauwens (2011).

2 Our focus here is on supervisory sanctions and measures as opposed to non-supervisory monetary penalties such as fines and restitution (see O'Malley, Chapter 18, this volume).

3 Based, at least in part, on a misreading of public opinion regarding criminal justice (see Roberts and Hough, 2011).

4 Of course, the term rehabilitation is highly ambiguous, and in one of its senses, rehabilitation does imply the restoration of citizenship's rights and duties (see Raynor and Robinson, 2009).

5 Carlen (1989: 120) argued that in some fractured and disadvantaged communities, idealistic community justice alternatives are simply not 'feasible'.

6 There are of course various conceptions of legitimacy from a range of social science disciplines. Suchman's analysis, on which we have drawn, derives from the organizational studies literature, rather than from the sociology, psychology or political science literatures on which criminological scholars have tended to draw (see Crawford and Hucklesby, 2011).

7 The success or failure of reparative CSM is judged principally in terms of the amounts, types and qualities of reparative acts and not in terms of reconviction rates. Reconviction rates 'sell' community sanctions on the basis of their role in reducing crime. A focus on reparation, however, 'sells' CSM in terms of delivering justice (McNeill, 2011). Showing that justice has been done, that debts have been settled, that redress has been provided, is in many ways an easier and more achievable measure of success for CSM.

8 The Festival here refers to the renowned Edinburgh International Festival that takes place in Scotland each summer. The Fringe started as a small, spin-off festival over 50 years ago, but has since grown to become much larger and more varied than the original Festival, albeit of more varied quality, ranging from the sublime to the frankly incompetent.

REFERENCES

Allen, F.A. (1981) *The Decline of the Rehabilitative Ideal: Penal Policy and Social Purpose.* New Haven, CT: Yale University Press.

Andrews, D.A. and Bonta, J. (1998) *The Psychology of Criminal Conduct*, 2nd edn. Cincinnati, OH: Anderson.

Bauman, Z. (1991) *Modernity and Ambivalence.* Cambridge: Polity Press.

Bauwens, A. (2011) 'The transformation of offender rehabilitation?'. PhD thesis, Vrije Universiteit Brussel.

Beccaria, C. (1764 [1963]) *On Crimes and Punishment,* trans. H. Pallouci. Indianapolis: Bobbs-Merrill.

Bell, D. (1973) *The Coming of Post-Industrial Society.* New York: Basic Books.

Beto, D.R., Corbett, R.P. and Dilulio, J.J. (2000) 'Getting serious about probation and the crime problem', *Corrections Management Quarterly,* 4: 1–8.

Bottoms, A.E. (1980) 'An introduction to "the coming crisis"', in A.E. Bottoms and R.H. Preston (eds), *The Coming Penal Crisis.* Edinburgh: Scottish Academic Press. pp. 1–24.

Bottoms, A.E. (1995) 'The philosophy and politics of punishment and sentencing', in C. Clarkson and R. Morgan (eds), *The Politics of Sentencing Reform.* Oxford: Clarendon Press. pp. 17–49.

Bottoms, A., Rex, S. and Robinson, G. (2004) 'How did we get here?', in A. Bottoms, S. Rex and G. Robinson (eds), *Alternatives to Prison: Options for an insecure society.* Cullompton: Willan. pp. 1–27.

Braithwaite, J. (1989) *Crime, Shame and Reintegration.* Cambridge: Cambridge University Press.

Braithwaite, J. and Pettit, P. (1990) *Not Just Deserts.* Oxford: Oxford University Press.

Canton, R. (2007) 'Probation in Europe', in R. Canton and D. Hancock (eds), *Dictionary of Probation and*

Offender Management. Cullompton: Willan. pp. 230–231.

Carlen, P. (1989) 'Crime, inequality and sentencing', in P. Carlen and D. Cook (eds), *Paying for Crime.* Milton Keynes: Open University Press. pp. 8–28.

Casey, L. (2008) *Engaging Communities in Fighting Crime: A Review (Casey Report).* London: Cabinet Office.

Cavadino, M. and Dignan, J. (2007) *The Penal System: An Introduction,* 4th edn. London: SAGE Publications.

Chapman, T. (2010) 'Revising the national outcomes and standards for criminal justice social work services in Scotland', in F. McNeill, P. Raynor and C. Trotter (eds), *Offender Supervision: New Directions in Theory, Research and Practice.* Cullompton: Willan. pp. 430–50.

Christie, N. (1977) 'Conflicts as property', *British Journal of Criminology,* 17: 1–15.

Clear, T. and Karp, D. (1999) *The Community Justice Ideal: Preventing Crime and Achieving Justice.* Oxford: Westview Press.

Cohen, S. (1985) *Visions of Social Control.* Cambridge: Polity Press.

Corbett, R.P. (2002) 'Reinventing probation and reducing youth violence: Boston's operation night light', in D. Karp and T. Clear (eds), *What is Community Justice? Case Studies of Restorative and Community Justice.* Boston, MA: Pine Forge. pp. 175–99.

Council of Europe (1992) Recommendation No. R (92) 16 of the Committee of Ministers to member states on the European rules on community sanctions and measures.

Crawford, A. and Hucklesby, A. (eds) (forthcoming) *Legitimacy and Compliance in Criminal Justice.* London: Routledge.

Cullen, F. (2005) 'The twelve people who saved rehabilitation: how the science of criminology made a difference', *Criminology,* 43 (1): 1–42.

Deleuze, G. (1995) 'Postscript on the societies of control', in G. Deleuze (ed.), *Negotiations: 1972–1990.* New York: Columbia University Press.

Dickey, W.J. and Smith, M.E. (1998) *Dangerous Opportunity: Five Futures for Community Corrections: The Report from the Focus Group.* Washington, DC: US Department of Justice, Office of Justice Programs.

Dignan, J. (2005) *Understanding Victims and Restorative Justice.* Maidenhead: Open University Press.

Diller, R., Greene, J. and Jacobs, M. (2009) *Maryland's Parole Supervision Fee: A Barrier to Reentry?* New York: Brennan Center for Justice.

Duff, A. (2001) *Punishment, Communication, and Community.* Oxford: Oxford University Press.

Durkheim, E. (1901 [1973]) 'Two laws of penal evolution', *Economy and Society,* 2: 278–308.

Durnescu, I. (2008) 'An exploration of the purposes and outcomes of probation in European jurisdictions', *Probation Journal,* 55 (3): 273–81.

Durnescu, I. (2011) 'Pains of probation: effective practice and human rights', *International Journal of Offender Therapy and Comparative Criminology,* 55: 530–45.

Ehlers, L. (2007) 'Probation in Africa', in R. Canton and D. Hancock (eds), *Dictionary of Probation and Offender Management.* Cullompton: Willan. pp. 228–229.

Eriksson, A. (2009) *Justice in Transition: Community Restorative Justice in Northern Ireland.* Cullompton, UK: Willan.

Etzioni, A. (1991) *A Responsive Society: Collected Essays on Guiding Deliberate Social Change.* San Francisco, CA: Jossey-Bass.

Farabee, D. (2005) *Rethinking Rehabilitation: Why Can't We Reform Our Criminals?* Washington: American Enterprise Institute Press.

Farrall, S. and Sparks, R. (2006) 'Introduction', *Criminology and Criminal Justice,* 6, 1: 7–17.

Feeley, M. and Simon, J. (1992) 'The new penology: notes on the emerging strategy of corrections and its implications', *Criminology,* 30: 449–74.

Feeley, M. and Simon, J. (1994) 'Actuarial justice: the emerging new criminal law', in D. Nelken (ed.), *The Futures of Criminology.* London: SAGE Publications. pp. 173–201.

Fitzgibbon, W. (2011) *Probation and Social Work on Trial.* London: Palgrave Macmillan.

Foucault, M. (1975/1977) *Discipline & Punish,* English trans. 1977. London: Allen Lane.

Garland, D. (1985) *Punishment and Welfare.* Aldershot: Gower.

Garland, D. (1990) *Punishment and Modern Society.* Oxford: Clarendon.

Garland, D. (1996) 'The limits of the sovereign state: strategies of crime control in contemporary society', *British Journal of Criminology,* 36 (4): 445–71.

Garland, D. (1997) 'Probation and the reconfiguration of crime control', in R. Burnett (ed.), *The Probation Service: Responding to Change (Proceedings of the Probation Studies Unit First Colloquium).* Oxford: University of Oxford Centre for Criminological Research. pp. 2–10.

Garland, D. (2001) *The Culture of Control.* Oxford: Oxford University Press.

Glaze, L.E. and Bonczar, T.P. (2009) *Bureau of Justice Statistics, Probation and Parole in the United States, 2008.* NCJ 228230. Washington, DC: US Department of Justice, December 2009.

Grattet, R., Petersilia, J., Lin, J., and Beckman, M. (2009) 'Parole violations and revocations in California: analysis and suggestions for action', *Federal Probation*, 73(1): 2–11.

Harding, J. (2000) 'A community justice dimension to effective probation practice', *Howard Journal,* 39 (2): 132–49.

Harding, J. (2003) 'Which way probation: a correctional or community justice service?', *Probation Journal,* 50 (4): 369–73.

Home Office (2006) *Rebalancing the Criminal Justice System in Favour of the Law-Abiding Majority: Cutting Crime, Reducing Re-offending and Protecting the Public.* London: Home Office.

Hulsman, L. (1976) 'Strategies to reduce violence in society: civilising the criminal justice system', an address to the annual meeting of the Howard League for Penal Reform (unpublished).

Hutchinson, S. (2006) 'Countering catastrophic criminology: reform, punishment and the modern liberal compromise', *Punishment and Society,* 8 (4):443–67.

Karp, D. and Clear, T. (eds) (2002) *What is Community Justice? Case Studies of Restorative and Community Justice.* Boston, MA: Pine Forge.

Kemshall, H. and Maguire, M. (2001) 'Public protection, partnership and risk penality: the multi-agency risk management of sexual and violent offenders', *Punishment and Society,* 3 (2): 237–64.

Kendall, K. (2004) 'Dangerous thinking: a critical history of correctional cognitive behaviouralism', in G. Mair (ed.), *What Matters in Probation.* Cullompton: Willan. pp. 53–89.

Lynch, M. (1998) 'Waste managers? The new penology, crime fighting and parole agent identity', *Law & Society Review,* 32: 839–69.

Lyotard, J.F. (1984) *The Postmodern Condition: A Report on Knowledge.* Manchester: Manchester University Press

Mair, G., Cross, N. and Taylor, S. (2007) *The Use and Impact of the Community Order and the Suspended Sentence Order.* London: Centre for Crime and Justice Studies.

Maloney, D., Bazemore, G. and Hudson, J. (2001) 'The end of probation and the beginning of community justice', *Perspectives,* 25 (3): 24–30.

Maruna, S. and Immarigeon, R. (eds) (2004) *After Crime and Punishment: Pathways to Offender Reintegration.* Cullompton: Willan.

Maruna, S. and King, A. (2008) 'Selling the public on probation: beyond the bib', *Probation Journal,* 55: 337–51.

Maruna, S. and LeBel, T. (2003) 'Welcome home? Examining the "re-entry court" concept from a strengths-based perspective', *Western Criminology Review,* 4: 91–107.

May, D.C. and Wood, P.B. (2010) *Ranking Correctional Punishments: Views From Offenders, Practitioners and the Public.* Durham, NC: Carolina Academic Press.

McCulloch, P. and McNeill, F. (2007) 'Consumer society, commodification and offender management', *Criminology and Criminal Justice,* 7 (3):223–42.

McEvoy, K. and Mika, H. (2001) 'Punishment, politics and praxis: restorative justice and non-violent alternatives to paramilitary punishment', *Policing and Society,* 11: 359–72.

McGuire, J. (ed.) (1995) *What Works: Reducing Reoffending.* Chichester: Wiley.

McIvor, G. (2010) 'Paying back: 30 years of unpaid work by offenders in Scotland', *European Journal of Probation,* 2 (1): 41–61.

McIvor, G., Beyens, K., Blay, E. and Boone, M. (2010) 'Community service in Belgium, the Netherlands, Scotland and Spain: a comparative perspective', *European Journal of Probation,* 2 (1): 82–98.

McNeill, F. (2011) 'Probation, credibility and justice', *Probation Journal,* 58 (1): 9–22.

Ministry of Justice (2010) *Breaking the Cycle: Effective Punishment, Rehabilitation and Sentencing of Offenders.* London: Ministry of Justice.

Morris, N. and Tonry, M. (1990) *Between Prison and Probation: Intermediate Punishments in a Rational Sentencing System.* Oxford: Oxford University Press.

Munden, D., Tewksbury, R. and Grossi, E. (1998) 'Intermediate sanctions and the halfway back program in Kentucky', *Criminal Justice Policy Review,* 9(1): 431–49.

National Audit Office (2008) *National Probation Service: The Supervision of Community Orders in England and Wales.* London: TSO.

National Probation Service (2005) *The NOMS Offender Management Model.* London: National Offender Management Service.

Nellis, M. (2000) 'Creating community justice', in S. Ballantyne, K. Pease and V. McClaren (eds), *Secure Foundations: Key Issues in Crime Prevention, Crime Reduction and Community Safety.* London: Institute for Public Policy Research. pp. 67–86.

Nellis, M. (2005) 'Dim prospects: humanistic values and the fate of community justice', in J. Winstone and F. Pakes (eds), *Community Justice: Issues for Probation and Criminal Justice.* Cullompton: Willan. pp. 33–51.

Nellis, M. (2010) 'Electronic monitoring: towards integration into offender management', in F. McNeill, P. Raynor and C. Trotter (eds), *Offender Supervision:*

New Directions in Theory, Research and Practice. Cullompton: Willan. pp. 509–33.

Padfield, N. and Maruna, S. (2006) 'The revolving door at the prison gate', *Criminology and Criminal Justice,* 6 (3): 329–52.

Padfield, N., van Zyl Smit, D. and Dünkel, F. (2010) *Release from Prison: European Policy and Practice.* Cullompton: Willan.

Payne, B.K. and Gainey, R.R. (1998) 'A qualitative assessment of the pains experienced on electronic monitoring', *International Journal of Offender Therapy and Comparative Criminology,* 42 (2): 149–63.

Pease, K. (1985) 'Community service orders', in M. Tonry and N. Morris (eds), *Crime and Justice.* Chicago: Chicago University Press. pp. 51–94.

Peters, A.G. (1986) 'Main currents in criminal law theory', in J. van Dijk, C. Haffmans, F. Rüter, J. Schutte, and S. Stolowijk (eds), *Criminal Law in Action.* London: Kluwer Law and Taxation Publishers. pp. 19–36.

Petersilia, J. (1990) 'When probation becomes more dreaded than prison', *Federal Probation,* 54: 23–27.

Petersilia, J. and Deschenes, E.P. (1994) 'Perceptions of punishment: inmates and staff rank the severity of prison versus intermediate sanctions', *The Prison Journal,* 74 (3): 306–28.

Pratt, J., Brown, D., Brown, M., Hallsworth, S. and Morrison, W. (eds) (2005) *The New Punitiveness: Trends, Theories, Perspectives.* Cullompton: Willan.

Raynor, P. (1988) *Probation as an Alternative to Custody.* Aldershot: Avebury.

Raynor, P. (2007) 'Community penalties: probation, "What Works", and offender management', in M. Maguire, R. Morgan and R. Reiner (eds), *Oxford Handbook of Criminology,* 4th edn. Oxford: Oxford University Press. pp. 1061–99.

Raynor, P. and Robinson, G. (2009) *Rehabilitation, Crime and Justice.* Basingstoke: Palgrave Macmillan.

Raynor, P. and Vanstone, M. (2007) 'Towards a correctional service', in L. Gelsthorpe and R. Morgan (eds), *Handbook of Probation.* Cullompton: Willan. pp. 59–89.

Roberts, J.V. and Hough, M. (2011) 'Custody or community? Exploring the boundaries of public punitiveness in England and Wales', *Criminology & Criminal Justice,* 11: 181–97.

Robinson, G. (2005) 'What works in offender management?', *Howard Journal of Criminal Justice,* 44 (3): 307–18.

Robinson, G. (2008) 'Late-modern rehabilitation: the evolution of a penal strategy', *Punishment and Society,* 10 (4): 429–45.

Robinson, G. and McNeill, F. (2004) 'Purposes matter: examining the "ends" of probation practice', in G. Mair (ed.), *What Matters in Probation.* Cullompton: Willan. pp. 277–304.

Robinson, G. and McNeill, F. (2008) 'Exploring the dynamics of compliance with community penalties', *Theoretical Criminology,* 12 (4): 431–49.

Roche, D. (2002) 'Restorative justice and the regulatory state in South African townships', *British Journal of Criminology,* 42: 514–28.

Rose, N. (2000) 'Government and control', *British Journal of Criminology,* 40: 321–39.

Ross, R.R., Fabiano, E.A. and Ewles, C.D. (1988) 'Reasoning and rehabilitation', *International Journal of Offender Therapy and Comparative Criminology,* 32: 29–35.

Sable, W.J. and Couture, H. (2008) *Prison Inmates at Midyear 2007.* Washington, DC: Bureau of Justice Statistics.

Scottish Prisons Commission (2008) *Scotland's Choice.* Edinburgh: Scottish Prisons Commission.

Sigler, R. T. and McGraw, B. (1984) 'Adult probation and parole officers: Influence of their weapons, role perceptions and role conflict', *Criminal Justice Review,* 9: 28–32.

Simon, J. (1987) 'The emergence of a risk society: insurance, law and the state', *Socialist Review,* 95: 61–89.

Simon, J. (1988) 'The ideological effects of actuarial practices', *Law & Society Review,* 22: 771–800.

Simon, J. (1993) *Poor Discipline: Parole and the Social Control of the Underclass 1890–1990.* London: University of Chicago Press.

Social Exclusion Unit (2001) *Reducing Re-Offending by Ex-Prisoners.* London: Home Office.

Suchman, M.C. (1995) 'Managing legitimacy: strategic and institutional approaches', *Academy of Management Review,* 20 (3): 571–610.

Sykes, G. (1958) *The Society of Captives: A Study of a Maximum-Security Prison.* Princeton, NJ: Princeton University Press.

Tonry, M. and Lynch, M. (1996) 'Intermediate sanctions', *Crime and Justice,* 20: 99–144.

Travis, J. (2005) *But They All Come Back: Facing the Challenges of Prisoner Reentry.* Washington, DC: The Urban Institute Press.

Tucker, S. and Cadora, E. (2003) 'Justice reinvestment: to invest in public safety by reallocating justice dollars to refinance education, housing, healthcare, and jobs. Ideas for an Open Society, Vol 3.

No. 3 (November). New York: Open Society Institute. Retrieved from: http://www.soros.org/resources/articles_publications/publications/ideas_20040106/ideas_reinvestment.pdf

Vanstone, M. (2004) *Supervision Offenders in the Community*. Aldershot: Ashgate.

Vass, A.A. (1990) *Alternatives to Prison*. London: SAGE Publications.

Von Kalmthout, A. and Durnescu, I. (eds) (2008) *Probation in Europe*. Nijmegen: Wolf Legal Publishers/CEP.

Wacquant, L. (2010) 'Prisoner reentry as myth and ceremony', *Dialectical Anthropology*, 34: 605–20.

Ward, T. and Maruna, S. (2007) *Rehabilitation*. London: Routledge.

Weber, M. (1922 [1946]) 'Class, status, party', in H.H. Gerth and C. Wright Mills (eds), *From Max Weber: Essays in Sociology*. New York: Oxford University Press. pp. 180–95.

Winstone, J. and Pakes, F. (eds) (2005) *Community Justice: Issues for Probation and Criminal Justice*. Cullompton: Willan.

Wodahl, E.J., Ogle, R. and Heck, C. (2011) 'Revocation trends: a threat to the legitimacy of community-based corrections', *The Prison Journal*, 91 (2): 207–26.

Zedner, L. (1994) 'Reparation and retribution: are they reconcilable?', *The Modern Law Review*, 57 (2): 228–50.

16

Youth Justice: In a Child's Best Interests?

John Muncie and Barry Goldson

INTRODUCTION

The gradual separation of systems of juvenile and youth justice from adult justice that was initiated in many Western jurisdictions from the mid- to the late-19th century onwards normally sought legitimation in a rhetoric of acting in a child's 'best interests'. The trajectory that such endeavour has followed, however, has never remained constant, has consistently been prey to over zealous paternalism and has characteristically been subjugated to the 'best interests' of adults. What may have begun as an attempt to prevent the 'contamination of young minds' by separating children and young people from adult offenders in prisons, has evolved into a complex of powers and procedures that are both diverse and multi-factorial. Typically systems of youth justice are beset by the ambiguity, paradox and contradiction of whether young offenders should be cast as children in need of help, guidance and support or as corrupt and undisciplined and thereby fully deserving their 'just deserts'. Traditionally this confusion has played itself out along the axis of 'welfare' or 'justice'. By the 1990s the parameters of such debate were, however, significantly altered by rapidly growing penal populations amidst a burgeoning USA-inspired 'culture of control'. Through various measures of 'adulteration' (Fionda, 1998) many young people have found that their special protected 'welfare' status (as in need of care and separate treatment) has been threatened. Rather, in many western jurisdictions it has become more common for the young to be held fully responsible for the consequences of any transgressive actions.

Such developments have, however, been far from universal. At the same time numerous counter movements have emerged that are designed to further rather than diminish children's rights. The restorative justice movement, for example, raises the possibility of less formal crime control and more informal offender/victim participation and harm minimization. The formulation of the United Nations Convention on the Rights of the Child in 1989 stresses the importance of incorporating a rights consciousness into all juvenile justice systems through, for example, the establishment of an age of criminal responsibility relative to developmental capacity, encouraging participation in decision making, providing access to legal representation, protecting children from capital or degrading punishment, and ensuring that arrest, detention and imprisonment are measures of last resort. Above all the Convention emphasizes that the 'best interests' of those aged under 18 should be a primary consideration.

By the 21st century, juvenile justice in many (western) jurisdictions has evolved into a significantly more complex state of affairs. Many systems are apparently designed to punish 'young offenders' while simultaneously, and paradoxically – in keeping with international children's rights instruments – ensuring that their welfare is safeguarded and promoted as a primary objective. The same systems are, at one and the same time, concerned with crime prevention *and* retribution, whereas the imperatives of restoration and reintegration are incongruously juxtaposed alongside some of the most punitive measures of surveillance, monitoring and penal confinement to be found in any 'justice' system, juvenile or adult (for a fuller discussion see Muncie and Goldson, 2006). Furthermore, children and young people perceived to be 'at risk' are targeted, as well as those arrested and convicted of offences. In this way, 'modern' juvenile justice systems increasingly appear to be concerned not simply with controlling crime but also with pre-emptively regulating all manner of behaviours deemed 'vulnerable', 'risky', 'nuisance' or 'anti-social'. Above all, a gradual accretion and incremental consolidation of myriad initiatives have emerged over two centuries. But the 'new' has never fully supplanted the 'old'. In the 21st century discourses of child protection, restoration, punishment, public protection, responsibility, justice, rehabilitation, welfare, retribution, diversion, human rights, and so on, intersect and circulate in a perpetually uneasy motion.

The presence of contradictory policies and practices both *between* and *within* territorial jurisdictions, renders contemporary youth justice both a complex and an engaging aspect in any broader study of punishment and society.

WELFARE TRADITIONS

Much of the 'best interests' principle in youth justice derives from the reforming zeal of philanthropists and 'child-savers' of the mid to late 19th century. Youth crime was thought best deterred by confining children in reformatories and subjugating them to disciplined labour and religious re-education. Such intervention was legitimized through a discourse of welfare and care. As a result, it was able to draw not only the offender, but also those thought likely to offend – the orphan, the vagrant, the runaway, the independent and those with a 'deviant' street lifestyle – into its remit. The prevailing argument that a child's age and/or the prospect of parental neglect should be taken into account when adjudicating on juveniles, subsequently opened the way for a plethora of welfare inspired legislation in the 20th century. For example, in England and Wales the Children Act 1908 created a separate and distinct system of justice based on the juvenile court; the Children and Young Persons Act 1933 statutorily required the court to consider the child's welfare and the Children and Young Persons Act 1969 initially provided for the phasing out of criminal, in favour of civil, proceedings. By the 1960s custodial and care institutions were also being criticized as stigmatizing, dehumanizing and criminogenic rather than as agencies capable of preventing further offending. In their place a range of preventive and rehabilitative treatment units located in the community was advocated (Miller, 1998). The welfare 'ideal' found a quite remarkable international consensus through the first 70 years of the 20th century.

Originating with the establishment of discrete juvenile courts in South Australia (1895), Illinois, USA (1899) and England

and Canada (1908), and developing through a wide corpus of protective statute in many jurisdictions, child welfare models of juvenile justice became paramount. Perhaps the exemplar of welfare-based approaches emerged in Scotland in the 1960s when the juvenile court was effectively abolished in favour of less formal tribunals in the shape of a children's hearing system (Kilbrandon Committee, 1964). More generally throughout this period, penal welfare, rehabilitation and 'meeting needs' were the watchwords and set the parameters of any debate over how to deal with the 'troubled and troublesome' young (Garland, 1985).

Welfarism though has never been universally accepted as the most propitious means of preventing youth crime. A strong law and order lobby has also ensured that a range of punitive custodial options always remained firmly in place. Consequently, it has been argued that the fate of welfarism has been one of simply adding to the range of interventions and disposals available to the court. Indeed during the 1970s welfarism was generally employed with a younger age group of, for example, low-school-achievers, 'wayward girls' and truants from 'problem' families designated as 'pre-delinquent', while the courts continued with the policy and practice of punishing more hardened 'offenders'. The two systems became vertically integrated. (Thorpe et al., 1980). At best welfare allows for an acknowledgement of the reduced culpability of children, but it has also served to justify early (pre-criminal) intervention against those considered to be 'at risk' and rarely, if ever, has it meant that children are dealt with more leniently (King and Piper, 1995).

By the 1980s liberal lawyers, civil libertarians and radical social workers were becoming increasingly critical of welfare-based discourse, procedures and sentencing. They argued that 'meeting needs' acted as a spurious justification for placing excessive restrictions on individual liberty, which were out of proportion either to the seriousness of the offence or to the realities of being in 'need of care and protection'. This was (and remains) particularly the case for girls and young women (Gelsthorpe and Worrall, 2009). Welfare-based approaches, it was claimed, not only preserved explanations of individual pathology, but also drew young people into the judicial process – from which there was rarely any escape – at an ever-earlier age. Young people were placed in double jeopardy sentenced for their background as well as for their offence – and as a result their movement up the sentencing tariff tended to accelerate (Morris et al., 1980).

PROGRESSIVE AND RETRIBUTIVE JUSTICE

The critique of welfare had three main elements that paradoxically signalled a convergence of otherwise divergent political positions. First, from the right, welfare and rehabilitative systems were condemned as evidence that juvenile justice was simply too 'soft on crime'. Second, radical social workers argued that the 'need for treatment' acted as a spurious justification for placing considerable and undue restrictions on the liberty of children. Third, civil libertarians and liberal lawyers maintained that welfarism denied juveniles access to full legal rights and that their 'protection' would be better served by removing aspects of discretionary decision making. In the USA the landmark Supreme Court *Gault* ruling of 1967 established that under the Fourteenth Amendment, juveniles accused of crimes in delinquency proceedings must be accorded essentially the same due process rights as adults. The most devastating critique of welfare as a reforming impulse, however, came from Martinson's (1974) analysis of 231 studies of treatment programmes in the USA. He concluded that 'with few and isolated exceptions the rehabilitative efforts that have been reported so far have had no appreciable effect on recidivism' (1974: 25). This conclusion was widely received as 'nothing works': that it was a waste of time and money to devote energy to the rehabilitative treatment of (young) offenders. It prompted a collapse of faith in correctionalism, initially in relation to prison-based 'treatment programmes' but subsequently expanded to include all manner of probation interventions and community corrections. Doubt was cast over the efficacy of many fundamental aspects of juvenile justice.

In the wake of such critique a justice-based model of corrections emerged in the 1970s, underpinned by the interrelated principles of: proportionality; determinacy; an end to judicial, professional and administrative discretion; protection of rights through due process and the diversionary imperative of minimum necessary intervention or 'least interference' (von Hirsch, 1976). Initially this progressive 'back to justice' movement appeared to be successful. Diversion from prosecution was encouraged through informal police cautioning (rather than prosecution) and diversion from custody was secured by the development of intensive community – based interventions. In some jurisdictions, such as in Massachusetts, USA, residential and custodial establishments were closed down (Miller, 1998). A focus on 'deeds' rather than 'needs' expunged many of the unaccountable aspects of welfarism from youth justice (Rutherford, 1992). In contrast to the free-ranging and 'needs' oriented interventions legitimized by reference to welfare, the concept of due process provided that the intensity of formal intervention should be proportionate to the severity/gravity of the offence, rather than the level of perceived 'need'. Formal intervention became conceived in terms of 'restrictions of liberty' that must be limited to the minimum necessary, in accordance with principles of *proportionality*.

Such liberal critique, however, coalesced with the concerns of traditional retributivists that rehabilitation was a 'soft option' and that its 'successes' were far from clear cut. For them, tougher sentencing was the only way of ensuring offenders received 'just deserts'. The language of 'justice' and 'rights' was appropriated, therefore, to imply 'individual responsibility' and 'personal obligation'. Accordingly Hudson (1987) has argued that the 'just deserts' or 'back to justice' movements that emerged in many western jurisdictions in the 1980s were evidence of a 'modern retributivism' rather than necessarily heralding the emergence of new liberal regimes and positive rights-based agendas. A rhetorical appeal to *punishment in the community* was emphasized in preference to community-based preventive measures. Moreover, renewed fears of persistent young offenders (for example, most famously in England following the political fallout from the murder of James Bulger by two 10-year-olds in 1993), enabled youth justice to take a decisively retributive turn. Custody was once more promoted as the key means to prevent re-offending. 'Get tough' slogans such as 'prison works', 'three strikes' and 'condemn more – understand less' gained political acceptability. Once more a legal discourse of guilt, responsibility and punishment resurfaced as the dominant discourse in the definition and adjudication of youth offending and youth justice (Goldson, 1999; Haydon and Scraton, 2000).

Fionda (1998) has also noted how a series of legislative changes and reformulations of policy from the 1980s onwards have constructed systems that now have 'an almost stubborn blindness' to welfare principles and the mitigating circumstances of age. Processes of 'adulteration' or 'adultification' became most marked in the USA via widespread dismantling of special court procedures that had been in place for much of the 20th century to protect young people from the stigma and formality of adult justice (Feld, 1993; Singer, 1997). Since the 1980s (but beginning in Florida in 1978), most American states expanded the charges for which juvenile defendants could be tried as adults in criminal courts, lowered the age at which such charges could be brought, changed the purpose of juvenile codes to prioritize punishment and resorted to more punitive 'training' interventions and boot camp regimes (Grisso and Schwartz, 2000). A renewed emphasis on public safety (rather than a child's best interests) also meant that the young person's conventional right to confidentiality in criminal proceedings was removed in most states with the names of juvenile offenders made public and in some cases listed on the internet. As Merlo et al. (1997) established, by the mid-1990s at least 23 states had some statutory or legislative waiver provisions so that some juveniles *had to be* adjudicated in adult courts thereby allowing the imposition of longer and more punitive forms of intervention. As a result around 200,000 children were processed as adults each year (Snyder, 2002). Moreover, before 2005 five US states, notably Texas and Florida, allowed execution for 17-year-olds and a further 17, notably Alabama and Louisiana, could authorize the death penalty for children who committed offences when they were aged 16. This practice was only abolished in March 2005 when the US Supreme Court ruled by a slim majority of 5 to 4 that it amounted to 'cruel and unusual punishment'.

HUMAN RIGHTS IMPERATIVES

During the 1980s and 1990s many jurisdictions not only developed specified *rights* in respect of children and young people in their domestic statutes; but also ratified a range of international conventions, standards, treaties and rules to protect children in conflict with the law. The United Nations Standard Minimum Rules for the Administration of Juvenile Justice (the Beijing Rules) were adopted by the United Nations in 1985 and provide guidance for the protection of children's rights in the development of *separate* and *specialist* juvenile/youth justice systems. The 'Rules' operate within a framework of two other sets of international juvenile/youth justice standards, both of which were adopted in 1990: the United Nations Guidelines for the Prevention of Juvenile Delinquency (the Riyadh Guidelines) and the United Nations Rules for the Protection of Juveniles Deprived of their Liberty (the JDL Rules). Perhaps most significantly, in 1989 the United Nations Convention on the Rights of the Child (UNCRC) set out comprehensive minimum standards for the treatment of *all* children. The UNCRC is the most widely adopted of all international conventions, having been ratified by 193 countries (the USA is the major exception). Although it does not relate exclusively to youth justice, many of its provisions ('articles') are directly focused upon children in conflict with the law.

Article 3 of the UNCRC provides that the 'best interests' of the child should be a primary consideration in *all* actions, courts and law. Although the UNCRC falls short of establishing a minimum age of criminal responsibility – Article 4.1 of the Beijing Rules states that the age of criminal minority should 'not be fixed at too low an age level, bearing in mind the facts of emotional, mental and intellectual maturity' and the UN has subsequently declared that setting the age of responsibility below 12 is not 'internationally acceptable' (UN Committee on the Rights of the Child, 2007). Further, the Beijing Rules 17.1(b) and 17.1(d) provide that: 'restrictions on the personal liberty of the juvenile shall … be limited to the possible minimum', and 'the well-being of the juvenile shall be the guiding factor in her or his case' (this is reiterated at Article 40.4 of the UNCRC). Indeed, the international instruments enshrine the concept of proportionality to offset the likelihood of over-zealous intervention and concomitant forms of injustice. In essence this important principle requires no more and no less than a fair and proportional reaction in any case where a child is convicted of a criminal offence. The UNCRC also specifies that detention of a child 'shall be used only as a measure of last resort and for the shortest appropriate period of time' and that 'every child deprived of liberty shall be treated with humanity and respect for the inherent dignity' (Article 37), taking into account 'the child's age and the desirability of promoting the child's reintegration and the child's assuming a constructive role in society' (Article 40(1)). Further, in 2006 The Commission of the European Communities published its own separate EU strategy on the rights of children affirming the issue as a 'priority' with the aim of promoting the EU as 'a beacon to the rest of the world'. Many of the latter's core principles of affording all children (those under 18 years) rights to protection, privacy, participation and material provision have subsequently been reiterated in the 2008 European Rules for Juvenile Offenders Subject to Sanctions or Measures.

To establish how far individual states are treating their young in the spirit, if not the word, of the UNCRC, the United Nations also established a separate Committee on the Rights of the Child that requires nation states to report periodically on their 'progress' and to receive recommendations for further action. However the Committee's 'General Comment' published in 2007, concluded that implementation of the UNCRC has often been piecemeal and that in juvenile justice reform the issue of children's rights frequently appears as an afterthought:

> ... many States parties still have a long way to go in achieving full compliance with CRC, e.g. in the areas of procedural rights, the development and implementation of measures for dealing with children in conflict with the law without resorting to judicial proceedings, and the use of deprivation of liberty only as a measure of last resort ... The Committee is equally concerned about the lack of information on the measures that States parties have taken to prevent children from coming into conflict with the law. This may be the result of a lack of a comprehensive policy for the field of juvenile justice. This may also explain why many States parties are providing only very limited statistical data on the treatment of children in conflict with the law'. (United Nations Committee on the Rights of the Child, 2007: 1)

In addition a United Nations report specifically on violence against children stated that in care and justice systems:

> Millions of children, particularly boys, spend substantial periods of their lives under the control and supervision of care authorities or justice systems, and in institutions such as orphanages, children's homes, care homes, police lock-ups, prisons, juvenile detention facilities and reform schools. These children are at risk of violence from staff and officials responsible for their well-being. Corporal punishment in institutions is not explicitly prohibited in a majority of countries. Overcrowding and squalid conditions, societal stigmatization and discrimination, and poorly trained staff heighten the risk of violence. Effective complaints, monitoring and inspection mechanisms, and adequate government regulation and oversight are frequently absent. Not all perpetrators are held accountable, creating a culture of impunity and tolerance of violence against children. (United Nations General Assembly, 2006: 16)

The UNCRC is persuasive but breach attracts no formal sanction. It may be the most ratified of all international human rights instruments but it is also the most violated. In most cases it has not been incorporated into domestic statute within nation states that have formally ratified it. Indeed, Abramson (2006) has concluded that the obligations of the UNCRC are received by many states as 'unwanted'. He notes how disproportionate sentences, insufficient respect for the rule of law, excessive use of custody and improper use of the juvenile justice system to tackle other social problems, are widespread. Similarly, analysis of the UN Committee's jurisdiction-specific reports with regard to several western European states, found that most states have failed to recognize that issues such as distinctive needs, dignity and humane treatment are absolutely core to the realization of children's rights (Muncie, 2008).

Significantly, most western Europe jurisdictions have been condemned for discriminating against minorities such as asylum seekers. The UN Committee in particular noted the disproportionate criminalization and incarceration of Roma and traveller communities (in Italy, Switzerland, Finland, Germany, Greece, the UK, Ireland, France, Spain, Portugal), of Moroccans and Surinamese (in the Netherlands) and of North Africans (in Belgium and Denmark). This raises the question of a fundamental racialization of youth justice in western societies generally. In the USA, for example, ethnic minorities make up about one-third of all juveniles in the general population but about two-thirds of those in secure detention. In some states almost all cases of juvenile waiver involve 'minorities'. There can be little dispute too that across Europe, ethnic and immigrant groups have been increasingly identified as a threatening 'underclass' and exposed to suspicion, neutralization and exclusion (Wacquant, 1999). For example, Europe's 8 million Roma – the largest ethnic minority group in the European Union – are widely reported as enduring systematic harassment, discrimination, forced eviction, ghettoization , detention and expulsion. In some jurisdictions, such as Switzerland, Austria, Belgium and Italy over one-third of their total prison populations are foreign nationals and over 100,000 prisoners in EU countries do not have citizenship of the countries in which they are incarcerated (Muncie, 2008).

In many countries it seems abundantly clear that it is possible to claim an adherence to the principle of universal rights while simultaneously pursuing policies that exacerbate structural inequalities and punitive institutional regimes. 'Cultural difference' and the absence of localized human rights cultures preclude meaningful adoption of international agreements (Harris-Short, 2003). The US case is indicative, whereby human rights violations appear to be intrinsic components of laws that allow for the prosecution of children in adult courts and which fail to specify a minimum age of criminal responsibility (Amnesty International, 1998).

RESTORATIVE APPROACHES

Although the principles of justice, welfare and rights continue to play themselves out in myriad complex and contradictory ways, some commentators have argued that the 'justice' afforded to young people should move beyond narrow interpretations of modern western legalism and to connect instead with broader conceptions of respect, reconciliation and restoration. For some, the time has indeed come to rethink the principles of juvenile justice through a lens of 'inclusion', 'reconciliation' or 'problem solving' (Smith, 2005; Allen, 2006) and to develop policies designed to both facilitate *conflict resolution* and offset the costs and the damage of excessively punitive responses to juvenile crime. The processes and cultural norms of a number of traditional indigenous societies across the Americas and Australasia, in particular, have seemingly made it possible to imagine fundamentally different responses to harms and conflicts.

Proponents of restorative justice claim that 'justice' can best be realized by *restoring* well-being to the 'victim' by some form of recognition or recompense, while the 'offender' is *restored* to membership of the community by both acknowledging and compensating for their transgression. Restoration may take many forms including an apology, a demonstration of full recognition of the harm done, reparation from the 'offender' to the 'victim' and/or some form of 'reintegrative shaming' designed to strengthen communitarian ideals. The processes may be ritual or ceremonial and often involve a public statement of apology from the 'offender' and forgiveness from the 'victim' or community leaders. For example, Family Group Conferences in New Zealand – based on traditional systems of conflict resolution within Maori culture – involve a professional coordinator, dealing with both civil and criminal matters, who calls the young person, their family and victims together to decide whether the young person is 'in need of care and protection' and if so what should be provided.

While most western jurisdictions have now adopted various forms of restorative justice their potential to provide a radical alternative to the conventional machinery of youth justice (be it derived from welfare, justice, retributive or rights-based discourses), is profoundly compromised by their coexistence with neoliberal discourses of remoralization, discipline and individual responsibility. The lack of accountability and the diminution of protection for the 'offender' – in terms of appeals to legality and due process – remain major areas of concern. Restorative justice can easily be corrupted as a set of apparent informal alternatives *within* otherwise formal systems of retributive justice (Daly and Immarigeon, 1998; Gelsthorpe and Morris, 2002; Cunneen, 2003; Cunneen and Hoyle, 2010). As a result the question remains of the extent to which restorative justice initiatives, administered in a criminal justice context, may simply act to extend the net of social control deeper into the community and to effectively reinforce the notion of individual responsibility. The general difficulty with restorative justice concerns its assumption that young people are autonomous, rational individuals able to make free moral choices for which they can be held to account. Ironically, such notions are also a core element of contemporary demands for increased responsibility, punishment and punitivity.

THE 'PUNITIVE TURN' AND REPENALIZATION

On the basis of our previous comparative research (Goldson and Muncie, 2006a; Muncie and Goldson, 2006; Muncie, 2008; Goldson and Hughes, 2010), arguments in support of a 'punitive turn' thesis appear unequivocal. Equally, the Children's Legal Centre/Y Care International (2006) campaign report is firmly based on the supposition that 'states all over the world have retained an overwhelmingly punitive response to young offending'. This is particularly evident within Anglo-American youth justice systems. In the USA, for example, juvenile incarceration increased by 43 per cent during the 1990s reaching an estimated 105,600 in 2006. Despite, or perhaps because of, the repeal of the death penalty, many states have retained powers of life imprisonment without parole. At least 2,225 child offenders were serving such sentences in 2005; 60 per cent of whom were African American (Human Rights Watch/Amnesty International, 2005). In contrast to the 'best interest' principle underpinning the establishment of the first juvenile court in Chicago in 1899, juvenile justice systems throughout America now give greater weight to punishment as an end in itself. Nevertheless we should also be mindful of distinct state differences and current pressures – economic, moral, pragmatic – to reverse this trend (Krisberg, 2006; Benekos and Merlo, 2008; Merlo and Benekos, 2010). The 'punitive turn' thesis also seems to hold true when considering policy trajectories over the past two decades in the UK and in particular in England (Goldson, 2009a). Not only has England been witness to a doubling of the population of children detained in the 'juvenile secure estate' between 1993 and 2008, it has also been witness to the adoption (symbolically or otherwise) of American-style experiments with curfews, naming and shaming responses, zero tolerance initiatives, dispersal zones, parental 'sin-bins', fast tracking schemes and the general targeting of pre-criminal disorder and incivility. Further, in 1998 the Crime and Disorder Act served to abolish the presumption of *doli incapax* that had provided that children between the ages of 10 and 13 years were presumed to be incapable of criminal intent. Before a child of this age could be convicted of a criminal 'offence' this core presumption had to be rebutted by the prosecution; by proving beyond 'reasonable doubt' that the child was aware that what they did was 'seriously wrong' as opposed to merely naughty or mischievous. Thus the doctrine of *doli incapax* – a long established principle of law dating back to the time of Edward III (1327–1377)– comprised an important legal safeguard for 10–13-year-old children; children, that is, who would be below the age of criminal responsibility in most other European countries. The abolition of *doli incapax*, together with the other punitive reforms signalled above, suggests a consolidating 'institutionalized intolerance' towards those aged under 18 (Muncie, 1999, 2008).

Furthermore, similar developments are evident in various European jurisdictions otherwise known for their progressive responses to juvenile crime. Van Swaaningen (2005) records how traditional cultures of penal tolerance in the Netherlands have become seriously compromised. Early intervention projects, such as STOP, have effectively lowered criminal responsibility from 12 to 10 years while juvenile detention rates have tripled since 1990 (uit Beijerse and van Swaaningen, 2006). Similarly, in Belgium public debate about insecurity and lack of safety has fuelled a fear of juvenile crime, legitimized police curfew and zero tolerance initiatives (Put and Walgrave, 2006) and bolstered an increasing tendency to refer juvenile offenders to adult courts (van Dijk et al., 2005).

In France, the right-wing government of Alain Juppé from 1993 to 1997 prioritized a zero tolerance police-led approach to crime prevention. The socio-economic conditions that produce youth marginalization and estrangement are no longer given central political or academic attention (Bailleau, 1998). In particular, attention has become increasingly directed towards identifiable groups of children – especially child migrants – as sources of trouble as distinct from objects of welfare-based concern. Special surveillance units have been established to repress delinquency in 'sensitive neighbourhoods'. Penalties for recidivism have been increased and the deportation of 'foreigners' has accelerated (Wacquant, 2001). New public safety laws have: expanded police powers of search, seizure and arrest; instituted prison sentences for public order offences (such as being disrespectful to those in authority); lowered from 16 to 13 the age at which young offenders can be imprisoned and introduced benefit sanctions for parents of offending children. Furthermore, the election of Nicolas Sarkozy as President of the French Republic in 2007, was swiftly followed by an assurance that 16-year-old children who re-offended would be treated as adults.

In 2008, Chancellor Angela Merkel in Germany announced plans to introduce boot camps and 'warning shot arrests' particularly for immigrant youth. Following an attack on a pensioner by two youths – one Greek and one Turkish – Merkel claimed that 'we have too many criminal young foreigners', despite statistical evidence showing that crime by non-Germans was in decline and that juvenile crime had remained stable – comprising approximately 12 per cent of all recorded offences – for the past 15 years.

Rechea Alberola and Fernandez Molina (2006) have argued that recent legislative reform in Spain has generally devalued 'best interest' principles in favour of tough responses to young offenders. Similarly, the reformed children's court in Ireland (Kilkelly, 2008a) and experimental youth courts for 16- and 17-year-olds in Scotland (Piacentini and Walters, 2006), each operate in a manner more akin to adult courts. Meanwhile, in Sweden, alarmism, zero tolerance and increased sanctioning of penal control has been expressed through both social democratic and conservative political discourse (Tham, 2001). According to Pratt (2008: 278), cuts in welfare benefits in the 2000s, the beginnings of privatization of state services and the marginalization of immigrants and the low-qualified has been reflected in a growing politicization of law and order. Attitudes to what constitutes acceptable levels of imprisonment appear to be changing. Similarly a 'return to law and order' (Balvig, 2004) in Denmark has meant that long standing welfare boards – alternative tribunals to court based systems for juvenile offenders – are also under threat by more repressive crime control initiatives (Jepsen, 2006).

Such commentaries suggest a major transformation in international juvenile justice, whereby punitive interventions are displacing traditional principles of child protection and welfare support. Governments of all persuasions appear to be increasingly turning to law and order as a means of providing symbols of security and to enhance their own chances of electoral success.

DECARCERATION

It would be erroneous to assume that such phenomena are being evenly applied on a global scale. In the same way that some youth justice jurisdictions manage to resist (or delay) processes of child criminalization, retain a progressive welfare ethic and locate youth crime and justice within forms of social-structural analysis and response, others sustain decarcerative priorities. Many jurisdictions in Australia, for example, witnessed substantial falls in child imprisonment in the early 21st century, seemingly as a result of extending diversionary options including the use of youth conferencing (Cunneen and White, 2006). Recent evidence from Canada also suggests a growing decarcerative movement (Smandych, 2006) whereas a number of European countries including Italy (Nelken, 2006) and Finland (Lappi-Seppälä, 2006), have been able to report significant *decreases* in their daily count of youth (aged under 21) incarceration throughout the age of 'new punitiveness' in the 1990s. According to UN data, Japan, Norway and Sweden similarly stand out as having been able to keep youth imprisonment to an absolute minimum and as maintaining such toleration at least up to the early 21st century (Muncie, 2005). Whether politically, pragmatically or economically inspired, a case establishing the damaging effects of custody on children (and the wider community) has repeatedly been made and acknowledged. Finland's experience, for example, seems to show that high incarceration rates and tough penal regimes do not control crime (Lappi-Seppälä, 2006). They are unnecessary. Decarceration can be pursued without sacrificing public safety. Indeed a progressive consensus appears to exist in Nordic countries (Iceland, Norway, Sweden, Finland and Denmark) such that 'forward looking' social and educational measures, together with mediation, take precedence over prosecution and punishment.

PRINCIPLES FOR YOUTH JUSTICE

Our analysis of international youth justice has established various trans-jurisdictional themes (both progressive and repressive) alongside prominent examples of political and cultural diversity. Our ultimate aim for youth justice research, though, is not limited to simply accounting for difference and/or similarity. Rather it is one of promoting those elements that offer the greater potential for systems to truly act in a child's 'best interests'. In our view, these lie in a hybrid of universal (non-criminalizing) welfare and children's rights imperatives. In general terms the most constructive youth justice systems appear to be situated in jurisdictions/countries in which there is a political willingness to sustain welfare protectionism or to subsume youth justice within alternative forms of conflict resolution. A cultural and political sensibility that imprisoning young people is not only harmful, but also self defeating, is crucial. Some of the key drivers of the more diversionary, decriminalizing and decarcerative youth justice systems are derived from restatements of a 'children first' philosophy; a commitment to pardon and to protect, but above all a preparedness to depoliticize youth crime and justice. In policy terms this involves the objective of removing all children from *prison service* custody and a greater commitment to suspending sentences and employing inclusionary and participative community based interventions as direct alternatives to incarceration. Compliance both with the spirit and the content of the international human rights framework is also pivotal (Kilkelly, 2008b).

We have formulated such an approach around six core principles (Goldson and Muncie, 2006b). Each necessitates a conceptual and organizational reframing of youth crime and youth justice and, paradoxically, a substantially reduced role for the conventional youth justice apparatus itself.

(1) Policy should *comprehensively* address the *social* and *economic* conditions that are known to give rise to conflict, harm, social distress, crime and criminalization, particularly *poverty* and *inequality*. It is no coincidence that youth justice systems characteristically serve to process (and punish) the children of the poor. Those children who are most heavily exposed to correctional intervention, surveillance and punishment, are routinely drawn from some of the most disadvantaged families, neighbourhoods and communities. Young people for whom the fabric of life invariably stretches across poverty; family discord; public care; drug and alcohol misuse; mental distress; ill-health; emotional, physical and sexual abuse; self-harm; homelessness; isolation; loneliness; circumscribed educational and employment opportunities; 'hollowed-out' communities and the most pressing sense of distress and alienation, are the very children targeted by the youth justice apparatus. The corrosive impact of poverty and structural inequality on children, families and communities is profound and is key to understanding and responding to the problems both experienced and perpetuated by identifiable sections of the young.

(2) The forging of the principles of *universality, comprehensiveness* and *re-engaging the 'social'* requires dispensing with forms of conditionality that bolster the 'deserving-undeserving schism' and instead providing holistic services that meet the needs and safeguard and promote the well-being of *all* children and young people. 'Normal' social institutions – including families (however they are configured), 'communities', youth services, leisure and recreational services, health provision, schools, training and employment initiatives – need to be adequately resourced and supported. The industrial-scale expansion of the youth justice system should be curtailed and resources re-directed to generic 'children first' services. Conversely, normalizing and decriminalizing approaches – intrinsic to the principles of universality, comprehensiveness and re-engaging the 'social' – are substantiated by robust research evidence. One of the most ambitious and comprehensive research analyses of youth crime prevention programmes in the world, for example, demonstrated that, even for 'serious, violent and chronic juvenile offenders', some of the most effective responses emanate from initiatives that are located *outside* of the formal criminal justice system (decriminalization), build upon children's and young people's strengths as distinct from emphasizing their 'deficits' (normalization) and adopt a social-structural approach rather than drawing on individualized, criminogenic and/or medico-psychological perspectives (contextualization) (Howell et al., 1995).

(3) Children and young people should be routinely diverted away from formal youth justice interventions. Of course, the most effective diversionary strategy is literally to remove children and young people from the reach of the youth justice system altogether, by significantly raising the age of criminal responsibility. There are strong grounds to support this proposition, not least evidence from jurisdictions where the age of criminal responsibility is set above the European mean, for example, and where there are no negative consequences in terms of crime rates (Goldson, 2009b).

(4) In the minority of cases where formal youth justice intervention is deemed unavoidable, it should be provided within a child-appropriate context. The intensity and duration of intervention should be proportionate to the severity of the offence and limited to the minimum that is absolutely necessary and its rationale should be explicit, evidenced-based and likely to provide positive outcomes for the 'young offender' and, where relevant, to any injured party. International human rights agencies are consistent in their critique of adulterized youth justice systems. It is imperative that such critique is constructively applied to inform a more child-appropriate youth justice system.

(5) Interventions that are ineffective or, more problematically, that violate international human rights obligations, are known to be damaging and harmful and/or aggravate the very issues that they seek to resolve should be abolished. This applies, in varying degrees to: over-zealous and criminalizing modes of early intervention; the net-widening effect of 'anti-social behaviour' initiatives and in particular, the practices of imprisonment. This is not to imply that nothing should be done with regard to youth offending, or that troubled and troublesome children and young people should simply be left to fend for themselves without the care, guidance, support and supervision that they may well need.

The central argument, however, is that the criminal justice apparatus is, in itself, singularly unfit for such purpose. Rather a critical rethinking of the conceptual origins, significances and meanings attributed to terms such as 'youth disorder', 'anti-social behaviour', 'youth crime' and 'young offender' is required. It offers an invitation to 'start from a different place'; to focus upon offending as a social harm to be resolved rather than simply punished (Hillyard and Tombs, 2007).

(6) The politicization of youth crime and justice, can only serve to demonise identifiable constituencies of the young, to legitimize 'ill-considered but attention grabbing tough-on-crime proposals' (Tonry, 2004: 2) and to 'institutionalize intolerance' (Muncie, 1999). Politicians repeatedly refer to an increasingly anxious, risk-averse and fearful public and selective constructions of 'public opinion' are mobilized and presented as primary legitimizing rationales for the 'tough on crime' agenda. Such reactive politicization not only negates evidence and distorts policy formation, however, it is also underpinned by a skewed reading of public opinion itself. A genuinely evidenced-based approach to youth crime and justice requires politicians and policy makers to remain cognizant of the complexities of public opinion. Moreover, senior politicians have a responsibility to *inform* public opinion as distinct from simply reacting to over-simplified and fundamentally erroneous interpretations of it. A principled youth justice, therefore, must transgress crude politicization and ultimately demand the de-politicization of youth crime and justice.

CONCLUSION

The antecedents of contemporary youth justice can be traced back to the 'invention' of 'juvenile delinquency' in the early 19th century, and the subsequent inception of a specific corpus of legislation, court structures, policies, procedures and practices for the processing of 'young offenders' at the beginning of the 20th. Throughout this period policy reform and practice development have not followed an even linear trajectory. Harris and Webb, for example, have noted that youth justice 'is riddled with paradox, irony, even contradiction … [it] exists as a function of the child care and criminal justice systems on either side of it, a meeting place of two otherwise separate worlds' (1987: 7–9). Similarly, Muncie and Hughes have reflected that: 'youth justice is a history of conflict, contradictions, ambiguity and compromise … [it] tends to act on an amalgam of rationales, oscillating around and beyond the caring ethos of social services and the neo-liberal legalistic ethos of responsibility and punishment' (2002: 1). The means by which 'two otherwise separate worlds' are reconciled or, to put it another way, the balance that is struck between the 'caring ethos' and the 'ethos of responsibility and punishment', is subject to the vagaries of political imperative and policy contingency. In short, youth justice systems are dynamic and ever-changing sites of contestation and change comprising, as we have argued, a mix of competing and/or intersecting thematic concepts including: welfare, justice (progressive and/or retributive), rights, restoration and retribution/punishment.

As a result it is difficult, if at all possible, to conceptualize juvenile/youth justice systems with reference to any totalizing rationale or even to compartmentalize them into discrete self-standing 'models' (Winterdyk, 2002; Cavadino and Dignan, 2006). Rather their core components are drawn from a variety of otherwise competing and contradictory thematic sources. Clearly, there are times and places when certain thematic priorities are more ascendant than others. In the final analysis, however, youth justice systems are dynamic, ever-changing, hybridized forms that are temporally and spatially contingent. Governments, formal administrations, judicial bodies and correctional agencies *choose* to construct and manage youth justice systems, in accordance with widely divergent ideological imperatives, political calculations, cultural priorities, judicial conceptualizations and operational strategies. Ultimately, similar acts can elicit quite different responses across time and space and, as a consequence, children's experiences of 'justice' are far from uniform but differentiated and diverse with their 'best interests' rarely, if ever, being fully realized.

REFERENCES

Abramson, B. (2006) 'Juvenile justice: the unwanted child', in E. Jensen and J. Jepsen (eds), *Juvenile Law Violators, Human Rights and the Development of New Juvenile Justice Systems*. Oxford: Hart. pp. 15–38.

Allen, R. (2006) *From Punishment to Problem Solving – A New Approach to Children in Trouble*. London: Centre for Crime and Justice studies.

Amnesty International (1998) *Betraying the Young: Children in the US Justice System*. AI Index AMR 51/60/98.

Bailleau, F. (1998) 'A crisis of youth or of juridical response?' in Ruggiero, V., South, N. and Taylor, I. (eds), *The New European Criminology*. London: Routledge. pp. 95–103.

Balvig, F. (2004) 'When law and order returned to Denmark', *Journal of Scandinavian Studies in Criminology and Crime Prevention*, 5(2): 167–87.

Benekos, P. and Merlo, A. (2008) 'Juvenile justice: the legacy of punitive policy', *Youth Violence and Juvenile Justice*, 6(1): 28–46.

Cavadino, M. and Dignan, J. (2006) *Penal Systems: A Comparative Approach*. London: SAGE Publications.

Children's Legal Centre/Y Care International (2006) *Youth Justice in Action: Campaign Report*. London: Y Care International.

Cunneen, C. (2003) 'Thinking critically about restorative justice', in E. McLaughlin, R. Fergusson, G. Hughes and L. Westmarland (eds), *Restorative Justice: Critical Issues*. London: SAGE Publications/ Open University. pp. 182–94.

Cunneen, C. and Hoyle, C. (2010) *Debating Restorative Justice*. Oxford: Hart.

Cunneen, C. and White, R. (2006) 'Australia: control, containment or empowerment', in J. Muncie and B. Goldson (eds), *Comparative Youth Justice: Critical Issues*. London: SAGE Publications. pp. 96–110.

Daly, K. and Immarigeon, R. (1998) 'The past, present, and future of restorative justice: some critical reflections', *Contemporary Justice Review*, 1: 21–45.

Feld, B. (1993) 'Criminalising the American juvenile court', in M. Tonry (ed.), *Crime and Justice*. Chicago: Chicago University Press. pp. 197–280.

Fionda, J. (1998) 'The age of innocence? – the concept of childhood in the punishment of young offenders', *Child and Family Law Quarterly*, 10 (1): 77–87.

Garland, D. (1985) *Punishment and Welfare: A History of Penal Strategies*. Aldershot, Gower.

Gelsthorpe, L. and Morris, A. (2002) 'Restorative justice: the last vestiges of welfare?', in J. Muncie, G. Hughes and E. McLaughlin (eds), *Youth Justice: Critical Readings*. London: SAGE Publications. pp. 238–54.

Gelsthorpe, L. and Worrall, A. (2009) 'Looking for trouble: a recent history of girls, young women and youth justice', *Youth Justice*, 9(3): 209–23.

Goldson, B. (ed.) (1999) *Youth Justice: Contemporary Policy and Practice*. Aldershot, Ashgate.

Goldson, B. (2009a) 'Child incarceration: institutional abuse, the violent state and the politics of impunity', in P. Scraton and J. McCulloch (eds), *The Violence of Incarceration*. Abingdon: Routledge. pp. 86–106.

Goldson, B. (2009b) 'Difficult to understand or defend': a reasoned case for raising the age of criminal responsibility', *Howard Journal*, 48(5): 514–21.

Goldson, B. and Hughes, G. (2010) 'Sociological criminology and youth justice: comparative policy analysis and academic intervention', *Criminology and Criminal Justice*, 10(2): 211–30.

Goldson, B. and Muncie, J. (2006a) 'Rethinking youth justice: comparative analysis, international human rights and research evidence', *Youth Justice*, 6 (2): 91–106.

Goldson, B. and Muncie, J. (2006b) 'Critical anatomy: towards a principled youth justice', in Goldson and Muncie (eds), *Youth Crime and Justice*. London, SAGE Publications. pp. 203–32.

Grisso, T. and Schwartz, R.G. (eds) (2000) *Youth on Trial*. Chicago: University of Chicago Press.

Harris, R. and Webb, D. (1987) *Welfare, Power and Juvenile Justice*. London: Tavistock.

Harris-Short, S. (2003) 'International human rights law: imperialist, inept and ineffective? Cultural relativism and the UN Convention on the rights of the child', *Human Rights Quarterly*, 25(1): 130–81.

Haydon, D. and Scraton, P. (2000) 'Condemn a little more, understand a little less: the political context and rights implications of the domestic and European rulings in the Venables-Thompson case', *Journal of Law and Society*, 27 (3): 416–448.

Hillyard, P. and Tombs, S. (2007) 'From 'crime' to social harm?', *Crime, Law and Social Change*, 48: 9–25.

Howell, J.C., Krisberg, B., Hawkins, J.D. and Wilson, J. (eds) (1995) *Serious, Violent and Chronic Juvenile Offenders: A Sourcebook*. London: SAGE Publications

Hudson, B. (1987) *Justice through Punishment*. London: Macmillan.

Human Rights Watch/Amnesty International (2005) *The Rest of Their Lives: Life without Parole for Child Offenders in the United States*. New York: Human Rights Watch.

Jepsen, J. (2006) 'Juvenile justice in Denmark: from social welfare to repression', in E. Jensen and J. Jepsen (eds), *Juvenile Law Violators, Human Rights and the Development of New Juvenile Justice Systems*. Oxford: Hart. pp. 213–62.

Kilbrandon Committee (1964) *Report of the Committee on Children and Young Persons*. Edinburgh: HMSO.

Kilkelly, U. (2008a) 'Youth courts and children's rights: the Irish experience', *Youth Justice*, 8 (1): 39–56.

Kilkelly, U. (2008b) 'Youth justice and children's rights: measuring compliance with international standards', *Youth Justice: An international journal*, 8 (3): 187–92.

King, M. and Piper, C. (1995) *How the Law Thinks About Children*. Aldershot: Ashgate.

Krisberg, B. (2006) 'Rediscovering the juvenile justice ideal in the United States', in J. Muncie and B. Goldson (eds), *Comparative Youth Justice*. London: SAGE Publications. pp. 6–18.

Lappi-Seppälä, T. (2006) 'Finland: a model of tolerance?', in J. Muncie and B. Goldson (eds), *Comparative Youth Justice*. London: SAGE Publications. pp. 177–195.

Martinson, R. (1974) 'What works? – questions and answers about prison reform', *The Public Interest*, 35: 22–54.

Merlo, A. and Benekos, P. (2010) 'Is punitive juvenile justice policy declining in the United States? A critique of emergent initiatives', *Youth Justice: An International Journal*, 10 (1): 3–24.

Merlo, A., Benekos, P. and Cook, W. (1997) 'Waiver and juvenile justice reform: widening the punitive net', *Criminal Justice Policy Review*, 8(2–3): 145–68.

Miller, J. (1998) *Last One Over the Wall. The Massachusetts Experiment in Closing Reform Schools*, 2nd edn. Columbus, OH: Ohio State University Press.

Morris, A., Giller, H., Geach, H. and Szwed, E. (1980) *Justice for Children*. London: Macmillan.

Muncie, J. (1999) 'Institutionalized intolerance: youth justice and the 1998 Crime and Disorder Act', *Critical Social Policy*, 19(2): 147–75.

Muncie, J. (2005) 'The globalization of crime control – the case of youth and juvenile justice: neo-liberalism, policy convergence and international conventions', *Theoretical Criminology*, 9(1): 35–64.

Muncie, J. (2008) 'The punitive turn in juvenile justice: cultures of control and rights compliance in western Europe and the USA', *Youth Justice: An International Journal*, 8(2): 107–21.

Muncie, J. and Goldson, B. (eds) (2006) *Comparative Youth Justice: Critical Issues*. London: SAGE Publications.

Muncie, J. and Hughes, G. (2002) 'Modes of youth governance: political rationalities, criminalisation and resistance', in J. Muncie, G. Hughes and E. McLaughlin (eds), *Youth Justice: Critical Readings*. London: SAGE Publications. pp. 1–18.

Nelken, D. (2006) 'Italy: a lesson in tolerance?', in J. Muncie and B. Goldson (eds), *Comparative Youth Justice: Critical Issues*. London: SAGE Publications. pp. 159–176.

Piacentini, L. and Walters, R. (2006) 'The politicization of youth crime in Scotland and the rise of the 'Burberry Court'', *Youth Justice*, 6 (1): 43–60.

Pratt, J. (2008) 'Scandinavian exceptionalism in an era of penal excess. Part II: does Scandinavian exceptionalism have a future?', *British Journal of Criminology*, 48 (3): 275–92.

Put, J. and Walgrave, L. (2006) 'Belgium: from protection to accountability', in J. Muncie and B. Goldson (eds), *Comparative Youth Justice*. London: SAGE Publications. pp. 111–126.

Rechea Alberola, C. and Fernandez Molina, E. (2006) 'Continuity and change in the Spanish juvenile justice system', in J. Junger-Tas and S. Decker (eds), *International Handbook of Juvenile Justice*. Dordrecht: Springer. pp. 325–350.

Rutherford, A. (1992) *Growing out of Crime: The New Era*. Winchester: Waterside.

Singer, S. (1997) *Recriminalizing Delinquency: Violent Juvenile Crime and Juvenile Justice Reform*. Cambridge: Cambridge University Press.

Smandych, R. (2006) 'Canada: Repenalialization and young offenders' rights', in J. Muncie and B. Goldson (eds), *Comparative Youth Justice*. London Sage Publications. pp. 19–33.

Smith, R. (2005) 'Welfare vs justice again!', *Youth Justice*, 5 (1): 3–16.

Snyder, H. (2002) 'Juvenile crime and justice in the United States of America', in N. Bala, J. Hornick, H. Snyder and J. Paetsch (eds), *Juvenile Justice Systems: An International Comparison of Problems and Solutions*. Toronto: Thompson. pp. 43–66.

Tham, H. (2001) 'Law and order as a leftist project?: The case of Sweden', *Punishment and Society*, 3 (3): 409–26.

Thorpe, D.H., Smith, D., Green, C.J. and Paley, J.H. (1980) *Out of Care: The Community Support of Juvenile Offenders*. London: Allen and Unwin.

Tonry, M. (2004) *Punishment and Politics: Evidence and Emulation in the Making of English Crime Control Policy*. Cullompton: Willan.

Uit Beijerse, J. and van Swaaningen, R. (2006) 'The Netherlands: penal welfarism and risk management', in J. Muncie and B. Goldson (eds), *Comparative*

Youth Justice. London: SAGE Publications. pp. 65–78.

United Nations Committee on the Rights of the Child (2007) *Children's Rights in Juvenile Justice,* 44th Session General Comment No 10. CRC/C/GC/10., United Nations, Geneva.

United Nations General Assembly (2006) *Report of the independent expert for the United Nations on Violence against Children*, 61st Session, A/61/299, United Nations, Geneva.

Van Dijk, C., Nuytiens, A. and Eliaerts, C. (2005) 'The referral of juvenile offenders to the adult court in Belgium', *Howard Journal*, 44 (2): 151–66.

Van Swaaningen, R. (2005) 'Public safety and the management of fear', *Theoretical Criminology*, 9 (3): 289–305.

Von Hirsch, A. (1976) *Doing Justice: The Choice of Punishments*. New York: Hill & Wang.

Wacquant, L. (1999) 'Suitable enemies: foreigners and immigrants in the prisons of Europe', *Punishment and Society*, 1 (2): 215–22.

Wacquant, L. (2001) 'The penalization of poverty and the rise of neo-liberalism' *European Journal on Criminal Policy and Research*, 9: 401–412.

Winterdyk, J. (ed.) (2002) *Juvenile Justice Systems: International Perspectives*, 2nd edn. Toronto: Canadian Scholars Press.

17

The Punishment Debate in Restorative Justice

Kathleen Daly

The relationship of punishment to restorative justice is uneasy. Many restorative justice promoters are 'against punishment', seeing little or no connection between it and restorative justice. Others see a complementary relationship in which restoration depends, in part, on punishment. Understanding the relationship of punishment to restorative justice (the 'punishment debate') is hampered by varied and imprecise use of key terms such as punitive, retribution, restoration and punishment itself.

In this chapter, I clarify and analyse the punishment debate in restorative justice. My focus is on domestic contexts of criminal justice in affluent democratic societies, as compared with transitional justice or international criminal justice contexts. The first section presents the early arguments that formed the basis for restorative justice, and how analysts construed punishment in making their case for justice alternatives. The second section examines contemporary work on restorative justice; it reveals differences in analysts' aspirations for restorative justice, what practices are called 'restorative', and how key terms are defined. In the third section, I present and assess different positions on the punishment debate; these turn on the meanings of 'punitive' and the role of punishment in restoration (or reparation).[1] I compare the arguments of three analysts – Lode Walgrave (2008), Ross London (2011) and Antony Duff (2003) – on punishment and restorative justice. Their arguments reflect differing aims and presuppositions: Walgrave is concerned with socio-ethical principles; London, with political pragmatism and empirical evidence, and Duff, with demonstrating the compatibility of restorative and retributive justice.

THE MAIN POINTS

Embedded in a selective history of restorative justice,[2] here are the main points. First, the early thinkers who are today associated with restorative justice were generally 'against punishment'. Eccentric and somewhat radical for their day, their views reflected the optimism of their times, the 1960s and 1970s, when it seemed possible to shift criminal justice toward a more constructive and less punitive direction. Such optimism spiralled downwards in the 1980s and 1990s, with rising imprisonment rates and a conservative turn in penal politics. Building on other proposed justice alternatives circulating at the time, the idea of restorative justice emerged as a new term in the late 1980s, consolidating in the 1990s. For many, it offered renewed hope and optimism for progressive change in criminal justice, despite a continuing conservative landscape.

Restorative justice has no agreed-upon definition. However, if we restrict the concept to one of several responses to common crime in the penalty or post-penalty phase of the criminal process, it has these common elements. Victims and admitted offenders are active participants and subjects of justice processes; and crime is addressed directly by the actions and words given by, or burdens imposed on, offenders directly to victims, and where relevant, to their supporters and a wider social group. These activities are intended to 'repair the harm' and 'restore' social relations broken by crime. Restorative justice is a form of informal justice, which means that emphasis is placed on dialogue, interaction and engagement of the protagonists, with relatively less reliance on strict notions of legal procedure or the involvement of legal professionals. At the same time, most proponents want clear legal standards and protocols in place, particularly to limit sanctions. The activities associated with restorative justice in domestic contexts are conferences, dialogues, circles and expanded types of victim-offender mediation (McCold, 2001). These take place at many points in the criminal process, as diversion from court, pre-sentence advice, supplemental to the court process and post-sentence. Restorative justice dialogues are also used to address wider political conflict, although these typically do not include criminal justice processes or sanctions.

It is important to emphasize that restorative justice occurs only in the *post-plea* or *penalty phase* of the criminal process.[3] There is as yet no 'restorative' or 'reparative' mechanism of adjudication; and thus, there is no complete justice system based on these ideas. Often it is said that restorative justice differs from conventional criminal justice in being consensually based, not adversarial. This sounds pleasing, but it is misleading. Conventional criminal justice is adversarial (whether the procedure is formally described as 'accusatorial' or 'inquisitorial') because the accused is put in the position of having to defend against an accusation by the state. There may be better ways to adjudicate crime, but no one believes that we should dispense with the right of individuals to defend themselves against a state's power to prosecute and punish alleged crime.

During the 1990s, restorative justice became immensely popular, eclipsing and overtaking other justice ideas circulating during the 1970s and 1980s – a range of restitution, reparation, reconciliation and informal justice projects. Restorative justice seemed to offer something for everyone, on both the left and right side of politics. With so many people involved, often with a partial view of the expanding literature, discussion flew in many directions. This leads to the second point: although most proponents put forward a general case 'against punishment', terms were not defined with precision. Instead, advocates wanted to move the idea onto the public agenda and to sell its benefits. Governments were attracted to the idea, rebranding some rehabilitation programs as 'restorative' and incorporating the term 'restorative justice' in new justice initiatives for youthful offenders. The pace of change and the thousands of people involved – academics, practitioners and faith-based community members, among others – created an ever widening field of knowledge.

Third, amid the diversity, simple metaphors seemed to bind people together. A significant one, introduced by Zehr (1985, 1990), is the contrast of retributive and restorative justice, which helped proponents to argue for the superiority of restorative justice over what was called retributive justice.

Some elements in the contrast are worth preserving, in particular, Zehr's effort to redefine crime and justice. However, at the time, anything to do with *retribution*, a term with many meanings, or *punishment*, as a social institution or 'a repertoire of penal sanctions' (Garland, 1990: 17), was eschewed by proponents as irrelevant or as being against the principles of restorative justice. The retributive-restorative oppositional contrast stalled a more sophisticated conceptual development of restorative justice in its formative years. Although some were critical of the contrast (Watson et al., 1989; Duff, 1992, 1996, 2001; Hampton, 1992, 1998; Zedner, 1994; Daly, 2000, 2002), at the time, such views were in the minority. Now, by contrast more considered attention is being given to the relationship of retribution and restoration (or reparation), and of punishment to restorative justice.[4] I identify three positions (not just two) on the punishment debate, and my analysis of the arguments by Walgrave, London and Duff shows that despite differences, there are many points of overlap.

KEY ARGUMENTS IN RESTORATIVE JUSTICE: FORMATIVE IDEAS

Among others, these key thinkers are associated with the development of restorative justice: Albert Eglash, Randy Barnett, Howard Zehr and Nils Christie. All say that conventional criminal justice is inadequate and accomplishes little for victims or offenders.

Eglash

Eglash is credited with first using the term restorative justice. A psychologist based in the USA, he worked in programs for youthful offenders and adult prisoners; and he drew from these experiences in outlining a 'creative' meaning of restitution (Eglash, 1957–58a, 1957–58b, 1959–60). Creative restitution varies depending on context, is offender self-determined but guided, and relates to constructive acts for a victim or others (Eglash, 1957–58a). Eglash distinguishes the 'first mile' of the return of property under court order or by the expectations of friends and family from the 'second mile' of restitution 'in its broad meaning of a complete restoration of good will and harmony ... [and] a situation left better than before an offense was committed' (1957–58a: 620). Restorative justice does not appear in this article or the two others appearing at the same time (1957–58b, 1959–60; but see note 5).

Almost two decades later Eglash (1977) explicitly used the term restorative justice.[5] He defined it as the 'technique of [creative] restitution' (1977: 91), contrasting it to retributive and distributive justice, which he associated with techniques of punishment and therapeutic treatment, respectively.[6] The elements of the 'restitutional act' are an 'active, effortful role', which is 'constructive [and] directed toward the victim, and ... reparative of the damage done to a person or property' (1977: 94). Eglash again includes 'the second mile', saying that creative restitution goes 'beyond coercion into a creative act' by leaving a situation better than before (1977: 95). He says that it 'fits best as a requirement of probation', but does not say how it relates to other sentence elements. He concludes by saying he is 'offender oriented', 'seldom thinks about the victim', and it has never occurred to him to ask victims what they thought of creative restitution (1977: 99).

Restorative justice, as defined by Eglash (1977), is some distance from principles and practices associated with the term today. However, these similarities can be discerned. Eglash makes a strong contrast between the failure of older justice forms (retributive and distributive) and the superiority of a new type (restorative). The latter form goes 'beyond coercion' by assuming an offender will take an 'effortful role' in redressing the damage and harm caused by an offence. He has a highly optimistic view of offenders' abilities and interests to want to go 'the second mile'.

Barnett

The elements in Randy Barnett's (1977) 'new paradigm' of restitutional justice are directly linked to current ideas in restorative justice. He defines crime as an offence of one person against another (rather than against the state), defines justice as a 'culpable offender making good the loss' caused, and is against punishment, which he equates with 'retributive justice'. In its place he proposes 'pure restitution', a 'non-punitive' form of restitution. This differs from 'punitive restitution', which Barnett defines as forced compensation or imposed fines.[7] The goal is 'reparations paid to the victim', which would be ordered, when an offender is 'sentenced to make restitution to the victim' (1977: 289). In Barnett's analysis, reparations (he uses the plural) and restitution refer to the same thing: financial payments. He considers a variety of ways of 'repaying the victim' (1977: 289–91), but concedes at the end of his paper that his proposed restitutional system collapses the distinction between crime and tort (1977: 299).

Barnett's argument is an early example of the 'civilization thesis' in two meanings of that concept: to bring offenders under civil, not criminal law; and to have a more enlightened response to acts called 'crime' (1977: 300).[8] His ideas raise questions for how elements of civil law could be incorporated within restorative justice (Johnstone, 2003: 8–14). However, he does not satisfactorily explain why 'we are not entitled to impose punishment upon offenders but are entitled to *force* them to pay restitution' (Johnstone, 2003: 21–2, 26 note 4, original emphasis). Furthermore, Barnett argues that 'pure restitution' is accomplished by sentencing an offender to make restitution, but it is difficult to see how this differs from sentencing an offender to pay compensation[9] or do work for the victim. Both are imposed on the offender in some way.

Zehr

Howard Zehr's (1985) contrast of retributive and restorative justice tracks Barnett's argument closely, but also departs from it. Zehr argues for a new paradigm, but names it restorative justice. Like Barnett, he redefines crime (an offence between two individuals, not just an offence against the state). For justice, he cites a variety of terms, including restoration, reconciliation, the process of making things right, right relationships measured by the outcome, repair of social injury and healing. Like Barnett, his preferred response to crime is restitution, which he sees 'as a means of restoring *both* parties' (Zehr, 1985: 81, original emphasis), not as a type of punishment. Zehr is also concerned to address the conflict between individuals: he calls for offenders and victims 'to see one another as persons, to establish or re-establish a relationship' (1985: 79). Compared to Barnett, who draws mainly from legal authority, Zehr draws from religious history and Judeo-Christian ideals. His work with the Victim-Offender Reconciliation Project, a Mennonite-based program that facilitated meetings between victims and imprisoned offenders, informs much of his thinking on restorative justice. Although the retributive-restorative justice contrast was an 'elegant and catchy exposition' at the time (Roche, 2007: 87), major restorative justice proponents acknowledge today that it was misleading because retribution can and should be part of restorative justice (Zehr, 2002; Walgrave, 2004, 2008; Van Ness and Strong, 2006).

Christie

Of the four authors detailed here, Nils Christie (1977) focuses more on the processes and procedures of optimal justice activities than sanctions alone. His article opens by taking us to a small village in Tanzania, where there is a conflict about property after a marital engagement broke off. He approves of the way the dispute (a civil matter) is settled: the protagonists are at the centre of attention, with family members and other villagers participating. They are the experts, not the judges.[10] Christie puts forward two related points. First, professionals, especially lawyers 'are particularly good at stealing conflicts' (Christie, 2003: 59) between individuals. Second, these conflicts should be seen 'as property' because they have great value. They offer a chance for people to participate in society, they provide 'opportunities for norm clarification', and they help protagonists to meet and get to know each other (2003: 61). His ideas for a model court go further than those of other analysts in that he shows how civil and criminal processes might be blended.

Christie's proposed court is victim-centred and lay-oriented, and it has four stages. The first is to establish that a law has been broken and the right person is identified. The second is to focus attention on the victim's situation and what can be done to address it, 'first and foremost by the offender' (2003: 63), then the local neighbourhood, and then the state. Christie has in mind repairing windows and locks, offenders paying compensation with money or by doing work for a victim, and in other ways, 'restoring the victim's situation' (2003: 64). After all of this occurs, the third stage is a judicial officer deciding if further punishment is required, 'in addition to those unintended constructive sufferings the offender would go through in his restitutive actions [for] the victim' (2003: 64). The last stage, which is post-sentence, is service to an offender, which includes addressing his or her social, medical, and educational needs.

Several observations can be drawn from these early works that are now linked to restorative justice. First, the authors all say that conventional criminal justice is a failure, and they propose different models of criminal justice. Second, they argue that admitted or convicted offenders should have a more direct and constructive role in 'repaying' victims for crime. This new role is variably termed creative restitution, pure restitution, restorative justice, or restoring the victim's situation; and its outcome is restoration, making reparations, healing, among other terms. Third, all struggle in imagining how this new role for offenders relates to conventional criminal justice. For all, there is a desire to identify 'non-punitive', more constructive responses to crime, and except for Christie, a rejection of the term punishment. Finally, for some (Zehr and Christie), there is also a new role for victims and others, who should be able to speak and participate in decisions about responding to crime.

RESTORATIVE JUSTICE TODAY

Restorative justice became immensely popular from the 1990s onwards and was viewed by many as a social movement of global dimensions. As increasing numbers of people got involved, conceptual and definitional problems emerged; and they remain today.

Defining restorative justice

Johnstone and Van Ness argue that restorative justice is not only a 'persistently vague concept, it is in fact a deeply *contested* concept' (2007: 6, original emphasis). There is no one definition, nor should this be expected, they say, because the restorative justice movement is not coherent or unified. Johnstone (2008) identifies five political agendas of advocates. Agendas 1 and 2 are the most familiar and widely used: changing the response to crime, and changing the way in which crime and justice are defined. Agenda 3 is concerned with widening the use of restorative justice to other organizational settings (e.g. schools, prisons, workplaces); and Agenda 4, with activities of political reconciliation (e.g. applications in post-conflict societies, among others). Agenda 5 is concerned with transforming social organization and one's personal life. Punishment is particularly relevant to Agendas 1 and 2, but relatively less so for the other agendas.

To make this discussion concrete, I turn to definitions of restorative justice by well-known recent advocates: Tony Marshall, Lode Walgrave and John Braithwaite. Marshall's definition is as follows:

> Restorative justice is a process whereby all the parties with a stake in a particular offense come together to resolve collectively how to deal with the aftermath of the offense and its implications for the future. (Marshall, 1998, reprinted in Johnstone, 2003: 28)

Marshall focuses on *the deliberative processes* of face-to-face negotiation and resolution of a criminal offence, and he gives passing reference to reparation in discussing practices. His definition is aligned with Agenda 1, a concern to change the response to crime. Walgrave's definition is aligned with Agenda 2; he is concerned with *the outcome* of restorative justice (restoration), and he defines restorative justice this way:

> an option for doing justice after the occurrence of an offence that is primarily oriented towards repairing the individual, relational, and social harm caused by that offence. (Walgrave, 2008: 21)

His definition is 'maximalist' because it may 'include non-deliberative interventions … or imposed restitution or community service if intended as a symbolic compensation for the harm to social life' (Walgrave, 2008: 20). He wishes to advance a 'revolutionary' understanding of crime and justice by asking 'how the harm can be repaired' rather than 'what should be done the offender'? He sees this difference as distinguishing restorative justice from 'punitive justice' and also from rehabilitation (2008: 23). Further he says that restorative justice is not the only way to respond to all types of crime, but it is an 'option'. He calls for a 'shift from the punitive apriorism to a restorative apriorism' in that the first task 'must be to assess what the harm is and how it can be repaired … not which punishment is to be inflicted on the offender' (2008: 24).

Walgrave argues for a restricted definition of restorative justice, one focusing on the way criminal offences are dealt with. Thus, he would exclude activities in Agendas 3, 4 and 5. Among his reasons are that restorative justice 'risks becoming empty of significance' by including other contexts, and the focus should centre on how the state uses coercion in responding to crime. Compared to Walgrave's restricted definition, others such as Braithwaite are more expansive.

Braithwaite's work has evolved from applications to youth crime in the early and mid-1990s (Braithwaite and Daly, 1994; Braithwaite, 1996) to broader mechanisms of regulation and societal transformation (Braithwaite, 1999, 2002, 2003). Indicative of his vision of 'holistic restorative justice', he argues that it is not just about 'reforming the criminal justice system, [but] a way of transforming our entire legal system, our family lives, our conduct in the workplace, our practice of politics' (Braithwaite, 2003: 1). He continues by saying that restorative justice is:

> about struggling against injustice in the most restorative way we can manage. … It targets injustice reduction [not merely crime reduction]. It aspires to offer practical guidance on how we can lead the good life as democratic citizens by struggling against injustice. It says we must conduct that struggle while seeking to dissuade hasty resort to punitive rectification or other forms of stigmatising response. (2003: 1)

This definition exemplifies Agenda 5 with its call for struggling against injustice and providing guidance to citizens to lead the 'good life'. In that struggle, 'punitive rectification' and 'stigmatizing responses' should not ideally be used.

Defining restorative practices

A significant question for the restorative justice field is what is to be considered a 'restorative' practice or response to crime. The term is often used to refer to any response that does not involve a prison sentence or that is 'non-punitive'. For instance, Pennsylvania's sentencing guidelines identify 'restorative sanction programs' as 'least restrictive, non-confinement intermediate punishments' (Section 303.12 (a) (5)). Roberts and Stalans (2004: 325–6) contrast 'punitive' and 'restorative' sanctions: the latter includes any type of community or non-custodial penalties. The problems here are twofold. First, many justice activities that would formerly be termed diversion from court, rehabilitative, or community-based penalties are now being termed 'restorative'. This is a simple rebranding that may have little to do with the principles and practices of restorative justice. Second, and importantly for this chapter, is how restorative justice sanctions can be distinguished from other types. Typically, 'non-punitive' is used to refer to a restorative response or outcome, but this begs the question: when is a response 'punitive' or 'non-punitive'? Is this in the mind of the decision maker, is it implied in any coerced sanction, is it how an offender experiences a sanction, or is it how a victim interprets a sanction? I turn next to consider these problems of definition.

Defining key terms

Restorative justice proponents define terms variably and imprecisely. Furthermore, key terms are not independently defined but collapsed on each other: thus, for example, retributive justice is associated with a punitive attitude, punitive sanctions, and punishment of the offender as the primary response. To understand and assess the punishment debates, we need to unravel these terminological knots. A key term is 'punitive'.

Punitive

Research on public punitiveness (Maruna, 2006) defines it as support for harsh sanctions of offenders.[11] Drawing from Maruna (2006), to be punitive implies an attitude of mind that sees offenders as 'bad persons', who require 'more harsh', 'tougher', or austere responses to crime, their suffering in some sense 'repaying' for the harm they caused another person. This contemporary understanding can be linked to earlier work on the idea of punitiveness. In the early 20th century, George Herbert Mead (1917–18, reprinted 1998) described two attitudes of mind in responding to crime: one, an 'attitude of hostility toward the lawbreaker' and the other, a 'reconstructive attitude'. Whereas the former 'brings with it the attitudes of retribution, repression, and exclusion' (1998: 47–48), the latter tries to 'understand the causes of social and individual breakdown, to mend ... the defective situation ... , not to place punishment but to obtain future results' (1998: 52). In the essay, Mead was defending the merits of the then emerging juvenile court; but his ideas are evident not only in the language and assumptions of the early figures of restorative justice (especially Eglash, Barnett and Zehr), but all those since.

If punitive is defined as an 'attitude of mind', associated with social exclusion and seeing no value in (or expectation of) attempts to change an offender, then a minority of criminologists in the world today would align with this position. Although members of the broader public may hold a punitive attitude of mind, I suspect that most criminologists (both advocates and critics of restorative justice) would say that they have a 'non-punitive' attitude of mind and that criminal justice decision makers should as well. 'Punitive' is rarely defined in the restorative justice literature except as a pejorative term to refer to any aspect of the conventional criminal justice system, or as a substitute name for that system (Walgrave [2008] on punitive justice compared to restorative justice). However, there can be greater conceptual precision if we define 'punitive' and 'non-punitive' as types of attitudes toward offenders. For example, in responding to crime, we may choose to distinguish (or not) an offending *person* from an offending *act*: a good person who committed a bad act (a non-punitive attitude), or bad person who committed a bad act (punitive attitude).

This distinction was made by Braithwaite (1989) in his theory of reintegrative shaming, an early theory in restorative justice: shame the act, but then reintegrate the person as a 'good person'. Braithwaite contrasted reintegrative shaming with stigmatizing shaming, in which both the act and person were shamed, and which he associated with conventional criminal justice. We can associate a non-punitive attitude with reintegrative shaming, and a punitive attitude with stigmatizing shaming. However, that does not tell us how we may distinguish between 'punitive' and 'non-punitive' *sanctions*. A prison sentence could be decided in a process that used reintegrative shaming, and compensating a victim could be imposed in a process that used stigmatizing shaming.

Retribution

According to Cottingham, philosophers have put forward at least nine theories of retribution to justify punishment, although he believes that there is a 'basic sense' of what the term means: repayment (1979: 238). Although the relationship between repayment and 'inflicting suffering' is 'left unexplained', it is 'both ancient and widely held' (1979: 238). For this reason, he says that the 'repayment sense' of retribution should be viewed as a metaphor more than a theory of punishment. Cottingham's observations help us to see why there are varied meanings of retribution in the restorative justice field. Some use the term to describe a *desert justification* for punishment (e.g. intended to be in proportion to the harm caused; see Walgrave and Aertsen, 1996), whereas others use it to describe a *form* of punishment. For the latter, some use retribution in a *neutral* way to refer to a censuring of harms (Duff, 1996), but most use the term to connote a *punitive* response, which is associated with the intention to inflict pain (Wright, 1991).

Punishment

Punishment conjures many images in people's heads, but for many restorative justice proponents, it is equated with prison and other forms of unacceptable ('uncivilized') pain infliction. More acceptable, they believe, are constructive efforts by an offender to do something for a victim (to mend, repair, or restore the harm caused by crime), whether by working directly for a victim or paying back money or property in some way. At issue is whether such sanctions or outcomes – which are intended to repair or restore – are (or should be viewed as) forms of punishment because they are coerced or imposed as a burden.

Some argue that incarceration and fines are punishments because they are *intended deprivations*, whereas probation or what are termed 'reparative measures' (such as doing work for a crime victim) are not punishment because they are *intended to be constructive* (Walgrave, 2004: 48–9). Others define punishment to include anything that is a form of suffering, is unpleasant, a burden, or an imposition; the intentions of a decision maker are less significant or irrelevant (Davis, 1992; Duff, 2001). Therefore, because any criminal justice process is coercive, outcomes from a restorative justice process are types of punishment (Crawford and Newburn, 2003: 46–7; see also Daly, 2000, 2002; Johnstone, 2003: 22), despite the benevolent intentions of restorative justice promoters (Levrant et al., 1999).

Are these word games and sleights of hand? At times, yes they are. For example, consider Barnett's (1977) contrast of *punitive* and *pure* restitution. In punitive restitution (punishment), an offender is forced to compensate a victim; in pure restitution (non-punishment), an offender returns stolen goods or money (or 'makes good' in some way), but the aim is not that the offender should suffer, but that a victim 'desires compensation' (Barnett, 1977: 289). The line Barnett draws is fine indeed: punitive restitution is forcing an offender to do something, but pure restitution does not involve force because the intent is to satisfy a victim. The intent to help a victim seems to magically remove the use of 'force' in punishment.

UNRAVELING THE KNOTS

A way forward is to observe that there are three positions in the punishment debate, not just two.

Position 1 Assumes a decision maker has a 'punitive' attitude, who sees the offender as a 'bad person', who should pay back the suffering caused to a victim. This position is associated with conventional criminal justice, although we know that it is a caricature because there are varied responses, including those intended to help and change an offender.

Position 2 Assumes a decision maker has a 'non-punitive' attitude, who sees the offender as a 'good person', who should repair or restore *the harm* caused to a victim. This position is associated with restorative justice promoters, who argue that because the intention of restorative justice decision makers is 'constructive', the outcomes are not punishment. Furthermore, the intent and outcome is to repair the harm – reparation or restoration – rather than to punish an offender (Walgrave, 2008).

Position 3 Assumes a decision maker has a 'non-punitive' attitude, who sees the offender as a 'good person', who should repair or restore *the wrong* of crime (Duff, 2003) or the *harm* (London, 2011) caused by crime. This position is associated those who see restorative justice (and restoration) and punishment as compatible.

The punishment debate today in restorative justice is between Positions 2 and 3, although most assume it is between Positions 1 and 2.[12] To unravel the knots further, we need to address these questions: how do analysts define restoration, and what do they see as the role of punishment in restoration? I examine Walgrave (2008) (Position 2) and London (2011) and Duff (2003) (Position 3) on the matter. I chose these authors because each has been engaged for some time in analysing the role of punishment in restorative justice and its relationship to restoration.[13]

The Appendix compares their arguments with respect to (1) the ideal aim of sentencing; definitions of (2) restoration and (3) punishment; the relationship of (4) retribution to restoration, (5) punishment to restoration, and (6) punishment to restorative justice; (7) key phrases that encapsulate the argument; (8) the analyst's unique contribution ; and (9) points of overlap and agreement. I sketch the core argument of each and then compare them.

Walgrave

> I look for a socio-ethical justification of punishment and do not find it. (2008: 66)
>
> If [a maximalist model of] restorative justice succeeds, it may represent a new step in human civilisation, [which] is a process of increasing control over spontaneous violence and of bringing violence under state monopoly (Elias 1939/1982). The next step … is to reduce state violence itself, by not taking for granted pain infliction after a crime. (2008: 57–8)

Walgrave is concerned with the socio-ethical problem of conventional criminal justice: at its core is 'intentional pain infliction'. He argues that 'punishment [as] the *intentional* infliction of suffering is not at all an appropriate tool in the pursuit of restoration' (2008: 49, emphasis added). He acknowledges that the 'obligation to repair is mostly painful for the offender, … [but] it is a *consequence* of a restorative process, not the objective (2008: 52, emphasis added). And although there is no intention to inflict pain, 'there must be an awareness of the painful effects, which must be taken into account' in a restorative process (2008: 48). Restoration and retribution are not opposites, 'but two sides of the same coin' (2008: 62). Common to both is to 'rebalance the consequences of wrong', but the difference lies in the way 'the balance is going to be restored'. Restorative justice does not 'add more hurt, but tries to take hurt away by inverting punitive retributivsm into a constructive restorative retributivism'. The latter takes a constructive approach to censuring crime, to the offender's responsibility for crime, and how the balance is to be restored (2008: 60–1). By contrast, 'punitive retributivism assumes that intentional pain infliction is indispensable to balance wrongful behaviour and to censure it' (2008: 62). Walgrave looks to the 'next step in human civilisation' of reducing 'state violence itself, by not taking for granted pain infliction after a crime' (2006: 57–8).

London

> Punishment *alone* is an extraordinarily poor way of restoring trust either in an offender or in society. … [Punishment may] operate as an instrumentality of healing … when it is administered *in combination* with all other means of restoring trust, including the expression of apology, the agreement to pay restitution, and … to undergo rehabilitation'. (2011: 105, 108, original emphasis)

> The claim that punishment is irrelevant or antithetical to healing lacks a firm empirical foundation. (2011: 99)

London is concerned with bringing restorative justice from the margins to the mainstream, that is, from a justice activity that responds to less serious forms of youth crime to one that can address more serious types of adult offending. The primary goal of sentencing is the restoration of trust. London's definition of trust is the 'presumption of reciprocity in others' (2011: 84, 87, 118), which operates at two levels: personal trust (trust in the offender) and social trust (trust in society). The restoration of trust 'replaces punishment as the primary goal of sentencing and regards punishment as simply one means – and not necessarily the most important means – to achieving the goal of restoring trust' (2011: 191). London proposes that the more an offender does to restore personal and social trust, 'the severity of punishment regarded as appropriate is correspondingly decreased' (2011: 319). Because punishment is one means of restoring trust ('especially if voluntarily accepted'), it cannot be eliminated, but it can be minimized (2011: 319).

The potential positive effect of punishment on victims' ability to recover from crime is pursued in a survey of 400 Rutgers University (Newark) college students.[14] Participants were asked to show their emotional reactions to several crime scenarios, and 'how their emotional well being in the aftermath of crime might be improved or impaired by apology, payment of restitution, and submission to a deserved punishment' (London, 2011: 111). He found that punishment was one of three major elements (the others were restitution and being treated with respect by the court) that would *aid* the imagined victims' recovery from crime. But when asked what would *harm* their recovery, the absence of punishment was the most important factor. Thus, punishment was important to (imagined) victims 'not so much as a means of promoting satisfaction as it was a means of avoiding further distress that would ensue from the failure to punish' (2011: 114). London tested three models of emotional recovery, based on differing combinations of punishment, apology and restitution: punishment only (the 'punitive model'); apology and restitution only (the 'non-punitive model'); and apology, restitution, and punishment (the 'comprehensive model'). The punitive model was least effective in promoting emotional recovery; and the comprehensive model was more effective than the non-punitive model (2011: 115–16). It is not, he argues, 'the accumulation of additional factors', but 'transforming the character of these very factors' when used in combination (2011: 117).

Duff

> [Restoration] requires retribution in that the kinds of restoration that crime makes necessary can be brought about only through retributive punishment. (2003: 43)

> We should recognize criminal mediation and reparation as punitive, indeed as a paradigm of retributive punishment … Criminal mediation and reparation

> [are] a kind of secular penance: as a burden undertaken by the wrongdoer, which aims to induce and express her repentant and apologetic understanding of the wrong she has done. (2003: 53)

Duff is concerned to reconcile the 'restorative paradigm' and 'punishment paradigm'. He argues that 'restoration is not only compatible with retribution', it *requires* retribution in that the kind of restoration that crime makes necessary can … be brought about only through retributive punishment' (2003: 43, original emphasis). Duff differs from London in that he views punishment as *necessary* for restoration. Although London sees 'the value of punishment in the processes of censure and penance', he views punishment as an 'instrumentality … that may be justifiably applied when other means are found to be inadequate' (2011: 172).

Duff observes a lack of precision in the definition and aims of restorative justice. He asks (rhetorically), what does it mean to 'repair' the 'harm' caused by crime, what are crime protagonists 'to deal with' in the 'aftermath of an offence', what is the nature of the 'conflicts', and what would it mean to 'resolve' them (Duff, 2003: 44)? He argues that the use of euphemistic language by restorative justice proponents obscures the public qualities of criminal law: crime not only *harms* a person, but it also *wrongs* him or her. Wrongs require a criminal (not civil) mediation response; and their repair requires something that 'only an offender can provide', which 'involves the offender's punishment' (2003: 48). This means to 'suffer remorse, … suffer censure, and [to take on] a burden of making reparation to a victim' (2003: 49). This is an 'appropriate kind of suffering, [which] is intrinsic to confronting and repenting one's own wrongdoing' (2003: 53–4); therefore, 'reparation must be burdensome if it is to serve its restorative purpose' (2003: 49).

Making comparisons

Common to the three analysts is identifying restoration as the aim of criminal sentencing, although London usefully identifies two levels of restoring trust (interpersonal and societal). Each understands punishment to be the intentional infliction of pain (or suffering) on another as a consequence of wrongdoing. Whereas London and Duff view punishment as compatible with restorative justice, Walgrave does not. Furthermore, Walgrave wishes to distinguish what is and is not punishment by the 'intention' of the decision maker: if it is constructive and not to inflict pain, then it is not punishment. At the same time, he recognizes that various types of reparative or restorative actions may be painful for an offender, although this is not the intent of the decision maker. Walgrave concedes that 'if every painful obligation … is called a punishment', then most initiatives in reparation may indeed be considered punishment' and that 'accepting coercive sanctions' (as Walgrave does) 'may leave no or very few distinctions from punishment' (2008: 45). Further, he says that if an offender does not accept the invitation of 'inverted constructive retributivism', a sanction will be imposed. Here, we see that punishment appears to have a role in Walgrave's restorative justice framework as an enforcement mechanism; however, later he says that such 'reparative sanctions are not punitive because they … are meant to serve a reparative goal' (2008: 153).

Differences are evident on the necessity of punishment to achieve restoration. For Walgrave, the 'a priori option of punishment is a serious obstruction' (2008: 49); and for London, restoration of trust is the overall aim, and punishment is one of several types of mechanisms to achieve it. In some cases, punishment may only be minimal or not needed, depending on what actions an offender undertakes to restore personal or social trust. For Duff, restoration can only be achieved by 'retributive punishment', which is not contingent or separate from an offender's actions (as London conceptualizes it), but rather embodies them. A key passage by London distinguishes his position from that of Duff.[15] He acknowledges 'the value of punishment in the processes of censure and penance', but he does not view punishment to be an 'essential communicative aspect of censure or a *necessary* inducement to penance' (2011: 172, original emphasis), as does Duff. Rather, punishment is 'an instrumentality ... that may be justifiably applied when other means are found to be inadequate' (London, 2011: 172). Thus, for London, the restoration of trust is the primary goal of sentencing, and punishment is secondary; whereas for Duff, restoration is achieved by punishment.[16]

Differences are evident in the degree to which each analyst is concerned with the public dimension of crime. Walgrave (like Barnett, 1977) wants to see an increased 'civilisation' (in both meanings of that term) in the state response to crime; its public dimension is relevant for the most serious offences and dangerous offenders (2008: 154–5). London and Duff, who also desire a more enlightened response to crime, differ from Walgrave in identifying a need to restore both personal and social trust (London) and defining crime as a public wrong – of concern to a victim and the 'whole political community' (for Duff, 2003: 47) – for all types of crime, not just the more serious.

The legacy of the earlier theorists is evident in Walgrave's and London's arguments, although they seem unaware of it. Walgrave's desire to identify a constructive approach to censuring crime with an offender taking 'active responsibility' and an 'active paying back role' is similar to that of Eglash (1977), and his concern that a sentencer have a non-punitive intent and not impose punishment is like that of Barnett (1977). London draws partly from Christie's (1977) ideal court in identifying punishment as a step that may be taken after apology or restitution, if it is required.

The points of overlap are of interest. Duff says he cannot 'justify our existing penal practices' (2003: 55), and Walgrave says that 'restorative justice cannot simply rule out criminal justice' (2008: 46). Retribution as 'rebalancing a wrong' is a common theme to all three, although London and Duff place more emphasis on the public dimension of retribution. For example, London says that 'retribution is imposed for the good of others yet unknown' (2011: 186), while Walgrave aims to 'invert' retributivism by focusing on what constructive actions an offender can take.

Distilling the punishment debate

At the risk of simplifying nuanced arguments, I distil the essence of the punishment debate, using Walgrave, London and Duff as examples. Walgrave is 'against punishment' because it offends socio-ethical principles about how a judge should relate to wrongdoers in a civilized society: there should be no judicial intention to inflict pain, even if the consequences may be painful. The ethical relationship toward an offender should be one of respect and solidarity, and an expectation of active responsibility. Walgrave contends that these virtues are not evident in the 'punitive apriorism' in criminal justice, which he equates with Duff's argument of imposed punishment intended to be painful and burdensome on an offender. However, Walgrave's point requires interrogation: what if an imposed punishment is made with a 'non-punitive' attitude of mind? My reading of London and Duff is that this is what they have in mind in contemplating the relationship of punishment to restorative justice (and to restoration): for London as a means of regaining trust in an offender and society; and for Duff, as a means of repentance to right a wrong. As such, ethical relationships of respect and solidarity, and active responsibility, are not compromised. Thus, by distinguishing punishment with punitive and non-punitive intent, apparent differences in their positions begin to dissolve.

Differences remain on what is required to achieve restoration. Walgrave focuses on an offender 'taking hurt away' by taking constructive actions, but so too does London (apology and restitution) and Duff (undertaking reparative measures). However, Duff assumes that wrongdoers must suffer remorse and censure, and that reparation must be burdensome – all elements he terms punishment; whereas London takes a more contingent position, and Walgrave imagines that in most cases, restoration can be achieved more effectively without a decision maker *intending* to cause suffering or burdens. Thus, differences turn on whether painful effects or burdens on offenders should be imposed and intended, or whether they should be invited and unintended, but nonetheless welcome consequences of restorative justice.

CONCLUSION

In the last decade, the punishment debate in restorative justice has matured. Analysts are increasingly reflecting with care on the relationship of restorative justice to retribution and punishment, rather than analysing retributive and restorative justice as oppositions in caricatured and simplified ways. My analysis of Walgrave, London and Duff shows that they have similar and differing ways of imagining the ideal relationship between a state official, an offender, a victim, and the public as participants and onlookers in a sanctioning process guided by restorative justice. Their arguments are informed by differing objectives: Walgrave, to create a new socio-ethical foundation; London, to bring restorative justice into the mainstream of criminal justice; and Duff, to identify the elements of retribution that make restoration possible. Walgrave, who in principle, is 'against punishment', recognizes that it cannot be completely excised from criminal justice. London is certain that if restorative justice is to be part of mainstream criminal justice, it will need to address more serious offences; thus, it must include punishment as one of several types of responses. Duff seeks to redefine the meaning and practice of punishment as a means to achieve restoration.

My view is that the civilizing project of reducing violence, including state violence, will not be achieved by being 'against punishment', even as a socio-ethical principle. The reason is that punishment itself is an evolving concept and practice. It will continue to change and perhaps to become 'more civilized'. However, changing its meaning and practice is not the same as being 'against' it. The latter is not practical or desirable because the moral intuition that an offender should 'repay' crime is too strong. We recognize today that most penalties imposed on offenders (fines, probation and other community-based penalties) are not corporeal forms of pain infliction, nor contrary to Walgrave's assumptions, are they likely to be imposed with the mere intent to inflict pain (although this is an empirical question). For some time, restorative justice proponents have recognized that the expression of a sincere apology can be painful for an offender, even if the intent of a decision maker or justice process is not to 'inflict pain'. Punishment therefore includes emotional forms of suffering, as well as physical forms or burdensome activities. In practice, it is difficult to separate the intent and consequences of an official's decisions, as Walgrave proposes we should; and in practice, the line between 'imposing' a sanction and 'inviting' an offender to take on a burdensome task is difficult to discern. In reflecting on the punishment debate in restorative justice, the different positions turn on what analysts imagine a state official intends to be doing, or what an official is or should be doing, when relating to an offender in redressing a wrong. They also turn on what the precise practices are (or should be) when restoration is the goal of sentencing. In all cases, punishment as an idea and practice is omnipresent, hovering: it cannot be willed away or made to disappear.

NOTES

1 Analysts in domestic criminal justice use 'reparation' and 'restoration' interchangeably; thus, for simplicity, I do so in this chapter.

2 For more on the history of restorative justice, its concepts, and popularity, see Bottoms (2003), Daly and Immarigeon (1998), Daly and Proietti-Scifoni (2011) and Johnstone (2002, 2003: 1–18).

3 It may also occur post-sentence and pre-release or independent of a legal process, but my emphasis here is on the adjudication and penalty phases of the criminal justice process.

4 A partial exception arises in the literature on justice in societies undergoing processes of political transition, classically from dictatorship to democracy or in the aftermath of civil conflict. With some exceptions (Combs, 2007), however, transitional justice analysts have a caricatured understanding of restorative justice and they often rely on the (now outdated) retributive-restorative justice contrast. This arises, in part, because justice can be bifurcated in transitional justice contexts, when distinguishing 'justice' (punishment of offenders) and 'reparation' (a variety of mechanisms for victims); and in part, because transitional justice analysts, as a new group to restorative justice, find the simple contrast attractive (for review, see Daly and Proietti-Scifoni, 2011).

5 The story is more complicated. Eglash says 'the relationship between offense and restitution is reparative, restorative' (1957–58b: 20). In Eglash (1959–60: 116), the term 'restorative justice' appears, but it is indented in the text as 'condensed' from Schrey et al. (1955), which is an English translation of a German text, *The Biblical Doctrine of Justice and Law*. Skelton (2005: 84–9) discovered that one of the authors, the Reverend Whitehouse, carried out a translation and adaptation of the original German text; and he created the term 'restorative justice' from the German expression *heilende Gerechtigkeit* ('healing justice'). Restorative justice was viewed as adding a 'fourth dimension' to justice, differing from secular forms of retributive, commutative, and distributive justice in that it 'can heal the ... wound of sin' (Skelton, 2005: 88). See Immarigeon (2005) and Van Ness and Strong (2006: 22) for additional background.

6 His linking of distributive justice to treatment (or rehabilitation) seems odd, but this is what he said.

7 In domestic criminal justice, analysts define and use key terms of restitution, reparation, and compensation in different ways; and there are also differences in usage by US and UK authors. Differences are also evident in the transitional justice literature, where authors use the term reparation (in the singular) and reparation*s*. In all cases, I preserve an author's use of terms, but would point out that key terms are not used consistently.

8 See Bottoms (2003) for discussion of the 'civilization thesis' and the problems it raises for restorative justice.

9 This is Campbell's (1984: 347) argument: reparation (which he defines as criminal justice schemes for victim compensation) is a 'form of punishment', not in opposition to it. In his view, 'the idea of compensation as punishment is, in general, a restoration of the moral breach between victim and offender created by the offence' (1984: 346).

10 See Bottoms (2003) for analysis and critique of Christie's romantic view of dispute resolution.

11 Maruna (2006) devised a punitive scale with items tapping a respondent's interest to toughen sentencing laws, bring back the death penalty, condemn offenders more, treat offenders harshly, use prison more, have more austere prisons (without television and gyms), and not support alternatives to prison or community sentences.

12 There may be some individuals who because of their particularly heinous offending are 'outside our moral and imaginative community [and] excluded from membership and beyond the reach of empathy' (Hudson, 2003: 204). For those offences, most everyone would take Position 1 and not view an offender as deserving of help or support of society, at least not until after a sentence has been served.

13 Others have done so (Barton, 2000; Daly, 2000, 2002; Dignan, 2003; Dolinko, 2003; Garvey, 2003; von Hirsch et al., 2003), but the arguments of three considered here are more recent and extensive.

14 Although research on samples of undergraduate students is limited, London (2006) finds that the responses of students who had experienced the incident and those who only imagined it were similar. Furthermore, the conceptualization of the survey appears sounds and could be extended to other populations.

15 London cites Duff's (2001) earlier, more extended analysis, which is encapsulated in Duff (2003).

16 These differences flow from the fact that whereas London's justification for punishment is consequentialist, Duff (2001: 89) attempts to create a unitary justification that combines retributive (backward-looking) and consequentialist (forward-looking) justifications.

REFERENCES

Barnett, Randall (1977) 'Restitution: a new paradigm of criminal justice', *Ethics*, 87: 279–301.

Barton, Charles (2000) 'Empowerment and retribution in criminal justice', in H. Strang and J. Braithwaite (eds), *Restorative Justice: Philosophy to Practice.* Aldershot: Dartmouth/Ashgate. pp. 55–76.

Bottoms, Anthony (2003) 'Some sociological reflections on restorative justice', in A. von Hirsch, J. Roberts, A.E. Bottoms, K. Roach and M. Schiff (eds), *Restorative Justice and Criminal Justice: Competing or Reconcilable Paradigms?* Oxford: Hart Publishing. pp. 79–113.

Braithwaite, John (1989) *Crime, Shame and Reintegration.* Cambridge: Cambridge University Press.

Braithwaite, John (1996) 'Restorative justice and a better future', *The Dalhousie Review,* 76 (1): 9–32. (Reprinted in Gerry Johnstone (ed.), *A Restorative Justice Reader.* Cullompton: Willan Publishing. pp. 83–97.)

Braithwaite, John (1999) 'Restorative justice: assessing optimistic and pessimistic accounts', in M. Tonry (ed.), *Crime and Justice: A Review of Research,* vol. 25. Chicago: University of Chicago. pp. 1–127.

Braithwaite, John (2002) *Restorative Justice and Response Regulation.* Oxford: Oxford University Press.

Braithwaite, John (2003) 'Principles of restorative justice', in A. von Hirsch, J. Roberts, A.E. Bottoms, et al. (eds), *Restorative Justice and Criminal Justice: Competing or Reconcilable Paradigms?* Oxford: Hart Publishing. pp. 1–20.

Braithwaite, John and Daly, Kathleen (1994) 'Masculinities, violence and communitarian control', in T. Newburn and E.A. Stanko (eds), *Just Boys Doing Business? Men, Masculinities and Crime.* New York: Routledge. pp. 189–213.

Campbell, Tom (1984) 'Compensation as punishment', *University of New South Wales Law Journal,* 7 (2): 338–61.

Christie, Nils (1977) 'Conflicts as property', *British Journal of Criminology,* 17 (1): 1–15. (Reprinted in Gerry Johnstone (ed.), *A Restorative Justice Reader.* Cullompton: Willan Publishing. pp. 57–68.)

Combs, Nancy (2007) *Guilty Pleas in International Criminal Law: Constructing a Restorative Justice Approach.* Stanford, CA: Stanford University Press.

Cottingham, John (1979) 'Varieties of retribution', *The Philosophical Quarterly,* 29 (116): 238–46.

Crawford, Adam and Newburn, Tim (2003) *Youth Offending and Restorative Justice.* Cullompton: Willan Publishing.

Daly, Kathleen (2000) 'Revisiting the relationship between retributive and restorative justice', in H. Strang and J. Braithwaite (eds), *Restorative Justice: Philosophy to Practice.* Aldershot: Dartmouth/Ashgate. pp. 33–54.

Daly, Kathleen (2002) 'Restorative justice: the real story', *Punishment and Society,* 4 (1): 55–79.

Daly, Kathleen and Immarigeon, Russ (1998) 'The past, present and future of restorative justice: some critical reflections', *The Contemporary Justice Review,* 1 (1): 21–45.

Daly, Kathleen and Proietti-Scifoni, Gitana (2011) 'Reparation and restoration', in M. Tonry (ed.), *Oxford Handbook of Crime and Criminal Justice.* New York: Oxford University Press. pp. 207–53.

Davis, Gwynn (1992) *Making Amends: Mediation and Reparation in Criminal Justice.* London: Routledge.

Dignan, James (2003) 'Toward a systemic model of restorative justice', in A. von Hirsch, J. Roberts, A.E. Bottoms, et al. (eds), *Restorative Justice and Criminal Justice: Competing or Reconcilable Paradigms?* Oxford: Hart Publishing. pp. 135–56.

Dolinko, David (2003) 'Restorative justice and the justification of punishment', *Utah Law Review,* 2003 (1): 319–42.

Duff, Antony (1992) 'Alternatives to punishment – or alternative punishments?', in W. Cragg (ed.), *Retributivism and Its Critics.* Stuttgart: Franz Steiner. pp. 44–68.

Duff, Antony (1996) 'Penal communications: recent work in the philosophy of punishment', in M. Tonry (ed.), *Crime and Justice: A Review of Research,* vol. 20. Chicago: University of Chicago Press. pp. 1–97.

Duff, Antony (2001) *Punishment, Communication, and Community.* New York: Oxford University Press.

Duff, Anthony (2003) 'Restoration and retribution', in A. von Hirsch, J. Roberts, A.E. Bottoms, K. Roach and M. Schiff (eds), *Restorative Justice and Criminal Justice: Competing or Reconcilable Paradigms?* Oxford: Hart Publishing. pp. 43–59.

Eglash, Albert (1957–58a) 'Creative restitution: a broader meaning for an old term', *Journal of Criminology and Police Science,* 48 (6): 619–22.

Eglash, Albert (1957–58b) 'Creative restitution: some suggestions for prison rehabilitation programs', *American Journal of Corrections,* 20: 20–34.

Eglash, Albert (1959–60) 'Creative restitution: its roots in psychiatry, religion and law', *British Journal of Delinquency,* 10: 114–19.

Eglash, Albert (1977) 'Beyond restitution: creative restitution', in J. Hudson and B. Galaway (eds), *Restitution in Criminal Justice.* Lexington, MA: DC Heath and Company. pp. 91–100.

Elias, Norbert (1939 [1982]) *The Civilising Process.* London: Blackwell.

Garland, David (1990) *Punishment and Modern Society.* Oxford: Oxford University Press.

Garvey, Stephen (2003) 'Restorative justice, punishment, and atonement', *Utah Law Review,* 1 (2003): 303–17.

Hampton, Jean (1992) 'Correcting harms versus righting wrongs: the goal of retribution', *UCLA Law Review,* 39 (6): 1659–1702.

Hampton, Jean (1998) 'Punishment, feminism, and political identity: a case study in the expressive meaning of the law', *Canadian Journal of Law and Jurisprudence,* 11 (1): 23–45.

Hudson, Barbara (2003) *Justice in the Risk Society.* London: SAGE Publications.

Immarigeon, Russ (2005) 'Search for restorative justice history leads back into the future', *VOMA Connections*, 19: (3–4): 10.

Johnstone, Gerry (2002) *Restorative Justice: Ideas, Values, Debates*. Cullompton: Willan.

Johnstone, Gerry (ed.) (2003) *A Restorative Justice Reader*. Cullompton: Willan.

Johnstone, Gerry (2008) 'The agendas of the restorative justice movement', in H.V. Miller (ed.), *Restorative Justice: From Theory to Practice*. Bingley: Emerald Group. pp. 59–79.

Johnstone, Gerry and Van Ness, Daniel (2007) 'The meaning of restorative justice', in G. Johnstone and D. Van Ness (eds), *Handbook of Restorative Justice*. Cullompton: Willan. pp. 5–24.

Levrant, Sharon, Cullen, Francis, Fulton, Betsy and Wozniak, John (1999) 'Reconsidering restorative justice: the corruption of benevolence revisited?', *Crime and Delinquency*, 45 (1): 3–27.

London, Ross (2006) 'The role of punishment in the emotional recovery of crime victims', *Restorative Directions Journal*, 2: 175–95.

London, Ross (2011) *Crime, Punishment, and Restorative Justice: From the Margins to the Mainstream*. Boulder, CO: Lynne Rienner Publishers.

McCold, Paul (2001) 'Primary restorative justice practices', in A. Morris and G. Maxwell (eds), *Restorative Justice for Juveniles: Conferencing, Mediation, and Circles*. Oxford: Hart Publishing. pp. 41–58.

Marshall, Tony (1998) *Restorative Justice: An Overview*. Minneapolis: Center for Restorative Justice and Peacemaking. (Excerpt reprinted in Gerry Johnstone (ed.) *A Reader in Restorative Justice*. Cullompton: Willan. pp. 28–45.)

Maruna, Shadd (2006) 'The state of redemption: do we believe that offenders can change ... and does it matter', paper presented to University of Sheffield, 11 October.

Mead, George (1917–1918) 'The psychology of punitive justice', *The American Journal of Sociology*, 23: 577–602. (Reprinted in Dario Melossi (ed.), *The Sociology of Punishment: Socio-Structural Perspectives* (1998). Aldershot: Ashgate/Dartmouth. pp. 33–60.)

Roberts, Julian and Stalans, Loretta (2004) 'Restorative sentencing: exploring the views of the public', *Social Justice Research*, 17 (3): 315–34.

Roche, Declan (2007) 'Retribution and restorative justice', in G. Johnstone and D. Van Ness (eds), *Handbook of Restorative Justice*. Cullompton: Willan. pp. 75–90.

Schrey, Heinz Horst, Walz, Hans Hermann and Whitehouse, Walter Alexander (1955) *The Biblical Doctrine of Justice and Law*. London: SCM Press, World Council of Churches.

Skelton, Ann (2005) 'The influence of the theory and practice of restorative justice in South Africa with special reference to child justice'. LLD thesis, University of Pretoria, Faculty of Law.

Van Ness, Daniel, and Strong, Karen (2006) *Restoring Justice: An Introduction to Restorative Justice*, 3rd edn. Cincinnati: Anderson Publishing. (1st edn, 1997.)

Von Hirsch, Andrew, Ashworth, Andrew and Shearing, Clifford (2003) 'Specifying aims and limits for restorative justice: a "making amends" model', in A. von Hirsch, J. Roberts, A.E. Bottoms, K. Roach and M. Schiff (eds), *Restorative Justice and Criminal Justice: Competing or Reconcilable Paradigms?* Oxford: Hart Publishing. pp. 21–41.

Walgrave, Lode (2004) 'Has restorative justice appropriately responded to retribution theory and impulses?', in H. Zehr and B. Toews (eds), *Critical Issues in Restorative Justice*. New York: Criminal Justice Press. pp. 47–60.

Walgrave, Lode (2008) *Restorative Justice, Self Interest and Responsible Citizenship*. Cullompton: Willan.

Walgrave, Lode and Aertsen, Ivo (1996) 'Reintegrative shaming and restorative justice: interchangeable, complementary or different?', *European Journal on Criminal Policy and Research*, 4: 67–85.

Watson, David, Boucherat, Jacky and Davis, Gwynn (1989) 'Reparation for retributivists', in M. Wright and B. Galaway (eds), *Mediation and Criminal Justice*. London: SAGE Publications. pp. 212–28.

Wright, Martin (1991) *Justice for Victims and Offenders*. Philadelphia, PA: Open University Press.

Zedner, Lucia (1994) 'Reparation and retribution: are they reconcilable?', *Modern Law Review*, 57 (2): 228–50.

Zehr, Howard (1985) *Retributive Justice, Restorative Justice*. Occasional paper No. 4, Mennonite Central Committee on Crime and Justice. (Reprinted in Gerry Johnstone (ed.), *A Restorative Justice Reader*. Cullompton: Willan. pp. 69–82.)

Zehr, Howard (1990) *Changing Lenses: A New Focus for Crime and Justice*. Scottdale, PA: Herald Press.

Zehr, Howard (2002) *The Little Book of Restorative Justice*. Intercourse, PA: Good Books.

LEGISLATION

The Pennsylvania Code (1982) *§ 303.12. Guideline Sentence Recommendations: Sentencing Programs*. http://www.pacode.com/secure/data/204/chapter303/s303.12.html

Appendix. The punishment debate in restorative justice: a comparison of arguments

Element	*Walgrave (2008: chapter 3)*	*London (2011)*	*Duff (2003)*
(1) Ideal aim of sentencing	Restoration [or reparation] of the harm to a victim	Restoration of trust	Restoration of the wrong
(2) How restoration or reparation is defined	'Reparation [or restoration] is an action to undo harm, which may ... be painful' (p. 65).	To restore two levels of trust: personal (trust in the offender) and social (trust in society). Restoration of trust 'replaces punishment as the primary goal of sentencing and regards punishment as simply one means – and not necessarily the most important means – to achieve the goal of restoring trust' (p. 191).	'We cannot separate the harm that needs repair from the wrong that was done' (p. 48). 'The meaning ... of reparative measures come to depend ... on who offers them; and there may be kinds of repair that only the offender can provide' (p. 46). 'What can "repair" or "restore" the wrong that has been done? ' ... Talk of apology, of shaming, even of "confession, repentance and absolution", becomes appropriate, [which] brings us into the realm of punishment' (p. 47). 'Reparation *must* be burdensome if it is to serve its restorative purpose' (p. 49, emphasis in original).
(3) How punishment is defined	'Hard treatment, the intention of inflicting it, and the link with the wrong committed' (p. 48). 'It is the painfulness in the intention of the punisher that counts, not in the perception of the punished. It is the punisher who considers an action to be wrong and who wants the wrongdoer to suffer it' (p. 48).	'Intentional inflection of suffering' (p. 165). 'One of several instrumentalities for regaining personal and societal level trust' (p. 189). 'Punishment (especially as voluntarily accepted) operates as a potential means of restoring trust, along with other means such as apology, payment of restitution, completion of rehabilitation ... Accordingly, as other indicia of trust are increased, the severity of punishment ... is correspondingly decreased' (p. 319).	'An activity that is intentionally painful or burdensome imposed on an offender for a crime' (p. 53). 'Criminal mediation and reparation [are] punitive ... a paradigm of retributive punishment' (p. 53). There are three types of suffering: 'to suffer remorse' by 'recognis[ing] and repent[ing] the wrong', to suffer censure from others ... and (c) 'a burden ... that of making reparation to a victim' (p. 49). Punishment can be 'self-imposed' (p. 54).
(4) Relationship of retribution to restoration	They are 'not opposites, but two sides of the same coin'. Both are concerned 'to rebalance the consequences of wrong', but they differ in the way 'the balance is going to be restored' (p. 62).	'Retribution is legal punishment ... its intention is not to demonise or destroy the personhood of an offender, but rather to control and condemn his behaviour. ... Retribution is imposed for the good of others yet unknown' (p. 186). '[It] is a means to address the legitimate needs of both the state and individual crime victim' (p. 185). '[It] is an essential component of reciprocal altruism and is necessary to maintain relations of trust' (p. 174).	Restoration is 'not only compatible with retribution, it *requires* retribution, in that the kinds of restoration that crime makes necessary can ... be brought about only through retributive punishment' (p. 43, original emphasis).

(5) Relationship of punishment to restoration	'The consequences of reparation may be painful, but it is not the intent' (p. 52, paraphrase). 'Punishment, the intentional infliction of suffering, is not at all an appropriate tool in the pursuit of restoration ... The a priori option of punishment is a serious obstruction' (p. 49).	'The potential ability of punishment to operate as an instrumentality of healing [restoration] is realized ... when it is administered in combination with all other means of restoring trust, including ... apology, ... restitution, and ... rehabilitation' (p. 180). 'Taken alone, the imposition of punishment on an unwilling ... offender does little to restore trust ... and little to repair the emotional wounds of the victim' (p. 108).	Restoration is achieved through 'appropriate retribution [punishment] ... [Restoration] is 'the proper aim of criminal punishment more generally' (p. 58).
(6) Relationship of punishment to restorative justice	'Even if there is no intention to inflict pain, there must be an awareness of the painful effects which must be taken into account' in a restorative justice process (p. 48).	'We need an end to dysfunctional hyperbole' ... and 'hypocrisy' (p. 315). Restorative justice already uses the idea of punishment as a 'means of enforcing agreements ... achieving accountability to society, ... and ensuring community security' (p. 189). '[My approach] does not reject the use of punishment, but would operate to minimize its use' (p. 301). 'Punishment is only one tool of restoring trust, ... and when trust is restored by other means, resort to [the use of punishment] may be minimized' (p. 109).	Restorative justice is defined vaguely (p. 44, paraphrasing). A victim has not only been 'harmed' but also 'wronged' (p. 46); thus, the response must be by some form of criminal mediation (pp. 49–53, paraphrasing). 'There is a kind of "repair" that only the offender can provide', and this 'involves the offender's punishment' (p. 48).
(7) Key phrases	'I look for a socio-ethical justification of punishment and do not find it' (p. 66). 'If [maximalist] restorative justice succeeds, it may represent a new step in human civilisation, [which] is a process of increasing control over spontaneous violence and of bringing violence under state monopoly (Elias, 1939[1982]). The next step ... is to reduce state violence itself, by not taking for granted pain infliction after a crime' (pp. 57–58).	'Punishment *alone* is an extraordinarily poor way of restoring trust either in an offender or in society' (p. 105, original emphasis). [It may] operate as an instrumentality of healing ... when it is administered *in combination* with all other means of restoring trust, including the expression of apology, the agreement to pay restitution, and ... to undergo rehabilitation' (p. 108, original emphasis).	'We should recognise criminal mediation and reparation as punitive, indeed as a paradigm of retributive punishment' (p. 53). 'Criminal mediation and reparation [are] a kind of secular penance: a burden undertaken by the wrongdoer, which aims to induce and express her repentant and apologetic understanding of the wrong she has done ...' (p. 53). 'The mediation process itself aims to confront the offender with what he has done and to bring him to repent it as a wrong: a process which must be painful. The reparation [he then undertakes] must be burdensome. ... Not to "make the offender suffer" for its own sake, but to induce an appropriate kind of suffering – the suffering intrinsic to confronting and repenting one's own wrongdoing and to make reparation for it' (pp. 53–54).

continued

Appendix. The punishment debate in restorative justice: a comparison of arguments

Element	*Walgrave (2008: chapter 3)*	*London (2011)*	*Duff (2003)*
(8) Original contribution	Defines restorative justice as 'inverted constructive retributivism' because it takes a constructive approach to censuring crime, to an offender taking active responsibility, and to an offender taking an active paying-back role (pp. 60–61). The offender is 'invited (under pressure) to take responsibility', but if this does not occur, 'a sanction will be imposed on the offender' (p. 61).	Identifies the restoration of personal trust (in the offender) and social trust (in society) as two levels of trust to be restored. From an empirical study of the importance of punishment to respondents' imagined sense of emotional healing in the aftermath of crime, he finds that the optimal outcome for emotional recovery is the 'comprehensive model' of apology, restitution, and punishment (p. 114). Punishment is important to victims 'not so much as a means of promoting satisfaction as it is a means of avoiding further distress than would ensue from the failure to punish' (p. 114).	Attempts to reconcile retribution and restoration in a unitary justification of punishment as a 'communicative enterprise', which looks backward and forward simultaneously (Duff, 2001: 89). Views criminal mediation and reparation as types of punishment, not alternatives to punishment.
(9) Points of overlap or agreement	'Accepting coercive sanctions may leave no or very few distinctions from punishment' (p. 45). 'A special category of "criminalisable" behaviours should be maintained ... Restorative justice cannot simply rule out criminal justice' (p. 46). 'If every painful obligation following the commission of a wrong is called a punishment, then most initiatives in reparation may indeed be considered punishment' (p. 47).	'We can agree [that] establishing the repair of harm [is] the overarching goal of criminal justice policy and practice ... Restorative justice is about restoration, and that is how it differs from conventional justice. The specific mechanisms of restoration are all secondary considerations' (p. 315).	'Criminal mediation ... is still very different from the criminal punishments typically imposed under our existing penal systems; and so it is and should be ... I believe that punishment is in principle a necessary and appropriate response to wrong-doing, but I am not seeking to justify our existing penal practices' (p. 55).

18

Monetized Justice: Money and Punishment in Consumer Societies

Pat O'Malley

KEY PROPERTIES OF MONEY SANCTIONS

Money is almost invisible in justice and criminology. Media frequently show offenders being hustled to and from jails in secure trucks, and certain prisons are iconic images in their own right. Executions, or at least the events surrounding them, are media events, and when corporal punishment was the norm, the marks on the body were a major feature of the spectacle of punishment. But who among members of the public has witnessed the convicted felon handing over a wad of cash or even knows if and when it occurs? What would be the point? And we can count on the fingers of one hand serious criminological attempts to come to grips with fines.

This point reveals some of money sanctions' almost unique properties as a sanction. Money is undifferentiated; we cannot tell one bundle of cash from another (Simmel, 1990). I can see the offender being lashed, or coming out of prison and know that this specific body has suffered loss of comfort or liberty. But whose money is being handed over? The parents', siblings', spouses', friends' or employers? The offenders' money looks like all other money. Money is anonymous. This is part of its secret to invisibility. At least equally important, it is behind the fact that criminal and civil justice pay little or no attention to who actually pays for the crime. Surely this is an extraordinary thing.

Money is invisible for other reasons, not least because the transfer of money is part of everyday life. Fines, fees, licenses, imposts, taxes, premiums, penalties, rents and prices blur into each other. As Jeremy Bentham (1780 [1962]) said over two centuries ago, the fine is a license paid in arrears. Many fines are regarded by states and the public merely as government revenue – states build fines incomes into their forward estimates. If I drive on a toll road without payment, I am issued a penalty notice that sets a price variously referred to as a 'fine' or 'penalty' or a 'fee'. Fines are increasingly just another vexing cost of living.

Here we have yet another remarkable characteristic. Unlike other punishments, money sanctions are not a subtraction from life, but a transfer of value. Imagine a ceremonial of court officials sombrely burning a heap of money collected from those fined. In the name of legal punishment bodies are destroyed and pain is inflicted, but nothing is exchanged. Of course we refer to the 'price' of crime and a 'debt' to society being paid by all manner of other sanctions. But money sanctions are *literally* prices – that can be paid in cash by anyone, even one unrelated to the wrong. And as neoliberals have remarked (Becker, 1974) with all other punishments the financial 'debt' to society is increased, only the fine actually repays. When a prisoner is incarcerated, his or her time is taken away but no-one gains this lost time or liberty. Yet money in punishment merely changes hands, from the offender to the state or sometimes to the victim. Among other remarkable associated consequences is that money is a sanction that is almost limitless in its application, for it costs the state almost nothing in net terms to inflict and generates income. These economic and political properties of money sanctions lie behind the modern state's capacity to have effected an enormous expansion of legal regulation over the past century. Without the money sanction the mass regulation that we now have may have been possible, but it would have required an economically feasible innovation that has not yet come to light.

These principal characteristics of money sanctions give rise to still others. First, almost all of us have paid fines, while only a small proportion of the general population has been to prison – although to study criminology would lead us to imagine the reverse. Second, fines are legally levied in almost every major context or institution as well as courtrooms – from libraries to freeways to factories. Last but not least, money sanctions, almost alone among punishments, can be digitized. Routinely, fines are issued and paid electronically, contributing still further to their ubiquity. In an age of informatics, this feature is at the heart of a revolution in justice arguably equivalent to the rise of the disciplinary prison in import: the emergence of what I will later term 'simulated justice'.[1]

FINES IN THE 19TH CENTURY

Before the turn of the 20th century, money sanctions were quite small business both in terms of the number of punishments inflicted, and in terms of the amounts of money involved. According to the Marxist theorists Rusche and Kirchheimer (1939), this was because the poor could not afford to pay a fine. In this view, the limits imposed on law by the relations of production kept fines in the role of a very marginal sanction until European advances in industrialization created sufficient surplus income among the masses. They document a rise in the use of fines from about 11 per cent of criminal justice punishments in the 1880s to almost 50 per cent by the 1930s (1939: 171–2). While attractive at first sight, there are many reasons to doubt this account.

To begin with, fines had been the principal sanction across western Europe until the last decades of the 18th century. In England during the 1700s, for example, they had represented up to 80 per cent of sanctions in the lower courts that dealt with the bulk of offenders (Sharp, 1990; King, 1996). This had been possible even though the mass of people were poorer in cash terms in these earlier times. Indeed, the money economy itself had not nearly taken on the reach and scale that became true by the early years of the 1800s – which strangely is just the time when fines were in decline. Rather, fines could be levied because they frequently were measured in quite small amounts, matters of a few shillings or even pennies (Briggs et al., 1996). Clearly fines of such amounts *could* have continued to be used in the 19th century. But poverty was not the force at work.

Fines' rapid slide into marginal status was due to the rise of the disciplinary prison (Seagle, 1948). A new age of penal enlightenment led by reformers such as Bentham and Howard regarded scientific correction in hygienic prisons as the way forward (King, 1996: 64). While of course the rise of the correctional prison has been outlined by Foucault (1977), he too forgot to mention fines, and gave the completely misleading impression that instead corporal and capital punishment had been the principal sanctions prior to the rise of corrections. In practice, the decline in the usage of fines from about 80 per cent of sentences to about 20 per cent almost exactly matched the rise in the utilization of imprisonment. No doubt this suggests some rethinking is in order order about the nature of 18th century 'sovereign' punishment, even if it alters little of our understanding of the disciplinary prison. The sovereign command did not require a declaration of war on every wrongdoer, and no society could have survived long were that the case.

A second reason to doubt Rusche and Kirchheimer's account is that as fines grew in popularity as a sanction, so too did ample evidence that the poor could not afford to pay them. Large numbers of fine defaulters were filling the prisons (Garton, 1982; Young, 1989). So pressing was this problem, that the early years of the 20th century were marked by attempts to render fines payable at the risk of reducing their punitive impact. Time to pay and payment by instalments were two such innovations. As well, magistrates and judges were instructed to take into account the means of the offender when setting the quantum of fines (O'Malley, 2009a). While it is clear this instruction has been routinely ignored, it does raise the question of why fines were not simply reduced to the small amounts previously levied that were more readily affordable.

A simple answer has to do with the fact that fines reappeared in the late 1800s because of mounting evidence that short periods of imprisonment were correctionally ineffective (Grebing, 1982: 8–9). Worse, by bringing minor offenders into contact with hardened criminals, they were seen to operate as training grounds for crime. While this revelation did not automatically bring an end to short terms of imprisonment, the enormous expense of prisons contrasted with the cheapness of fines led many jurisdictions across Europe to use fines far more frequently. Moreover, fines could no longer be for tiny sums because they had re-emerged as the equivalent to a short period of imprisonment and thus could not be set at a paltry amount without compromising the seriousness of incarceration. Hence the poor had problems paying such enlarged fines and ended up imprisoned in default. It is this transformation in sanctioning after about 1880 that Rusche and Kirchheimer registered but misunderstood. The return of the fine to its previous preponderance as a penal sanction in Europe registered discoveries of the limits to corrections, not the newly growing wealth of the poor.

MONEY DAMAGES AND PUNISHMENT BEFORE 1900

There is more to the mystery of the fines' (temporary) disappearance in the 19th century than even this suggests. While Bentham probably is best known for his advocacy of the Panopticon, he – and his Continental counterpart Beccaria – were even more in favour of 'pecuniary penalties'. Fines, Bentham argued, had a very large number of virtues as a sanction. They could be infinitely graduated to match the seriousness of the offence. They inflicted pain without touching the body – a liberal shibboleth of the time as Foucault has remarked. In the event of the discovery of a miscarriage of justice, unlike corporal punishment or incarceration, they could be completely reversed. They were cheap to administer and produced revenues to the state and/or financial compensation to the victim (Bentham, 1982: 579). Indeed, Bentham (1982: 580) advocated a victim compensation scheme of the sort that was not to come into being until quite recently. It speaks to the power of the faith in correctional prisons that money sanctions did not remain at the forefront of criminal justice throughout the 19th century. Even so, while fines declined sharply after 1780, it is misleading to suggest that money virtually disappeared as a punishment, because this would completely overlook monetary damages.

We are accustomed to thinking that civil law has nothing to do with punishment. But this is a 20th-century construction. Bentham did not believe that money damages were primarily compensation. Quite to the contrary, he included them in his discussion of penal law, and regarded the difference between fines and damages merely as procedural (1962: 392–4). In this view damages' primary function was to inflict pain – or take away the means of pleasure which he regarded as the same thing. Likewise, modern analysts (White, 2003) stress that compensation did not become the principal function of damages until the 20th century – when changing political visions and the rise of liability insurance were to centre the harms to workers and consumers. In the 19th century, their primary purpose could be understood as part of a wider punitive strategy aimed at creating a responsible liberal citizenry.

At the coercive end of this broad strategy were the Panopticon prisons and workhouses, intended to instil fear, as well as morality and prudence, into those dangerous classes who had to be 'civilized'. We are now familiar with the idea that these 'austere' institutions aimed at creating 'docile bodies', as Foucault (1977) argues. But the overall liberal strategy was equally intended to create individuals who took on what Bentham (1962: 307) referred to as 'the yoke of foresight' – the capacity and duty to look ahead and plan. For the poor, this meant frugality, diligence and thrift, an art in which the workhouse in particular provided grim schooling. But at the 'soft' end of the punitive spectrum there was a regime based on money sanctions other than fines. Payment of money damages at the time fell to the responsibility of the person at fault – there was no insurance industry to pay 95 per cent of damages as is now the case (Cane, 2006). In any case such an insurance arrangement would have subverted a primary logic of 19th-century tort law, which was to fine-tune lessons in the 'yoke of foresight' among those citizens too decent and civilized for the penal system (O'Malley, 2000).

One of the pivotal elements of this regime of damages was the principle of negligence, which made subjects liable for any harm they created and that they should have foreseen. Thus a worker who contributed to his own injury would not be able to recover any damages from the employer. Likewise, an employee who contributed to his fellow worker's injury would be liable to pay damages. At least in principle, this was a system of fines to be levied against those whose carelessness caused social injury, and in effect it was a primitive system of risk management (O'Malley, 2004). Certainly it was argued that making the workers responsible by holding the threat of money sanctions over them was rational in risk terms. After all, they were the subjects at the scene, the persons best-placed to know the details of the situation as it developed and thus best placed to act preventively. This is an argument of 'responsibilization' that has been resurrected by neoliberals today (O'Malley, 2004).

So, while fines had declined in the 1800s, money sanctions per se were present and active, assigned to effect a lesson in liberalism on workers and others through punishment. Of course, many contemporaries condemned the arrangement as based on a sham assumption that poor people could pay significant damages. These arguments have been continued by more modern scholars (Horwitz, 1977). But while denial of adequate recovery undoubtedly was an effect of this change, compensation was not the prime purpose of the law. As we know, courts have an amazing ability to ignore or disregard the empirically obvious if it does not fit their logic. Liability for damages remained the responsibility of the negligent parties regardless of their station in life – and thus regardless of their poverty. Hence it is even more unlikely that fines in the 19th century were marginalized simply because the poor could not afford to pay them. Making the negligent poor bear the uncompensated costs of injury due to their own negligence, and exposing them to the prospect of damages awarded against them for negligent harm (although this was of course hypothetical because few would bother suing a poor person) while simultaneously winding back the use of fines, was understood to reflect the most appropriate and effective means of punishment for producing liberal citizens. The evil would be subject to disciplinary corrections in prison, while those lesser wrongdoers who merely failed to exercise proper foresight would be the poorer for it. Then, as now, there was a core of criminal disciplinary institutions in place to deal with the hard cases, and a penumbra of 'soft' monetary penalties to deal with those whose deviance needed a lighter and less coercive intervention.

MONEY SANCTIONS AND THE RISE OF THE REGULATORY STATE

When in the early 20th century damages were being transformed from primarily a 'soft' punishment into a system of insurance-funded compensation, the fine was re-emerging as a principal sanction for minor offences and for offenders against the host of emerging regulations associated with the 'interventionist state'. Quite possibly this was coincidental. But an intriguing possibility remains that there was some form of connection, for fines did not merely re-emerge in their ancient form. Arguably their rationale had altered, and so too had their character. The (re)emerging fines had an historically new meaning attached to them, for now they were the punishment that dealt with those who did not require specifically *disciplinary* correction. Like damages – which by now were increasingly governed by an insurance principle – fines likewise were coming to be ordered in terms of a risk-based regulatory diagram. In key respects, both sets of money sanctions were moving toward a risk-based order of governance at a time when many states likewise were extensively being restructured around risk-based social insurance and related apparatuses.

Now, Rusche and Kirchheimer (1939: 176) made a singularly astute observation in this respect. They suggested that the fine was used where states had determined that it was not worth the cost and effort to extirpate a behaviour or to understand the pathologies of the offender. Fines, they argued, merely put a damper on the overall level of an unwanted activity. As such, fines are a tolerant sanction, for the implication is that a certain level of deviance is to be accepted as normal and to be lived with. In this view, fines are about governing distributions of action rather than about the correction of individuals. While the disciplinary apparatus created 'individuals' through examination, comparison with a norm, the assembling of a case history and a suitably tailored correctional regime, fines do none of these things. Fines, at least in most of the 20th century, work *through* the punishment of individuals in order to shape rates, distributions and flows of behaviour, and in this sense they are a form of what Foucault (1984) referred to as the orthogonal axis to discipline – 'regulation'.

It should be stressed that this transformation of the fine did not emerge full-blown or as part of a carefully plotted governmental plan to adopt new forms of power. At first, it was simply a matter of resurrecting an old sanction to fill a gap in the penal apparatus. In the late 1800s, most fines were still associated with the same court procedures – ceremonial and denunciation – as other criminal sanctions (O'Malley, 2009b). But as they became more frequently used and in relation to a wider array of minor offences and infringements, unexpected shifts began to occur. While the fine was meant to displace short periods of incarceration, state officials began to discover that the pressure on prison facilities was actually increasing. At first sight this was because so many of those fined were defaulting payment, and thus were being sent to prison. Yet a moment's reflection suggests a problem. If all that was happening was that those diverted from prison were ending up in prison after all, then why did pressure on prisons rise significantly rather than remain constant?

Stephen Garton (1982) shows that the answer has much to do with key properties of money. As fines became more frequently used, so did the sense that the penalty was 'only money' rather than loss of liberty or a flogging. As Simmel (1990) argued, in a liberal polity money does not carry the same level of political and moral meaning as liberty or pain. While money is not meaningless its everyday meaning nevertheless is lodged in the world of commodities (Zelizer, 1994). Where the penalties took on such a mundane character, where so little seemed at stake by comparison with incarceration of flogging, a field of summary justice began to be developed in which the ceremonials of justice were streamlined. And first to go were those time-consuming procedures associated with protection of the accused (Freiberg and Ross, 1999). The courts and police thereby had pressure on their time relieved. But the consequence was that more cases could be processed with the same resources, and as police and others still had to produce 'results' – and numbers of police were increasing at this time – the inputs into the criminal justice system increased. In turn, as the same proportion of this increased input defaulted on their fines, so the numbers of prisoners increased. It was this 'crisis' that created the impetus for the innovations of payment of fines by instalment, time to pay and taking the means of offenders into account (Garton, 1982).

An implicit lesson was soon learned: the 'it's only money' effect could routinely be deployed to allow a rationalization of procedure. This began to be generalized from the turn of the 20th century with the rise of regulatory agencies and enforcement. As their focus was largely the corporation or the company rather than an individual, money rapidly emerged as the appropriate sanction – all the more so because any individuals involved were seen as 'respectable' contributors to the common wealth for whom imprisonment was more or less out of the question (Carson, 1974; Paulus, 1976). As well, because such agencies tended to deal with what were constituted as 'technical' matters (something not divorced from the status of their targets), the vehicles for delivery of sanctions tended not to be courts but more bureaucratically structured tribunals that could operate more efficiently and rapidly. It was a model that was developed to an even greater degree with respect to a problem of government that was to swamp almost every other field of law, regulation and justice in the next half century: motor traffic.

As early as the turn of the 20th century, the rise of the automobile created considerable legal turmoil (Simon, 1999). While there was little disagreement that dangerous – or 'furious' – driving was a criminal offence, other traffic issues such as speeding were much more contentious. For many residents and local governments, the problem was one of nuisance – automobiles created dust and damaged dirt roads designed for more sedate vehicles. The faster the cars went, the worse these problems became. For drivers, however – and for their influential automobile associations – speeding was not a problem where it was not dangerous. And if it were dangerous then other laws already governed this. Rather, fines for speeding appeared to many as a 'tax on progress' (Plowden, 1971). The problem was especially fraught because the speedsters were not the usual clientele of the courts, but wealthy and respectable citizens. Courts often refused to convict for what seemed to them merely 'technical' offences. Consequently police often avoided enforcing speeding laws – so much so that in the UK the Home Office was forced to insist that the constabulary treat traffic offences seriously (Plowden, 1971). The picture was similar in the USA and elsewhere. For such status and political reasons, the courts and legislatures seem never to have considered anything other than fines as the appropriate sanction, although popular newspapers often called for much more punitive and draconian responses. As well, because the offenders were wealthy, the issue of imprisonment in default of payment seems never to have arisen even though it was a major issue with respect to more traditionally working class offences and offenders (O'Malley, 2009b).

In the UK, a response to the 'special' status of these traffic and regulatory offenders was that the courts invented a new procedure that allowed for the issue to be contested without this involving attendance in court. Of course it had always been the case that defendants might opt out of appearing, but then the case would proceed to conviction in absentia. Now a procedure was invented that eroded the moral and denunciatory ceremonial of court and introduced a more bureaucratic form of justice (Fox, 1996). In the USA, a parallel development was to be the emergence of special traffic courts that similarly were streamlined. As with other areas of justice at the time, bureaucratisation of justice was linked directly to the fact that money was the primary sanction in the overwhelming majority of cases. At the same time, of course, the economy of the justice apparatus emerged as a much more salient issue: it was not to be justice at any cost.

In this process individuals – the unique subjects that appeared as objects of governance at the intersection of disciplinary power and liberal government – have begun to slip out of sight. In its new form, the fine was emerging as a low-profile sanction appropriate to governing large volumes of unwanted actions performed by more or less unproblematic subjects. It was unnecessary and needlessly expensive to know much about the offenders and their complexities. Instead, the model of economics, insurance (and only incidentally of classical criminology) was mobilized. Offenders appeared as rational choice subjects – abstract and universal. Increasingly money sanctions would vary not because of the need to punish the morally bad, but because of a calculable economic model that would quite literally *price* transgression. The subjects of regulation would be governed as consumers.

THE 'MODERN FINE' AND CONSUMER SOCIETY

While it may be imagined that traffic offending is somehow marginal to criminology and penology, this would appear a decidedly perverse argument in the face of the likelihood that most of the business of law enforcement is taken up with traffic, and most citizens have contact with law and punishment through this domain. Nevertheless, it is important not to underemphasize the more traditional offences against persons, public order and property familiar to criminology, for key changes were also occurring in this respect. In one of only a handful of theoretical analyses of money sanctions, Anthony Bottoms (1983) also alluded to the fact that the fine is regulatory or distributional rather than disciplinary and individualized in nature. Moving beyond this, Bottoms asked why it was that throughout the twentieth century the fine had been becoming more central as a sanction even though apparently correctional thought and practice was such a prominent feature of the welfare state era. Although working from a broadly Foucaultian position, Bottoms nevertheless suggested that this shift was best understood as a reflex of changes in the relations of production.

During the 20th century, he suggested, the order of production had become sufficiently automated that the old model of the disciplinary factory had been overtaken. Discipline was no longer essential to the extent that the production line dictated the speed, quality and duration of labour's application. Rather, the environment of the factory was now based essentially on regulation: control that had become immanent in the environment rather than the disciplined 'soul' of the workers. Of course, Bottoms was aware that labour had not escaped discipline: the inefficient worker would stand out in this system, and disciplinary pressure would be brought to bear. But the same close management of individuals was less critical. Machines dictated the production and 'cared' only about a narrow band of performance.

In fairly familiar Marxist fashion, Bottoms suggested that as production relations changed toward a less disciplinary form so too did the relations in civil society. He pointed to the contemporaneous rise of the welfare state, that included such large-scale, risk-based distributional apparatuses as social insurance. Likewise, the politically fraught social environment of seething class tensions was being replaced by one in which relative affluence produced by automation created broad popular consent or at least conformity. It is an argument that parallels that of Jonathan Simon (1987) who suggested that once the working classes had been inured to the order of industrial society, they could be given more leeway to live under the looser constraints of risk or regulation. So for Bottoms it was not surprising to see that the place occupied by the disciplinary prison was becoming increasingly peripheral. It was not that the prison was less important, for it remained the backstop. But for most of the routine problems of police and criminal law, the fine offered a cheaper and more tolerant form of sanctioning that could now be afforded in a 'post disciplinary' society. Only those who present a more serious risk will be disciplined.

While Bottoms does not ignore Rusche and Kirchheimer's suggestion that the increasing wealth of the masses made the fine possible, his account ironically generates a somewhat more deterministic framework. After all, Rusche and Kirchheimer were content to suggest that the relations of production provided a material platform of economic surplus on which the edifice of monetary sanctions could be erected. Bottoms argues for a correspondence in form and function between industrial production and social control through fines. This confronts some serious problems. To begin with, the fine developed rapidly in countries of western Europe at a time well before the generalized automation of factories. Conversely, in the USA where automation developed fastest and farthest, at least until recently, the welfare state was stunted, and fines have been far less widely used as a sanction in criminal justice. While the case of the USA itself creates a mystery to which analysis will shortly turn, it is not the only difficulty.

Bottoms refers to what he calls 'the modern fine', as the fine that has come to be dissociated from imprisonment in default of payment, and regards this as an effect of the erosion of disciplinary society. He points out that fewer than 1 per cent of fines result in such imprisonment. But the difficulty is that this was something of a statistical artefact, for at the time Bottoms was writing, in the UK, for example, nearly one-half of all prison admissions were for non-payment of fines (Young, 1989). Together with the much larger numbers of traffic fines that are comparatively rarely are backed up by imprisonment, Bottoms collapsed fines for offences such as crimes against the person, property crimes and public order crimes, which then were frequently enforced by imprisonment in default.

Consequently, it appears quite possible that it is not so much changing relations of production that are critical to the growth and transformation of 'modern fines', but rather the appearance of mass ownership of automobiles. In turn, this is something that is itself an index of the emergence of consumer society, what Plowden (1971) referred to as the 'democratization' of automobile ownership. Likely, it is consumption rather than production alone that is key to understanding the growth of fines. In turn, this would make perfect sense of the fact that it is specifically the fine and not some other sanction that is the growing form of non-disciplinary punishment. It is the sanction that operates through the denial of pleasures of consumption in a society where surplus income and mass consumption have become life-defining.

Rusche and Kirchheimer's thesis thus reappears in a slightly different form. It was not the increase in mass surplus income that triggered the re-emergence of the fine. But in conjunction with the related formation of a consumer society it doubtlessly contributed to the growing use of fines thereafter and when the associated growth of traffic offences in included, it was more or less directly responsible for the massive expansion of modern fines on a scale that in 1939 Rusche and Kirchheimer could not foresee.

CONSUMPTION, RISK AND POLITICAL SPECIFICITY

As hinted at above, merely shifting attention from production to consumption still faces the enigma of the USA. If the consumption thesis is correct, surely the consumer society *par excellence* should not seemingly eschew fining. Yet with respect to such 'traditional' crimes as assault, theft, drug use and minor fraud, the fine continues to be relatively marginal in the USA. In 2004, at the federal level only four per cent of offenders were ordered to pay a fine (just 3.5 per cent received a fine only), and this was true for only 1 per cent of those convicted of felonies. The figure is especially striking because it includes corporate offenders, which were almost invariably fined. These figures compare with the fact that fines were the sentence for nearly a quarter of all indictable offences in England and Wales (O'Malley, 2009b). Even for misdemeanours, where the equivalent proportion in England and Wales was nearly 70 per cent, the proportion of US federal offenders fined was only 29 per cent. At the state level, the fine in the USA was hardly used as the sole sentence in relation to felonies, but was deployed as an additional penalty in about a quarter of all cases, most frequently as an add-on to a sentence of imprisonment (Bureau of Justice Statistics, 2004).

Despite this, in an important sense it is not true that fines play only a marginal role in the USA. After all, the USA almost invented fines as the default sanction for corporations, and has promoted the award of punitive damages as a form of quasi-fine against corrupt and egregious corporations (O'Malley, 2009a). Likewise, not only has the USA been a pioneer in the domain of traffic fines but it has been active in innovating new forms of fees and surcharges that sometimes dwarf the usual quantum of a fine, and that may also be used to augment the impact of fines (Dubber and Kelman, 2005: 74). Loïc Wacquant (2002) has shown that since the mid 1990s, prisoners have been charged for their room and board, for 'processing fees' at intake and release from prison, supplemental charges for medical care, laundry, electricity and so on. In Illinois, the Department of Corrections can charge, and if required sue, offenders up to US$16,070 per annum for the costs of incarceration. Of course, being governed by an increasingly monetized principle, such interventions have been poorly enforced precisely because the costs of collection exceed the revenues produced (Wacquant, 2002: 25). Harris et al. have argued that 'monetary sanctions are now imposed by the courts on a substantial majority of the millions of US residents convicted of felony and misdemeanor crimes each year' (2010: 1756). In California, a staggering 3100 separate fees, surcharges, fines, penalties and assessments may be levied in the criminal justice system, and in Washington State superior courts up to 17 fees and fines may be levied against offenders at the time of sentencing alone. Like Bentham, Harris et al. (2010: 1761) argue that it is more or less irrelevant that these may appear to have an administrative nature, because their impact is clearly punitive and they are justified on such grounds as increasing offender accountability. Much the same is true even with respect to traffic fines. The State of Virginia, for example, has introduced fees of up to US$3500 to be added to speeding fines, on the justification that speeders make it necessary for the state to build safer roads, and thus should contribute to their cost (O'Malley, 2010b).

In addition, Dubber and Kelman (2005: 40) point out that in the USA any reticence with regard to fines is not duplicated with respect to restitution orders. Federal Sentencing Guidelines specify that where there is an identifiable victim, the court should enter a restitution order for the full amount of the victim's loss. Even though in practice the courts use this order less frequently than might be imagined (no doubt because there is little point in making such an order against an unemployed pauper) the resulting fund had accumulated over US$5 billion even by 2002 (Dubber and Kelman, 2005: 40–2).

Thus it is not at all true to suggest the USA does not impose monetary sanctions. In light of this a determined argument could sustain the consumer society thesis – especially when traffic fines are included. But it would be ingenuous to ignore the fact that the USA jurisdictions do fine far less frequently than most European and other Anglophone societies with respect to 'traditional' criminal justice offences. How can this be squared with an argument that fines now reflect the rise of consumer society?

A number of explanations have been put forward for this American reluctance to fine. One of the least convincing is that the USA so emphasizes corrections, that it never took part in the early 20th century move back to fines in place of short terms of imprisonment (Gillespie, 1981: 201; Hillsman, 1990). It is not difficult to find examples of influential bodies arguing against fines on exactly these grounds (American Bar Association, 1971). Clearly it is the case that America has retained, and relies upon, jail terms of a few days or weeks far more than most other developed countries. But this incarceration has nothing to do with corrections because a majority of these sentences are served in lock-up facilities that have never pretended to offer correctional services. More to the point, it would be difficult to argue that US prison regimes are more correctionally oriented than those of, say the UK, Australia or Canada. It can also been suggested that the highly racialized nature of American society and criminal justice has meant that the poor Black population historically could never have paid fines. But this argument falls prey to parallel arguments made by Rusche and Kirchheimer, for the courts have been quite happy to ignore the poverty of offenders when levying fees and restitutions charges – and indeed have been instructed to do so by legislatures (Harris et al., 2010: 1766; see also Dubber and Kelman, 2005).

This leaves one rather more convincing account, which centres on the Fourteenth Amendment and its requirement for equal treatment before the law. Ratified during the 1860s, the Amendment predated the rebirth of the fine, and plausibly acted as a barrier to its reappearance in the USA. As a number of key federal cases have ruled, the fine is inequitable because poor people are far more likely to end up in prison in default than would a wealthy person (1971 *Tate* v. *Short* 401 U.S. 400; 1983 *Beardon* v. *Georgia* 461 U.S. 672). Precisely because these cases are prominent, the explanation cannot be discounted, although it has to be said that the case law on this point was not settled until the second half of the 20th century. Moreover, it is quite consistent with the practice of fining corporations, as corporations are wealthy and obviously cannot be imprisoned in default. Likewise, it could be argued that fining in respect of traffic offences fines has been accepted partly because it is so much less likely in such cases that imprisonment would follow in default. More to the point, it would be fairly obvious that a sentence of imprisonment for minor speeding and other traffic offences would be both draconian and logistically unfeasible. Finally, it could provide an account of why such a proliferation of fees, surcharges and the like has been levied against prisoners especially over the past few decades: for these do not appear as sentences nor formally as punishment, but simply as prices. In an era of neoliberalism, the economic register of justice, of 'monetized justice' in a consumer economy, has found its way around the stumbling block of the Constitution.[2]

Notwithstanding the plausibility of this latter argument, nonetheless it remains the case that US courts have used fines against those incarcerated – as an 'add-on' sanction, for many years, and with far less hesitation than against those not facing incarceration. The Constitution does not seem to have reared its head in opposition here. The distinct possibility emerges that there is an unspoken assumption in the US that imprisonment is the appropriate sanction in a country where liberty is such a political shibboleth, and that money sanctions' place is only as an adjunct. Perhaps this too explains the fact that reforms in Europe at the turn of the 20th century, which must have been known to US legislators and penologists, seemingly were ignored.

THE EMERGENCE OF 'SIMULATED JUSTICE'

During the 1930s, parking began to become a critical issue in the US, and elsewhere it reached a similar crisis point in the 1950s. As with speeding, parking violations were regarded as contentious (Fogelson, 2001). At first, many objected to the 'rent' charged for parking on the public roads, and resented the fine imposed if they stayed longer than allowed. Again, money appeared almost automatically as the appropriate response to infringements – and while we may now take this for granted, again it speaks to the special features of money that seemingly 'obviously' suit it to this role. Money is appropriate as the punitive currency of a justice that is not clearly criminal – just as was the case with damages in the 19th century. And it is appropriate to regulation of behaviours where the identity of the unique individual offender is not really the concern of law. Where the issue is, rather, the circulation or distribution of vehicles, and the number of violations is simply too great for correctional responses, money appears as the default punishment in a consumer society.

With such routine regulation, the quantum of the fine is set by increasing the 'price' levied in the fine until the point at which an acceptable balance is reached between the level of violations and the amount of work (or the cost) generated for the legal or regulatory apparatus (O'Malley, 2009b). Set the fine too high and many expensive contestations arise, set it too low and infringements rise. Rather than an exercise in individual justice, this reveals itself as an economic cost-benefit model of distributions of abstract universal rational choice subjects being shaped by an abstract universal money sanction. This takes place within an apparatus that does not seek to correct individuals or eliminate immorality but to strike the right balance between the costs of administration and the distributive benefits of key social processes. Money is central to this new economic model of monetized justice.

As the volume of traffic and other regulatory violations expanded in the post-Second World War era, so pressures increased to streamline procedure still further. And again because 'only money' was at stake, this streamlining could take revolutionary forms. The 1960s saw the invention of 'fixed penalty notices' or 'on the spot fines'. Developed at first in relation to traffic violations, although later spreading to a multitude of domains policed by a huge range of government and local government agencies, these instruments effectively created a fixed non-negotiable and non-discretionary penalty attached to each offence. Infringements were now priced (Fox, 1996)

Confronting a situation where courts and tribunals could not possibly deal with anything but the smallest fraction of even these notices, further procedures were instituted with the specific aim of keeping individuals out of the justice system. The order of development varies from jurisdiction to jurisdiction, but the trend is marked and unidirectional. Opting-out techniques, as seen above, developed almost at the rise of motoring offences. But from the 1960s these were displaced by opting-in provisions, whereby the assumption of a penalty notice is that the offender will not choose to contest. Opting-in requires a decision frequently accompanied by attendant costs and risks as a deterrent. For example, it is commonplace for a discount to be offered if the offender pays the fine before a certain date. As well, the penalties may increase if the case is contested and lost, especially through the imposition of 'administration' charges and fees. Notices came to be framed in such a way that the offences took the form of strict liability: for example the offence is to have a blood alcohol reading above a certain limit rather than to be driving in an impaired fashion. In practice there is little or no room for mitigation or even aggravation. Finally, with driving offences the assumption is made that the owner was the driver at the time of the offence, and the onus of proof is thrown upon the accused to disprove the charge and/or to challenge his or her identification as the driver concerned (Fox, 1996).

In this process much that was previously understood as 'justice' – and especially individual justice – was being eroded and displaced by a simple pricing mechanism. From about the 1970s, however, things took a still further turn away from traditional models of justice. I have suggested already that the category of the liberal-disciplinary 'individual' here is inappropriate. Penalty notices have been streamlined to the point where we are dealing with what Giles Deleuze (1995) has referred to as 'dividuals' – fragments of subjects that are used in information formats to govern distributions. The driver, the licensee, the operator, the owner – these and other dividuals become the subjects governed by penalty notices. The system has no interest in its subjects beyond this level. This is true even where such fixed penalty notices are attached to traditional rimes such as minor assault or drug offences (Duff, 1993; Fox, 1996). Proving the fine is expiated without challenge, there is no criminal conviction or other record made: the offender as individual is of marginal interest.

. And here we return again to money's characteristics. As noted, one of the critical features of money sanctions is that they need not be paid by the wrongdoers. This has annoyed courts in the past, but nothing has been done about it because of the obvious difficulties involved in establishing whose money is being used to pay a penalty. Equally, were this possible even trying to establish the 'real' source of the money would take up so much of the courts' time that the system would grind to a halt. In a strong sense, therefore, the operation of sanctioning across the bulk of law and regulation depends upon the fact that it does not matter who pays the penalty. One implication of this has been suggested already: what matters is not that a individual wrongdoer is punished so much as that the money is paid. As economists say, money prices things and thus puts friction into the system; increases in price drive down demand and divert action into preferred channels. Somewhere, someone pays, and aggregate demand falls – even if through such indirect pressures as an employer, spouse or parent bawling out the offender.

While Foucault (1984) refers to governance through distributions in such ways as 'regulation', more frequently in criminology is subsumed under the category of 'risk' – where governance is in terms of probabilistic reduction of future harms. Fines now appear as a central technology in the governance of risks. Indeed, from the 1970s, especially with respect to the traffic fines that make up 90 per cent of money penalties, the fine 'system' has been reframed piecemeal as a system of electronic and monetized risk management.

In this process, a first step came with the prioritization of risk as a discourse and technology. With respect to traffic, this appeared with the reframing of 'the road toll'. While the rising number of deaths from traffic accidents had been recognized since the first half of the twentieth century, in the 1970s the road toll was recast away from a discourse of unanticipated or negligent individual 'accidents'. Partly as a result of the Arab oil embargo of 1974, when many states – including the UK, the USA, Canada and Australia – lowered speed limits in order to conserve fuel, it was recognized that reductions in speed limits generated significant reductions in the road toll. Research following up on this showed clear correlations between speeding and rates of death and injury (Adams, 1994). Speeding now took on a new form: no longer merely a 'technical' infringement. It was no longer even a question of 'danger' – for it was not judged as an individual case as was dangerousness (Castel, 1991). Speeding was thereby transformed into 'objective' risk, its riskiness based on statistical facts. Now traffic offences could be subjected to a scientifically moralized discourse of truth and justice.[3]

In consequence, traffic regulation – and similar things were happening in areas such as public health and industrial health and safety – now appeared as *a measurable morality*. Advances in technologies for measuring speed and related 'risky' offences, such as running red lights and drink driving, rendered these calculably risk-bearing offences themselves more and more exactly and 'objectively' measurable. Indeed, often the offence was transformed in the process – as drink driving, for example, frequently was recast as having a blood alcohol content above the legal limit: the risk indicators became the offences. By the 1980s, speed cameras, hand held police 'radar' guns , red light cameras and the like, began to be developed and installed in many jurisdictions. Barcode readers in gantries or embedded in the road surface now check truck travel on major highways, to ensure drivers do not speed and do not exceed safe driving times. An electronically calculable morality of risk has been developed, and linked to an automated policing system which has virtually eliminated challenges to the judgment of the offence (O'Malley, 2010a).

Tying all these disparate developments together came to be a function allocated to computerization. In a new policing assemblage electronic devices record traffic offences and send messages to a central computer that compares the offence with a tariff of fixed penalties. The computer issues a penalty notice which is printed and mailed (or emailed) to the 'dividuals' concerned. We have what can be thought of as 'simulated policing'. Simulation here refers to the point at which the real and the virtual converge. Everything mentioned so far occurs in the realm of digitized or binary codes, but they are no less 'real' for that. Digital photographs or speed readings, digitized ownership identifiers and drivers' licenses, digitally generated penalty notices cannot be dismissed as 'virtual' in the sense of merely an electronic phantom. And at this point money reappears. It will be recalled that because of its undifferentiated character where money sanctions are concerned the law does not bother with the identity of who pays the penalty. This makes possible the anonymous and remote payment of the penalty. But in addition, money has that key attribute of itself being digitized (and real). The circle of justice can now be completed in the virtual space: detection, sentencing *and expiation* of sentence can all be disposed of in the form of electronic codes – by credit card or electronic banking – in a space that is both real punishment and yet within the domain of the virtual environment. Thanks to money, 'simulated justice' has arrived.[4]

Of course all this has not occurred simply through technological development, for a key driver of such change has been a growing assumption that legal regulation of everyday life is to be subjected to an economic rationality. From the late 19th century, many of the changes that streamlined justice to the point where simulated justice became possible, were driven by cost considerations. As regulation takes on an increasingly massive character, a cost-benefit logic – *the complete monetization of justice* – comes to be a principal driver of its form. It is not only that money is the form of justice, but money in the form of cost-benefit analysis is the primary shaper of the system of simulated justice. In this process, a mutated form of justice has driven 'individuals' to marginal spaces. In their place are machines speaking to each other. This justice targets 'dividuals' identified by their electronically codified traces. It is dividuals who pay their fines digitally. Individuals are expensive, whether enforcers or offenders, and no effort is spared to drive individuals out of this mass and monetized domain of governance (O'Malley, 2010b).

CONCLUSION: MONETIZED JUSTICE AND MONETIZED RISK

The emergence of simulated justice brings to the fore a number of key issues surrounding the expansion of monetized justice and regulation. Looking back at the characteristics of money sanctions, it seems all the more vital to recognize the extent to which money operates as a sanction that inflicts significant punishment while at the same time being of such low political profile that even criminologists barely recognize the existence – let alone the impact – of monetary sanctions (Harris et al., 2010). This is by no means to suggest that others have not noticed. In many jurisdictions there has been significant opposition to the expansion of simulated justice because of the inroads it makes into traditional legal assumptions about the presumption of innocence and the right to trial (Fox, 1996). Other prominent grounds for opposition include the belief that it is frequently a naked form of revenue collection. Arizona and Hawaii have opposed a program of speed cameras on such grounds, and popular resistance in Arizona has been such that fewer than one third of the 1.2 million tickets issued have been paid (Connolly, 2010). Ontario has banned red light cameras for the same reasons. In Melbourne, Australia cameras were removed from some freeways on the grounds that they were inaccurate; and in Sydney 38 cameras were removed because they were shown not to have improved safety. Even so, cameras are still becoming more widespread, and whatever the local opposition to which we can point in the USA, the principal private operator of speed cameras in America saw its revenues grow by 48 per cent in 2009 alone (Connolly, 2010).

Yet it is not only fines in 'simulated' justice that are on the march. The same is true for fines (and as we have seen, fees) as a sanction for 'traditional' criminal justice offences. True, during the 'punitive turn' of the past decade or so, fines have contracted in the face of demands for harsher penalties, at least in relation to more serious offending (O'Malley, 2009a). But it is still the case that in most jurisdictions outside the USA they make up about 70 per cent of all sanctions in the lower courts, and in numerical terms have been increasing more or less unchecked. Money has too many advantages ever to be seriously downgraded as a sanction in consumer societies.

However, if money appears as the 'soft' penumbra of justice, and simply a 'price' to be paid as a matter of course, this scarcely means that it is an inconsequential sanction. More precisely, this is how fines may appear to the middle classes. As late as the 1980s in the UK fine defaulters made up a substantial portion of prison intakes, indicating that that fines bit deeply enough into the lives of many poor people sufficiently hard that even in face of the imminent threat of incarceration they could not afford payment. For the poor, as Harris et al. (2010: 1792) document, take on significant and oppressive debts not only with respect to fines, but in the USA even more as a consequence of the array of fees and imposts levied for the costs of other punishment. So much is this the case, that they suggests that monetary sanctions in that country have effectively rendered the penal sector an inadequate supplier of social services to a poor that is forced pay for them. In practice, to the extent that the field of justice has been transformed by a logic of punitive risk-management (Feeley and Simon, 1994), the poor increasingly pay to govern the risks they are held to present to others.

Rather than inconsequential and peripheral, then, it would be better to regard monetized justice as a sanction that takes the form of monetized risk. Yet the monetization of risk has its limits. While economists advocate the use of fines even for the most serious of crimes (Becker, 1974), in practice high risk offenders cannot be governed in this fashion. In the domain of simulated justice, for example, this is registered in an array of back-up risk-based sanctions. Those who wish to speed or run red lights or commit minor offences punishable through fixed penalty notices, could do so with impunity as long as they were willing and able to pay the corresponding fine. For this reason, with respect to traffic especially, most jurisdictions have developed systems of cumulative demerit points such that, over and above the fine, drivers collect a number of points depending on the severity of the offence. In the case of speeding or example, each incremental increase in speed above the speed limit represents a certain increase in risk. In lockstep with increasing fines, a parallel metric measures risk in terms of demerit points. Those who accumulate more demerit points than the risk metric allows have demonstrated that their risk *cannot be governed by money* alone. In a sense, they are failed consumers. For such failures, the appropriate sanction itself is framed in terms of risk: license cancellation. License cancellation incapacitates that specific 'dividual' which causes the risk rather than incapacitating – at high social cost – the entire 'individual' through imprisonment. Only if the offender continues to drive without the license, or the offence is adjudged to risk-bearing to permit liberty (and drink-driving is considered this way in some jurisdictions) will the more draconian forms of incapacitation be considered.

Of course it is not only those caught in the electronic web of simulated justice who are classified with respect to their status as consumers. Those who are fined for 'traditional' offences are being judged as capable of being governed through the market. In such cases, if they pay their fine on time, they have proven themselves warrantable consumers. Continued reoffending or non-payment of the fine will exhaust the sanction, and the offenders will be returned to the court system for resentencing. Again, they have acted as failed consumers, and their risk is likely to be neutralized by some form of incapacitation.

The fine is thus a sanction of privilege that governs consumers through a graduated technology of risk. Only the failed consumers – the poor, the persistent or the dangerous offender – are ineligible for its 'gentle' way of punishment. It is for such reasons, rather than whether or not every singly consumer society governs its traditional offenders this way – that the fine appears as the sanction of consumer society. Fines govern through consumption, through the ability to demonstrate credentials as a consumer, and thus as licensed to be free. But as with all consumption, the cost may become a lifetime of debt and the terrible question we face is whether it is better to have a class in prison, or a class in debt.

NOTES

1 It should be clear that the focus of this chapter is on the governmental deployment of fines and their implications. As such the chapter does not raise questions in detail concerning social justice implications or the impact and 'effectiveness' of fines as such, which are beyond the scope of a single chapter. There is some literature on these matters, although again surprisingly little. Readers are directed to Harris et al. (2010) and Carlen and Cook (1989) for two key resources in this respect.

2 Of course, this could suggest, nevertheless, that no real effort has gone into finding solutions to the problem of imprisonment in default. The USA as shown only the barest interest in schemes such as day fines – that is, fines set at so many days income of the offender, thus holding wealth relatively constant. Day fines have been in existence since the middle of the 19th century, have been in more or less constant use in Scandinavia and other European countries. They were suggested by Bentham as a solution to the problem of inequitable punishment on the basis of wealth (O'Malley, 2009a). So it could be said that if the US federal and state legislatures were seriously interested in fines they could have made a greater effort in this direction. However, day fines confront one serious problem – and this certainly has been picked up as a central issue both in US trials of the scheme, and in other countries (such as Australia) where they have been considered but rejected. Day fines would probably fall foul of the

Fourteenth Amendment because the wealthy would be presented with fines in dollar amounts that greatly exceed those of the poor – after all, this is the aim of the scheme. But it is unlikely that such a system would survive a serious challenge, for it may well be that while a poor offender may pay tens of dollars, a wealthy manufacturer would pay thousands of dollars for an identical offence.

3 This is not to suggest that 'objectivity' is a truth rather than an effect of a certain discourse. As Adams (1994) argues, many of the so-called correlations on which such objective probabilities are based are likely spurious. This includes data on the risk reductions effected by the introduction of sat belts in the 1970s.

4 Note that in simulated justice non-monetary sanctions can be applied still within the virtual domain: license cancellation, for example, is issued by a computer based on the recorded number of demerit points. Nothing 'physical' need happen to the license itself, as its bar code will now indicate its null status to the next officer who swipes it through the police cruiser's reader.

REFERENCES

Adams, John (1994) *Risk.* London: UCL Press.

American Bar Association (1971) *Standards Relating to Sentencing Alternatives and Procedures.* Chicago: American Bar Foundation.

Becker, Gary (1974) 'Crime and punishment: an economic approach', in G. Becker and W. Landes (eds), *Essays in the Economics of Crime and Punishment.* New York: Columbia University Press. pp. 27–36

Bentham, Jeremy (1780 [1962]) *The Works of Jeremy Bentham*, Vol. 1, ed. John Bowring. New York: Russell and Russell.

Bentham, Jeremy (1782 [1982]) *An Introduction to the Principles of Morals and Legislation*, ed. James Burns and H.L.A. Hart. London: Methuen.

Bottoms, Anthony (1983) 'Some neglected features of contemporary penal systems', in D. Garland and P. Young (eds), *The Power to Punish.* London: Heinemann. pp. 83–125.

Briggs, John, Harrison, Christopher, McInnes, Angus and Vincent, David (1996) *Crime and Punishment in England.* London: UCL Press.

Bureau of Justice Statistics (2004) *State Court Sentencing of Convicted Felons 2004.* Washington DC: US Department of Justice.

Cane, Peter (2006) *Atiyah on Accidents, Compensation and the Law*, 7th edn. London: Butterworths.

Carlen, Pat and Cook, Dee (eds) (1989) *Paying for Crime.* Milton Keynes: Open University Press.

Carson, W.G. (1974) 'Symbolic and instrumental dimensions of early factory legislation', in W.G Carson and P. Wiles (eds), *Crime, Criminology, and Public Policy.* London: Heinemann. pp. 64–89.

Castel, Robert (1991) 'From Dangerousness to Risk', in Graeme Burchell, Colin Gordon and Peter Miller, (eds), *The Foucault Effect: Studies in Governmentality.* London: Harvester/Wheatsheaf. pp. 281–98.

Connolly, John (2010) 'Click go the cameras boys', *The Weekend Australian,* 31 July: 14.

Deleuze, Gilles (1995) *Negotiations 1972–1990.* New York: Columbia University Press.

Dubber, Marcus and Kelman, Mark (2005) *American Civil Law: Cases, Materials and Comments.* New York: Foundation Press.

Duff, Peter (1993) 'The prosecutor fine and social control,' *British Journal of Criminology,* 33: 481–503.

Feeley, Malcolm and Simon, Jonathan (1994) 'Actuarial justice. The emerging new criminal law.' in David Nelken (ed.), *The Futures of criminology.* New York: Sage. pp. 46–67.

Fogelson, Robert (2001) *Downtown, its Rise and Fall 1880–1950.* London: Yale University Press.

Foucault, Michel (1977) *Discipline and Punish.* London: Peregrine.

Foucault, Michel (1984) *The History of Sexuality. Volume 1.* London: Peregrine.

Fox, Richard (1996) *Criminal Justice on the Spot. Infringement Penalties in Victoria.* Canberra: Australian Institute of Criminology.

Freiberg, Arie and Ross, Stuart (1999) *Sentencing Reform and Penal Change.* Sydney: Federation Press.

Garton, Stephen (1982) 'Bad or mad? Developments in incarceration in NSW 1880–1920', in Sydney Labour History Group (ed.), *What Rough beast? The State and Social Order in Australian History.* Sydney: Allen and Unwin. pp. 89–110.

Gillespie, Richard (1981) 'Sanctioning traditional crimes with fines: a comparative analysis', *International Journal of Comparative and Applied Criminal Justice,* 5: 195–204.

Grebing, Gerhardt (1982) *The Fine in Comparative law: A Survey of 21 Countries.* Cambridge: Institute of Criminology Occasional Papers No.9.

Harris, Alexes, Evans, Heather and Beckett, Katherine (2010) 'Drawing blood from stones: legal debts and social inequality in the contemporary United States', *American Journal of Sociology,* 115: 1753–99.

Hillsman, Sally (1990) 'Fines and day fines', *Crime and Justice; A Review of Research,* 12: 50–98.

Horwitz, Morton (1977) *The Transformation of American Law*. Harvard, MA: Harvard University Press.

King, Peter (1996) 'Punishing assault: the transformation of attitudes in the English courts', *Journal of Interdisciplinary History*, 27: 43–74.

O'Malley, P. (2000) 'Uncertain subjects. Risk, liberalism and contract', *Economy and Society*, 29:460–484.

O'Malley, Pat (2004) *Risk, Uncertainty and Government*. London: Glasshouse Press.

O'Malley, Pat (2009a) 'Theorizing fines', *Punishment and Society*, 11: 67–83.

O'Malley, Pat (2009b) *The Currency of Justice: Fines and Damages in Consumer Societies*. London: Routledge Cavendish.

O'Malley, Pat (2010a) 'Simulated justice: risk, money and telemetric policing', *British Journal of Criminology*, 50: 795–807.

O'Malley, Pat (2010b) 'Fines, risks and damages', *Current Issues in Criminal Justice*, 21: 265–382.

Paulus, Ingeborg (1976) *The Search for Pure Food*. London: Martin Robertson.

Plowden, William (1971) *The Motor Car and Politics 1986–1970*. London: The Bodley Head.

Rusche, Georg and Kirchheimer, Otto (1939) *Punishment and Social Structure*. New York: Columbia University Press.

Seagle, William (1948) 'Fines', in E. Seligman and A. Johnson (eds), *Encyclopaedia of the Social Science*. New York: MacMillan. pp. 389–93.

Sharp, John (1990) *Judicial Punishment in England*. London: Faber and Faber.

Simmel, Georg (1990) *The Philosophy of Money*, enlarged edn. New York: Routledge.

Simon, Jonathan (1987) 'The emergence of a risk society: insurance, law, and the state', *Socialist Review*, 95: 61–89.

Simon, Jonathan (1999) 'Driving governmentality, automobile accidents. Insurance and the challenge to social order in the inter-war years 1919–1941', *Connecticut Insurance Law Journal*, 4: 522–88.

Wacquant, Loic (2002) 'Four strategies to curb carceral costs: on managing mass imprisonment in the United States', *Studies in Political Economy*, 69: 19–30.

White, Edward (2003) *Tort Law in America. An Intellectual History*, expanded edn. Oxford: Oxford University Press.

Young, Peter (1989) 'Punishment, money and a sense of justice', in P. Carlen and D. Cook (eds), *Paying for Crime*. Milton Keynes: Open University Press. pp. 101–27.

Zelizer, Viviana (1994) *The Social Meaning of Money*. New York: Basic Books.

PART IV

New Contexts

19

Punishment and Human Rights

Dirk van Zyl Smit

Is concern for human rights a recent development in the understanding of punishment? The invitation to write this chapter seemed to suggest that it was, for it placed the topic of punishment and human rights in the section of the Handbook dealing with 'new contexts'. At first glance this is extraordinary, for, at least since the Enlightenment at the end of the 18th century, a prohibition on certain forms of punishment has been recognized as a fundamental right and enshrined in foundational legal documents. However, what is relatively new is the development of these early prohibitions as part of a wider doctrine of human rights that purports to set boundaries on all aspects of the imposition and implementation of punishment and that claims universal validity for the limitations it contains.

This chapter sketches briefly the history of the development of human rights applicable to punishment before turning its attention more specifically to the impact that they have had on the practice of punishment. Practice is divided into two parts, namely the imposition of punishment and the implementation of punishment. The imposition part is subdivided into consideration of the forms of punishment that have come to be regarded as so heinous that they should never be imposed, and more subtle questions about the scope of the human rights-derived principles that would limit the imposition of forms of punishment that the same principles do not outlaw summarily. The section on implementation focuses on how human rights standards restrict the usage of those punishments that are (at least arguably) permitted by human rights norms. Finally, the chapter considers the wider issue of the current and future relationships between human rights and punishment.

HISTORY

Scholars of punishment, especially but not exclusively the lawyers among them, have long been aware that claims involving legal rights matter to those who are confronted by the state's power to punish. An academic generation ago they paid much attention to the work of historians, such as E.P. Thompson (1975) and Douglas Hay (1975; see also more critically, Langbein, 1983) who demonstrated that the poor in 18th-century England sought to rely on their legal rights to limit the penalties that could be imposed on them and the manner in which they were implemented. Although the law in which the poor placed their faith was often grossly flawed, they did not lose this faith, precisely because the law did sometimes work in their favour to an extent that made a real difference. In the early 18th century the legal and intellectual resources for critiquing the existing penal frameworks were limited, but certainly points of departure existed. As Hay demonstrated accused persons did call on the common law to support their claims for justice and mercy. They also had at their disposal the English Bill of Rights 1688, which laid down that 'excessive Baile ought not to be required nor excessive Fines imposed nor cruell and unusuall Punishments inflicted'.

Much of the major shift in the approach to punishment that took place towards the end of the 18th century sought to address the shortcoming in these legal guarantees. As Foucault recognised, it was driven by an attempt to answer the question: 'how are the two elements, which are everywhere present in demands for a more lenient penal system, "measure" and "humanity", to be articulated upon one another, in a single strategy?' (1977: 74). This was the question that Enlightenment theorists of punishment, such as Beccaria (1764 [1964]), sought to answer with their proposals for punishments that were proportionate to the crime and did not amount to torture. These penal ideals soon found direct reflection in the new constitutional orders that emerged at the end of the 18th century in the USA and France. In 1789 in America the Eighth Amendment to the US Constitution followed the wording of the English Bill of Rights, prohibiting both excessive fines and cruel and unusual punishments, while the French Declaration of the Rights of Man, adopted in the same year, also had the effect of guaranteeing human dignity.

The inclusion of these provisions in the two major constitutional documents of the age increased not only their legal salience but also their more general prestige. However, their impact was to be long delayed. In part this was because of the sometimes narrow interpretation given to these provisions that was limited to preventing new and excessively harsh punishments rather than evaluating them against wider standards.

The full flowering of the prohibition on certain forms of punishment as a key element in thinking about the rights of those subject to punishment is a much more modern phenomenon that goes together with the rise of the 20th-century movement for the recognition of universal human rights. While the broad human rights tradition has deep roots in both the ideas of natural law and the European Enlightenment, it flourished after the Second World War when, after the defeat of fascism, a determined effort was made to create a new world order in which the human rights of individuals were recognised and given legal force in international law.[1] Of course, their content, their relationship to each other and how they could be enforced was (and is) a matter of dispute. Initially, the focus was largely on civil and political human rights, such as the right to life, liberty and the integrity of the person, the freedoms of expression and religion, and legal due process. However, as a result of the efforts of Eastern Bloc and Third World countries in particular, attention was also paid to economic, social and cultural rights and their international recognition (Nowak, 2003). This legal significance of these latter, 'second generation', rights was initially denied by critics in the west in particular, as it was claimed that they were difficult if not impossible to enforce. Modern rights theorists accept, however, that the distinctions between different categories of human rights are somewhat artificial, as civil and political rights cannot be exercised effectively without at least a basic minimum of socio-economic provision: human rights, it is argued, are interdependent and indivisible (Van Boven, 2010).

Civil and political rights in particular were soon reflected in a range of international instruments with clear implications for punishment, as they tended to refer to it directly.

In 1946 the Universal Declaration of Human Rights recognized human dignity (Article 1) and a range of other rights, including the prohibition of torture and cruel, inhuman or degrading treatment or punishment (Article 5). This call was echoed in similar prohibitions on inhuman and degrading treatment or punishment in regional human rights conventions: in 1950, the European Convention on Human Rights (ECHR) (Article 3), in 1969, the American Convention on Human Rights (Article 5) and, in 1981, the African Charter on Human and Peoples' Rights (Article 3). The latter two regional conventions also recognized important economic, social and cultural rights, but did not relate them directly to questions of punishment.

At the international level, human dignity and the prohibition of torture and cruel, inhuman and degrading treatment or punishment were given significance as concepts underpinning the regulation of prison conditions by the International Covenant on Civil and Political Rights (ICCPR) adopted in 1966. The ICCPR was important both in terms of its careful limitation of the use of the death penalty (Article 6) and in terms of its recognition of prisoners' rights, which could only be achieved if adequate prison conditions existed. Not only did it provide that 'all persons deprived of their liberty shall be treated with humanity and with respect for the inherent dignity of the human person' (Article 10.1) and that 'no one should be subjected to torture or to cruel, inhuman or degrading treatment or punishment' (Article 7), but it also contained further provisions that could be interpreted as setting implicit requirements in respect of prison conditions. Of these the most important, from the point of view of the implementation of punishment, is the requirement in Article 10.3 that 'the penitentiary system shall comprise treatment of prisoners the essential aim of which shall be their social rehabilitation', which can be seen as an overarching requirement according to which the treatment of all sentenced prisoners and the prison conditions to facilitate it should be judged (Nowak, 2005).

The growing recognition of the human rights relevant to punishment was mirrored in a large number of national constitutions emerging in the same period that specified legally binding fundamental rights. By the early 1990s Bassiouni could report that 'the right to be free from torture and cruel and degrading treatment or punishment is provided for in at least eighty-one constitutions' (1993: 263). Even in the rare modern constitutions in which such a prohibition is not mentioned explicitly in a justiciable bill of rights, it is regarded as implicitly present: in India, where the constitution has no such prohibition, it has been deduced from the due process clause (Schabas, 1996), while the recognition of human dignity as the fundamental right in the German Basic Law has been held to encompass a prohibition not only on torture, but also on inhuman and degrading punishment (Streng, 2002). Indeed, in one specific area the German constitution goes further; by formally prohibiting the death penalty, it puts this form of punishment beyond legal and, to a large extent, even public debate.

The development of human rights that are directly applicable to punishment is, however, rarely undertaken in the primary international, regional or national instruments. In some instances these instruments are supplemented by protocols on specific penal topics, such as the protocols dealing with the death penalty discussed below. Such protocols have the status of binding treaties for the states that have ratified them. In other instances treaties, such as the 1989 United Nations Convention of the Rights of the Child, have a few provisions dealing specifically with penal matters in respect of the population to which they refer.

More characteristic of the post-Second World War period is that the general treaty level instruments are supplemented by a whole range of secondary material. These include international and regional rules, standards, resolutions and recommendations (the terminology is somewhat interchangeable), and the interpretations of the primary instruments by international or national courts, as well as the many reports of international and national inspecting and monitoring bodies that appeal to general human rights norms while developing standards that deal with specific manifestations of punishment. It is noteworthy that both the United Nations and the Council of Europe publish compendia of these rules that cover virtually every aspect of the penal process (UN Office on Drugs and Crime, 2006; Council of Europe, 2010). The human rights perspectives that these rules, recommendations and standards bring to bear on debates about punishment cannot be ignored. They are sometimes described as creating a form of 'soft law' of little legal significance, but that term may be misleading. In several instances bodies of rules may gain additional status by being referred to regularly in the interpretation of binding instruments. An example is the 1955 United Nations Standard Minimum Rules for the Treatment of Prisoners, which over the years, have grown in status to the point where it is recognised that 'some of their specific rules may reflect legal obligations' (Rodley and Pollard, 2009: 383). Thus, for example, the prohibition on placing a prisoner in a dark cell by Rule 31 is seen as a form of treatment that is specifically forbidden and therefore routinely regarded as a form of the cruel, inhuman or degrading treatment outlawed by Article 7 of the ICCPR. Even where this is not the case, the Standard Minimum Rules can provide guidance in interpreting and applying the ICCPR to prisoners.

IMPOSITION

Human rights can impact on the imposition of punishment in two ways. First, certain punishments may be declared contrary to human rights norms and, if this is accepted, excluded entirely from the range of options available to sentencers. Second, human rights may have something to say about the imposition of punishments that are not absolutely excluded.

Punishments that can never be imposed

It is easy enough to state in the abstract that torture and 'cruel and unusual' or 'inhuman and degrading' punishments may never be imposed, but what is meant by the terms 'torture', 'cruel and unusual' or 'inhuman and degrading'? As will become apparent this is a difficult question to answer in the abstract as interpretations of these terms may change over time. In this regard the US Supreme Court has famously referred, when interpreting the 'cruel and unusual' test of the Eighth Amendment to the US Constitution, to the necessity of bearing in mind the 'evolving standards of decency that mark the progress of a maturing society' (*Trop* v. *Dulles* (1958:100). The difficulty in applying this test has been that judges have had to decide for themselves what this 'standard of decency' is at any given time. On the one hand, this cannot be determined in isolation from a reflection on societal norms. On the other hand, a court cannot simply follow public opinion, as such opinion may support punishments that do not meet 'standards of decency'. In modern times the debate has been mostly about whether human rights norms absolutely forbid capital punishment and corporal punishment, but similar questions are increasingly being raised about persons sentenced to imprisonment with no prospect of ever being released.

Capital punishment

Arguments about the total abolition of capital punishment go back at least to the Enlightenment. However, historically, many of the arguments in favour of abolition were pragmatic rather than human rights based. Even Beccaria (1764 [1964]), whose work is associated most closely with the rise of moderate and proportionate punishment, opposed capital punishment on the grounds that it was not as effective a deterrent as harsh life imprisonment. Others argued that it was to be justified on retributive grounds as the only fitting punishment for very serious offences, and that this argument trumped any concern for the human rights of the offender sentenced to life imprisonment or, more rarely, not to be subject to an unacceptable form of punishment. However, there was a significant increase in the importance of human rights in this debate in the post-Second World War period. Hood and Hoyle describe this development:

> The dynamo for the new wave of abolition [of capital punishment] was the development of international human rights law. Arising in the aftermath of the Second World War ... the acceptance of human rights principles created a climate that advocated in the name of democracy and freedom, the protection of citizens from the power of the state and the tyranny of the opinions of the masses. Foremost among the factors that have promoted this new wave of abolition has been the political movement to transform consideration of capital punishment from an issue to be decided solely or mainly as an aspect of national criminal justice policy to the status of a fundamental violation of human rights; not only the right to life but the right to be free of excessive, repressive and tortuous punishments. (2008: 18–19)

It is important to note that the deployment of human rights arguments and more specifically those derived from international human rights law in national policy debates after the Second World War was a gradual process. At the international level the key provision dealing with capital punishment in a human rights treaty, Article 6 of the ICCPR, does not simply abolish it. Instead it reasserts the right to life of 'every human being' but then provides only that no one shall be deprived of life 'arbitrarily' (Article 6(1)). The rest of the Article then contains limitations on the death penalty: restricting it to serious offences, (Article 6(2)) and requiring due process and the possibility of pardon for all who may be sentenced to death (Article 6(4)). It outlaws the death penalty completely only for those under the age of 18 and pregnant women (Article 6(5)). Since then there have been attempts to strengthen the ICCPR, most significantly by the adoption of the Second Optional Protocol to the ICCPR, which provides for abolition of the death penalty.[2]

In Europe there was a similar evolutionary development. Zimring (2003) has noted that abolition of the death penalty in western Europe took place at the national level and that this preceded the development of strong human rights based campaigns against the death penalty at the level of European institutions such as the Council of Europe. The initial absence of a pan-European human rights dimension could be explained in part by the fact that the major European human rights instrument, the ECHR seemed to provide for the retention of the death penalty, for Article 2 of the ECHR contained an exception to the right of persons not to be deprived of life intentionally: 'save in the execution of a sentence of a court following his conviction of a crime for this penalty is provided by law'. However, once national abolition had taken place, a regional drive towards abolition, as part of a specific human rights agenda, began to take shape. The western European states, who were the initial members of the Council of Europe and signatories to the ECHR, sought to expand its scope to encompass the abolition of the death penalty. Two Protocols were added to the ECHR: Protocol 6 requiring the abolition of the death penalty in peace time and Protocol 13 requiring its abolition at all times. Both these protocols have now been ratified by the vast majority of European states. An important factor in this development was the requirement that new members agree to abolish the death penalty as a condition for joining the Council of Europe. This requirement was accepted by the eastern European states, including Russia, which joined the Council of Europe in the 1990s. Although Russia in particular has remained reluctant to comply fully with the requirements set initially for admission and has not acceded to the protocols to the ECHR, in practice the movement has been a great success as it has meant that the death penalty has not been implemented in Europe at all since the early 1990s.

The wider political developments were paralleled by a rethinking of the jurisprudence. Although Article 2 of the ECHR ostensibly exempted the death penalty from being regarded as an infringement of the right to life, the European Court of Human Rights (ECtHR) began to find against the death penalty by applying the ECHR more broadly: In *Soering* v. *United Kingdom* (1989), the ECtHR held that the complainant could not be extradited to the USA to face a possible death sentence because the delay in enforcing it could expose him to the angst of death row, which would be an inhuman punishment contrary to Article 3 of the ECHR. By 2005 when the Grand Chamber of the ECHR came to consider the death penalty again in the case of *Öcalan* v. *Turkey* (2005), it was prepared to hold that the mere threat of being subject to the death penalty was a form of inhuman and degrading treatment sufficient to infringe Article 3 and to raise the possibility that the exception allowing for the death penalty in Article 2 should be disregarded, at least in time of peace. This was made clear by the ECtHR in the recent case of *Al-Saadoon and Mufdhi* v. *United Kingdom* (2010:115) when it took as its explicit 'starting point … the right not be subjected to the death penalty'. It did so when holding that the UK government had a duty not to hand over, after its own withdrawal from Iraq, two Iraqi citizens that it had captured, for trial by Iraqi courts where they would face the possibility of being sentenced to death for the crimes they had allegedly committed.

Campaigns for the complete abolition of the death penalty have not been limited to Europe, or to Central and South America, where the death penalty has long been outlawed entirely (Hood and Hoyle, 2008), but have spread more widely, becoming part of the self image and the foreign policy of abolitionist states. Human rights campaigns against the death penalty have not always been successful. Notably, the death penalty has been retained in several states of the USA. This is of great symbolic importance because of the historical commitment of the USA to human rights, also in the sphere of punishment, and because of the huge influence of the USA in the modern world.

As in Europe, the major campaigns for the abolition of capital punishment in the USA were fought largely prior to the rise of the international human rights concern with the issue. The particular political structure of the USA long suggested that national abolition would come about through the intervention of the US Supreme Court. In this regard the decision of the Court in *Furman* v. *Georgia* (1972) was crucial. In that judgment a majority of the nine judges held that the death penalty as then applied in the US was unconstitutional. At the time it seemed as if this was a knockout blow. However a close reading of the judgment showed that only three judges argued directly that the death penalty was always unconstitutional because it amounted to an infringement of the basic human right to human dignity, the value that underlay the prohibition of cruel and unusual punishments. The remainder of the judges who made up the majority faulted the law then in force only on the basis that it did not provide the due process guarantees that offenders should have had as of right. The result was that retentionist states set out to amend their death penalty laws to meet these due process standards. Some of these new laws were subsequently upheld by the Supreme Court in *Gregg* v. *Georgia* (1976), with a majority of judges emphasising that public opinion still supported the death penalty and that under those circumstances a directly human rights-based argument that attacked the penalty as an automatic infringement of human dignity could not succeed. Since the mid-1970s therefore, the death penalty in the USA has largely been immune to direct challenge. Almost all subsequent strategies against the death penalty in the USA have challenged the procedural propriety of its imposition or have turned on it being disproportionately severe for a particular class of crimes or group of offenders (see below), rather than seeking its direct abolition.

In recent years direct abolition of the death penalty has continued to be a human rights issue but now with a considerable input from international human rights campaigns. There have been some notable legal victories. In 1990, that is before Hungary joined the Council of Europe, the Constitutional Court of Hungary relied heavily on international human rights law to inform its decision that the rights to life and human dignity, which are guaranteed by the constitution of Hungary, were to be interpreted as overriding a separate provision of the constitution that on the face of it allowed for the sentence of death as a lawful penalty. In 1995 the first judgment of the Constitutional Court of South Africa made similar use of international human rights developments to come to the conclusion that the national constitutional rights to life, human dignity and freedom from cruel, inhuman and degrading punishment meant that the death penalty was unconstitutional in the new South Africa (*S* v. *Makwanyane* (1995)).

Finally, it is noteworthy that the international criminal tribunals for the former Yugoslavia and for Rwanda, established by the United Nations Security Council in 1993 and 1994 respectively, as well as the 1999 Statute of the International Criminal Court make no provision for the death penalty, although these bodies were set up to try the most heinous crimes: genocide and crimes against humanity. At the very least this development signifies that a number of influential states will not tolerate the imposition of the death penalty at the international level. However, it does not mean that full international recognition that capital punishment is contrary to human rights, for some of the key countries were prepared to go along with these developments only if they could preserve the death penalty as a sentence in their domestic law. This is reflected in Article 80 of the Statute of the International Criminal Court, which carefully qualified the provision for penalties in the Statute by making it clear that they did not affect the application by states of penalties prescribed by their national law. This means that those states that continue to impose capital punishment would not be prevented by this Statute from doing so.

Corporal punishment

There is 'weighty evidence' that corporal punishment is contrary to international human rights law but its rejection, even as a punishment imposed by the state, is not universal (Rodley and Pollard, 2009: 427). In the European context the gradual shift away from corporal punishment as a sentence of the courts largely predates determination of the issue in overtly human rights terms. This is also largely true in the USA, where the US Supreme Court was never called upon directly to settle the issue, but a consensus emerged in the post-Second World War period that corporal punishment imposed by the state would be unacceptable. In Europe, the ECtHR was required to deal with the issue in one of its first decisions, handed down in 1978, *Tyrer* v. *United Kingdom* (1980). However, that case concerned corporal punishment imposed by a court on a juvenile on the Isle of Man, a small semi-independent territory under the control of the UK, and therefore subject to it in matters of international law. The UK had already abolished all forms of corporal punishment as court-imposed sentences. Nevertheless, it defended the Manx law vigorously. In the event, the ECtHR could draw on 'developments and commonly acceptable standards in the penal policy of member states of the Council of Europe' in coming to its conclusion that corporal punishment was a degrading punishment that infringed Article 3 of the ECHR.

Tyrer's case has had a wide impact outside Europe. Not only has it been followed by other international and regional human rights bodies,[3] but this has also happened at the national level outside Europe, most notably in southern Africa where the British tradition of corporal punishment had continued to be applied in an overtly discriminatory way by white dominated governments against a largely subservient black population. In relatively quick succession the supreme courts of Zimbabwe (*S* v. *Ncube* (1988)), Namibia (*Ex Parte Attorney-General Namibia: In re Corporal Punishment by Organs of State*

(1991)) and then the Constitutional Court of South Africa (*S* v. *Williams and others* (1995)), all relying directly on *Tyrer*, found that corporal punishment was a cruel, inhuman and degrading punishment that could not be imposed by a state that sought to uphold the human dignity of its subjects.

But just how far did the prohibition go? This issue was squarely raised before the South African Constitutional Court by a Christian group that wished to impose moderate corporal punishment on pupils in the private school that it ran but was prohibited from doing so by government regulation (*Christian Education South Africa* v. *Minister of Education* (2000)). The complainants argued that the prohibition infringed their constitutional and human right to freedom of religion as it prevented them from bringing up their children in a way that satisfied Biblical injunctions. In a subtle judgment the South African Constitutional Court conceded that the government regulation did limit the complainants' freedom of religion, but held at the same time that the regulation had a principled and symbolic function to uphold the dignity and physical and emotional integrity of all children. In such a case the South African constitution required an assessment of whether the limitation of the complainants' human right was proportionate to the wider objective of asserting other rights. The Court concluded that it was and upheld the power of the state to prohibit corporal punishment in all schools.

The ideas contained in western judgments such as *Tyrer* do not always transplant easily. In 1994 the sensitivities that underlie the assertion of an absolute right not to be subject to corporal punishment were highlighted when a young American, Michael Fay, was sentenced to corporal punishment for writing graffiti in Singapore. The Singaporean authorities responded strongly that this was a relative concept that should be applied with cultural sensitivity (Bahrampour, 1995). The penalty was reduced from 12 strokes to 4 on appeal, but it was carried out, in the face of protest from the USA that the punishment remained cruel and unusual.

This section has focused on corporal punishment imposed or sanctioned by the state, but it should not be forgotten that there is also a strong, human rights driven, campaign to abolish all forms of corporal punishment, including the physical chastisement of children by their parents. This has been encouraged by the Committee on the Rights of the Child (2006), the body of independent experts that monitors implementation of the Convention on the Rights of the Child. This movement is particularly strong in Europe where a number of countries outlaw this form of corporal punishment entirely. The campaign against it has been led by the Council of Europe and it can only be a matter of time before the ECtHR is asked to give a definitive ruling on whether standards of decency have evolved to the point where states have a duty to outlaw parental chastisement as it is regarded as inhuman or degrading punishment (Council of Europe, 2008).

Whole life imprisonment?

A third modern form of punishment that is gradually coming under increasing attack as inherently contrary to human rights is life imprisonment from which the offender has no prospect of release (Appleton and Grøver, 2007). The lead in this regard was taken by the German Federal Constitutional Court, which held that the right to human dignity meant that every prisoner must have a prospect of release (BVerfGE 21 June 1977). This meant that for a life sentence to pass constitutional muster it had to provide for such a prospect, and appropriate procedures that met requirements of due process for considering release had to be created. A vague prospect of a pardon was not enough.

The ECtHR has not gone as far. It does not require a specific release procedure, but in 2008 the Grand Chamber of the Court held in *Kafkaris* v. *Cyprus* (2009) that a life sentence from which de facto or de jure there was no prospect of release could conflict with the prohibition on inhuman or degrading punishment in Article 3 of the ECHR. It is likely that this doctrine will be developed further in the foreseeable future and whole life sentences outlawed decisively. In addition all life sentences will have to be accompanied by appropriate procedures to consider the release of the prisoners concerned (Van Zyl Smit, 2010b).

International human rights law, in the form of Article 37(a) of the Convention on the Rights of the Child declares a clear ban on life sentences without the prospect of release imposed on juveniles. Even the USA, which with Somalia is the only country in the world not to have acceded to this Convention, has shown some movement in this regard. In 2010 the US Supreme Court declared that so-called 'life without parole' sentences infringed the Eighth Amendment (*Graham* v. *Florida* (2010)). However, the Court excluded children convicted of murder from its judgment and thus reduced the ban on whole life sentences for juveniles from an absolute prohibition of a fundamentally unacceptable sentence to one based on its disproportionality to the relative seriousness of the offence.

Principles governing imposition

Even punishments that do not intrinsically breach human rights norms may involve severe limitations of human rights in practice. This applies most obviously to the most severe punishments such as the death penalty and life imprisonment, but lesser terms of imprisonment and other punishments also restrict human rights. It is thus an important part of the human rights agenda to see that in the imposition of punishments human rights standards are respected and conditions for limitations are met.

Legality

Procedural justice is a human right and in the sentencing context that means that offenders are entitled to a public hearing, legal representation and other aspects of the equality of arms during the sentencing stage. In the European context this means that Article 6 of the ECHR, which sets out the due process requirements of the Convention, applies to the sentencing stage as well, although rules of evidence may not be as strictly applied as at the trial stage (Emmerson et al., 2007).

Specific due process rules that are important at the stage of sentencing are those relating to precise definitions of penalties and the prohibition on retrospective penalties. Both relate to the civil right of legal certainty. Neither is as unproblematic as it may seem: for example, the ECtHR has ruled that a forfeiture that is imposed after conviction may be part of the penalty and, if it is, it cannot be imposed if there was not provision on the statute book for it at the time of the other commission of the offence (*Welch* v. *United Kingdom* (1995)).

An important part of the wider principle of legality is equality before the law. In this regard it is clear that offenders' human rights are infringed if at the sentencing stage they are subject to discrimination on, for example, grounds of ethnicity. However, proving the existence of such discrimination in a court of law is extremely difficult. Only in rare instances will it be possible to demonstrate that a particular sentencing body discriminated against someone who was being sentenced in a particular case. However, there is considerable evidence of structural discrimination in many systems, in that black offenders who commit crimes against white victims receive harsher sentences than white offenders guilty of the same crimes. Nevertheless, courts have been very reluctant to uphold arguments based on such general evidence. The leading case in this regard is the decision of the US Supreme Court in *McCleskey* v. *Kemp* (1987) which held, albeit by a bare majority of five to four, that even in a case where an offender had been sentenced to death it was not enough for him to prove that black persons were more likely to be sentenced to death than white persons for the same offence, for the sentence to be regarded as cruel and unusual and contrary to due process.

Proportionality

Perhaps the most important restriction that human rights law contains on the imposition of punishment is that the sentence should not be disproportionate to the offence or to the responsibility of the offender. An illustration of the potential impact of this limitation is the evolution of the jurisprudence of the US Supreme Court on the scope of the death penalty. Having set its face firmly against the total abolition of the death penalty, the Court has nevertheless held that it cannot be imposed for offences that are not of the highest degree of seriousness. It has thus held that it would be 'cruel and unusual' to impose the death sentence for rape (*Coker* v. *Georgia* (1977)), even for the rape of a child (*Kennedy* v. *Louisiana* (2008)). Moreover it has ruled that whole classes of offenders whose degree of responsibility for the offence is suspect may not be sentenced to death; prominent among these are those who are 'mentally retarded' (*Atkins* v. *Virginia* (2002)) and children below the age of 18 years at the time of the commission of the offence (*Roper* v. *Simmons* (2005)). For both groups the death sentence is always to be regarded as disproportionately severe and therefore as cruel and unusual punishment.

The case of *Roper* v. *Simmons* is also interesting as an example of the internationalisation of human rights concerns about punishment. In a brief put before the US Supreme Court the European Union argued against the constitutionality of the death penalty. The majority of the Court paid close attention to evidence of international trends against the death sentence for children and ignored the vociferous opposition from their colleagues in the minority against taking any notice of developments outside the USA in determining what should be regarded as evolving standards of decency in the early 21st century.

The proportionality of sentences of imprisonment, particularly sentences of life imprisonment, is usually regarded as a human rights issue too. In *S* v. *Dodo* ((2001): 403–404) the South African Constitutional Court explained clearly in human rights terms why this should be the case:

> The concept of proportionality goes to the heart of the inquiry as to whether punishment is cruel, inhuman or degrading, particularly where, as here, it is almost exclusively the length of time for which an offender is sentenced that is in issue …
>
> To attempt to justify any period of penal incarceration, let alone imprisonment for life … without inquiring into the proportionality between the offence and the period of imprisonment, is to ignore, if not to deny, that which lies at the very heart of human dignity. Human beings are not commodities to which a price can be attached; they are creatures with inherent and infinite worth; they ought to be treated as ends in themselves, never merely as means to an end. Where the length of a sentence, which has been imposed because of its general deterrent effect on others, bears no relation to the gravity of the offence the offender is being used essentially as a means to another end and the offender's dignity assailed. So too where the reformative effect of the punishment is predominant and the offender sentenced to lengthy imprisonment, principally because he cannot be reformed in a shorter period, but the length of imprisonment bears no relationship to what the committed offence merits. Even in the absence of such features, mere disproportionality between the offence and the period of imprisonment would also tend to treat the offender as a means to an end, thereby denying the offender's humanity.

In practice courts around the world have battled to apply the human rights based proportionality principle to actual sentences (van Zyl Smit and Ashworth, 2004). The US Supreme Court developed a tripartite test for disproportionality. When deciding whether a sentence was to be regarded as constitutionally disproportionate courts were asked to consider the seriousness of the offence, sentences imposed for the same offences in other (US) states, and sentences imposed for other similar offences in the same state. The Supreme Court applied this test in life imprisonment cases, ruling that a sentence of life without parole for passing a fraudulent cheque of US$100 was disproportionate in this sense, even if the offender had six previous convictions (*Solem* v. *Helm* (1983)). However it subsequently emasculated its own test by upholding a life sentence without parole for a first offender convicted of possession of (a large quantity of) drugs (*Harmelin* v. *Michigan* (1991)), as well as to offenders sentenced to life imprisonment with long minimum periods for relatively petty offences as a result of California's 'three strikes and you are out' laws (*Lockyer* v. *Andrade* (2003); *Ewing* v. *California* (2003)). The Court did so not by abandoning the notion of proportionality entirely, but by holding that if a sentence were proportionate to another rationale, such as incapacitation, its disproportionality to the offence could be ignored. Recently however, the proportionality test has been revived to exclude a whole class of offenders, children under the age of 18 years from life imprisonment without the prospect of parole for offences other than homicide (*Graham* v. *Florida* (2010)).

In Canada the proportionality test derived from the prohibition of cruel and unusual punishments has been applied to a wider range of prison sentences. In the leading case of *R* v. *Smith* (1987), which involved bringing illegal drugs into Canada, the Canadian Supreme Court held that a sentence should, where a statute set a mandatory minimum sentence, be regarded as unconstitutional if, on the basis of a hypothetical set of facts, it created the possibility that someone who infringed it could be sentenced to a term of imprisonment that could be regarded as grossly disproportionate. This meant that a statute dealing with the importation of drugs into Canada could not set a minimum sentence that would result in a disproportionate sentence for someone who imported a relatively small quantity of drugs. The Canadian statute in question failed this test. This assisted Smith, whose own offence was serious enough to warrant a sentence above the prescribed minimum, but who had to be resentenced in the light of the judgment striking down the minimum term. Subsequently however, the Canadian courts have watered down this test too, by requiring that the hypothetical sentence had to be 'reasonable' and setting such strict standards that it is of little practical significance (van Zyl Smit and Ashworth, 2004).

At the European level the ECtHR has generally insisted that the length of prison sentences is not a matter that falls within its remit. It has made exceptions only for those rights (such as the right to privacy or the right to freedom of expression) which are guaranteed by the ECHR but which may be limited by the state in some prescribed circumstances. In these instances it has emphasised that where criminal laws are used to limit human rights, sentences imposed in terms of them should be proportionately less severe. Thus, for example in a case where the complainant had insulted a judge by calling him a 'cretin' the Court held that it was legitimate to use the criminal law to limit freedom of speech in order to protect the judiciary (*Skałka* v. *Poland* (2004)). However the sentence of eight months imprisonment imposed in this case was not necessary for this purpose and was therefore disproportionately severe.

Paradoxically though, the ECtHR has not applied the same analysis to the right to liberty, which is protected particularly strongly in the Convention (Snacken, 2006). Article 5 of the ECHR guarantees the right of liberty to all persons, subject only to a closed list of narrowly defined exceptions, one of which is the 'the lawful detention of a person after conviction by a competent court'. Given that imprisonment negates liberty, that it limits so many other rights as well, and that longer prison sentences have more negative effect on prisoners than shorter sentences (van Zyl Smit and Snacken, 2009: 47–54), it is logical that imprisonment should only be regarded as not violating human rights if it is the shortest possible sentence that is proportionate to the crime and if it is used only as a measure of last resort, where no other, less severe infringement of the right to liberty would achieve the same result. In the absence of the adoption of such an argument by the ECtHR one must conclude that at the European level as elsewhere, the use of human rights standards to limit the imposition of imprisonment or the length of prison sentences has not been very successful.

IMPLEMENTATION

Human rights norms impact not only on the types of punishment that can be imposed and on the manner of their imposition but also on the way in which they are implemented. Of course where a form of punishment cannot be imposed at all, question of idolization do not arise. Issues of implementation may arise in the case of punishments that are strongly challenged on human rights grounds but have not been abolished everywhere. Thus, for example, opponents of the death penalty have sought to argue that, even if it is not accepted that a death sentence may never be imposed, the way in which it is implemented may be unacceptable. Some have gone as far as arguing that all conceivable forms of implementation are 'cruel and unusual' (Denno, 1997). More often challenges are brought against certain forms of implementation with varying degrees of success. In the USA, for example, attempts to challenge the use of lethal injections on the ground that they are 'cruel and unusual' have failed (*Baze* v. *Rees* (2008)). However, the Human Rights Committee of the United Nations, which interprets the ICCPR, has held that gas asphyxiation may prolong suffering and therefore be inhumane (*Ng* v. *Canada* (1994)). These challenges are, however, somewhat peripheral to the main human rights issue of whether the death penalty intrinsically infringes the human rights of the executed individual. Similarly, although regulation may seek to make corporal punishment compliant with human rights norms, for example, in the case of a whipping by limiting the number of strokes that may be imposed or the weight of the cane to be used, the question is usually whether corporal punishment infringes human rights per se or not.

The position is very different where a form of punishment, if imposed in appropriate cases, is widely recognized as acceptable, but human rights norms have developed about how it may be implemented. The prime contemporary example of such a punishment is imprisonment, and a sophisticated body of doctrine governing prisoners' rights has emerged as a specialized area of human rights law. However, the implementation of other 'acceptable' forms of punishment, such as community sanctions, may raise important human rights issues too.

Imprisonment

In respect of prisoners the major achievement of the human rights movement has been to establish as an undisputed fact that prisoners have rights and that they are not simply slaves of the state. This has been a long process that has proceeded in different ways in different jurisdictions. At the international level the 1955 United Nations Standard Minimum Rules for the Treatment of Prisoners has had a key role in spelling out the standards to which a prison regime should conform in order to meet basic human rights requirements. Regional instruments have played a similar role in Europe: for example the 2006 European Prison Rules, a more modern version of the UN Rules, refers explicitly to prisoners' human rights in Rule 1, which provides that: 'All persons deprived of their liberty shall be treated with respect for their human rights.'

The first question is therefore, what human rights do prisoners have? National courts around the world have produced general formulae: in England, for example, in 1982 the House of Lords held that: 'A convicted prisoner, in spite of his imprisonment, retains all civil rights which are not taken away expressly or by necessary implication' (*Raymond* v. *Honey* (1983): 10).

At the time this was an important statement of principle as it recognised authoritatively what the Dutch writer, Constantijn Kelk (2008), has called the *rechtsburgerskap* (the citizenship of rights) of all prisoners. Citizenship in this context should be understood as broadly encompassing not only civil rights in the narrow sense but all the human rights that inhabitants of modern democracies enjoy, whether they are citizens in the narrow legal sense or not.

The question remains: what rights can legitimately be taken away from prisoners? Here human rights law offers some primary guidance. Loss of liberty is the punishment and any deliberately added hardships would be unacceptable. This principle has been widely recognized. Even in Malaysia, where both capital and corporal punishment are still constitutionally permitted, the High Court has expressed the contrast starkly:

> A convicted prisoner is not sent to prison for punishment (excepting the death penalty or strokes with a rattan [cane]) but as punishment. (*Rajeshkanna Marimuthu v. Tuan Hj Abd Wahab Hj Kassim* (2004)).

In practice courts have found it very easy to assert that prisoners retain rights that can be granted without much cost or effort on the part of the authorities. The right to access to lawyers and to courts was recognised relatively early in Europe (*Golder* v. *United Kingdom* (1980)) and elsewhere.

More important perhaps has been the recognition that prisoners' human rights include the basic necessities of life: accommodation, food, clothing and medical care (Livingstone et al., 2008). In all these instances the typical form has been to argue that failure of the authorities to provide these things would amount to a form of treatment or punishment that was unacceptable in the sense of being 'cruel and unusual' or 'inhuman or degrading'. Determining when these boundaries were being exceeded has proved difficult. The typical form of reasoning adopted by the ECtHR and other bodies called upon to recognise the human rights of prisoners is to recognize that all imprisonment leads to some infringements of rights other than the simple loss of liberty, but to ask whether a particular infringement could be regarded as inhuman or degrading.

An important question is what can be expected of the authorities. Is the test simply whether objectively a right was being infringed or does the attitude of the authorities matter? In this regard there are important differences: in the USA for example, the Supreme Court has held that a failure to provide adequate medical treatment could only be regarded as cruel and unusual if the prison authorities were 'deliberately indifferent' to the needs of the prisoners (*Estelle* v. *Gamble* (1976)). In Europe in contrast, the ECtHR has held that the attitude of the authorities is not the determinate factor. If prisons fail to provide adequate accommodation because they are severely overcrowded, it is not a sufficient defence for the authorities to say that they tried their best but were unable to do more because of the restricted resources available to them. They can still be found to have treated prisoners in an inhuman or degrading way that is prohibited by Article 3 of the ECHR (*Kalashnikov* v. *Russia* (2003)).[4]

Arguments of this latter kind can provide a bulwark to defend the human rights of prisoners against the claim that they should not be better off than those in the worst position in free society, the so-called doctrine of less eligibility. This is well illustrated by the South African case of *Van Biljon* v. *Minister of Correctional Services* (1997), where a prisoner who was HIV positive and claimed that the prison authorities had a duty to provide him with anti-retroviral drugs which were essential for his survival. Failure to do so, he argued, would not only be a prohibited form of inhuman and degrading treatment but would also infringe his right to life, both fundamental human rights guaranteed by the South African constitution. The authorities countered that they could not afford the drugs, and that such drugs were not available free on the outside either, as the state could not afford to provide them for every indigent person who needed them. The South African court rejected this argument and held that when someone was taken into custody the state had a particular duty to ensure that his fundamental rights were not infringed.

A complex issue in the treatment of prisoners is deciding what imprisonment is for. Is it simply a matter of ensuring that sentenced persons lose their liberty for the time prescribed by the courts or should prison authorities attempt to do something more for those in their care? In this debate the German Federal Constitutional Court has famously taken sides and ruled that the authorities have a duty also to offer prisoners the opportunity to resocialize themselves. Significantly, this view rested squarely on human rights principles contained in the German Basic Law. As the German Court explained in the *Lebach* case:

> From the point of view of the offender, this interest in resocialization develops out of his constitutional rights in terms of Article 2(1) in conjunction with Article 1 of the Basic Law [i.e. the right to develop one's personality freely in conjunction with the protection of human dignity]. Viewed from the perspective of the community, the constitutional principle of the *Sozialstaat* requires public care and assistance for those groups in the community whom, because of personal weakness or fault, incapacity or social disadvantage were retarded in their social development: prisoners and ex-prisoners also belong to this group. (BVerfGE 5 June 1973: 236)

This pronouncement reflects the development of human rights arguments about how prisoners should be treated that go beyond the right *not* to be subject to unacceptable punishment to the recognition that they have a particular right to 'public care and assistance', a typical social right. In this case the latter right is derived in part from the constitutional status of the Federal Republic of Germany as not only a *Rechtsstaat* (a state governed by the rule of law) but also a *Sozialstaat* (loosely, a social welfare state).

This view has also been finding increasing favour at the European level where Rule 102 of the 2006 European Prison Rules provides that 'the regime for sentenced prisoners shall be designed to enable them to lead a responsible and crime-free life'. The Grand Chamber of the ECtHR has endorsed this principle in the case of *Dickson* v. *United Kingdom* ((2008): 29) in which it emphasised what it described as the recent and positive idea of 'resocialization through the fostering of penal responsibility'. This form of analysis has direct relevance for the human rights of the prisoner concerned. In the *Lebach* case quoted above, the German Court held that a prisoner's right to the opportunity to resocialize reinforced his right to privacy in a case where the media wished to report on his misdeeds for largely sensationalist ends. At the European level Mr Dickson was able to rely on the same right to compel the prison authorities to transport his sperm out of prison, thus exercising his right (and the right of his wife who was a co-applicant) to found a family and at the same time increasing the likelihood of his eventual resocialization.

There are advantages to having a clear statement of the purpose of imprisonment as it facilitates analysis of what sort of prison regime prisoners may expect as of right from the authorities (Lazarus, 2004), but there are also dangers as the purpose may be interpreted in a way that undermines prisoners' rights. As the official commentary to the European Prison Rules notes, Rule 102 avoids the terminology of rehabilitation and even resocialization as the former in particular has connotations of enforced treatment, which would be contrary to the human rights of the prisoners. If a substantive term is required, 'reintegration' as a way of preparing prisoners for release, inter alia, by consciously seeking to reduce the negative effects of imprisonment, is probably more neutral (van Zyl Smit and Snacken, 2009: 83–4).

The duty of protecting the human rights of prisoners that is placed on the State can be interpreted very widely. In various jurisdictions, as illustrated by the three examples below, courts have required not only that the rights of individual prisoners be protected but that institutions be structured in a particular way to ensure that this is done.

In Germany, the Federal Constitutional Court, in the course of ruling that new legislation was required to protect the human dignity of juvenile prisoners, stipulated that the legislator had a duty to rely on the best available information on how to do this. According to the Court, human rights standards on imprisonment were at the core of what was required. The Court warned that failure to take them into account could lead to it being held not have fulfilled its constitutional obligations: It explained that:

> It could be an indication that insufficient attention has been paid to the constitutional requirements of taking into account current knowledge and giving appropriate weight to the interests of the inmates if the requirements of international law or of international standards with human rights implications, such as the guidelines or recommendations adopted by the organs of the United Nations or the Council of Europe, are not taken into account or if the legislation falls below these requirements (Quoted in Dünkel and van Zyl Smit, 2007: 357).

In Israel, the Supreme Court has recently held that the privatisation of prisons is unconstitutional. It arrived at this conclusion not because it accepted that private prisons were necessarily worse at respecting the human rights of prisoners but because the use of private prisons to incarcerate persons sentenced by the state to loss of liberty was fundamentally incompatible with their human dignity. As the Court explained:

> [H]uman rights of prison inmates are violated *ipso facto* by the transfer of powers to manage and operate a prison from the state to a private concessionaire that is a profit-making enterprise. The denial of personal liberty is justified only if it is done in order to further or protect an essential public interest, and therefore the question whether the party denying the liberty is acting in order to further the public interest (whatever it may be) or is mainly motivated by a private interest is a critical question that lies at the very heart of the right to personal liberty. Therefore, [the Israeli law authorising private prisons] causes an additional independent violation of the constitutional right to personal liberty beyond the violation that arises from the imprisonment itself. When the state transfers power to manage a prison, with the invasive powers that go with it, to a private profit-making corporation, it violates the human dignity of the inmates of that prison, since the public purposes that give imprisonment legitimacy are undermined and the inmates becomes a means for the private corporation to make profits. (*Academic Center of Law and Business v. Minister of Finance* (2009): headnote)

In the USA, the Supreme Court, confronted by persistent evidence that, because of gross overcrowding over many years, the Californian prison system had not provided prisoners with a minimum standard of health care, which had led to their conditions of detention being 'cruel and unusual' and therefore an affront to their human dignity, upheld an order of a Federal Court for the state to produce for its approval a scheme for reducing the prison population by 46,000 prisoners within two years, so that it would be able to provide adequate health care for the remainder (*Brown* v. *Plata* (2011)). The Court explained that it had been driven to this extreme step by the consistent failure of the Californian state government to provide sufficient resources to produce prison conditions that were constitutionally acceptable for the many additional prisoners that its 'tough on crime' policies had incarcerated and had kept incarcerated for long periods. As the political process had demonstrated that it was incapable of taking the necessary steps, judicial compulsion was required.

Although these interpretations of what human rights principles require, may not apply equally in all jurisdictions, they demonstrate the potential power of these interventions. Since the German judgment, all new laws on the deprivation of liberty in that country routinely consider even soft law international standards; Israel is unlikely to be able to introduce private prisons without amending its constitution; and in California the State is now considering changes to both its sentencing and release policies as well as whether it returns offenders who have violated their parole conditions to prison.

Finally, it is worth remembering in the context of the implementation of sentences, also of imprisonment, that the human rights of others may also be involved. Thus, for example, family members of prisoners have a right to visit prisoners and to be treated with dignity when they do so (*Wainright* v. *United*

Kingdom (2007)). The rights of victims, and of society as a whole, must be protected too. In the case of *Mastromatteo* v. *Italy* (2002), where the temporary release of a prisoner resulted in re-offending that led to the loss of life of the victim, the Court reaffirmed that the authorities have a positive obligation, derived from Article 2 of the ECHR, to protect the right to life of its citizens. This did not mean, however, that the authorities had been able to prevent any potential violence, for, given the unpredictability of human conduct, early release invariably posed some danger to the public. In this instance the authorities were not held liable for the conduct of the prisoner, as for early release, all necessary precautions had been taken by the Italian authorities. However, in the more recent case of *Maiorano* v. *Italy* (2009) the outcome was different. A prisoner on day release had committed a double murder. The ECtHR found that, while the procedure followed in Italy for releasing prisoners temporarily was acceptable in principle, in granting day release to the prisoner despite his criminal record and behaviour in prison, together with the failure by the public prosecutor's office to forward information on his criminal activities to the sentence execution judge in the case, had constituted a breach of the duty of care required by Article 2 of the ECHR. These cases demonstrate that human rights based arguments may be used to protect the interests of potential victims as well as of offenders. However, given the drastic restriction that imprisonment places on the human rights of those subject to it, it should not be implemented for longer than necessary, unless the release of the offender poses a 'vivid danger' to potential victims (Bottoms and Brownsword, 1983).

Community sanctions and measures

Community sanctions and measures differ from imprisonment in that they are often seen as a lesser punishments for offenders who may otherwise be sentenced to imprisonment. Compared to imprisonment there is also far less jurisprudence involving instances in which offenders serving these sentences have sought to challenge they way in which they are implemented. This does not mean that they do not involve the human rights of those subject to them. On the contrary, as Boone (2000) has pointed out, their legal position is similar to that of prisoners in the sense that their sentence restricts their legal rights: even if it does not have the same impact on their right to liberty as imprisonment, the limitations that it does impose may be severe. The very informality and flexibility of these sanctions may make it more difficult to control the inroads that they make on the human rights of offenders.

As in the case of imprisonment there are some international instruments that shape their implementation against the background of general human-rights based prohibitions on cruel, inhuman and degrading punishment (van Zyl Smit, 1993; Morgenstern, 2009). Most prominent of these are the UN Standard Minimum Rules for Non-Custodial Measures (the Tokyo Rules) and the 1992 European Rules on Community Sanctions and Measures. Both of these contain some explicitly human rights based limits on the type of sanctions that can be imposed. Thus, for example, Rule 21 of the European Rules provides that '[n]o community sanction or measure restricting the civil and political rights of an offender shall be created or imposed if it is contrary to the norms accepted by the international community concerning human rights and fundamental freedoms' and Rule 22 adds that '[t]he nature of all community sanctions … shall be in line with any internationally guaranteed human rights of the offender'. However, as the official commentary to Rule 22 notes, these are general, hold-all provisions that do not indicate which rights may under no circumstances be restricted by a sanction.

More detailed indications of rights that may not be infringed by community sanctions may be found in national legal systems which have specific constitutional provisions for human rights which are not subject to statutory limitation. Thus German legal scholars are in agreement that a court could not, for example, attach a condition to a suspended sentence, compelling a defendant to marry the mother of his child as this would infringe the constitutional protection of the right to respect for private and family life; or to attend church services regularly, as this would infringe the right to freedom of religion, or order him not to join a particular society, as this would infringe the right to freedom of association (Streng, 2002). Nevertheless, there is merit in having some more abstract standard against which all sanctions that can be served in the community should be examined. The problem of setting limits in the light of the variability of community sanctions has been addressed at the level of ethical principle by Andrew von Hirsch (1990) who proposes that the general limit should be determined by what may be regarded as the 'acceptable penal content' of the sanction. Von Hirsch's point of departure is that community sanctions, like other forms of punishment, both deprive and censure. However, they should do so in a way that is designed to communicate a sense of shame to the offender, and not merely to humiliate. Sanctions should therefore 'be of the kind that can be endured with self-possession by persons of reasonable fortitude' (Von Hirsch, 1990: 167). To this end, they should be compatible with the human dignity of the offender, who is then in the position to reflect about the reason for the punishment and either to reject or, it is hoped, accept that he has transgressed. Sanctions served in the community are regarded as generally being particularly suitable for stimulating this process.

This positive view of community sanctions and measures is widely shared and their essentially reformative purpose is often stressed by the international instruments too. The Tokyo Rules in particular set out explicitly to promote the use of non-custodial measures. In this regard it is particularly important that there are sufficient controls in place, as both the Tokyo and European Rules require, in order to ensure that during the implementation of these sanctions or measures excessive demands are not placed on the offender in an attempt to increase their reformative efficacy, or to make the sanctions 'tougher' and thus more credible in the eyes of a sceptical public. This can be done by stipulating that the form the punishment should take be specified clearly, both in terms of what is required of the offender and its duration, so that this is beyond dispute at the implementation stage, for as Rule 3.10 of the Tokyo Rules provides: 'In the implementation of non-custodial measures, the offender's rights shall not be restricted further than was authorized by the competent authority that rendered the original decision.' Various process requirements can be set for the implementation stage to ensure that this does not happen. However, at the same time the system must have sufficient flexibility if the persons subject to the sanctions or measures are to benefit.

THE CHANGING RELATIONSHIP BETWEEN HUMAN RIGHTS AND PUNISHMENT

There can be no doubt that since the Second World War there has been a dramatic increase in the extent to which many aspects of the imposition and implementation of punishment are analysed in terms of human rights. But what has the impact of this been? The simple answer is that it varies. As far as the death penalty is concerned for example, there can be little doubt that human rights-based campaigns have contributed directly to the permanent abolition of capital punishment in several countries and ensured the continued desistance from this form of punishment among some waverers. A simple thought experiment underlines this; if *Furman* v. *Georgia* had been decided on the basis that the death penalty was inherently cruel and unusual in the sense that it was a constitutionally unacceptable affront to human dignity, as some of the judges in the majority in that case argued, then one can predict with some confidence that the death penalty would still be regarded as unconstitutional in the USA today.

The human rights-based improvement in the status of prisoners means something too. Sociological research has shown that, at very least, prisons are administered differently as administrators struggle to operate them in ways that allow for the recognition of those human rights of prisoners that are most strongly emphasised by courts and inspection bodies (Jacobs, 1977; Feeley and Rubin, 1998). What is particularly noteworthy is that some of the most impressive external regulatory systems consciously rely on human rights norms when developing their own independent standards for inspecting prisons for example, the 'expectations' of Her Majesty's Inspectorate of Prisons in England and Wales are explicitly derived from an amalgam of various prison human rights standards. Prisons are judged by the Inspectorate on whether they meet these expectations. Its public reports contribute both to the prison authorities having to engage with human rights standards and the public debate about prison being influenced by them (van Zyl Smit, 2010a).

Similarly, the Committee for the Prevention of Torture (CPT), which monitors European places of detention in order to seek to prevent inhuman or degrading treatment or punishment, has interpreted these terms in practical ways designed to achieve its objective. These interpretations, collated into a set of standards, have had a significant impact both on the judgments of the ECtHR and on European prison practice generally (Myjer, 2010). At the UN level a similar system has recently been created by the Optional Protocol to the Convention against Torture (OPCAT). It has the added strength that it seeks to combine monitoring by an international committee with the development of so-called National Preventive Mechanisms, which are designed to ensure by a variety of forms of inspection at a national level that no detainees are subject to torture or to cruel, inhuman or degrading treatment or punishment (van Zyl Smit, 2010a).

In other areas successes have been much more modest. Human rights driven arguments for the proportionate use of 'acceptable' punishments, and then only as a last resort, have not been successful in stemming the tide of imprisonment. However, even here some nuance is required. While prison numbers have increased rapidly in the USA this has not been true in Europe as a whole where increases in some individual western European countries have been compensated by decreases in many central and eastern European countries. Even in the west, patterns vary: Large increases in prison numbers in the Netherlands since the 1970s, for example, have been compensated to some extent by a recent decline, while in Germany prison numbers have remained constant. What is required is more analysis of what role human rights driven arguments about sentence played in these trends.

There is also a case to be made for arguing that, notwithstanding the increased emphasis on human rights in recent years, human rights activists, and lawyers in particular, have not engaged with all aspects of punishment. Thus, for example, Whitty (2011) points out that they have not engaged fully with the discourses about risk that are so prominent in decision making about various aspects of punishment, in particular prison practice and offender management. He also suggests that criminologists too are often surprisingly unaware of the potential of human rights as a normative basis for their work.

However, there are exceptions where courts have been prepared to weigh human rights directly against risk. For example, in a recent case the German Federal Constitutional Court had to deal with a difficult case of prisoner serving a life sentence whose release was delayed because the risk that he posed had not been considered at the appropriate time (van Zyl Smit, 2010c). Clearly there was a clash here between the right of the prisoner to be considered for release and that of the community to be protected against the risk he posed. The Court did not order the immediate release of the prisoner; but it did require a proportionality review in which the infringement of the liberty interest of the prisoner should be weighed against the legitimate concerns for protection of the community. The longer the detention continued, the greater the likelihood that it would outweigh the risk, even if the 'objective' level of risk had changed.

A more general exception that crosses the boundary between law and sociology is to be found in the work of the Utrecht School of Criminal Justice, which from the 1970s onwards adopted what van Swaaningen (1997) has identified as an approach of 'legal guaranteeism' within the wider framework of European critical criminology. Key to the work of this School, of whom Kelk (2008) and Boone (2000) are current exponents, is an attempt to link the legal principles associated with imposition and implementation of punishment systematically to both human rights norms and penal reality. As van Swaaningen explains, this allows them to avoid the trap of an abstract criminal jurisprudence in which norms are not related directly to social reality and to study empirically how successfully legal safeguards protect citizens against excesses of state power and give them a legal and social space to assert themselves.

Clearly much more research on the impact of human rights on punishment is needed. Research does not have to be limited to 'law in action' studies either. As Liebling notes, careful research on the 'moral performance' of prisons, which relies on the views of both prisoners and staff, is 'an additional way of deliberating on what the terms "inhuman" or "degrading" may mean' (2004: 453).

Finally, it is worth emphasising that what human rights demand of punishment and the social and political contexts in which they relate to each other keep changing. Good examples are the ostensible rise of populist punitiveness and a growing emphasis on security in many societies. Both of these are sometimes portrayed as the nemesis of a human rights approach to punishment. The reality is much more complex. Levels of punitiveness vary greatly across societies with different social welfare and economic models, and scope for policy choices remains (Snacken, 2010). In the European context, for example, if one analyses the increased emphasis on security in the European Union (Baker, 2010), it cannot be overlooked that the EU constantly finds it necessary to reiterate its concern for human rights as well. While cynics may dismiss this concern as mere rhetoric, it is significant that the authorities find it necessary to express it. The reality is that vital contemporary policy debates are being played out in a context in which 'human rights' remain a powerful concern. Analysis of punishment trends that overlooks this will be severely impoverished.

ACKNOWLEDGEMENT

I wish to thank Miranda Boone, Rob Canton, Julia Kozma and the editors for their comments on an earlier draft of this chapter.

NOTES

1 Whitman (2003) notes that Enlightenment concerns with human dignity had an ameliorating impact on punishment in Europe even before they were enshrined in (human rights) law.

2 All states that ratify this Protocol must abolish the death penalty in times of peace. However, at ratification states may choose to exclude death sentences imposed following conviction for a most serious crime of a military nature committed during wartime.

3 At the international level, see the decision of the Human Rights Committee applying the ICCPR in *Osbourne v. Jamaica* (2000). A similar approach has been adopted by the Inter American Court of Human Rights in *Caesar v. Trinidad and Tobago* (2005) and by the African Commission on Human and Peoples' Rights in *Doebbler v. Sudan* (2003).

4 It is noteworthy that these decisions in different jurisdictions are cast in terms of the civil and political right not be punished in an unacceptable way rather than in terms of wider social rights, such as 'the right of everyone to the enjoyment of the highest attainable standard of physical and mental health' which is

guaranteed by Article 12 of the International Covenant on Economic, Social and Cultural Rights.

REFERENCES

Appleton, C. and Grøver, B. (2007) 'The pros and cons of life without parole', *British Journal of Criminology,* 47: 597–615.

Bahrampour, F. (1995) 'The caning of Michael Fay: can Singapore's punishment withstand the scrutiny of international law?', *American University Journal of International Law and Policy,* 10: 1075–108.

Baker, E. (2010) 'Governing through crime – the case of the European Union', *European Journal of Criminology,* 7: 187–213.

Bassiouni, M.C. (1993) 'Human rights in the context of criminal justice: identifying international procedural protections and the equivalent protection in national constitutions', *Duke Journal of Comparative and International Law,* 3: 235–97.

Beccaria, Cesare (1764 [1964]) *Dei Delitti e Delle Pene.* Published as *Of Crimes and Punishments,* trans. Jane Grigson, collected with Alexandra Manzoni, *The Column of Infamy.* London: Oxford University Press.

Boone, M. (2000) *Recht Voor Commuun Gestraften.* Deventer: Gouda Quint.

Bottoms, A. and Brownsword, R. (1983) 'Dangerousness and rights', in J.W. Hinton (ed.), *Dangerousness: Problems of Assessment and Prediction.* London: George Allen and Unwin. pp. 9–24.

Committee on the Rights of the Child (2006) *General Comment No. 8.The Right of the Child to Protection From Corporal Punishment and Other Cruel or Degrading Forms of Punishment.* CRC/C/GC/8.

Council of Europe (2008) *Eliminating Corporal Punishment: A Human Rights Imperative for Europe's Children,* 2nd edn. Strasbourg: Council of Europe Publishing.

Council of Europe (2010) *Penitentiary Questions: Council of Europe Conventions, Recommendations and Resolutions.* Strasbourg: Council of Europe Publishing.

Denno, D. (1997) 'Getting to death: are executions constitutional?', *Iowa Law Review,* 82 (2): 319–464.

Dünkel, F. and van Zyl Smit, D. (2007) 'Preventive detention re-examined', *German Law Journal,* 5: 619–37.

Emmerson, B., Ashworth, A. and Macdonald, A. (2007) *Human Rights and Criminal Justice,* 2nd edn. London: Sweet and Maxwell.

Feeley, M.E. and Rubin, E.L. (1998) *Judicial Policy Making and the Modern State: How the Courts Reformed America's Prisons.* Cambridge: Cambridge University Press.

Foucault, M. (1977) *Discipline and Punish: the Birth of the Prison,* trans. A Sheridan. Harmondsworth: Penguin.

Hay, D. (1975) 'Property, authority and the criminal law', in D. Hay, P. Linebaugh, J.G. Rule, E. P. Thompson and C. Winslow (eds), *Albion's Fatal Tree: Crime and Society in Eighteenth-Century England.* London: Allen Lane. pp. 17–63.

Hood, R. and Hoyle, C. (2008) *The Death Penalty A Worldwide Perspective,* 4th edn. Oxford: Oxford University Press.

Jacobs, J.B. (1977) *Stateville: The Penitentiary in Mass Society.* Chicago: Chicago University Press.

Kelk, C. (2008) *Nederlands Detentierecht,* 3rd edn. The Hague: Kluwer.

Langbein, J.H. (1983) 'Albion's fatal flaws', *Past and Present,* 98 (1): 96–120.

Lazarus, L. (2004) *Contrasting Prisoners' Rights: A Comparative Examination of England and Germany.* Oxford: Oxford University Press.

Liebling, A. (2004) *Prisons and their Moral Performance: A Study of Values, Quality and Prison Life.* Oxford: Oxford University Press.

Livingstone, S., Owen, T. and MacDonald, A. (2008) *Prison Law,* 4th edn. Oxford: Oxford University Press.

Morgenstern, C. (2009) 'European initiatives for harmonisation and minimum standards in the field of community sanctions and measures', *European Journal of Probation,* 1 (2): 124–37.

Myjer, Egbert (2010) 'About human rights success stories of the Council of Europe. Some reflections on the impact of the CPT upon the case-law of the European Court of human rights', in M. Groenhuijsen, T. Kooijmans and T. de Roos (eds), *Fervet Opus; Liber Amicorum Anton van Kalmthout.* Apeldoorn: Maklu. pp. 161–74.

Nowak, M. (2003) *Introduction to the International Human Rights Regime.* Leiden: Martinus Nijhoff.

Nowak, M. (2005) *U.N. Covenant on Civil and Political Rights: CCPR Commentary.* Strasbourg: N P Engel.

Rodley, N. and Pollard, M. (2009) *The Treatment of Prisoners Under International Law,* 3rd edn. Oxford: Oxford University Press.

Schabas, W.A. (1996) *The Death Penalty as Cruel Treatment and Torture.* Boston: North Eastern University.

Snacken, S. (2006) 'A reductionist penal policy and European Human Rights Standards', *European Journal on Criminal Policy and Research,* 12: 143–64.

Snacken, S. (2010) 'Resisting punitiveness in Europe?', *Theoretical Criminology,* 14 (3): 273–92.

Streng, F. (2002) *Strafrechtliche Sanktionen*, 2nd edn. Stuttgart: Kohlhammer.

Thompson, E.P. (1975) *Whigs and Hunters: the Origins of the Black Act*. London: Allen Lane.

United Nations Office on Drugs and Crime (2006) *Compendium of United Nations Standards and Norms in Crime Prevention and Criminal Justice*. New York: United Nations.

Van Boven, T. (2010) 'Categories of rights', in D. Moeckli, S. Shah and S. Sivakumaran (eds), *International Human Rights Law*. Oxford: Oxford University Press. pp. 173–88.

Van Swaaningen, R. (1997) *Critical Criminology: Visions From Europe*. London: SAGE Publications.

Van Zyl Smit, D. (1993) 'Legal standards and the limits of community sanctions', *European Journal of Crime, Criminal Law and Criminal Justice*, 1 (4): 309–31.

Van Zyl Smit, D. (2010a) 'Regulation of Prison Conditions', *Crime and Justice*, 39: 503–64.

Van Zyl Smit, D. (2010b) 'Outlawing irreducible life sentences: Europe on the brink?', *Federal Sentencing Reporter*, 23 (1): 39–48.

Van Zyl Smit, D. (2010c) 'Release from life imprisonment: A comparative note on the role of pre-release decision making in England and Germany', in M. Groenhuijsen, T. Kooijmans and T. de Roos (eds), *Fervet Opus; Liber Amicorum Anton van Kalmthout*. Apeldoorn: Maklu. pp. 233–40.

Van Zyl Smit, D. and Ashworth, A. (2004) 'Disproportionate sentences as human rights violations', *Modern Law Review*, 67: 541–60.

Van Zyl Smit, D. and Snacken, S. (2009) *Principles of European Prison Law and Policy: Penology and Human Rights*. Oxford: Oxford University Press,

Von Hirsch, A. (1990) 'The ethics of community-based sanctions', *Crime and Delinquency*, 36: 163–73.

Whitman, J.Q. (2003) *Harsh Justice: Criminal Punishment and the Widening Divide between America and Europe*. New York: Oxford University Press.

Whitty, N. (2011) 'Human rights as risk: UK prisons and the management of risk and rights', *Punishment and Society*, 13 (2): 123–48.

Zimring, F. (2003) *The Contradictions of American Capital Punishment*. New York: Oxford University Press.

LIST OF CASES

Academic Center of Law and Business v. *Minister of Finance* HCJ 2605/05 27 19 November 2009.

Al-Saadoon and Mufdhi v *United Kingdom* (2010) 51 EHRR 9.

Atkins v. *Virginia* 536 US 304 (2002).

Baze v. *Rees* 553 US 35 (2008).

Brown v. *Plata* 563 US __ (2011).

Caesar v. *Trinidad and Tobago* IACHR Series C No 123(2005).

Christian Education South Africa v. *Minister of Education* 2000 (4) SA 757 (CC).

Coker v. *Georgia* 433 US 584 (1977).

Decision of the Hungarian Constitutional Court 23/1990 (X. 31.).

Dickson v. *United Kingdom* (2008) 46 EHRR 41.

Doebbler v. *Sudan* (AComHPR 236/2000 (2003)).

Estelle v. *Gamble* 429 US 97 (1976).

Ewing v. *California* 538 US 11 (2003).

Ex Parte Attorney-General Namibia: In re Corporal Punishment by Organs of State 1991 (3) SA 76 (NmSC).

Furman v. *Georgia* 408 US 238 (1972).

Golder v. *United Kingdom* (1979–1980) 1 EHRR 524.

Graham v. *Florida* 560 US __ (2010).

Gregg v. *Georgia* 428 US 153 (1976).

Harmelin v. *Michigan* 501 US 957 (1991).

Kafkaris v. *Cyprus* (2009) 49 EHRR 35.

Kalashnikov v. *Russia* (2003) 36 EHRR 34.

Kennedy v. *Louisiana* 554 U.S. 407 (2008).

Lebach case, BVerfGE 35, 203 of 5 June 1973.

Lockyer v. *Andrade* 538 US 63 (2003).

Maiorano v. *Italy* (ECtHR nr 28634/06) 15 December 2009.

Mastromatteo v. *Italy* (ECtHR nr 37703/97) 24 October 2002.

McCleskey v. *Kemp* 481 US 279 (1987).

Ng v. *Canada* (1994) UN Doc CCPR/C/49/D/469/1991.

Öcalan v. *Turkey* (2005) 41 EHRR 45.

Osbourne v. *Jamaica* HRC U.N. Doc. CCPR/C/68/D/759/1997(2000).

R v. *Smith* (1987) 34 CCC (3d) 97.

Rajeshkanna Marimuthu v. *Tuan Hj Abd Wahab Hj Kassim* [2004] 5 CLJ 328.

Raymond v. *Honey* [1983] 1 AC 1 (HL).

Roper v. *Simmons* 543 U.S. 551 (2005).

S v. *Dodo* 2001 (3) SA 382 (CC).

S v. *Makwanyane* 1995 (3) SA 391 (CC).

S v. *Ncube* 1988 (2) SA 702 (ZSC).

S v. *Williams and others* 1995 (3) SA 632 (CC).

Skałka v. *Poland* (2004) 38 EHRR 1.

Soering v. *United Kingdom* (1989) 11 EHRR 439.

Solem v. *Helm* 463 US 277 (1983).

Trop v. *Dulles* 386 US 86 (1958).

Tyrer v. *United Kingdom* (1979–1980) 2 EHRR 1.

Van Biljon v. *Minister of Correctional Services* 1997 (4) SA 441 (C).

Wainright v. *United Kingdom* (2007) 44 EHRR 40.

Welch v. *United Kingdom* (1995) 20 EHRR 247.

20

Punishment and Migration Between Europe and the USA: A Transnational 'Less Eligibility'?

Dario Melossi

Do migrants in Europe and ethnic minorities in the USA (such as, especially, African Americans), have something in common? On the one hand, one might think so, considering what we could call the 'overrepresentation' of both categories in the penal systems of the two societies. On the other hand, African Americans can hardly be described as 'immigrants', and migrants in Europe are for a good percentage perceived as 'white'.

At the end of this chapter, I would like to show a possible path in order to answer the question, by reconstructing the puzzle 'crime, punishment and migration' between the USA and Europe. A possible solution may be found perhaps by adapting, to the new era of globalization, the concept of 'less eligibility' placed by Georg Rusche and Otto Kirchheimer (1939) at the center of their reconstruction of the relationship between punishment and social structure. Thinking the idea of 'less eligibility', i.e. in a new transnational context.

MIGRATION AND PROCESSES OF CRIMINALIZATION IN THE USA

The relationship between immigration and various so-called 'social pathologies' (Lemert, 1951) has been of interest to sociologists and criminologists at least since the conjunction of mass migration with the emergence of a 'socio-criminological gaze' in North America, at the beginning of the 20th-century[1]. Such interest followed a trajectory that would reproduce itself in other settings when a similar conjunction also emerged. It seems increasingly likely that also today in Italy, and in Europe more generally, an intellectual and political development might unfold, that would be familiar to other countries and historical periods characterized by 'mass migrations'.

In the USA, at the beginning of the 20th century, a deep preoccupation about the pathology of migrations was linked to nativist positions tainted with racism and fear for the competition between native and immigrant workers on the labor market. Fear of immigrants has certainly played a historical role in the USA in promoting foreigners' criminalization during the 1920s and 1930s. Both the criminalization of alcohol in the period of prohibition and later on of drugs, were somehow connected to criminal representations strictly linked to 'non-American' peoples and habits (Rainerman and Levine, 1997). However, both socio-criminological research and various official commissions of inquiry, such as the Immigration Commission of the United States (1911) and the Wickersham Commission (1931), pointed out that the crime rates of the 'foreign born' were not significantly higher than the natives'. The Chicago School of sociology then produced a more balanced and 'normalized' view of the relationship between migration processes and deviance (Park et al., 1925; Park, 1928; Shaw and McKay, 1942; Bursik, 2006) according to which migrants' criminal behavior was the result of societal disorganization. This was not specific to immigrant groups but had to do with the very process of migration and thereafter of assimilation and integration into American society.

The Chicago school authors were also quick to point out that generally the 'first generation' of migrants tended to reproduce the criminal habits of the society of origin, whereas the second generations were in fact slowly assuming the levels and types of criminality typical of the environment where they were been raised. At this point, public preoccupations started to shift toward the issue of the generations successive to the immigrant ones, their integration, and their possible contribution to phenomena of deviance and crime. In fact, even very recently, Robert Sampson (2006), following in the footsteps of the Chicagoan tradition, noted that first generations are in a sense 'protected', by their relationships with their original families, within tried and true 'ethnic niches', which separate the migrant youth from the more obviously crime-prone currents of the context in which they find themselves. Their cultures of origin are often crime-adverse, and this is especially the case within so-called 'ethnic enclaves' (Martinez and Valenzuela, 2006; Sampson, 2006; Stowell, 2007; Stowell et al., 2009). However, when their offspring integrate within American society, one of the unfortunate consequences of the integration process is their participation within cultures that are characterized by a higher level of crime and violence. In fact, as the Chicago classic tradition teaches us, once they exit their ethnic enclaves, social controls decrease because of the new anonymity and heterogeneity.

It is after all not that surprising if immigrant first generations do their best to try and avoid what may be socially perceived as deviant or criminal behavior. After all, migrants have much more to lose than so-called natives. Generally criminal convictions carry with them, in the most serious cases, the danger of the additional sanction of deportation and, beyond that, there is always around the migrant, as Sayad (1999) suggested, a sort of 'double suspicion'. Therefore the 'punishment' is to the foreigner always quite more serious than to the native and it is reasonable that migrants are – contrary to stereotype – hyperconformists. Such is even more the case once they have established themselves in their new social settings. In the case of the various 'hyphenated-Americans', usually of European descent, after a few generations they not only started to feel more 'American' than the average member of the population. They also reached integration goals, in terms of wealth and social prestige (Jencks, 1983), which were higher than the average citizen.

However, between the latter and the first generations, there usually comes into being the rather peculiar condition of so-called 'second generations'. Socio-criminological literature usually connects such condition to the 'stress' caused by the unhappy position of the one who is 'between two cultures' – an analytical move first pioneered in a famous essay by Thorsten Sellin (1938).

It seems to me however that second generations' condition is a rather more complex affair and may be better captured in Jock Young's effort at understanding the action of youth who are, in his version of Merton, 'culturally integrated and structurally excluded' (1999: 81, 2003). The generations after the first are in fact educated to a culture that defines itself as 'democratic', therefore to an ideal of equality. For instance, as Thomas and Znaniecki famously remarked on the subject of the 'sexual immorality' of Polish immigrant 'girls' in Chicago in the 1920s:

> Perhaps the girl would settle down unrevoltingly to ... steady life, however dull, if the apparent possibilities of an entirely different life, full of excitement, pleasure, luxury and showing-off, were not continually displayed before her eyes in an American city. Shop windows, theatres, the press, street life with its display of wealth, beauty and fashion, all this forms too striking a contrast to the monotony of the prospect that awaits her if she remains a 'good girl.' If she felt definitely and irremediably shut off from this 'high life' by practically impassable class barriers, as a peasant girl in Europe feels, she might look at all this show of luxury as upon an interesting spectacle with no dream of playing a role in it herself. *But even aside from the idea of democracy – which though it does not mean much to her politically, teaches her to think that the only social differences between people are differences of wealth* – she feels that some small part at last of this gorgeousness actually is within her reach, and her imagination pictures to her indefinite possibilities of further advance in the future. Sooner or later, of course, she will be forced back into her destined channel by society, by the state, by economic conditions, will be forcibly 'reformed' and settled, not into a satisfied, positively moral course of life but to a more or less dissatisfied acceptance of the necessary practical limitations of her desires and of the more or less superficial rules of *decorum*. But before her dreams are dispelled she tries to realize them as far as she can. We have here, of course, only one specification of the unrest which characterizes America and American women. (Thomas and Znaniecki, 1918–20: 1820–1, emphasis added)

Not only therefore have second generation youth to bear witness to the fact that the people that – according to notions of filial piety one may generally find in every culture – they are expected to hold in the highest esteem, their parents, are treated as second-class citizens by the 'natives', or, when their skin color is perceived as different, even as naturally inferior human beings. Were this not, in and by itself, cause enough to make anybody loose his cool, they also realize that, whatever the solemn proclamations of democracy and equality, they themselves have to come to terms with being the objects of discrimination.

Often, such discriminatory attitude extends also to the police – the very agency which ought to be in charge of enforcing those political and legal principles of equality preached within the schools that the second generation migrant youth have attended. It may therefore happen that they come to perceive the necessity to form organizations that claim a purpose of self-defense. These are by some called 'gangs', by others 'street organizations' (Brotherton, 2008). In any case, they refer to the situation when, tired to be bullied around and left defenseless by those who would have the duty to protect them, these children take it onto themselves to defend their 'turf' from the assaults of other social groups, at first from native youth, but then, increasingly, from other migrants groups or young people from their very group but from other neighborhoods. Not much time goes by, though, before what was at first legitimized as a defense of their own community – especially in the absence of political conscious vanguards able to understand the complexity of the extant social processes[2] – turn into organizations which are parasitical on the very communities they claim to protect, forms of mafia-style organized crime (Venkatesh, 2008).

So, for instance, Daniel Bell, in a famous 1953 essay, would reconstruct organized crime as an essential aspect of the social climbing and the increasing integration of the various ethnic groups into an 'American way of life'. Whether Italian or Irish or Jewish or Polish, they organize in an increasingly deep complicity with the various urban power machines. Once reached satisfactory levels of integration within the conventional power structure, the children of the old gangsters, now become lawyers, engineers or small entrepreneurs, can afford to shed the rougher edges of their grandparents and enter the American middle class. Around the time when Daniel Bell was writing these pages, groups coming from other ethnic minorities – especially African Americans (who were also, in a sense, migrants, even if *internal* migrants coming from the South toward the urban centers of the mid-West and later of the West), Latin Americans, Asians – started replacing ethnic Europeans in the new gang formation process. Of course also with these newcomers – exactly as it had happened with the Italians, or the Irish – 'nativists' of all stripes, politicians, law and order officials, academics, sociologists and criminologists, linked the crime-prone character of the new groups to some innate feature in their constitutional or cultural make-up.

It is indeed to be noted that differently from what happened with ethnic-European groups, often it is much more difficult for these new gangs to cross the line of color, as it were, witness to it the horrendous overrepresentation of the new hyphenated Americans – especially African Americans – in the prison population. Furthermore things have changed quite a bit about immigration also in the USA and especially after the so-called 'US Patriot Act' 2001. The notorious new legislation passed by the state of Arizona in 2010,[3] which allows for the criminalization of unauthorized residence (Kil and Menjívar, 2006), and that spearheaded similar legislation by Georgia, Utah, Indiana and Alabama, is but the tip of the iceberg that followed an increasing role of state and local authorities on immigration issues which had traditionally been matter reserved to the federal government (Sassen, 2010).

IN ITALY AND EUROPE

European criminological discourse about migration took off instead between the 1950s and 1960s, and public discussion about migration flows from southern and eastern Europe toward the center and the north of Europe followed a roughly similar pattern (Ferracuti, 1968). The question of 'migration and crime' was again at the center of attention in the 1990s in Europe (Marshall, 1997; Tonry, 1997), this time also in southern Europe that, after the stop of the early 1970s linked to so-called 'oil crisis' and the transition from a 'Fordist' to a 'post-Fordist' type of economy, became a place of attraction for migratory in-flows from other Continents (De Giorgi, 2002; Calavita, 2005).

Also in Italy, and in Europe, today, it seems to me that we have followed a similar path to what had happened in the USA, probably with the only difference of the peculiar irrationality of immigration laws, that seem to have had a distinct 'criminogenic' effect. Here too the familiar complaint was raised that 'our data undoubtedly show that foreigners in our country commit a disproportionate amount of crimes relative to their number' (Barbagli, 2008: 104), even if this statement is immediately qualified by the circumstance that the authors of these crimes are for the great majority *undocumented* foreigners. The Caritas (2009) organization has shown that, also in Italy, foreigners' contribution to crime rates – measured by reports to the police – is very close to Italians' rate, especially if one takes into consideration the demographic profile of the two groups. If, by immigrants, one therefore means *documented* immigrants, also in Italy the preoccupation for their contribution to crime is certainly exaggerated. And as to the *undocumented* ones, one should remember that the connection to be established is between deviant behavior and the *condition* of lack of documents, not some kind of 'personal quality' of undocumented foreigners. Generally speaking, the latter are in fact people who entered legally (for instance on a tourist visa) or who acquired the proper documents for work, but subsequently lost the requirements to stay – a particularly critical problem in the current situation of economic crisis, given that work is one of the premises for maintaining the permit to stay legally in the country (in the EU). The problem is of course that the condition of being without documents places the foreign citizen within a set of conditions and constrictions that increase all the risk factors for criminal behavior enormously (besides making them more visible to official agencies of control).

In other words, the problem of the relationship between the documented status and the risk of deviant behavior is first of all a legislative and more generally normative one that concerns Italy, as well as many other countries members of the EU, because of the cumbersome nature of entry procedures. Especially in the case of unskilled labor (which is the kind of labor de facto on demand), until the beginning of the economic crisis, those who aspired to come and work in Europe would try to enter with every means possible to play thereafter a game of wait and see. The hunger for labor of European societies was such in fact that, sooner or later, some kind of individual or collective amnesty provision would be enacted[4] – thereby recognizing the rational, albeit unlawful, strategy of the migrants, not to mention the importance of their contribution to the welfare of the country. However, this situation is such to create a sort of 'gap' in the migrant's biography, when he or she has no chance to work legally therefore making them more likely to become prey to a variety of illegal or downright criminal 'occupations'.

The nature of the problems has somewhat changed with the economic crisis that started in 2008 and which has increased migrants' unemployment dramatically.[5] A report by the European Commission (2009) to the European Parliament showed that the rate of unemployment for third-country nationals (of course documented) had gone from 13.6 percent in 2008 to 18.9 percent in 2009 (8.4 percent for nationals) in the EU-27. It is very hard to guess what might have happened with undocumented workers. For the time being, we have some evidence on a declining flow of both legal and undocumented workers into the countries of the EU which, in the case of Italy, is probably connected also to the planned attitude of hostility which has been created by the previous government in both its more and less official aspects. For instance, according to the Italian research Institute ISMU, there has been a definite slowdown of new immigrant entries into Italy in 2010, about 100,000 fewer than in 2007, the last pre-crisis year (minus 40 percent).[6]

At the moment, as mentioned, we only have anecdotic evidence on a declining flow of both legal and undocumented workers into European countries. Exactly as it happened in the USA in the 1920s, first with the introduction of admission quota and then especially with the great depression of 1929, the changed scenario may be conducive to a shift of attention from first generations of migrants coming into the country, to the integration of so-called 'second generations', the children of those who made it in. To the traditional North American distinction between 'first' and 'second' immigrant generations is added, in Europe and especially southern Europe, a tripartite distinction among 'undocumented' migrants, first generation and second generation migrants (of course, undocumented migrants are present also in the USA but for reasons that we shall try to explore, this category seems to have been less important than in Europe vis-à-vis the issue of criminalization, even if, as we have seen, the Arizona law and populist anger about immigration has centered on the conflation between illegal immigration and criminal behavior). Whereas in Europe undocumented migrants (and their correspondent category among minors, 'unaccompanied minors') seem to suffer the bulk of the criminalization process, the relationship between first and second generations is similar instead to the one in the USA, as far as criminalization processes are concerned.

In fact, in a number of self-report delinquency studies we conducted of the relation between immigration and processes of criminalization in Italy, with particular reference to migrant minors enrolled in the eighth and ninth grades of a sample of high schools in the cities of Bologna, Sassuolo, and on the whole territory of the Emilia-Romagna

Region, concerning a total of about 6000 cases, we asked whether – after allowing for differences in sex, social class, and other relevant variables – significant differences in self-reported deviance would emerge between migrant minors and Italians (Melossi et al., 2009, 2011; Crocitti, 2011). Respondents were administered a questionnaire in the classroom, and asked to answer questions focusing on socio-biographical factors, socio-economic conditions, value-orientation and self-reported deviant behavior. The results offered no evidence of a higher frequency or seriousness of self-reported deviance among young 'first' or 'second-generation' immigrants compared to Italians (furthermore, whereas the results for 'second-generation' minors were very similar to the results for Italian minors, 'first-generation' children had a slightly lesser chance of involvement in deviant behavior). It seems, in other words, that integration within Italian society is accompanied by an increasing rate of deviance.[7] At the same time, both for Italian and immigrant respondents, self-reported deviant behavior appears to be strongly related to conflicts and problems with authority figures, in school and especially within the family. By and large, they support then those criminological studies, which deny any role of migration or national origin in the etiology of criminal behaviors.

One could therefore claim that the process of integration within Italian society takes place at the same time as a (slight) increase in deviant behavior. This is less surprising than what one would expect. Also based on the studies we have conducted, however, I think we should consider two other dimensions that have a bearing on second generations' destiny, so to speak. On the one hand, their increased deviance is probably also the product of racism and discrimination, because they are generally asked to integrate within a society – and in specific neighborhoods – that offer a mirror-image of their selves which is marked by exclusion and inferiorization. At the same time, second generation youth are more willing to take chances and break with the hyperconformism both of their families and of Italian society. They may be willing, in other words, to make innovative choices once they consider themselves to be full participants in Italian society, according to the promises of equality that we have already mentioned above. However, such 'innovative choices' may be met in a much differentiated manner as it was noted long time ago by William Chambliss (1973) in his famous article about the 'saints' and the 'roughnecks'. What applied to the roughnecks in terms of social class will certainly be true for migrant youth too (given that, demographically, immigration may very well be considered as a sort of mass import of a whole new section of the working class in a given society[8]).

The different condition of first and second generations is however something that should be kept completely separate, at least in Italy, from the issue of so-called 'unaccompanied minors', who certainly are 'first generation' but who also suffer from lack of documentation – until at least when (some of them) are taken in charge by social services. They are in fact the category which has been feeding juvenile penal institutions in large percentages, and who seem to be generally destined to a situation of exclusion, marginality and deviance. Their condition is drastically different from those first generations who came with their families or at least one of the parents and who are therefore protected both by that relationship and by the moral and customary norms of their original culture, often stricter than the Italian one.

In the case of second generations, I do not think we cannot discount – as Sampson notes for the USA – the 'drifting'[9] character of their path to integration within the larger 'Italian' group in which they are entering. At the same time I do not think that we can underestimate – beyond the rhetoric of 'culture conflict' *à la* Sellin (1938) – the role played by their specific kind of insertion into Italian society. Their is generally in fact the insertion of the one who, on the one hand, already belongs in terms of language, habits and customs, but, on the other hand, may find himself or herself even without citizenship – maybe with their parents' citizenship, the citizenship of a place they have never seen and the language of which they cannot even speak.[10] And all of this without even mentioning the peculiar show that the host society often offers them and their parents. The label of 'Balotelli generation' – referring to Black Italian (citizen) soccer champion Mario Balotelli who would often enter a stadium in Italy to see giant banners on which it was written 'THERE ARE NO ITALIAN BLACKS' – could not be more appropriate![11] Obviously this may mean, as it was observed by Jock Young (2003), a very strong cultural and emotional stress. It is difficult to discount in fact the peculiarly negative effects of the collective labeling of whole social groups and it may very well be that such negative effects may show up more openly once an older youth start to be more autonomous from his or her family. It may very well be at the same time that the prejudice and the racial and national profiling that are certainly at work also in Italy may cause some of these kids, once they are older, to try and do their best in order to show that they are indeed up to the image that is pictured of them.

EUROPE AND THE USA: THE IMPORTANCE OF LEGAL STATUS

As we have seen, many of such issues have now been played out not only in traditional immigration countries – such as for instance the USA – but also in countries that, until the 1970s, had been sending countries, like southern European countries. Starting in the 1980s, they too have become receiving countries, in some cases, like Italy and Spain recently, high-receiving countries (at least, before the crisis). Italian and Spanish immigration laws seem to 'welcome' immigrants exclusively as workers, their legal status contingent on temporary work permits that are difficult to get because of cumbersome and Byzantine procedures (Calavita, 2005). These laws therefore limit immigrants' ability to put down roots by denying them permanent residence. Immigrants are in fact useful as 'others' who are willing, or compelled, to work, under conditions and for wages that locals largely shun and that are part of a substantially 'post-Fordist' setting of social and economic circumstances. Racialization and criminalization are central elements of this immigrant marginalization.

Indeed, the emergence of Europe, and particularly southern Europe, as a pole of attraction, contributed to a rather unusual occurrence, as far as the linkage between migration and crime (or maybe we should say, migration and criminalization) is concerned. A striking difference has emerged between what has been going on in the USA and what has instead been going on in Europe. Something, which is quite apparent indeed if one looks at the number of foreigners imprisoned in the USA and in Europe – if this has to be taken as a measure of the criminalization process, if not of the criminal process. On the one hand, the total number of people imprisoned in the USA is staggering and the number of inmates in Europe, especially western Europe, is instead rather limited. The US imprisonment rate is above 700 per 100,000 whereas the European average is around 100 per 100,000 and even those countries where there has been recently quite an increase, such as the UK, Spain and the Netherlands, are anyway below 150 per 100,000 (Snacken, 2010: 274). On the other hand, if one considers the *percentages* of foreigners that are part of those larger numbers, the situation reverses itself. Their number is quite contained in the USA, as we are going to see, but is extremely high in Europe, so high in fact (see Table 20.1) to even overcome the American imprisonment's 'disproportionality' due to ethnicity (between five and six times for African Americans (Mauer and King, 2007)). In fact, in some countries, such as for instance Italy, foreigners' incarceration is more than enough to explain by itself the overall increase in incarceration rates in recent years.

On the contrary, the percentage of 'noncitizens' in prison in the US – at least the ones counted – is probably less than the number of noncitizens in the general population: on June 30, 2005, for instance, 91,117 noncitizens were in the custody of state or federal correctional authorities. Overall, 6.4 percent of state and federal inmates at midyear 2005 were not US citizens, whereas the percentage of the population which is foreign-born in the

Table 20.1 Overrepresentation of foreigners in European prison systems

	Percent of foreigners in prison pop.[i]	*Percent of foreigners / foreigners extra-UE in general pop.*[ii]	*Estimate of the rate of overrepresentation*[iii]
Austria	45.8	10.3/6.6	4.44-6.93
Belgium	41.1	9.1/2.9[iv]	4.51-14.17
Denmark	21.9	5.8/3.8	3.77-5.76
Finland	10.3	2.7/1.7	3.81-6.05
France	18.2	5.8/3.8	3.13-4.78
Germany	26.3	8.8/5.7	2.98-4.61
Greece	43.9	8.3/6.8	5.28-6.45
Ireland	13.1	11.3/3.1	1.15-4.22
Italy	36.2	6.5/4.6	5.56-7.86
Luxemburg	69.5	43.5/6	1.59-11.58
Netherlands	27.7	3.9/2.1	7.10-13.19
Norway	24.8[v]	6.3/2.9	3.93-8.55
Portugal	20.6	4.2/3.4	4.9-6.05
Slovenia	10.8	3.5/3.3	3.08-3.27
Spain	35.7	12.3/7.4	2.90-4.82
Sweden	28.5	5.9/3.2	4.83-8.9
Switzerland	69.7[vi]	21.7/8.3	3.21-8.39
United Kingdom (England and Wales)	13.1	6.6/3.9[vii]	1.98-3.35
European Union (27 countries)		6.4/4	

[i] At 10 June 2010 (source: International Centre for Prison Studies, King's College, University of London).

[ii] Percentage of foreigners/foreigners from countries outside the EU27 in the general pop. (on 1 January 2009; source: EUROSTAT).

[iii] I divided the number in the first column by both numbers in the second column: the result is the estimate in the third column, somewhere in between the two numbers. Why is that? Because we do not have a division of the percentages of inmates according to whether they are simply foreigners or foreigners from outside of the EU, an information that we have instead about the general population of foreigners. Now, most inmates are from countries outside the EU so the second term of the estimate is probably more precise. There are however two important exceptions to such rule of thumb: (1) the situation has changed with the entrance of Romania in the EU because the number of Romanians incarcerated in several countries is substantial, and (2) in many smaller countries, such as Belgium, Luxembourg or Switzerland (which is, like Norway, however not part of the EU!) a substantial number of inmates come from neighboring EU countries. Hence, the necessity of such an imprecise estimate!

[iv] Data 2008.

[v] Data 2008.

[vi] Data 2008.

[vii] Data 2008.

USA is about 12 percent (an unknown part of which have in the meanwhile become citizens). At midyear 2005, 35,285 Federal inmates were noncitizens, representing about 19 percent of all prisoners in Federal custody. California (16,613), Texas (9,346), New York (7,444), Florida (4,772) and Arizona (4,179) held over 75 percent of all noncitizens confined in state prisons. Noncitizen prisoners accounted for over 10 percent of the prison populations of Arizona, New York, Nevada and California. Using data on US imprisonment divided by place of birth, Rumbaut et al. (2006: 71) showed that in *all* American ethnic groups, the incarcerated foreign born males in each group are systematically lower than the incarcerated US born males in the same group.

Or could it be perhaps that there are no foreigners in prison in the USA – or at least many fewer than in Europe – because in the USA there are no undocumented migrants (given that they are, as we have seen, the bulk of criminalized migrants)? No, that is not the case, because the US government estimates that, as of January 2007, for instance, there were almost 12 million unauthorized immigrants living in the USA[12] and that is, in proportion to the population, more than in Italy.

Could it be perhaps that there are no foreigners in prison in the USA – or at least many fewer than in Europe – because they are all swiftly deported? Each year, about 300,000 foreigners are, in Saskia Sassen's words, 'incarcerated without trial only because officialdom considered it likely that they were illegal residents' (2010). Once again, if we listen to a statement by Gary E. Mead, Deputy Director of an ICE (DHS) office, 'Over the last four years more than a million people have passed through ICE detention facilities. During fiscal year 2007 alone, more than 322,000 illegal aliens passed through ICE detention facilities and approximately 280,000 of those were removed from the Unites States.'[13] That is during the year, which translates into an average presence of 30,000 illegal aliens in ICE detention facilities every single day. That is certainly many, however it is not comparable to the huge number of inmates in the USA. Furthermore, also in Europe there is a whole specialized sector of internment and detention for migrants, mostly outside the penal system, which has given birth to a reality often referred to with the moniker 'Fortress Europe'. And, as to penal prison population, we can see, in Table 20.1, that in Europe (and particularly in the European countries that first created the European Community) the overrepresentation of non-EU citizens in prison is many times their share of the general population (see also Melossi, 2003, 2005).

As we have seen, the immigrant group that is by far most criminalized in Europe, and especially in southern Europe, is the undocumented migrant, in the case of minors the so-called 'unaccompanied minor' (a number of studies have shown that between 70 and 80 percent of the migrants who are arrested, reported, convicted or detained in Italy are 'undocumented'[14]). One element, which is not often considered in American literature,[15] is the issue of the possession by recent immigrants of legal documentation that enables them to work. Work is an essential element of integration, and in many European countries, the possession of legal documents is a prerequisite for work. In Italy today, the process of criminalization is usually related not so much to the status of immigrant as to the status of 'undocumented' immigrant. This is true at the adult level but is also true for minors, in the sense that is crucial for the distinction, as we have seen, between what is called an 'unaccompanied' minor and a 'first' or 'second generation' minor. Whereas the former is essentially a young undocumented migrant who made it to Italy by himself or herself, the latter migrated to Italy within the larger unit of a family (entering the country at such an early age that the primary process of socialization took place in Italy) or, increasingly more often, was born in Italy of a family of first-generation migrants.[16] Growing up in a family in Europe (and especially in

Italy) seems to mean a situation that protects one from criminal involvement.

A very important aspect of all this is however how legal status is proved. Do we really know how many foreigners are in US prisons, for instance, given that this information seems to be at least in part derived from self-reporting (Hickman and Suttorp, 2008)? Beyond that, furthermore, it may be easier for a foreign citizen to integrate him- or herself in the USA because of the lack of a national identity document, which may facilitate hiring based on the false assumption of citizenship, and therefore increase the likelihood of employment and 'honest living'. I want to point out, in other words, what it would seem like a paradox: the greater ease of undocumented migrants' deception in the USA[17] might protect them – and American society – from the risk of crime,[18] whereas the European obsession with discovering migrant crime may increase the likelihood of its occurrence. This possibility is intensified by the fact that, in many European countries, it is the business of ordinary police forces to control and check on the dangerous stranger, something that is not yet as pervasive in the USA, although this is precisely what the Arizona law would encourage. (This, however, does not go uncontested: after all, in May 2010 the City Council of Los Angeles – a city where that kind of police behavior would be highly problematic – decided to boycott the state of Arizona because of its immigration bill, charged with going back to some of the discriminatory practices of the Second World War.) Indeed especially in Continental Europe, in the 19th century strangers were the original matter of police prevention powers together with prostitutes and vagrants and it is ingrained in much legislation and part of the public opinion that the stranger is dangerous by definition.

Laws of immigration are nowadays quite restrictive in Europe and Italy more specifically, because they are aimed at *contrasting* 'unlawful' immigration rather than at *regulating* immigration: the resources destined to combating illegal entries are enormously larger than those targeted at immigration services. Therefore, as we have seen, in a situation in which great parts of Europe, and specifically Italy, at least before the current economic crisis, are way below an offer of labor such to match demand, migrants come to Italy undocumented anyway and wait for the (at least in the pre-crisis era) unavoidable amnesty provision in order to be 'regularized'.[19] In between, a dangerous period of lack of documentation ensues, fraught with the necessity of all sorts of illegalities. In a recent article, Valeria Ferraris (2009) has shown how Italian immigration law forces foreigners to search for legal status through illegality. Because the annual entry quota has been transformed de facto into an amnesty for people already in Italy, due to an unrealistic system of matching supply and demand for labor, Italian immigration law produces 'institutionalized irregularity'. Foreigners enter illegally, find a job in the underground economy and then try to 'fix the papers' once in Italy. They use illegality – to the point of committing crimes – in order to become legal. Migrants implement strategies to overcome their precarious condition. True Mertonian innovators, they understand that the achievement of legal status is attractive because at least it means being safe from deportation. The success of the adopted strategies largely depends on the ability of migrants to understand the essential features of the host country and to exploit the available opportunities. Looking for a way to legality – Ferraris (2009) concludes – they reveal the essential features of the Italian way of life.

In other words, the easier the processes of legal integration in the host society (residency and naturalization) the lower the criminalization processes, conversely the harder the process of legal inclusion the higher instead the numbers of criminalized foreigners. In a comparative study, James Lynch and Rita Simon (1999) pointed out that 'immigrant nations', such as the USA, Canada and Australia have relatively open immigrant policies and high proportions of foreign born in the resident population. Germany[20] and Japan ('non-traditional immigrant nations') have restrictive immigration policies, strict policies for the control of resident aliens, and restrictive naturalization policies. France and the UK have restrictive admission policies based on race and national origin, but naturalization policies are relatively open. Comparing the incarceration rates, the pattern that emerges across the seven nations is that overall, immigrants in traditional immigrant receiving countries have lower criminalization rates than non-traditional immigrant nations. The apparent relationship between the inclusiveness of immigration policies and the criminal involvement of aliens suggests that the more restrictive the policy, the greater the criminalization of foreigners.

LESS ELIGIBILITY AND MIGRATION LAW

In their classic 1939 study, *Punishment and Social Structure*, Georg Rusche and Otto Kirchheimer stated the concept of 'less eligibility', according to which standards of living in prisons (and generally within the criminal justice system) ought to be lower than the standards of living allowed (by working) to the lowest stratum of the working class in order to preserve a principle of deterrence. Therefore they postulated a worsening of prison conditions in times of recession. They wrote however at a time of nation states and, characteristically, did not take into consideration the importance of migratory movements and of their regulation by nation states, movements and states that engage in a real struggle around the size of the labor force and the conditions of work. Economic crises, aided by the intensification of the artificial pressure of legal persecution, may produce in fact a truly 'Malthusian' elimination of increasing strata of the working class in host societies, by way of 'returns' forced sometimes by economic necessity and sometimes through legal means, such as rejections at the border, expulsions and deportations. For example, James Pendergraph, former executive director of ICE, happened to say, speaking at a Police Foundation National Conference on 21 August 2008, 'If you don't have enough evidence to charge someone criminally but you think he's illegal we [ICE] can make him disappear' (Amnesty International, 2008: 4). Similar policy attitudes (and outcomes) would of course be hard to fathom toward the 'native' working class, protected by its citizen status and by the remnants of a welfare tradition. Paradoxically, therefore, the number of imprisoned migrants may decrease in times of crises: if what we find inside prisons is a fraction of an 'industrial reserve army' of undocumented workers waiting in line for jobs (regular or otherwise), when such army is thinned, by choice or by force, also its imprisoned fraction will be thinned (even if, at the same time, it will probably be a greater fraction of a diminished total). Another way of looking at it, is that, if we want to take seriously those analyses which have maintained that the modern prison institution was created in relation to the ideal (more than the reality) of 'labor discipline' (Foucault, 1975; Melossi and Pavarini, 1977), then, if there is no work, neither there is going to be labor to be 'disciplined', at least not within the national borders of the host society. Rusche and Kirchheimer postulated in fact a worsening of prison conditions in times of recession,[21] but they wrote, as mentioned, at a time of nation states. These mechanisms should for migrants be articulated to legal status, not only because, as we have seen, the enforcers of the boundaries of a (national) legal order try, as it were, to regulate the size of the working class within those borders by means of the laws on citizenship and lawful residence, but also because, at the same time, both the success and the failure of that attempt usually ends up creating a sort of de facto multiplicity of access to the labor market by full citizens, lawful residents and unlawful residents, each group with specific claims in terms of rights and compensations.

The rules on residence end up therefore working in a way akin to an artificial wage ceiling keeping the condition of the lowest stratum of the working class – the migrant group and, within it, the undocumented migrant group – artificially low by law, as a sort of 'artificial' legal alteration of that 'situation of the lowest socially significant proletarian class which society wants to deter from criminal acts', which was for Rusche the 'inevitable limit' to all penal reform (Rusche, 1933: 4).

Does the principle of 'less eligibility' somehow work at the transnational level? On the one hand, migration seems to be a way by which whole sectors of a national working class manage to extricate themselves from the yoke of (their national) less eligibility by removing themselves from their national borders.[22] On the other hand, in their host countries, given that by assumption the latter are going to be characterized by better conditions and therefore by a higher threshold of less eligibility, a degree of less eligibility may be reconstituted only through mass expulsions. In a sense in fact mass expulsions constitute the neo-Malthusian policies through which it is possible to try and re-subject those strata of the working class to their old 'national' less eligibility. The only available alternative is instead lowering the less eligibility threshold for everybody through the compression of living standards for the working class of the host society (which is usually one of the goals of immigration policies anyway [see below]). For instance, this may explain the circulation, among Italian police or prison officers, of common places according to which immigrants would be 'accustomed' to 'lower standards' and that therefore in order to police or guard them effectively the standards in the host country should be lowered, or hardened.[23] More commonly, however, especially in a transitional period, what is created is a segmented multiplicity of access to the labor market by full citizens, lawful residents and unlawful residents, each group with its own specific claims and each group experiencing their own less eligibility threshold. There are however limits to how much the price of labor may express the value of men and women, and an important limit is set by norms on human rights, of the type enforced by the European Court of Human Rights[24] or the Committee for the Prevention of Torture (van Zyl Smit and Snacken, 2009; Snacken, 2010). They constitute limits of the kind that Georg Rusche had perceived in Weimar Germany where welfare institutions compensated for the ravages of the 1930s Depression years in a way that was impossible in the same period in the USA (Rusche, 1930).[25]

Migration laws seem in other words to work in the opposite direction of welfare, forcefully depreciating the value of labor instead of appreciating it. Because they help construct a secondary and even tertiary labor market of workers at the edge of legality whose wages are to be lower than minimum wage, they tend to depreciate the cost of labor in the same way in which welfare reforms – which, not surprisingly, are linked to concepts of *national* citizenship and lawful residence – seem to work in the opposite direction (the advantage of human right norms vis-à-vis welfare provisions is of course that human rights – when they are allowed to operate – are intended for every person, irrespective of his or her citizenship). Loïc Wacquant's (2009) dictum of a transition from the welfare state to the penal state should therefore be taken quite literally for migrants. Penality (or administrative detention) is in a sense one of the very few 'services' that are 'open' to undocumented foreigners. So, on the one hand, migration is strictly linked to the increasing imprisonment rates of the last few decades. On the other hand, however, both the development of migrations and the rising imprisonment rates constitute two mainstays of the whole neoliberal project that was started with the 'Reagan and Thatcher revolutions' between the 1970s and the 1980s. 'Revolutions' that had as their central point (as all capitalist revolutions do) the purpose of attacking the old working-class, which acquired such a 'dangerous' amount of power in the period culminating in the early 1970s.[26] Traditionally in fact, the importation of new, inexperienced potential working class from the countryside – which is the substance of most mass migration processes – is one of the pivoting elements around which political and economic elites organize their attack against the old working class. This attack usually extends against the very technological set-up of the old society together with political repression, anti-labor legislation, investment in new technological sectors (such as, in the specific case, the new information society). Furthermore, imprisonment is a classic instrument by which the resistance of the new imported working class is broken and new habits of subordination and compliance molded.

The legal regime of migration can therefore be understood – almost literally – as a quite traditional maneuver of authoritarian intervention on the labor market, similar to those we are familiar with from the infancy of working class movements, such as 19th-century workhouses or anti-union legislation. However, it may also be that it works in quite different ways in Europe and the USA, discharging itself on a *mix* of migrants *and* ethnic minorities in Europe (according to the age of migratory flows) and mostly on ethnic minorities – African Americans and second generation Latinos – in the USA. There is probably a process of representation and stigmatization here that is very hard to disconnect from the reality of a history of racism which ends up depicting a 'dangerousness' linked with specific images of 'otherness'.[27]

So, whereas pressure on the most destitute sectors of the working class in America is mostly of a socio-economic nature (with the recent and relevant exception of states such as Arizona and those that followed it), and has at its inner core a socially and culturally disenfranchised class held together by the working of the stigma (or the ban, as Matza would call it), in Europe the same result is held together by the working of legal restrictions that make migrants' existence ever more precarious. In both cases the stigma of criminalization may be thought as a cultural force (Garland, 1990: 193–212) that helps to create a specific pariah class. Calavita (2005) shows very effectively in her *Immigrants at the Margins: Law, Race, and Exclusion in Southern Europe,* how a lack of documentation, criminalization and racialization, reciprocally constitute and reinforce each other, as seen in Spain and Italy. Through the stigma of 'race', it may be that we are witnessing in Europe a slow move from the 'outsiderization' of migrants to that of groups within them, groups that are perceived as having certain 'racial' characteristics – we have seen the case of the 'Balotelli generation' in Italy. In countries such as France and the UK, with more long standing immigration, such mechanisms have already been in place for some time. Processes of criminalization are then co-terminus with the identification of Rusche's 'lowest stratum of the working class's social condition'. In short, in America, undocumented migrants are less apparent and harder to find. Could one fathom a Los Angeles police officer asking a passer-by to see his papers because he looks Central American or speaks Spanish? If indeed this is exactly what the new Arizona law requires, on the other hand we have seen how this has caused a boycott by the City Council of Los Angeles of the state of Arizona. And, at the same time, Levine and Peterson Small (2008) have shown how, in New York City, police officers did exactly that but to Blacks, in the 'marijuana arrest crusade' that started under Giuliani's 'zero tolerance' policy in the mid-1990s. Here, ethnic minorities are essentially still the culprits. In the European caste system instead, where citizens, denizens and quasi-slave statuses are found together in the same social formation,[28] the system of social subordination finds its victims in the least legally protected group. This may be a possible hypothesis in order to explain, at least in part, why, as we saw, the overrepresentation of migrants in the European criminal justice system is similar to the overrepresentation of minorities – but not of migrants – in the American one.

ACKNOWLEDGEMENTS

Previous versions of this chapter were presented at a Conference at the Monash University Prato Center in 2009, at the 2010 Annual Meeting of the American Society of Criminology, San Francisco, in the Distinguished Scholar Series Lecture of the Department of Sociology of the University of Hong Kong, in a Lecture in the Doctoral Program on Human Rights of the University of Palermo, at the London School of Economics Law Department's Interdisciplinary Seminar Series and at the University of Oxford COMPAS Michaelmas 2011 Seminar Series. It is impossible therefore to mention all the colleagues and students who have helped me with their comments and questions on these occasions. I would like therefore to thank them all wholeheartedly in a collective way. A very special thanks goes, however, to Kitty Calavita, Jonathan Simon and Nicola Lacey for their very close reading of the paper. Thanks also to the Center for the Study of Law and Society, University of California, Berkeley, where I was a guest in the Fall of 2010.

NOTES

1 Additionally, the case of Latin America would be well worth investigating (on Argentina see Sozzo, 2010).

2 And when this may happen, as it was the case with the Young Lords and especially the Black Panther Party in the 1960s, they became the target of a ruthless suppression by official agencies of control!

3 The new Arizona law – which, as we shall see, introduces many 'European' anti-immigration devices – has been spearheaded by the likes of Arizona Sheriff Joe Arpaio (Finnegan, 2009).

4 Routinely, Italian studies have shown that at least half of the regular, documented male immigrants witnessed to the fact that they found themselves without documentation for a period, whereas most women came to Italy based on family reunifications asked by those very immigrants (Melossi, 1999; Ambrosini, 2009).

5 It is a well-established fact of criminological research on the connections between criminal behavior and economic change – starting with Thorsten Sellin's time-honored pioneering effort (Sellin, 1937) – that, in a situation of deep recession, criminal behavior tends to increase, considering it on the side of criminal motivation, but tends at the same time to decline, considering it instead on the side of criminal opportunities, which become fewer and fewer.

6 16th Report on Migrations by ISMU ('La Repubblica', 13 December 2010).

7 A very recent similar study by Uberto Gatti and others (2010) show results in which second generation kids have slightly higher deviancy rates than both Italian and first generation kids.

8 I mean it literally: in our sample, half of the 'Italian' students' fathers could be described as 'middle class' and about one fourth as 'working class': those proportions were exactly inverted for the 'migrant' students' fathers and even more so if we look at the mothers' occupation (Melossi et al., 2011).

9 In Matza's (1964) sense.

10 Because of the Italian citizenship *ius sanguinis* (law of the blood) rule, according to the Caritas 2010 Yearbook, there are today in Italy almost 600,000 'foreigners' born in Italy!

11 The obvious reference, in terms of analysis, should be to the work of British Black intellectual Paul Gilroy who, working from Stuart Hall's Centre for Contemporary Cultural Studies at Birmingham University in the 1980s, authored the epoch-making book *There Ain't no Black in the Union Jack* (Gilroy, 1987). It is ironic that Balotelli is currently playing for the Manchester City team!

12 Michael Hoefer, Nancy Rytina and Bryan C. Baker, *Estimates of the Unauthorized Immigrant Population Residing in the United States: January 2007*, US Department of Homeland Security, Office of Immigration Statistics, Policy Directorate, available at: http://www.dhs.gov/xlibrary/assets/statistics/publications/ois_ill_pe_2007.pdf (Amnesty International, 2008: 4).

13 In a hearing before a Congressional Subcommittee on Immigration (13 February 2008).

14 I believe it would be interesting to compare the condition of undocumented migrants in Southern Europe to that of asylum-seekers in Central and Northern Europe.

15 See for instance the issue of *Criminology and Public Policy* (vol. 7, February 2008) partially devoted to this topic.

16 In the last few years, Italian sociological research on the relation between juvenile migration and deviance has concentrated mostly on the issue of *'unaccompanied minors'* (Melossi and Giovannetti, 2002) and this is also because immigration is a very recent phenomenon. However, with the establishment of immigrant communities, it can be easily foreseen that issues concerning social integration, cultural conflict and 'deviance', with reference to young immigrants, will increasingly tend to shift from the legal and cultural realm, with unaccompanied

children, towards the economic and social one, with first and second generations.

17 Is this myth or reality about the American immigration experience? Even if it were only myth however we know that myths have a deep influence on the ways in which people – last but not least control officers – perceive their role in society. It comes to mind that wonderful film by Elia Kazan, *America America*, where the protagonist, after having committed some horrendous crimes in a heroic effort to travel from his original Anatolia to the America he had so much longed for, finally in Ellis Island is christened a new man with a new name, Joe Arness! Or, out of fiction and more recently, the self-disclosure of an award-winning Filipino journalist who recently publicly revealed his irregular immigration status – lasted almost his lifetime – and the vicissitudes that made a successful life possible even under such circumstances, in a *New York Times Magazine* article (Vargas, 2011).

18 Whereas, 'as Massey, Durand, and Malone (2002) have noted, the [recent] stiffer immigration restrictions may have the unintended consequences of increasing the number of undocumented immigrants' (Kil and Menjívar, 2006: 167–8).

19 For the details of this process in Italy and Spain see once again Kitty Calavita's brilliant reconstruction.

20 At least until 1998 when the new red-green government proclaimed aloud that *Deutschland ist ein Einwanderungsland!* 'Germany is an immigration land!' (Monte, 2002).

21 But not an increase in imprisonment – this understanding of their theory was a development of 1970s quantitative analysts, such as Jankovic (1977), Greenberg (1977), Box and Hale (1982), Melossi (1985) and others, who tried to 'operationalize' Rusche and Kirchheimer's thesis using imprisonment rates!

22 So that, after the Italian unification, the Southern gentry saw in their peasants leaving to migrate to the Americas an act of defiance no less severe than taking to the mountains to become brigands (Teti, 1993).

23 Typically in Italy workers in penal institutions for youth – almost completely peopled by foreigners in the Center-North – tend to represent foreign youth who often come to Italy 'unaccompanied' as much 'older' and more 'mature' than their actual age!

24 To which, unsurprisingly, certain EU conservative governments, such as the UK government, are starting to object to and making noises to the effect of wanting to withdraw from it also in connection with the issue of immigrants' and asylum-seekers' rights.

25 Conversely, it is noteworthy that even nationality is not necessarily a protection from the workings of labor and human right compartmentalization. Exactly as it had happened in medieval Europe, today in China the norms about *hukou* (residence) produce a situation in which Chinese laborers without residence may find themselves in a situation very similar to that of undocumented foreign workers in Europe (Lee, 2007; Zhong, 2009).

26 I developed this overall argument, that I call 'the cycle of the canaille', in a number of essays (Melossi, 2006, 2008: 229–52, 2010).

27 Historian Aziz Rana (2010), in his *The Two Faces of American Freedom,* distinguishes between the republican and proto-democratic entitlement of the immigrants, assimilated into the original equalitarian commonwealth of the settlers, and the imperial attitude reserved instead toward the non-settlers, treated as colonized people. It is a historical variation on the 'internal colonialism thesis' (which would apply also to 19th-century Southern Italy!) which may offer a hint in the right direction here (I thank Peter Ramsey for bringing to my attention Rana's work). In the UK, the role played by Antillean African-American men looms large in the classic work *Policing the Crisis* (Hall et al., 1978).

28 This is probably a rather common condition of migration in many countries around the globe today!

REFERENCES

Ambrosini, Maurizio (2009) 'L'ennesima ultima sanatoria'. Available at: www.lavoce.info (accessed 1 September 2009).

Amnesty International (2008) 'Jailed without justice: immigration detention in the USA', Report.

Barbagli, Marzio (2008) *Immigrazione e Sicurezza in Italia*. Bologna: il Mulino.

Bell, Daniel (1953) 'Crime as an American way of life', *Antioch Review,* 13: 131–54. (Reprinted in Daniel Bell (2000) *The End of Ideology: On the Exhaustion of Political Ideas in the Fifties*. Cambridge, MA: Harvard University Press.)

Box, Stephen and Hale, Chris (1982) 'Economic crisis and the rising prisoner population', *Crime and Social Justice,* 17: 20–35.

Brotherton, David (2008) 'Beyond social reproduction: bringing resistance back in gang theory', *Theoretical Criminology,* 12: 55–77.

Bursik, Robert (2006) 'Rethinking the Chicago school of criminology: a new era of immigration', in R. Martinez Jr and A. Valenzuela (eds), *Immigration and Crime: Race, Ethnicity and Violence*. New York: New York University Press. pp. 20–35.

Calavita, Kitty (2005) *Immigrants at the Margins: Law, Race, and Exclusion in Southern Europe*. New York: Cambridge University Press.

Caritas/Migrantes (2010) *Immigrazione. Dossier Statistico 2010*. Roma: Idos.

Caritas/Migrantes, Redattore Sociale (2009) 'La criminalità degli immigrati: dati, interpretazioni, pregiudizi', in Agenzia Redattore Sociale (ed.), *Guida per l'informazione sociale. Edizione 2010*. Capodarco di Fermo: Redattore Sociale. pp. 580–603.

Chambliss, William (1973) 'The roughnecks and the saints', *Society*, November/December: 24–31.

Crocitti, Stefania (2011) 'I minori stranieri e italiani tra scuola, lavoro e devianza: un'indagine di self-report', *Studi Sulla Questione Criminale*, 6 (1): 65–106.

De Giorgi, Alessandro (2002 [2006]) *Re-Thinking the Political Economy of Punishment: Perspectives on Post-Fordism and Penal Politics*. Aldershot: Ashgate.

European Commission (2009) *Report from the Commission to the European Parliament and the Council: First Annual Report on Immigration and Asylum*.

Ferracuti, Franco (1968) 'European migration and crime', in M.E. Wolfgang (ed.), *Crime and Culture: Essays in Honor of Thorsten Sellin*. New York: Wiley. pp. 189–219.

Ferraris, Valeria (2009) 'Migrants' offside trap: a strategy for dealing with misleading rules and a hostile playing field', in J. Shapland and P. Ponsaers (eds), *The Informal Economy and Connections with Organized Crime: The Impact of National Social and Economic Policies*. Amsterdam: Boom Publishers.

Finnegan, William (2009) 'Sheriff Joe', *The New Yorker*, 20 July: 42.

Foucault, Michel (1975 [1977]) *Discipline and Punish*. New York: Pantheon.

Garland, David (1990) *Punishment and Modern Society: A Study in Social Theory*. Chicago: University of Chicago Press.

Gatti, Uberto, et al. (2010) 'Self-reported juvenile delinquency in Italy', in J. Junger-Tas,I.H. Marshall, D. Enzmann, M. Killias, M. Steketee and B. Gruszczynska (eds), *Juvenile Delinquency in Europe and Beyond: Results of the Second International Self-Report Delinquency Study*. Dordrecht, Springer. pp. 227–44.

Gilroy, Paul (1987) *There Ain't No Black in the Union Jack*. London: Hutchinson/Unwin.

Greenberg, David (1977) 'The dynamics of oscillatory punishment processes', *Journal of Criminal Law and Criminology*, 68: 643–51.

Hall, Stuart, Critcher, Chas, Jefferson, Tony, Clarke, John and Roberts, Brian (1978) *Policing the Crisis: Mugging, the State, and Law and Order*. London: Macmillan.

Hickman, Laura and Suttorp, Marika (2008) 'Are deportable aliens a unique threat to public safety? Comparing the recidivism of deportable and nondeportable aliens', *Criminology & Public Policy*, 7: 59–82.

Immigration Commission of the United States (1911) Report on 'Immigration and Crime', 61th Cong., 3d Session, Senate Document 750, Volume 36.

Jankovic, Ivan (1977) 'Labor market and imprisonment', *Crime and Social Justice*, 8: 17–31.

Jencks, Christopher (1983) 'Discrimination and Thomas Sowell', *New York Review of Books*, 3 March.

Kil, Sang Hea and Menjívar, Cecilia (2006) 'Criminalizing immigrants and militarizing the US-Mexico Border', in R. Martinez Jr and A. Valenzuela (eds), *Immigration and Crime: Race, Ethnicity and Violence*. New York: New York University Press. pp. 164–88.

Lee, Maggie (2007) 'Women's imprisonment as a mechanism of migration control in Hong Kong', *The British Journal of Criminology*, 47: 847–60.

Lemert, Edwin (1951) *Social Pathology: A Systematic Approach to the Theory of Sociopathic Behavior*. New York: McGraw-Hill.

Levine, Harry and Small, Deborah (2008) *Marijuana Arrest Crusade: Racial Bias and Police Policy in New York City, 1997–2007*. New York: New York Civil Liberties Union Report.

Lynch, James and Simon, Rita (1999) 'A comparative assessment of criminal involvement among immigrants and natives across seven nations', *International Criminal Justice Review*, 9: 1–17.

Marshall, Ineke (ed.) (1997) *Minorities, Migrants, and Crime*. London: SAGE Publications.

Martinez, Ramiro Jr and Valenzuela, Abel (eds) (2006) *Immigration and Crime: Race, Ethnicity and Violence*. New York: New York University Press.

Massey, Douglas, Durand, Jorge and Malone, Nolan (2002) *Beyond Smoke and Mirrors. Mexican Immigration in an Era of Economic Integration*. New York: Russell Sage Foundation.

Matza, David (1964) *Delinquency and Drift*. New York: Wiley.

Mauer, Marc and King, Ryan (2007) *Uneven Justice: State Rates of Incarceration By Race and Ethnicity*. Washington, DC: The Sentencing Project.

Melossi, Dario (1985) 'Punishment and social action: changing vocabularies of punitive motive within a political business cycle', *Current Perspectives in Social Theory*, 6: 169–97.

Melossi, Dario (ed.) (1999) *Multiculturalismo e Sicurezza in Emilia-Romagna: Prima Parte*. Quaderno n.15 del Progetto Città Sicure, Regione Emilia-Romagna.

Melossi, Dario (2003) '"In a peaceful life": migration and the crime of modernity in Europe/Italy', in Symposium Issue of *Punishment and Society* on 'Migration, Punishment and Social Control in Europe', 5/4: 371–97.

Melossi, Dario (2005) 'Security, social control, democracy and migration within the 'constitution' of the EU', *European Law Journal,* 11: 5–21.

Melossi, Dario (2006) 'The cycle of reproduction of 'La Canaille': on the permanent character of a correctionalist ideology', in R. Lévy, L. Mucchielli and R. Zauberman (eds), *Crime et Insécurité: un Demi-siècle de Bouleversements : Mélanges pour et avec Philippe Robert.* Paris: l'Harmattan. pp. 225–37.

Melossi, Dario (2008) *Controlling Crime, Controlling Society: Thinking About Crime in Europe and America.* Cambridge: Polity Press.

Melossi, Dario (2010) 'Il diritto della canaglia: teoria del ciclo, migrazioni e diritto', *Studi Sulla Questione Criminale,* 5 (2): 51–73.

Melossi, Dario and Giovannetti, Monia (2002) *I nuovi sciuscià. Minori stranieri in Italia.* Roma: Donzelli.

Melossi, Dario and Pavarini, Massimo (1977 [1981]) *The Prison and the Factory.* London: Macmillan.

Melossi, Dario, De Giorgi, Alessandro and Massa, Ester (2009) 'The "normality" of "second generations" in Italy and the importance of legal status: a self-report delinquency study', in W. McDonald (ed.), *Immigration, Crime and Justice. Sociology of Crime, Law, and Deviance,* Volume 13. Bingley: Emerald/JAI Press. pp. 47–65.

Melossi Dario, Crocitti, Stefania, Massa, Ester, Crocitti, Stefania and Prina, Franco (2011) *Devianza e Immigrazione: una Ricerca Nelle Scuole dell'Emilia-Romagna, Quaderni di Città Sicure* 37. Bologna: Regione Emilia-Romagna.

Monte, Michela (2002) 'Le politiche di immigrazione in Germania: la criminalità degli immigrati di ii e iii generazione'. Thesis in Criminology, Faculty of Law, University of Bologna.

Park, Robert (1928) 'Human migration and the marginal man', in R.E. Park (ed.), *On Social Control and Collective Behaviour.* Chicago: University of Chicago Press. pp. 194–206.

Park, Robert, Burgess, Ernest and McKenzie, Roderick (1925 [1967]) *The City.* Chicago: University of Chicago Press.

Rainerman, Craig and Levine, Harry (1997) *Crack in America: Demon Drugs and Social Justice.* Berkeley, CA: University of California Press.

Rana, Aziz (2010) *The Two Faces of American Freedom.* Cambridge, MA: Harvard University Press.

Rumbaut, Rubén, Gonzales, Roberto, Komaie, Golnaz, Morgan, Charlie and Tafoya-Estrada, Rosaura (2006) 'Immigration and incarceration. Patterns and predictors of imprisonment among first- and second-generation young adults', in R. Martinez Jr and A. Valenzuela (eds), *Immigration and Crime: Race, Ethnicity and Violence.* New York: New York University Press. pp. 64–89.

Rusche, Georg (1930 [1980]) 'Prison revolts or social policy: lessons from America', *Crime and Social Justice,* 13: 41–4.

Rusche, Georg (1933 [1978]) 'Labor market and penal sanction', *Crime and Social Justice,* 10: 2–8.

Rusche, Georg and Kirchheimer, Otto (1939 [2003]) *Punishment and Social Structure.* New Brunswick, NJ: Transaction.

Sampson, Robert (2006) 'Open doors don't invite criminals', *New York Times,* 11 March.

Sassen, Saskia (2010) 'Immigration: control vs governance'. Available at: http://www.opendemocracy.net

Sayad, Abdelmalek (1999 [2004]) *The Suffering of the Immigrant,* ed. Pierre Bourdieu. Cambridge: Polity Press.

Sellin, Thorsten (1937) *Research Memorandum on Crime in the Depression.* New York: Social Science Research Council.

Sellin, Thorsten (1938) *Culture, Conflict and Crime.* New York: Social Science Research Council.

Shaw, Clifford and McKay, Henry (1942) *Juvenile Delinquency and Urban Areas.* Chicago: University of Chicago Press.

Snacken, Sonja (2010) 'Resisting punitiveness in Europe?', *Theoretical Criminology,* 14: 273–92.

Sozzo, Maximo (2010) 'Migration, crime and the birth of criminology in Argentina (1887–1910)'. Paper presented at the Meetings of the American Society of Criminology, San Francisco.

Stowell, Jacob (2007) *Immigration and Crime: Considering the Direct and Indirect Effects of Immigration on Violent Criminal Behavior.* New York: LFB Scholarly Press.

Stowell, Jacob, Messner, Steven, McGeever, Kelly, and Raffalovich, Lawrence (2009) 'Immigration and the recent violent crime drop in the United States: a pooled, cross-sectional time-series analysis of metropolitan areas', *Criminology,* 47: 889–928.

Teti, Vito (1993) *La Razza Maledetta: Origini del Pregiudizio Antimeridionale.* Roma: Manifestolibri.

Thomas, William and Znaniecki, Florian (1918–20 [1958]) *The Polish Peasant in Europe and America.* Chicago: University of Chicago.

Tonry, Michael (ed.) (1997) *Ethnicity, Crime, and Immigration: Comparative and Cross-National Perspectives.* Chicago: University of Chicago Press.

Van Zyl Smit, Dirk and Snacken, Sonja (2009) *Principles of European Prison Law and Policy: Penology and Human Rights.* Oxford: Oxford University Press.

Vargas, José (2011) 'Two decades of living a lie in America', *International Herald Tribune*, 25–26 June.

Venkatesh, Sudhir (2008) *Gang Leader For A Day: A Rogue Sociologist Takes to the Streets*. New York: Penguin.

Wacquant, Loïc (2009) *Punishing the Poor. The Neoliberal Government of Social Insecurity*. Durham, NC: Duke University Press.

Wickersham Commission (1931) National Commission on Law Observance and Enforcement. *Crime and the Foreign Born*. Washington: US Government Printing Office. Report No. 10. (Republished in 1968 by Patterson Smith, Montclair, New Jersey).

Young, Jock (1999) *The Exclusive Society*. London: SAGE Publications.

Young, Jock (2003) 'To these wet and windy shores: recent immigration policy in the UK', *Punishment and Society*, 5: 449–62.

Zhong, Lena (2009) *Communities, Crime and Social Capital in Contemporary China*. Cullompton: Willan.

21

Amnesties, Transitional Justice and Governing Through Mercy

Kieran McEvoy and Louise Mallinder

INTRODUCTION

> It is the certainty of being punished and not the horrifying spectacle of public punishment that must discourage crime. (Foucault, 1977: 9)

The intersection between punishment and society explored in this chapter is in contexts where the 'certainty of punishment' (at least in a retributive sense) is explicitly suspended. Our central premise is that the decision not to prosecute in such contexts, and the legal, political and social processes involved, are of significant theoretical and practical interest beyond the ostensibly 'exotic' circumstances of post-conflict environments. Of course, there is a rich and interesting history of amnesty-like measures such as presidential pardons or the exercising of the Royal Prerogative of Mercy in settled democracies (Strange, 2001b; Crouch, 2009), but this is not the primary focus of this chapter. Rather, our analysis is upon societies that are in transition from violent political conflict and where amnesties are deemed necessary for 'the greater good' (Power, 2007: 419). Victims of the most egregious crimes are effectively asked to forego their individual desire for *punishment* – often too easily viewed as synonymous with retributive justice – in the interests of these broader collective objectives (Cullinan, 2001; Madlingozi, 2010). In such contexts, the relationship between punishment, politics and ideology is particularly keenly felt – indeed, it is expressly articulated, debated and understood as a central component of the emerging polity.

This chapter emerges from over a decade of fieldwork in transitional societies as well as from a major database of over 530 amnesty laws in 138 countries between 1945 and 2011 created by Mallinder.[1] Both of the authors are lawyers who work in the field of transitional justice, but McEvoy in particular has long been interested in and influenced by the criminological concerns that permeate the field of punishment and society. From a western vantage point, transitional justice has to date been largely concerned with 'exotic' locations, places often characterized by a history of extreme violence, a disregard for 'the rule of law' and a broad spectrum of differing levels of normative and practical attachment to democratic values and practices (Teitel, 2000; Bell, 2009; Arthur, 2009).[2] As such societies move out of violence, law emerges as a practical and symbolic break with the past and the commitment to human rights in particular becomes the key method of publicly demonstrating a new found commitment to legitimacy among the community of nations (McEvoy, 2007). In such contexts, in what is sometimes referred to as 'the triumph of human rights', accountability becomes synonymous with retribution and amnesties are a byword for impunity.

We begin the chapter therefore by exploring in a little more detail the notion of transitional justice and the historical and contemporary meanings of amnesties in the field. We then examine the outworkings of amnesties more closely through three of the key themes in the punishment and society literature, namely: retribution; deterrence; and restoration. The chapter concludes by examining the utility of the notion of the governance of mercy as a prism through which to explore the power relations at work in the design and implementation of an amnesty process.

THE TRANSITIONAL JUSTICE CONTEXT

The term 'transitional justice' can be traced to a series of debates in the late 1980s and early 1990s on how to deal with past violence in societies moving out of conflict or dictatorship (Teitel, 2000). Paige Arthur (2009) has well captured the plurality of influences that marked the emergence of the field as the result of a series of interactions between human rights activists, lawyers, legal academics, policymakers, journalists, donors and comparative policy experts. From the outset, in jurisdictions such as Chile, Argentina, South Africa, Guatemala and others, the field was marked by the inherent tensions between principle and pragmatism. On the one hand, there was and is a moral and political impetus towards punishing those who had visited 'extraordinary evil' on their victims (Orentlicher, 1991; Aukerman, 2002). On the other, the legal, practical and political difficulties inherent in following through on such impulses are manifest in such fraught contexts. These include circumstances where there may be no strong democratic tradition; where the military or intelligence services often remain powerful and suspicious of democracy in general, and oversight or accountability in particular; where the judiciary and police may be corrupt, incompetent or uninterested; where rebels or militia may retain their capacity for violence; and where political leaders are often faced with an array of pressing socio-economic challenges – in other words, the political conditions that journalists and the contemporary western commentariat have taught us to know as 'weak' or 'failed' states. Under such circumstances it is perhaps little wonder that the tensions between the demands of *justice* and the demands of peaceful *transition* are so prominent in such societies.

In the two decades since the term was first used, transitional justice has grown into a multidisciplinary field of scholarship, policy and practice. There are important documents produced by the United Nations (UNSC, 2004), a vibrant national and international non-governmental organization (NGO) sector (Backer, 2003), specialist journals, university courses, a plethora of books, heated debates and all of the other scholarly accoutrements that suggest a vibrant and energetic field of inquiry (Bell, 2009). We would argue that what has given the area a particular 'swagger' has been the expenditure of billions of pounds on the creation of ad hoc tribunals for the former Yugoslavia and Rwanda, the International Criminal Court and hybrid courts (involving local and international legal actors) in places such as Sierra Leone and Cambodia, designed to try those deemed most culpable for gross human rights violations (Schabas, 2006; De Guzman, 2008; Kelsall, 2009). The institutionalization of transitional justice in these new legal bodies, the development and codification of a new body of law (via the Rome Statute, which established the International Criminal Court and the jurisprudence of the other ad hoc tribunals) and the increased importance of regional human rights mechanisms such as the Inter-American Court have underlined the authority and political importance of the field. As noted above, the dominance of legalism does tend to narrow perspectives on what are deemed the most appropriate responses to human rights abuses towards predominantly retributive approaches.[3] Certainly, the vast bulk of expenditure in the field is spent on retributive trials and associated costs.[4] That said, transitional justice does encompass a range of non-punitive measures designed to deal with past violence including truth commissions, reintegration programmes for ex-combatants, reparations programmes for victims, a plurality of forms of commemoration and remembrance, and of course, amnesties (De Greiff, 2006; Mallinder, 2008; Keren and Herwig, 2009; Patel et al., 2009; Wiebelhaus-Brahm, 2010).

AMNESTIES PAST AND PRESENT

> Amnesty is organized forgetting ... it has nothing to do with the pacification that forgiveness can bring between two consciences. It is not by chance that there is a kinship between 'amnesty' and 'amnesia'. The institutions of amnesty are not all the institutions of forgiveness. They constitute a forgiveness that is public, commanded, and that has therefore nothing to do with a personal act of compassion. In my opinion, amnesty does wrong at once to truth, thereby repressed and as if forbidden, and to justice, at it is due to the victims ... Amnesty prevents both forgiveness and justice. (Ricoeur, 2005: 10)

The critique of amnesties advanced by the celebrated French scholar of memory Paul Ricoeur has become a key referent among many of those who work on the topic. His characterization of amnesties as 'commanded forgetting' and a denial of justice (2003: 353) well captures the dominant view of amnesties in the literature. Historically, amnesty laws were often described as 'acts of oblivion' or 'legal amnesia'. Indeed, as Ricoeur notes the word 'amnesty', like 'amnesia', can be traced to the Greek word 'amnēstia', meaning 'forgetfulness' (see also Orentlicher, 1991: 2543). Like the right to punish more generally, the capacity to grant an amnesty and (in Ricoeur's terms) to command forgetting and forgiveness has long been a key element of the power of the sovereign. As Parker notes, 'for as long as there have been written laws there has been an institutionalized power of mercy, pardon and amnesty' (2001: 76). Indeed, as is explored below, the capacity for mercy and benevolence from the sovereign through the granting of an amnesty was arguably at least as important an exercise of power as the ability to visit violence and retribution on the wicked or the vanquished (O'Shea, 2002).

The historical granting of amnesties, as a means to secure post-conflict peace and stability and its relationship to 'stateness', is therefore also relevant for current purposes. For example, the signing of the 1648 peace treaties at Westphalia, which were designed to end decades of sustained conflict in Europe,[5] included a provision that all 'insults, violent acts, hostilities, damages, and costs, without regard of the person or the issue' should be 'forgiven and forgotten in eternity' (Zepp-LaRouche, 1999: 1). At a practical level, the power to utilize amnesties, whether individualized or granted to designated groups after a war, evolved into a key element of post-conflict state-craft and governance (Weisman, 1972). In more recent times, in line with the changes in modern warfare, amnesties have increasingly been introduced in response to internal conflicts rather than international wars. At the symbolic level, however, the granting of amnesties has remained as a constant and powerful expression of state power and sovereignty, a key element of the process of what the anthropologist James C. Scott (1999) has described as 'seeing like a state'.[6]

Amnesties may be understood as the process by which states exercise their sovereign right to mercy by extinguishing criminal or civil liability for past crimes. In eradicating liability, amnesty essentially assumes that a crime has been committed but seeks to negate the possibility of prosecution. Amnesties therefore tend to be retroactive, applying only to acts committed before the relevant amnesty laws were passed (Bourdon, 1999).[7] Furthermore, amnesties are often limited in a variety of ways. For example, they may exclude certain categories of crimes (such as genocide or war crimes) or those who are considered leaders or key players in past policies of violence or oppression. In addition, an amnesty process may be conditional. It may require applicants to perform tasks such as surrender weapons, provide information on former comrades, admit the truth about past actions (discussed further below) or show remorse in order to benefit from the amnesty (Mallinder, 2008).

The exercise of state sovereignty in the guise of amnesties is not unqualified. Since the end of the Second World War, in what some commentators have referred to as 'the justice cascade' (Lutz and Sikkink, 2001), the rise of the international human rights movement and the elaboration of international human rights law has been linked closely with the 'fight against impunity' (Beigbeder, 2005). The *shape* of amnesties has been significantly influenced by the increased prominence of international human rights discourses. In the 1970s crude 'blanket amnesties' designed by the outgoing military dictatorships in Latin America and elsewhere were routinely afforded to the leaders, murderers and torturers of the *ancien régime*. However, these styles of unconditional amnesties enacted by repressive rulers and warlords to shield themselves from prosecution have increasingly come under attack from international and hybrid courts, universal jurisdiction proceedings, domestic legal challenges and civil society campaigns. Particularly within South America, these challenges have restricted the scope of previously broad amnesties so that today they shield far fewer perpetrators of serious human rights violations (Laplante, 2009; Collins, 2010).

In particular, as is discussed further below, it is now relatively common to see amnesties linked in some fashion to processes designed to incentivize former combatants to offer truth in return for non-prosecution. The strong gravitational pull exerted by the South African Truth and Reconciliation Commission in the field of transitional justice has seen versions of this model (exchanging amnesty for truth) reproduced in the mandates of truth commissions in Liberia, Timor Leste as well as (arguably) in commissions of inquiry such as the Bloody Sunday Inquiry in Northern Ireland where evidence given by witnesses could not be used in any subsequent criminal proceedings (Saville, 2010).[8] Where an amnesty is linked to truth-recovery mechanisms in such contexts, the traditional notion that the crime has been obviated is removed, and such crimes may be investigated, acknowledged, recorded and discussed in public discourse (Sarkin, 2007).

While the design of amnesties has been clearly affected by this 'justice cascade', their frequency has been largely unaffected. As Mark Freeman has argued, 'amnesties are as prevalent today as at any time in modern history … we are no more at the end of amnesties than we are at the "end of history"' (2010: 4). Freeman's assertion is supported by our own research. Drawing upon the database developed by Mallinder, between January 1979 and December 2010, an average of 14.7 amnesty laws were enacted each year around the world. Admittedly the global rate of amnesty laws has gone through a number of peaks and troughs. For example, following the end of the Cold War in 1989, the number of amnesty laws rose sharply as political transitions took place in the former communist states in eastern Europe – predominantly to benefit former dissidents whose actions had been criminalized by the previous regimes. This period also witnessed a reduction in the willingness of the superpowers to 'prop up' *some* dictatorial regimes or intervene in certain civil wars, which added impetus to local negotiated agreements that usually included amnesty provisions. Conversely, in places such as the former Yugoslavia where post-Cold War, newly independent states spiralled into civil war, again the final peace settlements often included a series of amnesties in the late 1990s (Binningsbø et al., 2005). In more recent times, the largest proportion of amnesties have been enacted in Sub-Sahara Africa, again associated with the myriad of post-colonial, inter-state and international conflicts in that region (Mallinder, 2012c).

In sum, a number of key points need to be borne in mind as we seek to explore how amnesties map onto some of the key themes in the punishment and society literature. First, in historical terms at least, amnesties have been associated with processes of 'commanded forgetting' where, not only were perpetrators 'not punished' but also victims and affected communities were in effect asked to erase the memory of what had occurred. Second, as with the power to punish itself, the power not to punish – to show 'mercy' – in the guise of an amnesty is intimately connected to the evolution of the modern state and the notion of sovereignty, and has long been an important tool of post-conflict governance and peacemaking. Finally, while the increased importance of human rights discourses and international criminal law has shaped the contours and contents of more recent amnesties – often linking them to processes of truth recovery – neither their usage nor political significance has diminished.

By far the most common rationale for punishing perpetrators in this field is retribution and so we begin with a necessarily detailed exploration of its outworkings in transitional justice. We then examine the closely linked claims that are advanced regarding the secondary justification for punishment in this context, namely deterrence. Finally, in order to explore some of their more potentially positive contributions, we examine amnesties from a restorative perspective.

AMNESTIES, RETRIBUTION AND THE LAW

As Henman has argued, the declared rationale (or in Hart's [1968] terms, the 'general justifying aim') for the creation of international penal processes remains 'predominantly retributive and marginally deterrent' (2004: 36). The ICTR has held:

> it is clear that the penalties imposed on accused persons found guilty by the Tribunal must be directed, on the one hand, at retribution of the said accused, who must see their crimes punished, and over and above that, on the other hand, at deterrence.[9]

The issue of deterrence is discussed below but as scholars of international criminal justice and transitional justice have detailed, retribution is the most obvious 'fit' for the often outrageous crimes to which transitional justice must respond (Mani, 2002; Roberts, 2003; Drumbl, 2007). As Beigbeder sums up, retribution is for many the 'primary object' of international justice. Its key role is to fight against the impunity hitherto enjoyed by those leaders most responsible for grave violations of human rights (Beigbeder, 2005: 226). Intuitively, at a very basic human level, individuals who have engaged in what Appadurai (2006) refers to as 'a surplus of rage'[10] or an extreme variant of what Kant discussed as 'radical evil', simply deserve to be punished.

There are a myriad of variants of historical and modern retributive justifications for punishment but we have chosen to focus on a few key thinkers for the purposes of this essay. Given the historical significance and durability of amnesties, some of the classic writings on retribution are instructive. In addition to the 'rightness' of retribution, the other elements of the retributive framework of most interest for our purposes are the centrality of law; questions of proportionality and selectivity; and the expressive functions of punishment.

The notion of retribution as meaning that criminals should be punished because they *deserve* it for what they have done is usually traced to Immanuel Kant (1785, 1796–7). For Kant the right to punish is 'the right a ruler has against a subject to inflict pain upon him because of his having committed a crime' (1796–7: 140). Punishment within the retributive framework is less concerned with the promoting of other social goals – 'for a man can never be treated as the means to the purposes of another' (Kant, 1796–7: 140) – thus mitigation of deserved sentence for a greater social good cannot be justified because such actions would represent a denial of *justice*, and indeed, a dereliction of duty on the part of the sovereign. For Kant, a community that fails to punish, as in the case of amnesty, will in effect be collaborating in the public violation of justice.

Like Kant, Hegel (1820) argues that justice requires decisions on whether to punish, whom to punish, how to punish and how much to punish based solely on 'the undeserved evil' of the criminal act itself, and not on other extraneous concerns. Hegel also talks of punishment as the annulment of crime – 'the annulling of crime ... is principally revenge, which is just in its content in so far as it is retributive' (1820: para. 102). However, for Hegel, revenge in this context is neither subjective nor arbitrary, but rather it must be rational, commensurate and legitimately delivered.[11] For Hegel the process of retributive punishment by the state reasserts the importance of the universal (or collective) right to punishment over the subjective claim to revenge by the individual victim.

For retributivists, the key mechanism for the delivery of such legitimate punishment is the law (Zaibert, 2006). Crime is a breach of the law and the response to that breach, punishment, must be *legal*. It must be authorized, delivered and regulated according to the law. While acknowledging the centrality of law does not offer easy solutions to issues such as unjust laws, contradictory laws or indeed behaviour that is manifestly wrong but not criminalized in a particular society, it is a useful axiom for this essay. If we accept that punishment must be done according to the law within the retributive framework, we must therefore examine the legality of amnesties.

As is noted above many states have introduced amnesty legislation thus rendering them lawful in domestic law (subject to constitutional challenge).[12] If constitutional challenges fail or are not viable even to lodge, most opponents of amnesties tend to resort to international law to argue that amnesties are impermissible. Many policymakers, scholars and human rights activists readily claim that international law does not permit amnesty laws for serious crimes (Bell, 2008). In fact, no international convention has explicitly prohibited amnesty laws (Slye, 2002). Indeed, on every occasion where an explicit prohibition or discouragement of amnesties has been mooted in the context of a multilateral treaty negotiation, states have demonstrated 'a resolute unwillingness to agree to even the mildest discouragement' (Freeman, 2010: 33). Without such an explicit prohibition, discerning whether amnesties violate international law is complex, requiring engagement with a number of distinct legal regimes: international humanitarian law, international human rights law and international criminal law and customary international law (Mallinder, 2012a).

The supposed 'duty to prosecute' under international law is usually invoked with regard to the most serious of 'international crimes' (Cryer, 2010) – namely, genocide, war crimes and crimes against humanity. Even within this category of crimes, there are divergences regarding the duty to prosecute. For example, with regard to genocide, the duty to prosecute has been described as 'absolute' and as creating a mandatory duty on states to prosecute (Scharf, 1996). At first blush, such a requirement would appear to render amnesty for such crimes a violation of states' obligation to punish. However, the definition of genocide contained in Article 2 of the Genocide Convention 1948 narrows this crime to actions that are taken with 'intent to destroy, in whole or in part, a national, ethnical, racial or religious group'.[13] The requirement for intent to destroy a substantial portion of a population is in practice quite a high threshold and rules out many conflicts. Similarly, the omission of acts directed against political groups – such as, for example, 'communists' or 'subversives' in South America's 'dirty wars' – would again place such mass killings beyond the scope of the Genocide Convention.

With regard to international humanitarian law (IHL), the 'laws of war' which govern war crimes the duty to prosecute under the Geneva Conventions 1949 and Additional Protocol I 1977 applies only to 'grave breaches' committed during international armed conflicts.[14] This obligation to prosecute is 'absolute', meaning 'that states parties can under no circumstances grant perpetrators immunity or amnesty from prosecution for grave breaches' (Scharf, 1996: 44). However, most conflicts since the Second World War have been internal armed conflicts, for which there is no explicit duty to prosecute contained in IHL treaties. Indeed, Article 6(5) of Additional Protocol II to the Geneva Conventions, which establishes the international humanitarian law framework for non-international armed conflicts, actually encourages states parties to enact 'the broadest possible amnesty' at the end of hostilities.[15] Since the 1990s, the International Committee of the Red Cross (ICRC) has sought to reinterpret this provision to cover only 'combat immunity', with the result that combatants who commit acts equivalent to grave breaches would be prohibited from receiving amnesty (Pfanner cited in Cassel, 1996: 218). In its 2005 study of Customary International Humanitarian Law, the ICRC argued that its interpretation of Article 6(5) has now become part of customary law (Henckaerts and Doswald-Beck, 2005: Rule 159). This interpretation has been echoed in the limited jurisprudence on amnesties emanating from the international and hybrid courts (Mallinder, 2010). However, it is based on only cursory examinations of state practice.

Crimes against humanity are not proscribed by international conventions and instead, like war crimes committed in internal conflicts, their criminalization is a product of customary international law. Recognizing the criminality of these crimes does not automatically imply a duty to prosecute (O'Shea, 2002: 205). Instead, Article 38 of the International Court of Justice Statute requires that determinations of whether such a duty exists under customary international law must be based on state practice and *opinio juris* (the belief that an action is required out of a sense of legal obligation). This can be found, for example, in the existence or absence of relevant domestic legislation (either granting amnesties or requiring prosecutions); state practice in relation to mediating peace agreements that include or exclude amnesty provisions; and state willingness to include provisions prohibiting amnesty in international conventions. As noted above, the data gathered in the Amnesty Law Database, and comparative research conducted by other scholars, highlights that states continue to enact amnesty laws even for the most serious crimes. In addition, some states continue to support peace negotiations in which amnesties are agreed,[16] and even provide financial, logistical or personnel support to the implementation of amnesty processes.[17] Furthermore, when negotiating the Rome Statute of the International Criminal Court 1998, delegates debated a range of proposals relating to amnesty laws, but were ultimately unable to reach a consensus on prohibiting them in the ICC Statute. As a result, the Statute contains no reference to amnesty legislation (Schabas, 2007: 87). These trends in state practice have encouraged several commentators to question the prohibition of amnesties for crimes against humanity and war crimes in internal conflicts under customary international law (Trumbull, 2007; Bell, 2008; Cryer, 2010; Freeman, 2010).

In short, there is a gap between some of the more grandiose rhetoric concerning the supposed duty to prosecute international crimes and the reality of state practice with regard to amnesties. International and domestic courts are by definition sites of contest and the tendency to overstate the clarity of international law as an element of social or political claims-making – a variant of what Michael Ignatieff (2003) has referred to as the 'human rights as trumps' argument – is perfectly understandable as part of broader efforts to combat impunity. However, both international and domestic law accepts a role for prosecution *and* amnesties in transitional justice settings, both can be and are introduced and implemented *legally*. We shall return to some of these arguments in the final section of this chapter.

Other significant challenges for advocates of an exclusively retributive approach to punishment in this field are with regard to *selectivity* and *proportionality*. Prosecutions in international justice are, by definition, selective. The politics of indictments issued by the ICC against particular rebels or brutal dictators have been discussed in detail elsewhere (Branch, 2007; Cayley, 2008). Similarly, the factors that contribute to the creation of an international or hybrid tribunal in the first place often appear to be influenced by a 'random confluence of political concerns' (Amann, 2002: 116). Why Yugoslavia, Rwanda or Sierra Leone, but not Guatemala or Sri Lanka? Even within the workings of such entities, the focus of resources are usually geared towards gathering evidence against so-called 'big fish' and the most winnable cases, not necessarily the ones which are most deserving (Drumbl, 2007). 'Small fish' who were not in leadership positions may well have been responsible for the most heinous of crimes which are, by any retributive standard, deserving of punishment. Yet punishment of all such actors is often legally, politically and practically impossible. In trying and sentencing a few 'officially guilty' perpetrators who clearly *deserve* to be punished because of their crimes, the practical translation of retributive principles also produces many more 'false innocents' (Steinhert, 1997) who deserve to be punished too.

With regard to proportionality, precisely because of the nature of the crimes involved, this too represents a test to the explanatory power of the retributive rationale. As Hannah Arendt has observed, the scale and the horror of the crimes of the Nazis was such that they 'explode the limits of law ... For these crimes, no punishment is severe enough' (1992: 54). As Mark Drumbl (2007: 157) has argued, a truly proportionate response to such crimes might involve torture or group elimination wherein survivors would be become as depraved as their tormenters. If, following Arendt we accept that the search for proportionality in such circumstances is 'inadequate and absurd' (1973: 439), then we would argue that this too weakens the case for an exclusive focus on retributive punishment in transitional context, and by extension, creates the space for exploring in a fairly cold-eyed and pragmatic fashion the restorative potential of amnesties (as detailed below).

Before moving to discuss the interrelated topic of deterrence, it might be useful at this juncture to deal with *expressive* functions of punishment. For contemporary retributivists in particular, the expression of societal disapproval of criminal behaviour is an intrinsic element of the punishment process. Although expressivism obviously departs from Kant's exclusion of ulterior rationales for punishing offenders, retributivists include it in their gaze by arguing that the primary focus for the message being sent remains the perpetrator. For example, Andrew Von Hirsch (1993) has suggested that retribution should also entail a public expression of *blame*, or *censure* – a proportionate quotient of 'public reproof' of wrongdoing, which serves to denounce the offence in such a way as to encourage the individual to recognize his or her own blameworthiness (see also Duff, 2001). This expressive function of punishment, demarcating the boundaries of acceptable and unacceptable behaviour as well as underlining the moral authority of law (Durkheim, 1933; Garland, 1990: esp chs 2 and 3), is intimately bound up with what Hay (1975) termed the 'majesty' of justice or what Douglas (2001) calls the 'spectacle of legality'. Of course, the expressivist messages of international trials may become distorted or blocked by entrenched cultures of violence, extreme nationalism or narratives of victimhood. For example, there is quite a lot of evidence to suggest that with regard to the trials of some of those who were prosecuted before the ICTY, war criminals were transmogrified into heroes (Klarin, 2009). That said, the issue of public censure remains one which must be regarded as central to contemporary discussion of the question of amnesties.

However, as we will argue below, other more restorative approaches such as carefully designed truth commissions (with amnesty available to incentivize perpetrators to come forward, tell the truth and engage in efforts to repair the damage done) may have an even greater expressive potential. To provide a concrete example, if the ICC's indictment against the Lord's Resistance Army leader, Joseph Kony, were ever to result in him being brought to court,[18] it is certainly arguable that the expressive power of his trial might well be 'muffled' by a trial possibly being conducted thousands of miles from the communities he terrorized, in, for example, the comparatively plush surroundings of The Hague (Keller, 2008: 266–70). If Kony adopted the position of many other mass murderers of denying or justifying his crimes, refusing to apologize or to seek to make amends, then the message might be all the more diluted. Alternatively, would a properly constituted truth commission in Uganda provide a more powerful spectacle as well as a more effective and impactive mechanism to deal with the past violence of that region? Such a scenario is at the very least debatable.

To recap before considering deterrence, while the retributive rationale remains the most commonly advanced in the field of transitional justice in favour of prosecution and as a bulwark against amnesties, we would argue it fails to retain its explanatory or justificatory power when subjected to even the most basic analysis. The obligation to prosecute under international law is less clear than is often argued and amnesties can be, if properly designed and implemented, perfectly lawful. Even for crimes such as genocide or grave breaches of humanitarian law where the duty appears clearer, it seems unlikely that the state's duty to prosecute requires the prosecution of all such crimes. This uncertainty could leave space for amnesties to coexist with limited prosecution strategies. Indeed, as we suggest further below, in sites where prosecutions are by definition selective and where punishments can rarely be truly proportionate, a lawful amnesty which requires the performance of certain obligations, such as occurs in a properly constituted truth commission, may in fact be preferable to de facto impunity where the vast bulk of perpetrators are untouched by any legal process. Finally, while the expressive functions of punishment must be taken seriously, we would argue that carefully crafted restorative institutions can achieve the same goal.

AMNESTIES, DETERRENCE AND THE RATIONAL ACTOR

Since crime and punishment have become serious areas of study, deterrence has been advocated as a key justification for inflicting punishment. Beccaria, for example, argued that the purpose of punishment was 'to prevent the criminal from inflicting new injuries and to deter others from similar acts' (1764: 42). In effect, his focus was upon what criminologists now term specific and general deterrence, punishing offenders so that they think again before re-offending, as well as sending a message to others who might be tempted towards crime in the future. Leaving crimes 'unpunished', as arguably is the case with amnesties, is highly imprudent from such a perspective. As Jeremy Bentham summed up:

> When we consider that an unpunished crime leaves the path of crime open, not only to the

same delinquent, but also to all those who may have the same motives and opportunities for entering upon it, we perceive that the punishment inflicted upon the individual becomes a source of security for all. (1830: 20)

For punishment to achieve both specific and general deterrence, theorists have suggested two characteristics must be present. First, it is more important that punishment is viewed by offenders to be *certain*, rather than severe, it if is to overcome 'the hope of impunity' in the offenders (Beccaria, 1764: 58). Second, offenders must be willing to incorporate the risk of punishment into their decision making in order to decide rationally whether the potential cost of punishment outweighs the benefits of engaging in criminality (Zimring and Hawkin, 1973). The utilitarian rationales of deterrence theory as preventing further crimes have been incorporated and adapted within the context of transitional justice. However, as this section will explore, transplantations of deterrence theory from individual crimes in ordinary criminal justice to situations of mass atrocity face several challenges.

In the field of international criminal justice, as noted above, deterrence is the second principal rationale deployed in support of prosecutions[19] and, either explicitly or implicitly, in opposition to amnesties. For example, when the UN Security Council established the ICTY, it explicitly linked prosecutions to the prevention of further violence by stating that a goal of the Tribunal was to 'put to an end' the widespread violations of international humanitarian law that were occurring within the former Yugoslavia.[20] Similarly, the preamble to the Rome Statute 1998 declares that the ICC is 'determined to put an end to impunity for the perpetrators' and 'thus to contribute to the prevention of [international] crimes'.[21] Since their creation, this objective of international tribunals has been recognized to varying degrees in their case law. For example, the Trial Chamber at the International Criminal Tribunal for Rwanda suggested the purpose of punishing those guilty of international crimes, 'over and above' the goal of retribution is 'deterrence, namely, to dissuade for ever others who may be tempted in the future to perpetrate such atrocities'.[22] To support these arguments, previous examples of a failure to punish and the consequent lack of deterrence to future generations are routinely made. For example, the former ICTY judge and prominent international law scholar Antonio Cassese has argued strongly that 'the impunity of the leaders and organisers of the Armenian genocide ... gave a nod and a wink to Adolf Hitler and others to pursue the Holocaust some twenty years later' (1998: 2).

In making assertions on the deterrent potential of prosecutions to address mass atrocity, policymakers and scholars have often gone beyond the traditional criminological focus on deterring specific offenders and other individuals from committing crimes in the future. Instead, transitional justice literature frequently links deterrence of communal violence to the achievement of broader social goals. In this way, the term specific (or 'immediate') deterrence is often used within transitional justice literature to denote the ability of courts to intervene in ongoing conflicts to contribute to the prevention of further violations and the peaceful resolution of the conflict. Vinjamuri explains that 'advocates of judicial deterrence' emphasize the particular contribution that courts can make 'in the absence of effective peace negotiations, economic sanctions, or the use of military force' (2010: 194–5). The salience of this rationale for prosecutions was vividly illustrated by the UN Security Council's unanimous referral in February 2011 of the situation in Libya to the ICC just weeks after the violence had erupted.[23]

Similarly, general deterrence has been linked within transitional justice literature to longer-term stabilizing objectives such as national reconciliation, democracy and the re-establishment of the rule of law (Akhavan, 2009). Furthermore, it has been used to convey ideas of deterrence that are 'neither confined to a particular individual or territory nor time-bound' (Vinjamuri, 2010: 194), but instead, seek to promote 'general deterrence vis-à-vis the world community' (Rodman, 2008: 559). Under this approach, even if prosecutions fail to end the violence within a particular context, advocates of trials assert that they can potentially influence the decisions of future perpetrators and thereby gradually contribute to greater compliance with human rights and humanitarian norms (Vinjamuri, 2010: 194). However, where human rights advocates make assertions about trials' deterrent capabilities, they rarely engage with criminological literature on deterrence.

Reflecting on the lack of engagement by international lawyers with matters criminological, Schabas has suggested (perhaps a little harshly) that many of their pronouncements on the theoretical rationales for punishment are 'marked by amateurishness … driven more by intuition than anything else' (2011: 349). Certainly, in reviewing some of the relevant judgements and academic materials, it would appear that there is often a tendency to overstate the certainty and impact of the deterrent effect. While claims with regard to the intellectual viability of deterrence continue to vary within criminology, generalized claims such as those which appear among international lawyers are now a rarity among serious criminologists. As overviews of the vast quantitative, qualitative and experimental literature on deterrence point out (Kennedy, 2008; Tonry, 2008; Jacobs, 2010; Apel and Nagin, 2010), determining which individuals may be deterred from which crimes and in what circumstances has remained a significant challenge for policymakers and scholars despite decades of research on the topic. Needless to say we would share this extreme tentativeness with regard to assertions about deterrent effects when it comes to the field of transitional justice, both due to uncertainty on deterrence in general, but also due to the specific challenges it faces in transitional contexts.

In recent years, transitional justice scholars have highlighted the existence of 'justice cascade' in which the number of persons facing prosecutions before national and international courts for crimes under international law has risen sharply (Kim and Sikkink, 2010). However, as Drumbl highlights, 'notwithstanding the fact that the prospect of getting caught is greater than it once was, it still remains tiny' (2007: 170). This reality has been acknowledged by then UN Secretary General Kofi Annan, who, in his influential 2004 report on 'Transitional justice and the rule of law' stated that '[i]n the end, in post-conflict countries, the vast majority of perpetrators of serious violations of human rights and international humanitarian law will never be tried, whether internationally or domestically' (UNSC, 2004: para. 46). In many of these cases, the absence of prosecutions will simply result from a failure to pursue accountability among domestic and international actors. However, in other instances, amnesty laws may be enacted to shield perpetrators from accountability. Where amnesties have been enacted they often apply to much greater numbers of offenders than trials, even where the prosecutions benefit from substantial international support.

For example, in Cambodia, the Extraordinary Chambers, a hybrid international/domestic court, has indicted five former leaders of the Khmer Rouge, but thousands of former Khmer Rouge members, including those who perpetrated serious violations, continue to benefit from an amnesty enacted in 1994 to encourage them to surrender and disarm.[24] Similarly, the hybrid Special Court of Sierra Leone, only indicted 13 individuals, two of whom died before being tried. The thousands of other perpetrators within Sierra Leone were processed by the TRC and Disarmament, Demobilisation and Reintegration (DDR) programmes, rather than put on trial.[25] Furthermore, in Timor Leste, the hybrid special panels were able to prosecute only 88 of 370 indicted individuals, four of whom were acquitted (Reiger and Wierda, 2006; Drumbl, 2007: 170), and all of those who were convicted benefited from a clemency law in 2008 that released them from serving the remainder of their sentences.[26] These examples illustrate that the 'certainty of punishment' that Beccaria (1764: 58) viewed as essential for effective deterrence to operate is in reality lacking for serious human rights violations. This clearly undermines arguments that rational offenders will be deterred from committing international crimes by the threat of punishment.

The application of deterrence theory to mass atrocity is further challenged by explorations of the extent to which assumptions of perpetrator rationality can be transferred to perpetrators of serious human rights violations (Drumbl, 2007: 171), both among political elites and their foot soldiers. The importance of deterring elites has been highlighted by former legal adviser to the ICTY prosecutor, Payam Akhavan, who makes the point that mass violence results from political choices made by elite leaders who promote and encourage warped views of the other and justify their extermination as an act of communal or national self-defence (2001: 10). In an important and closely argued paper, he reasons that in instances where leaders may be erratic or even psychotic, mass violence is usually linked to acquiring and maintaining power and still requires organized, rational cost-benefit calculations (Akhavan, 2001: 12). For Akhavan, the key aim of international justice is to make 'a credible threat of punishment' part of the rational calculation wherein the political censure and international stigma associated with even being indicted (never mind prosecuted) is factored in as a threat to sustained political power before deliberately unleashing murderous forces (2001: 12).

Of potential relevance to Akhavan's assertions regarding political and military leaders is the criminological literature on white-collar crime that suggests that 'deterrence is more likely to work for the powerful, as they are expected to act rationally' (Savelsberg, 2010: 104). However, the extent to which this applies in the intense context of mass violence or even sustained periods of political violence is explored by some scholars of international politics and international justice. While empirical studies are rare, two examples are instructive. John Wiseman's work on African leaders suggests that even for those who take on such positions, never mind engage in mass violence, the risks are high. Of Wiseman's (1993) database of 485 African leaders who came to power since 1945, over one-half were either killed, imprisoned or exiled. In similar work, Ku and Nzelibe (2006) question the assumptions that those who carry out human rights atrocities do so within a culture of impunity. In an interesting study, they track the fates of those who try to achieve political ends by violence across 17 countries in Africa through 348 coups or attempted coups. Twenty-eight per cent of the leaders involved in such coups were executed or otherwise murdered, 22 per cent were exiled or imprisoned, and another 16 per cent were arrested without any clear outcomes. As they point out, people involved in leading and directing the types of groups that often carry out the worst types of atrocities are already significant 'risk takers' who, given the intrinsic risks of their political and military activities, may be less likely to be deterred by the rigours of international justice which may appear less immediate and less onerous than the lives they already lead, and certainly than is sometimes assumed by international lawyers.

The relevance of deterrence theory to the 'foot soldiers' who do the dirty work of mass violence is, if anything, even more tenuous (Minow, 1998). As Drumbl puts it, do 'genocidal fanatics, industrialized into well-oiled machineries of death, make cost-benefit analysis prior to beginning work?' (2007: 171). Mégret asks the same question with regard to 'the average crazed nationalist purifier or abused child soldier' (2001: 203). Of course those engaged in violence maybe coerced, most obviously in the case of child soldiers, in which case their scope for rational calculation is all the more reduced. In addition, the argument that deterrence in the shape of punishment by a local or international court is a serious issue for those engaged in the suicidal terrorism of al Qaeda, the Taliban or similar groups is if anything even less persuasive. Even for groups who purport to act within a certain moral code in their violent activities, for example by seeking to distinguish between military and civilian targets, the threat of punishment may be of only marginal significance. In the case of Northern Ireland, for example, all new recruits to the IRA were told that the most likely consequences of joining up were either prison or death (McEvoy, 2001; English, 2005).

Certainly from our own experience of having interviewed hundreds of ex-combatants in over a dozen conflicted and transitional societies, the motivation for becoming involved in violence and the types of violence engaged in rarely map onto a neat rational calculation of personal gain versus potential punishment or other negative consequences. Once violence has been initiated, the mores, values and targeting strategies of armed groups or militias, their command structure and levels of discipline, the perceived 'justness' of the political or military cause and a range of other collective and environmental variables will often determine the nature of the 'crimes committed' (Nordstrum, 1997; Coady, 2008; Kalyvas et al., 2008).

In sum, the desire to deter the so-called 'big fish' from future offending in transitional justice is both understandable and laudable. It is hard to argue against making dictators, warlords and the like think twice about their murderous intentions for fear that they may be dragged to The Hague or a similar body at some future point. It is a different matter to claim definitively that such individuals will be so deterred or to claim that the deterrent effect of international punishment is so politically important that it rules out the potential of other arguably more creative and ambitious measures such as properly constituted amnesties.

Although amnesties are today commonly condemned for undermining deterrence and contributing to cultures of impunity, for centuries, proponents of amnesty laws argued that they were necessary to ease social unrest, prevent further human rights violations and encourage belligerent parties to sign peace agreements. This perspective is apparent in the title of the UN's first study of amnesty laws: 'Study on Amnesty Laws and their role in the safeguard and protection of human rights (UN Economic and Social Council, 1985). Although these views are greeted with some scepticism today, they continue to be invoked by some scholars and practitioners (Freeman, 2010), and have been supported by recent experiences in some conflicted and transitional states. For example, to return to the example of the Lord's Resistance Army, following the 2008 collapse of the Juba peace talks that aimed to find a peaceful settlement to the conflict between the Ugandan government and the LRA, concerns have been expressed that the arrest warrants issued by the ICC for the LRA leadership prevented Joseph Kony from signing the comprehensive peace agreement, and this argument was invoked by the LRA negotiators (Greenawalt, 2009: 107). Given the seclusion of Kony, it is impossible to understand accurately his decision to refrain from signing the agreement. However, it is apparent from the LRA's renewed crimes against humanity against civilians in the Democratic Republic of Congo that the arrest warrants have not deterred them from violence.[27]

Although demands for amnesty made by war criminals or repressive leaders in the midst of violence are clearly repugnant, where the threat of ongoing or renewed mass violations is genuine, Freeman has suggested that the international legal duty to *prevent* such horrific crimes, through measures such as amnesty laws, should be balanced against the duty to prosecute under international law. Where amnesty laws can be used to encourage combatants to surrender and disarm, or engage in peace negotiations, they have the potential to make immediate contributions to deterring future violations within the specific state. Furthermore, as the following section will explore, where amnesties are conditioned on individual offenders engaging in restorative and truth recovery processes, they can contribute to the reintegration of former combatants into society as well as broader peacemaking goals.

AMNESTIES, RESTORATION, REHABILITATION AND TRUTH

As noted above, amnesty laws are often framed by those who oppose them as a more or less straightforward denial of justice (Laplante, 2009). However, increasingly within transitional states, the realities of amnesty design and implementation are that they can and do coexist with or are component parts of broader restorative justice processes (Mallinder, 2012b). As is outlined below, we believe that the locating of amnesties within the restorative justice framework (through which we also discuss offender rehabilitation and the role of truth) offers the possibility that rather than denying justice, amnesties can in fact be used to facilitate and enhance compliance with the rule of law, strengthen justice norms as well as assist with broader processes of social and communal 'dealing with the past'.

Before exploring the utility of restorative justice more specifically with regard to the question of amnesties, we would suggest a couple of cautionary notes should be borne in mind. First, restorative justice advocates tend to be energetic, enthusiastic and visionary – all qualities to be admired when a default to cynicism is an easier response, albeit one less likely to provide a useful basis for praxis. That said, it is important not to promise too much in such contexts. As Llewellyn (2006) has argued, in deploying the approaches discussed below, particularly in transitional contexts, restorative justice cannot aim to 'restore' relationships to some idealized prior existing state. Loved ones who have suffered violent deaths cannot be returned, the emotional and psychological trauma experienced by victims (or indeed perpetrators) may never be fully healed, decimated communities cannot be magically rebuilt and so forth. Therefore, the restoration in such contexts may mean something as relatively modest as creating conditions where the fundamental rights of the other can be realized and where relations may be developed between citizens that make possible peaceful and lasting co-existence.

Second, as Chris Cunneen (2007) has argued, the contexts under discussion highlight the central role of the state in efforts to restore relations in such societies. Often the state and its actors have been key abusers in the past and it is important to bear in mind that the state has international legal obligations and will inevitably bear a considerable responsibility in resourcing, regulating and contributing to whatever restorative mechanisms are established.

Third, and relatedly, restorative justice is sometimes accused of narrowing the focus too much onto individual perpetrators, victims and communities. Not only must one bear in mind the role of the state and other powerful actors in past violence – what Mika (1992) and others have called the dangers of 'astructural bias' – but also that in deploying the necessary shorthand of victims and perpetrators, we remain cognisant that such identities are by definition simplified and may well change, coalesce or otherwise mutate in messy realities of transitional societies. This is an issue to which we return in the final section of this chapter.

The breadth of restorative justice theory and practice is discussed elsewhere in this collection by Daly. In this chapter, we are only drawing upon some key themes that are of direct relevance to the question of amnesties. Restorative justice is premised upon the belief that crime or anti-social behaviour is 'a violation of people and relationships' rather than simply law-breaking (Zehr, 2008). As a result, restorative approaches seek to identify the 'harms' caused by the offenders' actions to individual victims, their wider community, as well as the harm caused by the punishment and stigmatization to offenders themselves (Aukerman, 2002; Braithwaite, 2002). Restorative justice traces its roots to indigenous and tribal legal traditions in Australia, New Zealand, Africa, North America and elsewhere (Weitekamp and Kerner, 2002), antecedents that also feature in some of the amnesty ceremonies discussed below. Restorative justice was originally adopted as an element of juvenile justice in New Zealand and Australia from the 1980s onwards (Walgrave, 1998; Morris and Maxwell, 2003), and its practices have become gradually normalized as part of western adult systems albeit predominantly to deal with less serious crimes (Ventura Miller, 2008). In addition, and most pertinently for current purposes, restorative justice is now promoted by some of its most prominent advocates (Braithwaite, 2002; Braithwaite et al., 2010) to deal with the very worst crimes imaginable. Its often controversial and contested deployment to underpin, for example, the Truth and Reconciliation Commission in South Africa or post-genocidal *Gacaca* hearings in Rwanda, or indeed the restorative elements of some amnesty processes in different parts of the world speak directly to the increased political and practical importance of the framework.

In terms of its direct relevance to the topic of amnesties, a number of themes from the restorative justice framework are obvious. First, the fact that restorative justice has become increasingly prominent as a result of a widespread sense of exasperation at the failures of retributive punishment chimes with some of the discussions herein. Second, in terms of offenders, the focus within restorative justice theory and practice upon breaking cycles of offending and facilitating re-entry into the community (discussed below) are clearly among the key aims of any defensible amnesty process. Third, with regard to trying as much as possible to repair the damage done to victims and society, as we will examine further below, the linkage of amnesties to processes such as truth recovery, reparations, social healing and reconciliation is increasingly geared to achieving at least some of those objectives.

With regard to the failings of retribution detailed by many restorative justice scholars, as we have noted, there are strong resonances with some of the arguments outlined above with regard to amnesties. One important caveat is worth noting at this point. Both Daly and Duff have argued that restorative justice can in fact entail some form of 'punishment'. Daly has contended that restorative justice outcomes are 'alternative punishments' and not 'alternatives to punishment' (2000: 36). Her argument is that even well intentioned 'rehabilitative' measures (discussed further below) may well be viewed by those on the receiving end as 'unpleasant, a burden, or an imposition of some sort' and such methods should be viewed as punishment and can form part of a restorative process. Duff takes a similar view describing his approach as 'restoration through retribution' (2003: 393). By this, he too means that perpetrators can be compelled to partake in a mechanism that is at some level painful or burdensome, where the offender undertakes or undergoes a process of being confronted with his past wrongs, of being censured, and of making reparation. While such views are controversial in some restorative justice circles, for our purposes, we are quite comfortable with the notion of amnesties as including impositions upon perpetrators that may be painful or burdensome, which can entail forms of social censure for previous crimes, and which do require some efforts at practical or symbolic repair for the damage that has been done. The key challenge is ensure that this is done in ways that do not humiliate the offender and therefore render him or her liable to re-offend.

That challenge is famously referred to by John Braithwaite as 'reintegrative shaming' – finding mechanisms where offenders are subject to expressions of community disapproval which are in turn followed by 'gestures of reintegration into the community of law-abiding citizens' (1999: 55). The alternative – what Braithwaite terms disintegrative shaming, is a process that 'creates a class of outcasts' (1999: 55). In subsequent work, Braithwaite has explicitly held out the possibility of amnesties which are compatible with restorative justice so long as they contribute to ending a conflict, so long as all stakeholders are given a voice in the amnesty negotiations and so long as those who will benefit are willing to 'show public remorse for their crimes and to commit to the service of the new nation and its people and repair some of the harm they have done' (2002: 203).

Whether amnesties can fulfil Braithwaite's criteria might be best illustrated by some concrete examples. First, with regard to giving all stakeholders a voice in the amnesty negotiations, historically, amnesties such as those passed in Chile, El Salvador, France (in the wake of the Algerian conflict) and elsewhere tended to be crafted by and in the interests of the political or military elites with little if any heed given to the needs of victims (Mallinder, 2008). However, in recent years, the feasibility of meaningful participation by victims and affected communities has become more apparent. In Uganda, for example, the mobilization which led to the Amnesty Act 2000 actually came about in the wake of a lengthy campaign by religious, cultural and political leaders from the region worst affected by the conflict between the Ugandan government and the Lord's Resistance Army (LRA) (Khadiagala, 2001).[28] Once the legislation was introduced, the Amnesty Commission was required to co-ordinate a programme of public sensitization to the amnesty as well as to consider and promote appropriate reconciliation mechanisms in the conflict-affected areas.[29] In Timor Leste, following complaints from local leaders that the process was being dominated by international actors and political elites, the National Council for Timorese Resistance (the UN's local governing partner) created a steering committee comprising government officials, non-governmental organizations and international experts to consult on national reconciliation strategies including the local amnesty (Senier, 2008). In Uruguay, an amnesty that was originally negotiated in the wake of the handover of power by the military in the 1980s has twice been upheld by national plebiscites, most recently in the wake of very lively civil society-led debate in 2009 (Galain Palermo, 2010). In Northern Ireland, local NGOs including some prominent victims' organizations have been at the forefront of promoting ongoing debate and dialogue on whether non-prosecutions should be on offer in return for an inclusive truth process (McEvoy, 2012).

In addition to facilitating stakeholder participation in decisions to enact amnesty legislation, amnesty processes designed along restorative lines can also be specifically designed to include engagement with victims and affected communities during the implementation process. In doing this, such restorative processes can create a forum for the achieving of restorative justice goal of restoring relationships. In South Africa, there was some scope for the presence and participation of victims in the Amnesty Committee hearings (Sarkin, 2004). Victims' rights in these hearings included the right to be notified of the hearings, to provide evidence that was taken into consideration, to give formal testimony, to question amnesty applicants, either personally or through legal representatives, and to make impact statements, either orally or in writing (Du Bois-Pedain, 2007). These statements could include 'their feelings or intuition about the facts, how the events being related had affected them and their families, what their and their families' current needs were, requests for explanations of what had happened and sometimes statements of forgiveness' (Lax, 2004: 236–7). Finally, in addition to the Amnesty Committee's formal hearings, in exceptional cases following a victim request, the hearings were accompanied by 'behind the scenes interpersonal dialogues' between victims and perpetrators, facilitated by TRC staff (Chapman and Van der Merwe, 2007: 11). Overall, while it can be justifiably criticized for a range of failings including excessive legalism and a perceived pressure on victims to forgive (Mallinder, 2009), the South African amnesty process did offer victims more extensive participation rights than had featured in any previous amnesty around the world.

Other examples of amnesties have highlighted the potential for victim and community participation at a localized level, in the towns and villages most affected by past violence. For example, in both Northern Uganda and Timor Leste, traditional healing or reconciliation ceremonies have been used alongside or within amnesty processes. In Uganda, these localized ceremonies may include a cleansing ritual *nyono tong gweno* – the stepping on the egg ceremony – or two justice and reconciliation processes and ceremonies, *mato oput* (drinking of the bitter root) and *gomo tong* (the bending of the spears) (Rose, 2008). These rituals variously require public confession from the perpetrator, participation by victims' families, perpetrators and village elders, and some form of compensation – usually in the guise of livestock or small amounts of money. Although the Amnesty Act 2000 does not require compulsory participation in such ceremonies, some participants have argued that they were under orders from their local LRA commanders to participate, confess their crimes and ask for forgiveness (OHCHR, 2007: 57). In Timor Leste, individuals who wished to benefit from an amnesty had to take part in a Community Reconciliation Process (CRP) facilitated by the truth commission (Senier, 2008). During the CRP community members could listen to the statements of the victims and offenders, ask questions and contribute to decisions on the appropriate form of reparations including conducting carrying out community work (Stanley, 2009).

Of course, amnesty-related mechanisms that facilitate victim or community engagement are not a panacea for all ills. Processes which are in the end of the day designed primarily by elites as part of a political deal always run the risk of instrumentalizing victims or local communities (Madlingozi, 2010). Victims or local communities may have been so damaged by conflict that there are knowledge or capacity gaps that seriously inhibit meaningful participation (Allen, 2007). Other perennial problems of restorative justice remain such as determining how genuine is an apology or an act of remorse, how to prevent perpetrators from promising too much, or how to prevent acts of revenge in the wake of the ceremonies. If anything, these challenges are felt all the more acutely in post-conflict efforts to involve victims and violence-affected communities (Shaw and Waldorf, 2010). That said, as McEvoy (2007) has argued elsewhere, a criminologically informed view of transitional justice is alive to *seeing* challenges and to trying (at least) to meet them rather than simply defaulting to top-down formalism that would simply pass an amnesty act and make no effort to engage with either victims or communities.

The second criterion suggested by Braithwaite is does it 'contribute to ending a war' (2002: 203). We have interpreted this to mean not just 'is the amnesty part of process that brings violent conflict to an end?', but also does it 'work' in terms of 'identifying paths to prevention'?[30] In exploring these ideas in the space available, we will focus on complex issues related to offender or perpetrator 'rehabilitation'. A key element of the goal of restoring relationships is that offenders should be rehabilitated and reintegrated into society rather than being alienated and isolated through penal sanctions (Parmentier et al., 2008: 344). The complex and controversial history of how rehabilitation became a 'dirty word' in criminology, was rebranded, and at least partially re-emerged under different guises is beyond the purview of this chapter (see Ward and Maruna, 2007, for an excellent overview). However, rehabilitation of offenders is a commonly accepted rationale for punishment (Mani, 2002: 32), which is believed to benefit not just individual offenders, but also society by ensuring that the offender will no longer commit crimes (Aukerman, 2002). Although in the wake of mass atrocity, rehabilitation of torturers and war criminals may seem repugnant to large sectors of the population, particularly where it entails decisions to remove or reduce punishments, it nonetheless has become a feature of transitional contexts. In the context of transitional societies, for child soldiers at least, the responsibility to promote rehabilitation has been accepted within international criminal law.[31] For adults in transitional societies, the rehabilitation of former combatants is normally approached through the framework of DDR programmes that entail removing and/or destroying weapons, disbanding armed groups, and returning individuals to civilian life (Patel et al., 2009).

Amnesty laws can play an important role in reintegrating offenders by simply preventing the use of 'isolating punishment mechanisms' (Llewellyn, 2006: 98). However, they can also contribute to creating conditions in which offenders can fulfil their responsibilities to repair the harms they caused. At this basic level, this can entail requiring combatants to surrender their weapons and renounce violence within DDR programmes before they can benefit from the amnesty (Freeman, 2009). In other contexts, such as the Nepalese amnesty in 2006, Maoist guerrillas were paid on a sliding scale according to the weaponry that they surrendered.[32] Although the linkage between amnesties and DDR programmes does vary in terms of sequencing, the nature of the conditions attached and the extent to which any possible 'stick' is present (such as liability to future prosecution for non-compliance) (Waldorf, 2009), it has been broadly approved by the UN. In 2004, the Secretary General issued a report where he encouraged 'carefully crafted amnesties' as part of broader efforts to assist in the return and reintegration of former fighters (UNSC, 2004: para. 32).

The particular challenges with regard to the rehabilitation of those who have benefited from an amnesty mirror some of the debates in rehabilitation studies in general. In particular, the fact that rehabilitation appeared regularly to fail in its stated task of rehabilitating offenders (usually judged by recidivism rates) was crucial to the erosion of its credibility as an underpinning philosophy of punishment. In the realm of transitional justice, there is the beginning of something akin to a 'what works' movement in transitional justice (Van der Merwe et al., 2009; Backer, 2010; Dancy, 2010; Hamber et al., 2010; Olsen et al., 2010; Thoms et al., 2010). It is, however, yet in its infancy and is focused primarily on the contribution of transitional justice mechanisms to the achievement of broader social goals, such democracy and peace. With regards to recidivism rates, we are unaware of any meta-analysis on re-offending rates for those who been granted an amnesty. While there are sporadic local studies which are encouraging[33] we do not believe that there is sufficient robust data to say that amnesties either 'work' or do not 'work' in simple recidivism terms.

As Braithwaite has noted, what is defined as 'working' in a post-conflict context where the overall aim may be something as grand as 'the healing of a nation' is rather more complex than analyzing re-offending rates (2002: 69). While the engagement of former combatants who have benefited from amnesty or amnesty-like provisions in further acts of political violence or even ordinary criminality would certainly undermine the credibility of any settlement, we would argue that this is actually quite a low bar to assess success. A strong critique of DDR and its associated linkage with the notion of 'rehabilitation', and one which resonates with some of the literature on desistance discussed elsewhere in this collection by Maruna and colleagues, is the assumed *passivity* of the offender or ex-combatant in such terminology and practice. In this context – reintegration, resettlement, rehabilitation and the like – are processes that are done *to* or *for* those who attend such programmes. In our fieldwork in Northern Ireland and beyond over the past decade, we have frequently encountered strong resistance among ex-combatants towards such a worldview. Instead, as McEvoy (with Shirlow 2008) has argued elsewhere with regard to the Northern Ireland context where recidivism rates are so remarkably low, success should also be better measured by the extent to which ex-combatants exercise conspicuous agency and leadership in peacemaking work including healing relationships with victims and affected communities. 'Not re-offending' is simply not enough if amnesties are to be adjudged a success.

In the remainder of this section we will explore Braithwaite's final criterion that requires offenders 'to show public remorse for their crimes and to commit to the service of the new nation and its people and repair some of the harm they have done' by considering the link between amnesties and truth recovery. As noted above, although amnesty laws were historically perceived as acts of legal forgetting, in recent years, several truth recovery processes have been empowered to hear testimony from offenders and to offer incentives such as amnesty to encourage them to recount their crimes. Transitional justice scholars and activists commonly argue that such truth recovery is important for preventing a repetition of crimes and contributing to the healing of victims and society (Hayner, 2010; Wiebelhaus-Brahm, 2010). In addition, Parmentier et al. have contended that the process of testifying can potentially benefit offenders by enabling them 'to tell their own story and allow them to gain back the control over their position and their role in the conflict, and later also their place in the community' (2008: 347). From this perspective, the process of testifying may assist with offenders' reintegration into the community, and where their testimony is permitted to address the wider context in which their acts were committed, rather than just the facts of the case; it may contribute to greater social understanding of the causes of the violence. Gustafson argues that listening to such narratives can be important for preventing a recurrence of violence as '[t]hrough understanding the adversary becomes no longer an incomprehensible monster with no discernable connection to us' (1998: 78). Furthermore, through publicly answering for their actions, offenders are subjected to different forms of accountability (Mallinder and McEvoy, 2011). At a more general level, while an agreed version of the truth with regard to past violence may well be unobtainable, the process of assembling, presenting and testing the myriad versions of 'truth' does at least (to borrow a phrase from Ignatieff), 'narrow the range of permissible lies' in such societies (1996: 113). Amnesties are a central part of that process as by creating space for offender accounts, they can contribute to the development of richer, more inclusive narratives on which a shared history can be formed (Theissen, 2009).

The most high profile example of exchanging amnesty for truth occurred as part of the South African Truth and Reconciliation Commission. Under the legislation that established the TRC, perpetrators were required to disclose fully their political offences in order to obtain amnesty (Du Bois-Pedain, 2007). Following a challenge by the family of anti-apartheid activist Steve Biko who was murdered in police custody, the South African Constitutional Court underlined the amnesty's importance for overall truth recovery and national reconciliation in upholding the legality of the amnesty.[34] The procedures of the TRC's Amnesty Committee in receiving and processing offender testimony have been criticized for taking a narrow, legalistic and somewhat inconsistent approach towards what offenders were required to disclose. In turn, the unwillingness of large numbers of offenders to apply or to disclose certain crimes created further gaps in the information revealed (Simpson, 2002; Sarkin, 2004; Chapman and Van der Merwe, 2008). Despite the difficulties with the mandate, resources and proceedings of the Amnesty Committee, it is widely accepted that the process obtained more truth than would have been possible without the offer of amnesty (Sarkin, 2007). In its final report, the TRC argued that even if trials had been pursued, they 'would probably have contributed far less than did the amnesty process towards revealing the truth about what had happened to many victims and their loved ones' (SATRC, 2003: para. 66).

The truth-seeking role of the amnesty was challenged again in a recent case before the South African Constitutional Court that is worth outlining in a little more detail. The case concerned a controversial former member of Umkhonto we Sizwe (MK), the military wing of the African National Congress (ANC), Mr Robert McBride. McBride bombed a bar in Durban in 1986 in which three civilians were killed and 69 people injured, was convicted of murder and sentenced to death. He was subsequently released as part of the political negotiations, and applied for and was granted an amnesty by the TRC (Mallinder, 2009). In 2003, Mr McBride was in line for a senior policing appointment, and the *Citizen* newspaper (which was vehemently opposed to his appointment) published a number of critical articles and editorials referring to him as a murderer and a criminal. Mr McBride sued for defamation, arguing that the amnesty granted to him meant that he could not be so described. The Constitutional Court found against Mr McBride, arguing that 'The statute's aim was national reconciliation, premised on full disclosure of the truth. It is hardly conceivable that its provisions could muzzle truth and render true statements about our history false.'[35] He further concluded that while the amnesty in effect expunged the murder in terms of its impact on Mr McBride's civic right to employment, to run for office and so forth, it did not mean that newspapers or citizens had to conduct discourses on the past as if events had not happened. In short, the linkage of the amnesty to truth recovery in this context did not require or facilitate 'commanded forgetting' (as Ricoeur has suggested), quite the opposite. Rather, amnesties were one element of a broader architecture which while designed to achieve national reconciliation, did not impede a robust 'warts and all' public discussion about a violent past.

In sum, we would argue that viewed from the restorative perspective, amnesties can have a key role to play in transitional contexts. Carefully designed restorative amnesties can help foster the rebuilding of relationships shattered by mass violence, by facilitating an inclusive, participative dialogue both on the need for amnesty and on the implementation of amnesty processes. In particular, where the granting of amnesty is conditional upon individual offender participation in such processes they can contribute to offender rehabilitation by offering an alternative to penal sanctions, and by creating a forum for offender narratives to be told and incorporated into national truth recovery projects. In such contexts, rather than being a denial of justice, amnesty laws can complement restorative justice principles and objectives.

CONCLUSION: AMNESTIES AND THE GOVERNANCE OF MERCY

> The quality of mercy is not strained.
> It droppeth as the gentle rain from heaven
> Upon the place beneath. It is twice blest:
> It blesseth him that gives and him that takes.
> Tis mightiest in the mightiest; it becomes
> The throned monarch better than his crown.
> His sceptre shows the force of temporal power,
> The attribute to awe and majesty
> Wherein doth sit the dread and fear of kings.
> But mercy is above this sceptered sway.
> (Shakespeare, 1596)

In sketching some key elements of the relationship between amnesties, punishment and transitional societies, we are conscious that there are a range of issues that warrant closer examination. We have charted elsewhere the relationship between amnesties and accountability (Mallinder and McEvoy, 2011) but equally there is rich potential in further viewing amnesties through the prism of concepts such as risk, legitimacy, memory and other major themes in the social sciences and this we plan to do in future publications. In the space available in these concluding remarks, we would like to focus now upon the notion of mercy. As noted above, the historical antecedents of amnesties can be traced directly to this notion of mercy. We are drawn to the concept because of this historical linkage but also because it is an idea that points to the intersection between punishment, governance and law. As such, it offers rich potential for a more fully theorized account of the multiple functions of contemporary amnesties that we can at least point to here.

As noted above, much of the literature on mercy begins with the premise that it is closely associated with notions of state sovereignty and the exercise of state power. Schmitt, for example, refers explicitly to pardons and amnesties as examples of the 'omnipotence of the modern law giver' (1985: 38). Similarly, Weber describes mercy as combining rigid tradition with 'a sphere of free discretion and the grace of the ruler' (1970: 216). Douglas Hay's (1975) seminal work on late 18th and early 19th century England charted the relationship between England's infamous 'bloody code' in which the range and severity of its penal sanctions made its laws appear the most punitive in Europe. However, such excess was tempered in practice by a calibrated deployment of mercy so that such 'benevolence' was at least as important as terror in protecting the interests of the ruling elites. While the transition from absolute monarchy towards democracy has somewhat obscured the visibility of power in the exercise of mercy, as Strange has argued, it ultimately expresses 'the politics of rule' (Strange, 2001a: 5).

While we are drawn to the link between amnesties and the politics of rule, such relations are no longer (if indeed they ever were) an easy matter to chart. Certainly while amnesties remain intimately bound up with state power, the power relations at work in contemporary amnesties are much more complex than simply an expression of the will of the sovereign. Amnesties usually come in the wake of a direct challenge to the state's monopoly on the use of force. In such contexts, the exercise of power may be fragile, contingent and certainly contested. Indeed, in such contexts, amnesties may be more an effort to garner or consolidate state power rather than an expression of existing power.

Amnesties, like punishment, are arguably a particularly important realm of governance. As Garland (2001), Simon (2007), Loader and Walker (2007) and others have demonstrated in different ways over the last decade, it is precisely because notions of punishment, crime or security are so central to contemporary questions of governance that they have come to occupy an excessive space in the social, political and cultural lives of many societies. To paraphrase Simon (2007: 10), crime and related discourses on how to deal with it are much more than 'one social problem' among many in the modern era. Instead, these realms involve a range of actors and provide techniques, rationales and visions for governance that map onto much broader understandings of social and political relations in the material and 'imagined communities' in which they are located (Anderson, 1991). They offer points of resistance, acquiescence, mobilization and realignment in horizontal and vertical power relations, which are often much more subtle than the will of the most powerful political and military actors on the stage.

Amnesties, precisely because they are seen by some as an endorsement of past crimes, a denial of justice and a potential threat to future security (or because they encourage cultures of impunity, Laplante [2009]), occupy a similarly complex space in the political and social lives of many of the societies in which they are introduced. Decisions on whether or not an amnesty should be introduced; whose actions can be amnestied and whose excluded; the definitional wranglings on whether amnesty beneficiaries are combatants, perpetrators, criminals, heroes or victims; questions of the linkage to truth, reparations and all of the other discussions outlined above speak directly to fundamentally contested versions of the past and indeed often the future of transitional societies.

Mapping the outworkings of an amnesty in South Africa, Sierra Leone, Uganda or indeed Northern Ireland therefore requires a close grasp of local material and 'imagined' politics, a nuanced understanding of the rules (discussed below), and a feel for the key actors and in particular what Foucault (2004) referred to as grasping the 'technologies of the self' (the ways that different people and groups see themselves as both exercisers and subjects of power).[36] The design and implementation of amnesties can no longer be caricatured as the last act of the outgoing general as he signs the sweeping amnesty to protect now and forever all loyal assassins and toenail pullers just before departing the presidential palace. As well as being fettered by law, the shape and content of amnesties is also influenced by a myriad of other factors including the views and input of the international community; the level of organization of victims, ex-combatants, human rights activists and other civil society actors; the particular history of conflict; the relations between key political parties; the socio-economic context and various other factors. In short, understanding amnesties as mercy is useful because it directs us to the intersection between law, punishment and governance but it also demands a fully rounded grasp of the local power relations in order to do it justice.

Finally with regard to the 'rules', as David Garland reminds us in his panoramic discussion of punishment and its multiple meanings, at its core, punishment is 'the legal process whereby violators of the criminal law are condemned and sanctioned in accordance with specified legal categories and procedures' (1990: 17). Amnesties, as processes by which criminal and/or civil liability is extinguished by the state, are by definition, creatures of law. Amnesties usually require legislation. They must be compliant with international law (while acknowledging that this is somewhat less declaratory than is sometimes claimed). They often entail the creation of some kind of commission that must make decisions against declared criteria, weigh evidence and hear testimony; they may be subject to judicial scrutiny, and so forth. In short, the institutional requirements of establishing an amnesty process may be viewed as part of what Bourdieu (1987) has termed 'the force of law', its 'pull' wherein aspects of social or political life are shaped by what he terms the 'juridical field'. Although as commentators such as De Sousa Santos (2002) have argued this 'creeping legalism' is certainly not an unadulterated force for good, in the case of amnesties that were traditionally an example par excellence of unfettered state power, it is hard to argue against some checks and balances, or requirement for forms of restoration where previously there were none. More broadly, by legalizing this sphere, however loosely, one at least creates a structure or a process whereby those who would have hitherto enjoyed either complete de facto or de jure impunity from *any* legal process must subject themselves to a legal framework. Properly constituted, amnesties bring law to a previously *lawless* domain.

NOTES

1 Transitional or conflicted jurisdictions which have considered amnesty or amnesty-like measures studied by the authors have included Argentina, South Africa, Uruguay, Uganda, Colombia, Rwanda, Sierra Leone, Israel/Palestine and Northern Ireland. This work was variously funded by the Joseph Rowntree Charitable Trust, Atlantic Philanthropies and most recently the AHRC (Grant No. AHRC AH/E008984/1 Beyond Legalism: Amnesties, Transition and Conflict Transformation).

2 Although as we and others have argued, one can see an increased 'mainstreaming' of transitional justice discourses in settled democracies such as Ireland, Canada, Australia and even the USA where variants of truth commissions have been established or called for to deal with the institutional abuse of children, the legacy of colonialism, racism and even the abuses perpetrated by the Bush administration under the auspices of the War on Terror (Mallinder and McEvoy, 2010).

3 For a more detailed analysis of this phenomenon, see McEvoy (2007), and McEvoy and McGregor (2008).

4 As we have detailed elsewhere, in 2006 the United Nations estimated that the cost of 'a serious truth commission' is usually US$5–10 million. After significant lobbying and legal activism by victims' campaigners in South Africa, the reparations paid to victims of apartheid totalled US$71,375,000. In comparison, the total cost of the International Criminal Tribunal for the Former Yugoslavia (ICTY) up until 2011 was US$1,887,385,922. The International Criminal Tribunal for Rwanda (ICTR) appears to have stopped reporting their running costs in their annual reports from 2000 when the figure for that year was US$86,154,900. The budget for 2010/11 has risen to US$245,295,800. Since it was established in 2002, and having initiated a total of 12 cases, the

International Criminal Court has to date cost a total of €732,647,100. For further discussion, see Mallinder and McEvoy (2011).

5 The treaties were signed by the Holy Roman Emperor, Ferdinand III of the House of Habsburg, the Kingdoms of Spain, France, Sweden, the Dutch Republic, the Princes of the Holy Roman Empire, and sovereigns of the Free Imperial Cities. They followed a 30-year conflict within the Holy Roman Empire (involving at different times most of the countries of Europe) and the 80-year war between Spain and what is now the Netherlands. The treaties are widely viewed within political sciences as a key moment in the development of what we now recognise as the nation state. The notion of statehood which emerged, sometimes referred to as the Westphalian state, is usually defined by the sovereignty of the state being exercised within its national boundaries, the state has a monopoly on the use of force within those boundaries and a system of international relations which is based on the mutual recognition of such sovereignty. See Caporaso (2000).

6 The interplay between practical politics, claims-making and 'stateliness' has been well illustrated in Libya. Both the pro-Gaddafi and the rebel forces have proclaimed separate amnesties as part of their respective efforts to wean troops away from their counterparts while in turn demonstrating that they are the legitimate state authority in Libya. See e.g. 'Libya offers amnesty to soldiers who defected', *Radio Free Europe* (14 March 2011); 'Libya's opposition offers amnesty to Gaddafi regime', *Financial Times* (28 May 2011).

7 However, although the majority of amnesty laws apply to past crimes, Freeman highlights that 'there are many examples of defection-orientated amnesties, which are amnesties issued during the conflict as a device to encourage rebels, paramilitaries or terrorist organisations to abandon their cause, disarm and demobilize. By design, such amnesties do not apply only to past crimes. In countries such as Uganda, Algeria, Colombia and Afghanistan, such amnesties have been adopted, in each case allowing access to the law's benefits for eligible offences committed after the amnesty's entry into force' (Freeman, 2009: 16).

8 For a more detailed discussion, see Mallinder (2008).

9 *The Prosecutor* v. *Georges Anderson Nderubumwe Rutaganda* (Judgement and Sentence), ICTR-96–3-T, International Criminal Tribunal for Rwanda (ICTR), 6 December 1999, para. 456.

10 'The large scale violence of the 1990s appears to be typically accompanied by a surplus of range, an excess of hatred that produces untold forms of degradation and violation, both to the body and the being of the victim; maimed and tortured bodies, burned and raped persons, disembowelled women, hacked and amputated children, sexual humiliation of every type. What are we to do with this surplus, which has frequently been enacted in public actions, among friends and neighbours, and is no longer conducted in the covert ways in which the degradation of group warfare used to occur in the past?' (Appadurai, 2006: 10)

11 For further discussions on the distinction between retribution and revenge, see Nozick (1981).

12 See e.g. *Azanian Peoples Organisation (AZAPO)* v. *The President of the Republic of South Africa*, Many 1996, CCT 17/96 (8) BCLR 1015.

13 Convention on the Prevention and Punishment of the Crime of Genocide 1948, 78 UNTS 1021, art 2.

14 Each of the four Geneva Conventions requires states parties to respond to 'grave breaches' by searching for, prosecuting and punishing perpetrators of grave breaches, unless they extradite them for purposes of trial by another state party. Additional Protocol I extends the same obligations to punish to a wide range of 'grave breaches'.

15 Protocol Additional to the Geneva Conventions of 12 August 1949, and relating to the Protection of Victims of Non-International Armed Conflicts, 1977 art 6(5).

16 See e.g. 'Co-Chairs Of Sri Lanka Peace Process Urge Tamil Tigers To End Hostilities', RTT News (3 February 2009); 'Lay down arms, surrender – European Parliament tells LTTE', *The Colombo Times* (6 February 2009); 'U.N. Security Council Asks LTTE To Surrender', RTT News (22 April 2009).

17 See e.g. World Bank, 'Project Information Document: Uganda Emergency Demobilization and Reintegration Project' (23 January 2008); 'World Bank offers over sh3 billion to resettle former ADF, LRA Rebels' New Vision (Kampala 19 August 2008).

18 The ICC issued a warrant for the arrest of Kony and four other senior members of the LRA in 2005. The charges include crimes against humanity, murder, enslavement, sexual enslavement, rape, pillaging, inducing rape and forced enlisting of children into the rebel ranks.

19 For example, the ICTY has recognised achieving general and specific deterrence as one of the purposes that it can take into account when imposing sentences. See e.g. *Prosecutor* v. *Tihomir Blaskic*, Case No. IT-95–14-A, Judgement, para 678 (ICTY Ap. Ch. 29 July 2004).

20 UNSC Resolution 827, UN Doc S/Res/827 (1993) Preamble.

21 Rome Statute of the International Criminal Court (1998), 2187 UNTS 90, Preamble.

22 The *Prosecutor* v. *Georges Anderson Nderubumwe Rutaganda* (Judgement and Sentence), ICTR-96–3-T, International Criminal Tribunal for Rwanda (ICTR), 6 December 1999, para 456.

23 UNSC Resolution 1970, UN Doc S/Res/1970 (2011).

24 Loi relative à la mise hors-la-loi de la clique du Kampuchea democratique, art. 1 (1994) (Cambodia).

25 UN Department of Peacekeeping Operations, Disarmament, Demobilisation and Reintegration of Ex-Combatants in a Peacekeeping Environment: Principles and Guidelines (UN 1999) Annex 2B, 109.

26 Presidential Decree N° 53/2008, Presidential Pardon, art 2 (20 May 2008).

27 See e.g. 'UN says LRA Still Killing Civilians in DRC', *Voice of America News* (2 February 2010).

28 One of the key reasons behind the amnesty mobilization campaign in the Acholi region of Northern Uganda was that many of the perpetrators were child soldiers who had been kidnapped and conscripted into the LRA.

29 Interview with James Nyeko, Acholi Religious Leaders Peace Initiative (Gulu, 7 May 2008); Interview with Fr Joseph Okumu (Gulu, 8 May 2008); and interview with Haji B. Ganyana-Miiro, Amnesty Commissioner (Kampala, 9 May 2008).

30 The authors note, however, that recidivism rates are only one indicator than can be used to determine the impact or success of amnesty programmes. Other indicators may relate to particular features of specific amnesty processes or the needs of a transitional state. For example, the impact of the recent amnesty processes for insurgents in the Niger Delta has been discussed primarily in terms of levels of oil production. Alternatively, they could relate to procedural aspects of an amnesty process, such as were amnesty applications dealt with promptly, independently and transparently. Finally, as with the growing transitional justice literature on impact assessment, the success of amnesties could be measured in relation to broader social goals, such as peace and democracy.

31 e.g., Article 7 of the Statute of the Special Court of Sierra Leone states if 'any person who was ... between 15 and 18 years of age' when they committed their alleged crimes comes before the Court 'he or she shall be treated with dignity and a sense of worth, taking into account his or her young age and the desirability of promoting his or her rehabilitation, reintegration into and assumption of a constructive role in society', see SCSL Statute, Art 7.

32 Binaj Gurubacharya, 'Nepal offers amnesty, cash, land to surrendering rebels ahead of planned blockade', Associated Press (Kathmandu 13 March 2006); 'Nepal Government offers surrender bait as Maoists start blockade', Indo-Asian News Service (Kathmandu 14 March 2006). This amnesty was not implemented as Maoists declined to take advantage of the offer.

33 In Northern Ireland, for example, although there are debates as to whether it qualified as an amnesty, approximately 450 politically motivated prisoners belonging to organizations on ceasefire were released on license within two years of the signing of the Good Friday Agreement. As of July 2011, 23 prisoners have had their licences suspended and were returned to prison, 10 for alleged involvement in politically motivated offences, and 13 for involvement in 'ordinary' crime. This recidivism rate, just over 5 per cent after 13 years compares to one of 48 per cent for ordinary offenders within two years (see further Shirlow and McEvoy, 2008). Again, however, it should be stressed that these were prisoners rather than combatants 'still in the field' who had benefited from provisions of the Agreement.

34 *Azanian Peoples Organisation (AZAPO) and others* v. *the President of the Republic of South Africa and others* 1996 (4) SA 671 (CC), para 17.

35 See e.g. *Citizen* v *McBride*, Case CCT 23/10, Judgement of the Constitutional Court of South Africa, [April 2011] ZACC 11.

36 As Foucault argues, 'all jurists try to do the same thing, as their problem is to discover how a multiplicity of individuals and wills can be shaped into a single will or even a single body that is supposedly animated by a soul known as sovereignty.' Instead we should 'study the multiple, peripheral bodies, the bodies that are constituted as subject by power-effects' (2004: 29).

REFERENCES

Akhavan, Payam (2001) 'Beyond impunity: can international criminal justice prevent future atrocities', *American Journal of International Law,* 95 (1): 7–31.

Akhavan, Payam (2009) 'Are international criminal tribunals a disincentive to peace? Reconciling judicial romanticism with political realism', *Human Rights Quarterly*, 31: 624–54.

Allen, Tim (2007) 'The international criminal court and the invention of traditional justice in Northern Uganda', *Politique Africaine*, 107: 147–66.

Amann, Diane (2002) 'Group mentality, expressivism, and genocide', *International Criminal Law Review,* 2 (2): 93–143.

Anderson, Benedict (1991) *Imagined Communities: Reflections on the Origins and Spread of Nationalism.* London: Verso.

Apel, Robert and Nagin, Daniel (2010) 'General deterrence: a review of recent evidence', in J. Q. Wilson and J. Petersilla (eds), *Crime and Public Policy.* Oxford: Oxford University Press, pp. 411–36.

Appadurai, Arjun (2006) *Fear of Small Numbers: An Essay on the Geography of Anger.* Durham NC: Duke University Press.

Arendt, Hannah (1973) *The Origins of Totalitarianism.* New York: Harvest Books.

Arendt, Hannah (1992) *Hannah Arendt, Karl Jaspers: Correspondence 1926–1969.* San Diego, CA: Harcourt Brace Jovanovich.

Arthur, Paige (2009) 'How "transitions" reshaped human rights: a conceptual history of transitional justice', *Human Rights Quarterly*, 31 (2): 321–67.

Aukerman, Miriam J. (2002) 'Extraordinary evil, ordinary crime: a framework for understanding transitional justice', *Harvard Human Rights Journal*, 15: 39–97.

Backer, David (2003) 'Civil society and transitional justice: possibilities, patterns and prospects', *Journal of Human Rights*, 2 (3): 297–313.

Backer, David (2010) 'Watching a bargain unravel? A panel study of victims' attitudes about transitional justice in Cape Town, South Africa', *International Journal of Transitional Justice*, 4(3): 443–56.

Beccaria, Cesaria (1764 [1963]) *On Crimes and Punishment.* Indianapolis, IA: Hacket.

Beigbeder, Yves (2005) *International Justice against Impunity: Progress and New Challenges.* Leiden: Martinus Nijhoff.

Bell, Christine (2008) *On the Law of Peace: Peace Agreements and the Lex Pacificatoria.* Oxford: Oxford University Press.

Bell, Christine (2009) 'Transitional justice, interdisciplinarity and the state of the "field" or "non-field"', *International Journal of Transitional Justice*, 3: 5–27.

Bentham, Jeremy (1830) *The Rationale of Punishment.* London: Robert Heward.

Binningsbø, Helga Malmin, Elster, Jon and Gates, Scott (2005) 'Civil war and transitional justice, 1946–2003: a dataset', paper prepared for presentation at the Transitional Justice and Civil War Settlements workshop in Bogotá, Colombia.

Bourdieu, Pierre (1987) 'The force of law: toward a sociology of the juridical field', *Hastings Law Journal* 36: 805–13.

Bourdon, William (1999) 'Amnesty', in Roy Gutman and David Rieff (eds), *Crimes of War: What the Public Should Know.* Available at http://www.crimes-ofwar.org/a-z-guide/amnesty/ (accessed 23 March 2012).

Braithwaite, John (1999) 'Restorative justice: assessing optimistic and pessimistic accounts', *Crime and Justice* 25: 1–107.

Braithwaite, John (2002) *Restorative Justice and Responsive Regulation.* Oxford: Oxford University Press.

Braithwaite, John, Braithwaite, Valerie, Cookson, Michael and Dunn, Leah (2010) *Anomie and Violence: Non-truth and Reconciliation in Indonesian Peacebuilding.* Canberra: Australian National University Press.

Branch, Adam (2007) 'Uganda's civil war and the politics of ICC intervention', *Ethics and International Affairs*, 21 (2): 179–98.

Caporaso, James (ed.) (2000) *Continuity and Change in the Westphalian Order.* Oxford: Blackwell.

Cassel, Douglass (1996) 'Lessons from the Americas: guidelines for international response to amnesties for atrocities', *Law and Contemporary Problems*, 59: 197–230.

Cassese, Antonio (1998) 'Reflections on international criminal justice', *Modern Law Review*, 61 (1): 1–10.

Cayley, A. (2008) 'The prosecutor's strategy in seeking the arrest of Sudanese President Al Bashir on charges of genocide', *Journal of International Criminal Justice*, 6 (5): 829–40.

Chapman, Audrey and Van der Merwe, Hugo (eds) (2008) *Truth and Reconciliation in South Africa: Did the TRC Deliver?* Philadelphia, PA: University of Pennsylvania Press.

Coady, C.A.J. (2008) *Morality and Political Violence.* Cambridge: Cambridge University Press.

Collins, Cath (2010) *Post-transitional Justice: Human Rights Trials in Chile and El Salvador.* Philadelphia, PA: Pennsylvania State University Press.

Crouch, Jeffrey (2009) *The Presidential Pardon Power.* Lawrence: University of Kansas Press.

Cryer, Robert (2010) 'International criminal law', in Malcolm D. Evans (ed.), *International Law*, 3rd edn. Oxford: Oxford University Press. pp. 752–83.

Cullinan, Sarah (2001) *Torture Survivors' Perceptions of Reparation.* Available at: http://www.redress.org/downloads/reparation/TSPR.pdf (accessed 19 July 2011).

Cunneen, Chris (2007) 'Exploring the relationship between reparations, the gross violation of human rights and restorative justice', in Dennis Sullivan and Larry Tift (eds), *Handbook of Restorative Justice.* London: Routledge. pp. 355–69.

Daly, Kathleen (2000) 'Revisiting the relationship between retributive and restorative justice', in H. Strang and J. Braithwaite (eds), *Restorative Justice: Philosophy to Practice.* Aldershot: Dartmouth. pp. 33–54.

Dancy, Geoff (2010) 'Impact assessment, not evaluation: defining a limited role for positivism in the study of transitional justice' *International Journal of Transitional Justice*, 4(3): 355–376.

De Greiff, Pablo (ed.) (2006) *The Handbook of Reparations.* Oxford: Oxford University Press.

De Guzman, M.M. (2008) 'Justice in Cambodia: past, present, and future', *Criminal Law Forum*, 19 (2): 335–51.

De Sousa Santos, Boaventura (2002) *Towards a New Legal Common Sense*. London: Butterworths.

Douglas, Lawrence (2001) *The Memory of Judgment: Making Law and History in the Trials of the Holocaust*. New Haven, CT: Yale University Press.

Drumbl, Mark A. (2007) *atrocity, Punishment and International Law*. Cambridge: Cambridge University Press.

Du Bois-Pedain, Antje (2007) *Transitional Amnesty in South Africa*. Cambridge: Cambridge University Press.

Duff, Anthony (2001) *Punishment, Communication and Community*. Oxford: Oxford University Press.

Duff, Anthony (2003) 'Restoration and retribution', in Andrew von Hirsch, Julian Roberts, Anthony E. Bottoms, Kent Roach and Mara Schiff (eds), *Restorative Justice and Criminal Justice: Competing or Reconcilable Paradigms*. Oxford: Hart Publishing. pp. 43–60.

Durkheim, Emile (1933) *The Division of Labour in Society*, trans. G. Simpson. New York: Free Press.

English, Richard (2005) *Armed Struggle: The History of the IRA*. Oxford: Oxford University Press.

Foucault, Michel (1977) *Discipline and Punish*. London: Allen Lane.

Foucault, Michel (2004) *Society Must be Defended: Lectures at the Collège de France 1975–1976*, trans. D. Macey. Harmondsworth: Penguin.

Freeman, Mark (2009) 'Amnesties and DDR programs', in Ana Cutter Patel, Pablo de Greiff and Lars Waldorf (eds), *Disarming the Past: Transitional Justice and Ex-Combatants*. New York: Social Science Research Council. pp. 36–85.

Freeman, Mark (2010) *Necessary Evils: Amnesties and the Search for Justice*. Cambridge: Cambridge University Press.

Galain Palermo, Pablo (2010) 'The prosecution of international crimes in Uruguay', *International Criminal Law Review*, 10 (4): 601–18.

Garland, David (1990) *Punishment and Modern Society*. Oxford: Oxford University Press.

Garland, David (2001) *The Culture of Control*. Oxford: Oxford University Press.

Greenawalt, Alexander K.A. (2009) 'Complementarity in crisis: Uganda, alternative justice, and the international criminal court', *Virginia Journal of International Law*, 50: 107–62.

Gustafson, Carrie (1998) 'International criminal courts: some dissident views on the continuation of war by penal means', *Houston Journal of International Law*, 21: 51.

Hamber, Brandon, Ševčenko, Liz and Naidu, Ereshnee (2010) 'Utopian dreams or practical possibilities? The challenges of evaluating the impact of memorialization in societies in transition', *International Journal of Transitional Justice*, 4 (3): 397–420.

Hart, H.L.A. (1968) *Punishment and Responsibility*. Oxford: Oxford University Press.

Hay, Douglas (1975) 'Property, authority and the criminal law', in D. Hay, P. Linebaugh, J.G. Rule, E.P. Thompson and C. Wilson (eds), *Albion's Fatal Tree*. London: Allen Lane. pp. 17–63.

Hayner, Priscilla B. (2010) *Unspeakable Truths: Transitional Justice and the Challenge of Truth Commissions*, 2nd edn. Abingdon: Routledge.

Hegel, G.W.F. (1820) *Hegel's Philosophy of Nature*. Oxford: Oxford University Press.

Henckaerts, J.M. and Doswald-Beck, L. (eds) (2005), *Customary International Humanitarian Law. Vol 1: Rules*. Cambridge: Cambridge University Press.

Henman, Ralph (2004) 'Conceptualizing access to justice and victims' rights in international sentencing', *Social and Legal Studies*, 13 (1): 27–56.

Ignatieff, Michael (1996) 'Articles of faith', *Index on Censorship*, 25 (5): 110–22.

Ignatieff, Michael (2003) *Human Rights as Politics and Idolatry*. Princeton, NJ: Princeton University Press.

Jacobs, Bruce (2010) 'Deterrence and deterabilty', *Criminology*, 48 (2): 417–41.

Kalyvas, Stathis, Shapiro, Ian and Tarek Masoud (eds) (2008) *Order, Conflict and Violence*. Cambridge: Cambridge University Press.

Kant, Immanuel (1785) *The Metaphysics of Morals*. London: Routledge Classics.

Kant, Immanuel (1796–7) *The Philosophy of Law: An Exposition of the Fundamental Principles of Jurisprudence as a Science of Right*. (Reprinted 2002, Union NJ: The Lawbook Exchange Ltd.)

Keller, Linda M. (2008) 'Achieving peace with justice: the international criminal court and Ugandan alternative justice mechanisms', *Connecticut Journal of International Law*, 23 (2): 209.

Kelsall, Tim (2009) *Culture under Cross-Examination: International Justice and the Special Court for Sierra Leone*. Cambridge: Cambridge University Press.

Kennedy, David (2008) *Deterrence and Crime Prevention: Reconsidering the Prospect of Sanction*. New York: Routledge.

Keren, Michael and Herwig, Holger (eds) (2009) *War Memory and Popular Culture: Essays on Modes of Remembrance and Commemoration*. Jefferson, NC: McFarland and Co.

Khadiagala, Gilbert M. (2001) *The Role of the Acholi Religious Leaders Peace Initiative (ARLPI) in Peace Building in Northern Uganda*. Washington, DC: USAID.

Kim, Hunjoon and Sikkink, Kathryn (2010) 'Explaining the deterrence effect of human rights prosecutions for transitional countries', *International Studies Quarterly*, 54: 939–63.

Klarin, Mirko, (2009) 'The impact of the ICTY on public opinion in the former Yugoslavia', *Journal of International Criminal Justice*, 7: 89–96.

Ku, Julian and Nzelibe, Jide (2006) 'Do international criminal tribunals deter or exacerbate humanitarian atrocities?', *Washington Law Review*, 84 (4): 777–833.

Laplante, Lisa (2009) 'Outlawing amnesty: the return of criminal justice in transitional justice schemes', *Virginia Journal of International Law*, 49 (4): 915–84.

Lax, Ilan (2004) 'Amnesty, reparation and the object of reconciliation in the context of South Africa's truth and reconciliation commission,' in Erik Doxtader and Charles Villa-Vicencio (eds), *To Repair the Irreparable: Reparation and Reconstruction in South Africa*. Claremont: David Philip Publishers. pp. 224–41.

Llewellyn, Jennifer J. (2006) 'Restorative justice in transitions and beyond: the justice potential of truth telling mechanisms for post-peace accord societies,' in Tristan Anne Borer (ed.), *Telling the Truths: Truth Telling and Peace Building in Post-Conflict Societies*. Notre Dame: University of Notre Dame Press. pp. 83–113.

Loader, Ian and Walker, Neil (2007) *Civilizing Security*. Cambridge: Cambridge University Press.

Lutz, Ellen and Sikkink, Kathryn (2001) 'The justice cascade: the evolution and impact of foreign human rights trials in Latin America', *Chicago Journal of International Law*, 2: 1–34.

Madlingozi, Tshepo (2010) 'On transitional justice entrepreneurs and the production of victims', *Journal of Human Rights Practice*, 2 (2): 208–28.

Mallinder, Louise (2008) *Amnesty, Human Rights and Political Transitions: Bridging the Peace and Justice Divide*. Oxford: Hart Publishing.

Mallinder, Louise (2009) 'Indemnity, amnesty, pardon and prosecution guidelines in South Africa', working paper from Beyond Legalism: Amnesties, Transition and Conflict Transformation project, Queen's University Belfast.

Mallinder, Louise (2010) 'Amnesties', in William A. Schabas and Nadia Bernaz (eds), *Routledge Handbook of International Criminal Law*. Abingdon: Routledge. pp. 419–34.

Mallinder, Louise (2012a) 'Peacebuilding, the rule of law and the duty to prosecute: what role remains for amnesties?', in Faria Medjouba (ed.), *Building Peace in Post-Conflict States*. London: British Institute of International and Comparative Law.

Mallinder, Louise (forthcoming 2012b) 'Amnesties in the pursuit of reconciliation, peacebuilding and restorative justice', in Daniel Philpott and Jennifer Llewellyn (eds), *Restorative Justice, Reconciliation and Peacebuilding*. Oxford: Oxford University Press.

Mallinder, Louise (forthcoming 2012c) 'Amnesties' Challenge to the Global Accountability Norm? Interpreting Regional and International Trends in Amnesty Enactment', in Leigh A. Payne and Francesca Lessa (eds), *Amnesty in the Age of Human Rights Accountability: Comparative and International Perspectives*. Cambridge: Cambridge University Press.

Mallinder, Louise and McEvoy, Kieran (2010) 'Knowledge construction and the mainstreaming of transitional justice: truth, memory and dealing with the past in "settled democracies"', paper presented at International Studies Association Annual Conference, New Orleans.

Mallinder, Louise and McEvoy, Kieran (2011) 'Rethinking amnesties: atrocity, accountability and impunity in post-conflict societies', *Contemporary Social Science: The Journal of the Academy of Social Science*, 6 (1): 107–28.

Mani, Rama (2002) *Beyond Retribution: Seeking Justice in the Shadows of War*. London: Polity Press.

McEvoy, Kieran (2001) *Paramilitary Imprisonment in Northern Ireland: Resistance, Management and Release*. Oxford: Oxford University Press.

McEvoy, Kieran (2007) 'Beyond legalism: towards a thicker understanding of transitional justice', *Journal of Law and Society*, 34 (4): 411–40.

McEvoy, Kieran (2012) *The Trouble with Truth: Struggles with the Past in Northern Ireland*. London: Routledge.

McEvoy, Kieran and McGregor, Lorna (eds) (2008) *Transitional Justice from Below: Grassroots Activism and the Struggle for Change*. Oxford: Hart Publishing.

Mégret, Frédéric (2001) 'Three dangers for the international criminal court: a critical look at a consensual project', *Finnish Yearbook of International Law*, 12: 195–247.

Mika, Harry (1992) 'Mediation interventions and restorative justice: responding to the astructural bias', in H. Messmer and H.U. Otto (eds), *Restorative Justice on Trial: Pitfalls and Potentials of Victim-Offender Mediation – International Research Perspectives*. Dordrecht: Kluwer. pp. 559–68.

Minow, Martha (1998) *Between Vengeance and Forgiveness: Facing History after Genocide and Mass Violence*. Uckfield: Beacon Press.

Morris, Alison and Maxwell, Gabriel (2003) 'Restorative justice in New Zealand: family group conferences as a case study', in G. Johnstone (ed.), *A Restorative Justice Reader*. Cullompton: Willan. pp. 201–11.

Nordstrum, Carol (1997) *A Different Kind of War Story*. Philadelphia, PA: University of Pennsylvania Press.

Nozick, Robert (1981) *Philosophical Explanations*. Cambridge, MA: Harvard University Press.

O'Shea, Andreas (2002) *Amnesty for Crime in International Law and Practice*. The Hague: Kluwer Law International.

Office of the UN High Commissioner for Human Rights (OHCHR) (2007) *Making Peace our Own: Victims' Perceptions of Accountability, Reconciliation and Transitional Justice in Northern Uganda*. Gulu: OHCHR.

Olsen, Tricia, Payne, Leigh and Reiter, Andrew (2010) *Transitional Justice in Balance: Comparing Processes, Weighing Efficacy*. Washington, DC: United States Institute of Peace Press.

Orentlicher, Diane F. (1991) 'Settling accounts: the duty to prosecute human rights violations of a prior regime', *Yale Law Journal*, 100 (8): 2537–615.

Parker, Robert (2001) 'Fighting the siren's song: the problem of amnesty in historical and contemporary perspective', *Acta Juridica Hungaria*, 42 (1/2): 69–89.

Parmentier, Stephan, Vanspauwen, Kris and Weitekamp, Elmar (2008) 'Dealing with the legacy of mass violence: changing lenses to restorative justice', in Smeulers Alette and Haveman Roelof (eds), *Supranational Criminology: Towards a Criminology of International Crimes*. Antwerp: Intersentia. pp. 335–56.

Patel, Ana Cutter, de Greiff, Pablo and Waldorf, Lars (eds) (2009), *Disarming the Past: Transitional Justice and Ex-Combatants*. New York: Social Science Research Council.

Power, Jonathan (2007) *Conundrums of Humanity: The Quest for Global Justice*. Leiden: Martinus Nijhoff.

Reiger, Caitlin and Wierda, Marieke (2006) *The Serious Crimes Process in Timor-Leste: In Retrospect*. New York, International Center for Transitional Justice.

Ricoeur, Paul (2003) *Memory, History, Forgetting*. Chicago, IL: University of Chicago Press.

Ricoeur, Paul (2005) 'Memory, history, forgiveness: a dialogue between Paul Ricoeur and Sorin Antonhi', *Janus Head*, 8 (1): 4.

Roberts, Paul (2003) 'Restoration and retribution in international criminal justice: an exploratory analysis', in Andrew von Hirsch, Julian Roberts, Anthony E. Bottoms, Kent Roach and Mara Schiff (eds) *Restorative Justice and Criminal Justice: Competing or Reconcilable Paradigms?* Oxford: Hart Publishing. pp. 115–34.

Rodman, Kenneth A. (2008) 'Darfur and the limits of legal deterrence', *Human Rights Quarterly*, 30: 529.

Rose, Charlotte (2008) 'Looking beyond amnesty and traditional justice and reconciliation mechanisms in Northern Uganda: a proposal for truth-telling and reparations', *Boston College Third World Law Journal*, 28 (2): 345–400.

Sarkin, Jeremy (2004) *Carrots and Sticks: The TRC and the South African Amnesty Process*. Antwerp: Intersentia.

Sarkin, Jeremy (2007) 'An evaluation of the South African amnesty process', in Audrey Chapman and Hugo Van der Merwe (eds), *Truth and Reconciliation in South Africa: Did the TRC Deliver?* Philadelphia, PA: University of Pennsylvania Press. pp. 93–115.

SATRC (2003) *Final Report of the South African Truth and Reconciliation Commission*.

Savelsberg, Joachim J. (2010) *Crime and Human Rights: Criminology of Genocide and Atrocities*. London: SAGE Publications.

Saville of Newdigate, Lord (2010) *Report of The Bloody Sunday Inquiry*, London: The Stationery Office.

Schabas, William (2006) *The UN International Criminal Tribunals: The Former Yugoslavia, Rwanda and Sierra Leone*. Oxford: Oxford University Press.

Schabas, William (2007) *An Introduction to the International Criminal Court*, 3rd edn. Cambridge: Cambridge University Press.

Schabas, William (2011) 'Criminology, accountability and international justice', in M. Bosworth and C. Hoyle (eds), *What Is Criminology?* Oxford: Oxford University Press.

Scharf, Michael P. (1996) 'The letter of the law: the scope of the international legal obligation to prosecute human rights crimes', *Law & Contemporary Problems*, 59 (4): 41.

Schmitt, Carl (1985) *Political Theology: Four Chapters on the Concept of Sovereignty*. Chicago: University of Chicago Press.

Scott, James C. (1999) *Seeing like a State: How Certain Schemes to Improve the Human Condition have Failed*. New Haven, CT: Yale University Press.

Senier, Amy (2008) 'Traditional justice as transitional justice: a comparative case study of Rwanda and East Timor', *Praxis: Fletcher Journal of Human Security*, XXIII: 67–88.

Shakespeare, William (1596) *Merchant of Venice*. New York: Saddleback.

Shaw, Rosalind and Waldorf, Lars (eds) (2010) *Localizing Transitional Justice: Interventions and Priorities After Mass Violence*. Palo Alto, CA: Stanford University Press.

Shirlow, Peter and McEvoy, Kieran (2008) *Beyond the Wire: Former Prisoners and Conflict Transformation in Northern Ireland*. London: Pluto Press.

Simon, Jonathan (2007) *Governing Through Crime*. Oxford: Oxford University Press.

Simpson, Graeme (2002) '"Tell no lies, claim no easy victories": a brief evaluation of South Africa's truth and reconciliation commission', in Deborah Posel and Graeme Simpson (eds), *Commissioning the Past: Understanding South Africa's Truth and Reconciliation Commission*. Johannesburg: Witwatersrand University Press. pp. 220–64.

Slye, Ronald C. (2002) 'The legitimacy of amnesties under international law and general principles of Anglo-American law: is a legitimate amnesty possible?', *Virginia Journal of International Law*, 43 (1): 173.

Stanley, Elizabeth (2009) *Torture, Truth and Justice: The Case of Timor-Leste*. Abingdon: Routledge.

Steinhert, Heinz (1997) '*Fin de siecle* criminology', *Theoretical Criminology*, 1 (1): 111–29.

Strange, Carolyn (2001a) 'Introduction', in C. Strange (ed.), *Qualities of Mercy: Justice, Punishment and Discretion*. Vancouver: UBC Press. pp. 3–20.

Strange, Carolyn (2001b) 'Mercy for murderers? A historical perspective on the royal prerogative of mercy', *Saskatchewan Law Review*, 64: 559–72.

Teitel, Ruti G. (2000) *Transitional Justice*. Oxford: Oxford University Press.

Theissen, Gunnar (2009) 'Common past, divided truth: the truth and reconciliation commission in South African public opinion', in Susanne Karstedt (ed.), *Legal Institutions and Collective Memories*. Oxford: Hart Publishing. pp. 101–134.

Thoms, Oskar, Ron, James and Paris, Roland (2010) 'State-level effects of transitional justice: what do we know?', *International Journal of Transitional Justice*, 4 (3): 329–54.

Tonry, Michael (2008) 'Learning from the limitations of deterrence', *Crime and Justice*, 37: 279–312.

Trumbull, Charles P. (2007) 'Giving amnesties a second chance', *Berkeley Journal of International Law*, 25: 283–345.

UN Economic and Social Council (1985) *Study on Amnesty Laws and their Role in the Safeguard and Protection of Human Rights*, prepared by Louis Joinet. Sub-Commission on the Prevention of Discrimination and Protection of Minorities, UN Doc E/CN.4/Sub.2/1985/16.

UNSC (2004) *Report of the Secretary-General on The Rule of Law and Transitional Justice in Conflict and Post-Conflict Societies*, S/2004/616 (23 August 2004).

Van der Merwe, Hugo, Baxter, Victoria and Chapman, Audrey (eds) (2009) *Assessing the Impact of Transitional Justice: Challenges for Empirical Research*. Washington, DC: United States Institute of Peace Press.

Ventura Miller, Holly (2008) *Restorative Justice from Theory to Practice*. Bingley: Emerald Group Publishing.

Vinjamuri, Leslie (2010) 'Democracy, deterrence and the pursuit of international justice', *Ethics and International Affairs*, 24 (2): 191–211.

Von Hirsch, Andrew (1993) *Censure and Sanction*. Oxford: Clarendon Press.

Waldorf, Lars (2009) 'Linking DDR and transitional justice', in Ana Cutter Patel, Pablo de Greiff and Lars Waldorf (eds), *Disarming the Past: Transitional Justice and Ex-combatants*. New York: Social Science Research Council. pp. 14–35.

Walgrave, Lode (ed.) (1998) *Restorative Justice for Juveniles: Potentialities, Risks and Problems*. Leuven: Leuven University Press.

Ward, Tony and Maruna, Shadd (2007) *Rehabilitation: Beyond the Risk Paradigm*. London: Routledge.

Weber, Max (ed.) (1970) *From Max Weber: Essays in Sociology*. London: Routledge.

Weisman, Norman, (1972) 'A history and discussion of amnesty', *Columbia Human Rights. Law Review*, 4: 520–40.

Weitekamp, Elmar and Kerner, Hans (2002) *Restorative Justice: Theoretical Foundations*. Cullompton: Willan.

Wiebelhaus-Brahm, Eric (2010) *Truth Commissions and Transitional Societies: The Impact on Human Rights and Democracy*. Abingdon: Routledge.

Wiseman, John (1993) *Political Leaders in Black Africa: A Biographical African Dictionary of the Major Politicians since Independence*. Cheltenham: E. Elgar Publishing.

Zaibert, Leo (2006) *Punishment and Retribution*. Aldershot: Ashgate.

Zehr, Howard (2008) 'Doing justice, healing trauma: the role of restorative justice in peacebuilding', *South Asian Journal of Peacebuilding*, 1 (1): 1–16.

Zepp-LaRouche, Helga (1999) *The Treaty of Westphalia: A Precedent for Peace in the Balkans*. Schiller Institute. Available at: http://www.schillerinstitute.org/strategic/hzl_t_of_w_0599.html (accessed 23 March 2012).

Zimring, Frank and Hawkin, Gordon (1973) *Deterrence: The Legal Threat in Crime Control*. Chicago: Chicago University Press.

22

Control Without Punishment: Understanding Coercion

Liora Lazarus, Benjamin Goold and Caitlin Goss

In the case of serious harm, conventional punishment occurs too late.

(Zedner, 2007a: 174)

INTRODUCTION

This chapter explores the implications of terrorism and the recent global response, otherwise known as the 'war on terror', for punishment and the field of criminal justice. It argues that various domestic and international pressures have led to a significant shift away from the punishment model in the exercise of state coercion and have, in the most extreme cases, led to the use and legitimation of state-sponsored violence.

The chapter begins by examining a number of significant socio-legal changes that have taken place since the events of 9/11. It then goes on to examine various counter-terrorist measures, categorizing them along a spectrum beginning with substantive criminal law at one extreme, moving through a range of quasi-legal measures in the middle, and concluding with a series of extra-legal measures at the other end. These measures are explored from a variety of perspectives, with particular focus being paid to their coercive power, exceptional status, and adherence to the rule of law. The chapter then considers how disciplines such as sociology, criminology and penology have responded to this paradigm shift from punitive coercion to bare coercion, and examines various efforts aimed at ensuring these disciplines remain relevant to both the policy and practice of punishment.

Although acknowledging the important work that has been done by scholars in these fields, we argue that these efforts have so far failed to produce an effective response to the coercive practices arising from the 'war on terror', and remain hampered by the tendency to view these changes through what can best be described as a 'pre-9/11 lens'. The chapter concludes by arguing that a new analysis is needed, one that is based on an understanding of coercion that is neither framed within, or legitimated by, the existing criminal law or the moral and political justifications that underpin the imposition of state punishment. Such coercion includes not only measures so 'oppressive' as to 'entail pains comparable to that of punishment', (Ashworth and Zedner, 2010: 71) but also the infliction of pain or death that in many instances outstrips what we commonly associate with legitimate punitive coercion in contemporary Western states.

Hence, we will argue that highly burdensome state coercion that mimics and sometimes outstrips legally justified punitive practices is no longer simply an outcome of the formal processes of the criminal justice system.[1] Instead, it is increasingly being used by governments as a means of pre-empting criminal behavior and acts of terrorism, and justified in the name of exceptionalism rather than appeals to retributivism, deterrence or rehabilitation. Although such coercive messages may have a punitive element to them – especially when they are used against individuals the state regards as responsible for particular terrorist attacks – this is not their primary purpose. Expressions of state power at the more extreme end of our spectrum are more akin to military actions than to criminal justice penalties, despite the fact that they are often directed at individuals outside of the theatre of war. To the extent that these measures promote social solidarity by being aimed at the elimination of a 'common enemy', they may be said to be punitive in the Meadean sense (Mead, 1918). But these measures would certainly not constitute punishment within the meaning that liberal theories attribute to it, as such theories start from the assumption that punishment entails a formal system of criminal law, and a breach of that law, before it can be imposed (Bedau, 2010).

Studying these methods of coercion adopted in the name of counter-terrorism is therefore a challenge for the field of crime and punishment, precisely because it forces us to consider the meaning and limits of penality. Anthony Duff argues within the liberal tradition that 'legal punishment involves the imposition of something that is intended to be burdensome or painful, on a supposed offender for a supposed crime, by a person or body who claims the authority to do so'.[2] Moreover, 'legal punishment presupposes crime as that for which punishment is imposed, and a criminal law as that which defines crimes as crimes; a system of criminal law presupposes a state, which has the political authority to make and enforce the law and to impose punishments'.[3] If punishment is to be understood like this – as a sanction imposed for breaches of the criminal law – then many of the coercive practices which are deployed in the 'war on terror' cannot be described as punishment.

We believe there is an urgent need for the development of a normative critique that addresses the forms and use of such coercive techniques and violent oppressive strategies by states and private actors. Without such a critique, there is a danger that the current trend towards more pervasive and increasingly punitive forms of extra-legal coercion will continue to go unchallenged. The question, however, is whether this analysis is best undertaken within the field of punishment and society or whether, by conceding that such coercion constitutes a form of punishment, we risk inadvertently legitimating the coercive techniques that form the object of inquiry.

9/11 AND ITS CONSEQUENCES

Much has been written about the consequences of the terrorist attack on the World Trade Center on the morning of 11 September 2001 (Ackerman, 2004, 2006; Aradau and van Munster, 2009; Amoore and de Goede, 2008; Ashby Wilson, 2005; Beck, 2002, 2003, 2006; Bobbitt, 2008; Cole, 2003, 2004, 2009; Cole and Dempsey, 2006; Dershowitz, 2006; Dudziak, 2003; Ericson and Doyle, 2004; Forst, Greene and Lynch, 2011; Goold and Lazarus, 2007; Greenberg, 2006; Greenberg and Dratel, 2005; Gross, 2003; Gross and Ní Aoláin, 2006; Guiora, 2008; Ignatieff, 2004; Lyon, 2006b; Murphy, 2007; 9/11 Commission Report, 2004; Roach, 2007; Tribe and Gudridge, 2004; Waldron, 2010; Webb, 2007;

Zedner, 2010a). There is little doubt that this attack quickly came to be seen by many as the harbinger of a new era of 'super-terrorism',[4] and led to loud demands for 'exceptional' measures in response (Lazarus and Goold, 2007: note 1, pp. 1, 2–8). Despite the fact that countries such as Israel, India and the UK had been the targets of sustained terrorist activity in the decades leading up to 9/11 – and had developed sophisticated crime control strategies in response – the targeting of civilians on such a massive scale in New York, and subsequent terrorist attacks in other major cities, prompted politicians around the world to announce that 'the rules of the game had changed'.[5] According to then-Vice President Dick Cheney in an address to Republican Governors in October 2001, emergency is the 'new normalcy'.[6] The apparently exceptional nature of the 'super-terrorist' threat soon led to increased pressure being placed on the police, military and intelligence communities in countries such as the USA and the UK, and to calls for a more effective, coordinated and better resourced approach to national security. It also saw the introduction of range of so-called 'exceptional' coercive measures, typically justified with reference to their supposedly limited application to a range of emergency circumstances (Gross, 2003; Ackerman, 2004; Cole, 2004; Ignatieff, 2004; Tribe and Gudridge, 2004).

The responses were dramatic and widespread. Large-scale war began in Afghanistan in 2001 followed by Iraq in 2003, shifting conceptions of legal warfare, state sovereignty and the importance of intelligence gathering to military decision making. Alongside these formal military interventions, a consensus formed within the international community as to the need for 'collective security for all' in the face of what appeared to be a new type of terrorist threat.[7] Recognizing the 'profound implications' of the 'interconnectedness of contemporary threats to ... security' the United Nations promoted 'comprehensive' security strategies, calling on 'institutions to overcome their narrow preoccupations and learn to work across issues *in a concerted fashion*'.[8] Inter-institutional cooperation was promoted at an international and domestic level, often resulting in a fusion of 'criminal justice and national security' strategies (McCulloch and Pickering, 2009: 631), and heralding a time of spiraling securitization.[9] What was once seen as aid intervention or social welfare initiatives now became a way of shoring up failed States in pursuit of the international and domestic security of developed countries (Crawford, 2006, 2009).

However, the interconnected security strategies promoted at the international level were not accompanied by a consensus on the definition of terrorism for the purposes of international criminal law (Saul, 2006; Di Fillippo, 2008). As Cryer et al. have noted, 'no definition of terrorism has been agreed for the purpose of a global prohibition of terrorist acts in a legally binding instrument. None of the eleven global agreements defines terrorism except the Terrorist Financing Convention, and that is only for a secondary purpose' (2010: 342). No international court or tribunal exercises jurisdiction over the crime of terrorism under international law.[10] Earlier drafts of the statute for the International Criminal Court included terrorism as a 'treaty crime' under the Court's jurisdiction,[11] and the drafters of the *Rome Statute* considered, and deferred[12] until the Kampala Review Conference (2010), the possibility of bringing terrorism within the court's jurisdiction. However, while the Kampala Review Conference succeeded in defining the crime of aggression, at no stage was the possibility of including terrorism as a crime seriously considered. As such, acts associated with terrorism may only be brought before the ICC if they separately constitute, for example, war crimes, or crimes against humanity (International Council on Human Rights Policy, 2008: 35).

It might be argued that the lack of a universal definition of terrorism in international criminal law has suited the interests of certain key actors perfectly well. Going further, the lack of consensus around a definition of terrorism may also have been driven by a desire on the part of key players – such as the USA – to ensure that they retained control over the term, and to ensure that the line between crime and terrorism remained helpfully indistinct. It might also be argued that the failure to develop a framework for the prosecution of suspected terrorists in international law reflects a preference on the part of states for the language of war when dealing with acts of aggression, and a suspicion of criminal justice processes rooted in ideas of due process, open proceedings and legal representation.

Notwithstanding, or perhaps because of, the lack of consensus around the crime of terrorism at an international level, threatened states have embarked on a sophisticated, and sometimes secret, campaign against terrorism. This has quickly became referred to as the 'war on terror', a war that continues to this day. This campaign has relied on support from a wide range of institutions – such as domestic and international intelligence agencies, the police and the military – and has been marked by a blurring of the boundaries between traditional law enforcement techniques and strategies more commonly associated with open warfare and insurgency. Although the relationships between these different responses to terrorism are complex, many of the strategies associated with the war on terror share a common feature: they are highly coercive and pre-emptive in nature. Despite the name, the war on terror is not simply directed at terrorists. Crucially, it is also deeply concerned with anticipating and preventing grave threats to civilian life. As Zedner argues: 'the urge to avert the risks posed by the growth of terrorist activity has generated an emerging genre of preventive justice' (2007a: 174). These strategies soon became described *inter alia* as a 'new paradigm in prevention' (Cole, 2006, quoted in McCulloch and Pickering, 2009: 630), an 'aggressive preventive agenda', as 'radical prevention' (Janus, 2004: 2) and as signaling the emergence of a 'pre-crime' society (Zedner, 2007b: 261). At the same time, a trend has emerged which has seen the integration of 'national security into criminal justice along with a temporal and geographic shift that encompasses a blurring of the borders between the states' internal and external coercive capacities' (McCulloch and Pickering, 2009: 628).

As a consequence of these changes, a new paradigm of control and coercion has gradually begun to establish itself in many democratic states. Set against a backdrop of exceptionalism and appeals for greater emergency powers by governments in countries such as the USA and the UK (Aradau and van Munster, 2009), we have seen techniques more commonly associated with the regulatory state being used to criminalize a range of acts that might loosely be associated with terrorism. At the same time, we have also seen the logic of pre-emption and precaution spill into a whole host of other spheres and spaces, from airports and borders to political demonstrations and public protests. While it may be true that the use of pre-emptive strategies of control by the state is hardly new, the intensity with which they have been employed against citizens and non-citizens alike has intensified in the post-Second World War era. Furthermore, as the language of risk has evolved to encompass a range of dangers that go well beyond traditional actuarial concerns, ideas of pre-emption and prevention have become normalized, and increasingly viewed as entirely legitimate aims of government (Aradau and van Munster, 2007). As a result, while in the past pre-emption may have been reserved for only the most serious criminal threats to the state, over the past 20 years talk of precaution, risk management and preventive police action has increasingly become the norm within the criminal justice system. Since the events of 9/11, this trend has only continued, with increased speed and greater rhetorical momentum (Beck, 2002, 2003, 2006; Ericson and Doyle, 2004; Aradau and van Munster, 2007).

The rhetoric of exceptionalism and the logic of pre-emption have shifted the contours of criminal law and punishment (Beck,

2002, 2003, 2006; Ericson and Doyle, 2004; Aradau and van Munster, 2007), and in the process posed a serious challenge to our shared commitment to fundamental liberties and human rights. In addition, as modes of state power they have often stood outside the law altogether. There are a range of infamous examples of anti-terrorist activity which have taken place since 9/11 that have captured the public imagination and sparked serious concerns. Few of us will forget images of so-called 'enemy combatants' kneeling in their bright orange jumpsuits at Camp Delta in Guantanamo Bay. Similarly, few will be unaware of the international concern regarding the necessity or legality of the invasion of Iraq, the surveillance pictures used to back up a faltering Colin Powell (then US Secretary of State) in his address to the United Nations to justify the invasion, and the images of the first air strikes and the violence that ensued once the Hussein regime was toppled. Nor will they be unfamiliar with the pictures of grave abuse of detainees in Abu Ghraib prison in Iraq, or the mistaken killing of Jean Charles de Menezes at Stockwell Tube station by the London Metropolitan police and the subsequent De Menezes enquiry. More recently, the killing of Osama Bin Laden by US Special Forces in Pakistan – and the subsequent disposal of his body at sea – only serves to remind us that bringing suspected terrorists before a court of law is not a high priority for those perpetrating the war on terror. This act of state-sponsored execution was legitimated as an act of war (Bowcott, 2011), but widespread unease remains as to its legality (Tesón, forthcoming).

All of these disturbing images, brought to the homes of millions across the globe on an hourly basis, have had complex effects. On the one hand, they have cemented the idea that the war on terror has a special status. That it is a war of necessity conducted outside of the normal rules of the game, that any form of coercive or violent measures will be used in its pursuit, and that most of these interventions stand at best on the edge of justified legality. On the other hand, many if not most of these images have arguably served to delegitimize the war on terror in the eyes of a widening range of people it purports to serve. To this extent, a decade of relentless securitization, and the increasing extra-legal coercion of the 'common enemy' (Mead, 1918: n.4), may not have produced the public consensus that the 'war on terror' was originally intended to serve.

Of course, these public and evocative images represent a very small part of the activity carried out in the name of the 'war on terror'. The last decade has spawned a plethora of novel policing, intelligence, military and immigration control techniques, allegedly in response to the threat of terrorism. In this chapter, our aim is not to provide an exhaustive account of these measures, but rather to draw attention to their coercive force, exceptional status and proximity to (or distance from) the law and the criminal law in particular. In mapping out the forms of counter-terrorist state coercion, we necessarily engage in a degree of generalization and invoke some artificial distinctions. Some counter-terrorist measures may, for example, be both legal and extra-legal depending on their context. Equally, some extra-legal measures or extra-criminal measures may also travel into the legal or criminal realm through processes of normalization over time of previously exceptional measures (Zedner, 2010a: 394). Our overarching objective, however, is to draw attention to the full range of legal or extra-legal counter-terrorism measures, to highlight their highly coercive or violent character, and to raise questions about the relative lack of engagement with counter-terrorist activity from within the field of punishment and society. Our aim is to open up a debate within this disciplinary field as to the nature of coercive activity taken outside of the realm of formal or conventional notions of punishment. Our view is that facing up to this challenge will not only enrich the security debate, but will also expand the analytical power of punishment and society scholarship.

COERCIVE COUNTER-TERRORISM MEASURES WITHIN THE LAW

Many of the coercive counter-terrorism measures that have been on the increase since 9/11 involve the law – or are legitimated by law – in some way. Having a foundation in law does not, of course, mean that all of these measures are immune to procedural or human rights challenges in international or domestic courts, or that they do not invite legitimate normative criticism regarding the boundaries of legal frameworks. But these measures normally maintain a veneer of legality, or at least purport to be based on law. Such so-called legal measures manifest in a number of ways, some have survived in altered forms, and others have fallen foul of human rights legal challenges. Notwithstanding, our selection is chosen to exemplify coercive phenomena that ought to constitute an object of study for the field of punishment and society.

Criminal law and procedure

At one end of our coercive spectrum are those measures that are incorporated within the criminal law, and which invite many of the procedural safeguards and protections that arise in the process of enforcement and prosecution. The main manifestation here is the criminalization of individuals associated with, but not directly responsible for, terrorist activity. Here, states threatened by terrorism have generally sought an extension of the criminal law for the purposes of capturing preparatory acts through extensive use of inchoate offences. In the UK, the Terrorism Act 2006 (section 5) criminalizes 'any conduct in preparation' of terrorist acts, or any assistance to another in commission of such acts and attaches a maximum penalty of life imprisonment (Ashworth and Zedner, 2010). As McCulloch and Pickering argue 'many of the counter-terrorism laws enacted after 2001 criminalize conduct and label it, "terrorist-related" even where there is no evidence of harm or intention to do harm, such as giving money to a charity or associating with what are deemed to be terrorist organizations' (2009: 631).

Commentators generally refer to this tendency to extend criminal law as a process of *over-criminalization*. According to Husak (2008), although the criminal law should aim to both reduce harm and the risk of harm, it is vital that clear limits are placed on this preventative function of the criminal law. Unless the law adheres to a number of basic requirements – such as need for a substantial risk before criminalizing a particular action, as well as the need for an identifiable harm and an element of culpability – then there is a danger that there will be a significant expansion in 'crimes of risk prevention'. In addition, over-criminalization also threatens to undermine a variety of principles that lie at the heart of the criminal law, such as the requirement of proportionality and the rule against retroactivity. In its efforts to pre-empt terrorism and criminalize activities that raise a risk of harm, the state not only expands the ambit of the criminal law, but risks undermining the foundations that keep it – and the state's policing power – in check. As Ashworth and Zedner have observed, it 'is in recognition of the power that the criminal law bestows upon the state to take such extraordinary actions against its citizens that the safeguards of a fair criminal procedure are brought into play' (2010: 81).

Other counter-terrorist measures or actions may involve the criminal law in a different way, in that they rely on specified defenses to otherwise criminal acts. Here we speak not of the criminalization of acts done by individuals suspected of preparatory acts or acts associated with terrorism, but of the use of criminal defenses to legitimate state action in response to terrorism. A clear example here relates to the use of lethal force in self-defense in the context of policing imminent terrorist threats where individuals resist arrest or may pose, through suicide bombing or other forms of bombing, threats to the lives of others. Notably, the responses of human rights courts, such as the European Court of Human Rights, to human rights challenges take a context sensitive view of the gravity of response to the imminence of threat.[13] It is striking that in many of these cases, when considering the proportionality of the act in relation to the threat, the Court does not consider whether lethal force itself was a necessary element of the response in question, but focus rather on the imminence of the threat or the reasonableness of the apprehension of the threat in the assessment of the necessity of the exercise of lethal force.[14] To the extent that the criminal law and human rights courts may be more tolerant of self-defense claims from state actors than private individuals, this may be viewed as a form of *under-criminalization* that serves to extend the scope of coercive counter-terrorist activity. In addition, it also represents a substantial realignment of the very notion of self-defense, turning the exceptional case – the use of force in defense of another rather than oneself – into the central case.

In sum, within the criminal law realm, state coercion has been intensified through the over-criminalization of private actors, and the under-criminalization of lethal and other types of force by state actors. As we will see in the third section below, this intensification of the state's coercive reach is accompanied by an increase in civil law measures aimed at actions previously covered by the criminal law, with a resultant erosion of individual due process protections. This 'under-criminalization' of private actions aimed at the diversion of criminal procedure protections, and the over-extension of the criminal law's substantive reach, are two dimensions of the same pre-emptive thrust. They are all instances of what Ericson would have termed 'Counter Law I' measures – in the sense of laws acting against laws – legitimated by their exceptional status and aimed at the pre-emption of risk arising from terrorism. As he argued in 2008:

> Counter law I is law against law. New laws are enacted and new uses of existing law are invented to erode or eliminate traditional principles, standards, and procedures of criminal law that get in the way of preempting imagined sources of harm'. (2008: 57)

Police law

Still within the realm of criminal justice and procedure, but arguably of a lesser coercive gravity, are policing measures aimed at the prevention of terrorism. In the UK, for example, these measures have taken a variety of forms. Although the UK already had a formidable system of public surveillance prior to the events of 9/11 – established in part due to the continuing IRA threat during the 1980s and early 1990s, but also in response to growing public fear of crime in the late 1990s – since 2001 considerable resources have been devoted to upgrading the country's web of CCTV cameras (especially in urban centers such as London) and improving security in and around airports. As anyone who flies regularly in Europe can attest to, luggage restrictions and security procedures have become increasingly strict and intrusive over the past 10 years, while at the same time an increasing number of airports are making use of such devices as full body scanners and sophisticated bomb detection equipment (Lyon, 2003, 2006a,b; Neyland, 2006). Similarly, in the USA significant steps have been taken to strengthen border policing and airport security over the past decade, with a new government department – the Department of Homeland Security – being established to oversee the task of preventing another terrorist attack on US soil.

In addition to enhancing the architecture of surveillance and security, in many western democratic countries the police have been handed a range of new powers that are supposed to assist them in the fight against terrorism.[15] In Australia, for example, the Anti-Terrorism Act (No. 2) 2005 amended the Crimes Act 1914 (Cth) to give both state and federal police the power to stop, question and search persons for the purposes of investigating and preventing terrorism.[16] In addition, the 2005 Act gives the attorney the power to declare a 'prescribed security zone' if he or she believes that it will either prevent a terrorist act or make it easier for official agencies to respond to a terrorist act. Crucially, once a zone has been prescribed the police can then stop, search, and question any individual within the prescribed security zone, regardless of whether they reasonably suspect that the person has committed or is planning to commit a terrorist act.[17] Similar provisions have also been enacted in Canada. For example, under the Foreign Missions and International Organizations Act 2002, the police are empowered to take 'appropriate measures ... to the extent and in a manner that is reasonable in the circumstances' in their efforts to secure intergovernmental conferences.[18] Although the constitutionality of these sweeping powers has yet to be tested in Canada, to date the police have used them to justify closing city streets, undertaking warrantless searches of individuals in public, and subject citizens to warrantless searches, and establishing temporary security checkpoints in city centers.

By way of contrast, under Section 44 of the Terrorism Act 2000 chief constables in the UK already had the power to designate areas as 'authorization zones'. Once an area has been designated under the section, the police may stop individuals – as well as vehicles, drivers and passengers – and search them for items that might be used in connection with terrorist activities. Crucially, the police do not have to have any grounds for suspecting the presence of such items, and a failure to stop and submit to a search authorized under Section 44 is a criminal offence.[19] Following the enactment of the Anti-Terrorism, Crime and Security Act 2001, however, these powers were substantially expanded. Significantly, the Anti-Terrorism, Crime and Security Act 2001 amended the 2000 Act to give the police the authority to take fingerprints and photographs of individuals suspected of terrorism, with or without their consent.[20] More recently, these formal powers have also been supplemented by aggressive police tactics and crowd control strategies – such as 'kettling' – that are also highly pre-emptive in nature. The net effect of these changes in police powers and practices in the UK is the emergence of more authoritarian style of policing, at least in the context of threats to public safety and order maintenance.

In contrast, in the USA the expansion in police powers has tended to be in the area not of stop and search, but rather surveillance. Crucially, the US Patriot Act 2001[21] contained a range of provisions that substantially increased the surveillance powers of the police, and removed the need for judicial authorization and warrants for a variety of intrusive police activities. Most notably, the Act expanded the scope of warrants available under the Foreign Investigation and Surveillance Act 1978 and the Wiretap Act 1968, and made it possible for law enforcement agencies to undertake surveillance of unknown persons and track them across state borders and via different communications mediums.[22] In addition to these 'roving wiretaps', Section 218 of the US Patriot Act also expanded the circumstances under which a warrant can be granted under the Foreign Investigation and Surveillance Act 1978. According to the section, wiretaps, electronic surveillance and property searches of both citizens and non-citizens alike can be authorized provided that the gathering of 'foreign intelligence' is a 'significant purpose' of the surveillance.[23]

Although the US Patriot Act 2001 substantially increased police powers of surveillance in the USA, perhaps the most notorious example of US expansion in domestic surveillance in the wake of 9/11 was (ironically) achieved covertly. According to the *New York Times*, President Bush – ostensibly acting in his role as Commander in Chief of the Armed Forces under Article II of the US Constitution – issued an executive order in 2002 authorizing the National Security Agency to intercept and monitor communication between individuals in the USA and overseas (Lichtblau and Risen, 2005). As the

New York Times observed in 2005, when it first broke the story:

> The previously undisclosed decision to permit some eavesdropping inside the country without court approval was a major shift in American intelligence-gathering practices, particularly for the National Security Agency, whose mission is to spy on communications abroad. As a result, some officials familiar with the continuing operation have questioned whether the surveillance has stretched, if not crossed, constitutional limits on legal searches. (Lichtblau and Risen, 2005)

Although the surveillance practices sanctioned by the executive order were severely criticized when they eventually came to light,[24] the powers granted by President Bush have only been partially revoked. While the Foreign Investigation and Surveillance Act 1978 was eventually amended in 2008 to make it clear that the President does not have the power to authorize warrantless surveillance, the same amendment preserved some of the powers initially granted to the National Security Agency.[25] In addition to increasing the period during which surveillance without a warrant can be undertaken – from 48 hours to 7 days – the Act now also makes it possible for American citizens outside of the USA to be the subject of a wiretap or electronic surveillance by warrant. Taken together, these various changes constitute a major redrawing of the boundaries between lawful and unlawful surveillance in the USA, and have contributed to a significant expansion in the power of law enforcement agencies – both domestically and internationally – in the last decade.

Civil law and hybrid measures

At the next point on our coercive spectrum are measures that are inside the law but outside the criminal law or criminal justice process – often at the margins of criminal and civil law. Post-9/11 we have witnessed an increasing trend towards the use of anti-terrorist measures that mimic the coercive effects of the criminal law, yet are not subject to the same sorts of restrictions and the protections of criminal procedure. Such hybrid measures are commonly used where threatened states wish to control individuals suspected of being involved in terrorist activity. The most common examples are the various forms of highly restrictive house arrest that are referred to as 'control orders' in the UK[26] and Australia,[27] and Security Certificates in Canada.[28] In the UK, the use of control orders has been justified as on the grounds that they constitute a less burdensome form of preventive detention than that struck down by the UK House of Lords on human rights grounds in 2003.[29] Control orders impose liberty restrictions on their subjects that are generally as burdensome as punishment, but which attach very few of the procedural protections that criminal law affords:

> Those subject to Control Orders may be electronically tagged at all times; be required to abide by curfews (by remaining at home or in a specified place between specified times, in the initial orders for up to 18 hours per day); have their passports taken away; be denied access to rail stations, airports, and ports; have their telephone lines cut; have their contacts with others outside the home severely limited; and be subject at any time to unannounced visits and searches from the police and security services. They may be prohibited from using specified articles or substances (for example mobile phones, faxes, pagers, computers, and internet facilities); have their right to work or engage in other activities limited; and suffer restrictions on association with other people, on communication, movement, and residence. They may be required to report to a specified person at specified times and places; to have their photograph taken; to provide information on demand; and to permit anything to be removed from their home for the duration of the order. (Zedner, 2007a: 180)

Depending on the gravity of the liberty restrictions imposed, control orders are imposed either on the civil standard of proof (balance of probabilities), or simply on the basis of reasonable suspicion.[30] They normally involve an intricate procedure incorporating secret evidence, including special advocates to scrutinize such evidence without recourse to the suspect themselves. In jurisdictions such as Canada and the UK, such proceedings have been the subject of continuing fair trial challenges and their status, particularly in the UK, now remains in flux.[31] Notwithstanding human rights challenges, and recent moves for reform in the UK,[32] it is fair to say, that the 'penal character and impact' of control orders constitutes what Zedner (2007a) refers to as 'pre-punishment'.

The control order is only one species of 'pre-punishment' which gain increasing legal legitimacy within the preventive state (Steiker, 1998: 771; cf. Slobogin, 2003). Another variant can be found in asset freezing measures imposed under domestic law in compliance with United Nation Security Council Resolution 1373,[33] 1267[34] and their successors,[35] which require states to freeze assets of 'persons who commit, or attempt to commit, terrorist acts' (UNSC Res 1373) (Roach, 2007: 227, 230f). Again, a comprehensive account of national responses to the UNSC Resolutions cannot be provided here, but suffice to say that in the UK the measures have received limited parliamentary scrutiny, are imposed where there are 'reasonable grounds for suspecting that the person is or has been involved in terrorist activity', and have very onerous consequences for those subject to asset freezing orders as well as their families and dependents (Tomkins et al., 2010, 2011).

Similar human rights concerns were raised with respect to Canada's Anti-Terrorism Act 2001, and in particular to the introduction of preventative detention and special investigative hearings (Roach, 2007: 233). Although many provisions of the Act expired in 2007, it is significant that the Prime Minister Stephen Harper has taken steps to restore them. In April 2010, the government introduced Bill C-17 (also known as the Combatting Terrorism Act) that would have – had it been passed by parliament – both empowered the police to detain individuals suspected of terrorist activities, and given the courts the power to compel such individuals to provide any information they might have regarding such activities. Although Bill C-17 was not ultimately signed into law, the fact that the current government took steps to reintroduce powers originally established in the immediate aftermath of 9/11 suggests that the 'coercive turn' in Canadian law is far from over.

Across the border in the USA, a system of preventative detention has also been established under the auspices of the US Patriot Act 2001. Under Section 412, where the attorney general has 'reasonable grounds to believe' that a non-citizen has 'engaged in activity that endangers the national security of the United States', he or she can issue a certificate that authorizes their detention for up to 7 days.[36] Although the person must be charged with an offence or released once the 7-day period is over, if the person is charged or removal proceedings have been initiated, the detention can continue indefinitely provided that the attorney general or a court is satisfied that 'the release of the alien will threaten the national security of the United States or the safety of the community or any person'.[37] Although in recent years these provisions have been used far less frequently by the police, the fact there has been no attempt to dismantle these powers suggests, as in Canada and the UK, that the use of preventative detention has become increasingly accepted and normalized.

IMMIGRATION LAW

Central to immigration law is the ability to detain or deport non-citizens suspected of terrorist activity from a jurisdiction. While typically subject to limited human rights constraints – for example, where deportation would expose an individual to the prospect of torture in their 'home' country – in countries such as the UK and the USA immigration law has proved to be fertile ground for the development of new ways of coercing non-citizens suspected of terrorism. Immigration law was singled out as a means of countering terrorism in UN Security Council Resolution 1373, which called on states to create 'effective border controls' to 'prevent the movement of terrorists or terrorist groups'. In particular, the provisions included a requirement to strengthen existing immigration procedures to ensure that suspected terrorists could not easily claim asylum or refugee status. Partly as a result of the UN Security Council's initiative and partly at their own initiative, various jurisdictions (including the UK, USA and Canada) have increasingly used immigration law as a mechanism of counter-terrorism.[38]

The lower standards of proof in immigration law with respect to detention and deportation make this an ideal site for states to control and coerce suspected terrorists, without the due process protections or transparency of the criminal law (Zedner 2010a: 394f). Certainly, some states, such as the USA, have ignored the general human rights safeguards constraining deportation to jurisdictions engaged in torture.[39] Even where states have respected these constraints in the letter of the law, the use of immigration law to remove 'suspected terrorists' has proven an attractive technique for threatened states. Immigration law imposes considerable burdens on non-citizens. While Roach argues that 'the ultimate aim of immigration law [as anti-terrorism law] is removal, not punishment ...' (2007: 238), the long history of treating immigration controls as part of crime control belies such a distinction (Stumpf, 2006: 367). Immigration detention and removal are often as burdensome as penal sanctions, and in many cases more so. The recent death of an Angolan deportee, Jimmy Mubenga, at the hands of private security guards on the plane is an evocative example of just how coercive and even violent immigration regulation enforcement can become (Lewis et al., 2010). Similarly, the continuing battle to end the detention of child immigrants in the UK, raises serious questions about the extent to which we can distinguish between the coercive force of immigration regulation, and the sanctions that flow from breaches of the criminal law (Topping, 2011). Although these may be extreme cases, the hardship and gravity of immigration detention and controls in a range of jurisdictions tests the *de jure* distinction between immigration regulation and criminal law (Stumpf, 2006: 367).

Notwithstanding the continuing judicial acceptance of the cleavage between immigration law (civil law) and criminal law, the use of immigration law to regulate terrorism is problematic in a range of respects. For one, the processes surrounding the imposition of immigration controls allow for the development of novel techniques that would otherwise fall foul of criminal process protections. For example, in the USA immigration law was used in the immediate aftermath of 9/11 to 'detain suspects of terrorism, who were then subjected to closed hearings, denied access to counsel, and detained and removed on the basis of expressive and associational activities'. As Roach (2007) points out, however, very few criminal law charges or prosecutions for terrorist activity ever resulted from these immigration law detentions. Similarly, prior to a number of successful human rights challenges,[40] the UK used immigration law to justify the indefinite detention of foreigners suspected of terrorist activity, especially those who could not be deported to their home countries on the grounds of torture risk.[41]

Aside from having a direct effect on non-citizens, coercive techniques developed in the context of immigration law have a tendency to find their way into other areas of the legal system, and to eventually be applied to citizens in more mundane circumstances. This has proved to be the case with the special advocate system in the UK, which was first developed in the immigration arena and was soon utilized in control order proceedings (see above). Initially developed in 1997 as a means of providing foreigners with representation when appealing immigration or asylum decisions that engaged national security issues before the Special Immigration Appeals Commission (SIAC), special advocates are now imposed on citizens and non-citizens alike within the SIAC system and beyond. Hence, as Zedner argues special advocates which were 'targeted first against those at the very periphery of civil society, … serve as a template for the future of crime control more generally' (2010b: 22). Similar cross-overs can be seen with immigration detention, where critics have noted the increasing interdependence between the UK Border Agency and HM Prison Service (Bosworth and Guild, 2008; Bosworth, 2011). The movement goes both ways, as in the USA, the increasing criminalization of immigration law (even beyond the bounds of the regulation of terrorism) has now been famously described by Stumpf as the 'crimmigration crisis'. For her, the historical 'merger of the two areas … has created parallel systems in which immigration law and the criminal justice system are merely nominally separate' (2006: 376). It is small surprise therefore that the policing of terrorist activities through immigration law is so attractive, where similarly coercive interventions can be undertaken with few of the procedural constraints of the formal criminal law system.

Exacerbating the tendency for immigration law techniques to taint the due process foundations of other areas of law, and the parallel criminalization of immigration law itself, is the fact that the entire system rests on a fundamental distinction between the rights of citizens as opposed to non-citizens (Calavita, 2005; Stumpf, 2006; Bosworth and Guild, 2008). There is little question that the inherent 'othering' process entailed in this distinction has underpinned the logic of various responses to terrorism, including the establishment of Guantanamo Bay and the development of increasingly restrictive (and discriminatory) border controls and security. The war on terror was thus able to build upon a pre-existing system of 'crimmigration' premised upon a fundamental distinction between citizenship and outsiders. As a consequence, Cole (2003) makes a powerful constitutional and pragmatic case in the US against the trading off of non-citizens rights in favor of the rights to security of citizens. The due process, constitutionality and human rights arguments raised by Cole regarding the treatment of non-citizens clearly resonate beyond the US borders, and have been picked up by many others with respect to jurisdictions such as the UK and Canada, respectively.

COERCIVE EXTRA-LEGAL COUNTER-TERRORISM MEASURES

Up to this point we have laid out a range of coercive mechanisms which have been developed within the law and which range in their proximity to criminal law and their procedural safeguards. We have shown that many of these instruments form part of a coercive strategy aimed at preventing terrorist activity. In this section we lay out an alternative field of coercion, one that at times carries a thin veneer or 'colour' of legality,[42] and at other times is conducted in covert operations outside of the law. This field is also characterized by violent, lethal and highly oppressive techniques.

Extra-legal imprisonment

> A Presidential Military Order, declaring an extraordinary emergency for national defence purposes, passed by United States President George W Bush in November 2001 allowed the arrest, detention and possible military trial of non-United States citizens by the United State's Defense Department, regardless of their location. It is estimated that 70,000 people have been detained in the United States' extraterritorial penal camps around the world. There is now a real possibility that the mass incarceration and the brutality that accompanies it, an outstanding feature of the past decades in the United States, is central to its continuing global ambition. (Scraton and McCulloch, 2009: 16)

The war on terror has been characterized by widespread detention of so-called enemy combatants or terrorist suspects. This is not necessarily a new phenomenon. Mass detention as a response to real or imagined security threats long pre-dates 9/11, having been used *inter alia* as a colonial defense by the British (as in Malaysia and South Africa); by the US authorities towards the Native American Indians in the 1830s, the Philippine-American War, and the Japanese in the Second World War, and the Israelis in the first intifada. What distinguishes the internment of terrorists globally is the diffuse, global and indeterminate nature of the so-called conflict that is used to legitimate the detention in question.

In the sites we know about presently – Guantanamo Bay, Abu Ghraib and Bagram – the style of military detention is brutal and highly oppressive and designed to humiliate and break the spirit of detainees. There is ample evidence now produced that torture and abusive techniques were routinely deployed in sites around Iraq and Afghanistan and received official authorization.[43] While detention might arise in active military combat, the means adopted were in flagrant breach of the Geneva Conventions and of many other norms of customary international law. The suspension of these norms, and the basic protections of the US constitution, was made explicit by the US government in the case of Guantanamo Bay.

While the use of torture is examined below, it is important to highlight the concerted effort on the part of the Bush administration to avoid any application of habeus corpus to the detainees at Guantanamo (Endicott, 2007). This approach was replicated in the UK with respect to the foreign detainees in Belmarsh prison. In the first part of this decade both the US and UK governments were clear that such protections should be suspended in the case of terrorist suspects. The US and UK Supreme Courts did not agree with their government's positions, and these particular detention regimes have now also lost political support. Nevertheless, prisoners remain in Guantanamo Bay, and military detention continues. Moreover, there are clearly other mechanisms being deployed within the context of extraordinary rendition that entirely undermine the liberty and dignity of those detained or rendered.

Penologists have been quick to identify the continuity between the techniques deployed in military detention, and those that occur in the context of high security civilian imprisonment. Highlighting the 'normalcy of exceptional brutality', Gordon points to the fact that the continuity exists both in 'personnel, punishment regime, law and geopolitics' (Gordon, 2009: 167). Similarly, Davis argues that the 'permissive, "barbaric" practices adopted were a reflection and extension of the 'normalisation of torture within domestic prisons' (Davis, 2005). Such is the extent of the overlap, that some argue that to understand 'the abuses at Abu Ghraib as exception aberrations requires a denial of the everyday "cruel but usual punishments" of contemporary incarceration in liberal democracies' (Scraton and McCulloch, 2009: 131).

These parallels fail to pick up on contrasts between many liberal democracies as regards the treatment of non-terrorist prisoners. Since 1945 the international law on prisoners' rights has developed at an intense pace, with prohibitions on torture and the development of prison standards being articulated and entrenched. Since the early 1970s, in Northern Europe in particular, prisoners' rights have been increasingly recognized by legislatures, courts, prison enquiries and prison management. The excesses of punishment are now more and more constrained by values such as dignity and autonomy, which have not only been espoused in law, but also more and more in administrative practice (Lazarus, 2004). This is however less the case in the USA which has been particularly resistant to dignity as a restraining value on punishment (Whitman, 2004). To this extent, the distinction between the treatment of terrorist and non-terrorist offenders in the USA may be less stark than some European counterparts.

Notwithstanding, fear of terrorism, and the search for security, risks undermining the values of dignity and liberty within the penal system in Europe. The 'war on terror' may contaminate criminal justice in insidious ways that are harder to identify and restrain. One particular dimension of this process is the way that human rights safeguards have been weakened in territories beyond the borders of the state in question. While the robust jurisprudence of the European Court of Human Rights on the extraterritorial application of human rights standards is to be welcomed, there is still limited accountability where states violate the human rights of individuals beyond cases where the Court considers that jurisdiction applies.[44] A further dimension to this process – internal to domestic prison systems – is the way in which the treatment of terrorist offenders and suspects within high security prison institutions contaminates the administration of the system as a whole (Liebling et al., 2010). Suffice it to say, that despite the complexity and diversity among various leading liberal democracies, the impact of extra-legal imprisonment on normal conditions of imprisonment may be more insidious than previously understood. As Waldron argues about torture:

> The warning has been sounded often enough: 'Don't imagine that you can maintain a firewall between what is done by your soldiers and spies abroad to those they demonize as terrorists or insurgents, and what will be done at home to those who can be designated as enemies of society'. (2010: 249)

Torture

The prohibition of torture is a *jus cogens* norm of international law,[45] the subject of international and regional treaties,[46] prohibited in almost every universal, regional or domestic declaration of human rights[47] and constitutes a criminal offence in most civilized nations including the USA. The European Court of Human Rights is unambiguous in its view that torture is forbidden in all circumstances. It has argued clearly that 'Article 3 [prohibition of torture, inhuman and degrading treatment] enshrines one of the most fundamental values of democratic society … The Court is well aware of the immense difficulties faced by States in modern times in protecting their communities from terrorist violence. However, even in these circumstances, the Convention prohibits in absolute terms torture or inhuman or degrading treatment or punishment, irrespective of the victim's conduct. Unlike most of the substantive clauses of the Convention and of Protocols Nos. 1 and 4 (P1, P4), Article 3 makes no provision for exceptions and no derogation from it is permissible under Article 15 even in the event of a public emergency threatening the life of the nation.'[48]

Notwithstanding the universal acceptance that torture is prohibited under international or domestic law, torture formed a central technique of US intelligence in the early years on the war on terror (Levinson, 2004; Greenberg and Dratel, 2005; Greenberg, 2006). The 'enhanced interrogation techniques' (which included repeated waterboarding in many instances, as well as physical and mental deprivation) conducted in Camp Delta in Guantánamo Bay and in other occupied sites by the CIA in Afghanistan and Iraq, were initially justified by the US government in the now infamous 'torture opinions' in 2002.[49] This set the bar for 'torture' very high, incorporating 'deliberate and calculated act[s] of an extremely cruel and inhuman nature, specifically intended to inflict excruciating and agonizing physical or mental pain or suffering'.[50] The legal justifications provided by the Bush administration are now generally regarded as 'dishonorable' and implausible. The memos reveal:

> [A] carefully orchestrated legal rationale, but one without legal or moral foundation. The threshold premise [of the memos], that Guantanamo Bay is outside the jurisdiction of the U.S courts, was soundly rejected by the Supreme Court last June in *Rasul v Bush*, and the successive conclusions built upon that premise will, like the corrupted dominoes they are, tumble in due course. There they will join the other legally instituted but forever discredited stains upon U.S. legal history: the internment of Japanese during World War II, the treatment of Native Americans, and slavery. (Waldron, 2010, quoting Dratel)

To this extent, we classify the use of torture on our coercive spectrum, whether it attracted attempts at legal justification, on the extra-legal, if not outright illegal, end of our coercive spectrum.

It goes without saying that torture conducted in the course of the 'war on terror' raises grave moral concerns. As with extra-legal imprisonment, torture is very rarely conducted inside the borders of established liberal democracies. But many of these jurisdictions remain connected to acts done outside their borders in highly opaque circumstances that we do not yet know about. The public images of Abu Ghraib and Guantanamo Bay, not to mention John Yoo's torture memo to the Bush administration,[51] indicate, however, the extent of the depraved treatment dispensed to those suspected of involvement in terrorist networks. Acts of state punishment, forcefulness or violence, are normally constrained in most established liberal democracies by prohibitions on torture, and cruel and inhumane treatment. Even in the USA, where the death penalty and indeterminate life sentences remain in place and prison conditions frequently test European prison standards,[52] torture (as an act of 'specific intent' [Waldron, 2010: 206]) is constitutionally prohibited. That torture violates almost every human rights standard or criminal justice value held dear by liberal democracies, and represents an abomination and shameful exercise of the State's monopoly on violence, is indisputable.

But torture does something more insidious. It undermines the 'general principle of non-brutality' in state treatment (Waldron, 2010: 247), and raises the benchmark against which other acts of state coercion, such as legal punishment, are measured. The danger that torture will taint the ordinary values and standards of criminal justice, or corrupt the character of our legal system more generally, are equally present here as they are with respect to extra-legal imprisonment. Waldron makes the case very well when he argues that the rule against torture constitutes an 'archetype' of the liberal legal tradition as a whole and its 'determination to draw a line between law and savagery or between law and brutality' (Waldron, 2010: 234). The prohibition of torture demonstrates that law's coercive force can only operate 'without compromising the dignity of those whom it constrains and punishes' (Waldron, 2010: 234). Engaging in torture is then to tamper with the order of principles and archetypes upon which law and punishment in the liberal tradition is built. Waldron draws a direct relationship between torture and our views on punishment or other forms of state forcefulness:

> Our beliefs that flogging in prisons is wrong, that coerced confessions are wrong, that pumping a person's stomach for narcotics evidence is wrong, that police brutality is wrong – these beliefs may each of them be uncertain and a little shaky, but the confidence we have in them depends partly on analogies we have constructed between them and torture on a sense that what is wrong with torture gives us some insight into what is wrong with these other evils. If we undermine the sense that torture is absolutely out of the question, then we lose a crucial point of reference for sustaining these other less confident beliefs. … The *archetypal* character of the prohibition on torture means that it plays a crucial and high-visibility role in regard to the principle. As we have seen, the prohibition on torture is a point of reference to which we return over and over again in articulating legally what is wrong with cruel punishment or how to tell a punishment which is cruel from one which is not: we do not equate cruelty with torture, but we use torture to illuminate our rejection of cruelty. (Waldron, 2010: 234, 247)

In short, despite torture's extra-legal status, it bears a direct and strong relationship to the nature of legal punishment, and has the potential to taint or undermine all that liberal theories of punishment entertain.

Targeted killing

In May 2010, Philip Alston submitted a report to the UN General Assembly and Human Rights Council on the subject of extrajudicial, summary or arbitrary executions. The report begins with a definition and a blunt observation:

> A targeted killing is the intentional, premeditated and deliberate use of lethal force, by States or

> their agents acting under colour of law, or by an organized armed group in armed conflict, against a specific individual who is not in the physical custody of the perpetrator. In recent years, a few States have adopted policies, either openly or implicitly, of using targeted killings, including in the territories of other States.[53]

As Alston goes on to note, such policies have been justified by states on the grounds that they are a legitimate response to the threat of terrorism, and an inevitable outcome of a new style of asymmetric warfare. Tellingly, states have argued that targeted killing is outside of the scope of domestic criminal – or even international – criminal law, and instead governed by the law of armed conflict. This is worrisome for a variety of reasons. On the one hand, it frees states from the procedural constraints typically imposed by the criminal law, and leads to a 'highly problematic blurring and expansion of the boundaries of the applicable legal frameworks – human rights law, the laws of war, and the law applicable to the use of inter-state force'.[54] More disturbingly, the move to place targeted killing outside of the scope of the criminal law has been accompanied by a deep unwillingness on the part of states to disclose any information about the use of such tactics. As Alston notes:

> [T]he States concerned have often failed to specify the legal justification for their policies, to disclose the safeguards in place to ensure that targeted killings are in fact legal and accurate, or to provide accountability mechanisms for violations. Most troublingly, they have refused to disclose who has been killed, for what reason, and with what collateral consequences. The result has been the displacement of clear legal standards with a vaguely defined licence to kill, and the creation of a major accountability vacuum.[55]

It is hard to imagine a more chilling example of a coercive, extra-legal measure than targeted killing. Pre-emptive and unfettered by the constraints imposed by due process or the need for transparency, it is a counter-terrorism technique that – even if it can somehow be justified as a legitimate exercise of state power – is ripe for abuse. In addition, in attempting to publicly justify such practices, states have begun to undermine a well-established norm against the use of such techniques. While it is almost certainly true that many states have carried out targeted killings in the past, for the most part they have always strenuously denied such activities. The use of assassination techniques by the CIA against Fidel Castro in the 1960s were, for example, formally denied for decades, as was the use of targeted killing in Vietnam and Chile during the 1970s.[56]

Since 9/11, however, not only have successive US administrations gradually come to acknowledge such practices, but they have also demonstrated a willingness to extend targeting to US citizens engaged in terrorist activities directed against the USA (Priest, 2010). As the *Economist* (2011) has reported, in 2004 there were below 10 drone strikes on terror suspects, and in 2011 this figure rose to just below 50. There is no question that the rapid rise of state sanctioned 'targeted killing' is attracting serious criticism. Alston is joined by a range of critics, who have voiced very grave concerns both at the level of strategy, but also about the legal and moral legitimacy of these actions (Waldron, 2011: Altman et al., forthcoming).

What is perhaps most disturbing is not just that states have begun to openly acknowledge the use of such measures, but rather that they have begun to develop their own normative frameworks to justify such activities at home and abroad. Typically based on claims to exceptionalism – the threat faced is uniquely dangerous, and the state in question is justified in acting differently from other countries – such arguments are usually couched in language that suggests they are not meant to have universal application. As more and more states avail themselves of similar arguments in favor of targeted killing, there is a very real danger that this form of extra-legal action will become a regular practice, and will only serve to reinforce the belief that there is little room for the law when it comes to pre-emptive efforts to protect the state from the threat of terrorism.

Perhaps the most illustrative example of this can be seen in the recent assassination of

Osama Bin Laden, and how his death was presented to the US public by the Obama administration. Although initially the media was told that Bin Laden died in a firefight with US Special Forces, US officials quickly began to downplay any suggestion that he was killed in self-defense or out of necessity. Within a week of his death and the disposal of his body, the administration was unapologetically presenting his killing as a deliberate act. This alone represents a significant shift in the politics and legitimacy of targeted killing. Furthermore, the fact that Bin Laden was located and killed by US forces in Pakistan without the knowledge of the Pakistani government – and that no attempt appears to have been made to capture him alive – clearly marks a major shift in the use of such extra-legal, coercive measures by western democratic states. Not only was there no pretense that Bin Laden should be given a trial or imprisoned for his crimes, but little effort was made to cover up the fact that his killing was a form of state-sanctioned punishment.

Public reaction to the killing of Osama Bin Laden suggests that the real threat may lie in the very satisfying populist quality of targeted killing, which will lead states to exaggerate its necessity and further undermine public recognition of criminal law protections as a requirement of justice. Similarly, the positive reception of the targeted killing of Osama Bin Laden in many parts of the world appears to reflect a kind of approval of vigilante-style justice. While clearly without prior process, there was little doubt that the killing of Bin Laden was equated in many people's minds as a form of punishment in the form of retributive justice. The question remains therefore whether targeted killing will be a more pernicious form of punishment than the death penalty, free of all associated due process and evidential standards, and randomly executed.

Illegal use of force

The boundaries of the prohibition on the use of force encapsulated in Article 2(4) of the UN Charter, and in customary international law, have been challenged by states engaged in the 'war on terror'. Article 2(4) of the UN Charter provides that 'Members shall refrain in their international relations from the threat or use of force against the territorial integrity or political independence of any state, or in any manner inconsistent with the Purposes of the United Nations.' The prohibition on the use of force has been described as the 'cornerstone'[57] of the UN Charter, and has been found to represent customary international law.[58] The only exceptions to this prohibition on the use of force arise from the right of states to individual or collective self-defense under Article 51 of the UN Charter, or where authorized by the Security Council in order to preserve international peace and security.

The debate concerning the use of force in relation to terrorism contains three key points of tension: the legality of using force in anticipation of an attack that has yet to occur; the legality of a state or group of states using force against non-state actors; and the necessity and proportionality of military responses to terrorist threats. The first of these debates, about the legality of a state acting in self-defense prior to or in anticipation of a terrorist attack reflects the debate concerning the use of pre-crime or non-punishment oriented coercive measures.

In its 2002 National Security Strategy, the USA asserted that:

> It is an enduring American principle that this duty obligates the government to anticipate and counter threats, using all elements of national power, before the threats can do grave damage. The greater the threat, the greater is the risk of inaction – and the more compelling the case for taking anticipatory action to defend ourselves, even if uncertainty remains as to the time and place of the enemy's attack. There are few greater threats than a terrorist attack with WMD.

While international law has never required that a state wait until it has already been attacked before acting in self-defense, there is a requirement that the threat of attack be *imminent*.[59] In recent years, as reflected in its 2002 National Security Strategy, the USA has sought to cast what has traditionally been viewed as a limited right to anticipatory self-defense as a broader right to pre-emptive or preventive self-defense.

In contrast to the USA, the UK has maintained a more cautious position, at least in terms of its official legal position. The attorney-general stated that if anticipatory self-defense 'means more than a right to respond proportionately to an imminent attack this is not a doctrine which, in my opinion, exists or is recognised in international law'.[60]

There are three possible ways to view the claims of the USA about the scope of anticipatory self-defense under international law: first, that they represent a continuation of the existing law on self-defense under international law, perhaps extended in light of new forms of warfare, and the role of non-state terrorist actors; second, that they reflect a shift in customary international law allowing states increased rights in relation to pre-emptive self-defense measures; and third, that these measures are illegal, and represent a violation of the prohibition on the use of force.

The debate and uncertainty surrounding the precise scope of anticipatory self-defense is reflected to some extent in the debate about the use of force against non-state actors. The USA argues that the right of self-defense against non-state actors pre-dates – and is contained within (due to the reference in Article 51 to the recognition of states' 'inherent' right to self-defense) – the UN Charter.[61] Supporters of the right of self-defense against non-state actors have argued that it is a right which may be justified on a plain reading of the text of Article 51, and that sufficient state practice exists, beginning with the Caroline Incident and including a series of actions by Israel,[62] to establish this right under customary international law.

Other supporters of this right argue that it is a new, or emerging right, which has evolved in response to modern terrorism, and in particular, the advent of 9/11. Proponents of this position point to the International Court of Justice's ruling in the Nicaragua case against the right of self-defence of non-state actors, as well as a lack of sufficient state practice, but cite Security Council Resolutions 1368[63] and 1373, recognizing the 'inherent right of self-defence' in the context of an attack by a non-state actor as representing a shift following the 9/11 terror attacks. Some have described this as representing an instance of 'instant customary law'; or a 'Grotian moment'.

Others argue simply that there is no right of self-defense against non-state actors, and that the developments since 9/11 have not changed customary international law.

Nonetheless, the USA has (as discussed in relation to targeted killing) used force on foreign soil against non-state actors as part of its response to terrorism. Such actions may have the 'colour' of legality, but ultimately the legality of these actions is still subject to debate under international law.

Extraordinary rendition

The phrase 'extraordinary rendition' refers to a range of practices associated with the transfer of individuals between jurisdictions without legal authority. Rendition in the form of extradition is a valid legal process, governed by extradition treaties and domestic laws.[64] extraordinary rendition refers to rendition that occurs *outside* of these laws. Since 9/11, extraordinary rendition and the practices associated with it – capture, detention and interrogation in covert circumstances – have come to encompass a range of extra-legal measures adopted as part of the 'war on terror'. In particular, practices of extraordinary rendition have become intimately connected to torture and enhanced interrogation conducted by US officials outside of US territory, or by third parties in countries such as Egypt, Jordan, Morocco, Saudi Arabia, Syria, Uzbekistan and Yemen, who receive rendered individuals (Weissbrodt and Bergquist, 2006: 590). Although versions of extraordinary rendition pre-date 9/11, the practice has 'expanded dramatically' since then, and the methods and purposes associated with it have also changed.[65]

The practices associated with extraordinary rendition have a veneer of legality. In the USA, presidential (executive) orders have supported extraordinary rendition,[66] although the practice has not been recognized in US legislation or by Congress. The measures associated with extraordinary renditions are at times denied by government officials and intelligence operatives, and at times adopted and endorsed. As such, they have come to occupy a peculiar legal and political space, being an 'officially recognized but covert policy' (Weissbrodt and Bergquist, 2006: 586). Moreover, courts have held that even where an individual defendant has been subject to illegal rendition, this breach of international law does not prevent that individual from being tried in the same jurisdiction.[67]

The current approach to extraordinary rendition diverges from the procedures of the pre-9/11 period (Weissbrodt and Bergquist, 2006: 589). Rather than being a process of questionable legality designed to bring suspects within the jurisdiction of the USA or its allies, extraordinary rendition is now directed more at the interrogation of suspects and the gathering of intelligence in covert settings, without a view towards the trial and sentencing of these suspects. As Weissbrodt and Bergquist contend:

> This new form of extraordinary rendition typically targets a person who is not formally charged with any crime in the United States. Instead, U.S. agents or their proxies seize the person abroad for transport to the custody of a third country. Today, the term 'extraordinary rendition' is used exclusively as a euphemism to describe abduction of terror suspects not in order to bring them to justice in the United States, but rather to transfer them to a third country. (2006: 588–9)

The process of extraordinary rendition is closely linked with the use of torture, or 'enhanced interrogation techniques'. Tellingly, a Department of Justice (DoJ) memo from December 2004 deals with enhanced interrogation techniques and rendition of 'high value detainees' in concert. Rendition is the first step of a process of interrogation that may involve techniques described as 'conditioning' (nudity, sleep deprivation, dietary manipulation), 'corrective' ('insult slap, abdominal slap, facial hold and attention grasp') and 'coercive' ('walling, water dousing, stress positions, wall standing, and cramped confinement').[68] Prior to interrogation, however, the rendition will involve, the DoJ memo states, the High Value Detainee (HVD) being flown to a 'black site' where the detainee is 'securely shackled and deprived of sight and sound through the use of blindfolds, earmuffs and hoods'; on reception, the 'HVD's head and face are shaved', nude photographs of the detainee are taken, and physicians and psychologists undertake examinations to determine whether there are 'any contraindications to the use of interrogation techniques'. The HVD is then interviewed in what is initially a 'relatively benign environment', with conditions and coercion escalating in the interrogation process. Significantly, the DoJ memo states that 'the purpose of interrogation is to persuade [HVDs] to provide threat information and terrorist intelligence in a timely manner, to allow the US Government to identify and disrupt terrorist plots and to collect critical intelligence on al-Qa'ida.'[69] Nowhere in this memo is the trial or punishment of the individual detainee mentioned as a goal, or even a possibility.

As with other practices that involve coercion and mistreatment outside of a criminal justice or even legal framework, the practice of extraordinary rendition involves subjecting suspects to a highly punitive process, without any of the safeguards of the criminal law. The phrase 'erroneous rendition' has emerged to refer to innocent persons mistakenly abducted or subjected to rendition and associated interrogation techniques. The most infamous case of erroneous rendition is that of German national Khaled El-Masri who was taken from Macedonia to a detention center in Afghanistan. A civil suit brought by El-Masri against the US government was dismissed on the grounds of national security, without regard to the merits, but is widely regarded as being an example of an illegal and mistaken rendition (Weisbrodt and Bergquist, 2006: 644; Garcia, 2009). A similarly shocking example can be found in the rendition of Maher Arar, a Canadian citizen and qualified computer engineer who was arrested at JFK airport and then sent to Syria where he was imprisoned and tortured for nearly a year.[70] Both of these cases of mistaken rendition have given rise to serious popular concern, and may well result in a growing delegitimization of this sort of preventive control.

Despite these issues, the USA has attempted to justify extraordinary rendition in a range of ways, including as argued by then Secretary of State Condoleeza Rice:

> The captured terrorists of the 21st Century do not fit easily into traditional systems of criminal or military justice, which were designed for different needs. We have to adapt. Other governments are now also facing this challenge.
>
> We consider the captured members of al-Qaeda and its affiliates to be unlawful combatants who may be held, in accordance with the law of war, to keep them from killing innocents.[71]

It is relatively clear, however, that extraordinary rendition violates laws relating to extradition and trial, and, as discussed in relation to torture techniques, the various provisions of international law and treaties prohibiting the use of torture. Extradition in its ordinary sense is based on treaties between nations that govern the process by which a person who is accused of committing a crime in a jurisdiction may be returned to that jurisdiction by a second country. Those subjected to extraordinary rendition, however, do not have the protection of, for example, US Constitutional guarantees concerning due process, and are potentially subject to torture in third states. Even if the US's characterization of terror suspects as combatants (of any kind) is correct, it seems that the US's policies violate 'well-established norms of international human rights law and international humanitarian law' (Sadat, 2006: 106). Notably, the Convention Against Torture (CAT)[72] prohibits the transfer of individuals to countries where there is a substantial likelihood they may be tortured.[73]

Finally, it should be noted that the action of states in employing the coercive power of extraordinary rendition and associated interrogation is not limited to those states directly involved in the process. A number of European states have been implicated either in the provision of airspace, the location of 'black sites', and the feeding of questions to US or third-party interrogators with a view to gaining intelligence insights.[74] Although many of these 'black sites' effectively serve as prisons for individuals captured in the ongoing war on terror, the fact that they are not designated as such and have been kept secret has meant that such sites have largely operated outside the law. States that use these facilities do not have to ensure that they are compliant with their own domestic prison laws or human rights requirements, or even with the demands of due process and access to legal counsel. As a consequence, they are a striking example of an institution of coercion that has emerged as a response to terrorism in recent years, and which has been deliberately placed beyond the scope of domestic or international law.[75]

PUNISHMENT AND SOCIETY AND THE WAR ON TERROR

In this chapter, we have examined a variety of counter-terrorism techniques that have been used by states in the wake of 9/11. Although these techniques vary considerably in terms of their focus and approach, they share a common feature: they are all forms of coercion that operate on the margins – or outside – of the scope of the criminal law. However, interestingly these practices do not operate on the margins of what most would recognize as penal practices, and in many instances a gross violation of what all liberal democracies (including the USA) would recognize as the standards of civilized punishment (Elias, 1969, 1982). This raises the important dimension that punishment and society scholarship needs to address, namely that almost all of these preventive control measures constitute punishment (often entirely inhumane and undignified) without any relationship to the criminal law.

Although it may be tempting to try to characterize these new counter-terrorism measures as an extension of existing domestic and international law, we believe that the twin emphasis on pre-emption and extra-legal coercion or violence marks them out as something altogether new. Whereas in the past states may have engaged in such activities behind the cloak of secrecy or carefully crafted public denials – or sometimes relied on justifications based on the demands of war – over the past decade these techniques have not only become more visible, but also subject to an entirely different set of justifications and explanations. Far from being the hidden face of the war on terror, coercive counter-terrorism techniques have begun to take center stage in discussions about security and the responsibilities of the state.

The emerging use of these techniques has important implications for the way in which we see and understand the role of the state, and in particular the state's use of coercion, violence or aggression. From the perspective of a liberal punishment theory, one of the reasons why we let the state inflict pain, coercion or violence upon individuals is because we believe that state involvement provides a vital sense of legitimacy and independence. Punishment then can be distinguished from bare coercion or state violence in that it exists within the framework of the criminal law. Supposedly impartial and governed by strict rules, the liberal punishment model is designed to protect individuals from arbitrary or capricious sanctions. State punishment is hence frequently contrasted with other, allegedly less desirable forms of coercion or violence – such as personal vengeance and, ironically, acts of terrorism. If, however, the state is able to use coercive techniques that stand outside the criminal law, then where does this leave the institution of punishment or our commitment to the state's monopoly on violence? If the state is able to use force pre-emptively to avert an alleged threat without regard to due process, why should individuals and organizations not be allowed to do the same?

In part, one of the reasons why the liberal state is allowed to punish is because the state's hands are tied by a commitment to the rule of law. Once we remove those ties, however, much of the legitimacy that accompanies state punishment vanishes, and the state simply becomes yet another body capable of acts of coercion and violence. It is for this reason that the emerging use of techniques such as extraordinary rendition, targeted killing and enhanced interrogation or torture presents a fundamental challenge to the way in which we understand the state, and how state coercion might be framed in a liberal democratic society committed to democratic accountability and the rule of law. If pre-emptive coercion in the name of counter-terrorism is a new form of state coercion, then how should the law respond? What is the relationship between the criminal law and the laws of war? What are the implications for the way in which we see punishment? Is punishment now displaced by this kind of punitive coercion altogether? Or, as Gordon argues, are the techniques of non-punitive coercion merely an extension and mirror of the normalcy of cruelty that legal punishment involves (Gordon, 2009). If forms of punishment, such as high-security and mass incarceration are themselves illegitimate, what difference is there between legal punishment and the kind of abuse that takes place in the name of the war on terror?

As a quick perusal of the Reference section at the end of this chapter will show, to date the field of counter-terrorism has been captured by human rights lawyers, moral philosophers, international relations scholars, international lawyers and war studies scholars. In contrast, with some notable exceptions, social sciences such as criminology and penology have been relatively marginal to the debate on the 'war on terror'.[76] As discussed above, criminal law theorists, such as Ashworth and Zedner, have sought to engage with questions of the boundaries of the criminal law and the criminal process linked to preventive measures in the context of counter-terrorism (Ashworth, 2008; Ashworth and Zedner, 2008; Zedner, 2010a,b). Moreover, penologists such as Scraton and McCulloch have sought to highlight the continuity between the techniques adopted in military detention and that arising in high security imprisonment, and have in turn linked this to the centrality of mass violent incarceration in neo-liberal democratic states. The war on terror, in their view, is simply more of the same (Scraton and McCulloch, 2009: 13).

Aside from these and criminologists whose work is focused on the relationship between human rights and criminal justice – penology has yet to produce a compelling theoretical debate of the emerging forms of state coercion or violence that sits either within the law but outside criminal law, or outside of the law altogether. Although hardly conclusive evidence, it is interesting to note that many university courses on criminology and penology have been left relatively untouched by the 'war on terror' and its consequences. Although some courses may engage with the idea of terrorism as a crime, few consider the possibility that we are witnessing a displacement of legal punishment as the primary mode of delivery of state coercion, or the emergence of new discourse of extra-legal coercion that stands outside traditional domestic and international systems of criminal justice.

The absence of a positivist criminological voice in studies of terrorism has been noted most recently by Brian Forst (and others, 2011: 1) in *Criminologists on Terrorism and Homeland Security* :

> The accumulated writings and discussions on terrorism have been strikingly deficient in one important respect: Although often acknowledging that acts of terror are acts of crime in most places where they occur, most writings overlook the substantial body of pertinent knowledge that has been produced over the past several decades by criminologists and criminal justice scholars on the nature and sources of crime and aggression, and what works to prevent crime and intervene effectively against it.

While this book seeks to address the balance, including some notable attempts to include crime prevention knowledge and regulatory theory to the question of terrorism, it notably does not include any chapters on the relationship between punishment and the 'war on terror' (Amoore and Goede, 2008).

An important question posed by Zedner then is whether a discipline focused on the criminal justice practices that arise post-crime is capable of engaging with the radically preventive state. Significantly, she resists the temptation to view counter-terrorist measures outside of the criminological realm (Zedner, 2007), and instead urges the discipline to theorize itself more pertinently around the idea of 'pre-punishment' and the realm of 'security':

> The temporal shift denoted by the war on terror poses a powerful challenge to the historic precincts of criminological scholarship. Where once terrorism and counter-terrorism stood outside the normal boundaries of criminological knowledge, they now demand criminological attention ... Together these temporal and sectoral shifts pose a powerful challenge to criminology's raison d'être. (Zedner, 2007: 264)

Zedner's (2007) solution is for criminology to draw more openly on fields already associated with the pursuit of security, namely economic analysis, international relations, moral philosophy and political theory. In this sense, terrorism and measures in pursuit of its elimination may be said to have generated a new paradigm for criminology in which the study of security, 'pre-punishment' and the pre-crime field it generates take center stage. In short, the study of preventive or pre-emptive counter-terrorist techniques must become central if criminology is to adjust to the changing world around it and remain a relevant field of enquiry. The question that arises however, is what this shift means in particular for the field of punishment and society?

Should punishment and society scholarship shift its temporal focus to actions taken prior to crime breaches and the punishment that arises from such breaches? Should it view mechanisms of prevention, pre-emption or radical prevention as its focus of enquiry? To do so would, in our view, constitute only a partial response and present a wasted opportunity. As a field that studies the forms, mechanisms and techniques of coercion that take place within the penal realm, punishment and society is uniquely placed to engage with the coercive strategies deployed outside the punishment framework in the 'war on terror'. However, the absence of the legal or moral frameworks that distinguishes the bare coercion undertaken in the name of counter-terrorism from the coercive activities undertaken in pursuit of legitimate and legal punishment represents a disciplinary and moral conundrum. Does engaging with bare coercion of this kind from within the field of punishment and society risk inadvertently casting counter-terrorist coercion as legitimate punishment? Or should punishment and society actively declare such coercive activity outside of the penal realm, and outside of the disciplinary reaches of this field? In other words, should the discipline of punishment and society declare itself wedded to the limits of legitimate penality?

We do not seek here to suggest a resolution of these dilemmas, but rather to highlight the fact that punishment and society as a field collectively has thus far had very little to say about terrorism. Once theorized as bare coercion, however, counter-terrorism may well invite a fuller penological response. While this shift will require a commitment from punishment and society scholars to engage with the other disciplines such as international relations, war studies and human rights, it may well be a shift worth making.

NOTES

1 'Punishment is an authorized act, not an incidental or accidental harm. It is an act of the political authority having jurisdiction in the community where the harmful wrong occurred' (Bedau, 2010). See also Merriam-Webster Dictionary: 'punishment is a penalty inflicted on an offender through judicial procedure (http://www.merriam-webster.com/dictionary/punishment). J Rawls in *Theory of Justice* derived his conception of deserved punishment from his conception of the justice of the institutions which imposed it: 'deserved punishment, insofar as it exists at all, thus emerges as a result of "pure procedural justice"' (Bedau, 2010 referring to Rawls, 1971).

2 See: http://plato.stanford.edu/entries/legal-punishment/

3 See: http://plato.stanford.edu/entries/legal-punishment/

4 'Super-terrorism' has been characterized as having 'global aims', an 'apocalytic' ideology and 'war-like' means. It is described as a form of terrorism which precludes political negotiation (M. Freeman, 'Order, rights and threats: terrorism and global justice' in R. Ashby Wilson (2005) 37 at 38.

5 http://www.guardian.co.uk/uk/2005/aug/05/july7.uksecurity5

6 Remarks to the Republican Governors Association, Washington, DC on 25 October 2001.

7 Note by the Secretary General of the United Nations (2 December 2004, A/59/565) para. 1.

8 Note by the Secretary General of the United Nations (2 December 2004, A/59/565) para. 5. Original emphasis.

9 See Loader, 2004a,b. As Rita Taureck has observed: 'by stating that a particular referent object is threatened in its existence, a securitizing actor claims a right to extraordinary measures to ensure the referent object's survival. The issue is then moved out of the sphere of normal politics into the realm of emergency politics, where it can be dealt with swiftly and without the normal (democratic) rules and regulations of policy-making (2006: 55). See also Murphy (2007).

10 Note that the Lebanon Tribunal has jurisdiction over terrorism as a crime against Lebanese, rather than international law; it is the only tribunal before which terrorism *per se* is prosecuted. See Cryer et al. (2010: 338).

11 Draft Statute for an International Criminal Court, *Yearbook of the International Law Commission*, vol. II (Part Two) 1994, (b) Annex, (d) Appendix II. http://untreaty.un.org/ilc/texts/instruments/english/draft%20articles/7_4_1994.pdf

12 See Final Act of the United Nations Diplomatic Conference of Plenipotentaries on the Establishment of an International Criminal Court (17 July 1998), UN Doc. A/CONF.183/10. Available at http://untreaty.un.org/cod/icc/statute/finalfra.htm, Part E.

13 See for example: *McCann and others* v. *UK* (1996) 21 EHRR 97; *Andronicou and Constantinou* v. *Cyprus* (1998) 25 EHRR 491; *Gül* v. *Turkey* (2002) 34 EHRR 28. See also Leverick (2002).

14 Note, however, the reasoning in *McCann and others* v. *UK* (1996) 21 EHRR 97 para 203f.

15 See: Australian Anti-Terrorism Act 2005; Canadian Anti-Terrorism Act 2001; the UK Prevention of Terrorism Act 2005 (which replaced the Anti-Terrorism, Crime and Security Act 2001); and the US Patriot Act 2001.

16 See sections 3UA–UK of the Crimes Act 1914 (as amended).

17 For a full discussion of Australia's counter-terrorism laws, see Australian Human Rights Commission (2008). As the Guide notes, a police officer can also use the stop, search, questioning and seizure powers in a Commonwealth (i.e. federal) place that has not been declared a 'prescribed security zone', provided the officer suspects on reasonable grounds that the person might have just committed, might be committing, or might be about to commit a terrorist act.

18 Section 10.1(2).

19 Note that in January 2010, the European Court of Human Rights declared that Section 44 constituted a violation of Article 8 of the European Convention on Human Rights on the grounds that the powers conferred by the section were 'not sufficiently circumscribed' and lacked 'adequate legal safeguards against abuse'. See: *Gillan and Quinton* v. *United Kingdom* (Application no 4158/05).

20 Anti-Terrorism, Crime and Security Act 2001, Part 10.

21 Uniting and Strengthening America By Providing Appropriate Tools Required to Intercept and Obstruct Terrorism (USA Patriot Act) 2001.

22 The US Patriot Act 2001, sections 206, 207, 214, and 216.

23 Prior to the amendment, law enforcement agencies were instead required to show that the gathering of foreign intelligence was the 'primary purpose' of such surveillance. For further discussion of the surveillance powers introduced by the Patriot Act, see Kennedy and Swire (n.d.).

24 Dworkin et al., 2006. Questioning the power of the NSA domestic surveillance program, the authors of the letter observed that: '[i]f the administration felt that FISA was insufficient, the proper course was to seek legislative amendment, as it did with other aspects of FISA in the Patriot Act, and as Congress expressly contemplated when it enacted the wartime wiretap provision in FISA. One of the crucial features of a constitutional democracy is that it is always open to the President or anyone else to seek to change the law. But it is also beyond dispute that, in such a democracy, the President cannot simply violate criminal laws behind closed doors because he deems them obsolete or impracticable.'

25 Foreign Surveillance Act of 1978 Amendments Act of 2008, H.R. 6304.

26 Prevention of Terrorism Act 2005, Section 1.

27 Australian Anti-Terrorism Act 2005.

28 Public Safety Canada, 'Security Certificates', http://www.publicsafety.gc.ca/prg/ns/seccert-eng.aspx. It is important to note that these certificates can only be issued in the case of individuals who are not citizens or permanent residents.

29 *A* v. *Secretary of State for the Home Department* [2003] 1 All E.R. 816. Preventive detention mechanisms were used extensively in the earlier part of the decade in the UK's Belmarsh prison (and of course in the infamous Guantanamo Bay). Although the indefinite detention of foreign nationals suspected of terrorism did not survive human rights challenge in the UK, the existence of preventive detention as a state coercive mechanism will be discussed further below as a matter of special interest to those engaged in the field of 'punishment and society'.

30 UK: Prevention of Terrorism Act 2005; Canada: Immigration and Refugee Protection Act 2001.

31 Key cases with regard to the UK system include: *A* v. *United Kingdom* (3455/05) European Court of Human Rights (Grand Chamber), 19 February 2009; *AF* v. *Secretary of State for the Home Department* [2009] UKHL 28. In Canada, in the landmark case of *Charkaoui* v. *Canada (Minister of Citizenship and Immigration), 2007 SCC 9* 23 February 2007 the Supreme Court found that the security certificate process was unconstitutional and in October of 2007 introduced amending legislation based on the British control order system, in an attempt to bring the security certificate procedures in line with Canadian constitutional protections (see Bill C-3, An Act to amend the Immigration and Refugee Protection Act (certificates and special advocates).

32 The UK Government has announced plans to replace Control Orders with Terrorism Prevention Investigation Measures (TPIMs). These would be subject to tighter safeguards and would be viewed as part of a criminal investigation into the suspect. See Lord MacDonald, *Review of Counter-Terrorism and Security Powers* (Cm 8003).

33 UNSC Res 1373 (28 September 2001) UN Doc S/RES/1373.

34 UNSC Res 1267 (15 October 1999) UN Doc S/RES/1267.

35 UNSC Res 1456 (20 January 2003), UN Doc S/RES/1456; UNSC Res 1566 (8 October 2004), UN Doc S/RES/1456.

36 US Patriot Act, *supra*, note x, section 412(a), adding 236A(3)(A) to 8 U.S.C. 1101.

37 According to David Cole, at least 5000 individuals were detained under this provision in the two years following 9/11 (2003: 25–6).

38 USA: US Patriot Act; Canada: Anti-Terrorism Act 2001; Immigration and Refugee Protection Act 2001; UK: Anti-Terrorism, Crime and Security Act 2001.

39 Commission of Inquiry into the Actions of Canadian Officials in Relation to Maher Arar, *Report*

of the Events Relating to Maher Arar: Analysis and Recommendations (CP32–88/1–2006E) (http://www.sirc-csars.gc.ca/pdfs/cm_arar_rec-eng.pdf#53). See also: Editorial, 'The Unfinished Case of Maher Arar' *The New York Times* (17 February 2009) – http://www.nytimes.com/2009/02/18/opinion/18wed2.html

40 *A* v. *Secretary of State for the Home Department* [2003] 1 All E.R. 816.

41 Anti-Terrorism, Crime and Security Act 2001, Part 4.

42 P Alston *Report of the Special Rapporteur on extrajudicial, summary or arbitrary executions* (UN General Assembly, Human Rights Council 14th Session) A/HRC/14/24/Add.6 (28 May 2010) para. 1.

43 Human Rights Watch, *No Blood, No Foul*, 22 July 2006; Golden (2005) and Guiora and Page (2006).

44 There is some ambiguity as to when such jurisdiction may be said to arise. Some cases apply the 'effective control' test (*Bankovic and others* v. *Belgium* and others, no. 53307/99, 12 December 2001, (2007) 44 E.H.R.R. SE5), while others are more progressive in their approach (*Al-Skeini et al.* v. *UK*, appl. no. 55721/07, 7 July 2011).

45 Article 7 (and 4) ICCPR; Art. 3 ECHR; *Prosecutor* v. *Anto Furundžija* IT-95–17/1-T. [144] : 'It should be noted that the prohibition of torture laid down in human rights treaties enshrines an absolute right, which can never be derogated from, not even in time of emergency (on this ground the prohibition also applies to situations of armed conflicts). This is linked to the fact, discussed below, that the prohibition on torture is a peremptory norm or jus cogens. This prohibition is so extensive that States are even barred by international law from expelling, returning or extraditing a person to another State where there are substantial grounds for believing that the person would be in danger of being subjected to torture' (available at http://www.icty.org/case/furundzija/4). Association of the Bar of the City of New York Committee on International Human Rights, Committee on Military Affairs and Justice, April 2004, in Greenberg and Dratel: 'The prohibition of torture is, moreover, one of the few norms which has attained peremptory norm or *jus cogens* status, and is recognized as such by United States courts. ... *Jus cogens* is defined as a peremptory norm "accepted and recognized" by the international community of states as a whole as a norm from which no derogation is permitted and which can be modified only by a subsequent norm of general international law having the same character' (2005: 598).

46 United Nations Convention against Torture and Other Cruel, Inhuman or Degrading Treatment or Punishment (1984); European Convention for the Prevention of Torture and Inhuman or Degrading Treatment or Punishment (1987).

47 Section 12, South African Constitution; Eighth Amendment, US Constitution; Section 12, of Canadian Charter of Rights and Freedoms.

48 *Chahal* v. *the United Kingdom*, 15 November 1996, § 79; see also *Gafgen* v. *Germany* 22978/05 [2010] ECHR 759 (1 June 2010).

49 J Yoo and R Delahunty, 'Application of Treaties and Laws to Al Qaeda and Taliban Detainees', Memorandum for William J. Haynes, General Counsel, Department of Defense, January 9, 2002; Memo: 'Re: Standards of Conduct for Interrogation under 18 U.S.C. 2340–2340A,' from the Justice Department's Office of Legal Counsel for Alberto R. Gonzales, counsel to President Bush. Dated August 1, 2002 (Bybee memorandum') Amended in 2003 by William J. Haynes II, Action memo: 'Counter-Resistance Techniques,' (for Secretary of Defense, from General Counsel of the Department of Defense), November 27, 2002. For discussion of the relation between the Bybee and the Haynes memoranda, see Herman Schwartz, Judgeship Nominees; Twisting the Law on Interrogating Detainees, Newsday, August 18, 2004, p. A39. All available in Greenberg and Dratel (2005).

50 Bybee memorandum, p. 16 (citing S. Treaty Doc. 100–20 at 4–5) ; Dratel, xxii–xxiii.

51 J Yoo and R Delahunty, 'Application of Treaties and Laws to Al Qaeda and Taliban Detainees', Memorandum for William J. Haynes, General Counsel, Department of Defense, January 9, 2002.

52 The European Court of Human Rights is clear that the death penalty violates Article 3 on the ECHR (*Soering* v. *UK*, appl. no. 14038/88, 7 July 1989, (1989) 11 E.H.R.R. 439). Similarly, the UK courts have grappled with whether the indeterminate life sentence is compatible with the prohibitions of Article 3 (*Wellington* v. *Secretary of State for the Home Department* [2009] 2 All E.R. 436).

53 P Alston *Report of the Special Rapporteur on extrajudicial, summary or arbitrary executions* (UN General Assembly, Human Rights Council 14th Session) A/HRC/14/24/Add.6 (28 May 2010) para. 1.

54 P Alston *Report of the Special Rapporteur on extrajudicial, summary or arbitrary executions* (UN General Assembly, Human Rights Council 14th Session) A/HRC/14/24/Add.6 (28 May 2010) para. 1.

55 P Alston *Report of the Special Rapporteur on extrajudicial, summary or arbitrary executions* (UN General Assembly, Human Rights Council 14th Session) A/HRC/14/24/Add.6 (28 May 2010) para. 1.

56 For a discussion of early use of targeted killing by the US military, see Tovy (2009).

57 Judge Koroma, *Armed Activities Case* [148].

58 Nicaragua, [187–201].

59 The Caroline Incident 29.B.F.S.P. 1137–1138; 30 B.F.S.P. 195–196, Secretary of State Mr. Webster to Mr. Fox (1841), 'a necessity of self-defence, instant, overwhelming, leaving no choice of means, and no moment for deliberation.'

60 Lord Goldsmith, 'Secret: Advice to Prime Minister: Iraq: Resolution 1441', http://news.bbc.co.uk/1/shared/bsp/hi/pdfs/28_04_05_attorney_general.pdf Accessed: 7 March 2003.

61 See Gray (2004), 114–128, who characterises this as the 'wide' reading, discussing arguments by Derek Bowett and others.

62 In 1982, Israel in Lebanon with regard to the PLO; in 1985, Israel in Tunisia with regard to the PLO; in 1986, the US bombing of Libya in response to the bombing of a German nightclub.

63 S.C. Res. 1368, U.N. Doc. S/RES/1368 (Sept. 12, 2001).

64 See summary in Garcia (2009: 1).

65 American Civil Liberties Union, 'Fact Sheet: Extraordinary Rendition', 6 December 2005, Available at: http://www.aclu.org/national-security/fact-sheet-extraordinary-rendition. Although numerous sources assert a marked increase in rendition, there are, of course, no published statistics on the matter. Garcia, writing in 2009, said: 'Although there are some reported estimates that the United States has rendered more than 100 individuals following 9/11, the actual number is not a matter of the public record.' Other sources suggest that close to 3000 individuals may have been illegally rendered, and the report of the European Parliament notes that more than 1200 flights associated with the extraordinary rendition program involved European airspace; see discussion in Leila Sadat, 'Extraordinary Rendition, Torture and Other Nightmares from the War on Terror', *The George Washington Law Review*, Vol 75:05/06, 105.

66 Presidential Decision Directive 39, 'US Policy on Counterterrorism', signed by William J Clinton 21 June 1995, Available at: http://www.fas.org/irp/offdocs/pdd39.htm: building on National Security Directive 77, Classified Title, signed by George H.W. Bush, January 1993.

67 *Attorney-General of Israel* v. *Eichmann* [1961] IsrDC 45(3), translated in 36 INT'L L. REP. 5 (1968), aff'd *Attorney-General* v. *Eichmann* [1962] IsrSC 16(2033), translated in 36 INT'L L.; *United States* v. *Alvarez-Machain* 504 U.S. 655 (1992), cited in Weissbrodt and Bergquest (1996: 586–7). REP. 277 (1968).; Alvarez.

68 DoJ Memo, 7–8.

69 DoJ Memo, 1.

70 Commission of Inquiry into the Actions of Canadian Officials in Relation to Maher Arar, *Report of the Events Relating to Maher Arar: Analysis and Recommendations* (CP32–88/1–2006E) (http://www.sirc-csars.gc.ca/pdfs/cm_arar_rec-eng.pdf#53). See also: Editorial, 'The Unfinished Case of Maher Arar' *The New York Times* (17 February 2009) – http://www.nytimes.com/2009/02/18/opinion/18wed2.html

71 BBC News, 'Full Text: Rice defends US policy', 5 December 2005, http://news.bbc.co.uk/1/hi/4500630.stm

72 Convention Against Torture and Other Cruel, Inhuman or Degrading Treatment or Punishment (CAT), G.A. Res. 39/46, Annex, 39 U.N. GAOR Supp. No. 51, U.N. Doc. A/39/51 (1984).

73 Article 2(1), ibid.

74 Binyan Mohamed case – UK.

75 For an overview of black sites and their role in extraordinary rendition, see Sadat (2006).

76 See, for example: Lyon (2006b) and Webb (2007). Equally, human rights scholars have also been extremely prolific when it comes to the subject of September 11 and its effects on fundamental liberties (Cole, 2009).

REFERENCES

Ackerman, B. (2004) 'The emergency constitution', *Yale Law Journal*, 113: 1029–43.

Ackerman, B. (2006) *Before the Next Attack: Preserving Civil Liberties in an Age of Terrorism*. New Haven, CT: Yale University Press.

Altman, A., Finkelstein, C. and Ohlin, J. (eds) (forthcoming) *Using Targetted Killing to Fight the War on Terror*. Oxford: Oxford University Press.

Amoore, L. and de Goede, M. (2008) *Risk and the War on Terror*. London: Routledge.

Aradau, C. and van Munster, R. (2007) 'Governing terrorism through risk: taking precautions, (un)knowing the future', *European Journal of International Relations'*, 13 (1): 89–115.

Aradau, C. and van Munster, R. (2009) 'Exceptionalism and the "war on terror": criminology meets international relations', *British Journal of Criminology*, 49: 686–701.

Ashby Wilson, R. (ed.) (2005) *Human Rights in the 'War on Terror'*. Cambridge: Cambridge University Press.

Ashworth, A. (2008) 'Conceptions of overcriminalization', *Ohio State Journal of Criminal Law*, 5: 407–425.

Ashworth, A. and Zedner, L. (2008) *Defending the Criminal Law: Reflections on the Changing Character of Crime, Procedure and Sanctions*. Criminal Law and Philosophy.

Ashworth, A. and Zedner, L. (2010) 'Preventive orders: a problem of undercriminalization?', in R.A. Duff, L. Farmer, S. Marshall, M. Renzo and V. Tadros (eds), *The Boundaries of the Criminal Law*. Oxford: Oxford University Press.

Australian Human Rights Commission (2008) *A Human Rights Guide To Australia's Counter-Terrorism Laws*. Available at: http://www.hreoc.gov.au/legal/

publications/counter_terrorism_laws.html (Accessed 20 March 2012).

Beck, U. (2002) 'The terrorist threat : world risk society revisited', *Theory Culture Society*, 19: 39.

Beck, U. (2003) 'The silence of words: on war and terror', *Security Dialogue*, 34 (3): 255–267.

Beck, U. (2006) 'Living in the world risk society', *Lecture at the London School of Economics*, 15 February.

Bedau, H.A. (2010) 'Punishment', *Stanford Encyclopedia of Philosophy*. Available at: http://plato.stanford.edu/entries/punishment/

Bobbitt, P. (2008) *Terror and Consent: The Wars for the Twenty-First Century*. New York: Knopf.

Bosworth, M. (2011) 'Deportation, detention and foreign-national prisoners in England and Wales', *Citizenship Studies*, 15 (2): 583–595.

Bosworth, M. and Guild, M. (2008) 'Governing through migration control: security and citizenship in Britain', *British Journal of Criminology*, 48: 703–719.

Bowcott, O. (2011) 'Osama bin Laden: US responds to questions about killing's legality', *Guardian*, 3 May. Available at: http://www.guardian.co.uk/world/2011/may/03/osama-bin-laden-killing-legality (Accessed 20 March 2012).

Calavita, K. (2005) *Immigrants at the Margins: Law, Race, and Exclusion in Southern Europe*. Cambridge: Cambridge University Press.

Carlton, B. (2006) 'From H division to Abu Ghraib: regimes of justification and the historical proliferation of state-inflicted terror and violence in maximum security', *Social Justice*, 33: 15–36.

Cole, D. (2003) *Enemy Aliens: Double Standards and Constitutional Freedoms in the War on Terrorism*. New York: The New Press.

Cole, D. (2004) 'The priority of morality: the emergency constitution's blind spot', *Yale Law Journal*, 113: 1753–1800.

Cole, D. (2009) *The Torture Memos: Rationalizing the Unthinkable*. New York: The New Press.

Cole, D. and Dempsey J. (2006) *Terrorism and the Constitution: Sacrificing Civil Liberties in the Name of National Security*. New York: The New Press.

Corn, G. and Jensen, E. (2008) 'Untying the Gordian knot: a proposal for determining applicability of the laws of war to the war on terror', *Temple Law Review*, 81: 787.

Crawford, A. (2006) 'Networked governance and the post-regulatory state? Steering, rowing and anchoring the provision of policing and security', *Theoretical Criminology*, 10: 449–79.

Crawford, A. (2009) *Crime Prevention Policies in Comparative Perspective*. Cullompton: Willan.

Cryer, R., Friman, H., Robinson, D. and Wilmshurst, E. (2010) *International Criminal Law and Procedure*, 2nd edn. Cambridge: Cambridge University Press.

Davis, A. (2005) *Abolition Democracy: Beyond Empire, Prisons and Torture*. New York: Seven Stories Press.

Dershowitz, A. (2006) *Preemption: A Knife That Cuts Both Ways*. New York: WW Norton.

Di Fillippo, M. (2008) 'Terrorist crimes and international cooperation: critical remarks on the definition and inclusion of terrorism in the category of international crimes', *The European Journal of International Law*, 19 (3): 533.

Dudziak, M. (ed.) (2003) *September 11 in History: A Watershed Moment?* Durnham and London: Duke University Press.

Dworkin, R. (2003) 'Terror and the attack on civil liberties', *The New York Review of Books*, 50 (17): 37.

Dworkin, R., Sullivan, K., Tribe, L., et al. (2006) 'On NSA spying: a letter to Congress', *New York Review of Books*, 9 February.

Economist (2011) 'Editorial: drones and the law: America's attack on suspected terrorists should be more closely monitored', *Economist*, 8 October.

Elias, N. (1969) *The Civilizing Process, Vol. I. The History of Manners*. Oxford: Blackwell.

Elias, N. (1982) *The Civilizing Process, Vol. II. State Formation and Civilization*. Oxford: Blackwell.

Endicott, T. (2007) '*Habeas corpus* and Guantanamo Bay: a view from abroad', *Oxford Legal Studies Research Paper* No. 6/2007.

Ericson, R. (2008) 'The state of preemption: managing terrorism through counter law', in L. Amoore and M. de Goede (eds), *Risk and the War on Terror*. Abingdon: Routledge.

Ericson, R. and Doyle A. (2004) 'Catastrophe risk, insurance and terrorism', *Economy and Society*, 33 (2): 135–173.

Forst, B., Greene, J. and Lynch, J. (eds) (2011) *Criminologists on Terrorism and Homeland Security*. Cambridge: Cambridge University Press.

Garcia, M.J. (2009) 'Renditions: constraints imposed by laws on torture', Congressional Research Service – CRS Report for Congress, 8 September.

Golden, T. (2005) 'In US Report, Brutal Details of 2 Afghan Inmate Deaths', *New York Times*, 20 May.

Gordon, A. (2006) 'Abu Ghraib: imprisonment and the war on terror', *Race and Class*, 48.

Gordon, A. (2009) 'The United States military prison: the normalcy of exceptional brutality', in P. Scraton and J. McCulloch (eds), *The Violence of Incarceration*. London: Routledge.

Gray, C. (2004) *International Law and the Use of Force*. Oxford: Oxford University Press.

Greenberg, K. (2006) *The Torture Debate in America.* Cambridge: Cambridge University Press.

Greenberg, K. and Dratel, J. (eds) (2005) *The Torture Papers: The Road to Abu Ghraib.* Cambridge: Cambridge University Press.

Gross, O. (2003) 'Chaos and rules: should responses to violent crises always be constitutional?', *Yale Law Journal*, 112: 1011–1034.

Gross, O. and Ní Aoláin, F. (2006) *Law in Times of Crisis: Emergency Powers in Theory and Practice.* Cambridge: Cambridge University Press.

Guiora, A. (2007) *Global Perspectives on Counterterrorism.* Aspen Publishers.

Guiora, A. (2008) *Fundamentals of Counterterrorism.* Aspen Publishers.

Guiora, A. (forthcoming 2011) *Homeland Security: What Is It and Where Are We Going?* CRC Press/ Taylor & Francis Publishers.

Guiora, A. and McNeal, G. (forthcoming 2011) *Counterterrorism Law Across Borders: Differing Perspectives on Rights and Security.* Aspen Publishers.

Guiora, A. and Page, E. (2006) 'The unholy trinity: intelligence, interrogation and torture', *Case Western Research Journal International Law*, 37: 427–447.

Husak, D. (2008) *Overcriminalization: The Limits of the Criminal Law.* Oxford: Oxford University Press.

Ignatieff, M. (2004) *The Lesser Evil: Politics in an Age of Terror.* Princeton, NJ: Princeton University Press.

International Council on Human Rights Policy (2008) *Talking About Terrorism: Risks and Choices for Human Rights Organisations. Geneva:* ICHRP.

Janus, E. (2004) 'The preventive state, terrorists and sexual predators: countering the threat of a new outsider jurisprudence', *Criminal Law Bulletin*, 40: 576.

Kennedy, C.H. and Swire, P.P. (n.d.) 'State wiretaps and electronic surveillance after September 11'. Available at: http://papers.ssrn.com/sol3/papers.cfm?abstract_id=416586 (accessed 2 April 2012)

Kramer, R. and Michalowski, R. (2005) 'War, aggression and state crime: a criminological analysis of the invasion and occupation of Iraq', *British Journal of Criminology*, 45: 446.

Lazarus, L. (2004) *Contrasting Prisoners' Rights.* Oxford: Oxford University Press.

Lazarus, L. and Goold, B. (2007) 'Introduction', in Goold, B. and Lazarus L. (eds), *Security and Human Rights.* Oxford: Hart Publishing. pp. 1–8.

Leverick, F. (2002) 'Is English self-defence law compatible with Article 2 ECHR?', *Criminal Law Review* 347–362.

Levinson, S. (2004) *Torture: A Collection.* Oxford: Clarendon Press.

Lewis, P., Taylor, M. and de Comarmond, C. (2010) 'Security guards accused over death of man being deported to Angola', *Guardian*, 14 October. Available at: http://www.guardian.co.uk/uk/2010/oct/14/security-guards-accused-jimmy-mubenga-death (accessed 29 March 2012).

Lichtblau, E. and Risen, J. (2005) 'Bush lets US spy on callers without courts', *New York Times*, 16 December.

Liebling, A., Arnold H. and Straub, C. (2010) 'Power and Vulnerability in Prison: Updating the Findings from HMP Whitemoor Ten Years on – June 2009 to November 2010', in Institute of Criminology, Cambridge, *Prisons Research Centre: Annual Report on Research Findings 2010* Available at: http://www.crim.cam.ac.uk/research/prc/prcrep10.pdf (Accessed March 2012).

Loader, I. (2004a) 'Policing unlimited? Security, civic governance and the public good', in K. van der Vijver and J. Terpstra (eds), *Urban Safety: Problems, Governance and Strategies.* Enschede: IPIT. pp. 55–64.

Loader, I. (2004b) 'Policing, securitisation and democratisation in Europe', in T. Newburn and R. Sparks (eds), *Policing, Securitisation and Democratisation in Europe.* Cullompton: Willan. pp. 49–79.

Lyon, D. (2003) 'Airports as data filters: converging surveillance systems after September 11', *Information, Communication and Ethics in Society*, 1(1): 13–20.

Lyon, D. (2006a) 'Airport screening, surveillance and social sorting: Canadian responses to 9/11 in context', *Canadian Journal of Criminology and Criminal Justice*, 48 (3): 397–412.

Lyon, D. (2006b) *Surveillance after September 11.* London: Polity.

MacMaster, N. (2004) 'Torture: from Algiers to Abu Ghraib', *Race and Class*, 46: 1.

McCulloch, J. and Carlton, B. (2006) 'Preempting justice: suppression of financing of terrorism and the war on terror', *Current Issues in Criminal Justice*, 17: 397.

McCulloch, J. and Pickering, S. (2009) 'Pre-crime and counter terrorism ', *British Journal of Criminology*, 49: 628–645.

Mead, G.H. (1918) 'The psychology of punitive justice', *American Journal of Sociology*, 23: 577–602.

Murphy, C. (2007) '"Securitizing" Canadian policing: a new policing paradigm for the post 9/11 security state?', *The Canadian Journal of Sociology*, 32 (4): 451–477.

National Commission on Terrorist Attacks upon the United States (9/11 Commission) Report (2004)

Available at http://www.9–11commission.gov/report/index.htm

Neyland, D. (2006) *Privacy, Surveillance and Public Trust.* Basingstoke: Palgrave Macmillan.

Pickering, S. McCulloch, J. and Wright-Neville, D. (2008) *Counter-Terrorism Policing: Community, Cohesion and Security.* New York: Springer.

Priest, D. (2010) 'US military teams, intelligence deeply involved in aiding Yemen on strikes', *Washington Post,* 27 January. Available at: http://www.washingtonpost.com/wp-dyn/content/article/2010/01/26/AR2010012604239.html?sid=ST2010012700394

Roach, K. (2007) 'Sources and trends in post-9/11 anti-terrorism laws', in B. Goold and L. Lazarus (eds), *Security and Human Rights.* Oxford: Hart. pp. 227–256.

Sadat, L. (2006) 'Ghost prisons and black sites: extraordinary rendition under international law', *Case Western Reserve Journal of International Law,* Washington U. School of Law Working Paper No. 06–02–01. Available at SSRN: http://ssrn.com/abstract=886377

Sadat, L. (2007) 'Extraordinary rendition, torture and other nightmares from the war on terror', *George Washington Law Review,* 75: 101.

Saul, B. (2006) *Defining Terrorism in International Law.* Oxford: Oxford University Press.

Scraton, P. and McCulloch, J. (eds) (2009) *The Violence of Incarceration.* London: Routledge.

Slobogin, C. (2003) 'A jurisprudence of dangerousness', *Northwestern University Law Review,* 98: 1–62

Steiker, C. (1998) 'The limits of the preventive state', *Journal of Criminal Law and Criminology,* 81: 771–808.

Stumpf, J. (2006) 'The crimmigration crisis: immigrants, crime, and sovereign power', *American University Law Review,* 56 (2): 367–419.

Taureck, R. (2006) 'Securitization theory and securitization studies', *Journal of International Relations and Development,* 9 (1): 53–61.

Tesón, FR (forthcoming) 'The morality of targeted killing', in A. Altman, C. Finklestein and J. Ohlin (eds), *Using Targeted Killing to Fight the War on Terror.* Oxford: Oxford University Press.

Tomkins, A., Lazarus, L. and Fenwick, H. (2010) 'Submission in response to HM Treasury: Public Consultation: Draft Terrorist Asset-Freezing Bill (Cm 7852)'. Unpublished report.

Tomkins, A., Fenwick, H. and Lazarus, L. (2011) 'Terrorist asset-freezing – Continuing flaws in the current scheme', *International Review of Law, Computers and Technology,* 25: 117–28.

Topping, A. (2011) 'UKBA accused of breaking pledge to end child detention', *Guardian,* 16 October. Available at: http://www.guardian.co.uk/uk/2011/oct/16/ukba-childrens-society-child-detention (Accessed 2 April 2012).

Tovy, T. (2009) 'The theoretical aspect of targeted killings: the Phoenix Program as a case study', *Journal of Military and Strategic Studies,* 11 (4): 1–24.

Tribe, L.H. and Gudridge, P.O. (2004) 'The anti-emergency constitution', *Yale Law Journal,* 113: 1801.

Waldron, J. (2010) *Torture, Terror and Trade-Offs: Philosophy for the White House.* Oxford: Oxford University Press.

Waldron, J. (2011) 'Can targeted killing work as a neutral principle', NYU Public Law and Legal Theory Research Paper Series Working Paper No. 11–20.

Walker, C. (2007) 'Keeping control of terrorists without losing control of constitutionalism', *Stanford Law Review,* 59: 1395–1463.

Webb, M. (2007) *Illusions of Security: Global Surveillance and Democracy in the Post-9/11 World.* San Francisco, CA: City Lights Publishers.

Weissbrodt, D. and Bergquist, A. (2006) 'Extraordinary rendition and the torture convention', *Virginia Journal of International Law,* 46 (4): 587.

Weissbrodt, D. and Bergquist, A. (2007) 'Extraordinary rendition and the humanitarian law of war and occupation', *Virginia Journal of International Law,* 47 (2): 295.

Whitman, J. (2004) *Harsh Justice: Criminal Punishment and the Widening Divide between America and Europe.* Oxford: Oxford University Press.

Zedner, L. (2007a) 'Preventive justice or pre-punishment? The case of control orders', *Current Legal Problems,* 59: 174–203.

Zedner, L. (2007b) 'Pre-crime and post-criminology?', *Theoretical Criminology,* 11 (2): 271–275.

Zedner, L. (2010a) 'Security, the state, and the citizen: the changing architecture of crime control', *New Criminal Law Review,* 13: 379–403.

Zedner, L. (2010b) 'Pre-crime and pre-punishment: a health warning', *Criminal Justice Matters,* 81(1): 24–25.

Index

Introductory Note

References such as "138–9" indicate (not necessarily continuous) discussion of a topic across a range of pages. Wherever possible in the case of topics with many references, these have either been divided into sub-topics or only the most significant discussions of the topic are listed. Because the entire volume is about "punishment", the use of this term (and certain others occurring throughout the work) as an entry point has been restricted. Information will be found under the corresponding detailed topics.